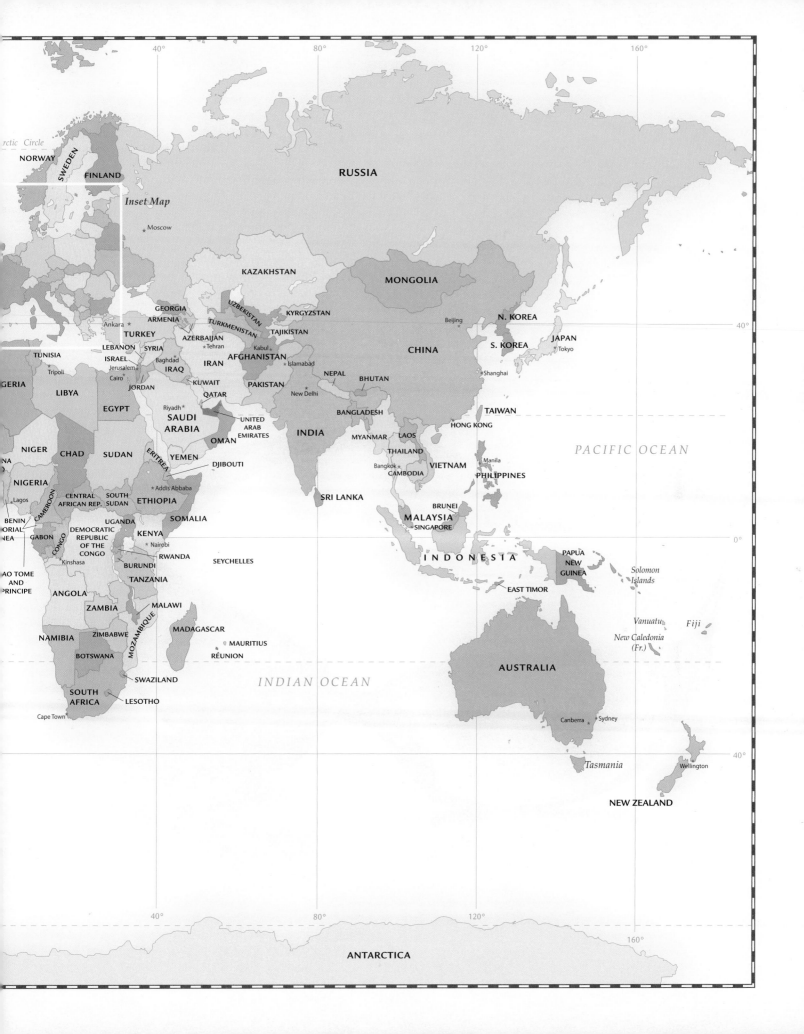

EXPERIENCE

SOCIOLOGY

SECOND EDITION

DAVID CROTEAU
WILLIAM HOYNES

EXPERIENCE SOCIOLOGY, SECOND EDITION

Published by McGraw-Hill Education, 2 Penn Plaza, New York, NY 10121. Copyright ©
2015 by McGraw-Hill Education. All rights reserved. Printed in the United States of America.
Previous edition © 2013. No part of this publication may be reproduced or distributed in any
form or by any means, or stored in a database or retrieval system, withoutthe prior written
consent of McGraw-Hill Education, including, but not limited to, in any network or other
electronic storage or transmission, or broadcast for distance learning.

Some ancillaries, including electronic and print components, may not be available to
customers outside the United States.

This book is printed on acid-free paper.

1 2 3 4 5 6 7 8 9 0 DOW/DOW 1 0 9 8 7 6 5 4

ISBN: 978-0-07-802673-7
MHID: 0-07-802673-3

Senior Vice President, Products & Markets: *Kurt L. Strand*
Vice President, General Manager, Products & Markets: *Michael Ryan*
Vice President, Content Design & Delivery: *Kimberly Meriwether David*
Managing Director: *Gina Boedecker*
Brand Manager: *Courtney Austermehle*
Director, Product Development: *Meghan Campbell*
Product Developer: *Briana Porco and Sylvia Mallory*
Marketing Manager: *Philip Weaver and Kimberli Brownlee*
Lead Product Developer: *Rhona Robbin*
Digital Product Analyst: *John Brady*
Director, Content Design & Delivery: *Terri Schiesl*
Program Manager: *Marianne Musni*
Content Project Managers: *Susan Trentacosti, Emily Kline*
Buyer: *Carol A. Bielski*
Design: *Matthew Backhaus*
Content Licensing Specialists: *John Leland, Beth Thole*
Cover Image: *Peter Dazeley/GettyImages*
Compositor: *Aptara®, Inc.*
Typeface: *Janson Text LT Std*
Printer: *R. R. Donnelley*

Library of Congress Cataloging-in-Publication Data

Croteau, David.
    Experience sociology / David Croteau.—Second edition.
        pages cm
    ISBN 0-07-802673-3 (alk. paper)
1.   Sociology.   I.   Title.
    HM585.C773 2014
    301—dc23

                                          2014029127

The Internet addresses listed in the text were accurate at the time of publication. The inclusion
of a website does not indicate an endorsement by the authors or McGraw-Hill Education,
and McGraw-Hill Education does not guarantee the accuracy of the information presented
at these sites.

DEDICATION

To all the dedicated instructors of
introductory sociology courses and
to the students who inspire them.
—DAVID CROTEAU

To Ben and Nick Hoynes, who have
taught me more about sociology
than they know.
—WILLIAM HOYNES

About the AUTHORS

DAVID R. CROTEAU earned a B.A. in sociology from Brandeis University and a Ph.D. in sociology from Boston College. Over the years he has taught a diverse range of students at Boston College, Clark University, Keene State College, and the University of Mary Washington. As an associate professor at Virginia Commonwealth University, he taught introductory sociology as well as both undergraduate and graduate courses in theory, methods, stratification, movements, and media. He continues to teach there and works at the Academic Learning Transformation Lab (ALT Lab). You can follow him on Twitter @DavidRCroteau and he blogs about sociology and education at DavidRCroteau.net.

In addition to various journal articles and book chapters, David Croteau is the author of *Politics and the Class Divide*, a finalist for both the C. Wright Mills Award from the Society for the Study of Social Problems and the Transformational Politics Book Award from the American Political Science Association.

WILLIAM HOYNES earned a B.A. in history and political science from Tufts University and a Ph.D. in sociology from Boston College. He is Professor of Sociology at Vassar College, where he teaches Introductory Sociology as well as courses on media, culture, research methods, and social theory. During his more than 20 years at Vassar, Professor Hoynes has served as chair of the Sociology Department and director of both the Media Studies Program and the American Studies Program.

In addition to various journal articles and book chapters on public broadcasting in the United States, Professor Hoynes is the author of *Public Television for Sale: Media, the Market, and the Public Sphere*, which was awarded the Goldsmith Book Prize from the Shorenstein Center on Media, Politics and Public Policy at Harvard University's John F. Kennedy School of Government.

CROTEAU and HOYNES are coauthors of *Media/Society: Images, Industries, and Audiences*, which was published in a revised fifth edition in 2014; *The Business of Media: Corporate Media and the Public Interest*, which won the Robert Picard Award for best new book in media economics by the Association for Education in Journalism and Mass Communication; and *By Invitation Only: How the Media Limit Political Debate*. They are also coeditors, with Charlotte Ryan, of *Rhyming Hope and History: Activists, Academics, and Social Movement Scholarship*.

Dear Colleagues

Like all of us who teach sociology, we want to help a diverse range of students grasp the basic concepts of the discipline, see the relevance of those concepts to their everyday lives, and apply what they learn to the world around them. We want students to experience that aha! moment when they see the familiar in a new way and realize that sociology's tools can help them better understand their rapidly changing social world. In other words, we want students to see the world from a sociological perspective and to actively use their sociological imagination. We want them to experience sociology.

What's unique about the second edition of *Experience Sociology*?

CULTURE. STRUCTURE. POWER. *Experience Sociology* engages students with a clear framework for understanding their world based on three familiar terms at the heart of sociology: culture, structure, and power. Through the lenses of these three concepts, students learn from their first class to see the world from a sociological perspective and to grasp the significance of sociology for their own lives. For every topic in the book—from the family to the economy to the environment—they learn to recognize the effects of the culture they have been taught, see the structures that constrain or empower them, and notice how power operates at every level of society.

How is theory covered?

Theory has a role in every chapter in *Experience Sociology*. We know how important it is for students not only to be able to apply concepts to their lives, but also to understand and be able to apply sociological theory. With its innovative organization around primary sociological concepts, *Experience Sociology* emphasizes the common ground that informs a basic sociological perspective. But every chapter also addresses the way differing theoretical perspectives illuminate various facets of these key sociological concepts, letting instructors and students go beyond conventional theoretical boundaries and the either-or framing of theoretical perspectives to see how each can contribute to our understanding of the social world.

What's the full Experience?

The second edition of *Experience Sociology* is much more than this textbook alone. Incorporating the work of many sociology instructors, it is instead a comprehensive instructional program that combines digital and print resources to promote student learning. Featuring Connect Sociology assessments tied to learning objectives, and the adaptive LearnSmart suite that generates a study plan specifically designed to address students' individual strengths and weaknesses, *Experience Sociology* helps you manage assignments and makes learning and studying more engaging and efficient for your students.

We wrote *Experience Sociology* because we want students to be able to do just that: experience their world differently through the insights of sociology. We hope these resources will help you in introducing your students to the excitement of sociology.

Sincerely,

BRIEF CONTENTS

CONTENTS

PART 3
THE SOCIAL SELF

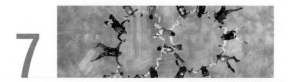

6

SOCIALIZATION 134

7

INTERACTION, GROUPS, AND ORGANIZATIONS 160

8

DEVIANCE AND SOCIAL CONTROL   190

PART 4
IDENTITY AND INEQUALITY

9

CLASS AND GLOBAL INEQUALITY   222

10 RACE AND ETHNICITY 254

11 GENDER AND SEXUALITY 288

PART 5
SOCIAL INSTITUTIONS AND SOCIAL ISSUES

12
FAMILY AND RELIGION 320

13
EDUCATION AND WORK 350

14

MEDIA AND CONSUMPTION 382

15

COMMUNITIES, THE ENVIRONMENT,
AND HEALTH 412

Experience the power of data in your classroom

Experience Sociology transformed the way your students consider the world around them, using the lenses of culture, structure, and power. The second edition will transform the way you teach.

THE HEAT MAP STORY

Over the past two years, data points showing concepts that caused students the most difficulty were anonymously collected from Connect Sociology's LearnSmart for *Experience Sociology*. The data from LearnSmart were provided to the authors in the form of a heat map, which illustrated troublesome "hot spots" in the text. The authors used this empirically based heat map data to refine the content and reinforce student comprehension in the second edition.

 **New! Connect Sociology, now with Insight!**

Connect Sociology, the integrated assignment and assessment platform that makes learning more motivating and accessible for students, now makes teaching easier and more efficient for instructors. The first and only analytics tool of its kind, Connect Insight™ is a series of visual data displays—each framed by an intuitive question—to provide real-time, at-a-glance information regarding how your class is doing. Available at a moment's notice from your tablet device.

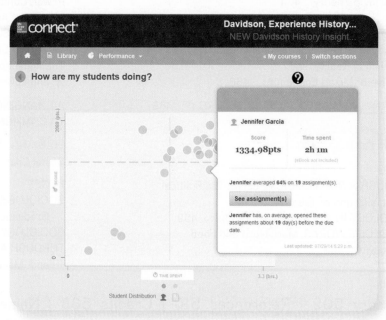

⧈ℍ LEARNSMART®

LearnSmart Advantage is a new series of adaptive learning products fueled by **LearnSmart**—a widely used, adaptive learning resource that has been proven to strengthen memory recall, increase retention, and boost grades. Data collected from over 1.5 million student users and more than 1 billion questions answered are used to make the LearnSmart Advantage products intelligent, reliable, and precise.

SmartBook™ is the first and only adaptive reading experience designed to change the way students read and learn. It creates a personalized reading experience by highlighting the most impactful concepts a student needs to learn at that moment in time. As a student engages with SmartBook, the reading experience continuously adapts by highlighting content based on what the student knows and doesn't know. This ensures that

the focus is on the content he or she needs to learn, while simultaneously promoting long-term retention of material. Use SmartBook's real-time reports to quickly identify the concepts that require more attention from individual students—or the entire class.

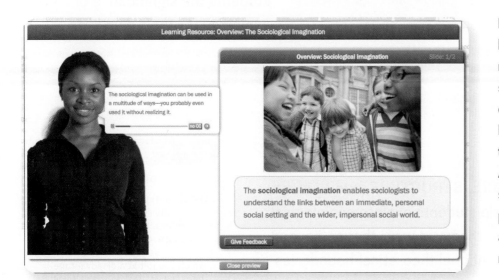

New! **LearnSmart Achieve** is a learning system that provides resources to enhance under-standing of important learning objectives. Powered by LearnSmart's proven adaptive technology, LearnSmart Achieve identifies what a student should study and provides learning resources at the moment he or she needs them the most.

Make the familiar a new experience for you and your students

WHY THE 3D GLASSES?

We want students to see their familiar world in a new way. *Experience Sociology*, Second Edition, uses the lenses of culture, structure, and power to empower students to move beyond an individual perspective to gain a sociological perspective.

How were you socialized into your society's **culture**?

How do agents of socialization reproduce social **structure**?

How does **power** shape your daily life and your sense of self?

Using the lenses of **CULTURE**, **STRUCTURE**, and **POWER**, *Experience Sociology* shows students the significance of sociology for their own lives.

CULTURE, **STRUCTURE**, and **POWER** help students explore sociological theory in ways that go beyond conventional theoretical boundaries.

S P O T L I G H T
on social theory

Symbolic interactionism stresses the role of interpersonal interactions in reproducing culture and social structure. Have you ever been in a situation in which you felt at a disadvantage because you lacked the cultural capital to know what behavior was expected of you?

EXPERIENCE SOCIOLOGY includes a variety of boxed features and in-text learning aids to help students appreciate the range of sociology's insights and their relevance to today's fast-changing social world, and to apply sociology's concepts and theories to their own lives.

BOXED FEATURES

 Sociology in Action boxes highlight the contributions of sociological research to public policy and to the efforts of public interest organizations, social movements, and others to effect social change.

 Sociology Works boxes profile people who studied sociology in college and are now using sociology's insights in diverse work settings. These high-interest stories feature people working in fields such as health care, criminal justice, social work, business, mass media, government, and the military.

 Through a Sociological Lens boxes demonstrate how sociology can provide distinctive insights into contemporary social issues. Students can see how sociological research reveals information that can both surprise and empower them in their everyday lives.

FF **Fast-Forward** boxes illuminate the ever-evolving nature of our social world. These brief, engaging features—illustrated with photographs, advertisements, or other images—show students how change has been a constant feature of social life.

CW **A Changing World** sections conclude each chapter with a look at the influence of changing social conditions on some aspect of the chapter topic. Examples include culture and globalization, increasing inequality in the United States, social structure and privacy, and convergence in gender and sexuality.

IN-TEXT LEARNING AIDS

think **Thinking About** notes help students connect chapter content to their own experience. These brief notes, found at the bottom of text pages, prompt students to consider how the three core concepts of **culture, structure,** and **power** apply to their own lives and views on issues, thus encouraging students to think sociologically.

CCC **Core Concepts Challenge** questions encourage students to apply their sociological imagination to what they are learning. Appearing with selected figures, tables, and photographs, these questions prompt students to apply **culture, structure,** and **power** in thinking about an issue as well as to think critically about the graphic, table, or image.

 Spotlight notes prompt students to consider social theories that are discussed within the text. These notes help students use the three concepts to apply theory to their own lives.

Highlights of the second edition

✔ Indicates revisions based on student heat map data.

CHAPTER 1

- New chapter-opening vignette using Nelson Mandela's life story to illustrate how, in a single lifetime, people working together can change the world in meaningful ways
- New figure to illustrate the dimensions of social theory
- Boxed features revised and updated

CHAPTER 2

- New chapter-opening vignette spotlighting the scientific method through analysis of a recent study on whether teenage troublemakers encourage friends to engage in criminal or delinquent behavior
- Updated data on voting patterns
- New Through a Sociological Lens box, "Correlation, Causation, and Spuriousness"
- New Fast-Forward selection, "Change Research"
- Significantly revised "A Changing World" section, "Technology and Social Research"

CHAPTER 3

- Updated data for maps and figures throughout
- New material explaining taboos
- New discussion on folk culture
- New "A Changing World" section, "Culture and Globalization," featuring the Nigerian film industry

CHAPTER 4

- New chapter-opening vignette showcasing the benefits to college students when there are constraints on the structure of academic programs
- Updated "Through a Sociological Lens" box integrating new material on school violence (Newtown, Connecticut)
- Updated "A Changing World" section, "The Evolving Structure of News Production"
- Updated data throughout

CHAPTER 5

- Comprehensively revised "A Changing World" section, "Money, Power, and Politics," featuring updated data and new discussion on electoral campaign spending
- New figures on campaign contributions and spending

CHAPTER 6

- New section, "Epigenetics: Genes and the Environment"
- Revised Ngram figure on use of the terms *teenage* and *adolescent*
- Updated data and figures throughout

CHAPTER 7

- New chapter-opening vignette looking at the recent change in Yahoo corporate policy regarding telecommuting, to illustrate the importance of social interaction
- Major reorganization of the text sections on networks, groups, and organizations for enhanced flow and clarity ✔
- New Table 7.1: Groups versus Networks: Some Differences
- New "A Changing World" section, "Social Structure and Privacy"
- Updated data throughout

CHAPTER 8

- Extensive new section: "Surveillance and Social Control in the Digital Age"
- Updated data, text, and examples throughout ✔

CHAPTER 9

- Addition on government regulation of corporations
- Addition on inherited wealth
- New/updated discussion of income and wealth inequality
- New and revised figures, tables, and maps on income, job growth, unemployment, poverty throughout
- Updated data on wages, unionization, and tax rates
- Updated discussion of public assistance, noting the 2008–2009 bank bailouts

CHAPTER 10

- Revised chapter-opening vignette related to ongoing debates in the United States over immigration policy and citizenship
- Updated material and data on racial and ethnic groups today
- Updated material on immigration and unauthorized immigration
- Substantially revised section, "Changing Population Trends"

- Revised and reorganized section, "Culture, Structure, and Power: The Nature of Racial and Ethnic Inequality Today" ✔
- New section, "The Death of 'Old Racism': Changing Practices and Attitudes"
- Revised section, "Enduring Inequality"
- Revised section, "The Legacy of Past Discrimination: The Black-White Wealth Gap" ✔
- Revised section on color-blind racism ✔
- Updated data and figures on inequality, racial demographics, and intermarriage

CHAPTER 11
- New section, "Sexuality and the Internet"
- Updated discussion of same-sex marriage ✔
- Additional material on Engels regarding the economic roots of gender stratification
- New and updated data and figures on gender stratification, education, women in government, and same-sex marriage
- Updated data on the gender pay gap
- Updated material on women among executives at *Fortune* 500 companies and women among U.S. political leaders

CHAPTER 12
- Updated Through a Sociological Lens box, "Delaying Adulthood"
- Updated data and figures on marriage, cohabitation, divorce, families, and religious traditions
- Updated discussion of same-sex marriage ✔
- New Sociology in Action box, "Research, Public Policy, and the Law"
- Updated data on interracial and interethnic families, world religions, and religious adherence in the United States

CHAPTER 13
- New section, "Cyberbullying"
- New material on the Common Core Standards Initiative
- Updated "A Changing World" section, "Uncertainty in the Twenty-first-Century Workplace," including a new discussion of precarious work
- Updates to Sociology in Action box, "Challenging the Structure of School Financing"
- Updated discussion of the gender wage gap
- New and revised figures and tables on wages, school enrollment, educational attainment, student debt, and unionization throughout

- Updated data on school segregation, charter schools, and global adult literacy

CHAPTER 14
- New chapter-opening vignette on the phenomenon of the selfie and how it embodies developments that are unique to contemporary media
- Revised section on new media ✔
- Updated discussion of trends in the media industries
- Updated data and figures on the digital divide and news corporations
- Revised discussion of consumer culture and credit card debt among college students
- Revised section on product placement ✔
- Revised Through a Sociological Lens box, "Examining the Commercialization of Childhood"

CHAPTER 15
- Revised discussion of suburban sprawl ✔
- Revised definition of environmental sociology and what makes it a distinctive approach ✔
- Additional discussion of the sociology of health and the social construction of illness
- Updated data on global urban population growth, commuting, and death rates due to poor sanitation

CHAPTER 16
- New chapter-opening vignette on economic insecurity in the contemporary United States, related to factors like military service, corporate actions, and continuing unemployment
- Revised section on the structure of politics ✔
- Fine-tuned definitions of the meaning of the terms *politics* and *government* ✔
- Updated section on the national security state
- New and revised figures, maps, and tables on political parties, campaign spending, voter turnout, lobbying, taxation, and government spending throughout

CHAPTER 17
- New chapter-opening vignette on China's controversial one-child policy and abuses of state power that are connected to it
- Revised Sociology Works box, "Sociology Majors After Graduation"
- New and updated data and figures on globalization, demographics, social change, and same-sex marriage
- Revised Sociology in Action box, "The U.S. Census Bureau"

Teaching and Learning with *Experience Sociology*

TEACHING RESOURCES

Instructor's Manual. The instructor's manual incorporates tips for both new and experienced instructors and includes learning objectives, brief and detailed chapter outlines, chapter summaries, lecture outlines, lecture ideas, and topics for class discussion.

Test Bank. This resource offers 100 multiple-choice and true/false questions for each chapter. McGraw-Hill's computerized EZ Test allows instructors to create customized exams using the publisher-supplied test items or instructors' own questions.

PowerPoint Slides. The PowerPoint slides include bulleted lecture points, figures, and maps. They can be used as is or modified to meet the needs of individual instructors.

 **CREATE**, because customization for your course needs matters. Design your ideal course materials with McGraw-Hill's Create, **www.mcgrawhillcreate.com!** Rearrange or omit chapters, combine material from other sources, upload your syllabus or any other content you have written to make the perfect resource for your students. Register today at **www.mcgrawhillcreate.com,** and get a complimentary review copy in print or electronically.

 **McGraw-Hill Campus** is a new one-stop teaching and learning experience available to users of any learning management system. This institutional service allows faculty and students to enjoy single sign-on (SSO) access to all McGraw-Hill Higher Education materials, including the award-winning McGraw-Hill Connect platform, from directly within the institution's website. With this program enabled, faculty and students will never need to create another account to access McGraw-Hill products and services.

 **Tegrity Campus** is a service that makes class time available all the time by automatically capturing every lecture in a searchable format for students to review. With a simple one-click start-and-stop process, you capture all computer screens and corresponding audio. Students can replay any part of any class with easy-to-use browser-based viewing on a PC or Mac. Help turn all of your students' study time into learning moments immediately supported by your lecture. To learn more about Tegrity, watch a 2-minute demo at **http://tegritycampus.mhhe.com.**

 **CourseSmart** offers thousands of the most commonly adopted textbooks across hundreds of courses from a wide variety of higher education publishers. It is the only place for faculty to review and compare the full text of a textbook online, providing immediate access without the environmental impact of requesting a printed exam copy. At CourseSmart, students can save up to 50% off the cost of a printed book, reduce their impact on the environment, and gain access to powerful web tools for learning, including full text search, notes and highlighting, and email tools for sharing notes among classmates. Learn more at **www.coursesmart.com.**

ACKNOWLEDGMENTS

Writing *Experience Sociology* has been a multiyear journey for us, a journey we could not have completed without the support of many people along the way. We would like to thank Sherith Pankratz, our initial editor at McGraw-Hill, for encouraging us to begin the project in the first place. Thanks to the many folks at McGraw-Hill who have helped us complete the book. In particular, we benefited from the hard work of Rhona Robbin, Sylvia Mallory, and Briana Porco throughout the writing and editing process. We would also like to thank Courtney Austermehle, brand manager; Philip Weaver, marketing manager; Gina Boedeker, managing director for social sciences; and Mike Ryan, VP and general manager, for their support on the project. Susan Trentacosti, our project manager, shepherded the project from manuscript to finished product. Margarite Reynolds and Matthew Backhaus oversaw the project's design and John Leland managed photo research. And thanks to Meghan Campbell and John Brady for overseeing *Experience Sociology*'s wealth of digital resources.

Many thanks to our colleagues who have helped us think about teaching sociology, including Mike Malec and William Gamson at Boston College; Joe Marolla at Virginia Commonwealth University; Steve Lyng at Carthage College; and Eileen Leonard, Bob McAulay, and Marque Miringoff at Vassar College. We appreciate the contributions of our various research assistants, including Meg Burns, Kelly Capehart, Rachel Cerlen, Corrina Regnier, Mollie Sandberg, Jacinthe Sasson-Yenor, and Shawna Seth. More generally, we are grateful to our students, from whom we have learned a great deal about sociology and pedagogy over the past two decades.

Finally, David would like to thank Cecelia Kirkman—again—for everything. William would like to thank his family, Deirdre, Ben, and Nick, for their support, encouragement, and patience throughout the years required to produce this book.

BOARD OF ADVISORS

We would like to thank our board of advisors for their invaluable insights to this project, particularly its digital components.

Curtis Hosier, Indiana University—Purdue University Fort Wayne
Jennifer Jacobson, Yavapai College
Marjorie Jolles, Roosevelt University
Jenny Kosinski, Rock Valley College
Lori Maida, Westchester Community College
Matthew Reynolds, College of Southern Idaho—Twin Falls
LaTasha Sarpy, Bunker Hill Community College
Karrie Snyder, Northwestern University
Rose Suggett, Southeast Community College
Lisa Weinberg, Florida State University

ACADEMIC REVIEWERS

Thanks to the following for their thorough and thoughtful evaluations of various portions and drafts of *Experience Sociology*.

Cawo Abdi, University of Minnesota–Minneapolis
Wesley Abercrombie, Midlands Technical College
Donna Abrams, Georgia Gwinnett College
Doug Adams, University of Arkansas–Fayetteville
Isaac Addai, Lansing Community College
Adansi Amankwaa, Albany State University
Trudy Anderson, Texas A&M–Kingsville
Robert Aponte, Indiana University–Purdue University Indianapolis
David Arizmendi, South Texas College
Bryan Auld, Indiana University—Purdue University Fort Wayne
Robert Baker, Sandhills Community College
Sergio Banda, Fullerton College

Baishakhi Banerjee Taylor, University of Kentucky–Lexington
Nadine Barrett, University of Central Florida
Joshua Bass, Portland State University
Lance Basting, Chippewa Valley Technical College
John Batsie, Parkland College
James Bazan, Central Piedmont Community College
James Becker, Pulaski Tech College
Joseph Beczak, San Diego City College
Janice Bending, University of Cincinnati–Cincinnati
Claudette Bennett, Howard University
Todd E. Bernhardt, Broward College–Central
Terry Besser, Iowa State University
Gary Bittner, York College of Pennsylvania
Amy Blackstone, University of Maine
Michelle Blake, University of Evansville
Carolyn Bond, Boston University
Karyn Boutin, Massasoit Community College
Christophe Bradley, Indiana University–Purdue University Fort Wayne
Judith Brake, Ozarks Technical Community College

John Brenner, York College of Pennsylvania
Helen Brethauer-Gay, Florida A&M University
Daniel Brewster, West Virginia University–Morgantown
David L. Briscoe, University of Arkansas–Little Rock
Rebeca Brittenham, College of Southern Nevada–West Charles
Scott Brooks, University of California–Riverside
Richard Bucher, Baltimore City Community College
Jonathan Bullinger, Camden County College
Mary L. Burns, Michigan State University–East Lansing
Paul Calarco, Hudson Valley Community College
Allison Camelot, Saddleback College
Roberta Campbell, Miami University
Elaine Cannon, El Camino College
Marketa Cawood, Hopkinsville Community College
Edwin Chambless, El Paso Community College–Valle Verde
Gina Chance, Central New Mexico Community College

Nina Chapman, Golden West College

Adrian Cheatwood, University of Texas–San Antonio

Adrian Chevraux-FitzHugh, Sacramento City College

Andrew Cho, Tacoma Community College

Margaret Choka, Pellissippi State Technical Community College

Bridget Christensen, Southeast Community College

Sue Ciriello, Naugatuck Valley Community College

Rodney Clayton, Central Community College–Hastings

Susan Cody, Georgia Perimeter College–Dunwoody

Charles Combs, Sinclair Community College

Ida Cook, University of Central Florida

Lisa Coole, Massasoit Community College

Mary Kay Cordill, Cape Cod Community College

Linda Cornwell, Bowling Green State University

Carolyn Corrado, State University of New York at Albany

Mary Croissant, Front Range Community College–Fort Collins

April Cubbage, Saddleback College

Larry Curiel, Cypress College

Cloyis Daughhetee, Arkansas State University

Robert Scott Davis, Treasure Valley Community College

Rhett Davy, North Central Texas College

Susan Day, Texas State University

Rohan De Silva, Milwaukee Area Technical College–Milwaukee

Kelly Dever, University of Florida at Gainesville

Aimee Dickinson, Lorain County Community College

Nancy Dimonte, Farmingdale State College

Greg Donnenwerth, University of Memphis

Joe Donnermeyer, Ohio State University–Columbus

Brian Donovan, University of Kansas–Lawrence

Sue Dowden, El Camino College

Lilli Downes, Polk State College

Michael Dreiling, University of Oregon

Adam Driscoll, University of North Carolina–Charlotte

Susan Dumais, Louisiana State University

Gianna Durso-Finley, Mercer County Community College

Shelly Dutchin, Western Tech College

Isaac W. Eberstein, Florida State University

Samuel Echevarria-Cruz, Austin Community College–Riverside

Martin Edelstein, Baruch College

Sherwood Edwards, College of Dupage

John Ehle, Jr., NOVA Community College–Annandale

Susan Eichenberger, Seton Hill University

Richard Ellefritz, Oklahoma State University

Jim Elliott, University of Oregon

David Embrick, Loyola University–Chicago

Graves Enck, University of Memphis

Kevin Ervin, Northern Illinois University

Kathryn Feltey, University of Akron

Catherine Felton, Central Piedmont Community College

Leticia Fernandez, University of Texas at El Paso

Richard Fey, Arizona State University

Lauralee Finley, Florida Atlantic University

Kevin Fitzpatrick, University of Alabama at Birmingham

Dona Fletcher, Sinclair Community College

Martha Flores, El Paso Community College–Valle Verde

Tammie Foltz, Des Moines Area Community College–Boone

Murray Fortner, Tarrant County College Northeast

Tony Foster, Lone Star College–Kingwood

John Gannon, College of Southern Nevada–North Las Vegas

Beverly Gartland, Youngstown State University

David Gay, University of Central Florida

Marie L. Germain, City College–Miami

Steve Glennon, Iowa Western Community College–Council Bluffs

Sergio Gomez, Chaffey College

Natasha Gouge, Cape Fear Community College

Kyra Greene, San Diego State University

Mike Greenhouse, Middlesex County College

Sara Grineski, University of Texas at El Paso

Elke Grogg, Ivy Tech Community College of Indiana

Heather Guevara, Portland Community College–Sylvania

Jeffrey Hall, University of Alabama at Birmingham

Bram Hamovitch, Lakeland Community College

Carl Hand, Valdosta State University

Sara Hanna, Oakland Community College–Highland Lakes

Peggy Hargis, Georgia Southern University

Kalynn Heald, Northwest Arkansas Community College

Nina Heckler, University of Alabama at Tuscaloosa

Garrison Henderson, Tarrant County College Southeast

Kimberly Hennessee, Ball State University

Marta T. Henriksen, Central New Mexico Community College

Pablo Hernandez, Lansing Community College

Teresa Hibbert, University of Texas at El Paso

Carmon Weaver Hicks, Ivy Tech Community College of Indiana

Tonya Hilligoss, Sacramento City College

Candace Hinson, Tallahassee Community College

Caroll Hodgson, Rowan-Cabarrus Community College

Donna Holland, Indiana University–Purdue University

Kathleen Holmes, Darton College

Mark Horowitz, University of Texas at Brownsville

Nils Hovik, Lehigh Carbon Community College

Erica Hunter, State University of New York at Albany

Ronald Huskin, Del Mar College

Creed Hyatt, Lehigh Carbon Community College

Peter Iadicola, Indiana University–Purdue University Fort Wayne

Denise Ingram, Mercer County Community College

Michael Itagaki, Fullerton College

Jennifer Jackson, Cincinnati State Technical & Community College

Timothy Jacobs, Naugatuck Valley Community College

Jennifer Jacobson, Yavapai College

Laura Jamison, Parkland College

Randy Jarvis, South Texas College

J. Craig Jenkins, Ohio State University–Columbus

Mark Jepson, University of California–Los Angeles

Dennis Johnson, Craven Community College

Jim Jones, Mississippi State University

Ali Kamali, Missouri Western State University

Irwin Kantor, Middlesex County College

Michael Kaune, Saint Francis College

Henry Keith, Delaware Technical Community College

Margaret Kelly, University of Minnesota–Minneapolis

Paul Ketchum, University of Oklahoma–Norman

Steve Keto, Kent State University

William Kimberlin, Laini County Community College

Brian Klocke, State University of New York at Plattsburgh

James Knapp, Southeastern Oklahoma State University

Michelle Knoles, Cowley County Community College

Jamee Kristen, University of Nebraska–Lincoln

Lorien Lake, University of Arizona

Judy Lasker, Lehigh University

Terina Lathe, Central Piedmont Community College

Jodie Lawston, Depaul University

Rebecca Leichtfuss, Moraine Park Tech College

Jason Leiker, Utah State University

Joe Lengermann, University of Maryland–College Park

Troy Lepper, Colorado State University

David Liu, Harrisburg Area Community College

David Locher, Missouri Southern State University

William Lockhart, McLennan Community College

Nicole Loftus, Saddleback College

Royal Loresco, South Texas College

Joleen Loucks, Kutztown University of Pennsylvania

Michael Loukinen, Northern Michigan University

Bradford Lyman, Baltimore City Community College

Jean Lynch-Brandon, Lansing Community College

Joanna Maata, Pennsylvania State University

Anne MacLellan, Community College of Baltimore County–Catonsville

I. Ross Macmillan, University of Minnesota–Minneapolis

Sherry Mader, Western Technical College

M. Wilbrod Madzura, Normandale Community College

Cheryl Maes, University of Nevado–Reno

Lori Maida, Westchester Community College

Farshad Makek-Ahmadi, Naugatuck Valley Community College

Susan Mann, University of New Orleans

Nick Maroules, Illinois State University

Ronald Matson, Wichita State University

Deborah McCarthy, College of Charleston

Dorothy McCawley, University of Florida

Karen McCue, Central New Mexico Community College

Victor McCullum, Triton College

Marian McWhorter, Houston Community College–Central College

Ronald Meneses, University of Florida

Chadwick L. Menning, Ball State University

Melinda Messineo, Ball State University

Janet Michello, LaGuardia Community College

Harvest Moon, University of Texas at Arlington

Mel Moore, University of Northern Colorado

Marcillino Morales, East Los Angeles College

John Morra, Quinnipiac University

Edward Morris, University of Kentucky–Lexington

Kelly Mosel-Talavera, Texas State University–San Marcos

Brian Moss, Oakland Community College–Highland Lakes

Sepandar Mossadeghi, Palm Beach State College–Eissey Campus

Dan Muhwezi, Bulter Community College

Lynn Newhart, Rockford College

Bruce Nicometo, Northwest Arkansas Community College

Claire Nivens-Blower, Cape Cod Community College

Nelda Nix, Community College of Baltimore County–Essex

Cheryl North, Tarrant County College Northeast

Kwaku Obosue-Mensah, Lorain County Community College

Patricia O'Brien, Elgin Community College

Bob O'Neil, Louisiana State University–Baton Rouge

Jacob Oni, Cape Cod Community College

Robert Orrange, Eastern Michigan University

Diane Owsley, Elizabethtown Community College

Bruce Pabian, Delaware Technical Community College–Stanton

Frank Page, University of Utah–Salt Lake City

Chris Papaleonardos, Ohio State University–Columbus

Caroline Parham, Craven Community College

Kevin Payne, Park University–Parkville

Douglas Peck, Stark State

Lisa Pellerin, Ball State University

Jane Penney, Eastfield College

Narayan Persaud, Florida A&M University

Nancy Pietroforte, Rockland Community College

Peggy Preble, Thomas Nelson Community College

Paul C. Price, Pasadena City College

William Price, North Country Community College

Ariane Prohaska, University of Alabama at Tuscaloosa

Adrian Rapp, Lone Star College–North Harris

Todd Rasner, Hudson Valley Community College

Kent Redding, University of Wisconsin–Milwaukee

Nancy Reeves, Gloucester County College

John Rice, University of North Carolina–Wilmington

Ray Rich, College of Southern Nevada–West Charles

Cecelia Rivers, Northwest Florida State College

Gregg Robinson, Grossmont College

Christine Rodriguez, East Los Angeles College

Fatima Rodriguez, Rutgers University

Robyn Rodriguez, Reedley College

Luis Rodriguez-Abad, University of Texas at Brownsville

Richard Rosell, Westchester Community College

Olga Rowe, Oregon State University

Alan Rudy, Central Michigan University

Amy Ruedisueli, Tidewater Community College

Igor Ryabov, Ohio University–Athens

Charlotte Ryan, University of Massachusetts–Lowell

Ivanka Sabolich, Kent State University

George Saunders, Ball State University

Peter Sawyer, Hudson Valley Community College

David Schall, Milwaukee Area Technical College

Jon Schlenker, University of Maine–Augusta

Rachel Schneider, University of Akron

Andreas Schneider, Texas Tech University

David Schjott, Northwest Florida State College

Sarah Bill Schott, North Central College–Naperville

Terri Schrantz, Tarrant County College

Ron Schultz, Gateway Technical College

Jeff Schulz, Central Community College–Grand Island

Megan Seely, Sierra College

Lystra Seenath, Palm Beach State College–Lake Worth

Barbara Seiter, Raritan Valley Community College

Patricia Seitz, Central New Mexico Community College

Charles Selengut, County College of Morris

Monissa Shackleford, Pensacola Junior College

Robert Shelly, Ohio University–Athens

Anson Shupe, Indiana University–Purdue University Fort Wayne

Denise Shuster, Owens Community College

Edward Silva, El Paso Community College–Valle Verde

Toni Sims, University of Southwestern Louisiana

Amy Slater, MCC–Blue River Community College

Steven Sloan, Gateway Technical College

Michael Smith, Lakeland Community College

Michelle Smith, Southwestern Illinois College

Karrie Snyder, Northwestern University

Tomecia Sobers, Fayetteville Technical Community College

Stephanie Southworth, Clemson University

Ryan Spohn, Kansas State University

Johnnie Spraggins, University of Texas at San Antonio

Dan Stalder, University of Wisconsin–Whitewater

Rachael Stehle, Cuyahoga Community College Western–Parma

Lawrence Stern, Collin County Community College–Plano

Terrence Stewart, Mott College

Michelle Stewart Thomas, Mt. San Antonio College

Jill Stiemsma, Moraine Park Tech College

Beverly Stiles, Midwestern State University

Randolph Ston, Oakland Community College–Auburn Hills

Michael Stupak, Milwaukee Area Technical College

Holly Suarez, University of North Carolina–Charlotte

Rose Suggett, Southeast Community College

Deborah Sullivan, Arizona State University–Tempe

Richard Sweeny, Modesto Junior College

John Szivos, Mount Wachusett Community College

Margaret Taylor, Greenville Technical College

Sara Thompson, Laredo Community College

Ruth Thompson-Miller, Texas A&M University

Bob Transon, Milwaukee Area Technical College

Tim Tuinstra, Kalamazoo Valley Community College

Toby Vance, El Paso Community College–Valle Verde

Melinda Vandervis, Orange Coast College

Steven Vassar, Minnesota State University–Mankato

Ray Von Robertson, Lamar University

Vu-Duc Vuong, De Anza College

Sally Vyain, Ivy Tech Community College of Indiana

Florence Wakoko, Columbus State University

Glenda D. Walden, University of Colorado–Boulder

Marie L. Wallace, Pima Community College–West

Suzan Waller, Franklin University

Gina Walls, Parkland College

Sheryl Walz, Citrus College

Martha Warburton, University of Texas at Brownsville

Elizabeth Watts Warren, Gordon College

Sandra Way, New Mexico State University–Las Cruces

Sharon Wettengel, Tarrant County College Southeast

Shonda Whetstone, Blinn College

Amanda White, St. Louis Community College–Meramec

Debbie White, Citrus College

Gailynn White, Citrus College

Gordon Whitman, Tidewater Community College–Norfolk

Cindy Whitney, Kansas State University, College of Technology & Aviation

Linda Wicks, Stony Brook University

Cleon Wiggins, Kansas City Kansas Community College

Marion Willetts, Illinois State University

L. Sue Williams, Kansas State University

Gerald Williams, Camden County College

Bryan Williamson, Lorain County Community College

Beate Wilson, Western Illinois University

Charles Wilson, Kansas City Kansas Community College

Rowan Wolf, Portland Community College–Sylvania

Amy Wong, San Diego State University

Robert E. Wood, Rutgers University

Peter Wood, Eastern Michigan University

Timothy Woods, Manchester Community College

Diane Wysocki, University of Nebraska–Kearney

Marik Xavier-Brier, Houston Community College

Pat Yeager, Ivy Tech Community College of Indiana–Evansville

Andrew Ziner, Kutztown University of Pennsylvania

John F. Zipp, University of Akron

CONNECT REVIEWERS AND CONTRIBUTORS

The following instructors contributed to Connect Sociology with their thoughtful evaluations, their direct creation, or both:

Marketa Cawood, KCTS Hopkinsville Community College

Sue Ciriello, Naugatuck Valley Community College

Susan Cody, Georgia Perimeter College–Dunwoody

Joe Donnermeyer, Ohio State University–Columbus

Gianna Durso-Finley, Mercer County Community College

Shelly Dutchin, Western Technical College

Isaac W. Eberstein, Florida State University

Samuel Echevarria-Cruz, Austin Community College–Riverside

David Embrick, Loyola University–Chicago

Dona Fletcher, Sinclair Community College

Tammie Foltz, Des Moines Area Community College–Boone

Carmon Weaver Hicks, Ivy Tech Community College of Indiana

Erica Hunter, State University of New York at Albany

William Kimberlin, Laini County Community College

Jamee Kristen, University of Nebraska–Lincoln

Terina Lathe, Central Piedmont Community College

Melinda Messineo, Ball State University

Dan Muhwezi, Butler Community College

Lynn Newhart, Rockford College

Douglas Peck, Stark State College

Sarah Bill Schott, North Central College–Naperville

Megan Seely, Sierra College

Karrie Snyder, Northwestern University

Tomecia Sobers, Fayetteville Technical Community College

Margaret Taylor, Greenville Technical College

Marie L. Wallace, Pima Community College–West

Gerald Williams, Camden County College

Pat Yeager, Ivy Tech Community College of Indiana–Evansville

1

Sociology in a Changing World

looking AHEAD

How can sociology and the sociological perspective help us understand society and our place in it?

How can three of sociology's core concepts—culture, structure, and power— and its diverse theories help us understand ourselves and our world?

How can sociology, which emerged in a period of revolutionary change, help us understand our own rapidly changing world?

The death of former South African president Nelson Mandela in December 2013 brought a staggering global response. More than 90 heads of state were among the tens of thousands who attended the memorial service in Soweto in the pouring rain. The service was a powerful commemoration of a courageous individual's life and also a testament to how much had changed during this one man's lifetime.

Millions of viewers worldwide watched Mandela's memorial service live on television. But when Mandela was born in 1918, television had not even been invented. When he died at age 95, Mandela's native country of South Africa had a democratically elected government and a black president. But Mandela had grown up in a society characterized by apartheid, or legalized racial segregation; blacks could not vote or hold skilled jobs, and they could live only in racially restricted neighborhoods. As a young man, Mandela joined the African National Congress, a movement that challenged the government and its apartheid policies, first through nonviolent protest and later through armed struggle. He was arrested in 1962, convicted of sabotage, and given a life sentence. Released from prison more than 27 years later, he was elected president of South Africa in 1994. Mandela, a vibrant symbol of perseverance and the possibility of social change, helped pave the way for a peaceful transition from a white-dominated apartheid regime to a multiracial government.

Mandela's contemporaries in the United States—your grandparents or great-grandparents— similarly experienced dramatic social change during a single lifetime. Women born before 1920 came into a world that did not permit them to vote. But for decades now, women not only have voted but have done so at a higher rate than men. Many African Americans of Mandela's generation grew up with their own version of apartheid in the South's legal racial segregation that mandated separate schools and separate seating on public transportation until the 1960s. The civil rights movement helped abolish legal segregation, and the idea of separate black and white seats on a bus is hard to imagine today. When Mandela was born, the American labor movement was working to outlaw child labor and establish basic rights such as a minimum wage. Today, the minimum wage and the abolition of child labor are well-established norms.

Mandela's story has a powerful message. It reminds us that in a single lifetime, people working together can help change the world in countless ways.

Social change has long been a topic of interest to sociologists. Sociology originated in the late 1800s, a time of breathtaking change, when Europe and the United States were shifting from a rural agricultural economy to an urban industrial economy. Early sociologists were trying to understand the impact of this and other social changes on how people lived, how they earned a living, and how families were organized.

Today's sociologists are doing much the same thing, except that now they are grappling with contemporary changes related to our global economy, the expansion of media and technology, a rapidly changing population, and enduring cultural conflicts, to name just a few focal points. *Experience Sociology* introduces you to a sociological perspective on these sorts of contemporary developments. Amid continuing shifts in the social landscape, the sociological perspective provides valuable tools for helping you navigate our changing world.

This chapter introduces sociology, its unique perspective, and its early development as a discipline. It examines some of sociology's diverse theories and the core concepts that unite the field, along with a number of key concerns of sociology—indeed, of all of us today. We will see how sociology offers insight into the forces that are shaping our lives and, at the same time, how it helps us recognize our own capacity to bring about change.

A motorcycle-riding Texan, C. Wright Mills wrote a classic description of the sociological perspective called *The Sociological Imagination* (1959) and a series of books focused on social class and power in the United States (1948, 1952, 1956). He taught at Columbia University from 1946 until 1962, when he died of a heart attack at age 45. Mills's critique of the concentration of power in the United States inspired a generation of activists in the 1960s to promote a more inclusive and democratic society, themes that continue to resonate today.

What Is Sociology?

Sociology is *the systematic study of the relationship between individuals and society.* The approach used in sociology can be thought of as a perspective, a way of looking at the world. To take a **sociological perspective** is *to see and understand the connections between individuals and the broader social contexts in which they live.* You can understand your own life—including the forces that have shaped your current daily routines and the options you have in your future—only by considering the broader social contexts within which you live. Your identity (including your race, ethnicity, class, gender, and nationality) as well as the social environment in which you live (including your family, neighborhood, country, culture, and historical period) influence who you are and who you can be. Understanding those connections is at the heart of a sociological perspective.

The Sociological Perspective

Writing in 1959, U.S. sociologist C. Wright Mills provided the best-known description of the sociological perspective (or, as he called it, the *sociological imagination*). According to Mills, "The sociological imagination enables us to grasp history and biography and the relations between the two within a society" (p. 6). In other words, our individual condition (what Mills calls "biography") depends, in part, upon larger forces in society ("history").

Do you live in a prosperous, peaceful society with democratic freedoms or in one where survival is a challenge, violence is a constant threat, and people's basic civil rights are suppressed? Is your mother or father a retail clerk, an auto worker, a school teacher, an engineer, in the military, a business executive, or unemployed? Are you African American, Latino, Asian, white? Are you male, female, or transgendered? Are you gay or straight? Are you from a rural community, the suburbs, or a major city? Were you raised as a Christian, a Jew, a Muslim, a Hindu, or a nonbeliever? Although we often like to think of ourselves as rugged individuals responsible for our own lives, characteristics and circumstances like these influence who we are and the options we have. And as Mills (1959) points out (using the gendered language of his day), as social conditions change, so do the lives of individuals:

> When a society is industrialized, a peasant becomes a worker; a feudal lord is liquidated or becomes a businessman. When classes rise or fall a man is employed or unemployed; when the rate of investment goes up or down, a man takes new heart or goes broke. When wars happen, an insurance salesman becomes a rocket launcher; a store clerk, a radar man; a wife lives alone; a child grows up without a father. Neither the life of an individual nor the history of a society can be understood without understanding both. (p. 3)

We need only consider the economic recession of recent years, the wars in Iraq and Afghanistan, the rapid growth of

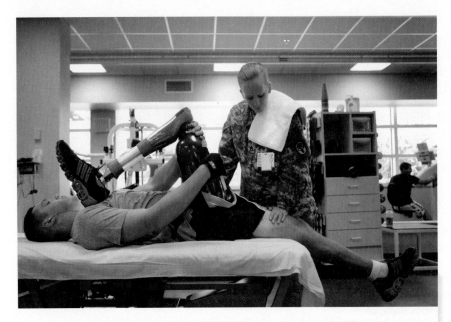

Personal choices—especially deciding to volunteer for the armed forces—contributed to this Iraq war veteran's current situation. But those decisions were made in the context of broader social conditions, including economic pressures to earn a living, a culture of popular patriotism, key decisions made by those with political power, and events that transformed international relations. The connections between individual lives and larger social processes are rarely so explicit or so poignant.

to play the cards you're dealt in life." The card game metaphor makes the point that from the beginning, our options in life have been shaped by social conditions that we did not get to pick ourselves. Such factors can heavily influence the opportunity people have for good health, education, material comfort, and overall well-being.

You don't get to choose the cards you are dealt, but you do get to decide how you will play them. For example, you no doubt decided to go to college with the hope that doing so could positively influence your future. Others may have had the option of attending college but chose not to exercise it. Many more people, of course, never had the option of attending college in the first place; they were dealt a very different hand in life.

The idea that people must play the cards they are dealt in life is consistent with a sociological perspective. But the problem with relying on commonsense folk wisdom to understand the world is that, however insightful it may sometimes be, it can produce a bewildering array of contradictory claims. The maxim about playing the cards you are dealt in life would seem to contradict another popular saying, "Life is what you make of it," which suggests that individuals have total control over their fate. Or perhaps you agree with the maxim, "The apple doesn't fall far from the tree," suggesting that our social origins largely predetermine our character. Without some way of gauging their accuracy, such wildly contradictory claims provide no insight at all.

In addition, an understanding of the world based only on our own individual experience may not be helpful in unfamiliar circumstances. This is especially true in a world in which communications, media, immigration, and international travel are bringing together people of vastly different backgrounds as never before. To operate in such a diverse society we need to understand not only how *we* make sense of the world, but how other people do so as well.

If we are to understand our connection to the social world beyond our own limited experience and be able to sort through competing claims about that world, we need a more systematic way to comprehend the patterns of behavior and the processes that make up social life. We need the discipline of sociology.

technology, and accompanying social developments to see that Mills's observations are as relevant today as they were more than half a century ago.

However, Mills and other sociologists do not argue that people are simply the passive victims of their social circumstances. Rather, as the sociological perspective reveals, interplay exists between the social conditions that shape our lives and the actions we take as individuals. We don't get to choose the conditions under which we live, the opportunities we enjoy, or the barriers we face, but we do have choices about how we respond to those circumstances, both individually and collectively. Deciding to join the military, have children, attend college, or move to another city are among the many individual decisions a person can make that have a major impact on his or her future. Mills himself was a strong advocate for collective action to strengthen democracy and help change the difficult and often unequal conditions that face people in society. That idea, too, is as relevant today as ever.

Sociology and Common Sense

You do not have to be a professional sociologist to look at the world from a sociological perspective. Indeed, many popular expressions reflect a kind of commonsense folk wisdom that assumes a sociological perspective. You have probably heard some version of the expression, "You've got

Sociology as a Discipline

Sociologists combine the sociological perspective with a variety of research methods (discussed in Chapter 2) to study in a systematic way how our actions shape, and are shaped by, broader social forces. Because the sociological perspective can apply to any aspect of people's lives and any social issue,

These children's life chances—their opportunities for good health, education, material comfort, and overall well-being—are significantly influenced by the social environment into which they were born. What differences are evident from these photographs? What elements of your social environment influenced your development?

the discipline of sociology addresses an especially broad array of topics, as we will see throughout this book.

Sociology is one of the *social sciences*, a group of research-based disciplines that gather and evaluate evidence in order to study human society. This focus on human society distinguishes the social sciences from the *natural sciences*, which focus on the physical aspects of nature. In addition to sociology, the social sciences include political science, economics, psychology, and anthropology. Each of these disciplines highlights different aspects of social life.

Take crime, for example. *Political scientists* might study how politicians use the issue of crime in their campaigns. *Economists* might examine the financial impact of crime on society. *Psychologists* might look at the individual features of criminals, perhaps suggesting personality traits associated with certain types of criminal behavior. *Anthropologists* might compare how different societies define crime and respond to it. *Sociologists* emphasize the interrelationship between individuals and larger social forces, as well as the interactions between various social institutions such as government, economy, media, schools, and family. They explore why crime rates vary over time and are often linked to social trends such as changes in the age of the population (since younger people commit crimes at a higher rate than older ones). They examine the role of media in helping shape people's perception of crime and the criminal justice system through both news coverage and entertainment dramas. They examine the effectiveness of government efforts to reduce crime. Such topics illustrate the broad range of sociological research.

Sociologists have many interests, and the discipline as a whole has many areas of specialization, including medical sociology, sociology of the family, sociology of religion, political sociology, the sociology of race and ethnicity, the sociology of work, the sociology of gender, the sociology of media, and the sociology of social movements. As a result, sociology courses can provide a foundation for further study in any of these fields. As the Sociology Works box suggests,

SOCIOLOGY WORKS

The Sociology Major and the Job Market

People, culture, social problems, social change—these fascinating topics help explain why students often enjoy sociology. However, practical concern about the future might lead some to ask, "What can I *do* with a degree in sociology?"

The answer is, "Plenty." By majoring in sociology you not only learn to better understand yourself and your world, but you also develop important skills that can prepare you for entry-level positions in a variety of employment settings, including business, education, social services, health care, government, media, and criminal justice. Sociology can also be an excellent choice for students who plan to go on to graduate school.

Here are four key advantages of majoring in sociology:

1. *A sociology degree is flexible.* Because sociology can be applied to virtually any aspect of social life, you can major in sociology with an eye toward your own particular interests. For example, if you are interested in health and medicine, you can take a course in medical sociology; if you are interested in social work, you can take courses related to the social problems you wish to address or the populations you wish to serve. Sociology can help you understand the issues related to your field of interest.

2. *Sociology focuses on the critical use of information.* As part of a liberal arts education, a sociology degree prepares you to find, understand, analyze, use, and communicate information. These fundamental critical-thinking skills apply to an array of work settings and will not become obsolete; they are highly valuable in today's rapidly changing, information-based job market. Since most people change jobs—and even careers—during their lives, mastering such information-based skills is crucial for success. The ability to work with social science data found in government reports, marketing surveys, and other information sources is particularly important.

3. *Sociology provides insights into diversity.* Success in many fields of employment requires understanding people from different backgrounds. Sociology majors have an advantage in understanding diversity. As a result, they are more likely to work effectively in multicultural workplaces such as schools, hospitals, and businesses as well as in any field in which the players may be from diverse social backgrounds.

4. *Sociology explores the source of social problems.* Are you interested in a field that addresses social problems, such as social work, criminal justice, or health care? Do you plan to work with community organizations, international aid agencies, or social movements to bring about social change? If so, studying sociology can be particularly relevant. By focusing on the relationship between individuals and their social context, sociology helps you understand the roots of social problems.

> Majoring in sociology allows you to study a subject area that interests you *and* helps you prepare for your future.

The Sociology Works boxes throughout this book highlight how former sociology students are using the insights of sociology in a variety of fields. If you are considering majoring in sociology, talk with your instructor, who can tell you about the programs available at your school.

think about it

1. *Do you have any tentative ideas about the kind of work you'd like to do when you complete school? What kinds of classes do you think will help you prepare for the future? Why?*

2. *Take a look at your school's course listings. Do you see any sociology courses that you think you may want to take? What interests you about the topics covered in these courses?*

Sociology majors in many occupations have made contributions to their professional fields. A few well-known majors have had an impact across society. Pictured here, from left to right, are former U.S. president Ronald Reagan, civil rights leader Martin Luther King Jr., First Lady Michelle Obama, Hall of Fame quarterback and broadcaster Troy Aikman, and actor Kal Penn.

the study of sociology can also provide valuable skills for many careers, including some that may seem completely unrelated to sociology itself.

Sociology's Historical and Social Context

Imagine a society in which scientific discoveries reveal more and more about the world, political unrest sparks calls for social change, and economic crises and new technologies transform daily life. You might suspect this was a description of today's United States, but similar upheavals disturbed Europe in the 1800s, which is where and when the formal discipline of sociology first emerged. To better understand the origins of the discipline, we need to consider that historical and social context.

The Rise of Modernity

In the 1700s, European society entered a new historical era, **modernity,** *characterized by the growth of democracy and personal freedom, increased reliance on reason and science to explain the natural and social worlds, and a shift toward an urban industrial economy.* Earlier, during the Middle Ages (roughly 400–1400), religious explanations of the natural and social worlds dominated intellectual life, the land-owning aristocracy and clerical elite dominated political life, and the economy rested on a rural, agricultural base. (Our romanticized images of kings in castles and knights in battle come from this period.) During the transitional Renaissance and Early Modern periods (from roughly the 1400s to the 1600s), scholars laid the foundation of modern science with pioneering works in astronomy, anatomy, and other fields of knowledge; uprisings challenged traditional political authority; and technological advances improved agricultural production.

The rise of modernity in the eighteenth and nineteenth centuries was marked by revolutionary change (Table 1.1). Early sociologists sought to understand the dramatic shifts they were witnessing and to suggest what might be done to deal with the social problems that resulted from them.

Cultural Revolution: Science and the Enlightenment

During the Middle Ages the Church and its clergy dominated European intellectual life, controlling the era's limited number of books, libraries, and schools. Because religious doctrine formed the basis for acceptable social thought, heretics—those who held beliefs contrary to Church teaching—were often persecuted and even killed for questioning the accepted order. This intellectual climate was not hospitable to the open and free inquiry required for **science,** which *uses logic and the systematic collection of evidence to support knowledge claims.*

The dominance of the Church slowly eroded, however, as scientific research exposed the shortcomings of religious explanations of the natural world. For example, proof that the earth orbited the sun contradicted Church doctrine that the earth was at the center of the universe. Writers and philosophers seized on these advances in the natural sciences to promote the *Enlightenment,* an eighteenth-century intellectual movement that combined a belief in individual freedom and respect for individual rights with the calculated logic of the natural sciences. These Enlightenment thinkers, who were among the first intellectuals independent of the Church, argued that neither the physical nor the social world should be taken on faith. Instead, both should be open to questioning and examined through reason; claims to knowledge should be subject to testing through the collection of evidence, and explanations should be based in natural causes and events. German philosopher Immanuel Kant summed up this revolutionary way of thinking in the motto "Dare to know" ([1784] 1999). This new emphasis on reason and science created the cultural conditions needed for the emergence of sociology.

Political Revolution: The Rise of Democracy

Enlightenment thinkers believed that the open debate of ideas would promote tolerance, individual rights, equality, and democracy. They suggested that applying reason and science to questions of social significance would inevitably advance individual rights and freedom. Enlightenment

| TABLE 1.1 | SOCIOLOGY AND REVOLUTION |

SOCIOLOGY AROSE IN THE CONTEXT OF REVOLUTIONARY CHANGE

Cultural Revolution	Political Revolution	Economic and Social Revolution
The declining influence of religion	Declining power of monarchies; American and French revolutions	Decline of agricultural life; industrialization and rise of consumer society
The rise of scientific thought		
The Age of Enlightenment	Uprisings of 1848	Capitalism
	Growth in democracy and individual rights	Urbanization

The rise of modernity introduced rapid social change. Work life shifted from fields to factories. Home and community life was transformed as people moved from small rural villages to rapidly expanding urban centers. What effect do you think the shift from rural village life based on farming to urban life based on wage labor had on family life?

ideas provided the intellectual basis for both the American (1775–1783) and French (1789–1799) revolutions, as well as for a series of uprisings that swept through Europe in 1848, challenging traditional rulers and promoting democratic ideals. These revolutions stimulated much interest in achieving a more equal society and improved living conditions, but they provoked condemnation from conservatives who saw them as a threat to stability, traditional values, and social order. Thus controversies about the nature and desirability of social order versus social change were among the first topics addressed by early sociologists.

Economic and Social Revolution: Industrial Capitalism and Urbanization

The term *Industrial Revolution* refers to a collection of major developments that transformed rural agricultural societies into urban industrial societies. This process began in Great Britain and spread through Europe and the United States in the nineteenth century.

The practical application of scientific developments, such as the creation of the steam engine, paved the way for **industrialization,** *the use of large-scale machinery for the mass manufacture of consumer goods.* Industrialization required a major investment in factories and mills with complex machinery—such as mechanized looms—at a cost that was often beyond the reach of a single owner. Thus industrialization became linked to the rise of *capitalists,* people who pursued profits by investing in and owning businesses. Mass manufacturing relied on a new type of relationship between workers and owners in which the workers sold their labor for a wage. They used their wages to buy food, clothing, and shelter, unlike rural peasants who produced many of their own

material goods and met their basic needs by farming. The result was the birth of both wage labor and *consumerism,* a way of life that depends on the purchase and use of commercial goods and services. These developments fueled the rapid expansion of *capitalism,* an economic system in which the machinery used for production is owned privately, workers are paid a wage, and markets facilitate the exchange of goods and services.

Economic changes fueled changes in social life. An agrarian economy requires farmers to work and live in rural areas. An industrial economy requires workers to congregate near centralized sites of production. Large-scale mass manufacturing operations were housed in factories and mills, often located along riverbanks to harness water power. As the Industrial Revolution took hold, many people left their rural homes and traveled to newly emerging cities for jobs they hoped would mean a better life. This migration contributed to **urbanization,** *the growth of cities.* Before 1800, more than 90 percent of Europeans lived in rural areas; by the 1890s, more than half lived in cities.

Urban life dramatically changed how people lived. In the agricultural economy of the Middle Ages, peasants worked the fields and lived in tiny rural villages among people mostly like themselves. Children could expect to grow up and live in the village they were born in and to do the same sort of work their parents and grandparents did. In contrast, the modern industrial economy required wage laborers to work the machinery in the factories of rapidly expanding cities. These bustling cities featured considerable diversity and rapid social change, some of which contributed to growing social problems.

Early industrial capitalism was highly productive, but it also created great inequalities, generating tremendous profits for a few wealthy owners from the labor of many overworked and underpaid workers. Disease (linked to poor sanitation), overcrowded and unsafe housing, inadequate transportation, and crime plagued the rapidly growing cities. Staggering inequality and growing social problems caused great concern among political and social thinkers, inspiring calls for reform and igniting revolutionary movements.

The rise of modernity produced rapid and immediately visible changes that showed traditional ways of life were not inevitable; the fate of individuals was tied to broader social changes beyond their control; and human action could transform the world through new ideas, political reform, and technological innovation. Faced with the challenge of understanding these dramatic transformations, social thinkers began applying reason and scientific techniques to study social life systematically and to suggest ways that society might be improved. The resulting ideas became the foundation of sociology.

Foundations of Sociological Thought

Sociology today has its roots in the ideas developed by early sociologists more than a century ago. Some of these thinkers asked profound questions of enduring relevance and are still widely read (Calhoun 2012; Ritzer and Stepnisky 2013). Their work on the rapidly changing world of the late eighteenth and early nineteenth centuries continues to provide insight into our own social world today.

Defining the Terrain of Sociology: Comte and Spencer

Auguste Comte (1798–1857) and Herbert Spencer (1820–1903) helped establish the idea that the social world could be the subject of systematic, scientific investigation.

AUGUSTE COMTE: STABILITY AND CHANGE   Auguste Comte, a French intellectual with wide-ranging interests, coined the term *sociology* in the early nineteenth century. Comte sought to establish sociology as a rigorous science of society—modeled on the natural sciences—that would identify the laws that govern human behavior.

At the core of Comte's new field of study were two fundamental questions about social life: "How and why do societies change?" (social dynamics) and "What is the basis of social stability at a specific historical moment?"

(social statics). He was interested in how society had developed from humanity's earliest small-scale bands of hunters and gatherers to his own nineteenth-century European society. He theorized that throughout history societies progressed in a straight line through several stages: the theological (ruled by religion), the metaphysical (ruled by philosophy), and the positivist (ruled by science). For Comte, **positivism,** *a belief that accurate knowledge must be based on the scientific method*, enabled a deeper understanding of human life and was the key to solving persistent social problems.

Comte's efforts to build a science of society were crude by today's standards. Few of his ideas have withstood the test of time, but the focus of his interest—the nature of social stability and social change—continues to be a major concern in sociology.

HERBERT SPENCER: SOCIETY AS A SOCIAL ORGANISM   The British intellectual Herbert Spencer was another early adopter of the term *sociology*. Taking a cue from the biological sciences, Spencer argued that society is a "social organism," much like a human organism. He theorized that, like its biological equivalent, society is made up of separate parts, each with a unique function, that work together to sustain the entire organism. Thus Spencer's theory emphasized the overall structure of society, the functions served by the various elements of society, and the interactions among these elements. Spencer also theorized that when societies evolve, their component parts—and the functions they serve—change as well.

Spencer believed that society progresses as it evolves. Therefore, evolution should be allowed to take place without interference from government. Rather than intervene with reforms in the face of the growing inequality created by unregulated industrial capitalism, Spencer believed in the "survival of the fittest," a phrase he devised before Charles Darwin's work on natural selection and the theory of evolution was published. Spencer's application of the survival of the fittest to human society is today known as *social Darwinism*. Spencer later recanted some of his more extreme views, but in recent years, those who wish to minimize the role of government in social and economic affairs have revived some of Spencer's ideas.

The Key Founders: Marx, Durkheim, and Weber

Spencer and Comte helped define the terrain of sociology in its earliest years. But the thinkers who are widely seen as the founders of sociology and who set the agenda for the next century of sociological theory were Karl Marx, Emile Durkheim, and Max Weber.

	Karl Marx	**Emile Durkheim**	**Max Weber**
Biography	1818–1883	1858–1917	1864–1920
	German	French	German
	Writer and activist	Academic	Academic
Key issues and key work	The nature of capitalism	The nature of social solidarity	Decline of tradition
	Conflict and inequality	Shared values and morals	Rationalization of society
	Capital	*Suicide*	*The Protestant Ethic and the Spirit of Capitalism*

KARL MARX: THE EFFECTS OF CAPITALISM

The German-born Karl Marx (1818–1883) is best known as a revolutionary thinker who advocated radical change to advance the interests of workers. Marx combined writing with political activism, and much of his life was spent escaping political repression. Because of his writings, Marx was expelled from France (twice!) and Belgium. In Germany he was arrested, tried, acquitted, and also expelled. Finally, in 1849 he went to London, where he spent the rest of his life in exile. He lived in poverty while he wrote his greatest works, including *Capital*, his comprehensive analysis of the history and dynamics of capitalism.

Marx recognized that industrial capitalism was remarkably productive and thus capable of doing away with hunger and poverty for all. But instead, industrial capitalism was used to produce huge fortunes for a few owners, while leaving workers to labor in dangerous conditions and often live in poverty. In much of his work, Marx sought to explain how and why so much wealth and productivity could coexist with such widespread poverty and misery.

For Marx, the answer could be found in the relationship between capitalists, who owned the means of production, and workers (the proletariat), who sold their labor power to the capitalists. The dynamics of capitalism, said Marx, encouraged owners to pay the lowest wages possible because lower labor costs mean higher profits. This dynamic explained the simultaneous creation of enormous fortunes and devastating poverty.

Capitalists accumulated great wealth precisely because they were able to exploit the workers who toiled in their factories. This wealth gave owners great power, which they used to control governments and cultural institutions (Marx [1867] 1976).

To Marx, conflict between owners and workers was an inevitable feature of capitalism. As a result, he argued that capitalism—like earlier economic forms based on inequality—had within it the seeds of its own destruction. He theorized that the exploitation of workers would eventually become so extreme that wage laborers would rise up and overthrow the capitalist system. In its place, they would adopt *socialism*, a system in which ownership of the major means of production—such as factories, utilities, and railways—is in public, rather than private, hands, and government directs the use of the productive forces of industry for the public good. The goal of socialism would be a society without the extreme inequalities that characterized capitalism. (We explore the nature of capitalism and socialism more closely in Chapter 16.)

Marx's analysis of industrial capitalism was insightful in specifying the connection between wealth and poverty. He accurately predicted that the search for cheap labor would lead to the expansion of capitalism around the globe. He also correctly predicted the growth of labor movements demanding an end to unregulated capitalism. But he failed to appreciate the ability of capitalism to accommodate reform or the important role markets play in stimulating innovation and efficiency. The revolutionary worker movements Marx supported in recently industrialized countries like Great Britain, France, and Germany ultimately reformed, rather than overthrew, capitalism. Meanwhile, the socialist revolutions that did occur, most notably in Russia and China, took place in primarily agricultural societies that did not have the capacity to produce an abundance of material goods. Even though the brutal totalitarian states that emerged after these revolutions invoked Marx's name in their official ideology, they bore almost no resemblance to the humanist egalitarian vision that Marx had promoted.

Beyond the specific analysis of capitalism, Marx's work highlighted a core concept in sociology: in this case, economic power and its role in enforcing inequality. Marx argued that economic power could be used to influence other aspects of social life, including government and cultural institutions, such as schools and the media. Marx's work also stressed the interplay between structure and action that is at the heart of the sociological perspective. "Men make their own history," he wrote, "but they do not make it just as they please; they do not make it under circumstances chosen by themselves, but under circumstances directly found, given and transmitted from the past" (Marx [1852] 1978, 595).

The issues Marx explored continue to be important today. Questions about the nature and direction of our economy are among the most significant ones addressed by sociologists. For example, how has globalization changed our economy? How are the most recent economic crises linked to the dynamics of capitalism? How has the nature of work been changing? How have the labor movement and social welfare programs—both examples of attempts to moderate the excesses of capitalism—affected the lives of workers?

EMILE DURKHEIM: SOCIAL SOLIDARITY

Emile Durkheim (1858–1917), who lived a generation after Marx, was also concerned with understanding social change in the modern world, but Durkheim's life could hardly have been more different from Marx's. The descendant of a long line of rabbinical scholars in France, Durkheim studied to be a rabbi but rejected religion in his teens and became agnostic, believing there was no way to know whether or not God existed. However, he retained a lifelong interest both in the role of religion in social life and in the scientific study of morality.

Durkheim is perhaps the single individual most responsible for establishing sociology as an academic discipline. He

held the first academic position in sociology; wrote a book laying out the methods of the discipline, *The Rules of Sociological Method* (Durkheim [1895] 1982); and established a well-respected academic journal devoted to the new field.

Like many social thinkers who witness dramatic change, Durkheim was concerned with how to maintain social order. He was particularly interested in the question of **social solidarity,** *the collective bonds that connect individuals.* At the core of his theory was the proposition that society is held together by shared cultural values. As we explore in more detail in Chapter 3, cultural *norms,* or shared expectations about behavior associated with a society's values and morals, are promoted informally through custom and tradition and are spelled out more systematically in laws. When internalized by individuals, shared values and morals become the foundation for social solidarity.

Durkheim observed that traditional agricultural societies were often tight-knit communities. They shared social bonds across generations because people did the same sort of work, shared a common religion, and followed similar customs. These similar experiences resulted in *mechanical solidarity*—social cohesion based on shared experience and a common identity with limited individuality. As European societies grew and became urbanized and industrialized, however, people increasingly differed from one another. A more complex economy required an increasing **division of labor,** in which *people specialize in different tasks, each requiring specific skills.* As cities developed, a diverse array of people coexisted, often with different religions and cultural traditions. Given this increasing social complexity and diversity, how could social solidarity be maintained?

Durkheim's answer was *organic solidarity*, a new form of social cohesion, characteristic of modern industrial societies, that is based on interdependence. In the tradition of Spencer's "social organism," Durkheim argued that the social glue that holds together modern societies mirrors the way living organisms depend on multiple, specialized components operating in unison. Social cohesion is possible because we are dependent on one another. With its increased division of labor, modern urban industrialized society requires doctors, construction workers, sales clerks, police officers, factory workers, janitors, and thousands of other specialists to keep operating. Durkheim's theory helped explain why rapid growth and social differentiation in European societies did not lead to the breakdown of social solidarity, but instead produced a new and, Durkheim thought, even stronger form of solidarity that would

Explaining the Social Basis of Suicide

Why do people intentionally kill themselves? At first glance, suicide seems to be the ultimate example of a private individual act, best explained by psychologists, not sociologists. But sociologist Emile Durkheim broke new ground: he made suicide the subject of the first sociological study to use large-scale data analysis. After examining official government records of suicide cases, Durkheim theorized that certain groups are more or less likely to commit suicide because of their relationship to society. This was a fundamental sociological insight.

Durkheim's study, *Suicide,* showed that a sociological perspective could help explain how individuals are affected by the quality of their relationship with larger social groups, even to the extent of taking their own lives. His research revealed, for example, that unmarried adults had higher rates of suicide than married adults, and Protestants had higher rates than Catholics or Jews. Durkheim explained these differences through an analysis of social *integration,* the strength of social ties that allow people to feel they belong to a group, and social *regulation,* the strength of social norms that control people's behavior. Too much or too little of either would increase the likelihood of suicide. Thus Durkheim identified four types of suicide—egoistic, anomic, altruistic, and fatalistic.

Egoistic suicides result from too little social integration and are committed by people who feel isolated and detached from society. For example, married couples are likely to have a strong bond with one another, whereas divorced, widowed, and unmarried people are more likely to lack a strong social connection; thus suicide rates among these latter groups are higher. Protestants lack the intense communal rituals associated with Catholicism and Judaism, which helps explain their higher rates of suicide. At the other extreme, *altruistic* suicides result from too much social integration, leading individuals to sacrifice themselves for the sake of the collective. Consider, for example, the Japanese kamikaze pilots who volunteered to fly suicide missions for their country during World War II.

The absence of regulation in the form of social norms and boundaries is also associated with higher suicide rates. *Anomic* suicide often results from a sudden and dramatic change in the level of social regulation, which leaves the individual without clear rules about how to adapt. These changes can be negative, such as with the death of a spouse or the loss of a job. Ironically, the changes can also be positive, as when entertainers become "overnight successes" and suddenly have access to endless amounts of money and attention. The self-destructive behavior and suicides of many celebrities, such as musician Kurt Cobain and actor and reality television star Gia Marie Allemand, fit into this category. Conversely, too much regulation can result in *fatalistic* suicide, as in the case of slaves, prisoners, or invalids who see no hope or way to escape their desperate conditions.

Today, the issue of suicide remains a poignant one, and Durkheim's work remains a touchstone. News outlets have been filled with stories about the alarmingly high suicide rate among returning U.S. veterans. In 2013, medical researchers launched a suicide prevention study that monitors Facebook profile content and Twitter posts of veterans who have volunteered to share their social media activity, with the aim of providing clinicians with real-time assessments of risk factors for suicide and other dangerous behaviors. The study's name? The Durkheim Project.

Suicide and Social Integration

	Too Little	Too Much
Integration	Egoistic	Altruistic
Regulation	Anomic	Fatalistic

think about it

1. *Using Durkheim's insights about suicide, consider which of the four types of suicide seems to best apply to suicide bombers who act to advance a cause. Explain your reasoning.*

2. *Based on Durkheim's analysis, what positive steps could be taken to help reduce the risk of suicide for any particular individual?*

permit a balance between individuality and a commitment to the group.

Durkheim's work highlights the interplay between social structure and cultural values, especially as they relate to social solidarity. Much of Durkheim's sociological work builds upon this central concern with social solidarity. Indeed in *Suicide,* one of his most influential works and one of the first to show the potential of the sociological perspective combined with systematic research, Durkheim argued that suicide rates could be explained by the strength of the social ties people have with larger social groups (Durkheim [1897] 1951). (See the Through a Sociological Lens box.)

Durkheim also argued that crime and punishment are fundamentally about solidarity (see Chapter 8). Crimes, for Durkheim, are acts that offend the **collective conscience,** or *shared values of a society.* Punishment serves as a means to reinforce social solidarity in the face of such antisocial actions. Without the moral constraints provided by the collective conscience, Durkheim argued, people—and society as a whole—would descend into a chaotic state of **anomie,** or *normlessness, without moral guidance.*

Today, close to a century later, people are still debating the proper role of values and religion in public and private life. How might Durkheim's ideas help explain the resurgence of traditional religious belief? Can the increasing diversity of our society serve as a source of strength, rather than division? How can people maintain healthy social ties in a world where they regularly move from one community to another? How can we affirm people's individuality while maintaining a sense of common identity? As sociologists investigate such twenty-first-century questions, Durkheim's theories continue to be relevant.

MAX WEBER: THE PROTESTANT ETHIC AND THE RATIONALIZATION OF MODERN LIFE

Like Durkheim, German theorist Max Weber (pronounced "VAY-ber") (1864–1920) was also trying to make sense of the shift from traditional to modern society. The son of a high-ranking government bureaucrat, Weber took a series of university positions as a young man, carried out major research projects, and served as a consultant for government agencies. By his mid-thirties, Weber was in a state of exhaustion and suffered a nervous breakdown that left him incapacitated for nearly seven years. When he was able to return to his writing full time, Weber produced his best-known work, *The Protestant Ethic and the Spirit of Capitalism* (Weber [1905] 1958).

In *The Protestant Ethic,* Weber argued that culture—in the form of Protestantism—had helped promote the early development of capitalism in northern Europe. Traditionally, the Catholic Church had encouraged the rejection of worldly affairs and wealth, promising everlasting life to those who were faithful and participated in the Church's defining rituals such as baptism and communion. However, after the Protestant Reformation, some sects—particularly Calvinists—rejected this approach to salvation and instead maintained that people's fate in the afterlife was predetermined before birth and could not be changed by actions they took on earth. But how could a person know whether he or she was going to heaven or hell? Some believers thought that wealth, accumulated through diligent work, was a sign of God's favor, indicating likely salvation. This cultural belief encouraged hard work, investment, and the accumulation of wealth—the essential requirements for success in a capitalist economy. Marx had focused on the economy's role in influencing other aspects of social life—including culture. With *The Protestant Ethic and the Spirit of Capitalism,* Weber argued that cultural beliefs could influence economic development.

As *The Protestant Ethic* illustrates, Weber sometimes tried to understand social action by viewing it from the perspective of the actor, an approach known by the German word *verstehen,* which means "understanding." Understanding why someone behaves the way he or she does also provides insight into the broader culture in which the action is taking place. As we will see, this approach was an important precursor to later sociological theory that focused precisely on how people make meaning of the social world.

Weber also contributed to sociological theory through his effort to explain the shift from traditional to rational action. One of his central theoretical propositions was that, in earlier societies, *tradition*—beliefs and customs often charged with emotional significance that are passed on from generation to generation—primarily influenced the actions of people. However, in newly industrialized capitalist societies, *rationality*—the use of reason and logical calculation to achieve a goal as efficiently as possible—was much more likely to influence people's actions.

Weber argued that the **rationalization of society**—*the long-term historical process by which rationality replaced tradition as the basis for organizing social and economic life*—propelled the social change of his day. The influence of rationalization went beyond individual human action to include broader social institutions. For example, Weber argued that whereas rulers had previously claimed authority based solely on their claim to descent from previous rulers, the authority of government officials now rests increasingly on such rational-legal foundations as elections or specific training and certification. In addition, Weber argued that the principle of rationality was responsible for the formation of bureaucracies within large organizations—government agencies, political parties, industrial companies—that manage economic and political life.

Weber could see that rationalization might be productive for society, since it focused on specifying procedures, training officials, and pursuing efficiency. But he also saw that as rationalization permeated all aspects of social life it would create cold and impersonal societies. Weber believed that bureaucracy was self-perpetuating and becoming the dominant type of social organization. He worried it would constrain human action and imprison us in an "iron cage of bureaucracy."

Ultimately, Weber feared that in modern society humans could engage in meaningful action only in large organizations, in which they were allotted narrowly defined tasks and sacrificed their personal goals to the impersonal goals of the whole. And although he agreed with much of Marx's critique of industrial capitalism, Weber's theory of rationalization led him to predict that postcapitalist societies would not produce the kind of egalitarian future that Marx predicted, but would instead be even more highly rationalized, with more layers of bureaucracy. In this way, Weber was perhaps the most prophetic of the three major founders of sociology. He did not share in the pure optimism for science and rational thought that emerged from the Enlightenment. Instead, he saw the early signs of a dark side to rationality that has now become a cautionary element of contemporary sociological thought.

Weber's sociological theory applies to a wide range of contemporary concerns. Rationalization continues to pervade our lives at home, school, and work in a variety of ways. Do the large lecture halls of the large university and the even larger online courses represent the rationalization of higher education? How do the bureaucracies of governments and corporations assist in—and interfere with—the work of those organizations? Are such bureaucracies a threat to our privacy and freedom? Weber gives us valuable tools for analyzing the role of rational thought and practice in many areas of our lives.

forceful critique of the failure of the United States to live up to its democratic promise in its treatment of both slaves and women. At this time, she also wrote about the methods of social research in *How to Observe Morals and Manners* ([1838] 2009). Finally, Martineau made an important contribution to sociology by translating the work of Auguste Comte for English-speaking audiences.

Recovered Voices: Harriet Martineau, W.E.B. Du Bois, Jane Addams

Because of the prevailing discriminatory attitudes toward women and racial minorities during the early years of sociology, a variety of social thinkers were excluded from or marginalized in the academic world. Instead of writing for a strictly academic audience, they wrote for popular publications, authored novels, and spoke out as activists advocating social change. In many ways, they were ahead of their time. Although often at the margins of academic sociology while they were alive, these thinkers are now appreciated more widely for the contributions they made to our understanding of social life. Among these voices are Harriet Martineau, W.E.B. Du Bois, and Jane Addams.

HARRIET MARTINEAU: GENDER DISCRIMINATION
Many consider Harriet Martineau (1802–1876), born into an affluent English family, to be the first female sociologist. Her work delved into issues of gender discrimination and slavery that many of the white male sociologists of her time had largely ignored. She also agitated for women's suffrage and the expansion of women's rights in England.

Self-taught and—like other women at the time—excluded from an academic appointment, Martineau began by writing magazine articles and then a series of books on economics and politics that were geared toward the general public rather than an academic audience. Her books were highly successful, making her independently wealthy as well as a literary celebrity. After traveling in the United States for two years, she wrote two books based on her observations, most notably *Society in America* (Martineau [1837] 2009), a

W.E.B. DU BOIS: RACIAL INEQUALITY
W.E.B. Du Bois (pronounced "doo-BOYS") (1868–1963) made important contributions to sociology with his groundbreaking research on race in America as well as with his efforts to promote racial justice. Du Bois, a descendant of African, French, and Dutch ancestors, came from a comfortable middle-class Massachusetts family that provided him with a solid early education and insulated him from the worst effects of racism. When he traveled south to Nashville to study at Fisk University in the 1880s, however, he encountered a rigidly segregated world in which African Americans were frequently the targets of beatings and lynchings. This injustice strengthened his interest in race as a subject of sociological study. In 1895, Du Bois became the first African American to obtain a Ph.D. from Harvard University. He went on to teach sociology and to write a series of studies that elevated race to a place of prominence in sociology. Du Bois published the first sociological study of a black community, *The Philadelphia Negro* ([1899] 1996), followed by the widely read *The Souls of Black Folk* ([1903] 2005). Both works explored the complexity of race relations in turn-of-the-century American society.

Throughout his life, Du Bois combined scholarship with activism. He played an important role in the founding of the National Association for the Advancement of Colored People (NAACP), arguably the leading civil rights organization of the twentieth century. He founded—and for a quarter century edited—the NAACP's influential magazine, *The Crisis*, which is still published today (thecrisismagazine.com). He also nurtured efforts to promote unity among people of African descent worldwide. As an agent of change, he faced opposition from powerful forces. During the Cold War anticommunist hysteria of the 1950s, the U.S. Justice Department accused Du Bois of being an agent of the Soviet Union because of his peace activism and promotion of nuclear disarmament. Although he was acquitted, the FBI continued to harass him and the government revoked his passport. Eventually, he was allowed to travel abroad and he moved to Ghana, where he became a citizen. He died there at the age of 95 on August 27, 1963, the day before the civil rights march on Washington,

Harriet Martineau

W.E.B. Du Bois, as portrayed on a U.S. postage stamp honoring his social activism

Jane Addams with some of the youngsters who frequented Hull House

Biography	1802–1876	1868–1963	1860–1935
	English	American	American
	Writer and activist	Scholar and activist	Scholar and activist
Key issues and work	Gender, slavery, and discrimination	Race and discrimination	Urban social problems
		NAACP cofounder	Hull House founder
	Society in America	*The Philadelphia Negro; The Souls of Black Folk; The Crisis* magazine	*Hull House Maps and Papers*

D.C., where Martin Luther King Jr. gave his famous "I Have a Dream" speech.

JANE ADDAMS: URBAN SOCIAL PROBLEMS

Jane Addams (1860–1935) is best known as a social reformer and the founder of Hull House, which provided a wide range of social services in the poor immigrant communities of Chicago and served as a model for later similar establishments, known as settlement houses, in other cities. Addams was the first American woman to win the Nobel Peace Prize, awarded to her in 1931 for her long-standing work in building an international women's coalition to promote peace and prevent war. But Addams also made an important contribution to the development of sociology. Her social reform work and her research on social life on the south side of Chicago had a significant influence on the development of urban sociology at the University of Chicago, the home of the first sociology department in the United States.

However, unlike some University of Chicago sociologists, who limited their work to understanding urban life, Addams believed that social theory and research should be linked to action promoting social change. Working to address social problems enabled her to contribute to social reform while developing and testing theories about how society worked. In

doing so, she often challenged those in power, advocating for the poor and others at the margins of society.

In *Hull House Maps and Papers* ([1895] 2007), Addams chronicled life in the immigrant communities around Hull House, producing data that were used to promote reform. In *Democracy and Social Ethics* ([1902] 2002), she linked democracy with diversity, explaining that a well-functioning democratic society requires an understanding of a wide range of experiences and perspectives, something that early sociology was well equipped to provide. In addition, Addams foreshadowed the development of feminist social theory by critiquing the way male sociologists often based their generalizations about society on men's experiences only. She argued that for researchers to fully understand social problems, they needed to have a sympathetic connection with the people affected by those problems. Her collaboration with poor immigrants informed her sociological understanding that people actively seek to improve their conditions, even when facing great odds in extremely difficult situations.

Although the works of Martineau, Du Bois, Addams, and others may have been underappreciated when they wrote them, those works have since had a significant impact on sociology, encouraging sociologists to pay careful attention to the social complexities of gender, race, class, and power.

Foundations of Sociological Thought

Sociology's Diverse Theories

The work of early sociologists served as the source for the development of later sociological theory. In the chapters to come, we consider different theories regarding specific social phenomena. In this section, we examine some of the general approaches to theory that have developed over the years. First, though, we consider what theory is and examine some basic ways that sociological theories vary.

Understanding Theory

The film *Avatar* sold nearly $3 billion in movie tickets, making it the biggest box office hit in history. Why do you think the film has taken in so much money? Perhaps the story is compelling, the actors superb, or the special effects well worth the price of admission. Or maybe the studio advertised and promoted the film especially well. Or perhaps the film's success is due to the growing number of movie theaters worldwide, which translates into more ticket sales.

Each possible explanation for the financial success of *Avatar* is, in effect, a theory because it tries to explain an observation. Accurate evidence and data—such as *Avatar*'s $3 billion in ticket sales—*describes* the world and helps us see "what" has occurred. Theories answer "why?" questions and help *explain* the data or evidence: "Why did this happen?" "Why is this so?" More formally, a **social theory** is *a set of principles and propositions that explains the relationships among social phenomena*. Through their explanations, theories also alert us to the sorts of questions we should be asking in future research.

Of course, sociologists don't ask about just box office hits—although media sociologists would be able to offer some likely explanations for *Avatar*'s success. Instead, sociological theorists address broad questions, such as, "Why don't complex societies fall apart?" and "Why do wealth and poverty coexist?" as well as more narrowly defined questions, such as, "Why do some schools succeed while others fail?" or even "Why do students who sit in the back of the class tend to have lower grades than those who sit up front?" When we speak of approaches to sociological theory, therefore, we are referring to broad explanations sociologists have for why society operates the way it does. Although thinking about theory can seem intimidating at first, it actually is fairly straightforward and involves answering the most interesting question of all: Why?

A few other characteristics of theories are important to remember:

- *A theory is not just a hunch or personal opinion.* It may start off that way—just as our explanations for *Avatar*'s success did—but to be useful, theories have to be put to the test to see if they are consistent with the evidence; that's the nature of science. Sociological theory is linked to research and evidence in ways that we explore in Chapter 2.

- *Theories evolve and are sometimes rejected, leaving the most useful to survive.* When evidence repeatedly contradicts a theory, the theory is either revised or discarded. The most useful theories are those that endure, some of which we discuss later in this chapter.

- *Multiple theories often give us a more complete picture than any single one.* Just as many factors likely contributed to *Avatar*'s success, many factors similarly contribute to most aspects of social life. Considering different theories can alert us to a variety of possible explanations for a social phenomenon and to a range of factors that can contribute to it.

Finally, theories tend to vary along a few key dimensions, which we now consider.

Key Dimensions of Theory

How do professional football teams vary? Some focus on offense, others on defense. Some rely on skilled veteran players, whereas others groom the abilities of younger team members. Some teams get most of their points by running the ball, whereas others generate most of their offense by passing. These are among the key dimensions on which teams vary.

Sociological theories, too, vary along key dimensions, including consensus and conflict, subjective and objective reality, and micro-level and macro-level analyses (see Figure 1.1). Think of each dimension as a continuum rather than an either-or division. Knowing where a theory lies on each continuum can help you understand how it fits into the larger picture of sociological thought.

CONSENSUS AND CONFLICT *Conflict* refers to tensions and disputes in society, often resulting from the unequal distribution of scarce resources, which can contribute to social change. *Consensus* refers to solidarity and cooperative interaction, often due to shared values and interests, which can contribute to social stability. Although different theories focus more on one or the other, both consensus and conflict coexist in every society, institution, and organization—indeed, in all social life.

In some instances, conflict can produce certain kinds of consensus (Coser 1956). When countries go to war, a dramatic example of conflict, citizens in each nation often feel a renewed sense of solidarity, which they express through increased patriotism and nationalism. On the other hand, sometimes apparent consensus masks simmering tensions that become evident only when they erupt into full-blown conflict. For example, the ordinary daily routines of some cities have sometimes concealed underlying racial tensions that exploded into broad urban riots sparked by a specific incident.

OBJECTIVE AND SUBJECTIVE REALITY *Objective conditions* are the material aspects of social life, including the physical environment, social networks, and social institutions. All of these exist outside of us, and collectively they make up the objective dimension of social life. In contrast, the *subjective dimension* of social life involves the world of ideas, including our sense of self, social norms,

FIGURE 1.1 | DIMENSIONS OF SOCIOLOGICAL THEORY

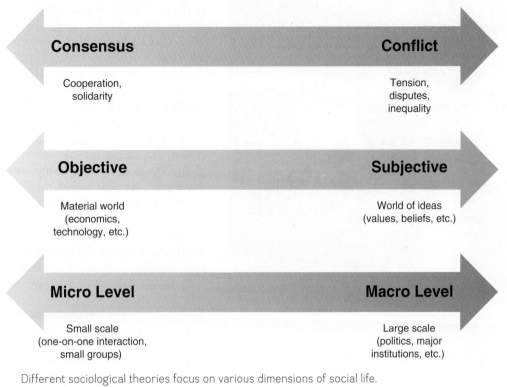

Consensus
Cooperation, solidarity

Conflict
Tension, disputes, inequality

Objective
Material world (economics, technology, etc.)

Subjective
World of ideas (values, beliefs, etc.)

Micro Level
Small scale (one-on-one interaction, small groups)

Macro Level
Large scale (politics, major institutions, etc.)

Different sociological theories focus on various dimensions of social life.

values, and belief systems. These all exist "in our head," so to speak, and are part of the cultural aspect of social life.

Both the objective physical world we live in and our subjective interpretations of that world have a significant impact on our lives and our society. For example, we have seen that Marx emphasized the impact of economic life (an objective factor) whereas Weber's theory regarding the Protestant Ethic highlighted the role of cultural beliefs (a subjective factor).

MICRO-LEVEL AND MACRO-LEVEL ANALYSES

The third dimension of sociological theory relates to different levels of analysis—as well as to different levels of society itself. Theories that focus on small-scale, usually face-to-face, social interaction are operating at the **micro level of analysis.** ("Micro" means small.) Theories that focus on large-scale social systems and processes such as the economy, politics, and population trends operate at the **macro level of analysis.** ("Macro" means large.) Theories that focus somewhere between very large and very small social phenomena—on organizations or institutions, for example—are using a **meso level of analysis.** ("Meso" means middle.) Often, sociological work focuses on the interaction between these various levels of social life.

Now that you are equipped with a better understanding of what theory is and how theories vary, let's take a closer look at some major theoretical traditions. Since the mid-twentieth century, sociologists have sometimes grouped varied sociological theories into three broad categories: *structural-functionalist theories*, *conflict theories*, and *symbolic interactionist theories*.

Structural-Functionalist Theories

Structural-functionalist theories *focus on consensus and cooperative interaction in social life, emphasizing how different elements that make up a society's structure contribute to its overall operation.* The roots of this tradition can be found in the work of Spencer and Durkheim. Structural-functionalist theories—often referred to simply as **functionalist theories**—were dominant in the United States in the middle of the twentieth century, when its leading proponent was Talcott Parsons (1902–1979). Parsons saw societies as complex systems made up of interdependent parts—for example, families, courts, schools, the economy—that work together to produce social stability. Because the systems are balanced, they tend to move toward normal states of equilibrium; a change in one part of the system results in a change in another part to compensate. Individuals are integrated into the social structure through culture, especially in the form of shared values. A consensus on basic values results in a moral commitment to society, which helps enable its smooth functioning.

To endure, a social institution must meet a need of the system as a whole; institutions that do not contribute adapt or disappear. Parsons argued that any social organization—whether a small group or a large and diverse society—must perform several key functions to survive, including teaching group members core community values, integrating members into productive participation in social life, defining and attaining community goals, and adapting to a changing environment.

Individuals are embedded within larger social structures that correspond to different levels of sociological analysis. These drummers at the 2008 Beijing Olympics, for example, brought their individual talents to the performance (micro level), but their efforts were coordinated by the organization behind the Beijing Olympics (meso level), which was, in turn, one project of the global International Olympic Committee (macro level).

In an important contribution to functionalist theory, Robert K. Merton (1910–2003) distinguished between **manifest functions,** *the recognized and intended consequences of social phenomena,* and **latent functions,** *their largely unrecognized and unintended consequences.* A manifest function of schools, for example, is to help prepare people for future employment, whereas a latent function is to serve as a dating pool or marriage market. Merton also reminds us that even though some phenomena are persistent, they can be **dysfunctional,** *inhibiting or disrupting the working of a system as a whole.* The persistent overcrowding in many schools, for example, is dysfunctional.

Consider how one might study the family as a social institution using functionalist theories. Families serve a number of functions, including the raising of children (though some societies raise children communally outside of the family and many families do not include children). In recent decades, a changing economy (another part of the social system) and changes in cultural values have contributed to changes in the family, including the rise of two-wage-earner families, single-parent families, blended families, and families with same-sex parents. Despite such changes, shared values continue to tell us how to raise children and maintain family life. Families can be dysfunctional, too—for example, by harboring child abuse or domestic violence.

Conflict Theories

Conflict theories *focus on issues of contention, power, and inequality, highlighting the competition for scarce resources.* The roots of this approach can be found in the work of Marx and Weber. Today, work that focuses on class, race, gender, and other forms of inequality is often based in this tradition, drawing on the work of Martineau, Du Bois, Addams, and others. The conflict approach emphasizes that, to meet common needs, people attempt to acquire scarce and valuable resources. These include material goods—such as food, housing, and good jobs—as well as less tangible resources, such as social respect and freedom. Because these resources are often limited, people compete for them, bringing different groups into conflict. Even when conflict is not visible, it is often present but repressed by the dominance of the powerful over the less powerful.

Conflict theories, then, see power at the core of social life. Power enables some people to gain an advantage over others and acquire more resources; more resources, in turn, give them more power. In this ongoing struggle, different groups use culture's values and ideas as weapons to advance their own positions. The dominant culture supports and justifies existing inequalities. Various countercultures articulate different values in their challenge to the existing condition.

How would one study the family with conflict theory? Conflict theories explain that tension and disagreement within families are routine and ordinary. Some of this discord emerges because of differences in power between women and men. Historically, the extensive legal, economic, and social inequalities between women and men reflected the different amounts of power each possessed. This inequality had been justified by a dominant culture that viewed men as naturally superior to women. Such cultural beliefs traditionally kept women in restricted family roles and prevented them from pursuing ambitions they might have had for themselves, topics we explore in Chapter 12. Inequalities continue to exist around family life today, both within families, where power may not be shared evenly, and within broader society, where some forms of family, such as same-sex unions, do not yet have universal legal recognition.

Symbolic Interactionist Theories

Symbolic interactionist theories *focus on how people use shared symbols and construct society as a result of their everyday interactions.* Weber's approach of *verstehen,* in which the researcher tries to understand action from the perspective of the actor, laid some groundwork for these theories, as did early work by Georg Simmel (1858–1918), who wrote insightful essays on the dynamics of daily life. However, symbolic interactionist theories were fully developed in the United States, building on work by social psychologists in the early and mid-twentieth century. George Herbert Mead (1863–1931), for example, wrote about how we develop a sense of self through our interaction with others and by self-reflection (see Chapter 6). In his dramaturgical theory, Erving Goffman (1922–1982) showed how social life was very much like a play, with people adopting roles, complete with props and scripts (see Chapter 7).

Symbolic interactionist theories are strongly associated with the subjective and micro-level dimensions of social life. They explain social life by highlighting that the social world is based on interaction between people using cultural symbols, such as words and nonverbal body language. Through interaction, individuals develop a sense of self and create a shared understanding of reality with others. People with more power are typically better able to influence this interpretation of reality. This common interpretation of reality leads to patterns of social interaction within groups that form the basis of social structure. But everyday interaction is also constantly recreating or changing these patterns, so society itself is inherently unstable and constantly in flux. Always under construction, the social world is therefore always capable of change. In this way, the symbolic interactionist theories explain social life by highlighting the active role people take in constructing shared understandings of social reality and creating society.

Applied to the family, the symbolic interactionist approach directs our attention to micro-level interactions between family members. As they interact, they develop an understanding of who they are and what their role is within the family. What does it mean to be a "good parent" today? Who will work to earn money? Who will care for children? What responsibility does a child have for an aging parent? Family members must come to some mutual understanding about what is expected from each of them. This shared interpretation of reality produces patterns of behavior that provide a routine structure to family life. But these interpretations and arrangements are not static; they are continuously reexamined and thus subject to change. The changes in family structure over the past half century illustrate the cumulative effect of individual-level decisions. People in different types of family—including two-parent families, one-parent families, childless couples, families with same-sex parents, and step-families—actively interpret the meaning of "family" and act accordingly.

Feminist Theories and Theoretical Diversity

As we see throughout this book, sociological theory has developed considerably since the mid-twentieth century, when some sociologists grouped the field's varied theories into the categories of functionalist, conflict, and symbolic interactionist perspectives. Newer perspectives often do not fit neatly into these older categories. Among the most important contemporary perspectives is feminist theory. Feminist theories focus on inequality between women and men and could be considered in the tradition of conflict theories. But feminist theories also provide insight into how those inequalities are created and reinforced in daily interactions, placing these insights squarely in the tradition of symbolic interactionism (see Chapter 11).

As with other theoretical traditions, there is no single feminist theory. Instead, a variety of feminist theories emphasize the importance of women's experience, analyze gender inequality, and advocate gender equality (Anderson and Witham 2010; Taylor, Rupp, and Whittier 2008). As we saw earlier in the chapter, feminist ideas from Harriet Martineau, Jane Addams, and others were present during the early years of sociology but were often marginalized in the male-dominated world of academia. The women's movement of the 1960s and 1970s, however, helped create a space for the emergence of feminist scholars who transformed many academic fields, including sociology. Often working across disciplinary boundaries and in newly established women's studies departments, feminist theorists challenged male assumptions about the world and about how social research should be done (Harding 1991; Reinharz 1992).

Historically, men had dominated the analyses of social life and often assumed that their understanding and perspective applied to everyone. Feminist "standpoint theory" rejected this notion, instead emphasizing that all knowledge is constructed from a particular perspective and that women's different experiences need to be included to produce an accurate understanding of social life (Harding 2004; Smith 1974, 1989). In the years that followed, this basic insight was extended to include the recognition that women's experiences vary depending on their class, race, and sexual orientation (Collins 2009; hooks 2000). This understanding has contributed to a wider recognition that the effects of gender, class, race, and sexual orientation intersect in shaping social life (Anderson and Collins 2013; Rothenberg 2014) and that women's lives vary across different societies (Mohanty 2003). Feminist theory has also contributed to a focus on women's bodies as a site of social struggles involving sexuality, beauty norms, violence, reproductive rights, and health (Lorber and Moore 2010). Finally, feminist theory has informed work on men, gender, and sexuality, revealing how our ideas about masculinity are socially constructed (Kimmel and Messner 2013; Pascoe 2011).

In addition, various recent theories—under the umbrella term *postmodernism*—have highlighted how shared meanings and assumptions about the world have fragmented, as different groups in society come to understand social reality differently. Meanwhile, rational choice theories have introduced a sort of economic analysis, suggesting that social interaction be understood as exchanges between rational individuals. And queer theory challenges the stability of basic identity categories—such as straight or gay, male or female—highlighting the fluidity and complexity of identity in contemporary society.

One of the great strengths of sociology is that it contains a variety of theories about the workings of social life that reach well beyond the three traditional approaches. But what unites sociology? What is the common ground that enables people using such disparate theories to identify as sociologists? That common ground is the sociological perspective and the core concepts that are at its heart.

Sociology's Common Ground: Culture, Structure, and Power

Diverse sociological theories are united by the core concepts that are central to a sociological perspective, including culture, structure, and power. As we have already seen, these concepts were used extensively by sociology's early thinkers and they have been at the heart of sociology ever since.

To varying degrees, all theoretical approaches rely on sociology's core concepts. For example, functionalism highlights culture's role in providing society with common values, such as

love of family. Conflict theory emphasizes how competing groups can manipulate cultural ideas and symbols to their advantage, as when politicians attach the idea of "family values" to their legislative initiatives and suggest opponents are anti-family. Symbolic interactionism emphasizes the process by which individuals create culture, as when people redefine "family" to incorporate a broader range of relationships. Although these approaches differ in their interpretations and emphases, they all agree that culture is a significant feature of social life worthy of close attention. Similarly, structure and power are important to all sociological theories. Table 1.2 summarizes how these core concepts provide the common ground that links the major approaches to sociological theory.

This section presents a brief overview of sociology's three core concepts. Each concept is later covered in depth in a separate chapter. By learning to use these three concepts to analyze and understand social life, you will succeed in developing a sociological perspective.

Culture

Culture is *the collection of values, beliefs, knowledge, norms, language, behaviors, and material objects shared by a people and socially transmitted from generation to generation.* Culture operates at all levels of society: through everyday interactions

TABLE 1.2	CORE CONCEPTS AND APPROACHES TO SOCIOLOGICAL THEORY		
	Functionalist Theories	**Conflict Theories**	**Symbolic Interactionist Theories**
Key questions	How is society held together? What function do the parts of society serve?	How is inequality structured in society? How are power relations maintained; how can they be changed?	How do people interpret and understand the social world in their interactions? How do they help shape the reality they experience?
Culture	Culture represents the consensus values and norms of a society into which individuals are socialized.	Conflicting parties use culture to advance their interests. Those in power perpetuate their privilege by socializing people into dominant values and norms. Those who are oppressed develop countercultures that challenge the dominant world view.	Through the use of symbols, people create culture based on their interpretation of social reality. They pass on these ideas and values in the socialization process.
Structure	Society is a stable system made up of interconnected structures. People act within structural constraints so that change is typically gradual and temporary, returning societies to a stable equilibrium.	Structure is the social order maintained by dominant groups primarily through coercion and the threat of force. Collective action challenging the existing order is often the source of structural change.	Social structure is produced through recurring individual actions that create a pattern. Structure is inherently unstable and changeable since it must be reproduced continually through individual action.
Power	Power is the ability of a social system to achieve its collective goals. Inequalities between groups serve a positive function in society by motivating the most qualified to fill the most important positions.	Power is often concentrated in the hands of a dominant group that uses it to exploit or oppress others. Inequality is the result of struggle between groups for scarce resources.	Power is rooted in the social relationships between people. Inequality results from the actions of individuals and therefore can be changed.

between individuals; through organizational norms in schools, businesses, and other groups; and through society-wide mechanisms such as the media and religion. At its broadest, culture is a way of life.

We tend to take our own culture for granted since we have internalized its basic customs and assumptions. For example, most of us, most of the time, have a fairly good understanding of what to expect from routine social interactions and what is considered appropriate behavior in those settings. We know when we are expected to be more formal and polite (perhaps with authority figures) and when we can relax and be casual (perhaps with close friends and family). We know that raising a hand to speak when hanging out with friends is unnecessary and that cracking open a beer in class is unwise. These unwritten "rules"—and the ideas about courtesy and respect that inform them—are part of our culture that we have learned.

Consider, for example, the simple matter of where to look when speaking with someone. Most Americans look people in the eye since in American culture direct eye contact signals honesty and forthrightness, whereas avoiding eye contact suggests that one has something to hide. But in some Asian societies, extended direct eye contact is often considered rude and impertinent, whereas averting one's gaze is a sign of deference and respect. Imagine the potential miscommunication if, say, an Asian and an American business executive, unaware of these cultural differences, were assessing each other as potential business partners. The American might think her Asian colleague had something to hide, whereas the Asian executive might think his American colleague was being rude and disrespectful. Understanding the concept of culture helps us interact in a world of diversity and allows us to critically examine beliefs and behaviors we might otherwise view as "natural."

Culture is not "natural" or biologically based because it must be taught and learned through the process of socialization (see Chapter 6). Since people must reproduce culture for it to survive, people can also change culture by adopting new values, beliefs, and behaviors and abandoning older ones. This process of cultural evolution can create conflict as some people seek to hold on to more traditional values and ways of life, while others embrace new ideas and behaviors. As a result, cultural conflicts are common. Clashes in values, beliefs, and ways of life help fuel conflict, sometimes even contributing to warfare. On the other hand, culture is often something to celebrate, and our identity comes, in part, from the elements of culture that we choose to embrace. Our tastes in music, our dress and appearance, our religious beliefs or nonbeliefs, our language, our family's ancestry, among other things, are all cultural features that help make us who we are.

FIGURE 1.2 | THE INTERPLAY BETWEEN PEOPLE AND SOCIAL STRUCTURE

Social Structure

Social structures influence how people act.

People act, thereby creating, reproducing, or changing social structures.

Individuals

Culture, therefore, is woven into the fabric of social life and is an essential element of a sociological analysis of society.

Structure

Structure refers to *the recurring patterns of behavior in social life*. These patterns occur at all levels of society, from our daily interactions with others to the global economy. Structures range from highly informal patterns, such as where and when we routinely meet up with friends, to much more formal organizations and institutions, such as schools and government.

People create structures to help them accomplish their goals, but, in turn, structures come to constrain what they can do (see Figure 1.2). For example, imagine that you and your friends decide to form a new group to advocate for better student life, including more parking spaces on campus. In establishing your group, you have to decide things like: Will there be formal leadership positions, such as president and secretary? How will those be chosen? How do you become a member? How will decisions be made? How you answer such questions will determine the structure for your organization. You would hope that the structure you create will help the group function smoothly and promote its goal effectively. But the rules that define the structure will also constrain the behavior of group members because they regulate how members are supposed to behave. As new members join your group, they will experience the rules as an already-existing reality that constrains their actions. They may choose to comply with the rules, thereby reproducing the structure of your group, or work to change them in some way, thereby modifying the structure.

thinking about the core concepts

Review the description of sociology's early thinkers. What roles did culture, structure, and power play in their work?

Social Change and Urbanization

Social change influences the lives of individuals and communities alike. These photos show the rapid development that has occurred in a portion of Shanghai, China, between 1987 (*top*) and 2013 (*bottom*). Just as the fast growth of industrial cities more than a century ago prompted early sociologists to study urbanization, such quick expansion in contemporary cities has led sociologists to examine how culture, structure, and power are changing today.

Daily life tends to be ordered by various informal patterns of behavior, or *social structures*. We can talk about "family structure," for example, even though there are no formal organizational by-laws that regulate the behavior of such groups. There are, however, legal standards, social norms, and common practices that establish the "rules" of family life, something we explore later in the book.

Similar to how culture must be reproduced—and can be changed—structures must be reproduced through continuing patterns of behavior or they can be changed through changes in that behavior. History provides examples of how people can act collectively to change social structure. In the nineteenth century, six-day workweeks were the norm in industrial societies, and workers usually labored for 10 or 12 hours a day. By the early twentieth century, however, a growing number of people joined the labor movement, which promoted the then-radical ideas of an eight-hour workday and a five-day workweek. With great difficulty, labor unions struggled successfully to establish this new standard, thus creating the much-beloved weekend with its two-day reprieve from work. This resulted in a fundamental change in the social structuring of time in our society. (See the Sociology in Action box for an example of the role sociology can play in helping change social structures today.)

Power

Power is *the ability to bring about an intended outcome, even when opposed by others.* Power, too, operates at all levels of society, including in families (parents have power over their children), in organizations (managers have power over the people who report to them), and in national and international relations (leaders exercise military and economic power to achieve national goals). Sometimes people *empower* themselves to achieve a goal (as when a student completes a degree to qualify for a particular career). Other times power is used to influence the thinking and behavior of others and even to dominate others. For example, an employer can dictate the rules that employees must follow during work hours.

Power is commonly used to allocate resources (economic power), make rules and decisions (political power), and help define reality (cultural power). It is thus closely tied to *inequality*, the systematic and unequal distribution of resources among various groups of people. All societies have some form of inequality; it just varies by type and degree. Those who have more economic, political, and cultural resources have a better chance to achieve their goals and overcome hurdles and opposition. In other words, they have more power.

Paying attention to power allows us to see connections and similarities between different forms of inequality, which coexist and interact. Considering the intersections of race, class, gender, and sexuality has proven to be especially important in understanding power and inequality.

SOCIOLOGY in ACTION

The Arab Struggle for Democracy

In January 2011, a wave of protests erupted in the Arab world against the region's dictatorial regimes. In Egypt, the most populous Arab country, young people, many of them college students or recent graduates, used Facebook, Twitter, and other social media to coordinate protests against the U.S.-backed regime of Hosni Mubarak, who had ruled with an iron hand since 1981. Labor unions and other groups brought workers out into the streets by the hundreds of thousands. When the military sided with the protesters, the regime was doomed. The revolution was followed by an election, widespread protests, and a military coup, events making clear that Egypt's future remains uncertain. Though the revolution and subsequent developments took many people by surprise, the struggle for democracy in Egypt began decades ago, and in one little-known way, social scientists played a role in it.

Sociologist Saad Eddin Ibrahim is the founder of the Ibn Khaldun Center for Development Studies in Cairo, which is named for Abd al-Rahman Ibn Khaldun (1332–1406), who pioneered the formal study of society centuries before the discipline of sociology emerged in the nineteenth century. The center's researchers study and advocate for economic development, democratization, and the strengthening of the agents of civil society—voluntary organizations such as unions, charities, professional associations, and advocacy groups that are neither government nor for-profit businesses. Ibrahim's work led him to conclude that the Arab world would not enjoy peace or widespread prosperity until democracy flourished in the region. He and his colleagues have worked relentlessly for democratic freedom and championed the inclusion of women and minorities in the political process.

A vocal critic of repressive Arab regimes and the U.S. policy of supporting them to promote stability and steady access to Mideast oil, Ibrahim made himself unpopular with the Mubarak government. In 2000, when Mubarak announced elections, Ibrahim and his colleagues said they would conduct independent surveys of voters and publish the results, which threatened to embarrass an unpopular dictator planning a sham election. Ibrahim also explained in a foreign magazine article that he believed Mubarak had no intention of submitting to fair elections and instead was grooming his son to take over the regime as the new president-for-life.

The reaction was swift. The same day the article was published, the Ibn Khaldun Center was looted by State Security guards and Ibrahim and twenty-six of his colleagues were arrested. Ibrahim was convicted and sentenced to seven years' hard labor for "tarnishing" Egypt's image abroad. The imprisonment drew outcries from human rights organizations, the United Nations, social scientists (including the American Sociological Association), and, eventually, the U.S. government. After three years in isolation, Ibrahim was acquitted of all charges on appeal. He suffered permanent nerve damage in one leg from torture he endured while in prison. A former marathon runner, he needed multiple surgeries before he could walk again, and then only with a cane.

Upon Ibrahim's release, the Ibn Khaldun Center reopened and he and his colleagues resumed their work. In 2007, however, facing a new round of charges, Ibrahim chose to go into exile in the United States rather than risk another prison term. He continued his work on Arab democracy from abroad while his colleagues at the center helped train observers to monitor the polling stations in Egypt's 2010 elections. The fraud they witnessed fed growing public disillusionment that contributed to the 2011 revolution.

When the revolution's success appeared imminent, Ibrahim risked returning to his homeland. The country's first election brought the Muslim Brotherhood to power, but economic turmoil and political discord continued. Once again, Ibrahim became a vocal critic of the new government's unwillingness to work with political minorities and has continued to engage that country's evolving situation.

Like the founders of sociology who were public intellectuals engaged in the political debates of their day, who advised governments on public policy, and who worked with social movements to promote change, Ibrahim and his fellow scholars at Egypt's Ibn Khaldun Center embody one version of sociology in action.

Sources: Goodman (2007); Alan Johnson (2007); Stockman (2011); Ward (2010); Weiss (2011); and the Ibn Khaldun Center for Development Studies (eicds.org).

think about it

1. *Why can social science research, such as surveying citizens, pose a threat to an autocratic government?*
2. *With the political freedoms they enjoy, do you think young people in the United States feel empowered to help shape the future of their country, as the young people in Egypt did? Why or why not?*

Culture, structure, and power are not unchanging features of social life; they are part of ongoing social processes. Culture is reproduced and changed through socialization. Structures are created and altered through action. Power can be used to produce or reduce inequalities, which in turn can alter the distribution of power. These dynamics are at the heart of a sociological analysis that recognizes the ever-changing nature of social life.

A Changing World

FROM MODERN TO POSTMODERN SOCIETY

Sociology arose over a century and a half ago during a period of transition that marked the emergence of modernity in the eighteenth and nineteenth centuries. Early sociologists, drawing on the core concepts of culture, structure, and power, sought to explain that transition and the social turmoil that often accompanied it. Today, we are living through another period of transition, this time from modernity to an as-yet-uncertain postmodernity, and sociologists are studying the nature and consequences of these changes.

Modernity was a period associated with the rise of industrialization, democracy, and science. In contrast, **postmodernity** is *a historical period beginning in the mid-twentieth century characterized by the rise of information-based economies and the fragmentation of political beliefs and ways of knowing.* Because we are in the midst of this transition, it is difficult to summarize neatly what postmodernity will look like or what long-term impact it will have. Nonetheless, we can point to certain features of this transition to the postmodern world (see Table 1.3).

Classical theorists were concerned with the rise of an industrial economy; today's sociologists are interested in the relationship between so-called postindustrial economies, in which information-based and service-sector jobs predominate, and the developing industrial economies that now produce the bulk of the world's manufactured goods. Classical sociologists studied the rise of urban life that accompanied industrialization; contemporary sociologists have examined the emergence of suburban life as a new social reality in advanced economies while documenting continued urbanization in the developing world and the growth of "mega-cities." The modern era was marked by a great faith in democratic governments as a means to human progress; in postmodern times, distrust of government and a loss of faith in political ideologies have often led to stalemated conflicts, political disengagement, and widespread cynicism. Finally, classical theorists highlighted the declining influence of religion, the rise of science, and the rationalization of modern life. Contemporary sociologists have studied our highly fragmented culture, which includes everything from the rise of multiculturalism and rejection of universal truths to a resurgence of fundamentalist religions and reaffirmation of universal truths.

Ten Features of Postmodern Society

Beyond such broad changes, a number of significant developments are transforming our way of life. These changes tend to affect the wealthier societies of the world most.

	TABLE 1.3	KEY FEATURES OF PREMODERN, MODERN, AND POSTMODERN SOCIETIES

	Premodern	Modern	Postmodern
Economy	Agricultural	Industrial	Information based Service oriented
Social life	Rural	Urban	Suburban Mega-cities
Politics	Religiously sanctioned leaders	Democracy	Disengagement Cynicism
Dominant culture	Religion	Rationality and science	Fragmented Multicultural

Throughout this book, we use a sociological perspective to better understand these aspects of postmodern society. As you read the list of changes below, consider how they have affected—or will affect—your life:

1. ***The expansion of media and commercial culture.*** In postmodern society, media technologies have dramatically expanded into all aspects of social life, creating new opportunities for communication and new dilemmas. The boundaries between the Internet, television, smartphones, video games, and other media continue to blur, resulting in the all-encompassing and commercialized media environment in which we live. Closely connected to this expansion has been unprecedented growth in advertising and the promotion of consumption. How is the saturation of society by the media influencing social life? How often do you check or send texts or check your Facebook page? How many advertisements have you seen today? (See especially Chapter 14.)

2. ***The threat to the natural environment.*** The ever-increasing production and consumption of consumer goods have taken a serious toll on the environment in the form of resource depletion, pollution, climate change, and an ever-growing accumulation of waste. How can we balance the desire for material comfort with the need to protect diminishing resources? How are environmental changes potentially affecting our health and our way of life? (See Chapter 15.)

3. ***The decline of U.S. cities and the rise of suburbs.*** In the postmodern era, corporations have moved many industrialized manufacturing jobs to developing nations with lower-wage workers. As industrial jobs in U.S. cities disappeared, the economic base of major urban areas crumbled, leaving behind unemployment, poverty, and crime in many inner cities. Meanwhile, rapid suburban growth has permitted more people to own

homes in relatively safe and tranquil surroundings. But suburban life can leave people feeling socially isolated and require lengthy commutes to work in heavy traffic. How can U.S. cities remain vital in postmodernity? How have the suburbs changed the rhythms of daily life, and what is their effect on people's sense of community? How will the expansion of urban life in developing nations affect those societies? (See Chapter 15.)

4. *The global economy.* You need only consider the route traveled by the ingredients of your morning cup of coffee—from the plantations of Brazil, Colombia, or Vietnam to your local coffee shop or grocery store— to realize that we are inextricably part of a global system of production and consumption. The global economy is transforming societies around the world, and the debate over the nature of this change has been an important topic in sociology recently. How does a global economy affect the inequality between rich and poor nations? How has the growth of a global economy impacted employment patterns, educational requirements, and family life? (See Chapters 9 and 16.)

5. *The aging population.* We are living longer and healthier lives thanks to advances in health information and medical technology. Now society must adjust to the new reality of an aging population. The U.S. Census Bureau reports that the number of Americans aged 90 and over increased from 720,000 in 1980 to 1.9 million in 2010, and projects the 90+ population to grow to more than 10 million by 2050 (He and Muenchrath 2011). How will the need to care for aging parents and grandparents affect future American families? How will social services and the health care system cope with an aging population? (See Chapter 17.)

6. *The changing family.* Effective contraception, divorce, blended families, two-wage-earner families, single-parent families, same-sex marriage, and surrogate parenting, among other developments, have changed the definition of the family and its role in society. How does today's family differ from yesterday's? How have recent social changes affected the nature and function of the family? What is in store for the family in the future? (See Chapter 12.)

7. *Troubled political institutions.* In many parts of the world today, the prospect of democracy holds great promise as a substitute for repressive political regimes. But long-established democracies often seem to have their own troubles. Why do some well-established democracies stagnate? What threats challenge the vitality of our democratic institutions? (See Chapter 16.)

8. *Increased diversity and multiculturalism.* A recent influx of immigrants has been a catalyst for change as well as conflict in the United States, just as was an earlier wave of immigrants who arrived in the early twentieth century. In addition, the global economy and the relative ease of modern travel have begun to erode the significance of national boundaries. Do the fragmentation and juxtaposition of cultural experiences—in music, food, film, and more—point to a new cultural mash-up? Does the presence of such cultural diversity threaten societies with fragmentation? How can the distinct contributions of different cultures be preserved in a world in which cultural traits are increasingly blended? (See Chapters 10 and 14.)

9. *The changing nature of violence and warfare.* Powerful and wealthy countries, including the United States, possess advanced weapons that can destroy humanity many times over. Some smaller nations and various nonstate actors have developed low-tech but deadly weapons and tactics. The result is a world bristling with arms, threatened by violence, and locked in political and military stalemates. How can societies reduce violence? What factors contribute to the recent rise in terrorist activity? What is the future of warfare? (See Chapter 16.)

10. *The changing role of religion.* To varying degrees, the world's wealthy industrialized nations have become increasingly secular—that is, religion plays a much less significant role in public and daily life in those nations than it once did. But in other parts of the world, religious beliefs continue to inform and drive many aspects of social life. Because of the increased contact among cultures, differences in religious beliefs now fuel some of the world's major conflicts, as well as divisive political issues at home. Will secularization continue to expand, or will religious revivals spread? Can different cultures coexist even with fundamental religious differences? (See Chapter 12.)

The Challenge and Hope of Sociology

Sociology holds great promise. As C. Wright Mills pointed out, it can help us understand the connections between ourselves and the larger social world. In studying society, we learn more about who we are as individuals, why we face the conditions that we do, and how we are connected to others. At its best, sociology promotes an understanding of the social world and our place in it and suggests ways that we might act to improve our lives, our community, and our world.

But sociology comes with some challenges, too. Because it addresses serious problems that face society, it can lead us to some disturbing discoveries about society and ourselves. Issues such as how to care for an aging population, how to balance human needs with environmental concerns, how to address persistent poverty, how to combat racism and sexism, how to respond to extremist violence, and how to accommodate diversity in society are not easy to think about, but they are important and must be faced. Also, looking at our experiences in a broader social context sometimes reveals disconcerting insights about our relative privilege, or lack of it, due to the effects of class, race, gender, sexual orientation, or nationality. Achieving a better understanding of our place in the world's hierarchy of privilege can be enlightening, but also unsettling.

As you will see throughout this book, sociology can force us to move outside our comfort zone and challenge us to think in new ways about things that we take for granted. If we live in relative comfort and freedom, we might find it easy to ignore difficult issues that face society, and hope they won't affect us personally. If we are struggling to get by, we might prefer to focus solely on taking care of our private lives, hoping that eventually we can insulate ourselves from economic upheaval, crime, and other social problems. But sociology reminds us that in taking either position we are, by default, helping reproduce the society in which we live, with all its problems. Whether we realize it or not, whether we like it or not, we are part of the broader social world.

In the face of our changing world, sociology offers hope. It is not a fearful hope that we can somehow manage individually to escape the world's problems. Instead, it is the hopeful realization that societies—and the issues that confront them—are largely created by human beings. That means people working together also have the capacity to change and improve those societies, as well as their own lives. We invite you to take up the challenge to use sociology to better understand the world and your place in it. And we hope that from this understanding, you'll be inspired and better equipped to act—in whatever way you see fit—to make a positive difference in your life and in our rapidly changing world.

REVIEW, REFLECT, AND APPLY

Looking Back

1. The sociological perspective is a way of looking at the world that focuses on the relationships between individuals and larger forces in society. Sociology as a discipline couples this perspective with systematic study and research using the methods of social science.

2. The discipline of sociology emerged in the late 1800s, in part as a response to the dramatic economic, political, cultural, and social changes taking place in the modern world.

3. Karl Marx, Emile Durkheim, and Max Weber were the three most influential classical sociological thinkers. Marx is best known for his work on capitalism and on the role of conflict in society. Durkheim's work focused on social solidarity. Weber is best known for his work on the rationalization of society, including the rise of bureaucracy.

4. Because of the sexism and racism of the day, the contributions of other social thinkers such as Harriet Martineau, W.E.B. Du Bois, and Jane Addams were not fully recognized or accepted within the discipline of sociology in their time. However, they made a major contribution, especially in spotlighting issues of gender- and race-based inequality.

5. Sociological theories seek to explain the workings of society by explaining why things happen as they do. These theories vary along three key dimensions: consensus and conflict, subjective and objective reality, and micro-level and macro-level analyses. Diverse theories are sometimes grouped into the functionalist, conflict, and symbolic interactionist approaches.

6. The foundational work in sociology highlighted a number of core concepts that still serve as sociology's common ground. Among these enduring concepts are culture, structure, and power. These concepts are used throughout the book to help analyze social issues and phenomena.

7. Today, sociologists continue to study the social changes taking place as modernity gives way to the postmodern era. In many respects, the postmodern world is distinctly different from the one studied by the classical sociologists. But the enduring core concepts and theoretical insights of those early sociological thinkers—combined with new ideas and theories—can help us better understand our contemporary society. That is the focus of this book.

Critical Thinking: Questions and Activities

1. What is sociology and what is the sociological perspective? How does the sociological perspective apply to your own life?

2. The use of indiscriminate deadly violence against civilians, often referred to as terrorism, is a topic of intense interest to social scientists. What sorts of issues and questions would someone using a sociological perspective focus on

in addressing this topic? What sorts of questions might researchers in other social science disciplines—such as economics, psychology, anthropology, and political science—focus on when considering this phenomenon?

3. What do you see as some of the advantages and disadvantages of the rise of modernity?

4. Of the 10 changes in contemporary society listed on pages 26–27, which one do you think is the most significant? Why? What important changes, if any, would you add to the list? Why do you feel they should be included?

5. What cards have you been dealt? Consider, for example, these questions about your childhood: Did you regularly have access to adequate food and clean drinking water? Did you live in a neighborhood that was relatively safe and free of crime? Did you have access to a good education? Did you answer no to one or more of these questions, you no doubt had to overcome some hurdles while growing up. If you answered yes to these questions, you have enjoyed privileges that are unavailable to others. Using your sociological imagination, list 10 more questions that could help determine whether people have enjoyed access to privileges in their lives.

Key Terms

anomie (p. 15) social normlessness, without moral guidance or standards.

collective conscience (p. 15) the shared values of society.

conflict theories (p. 20) social theories that focus on issues of contention, power, and inequality, highlighting the competition for scarce resources.

culture (p. 22) the collection of values, beliefs, knowledge, norms, language, behaviors, and material objects shared by a people and socially transmitted from generation to generation.

division of labor (p. 13) the way people specialize in different tasks, each requiring specific skills.

dysfunctional (p. 20) inhibiting or disrupting the working of a system as a whole.

functionalist theories (p. 19) see "structural-functionalist theories."

industrialization (p. 10) the use of large-scale machinery for the mass manufacture of consumer goods.

latent functions (p. 20) the largely unrecognized and unintended consequences of social phenomena.

macro level of analysis (p. 19) a focus on large-scale social systems and processes such as the economy, politics, and population trends.

manifest functions (p. 20) the recognized and intended consequences of social phenomena.

meso level of analysis (p. 19) a focus somewhere between very large and very small social phenomena—on organizations or institutions, for example.

micro level of analysis (p. 19) a focus on small-scale, usually face-to-face social interaction.

modernity (p. 9) a historical era beginning in the 1700s characterized by the growth of democracy and personal freedom, increased reliance on reason and science to explain the natural and social worlds, and a shift toward an urban industrial economy.

positivism (p. 11) a belief that accurate knowledge must be based on the scientific method.

postmodernity (p. 26) a historical period beginning in the mid-twentieth century characterized by the rise of information-based economies and the fragmentation of political beliefs and ways of knowing.

power (p. 24) the ability to bring about an intended outcome, even when opposed by others.

rationalization of society (p. 15) the long-term historical process by which rationality replaced tradition as the basis for organizing social and economic life.

science (p. 9) a method of inquiry that uses logic and the systematic collection of evidence to support knowledge claims.

social solidarity (p. 13) the collective bonds that connect individuals.

social theory (p. 18) a set of principles and propositions that explains the relationships among social phenomena.

sociological perspective (p. 5) a view of the social world that focuses on discovering and understanding the connections between individuals and the broader social contexts in which they live; what C. Wright Mills called the *sociological imagination*.

sociology (p. 5) the systematic study of the relationship between individuals and society.

structural-functionalist theories (p. 19) theories that focus on consensus and cooperative interaction in social life, emphasizing how different elements that make up a society's structure contribute to its overall operation. Often referred to simply as "functionalist theories," or "functionalism."

structure (p. 23) the recurring patterns of behavior in social life.

symbolic interactionist theories (p. 20) social theories that focus on how people use shared symbols and construct society as a result of their everyday interactions.

urbanization (p. 10) the growth of cities.

Understanding the Research Process

How do social science researchers know what they claim to know?

What special challenges might confront you as a social science researcher?

How can you become a more informed consumer of social science research?

SOCIOLOGY in ACTION

Participatory Action Research: Media Coverage of Domestic Violence

Leaders of the Rhode Island Coalition Against Domestic Violence had long been frustrated by local press coverage of their issue, especially domestic murders. Even reporters with good intentions often wrote stories that helped perpetuate what coalition leaders saw as destructive myths about domestic violence, including the notion that it is caused by substance abuse, that perpetrators are "out of control," and that domestic violence is just a private family problem. From their many years of working with survivors of such violence, coalition leaders knew that the larger story behind domestic violence tended to be invisible in the news. They felt that if they had a better understanding of how reporters gathered their information, they could work with local journalists to improve their coverage and draw attention to the need for better resources to combat domestic violence.

The coalition partnered with sociologist Charlotte Ryan to develop a study that used *participatory action research,* a form of applied research to address this problem. In this type of research, community members and sociologists work together to identify the key research questions and design the research project—and sometimes even to carry out the research.

Ryan began by examining local newspaper coverage of twelve domestic violence murders in Rhode Island between 1996 and 1999. In her analysis of eighty-eight articles, Ryan found that the reporters' sources played a key role in shaping the story. Neighbors and on-the-scene witnesses generally emphasized the tragedy of the particular event. Police sources focused on the details of the crime. Only the few reporters who turned to experts in domestic violence—including shelter providers, public health workers, and advocates—included information linking the murders to domestic violence and the need for community resources to deal with it. Ryan concluded: "With a few notable exceptions, the media reinforced the perception that domestic violence murders are isolated family tragedies and did not challenge common myths about domestic violence. In doing so, reporters missed opportunities to broaden the public's understanding of domestic violence, its warning signs and possibilities for prevention and community

intervention" (Rhode Island Coalition Against Domestic Violence 2000, 5-4).

As part of the research project, the Rhode Island Coalition also conducted a series of conversations with two key groups: local news reporters, to learn how reporters understand their responsibilities and goals; and survivors of domestic violence, to gather their recommendations about how reporters should cover domestic violence stories.

Once all the research was complete, Ryan and the Rhode Island Coalition developed an action strategy with two main components. First, Ryan and the coalition produced *Domestic Violence: A Handbook for Journalists* and distributed it to reporters throughout the state (Rhode Island Coalition Against Domestic Violence 2000). The handbook provides a wide range of resources, including background information, statistical data on domestic violence, a summary of Ryan's study, and recommendations from survivors of domestic violence. In addition, it gives tips on how to cover domestic violence, identifies "best practices" for crime reporters, and directs them to reliable news sources about this issue. Second, the Rhode Island Coalition began training survivors and advocates about how reporters work so that they could become more effective news sources when communicating with them.

As a result of this collaborative research project, the Rhode Island Coalition is now one of the principal sources for reporters in covering cases of domestic violence in the state. In addition, news reporting has changed in ways that reflect the coalition's emphasis on understanding domestic violence as a social problem, not just a private tragedy.

think about it

1. *Find a detailed news story online or in a newspaper about a recent domestic violence case. Does the coverage characterize the violence more as a private issue or a broader social problem?*

2. *What might be some of the strengths and weaknesses of participatory action research?*

---

evidence to a child that he must be real. What else would account for all those Santa decorations, greeting cards, and television specials? Ideas that have withstood the test of time deserve our attention. But beware: just because a belief has been around for a long time doesn't make it true. As with our approach to authorities, we need to temper our respect for tradition with a healthy skepticism that demands knowledge claims be backed by evidence.

■ *Generalizations based on personal experience.* Some children have the ultimate evidence: personal experience. They have seen, heard, touched, and even talked to Santa at the local mall. After all, "Seeing is believing." Well, maybe not. In some cases, personal experience can be very useful, but relying on it can also be misleading. We may misunderstand or misinterpret an experience. Or our experiences may not be typical; we may overgeneralize from them. We need broader sources of evidence, especially when we are talking about the social world.

- **Reliance on selective observation.** Using *selective observation*, anyone can find evidence that might appear to confirm the existence of Santa. For example, the milk and cookies left for Santa disappear. A more accurate picture of the world requires us to remain open-minded, however, willing to take seriously evidence that contradicts our initial inclinations and to consider alternative explanations for the evidence we have. In other words, we must gather and evaluate evidence systematically to increase the chances that we will reach an accurate conclusion.

- **Biased observation and interpretation.** One final barrier to clear thinking about Santa may be *bias*: a child has a vested interest in believing the story. Who wants to mess with a legend that delivers such generous benefits? In assessing what someone believes, it is helpful to keep in mind the potential interests that this person has in promoting certain ideas. By itself, a person's bias is not a reason to reject a claim, but if someone benefits substantially from interpreting evidence one way or another, we certainly should pay especially close attention to how he or she has gathered and explained the evidence.

Our Santa example may seem trivial, but the problems it illustrates are serious. When adults reach conclusions based solely on a belief in authority, common sense, tradition,

personal experience, or selective observation—or when they allow their personal bias to influence their conclusions—they are likely to wind up with a distorted and inaccurate picture of the world. Acting on the basis of such misjudgments can be disastrous for people, public policy, and societies. People can avoid these mistakes by using an approach to knowledge based on social scientific principles, which we discuss next.

The Elements of Social Science Research

Four key elements distinguish social science research: identifying and understanding patterns in social life, gathering empirical evidence, explaining how the evidence was collected and analyzed, and viewing the resulting research claims as provisional knowledge.

PATTERNS IN SOCIAL LIFE Social science focuses on the patterns in social life—identifiable, repeating patterns in human thought and action. Of course, each human being makes independent decisions, and as a result an individual's behavior is not entirely predictable. On the other hand, social life is not merely a chaotic series of random events. Research shows that there *are* recurring patterns to human perception, behavior, and experience. Social science research largely consists of identifying and understanding these patterns in social life.

For example, social science research can tell us the probability that certain categories of people will or will not vote. Figure 2.1 provides some data from the U.S. Census Bureau

" I'm feeling a bit cynical this year. Just bring me cash."
© www.cartoonstock.com

A belief in Santa Claus can be lucrative for children, but it involves some common errors in everyday thinking.

FIGURE 2.1 | VOTING IN THE 2012 ELECTION, BY AGE

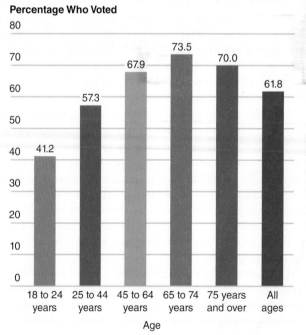

Percentage Who Voted

Age	Percentage
18 to 24 years	41.2
25 to 44 years	57.3
45 to 64 years	67.9
65 to 74 years	73.5
75 years and over	70.0
All ages	61.8

Source: U.S. Census Bureau, Current Population Survey, November 2012.

on the percentage of U.S. citizens aged 18 years or older who said they voted in the 2012 election.

Do you see the pattern? The older the age group, the more likely its members were to vote. Although there is a slight drop in turnout for those aged 75 or older, the overall pattern is clear.

Social scientists use a variety of techniques to describe and measure the patterns in social life. Some of these efforts involve the use of sophisticated statistical techniques. But even a straightforward analysis of the simplest data, such as that presented in Figure 2.1, can provide us with insight about the social world.

EMPIRICAL EVIDENCE To describe patterns in social life, sociologists depend on gathering relevant **empirical evidence**—*evidence that can be observed or documented using the human senses.* Empirical evidence can be categorized broadly as quantitative or qualitative. **Quantitative data** are simply *evidence that can be summarized numerically.* Quantitative data are presented in the form of **variables,** *measures that can change (or vary) and thus have different values.* Figure 2.1 includes quantitative data with two variables—age and voting. The value for age varies depending on how many years a person has lived; the value for voting varies depending on whether or not a person said he or she voted. Researchers must **operationalize** their terms, that is, *define clearly the variables to be studied.* In this case, age is measured in terms of years, and the voting variable is based on whether or not a person says that he or she has voted.

Variables are often categorized as independent or dependent. The **independent variable** is *associated with and/or causes change in the value of the dependent variable.* The **dependent variable** *changes in response to the independent variable.* In our example, age is the independent variable (because it is associated with the likelihood of voting), whereas voting is the dependent variable (because it varies with age). Thus our data show that people are more likely to vote as they get older; voting doesn't make them grow old.

When the independent variable is *associated with* the change in value of the dependent variable, it is known as **correlation,** *a relationship in which change in one variable is connected to change in another variable.* But correlation is not the same as causation. (See the Through a Sociological Lens box.) Age is *correlated* with voting, but age doesn't *cause* voting. Instead, age is associated with a variety of factors

that influence the likelihood of voting, such as living in a community longer. In 2012, 76 percent of eligible voters who had lived in the same location for five or more years said they voted in 2012, while only 41 percent of those who had been in their residence less than a month say they voted (U.S. Census Bureau, 2012b).

As a starting point for quantitative research, researchers often pose a **hypothesis,** *a statement about the relationship between variables that is to be investigated.* In addition to age, for example, we might hypothesize that the more education people have, the more likely they are to vote. Researchers would have to investigate this relationship to either confirm or reject the hypothesis.

Qualitative data are *any kind of evidence that is not numerical in nature, including evidence gathered from interviews, direct observation, and written or visual documents.* Whereas researchers using quantitative data focus on measuring variables, those who use qualitative data usually focus on describing social processes. In presenting qualitative data, researchers often organize their evidence around central themes that have emerged in their study and use direct quotations or vivid descriptions to illustrate their points. For example, to understand why a smaller percentage of people between the ages of 18 and 24 tend to vote than do people in older age groups, you might interview segments of this population. A qualitative approach can provide valuable insights into the specific experiences and attitudes of this group.

To take another example, one study used qualitative data as a tool to evaluate how clients are served by social service agencies. Researchers examined interviews with homeless men and women in Portland, Oregon, that focused on their experiences in shelters and soup kitchens and with other agencies (Hoffman and Coffey 2008). One common theme in the interviews was the experience of being disrespected and treated like children by service providers. One 37-year-old woman noted that "they treat everyone the same . . . like they are in elementary school," and a 27-year-old man said that he "tried the Salvation Army program they had up there but I had too much personal pride to be talked down to and to be treated like a child" (pp. 213–14).

Personal stories of this sort, as well as other types of qualitative data, allow researchers to see *how* people experience the social world and how they understand their own experiences. This kind of qualitative data can be extremely important, revealing complexities that statistical data cannot capture. In the study of homelessness, for example, the authors make

Correlation, Causation, and Spuriousness

Imagine you visit your favorite online news site and are greeted by this headline: "Ice Cream Can Kill You!" It turns out that a reporter investigating why people drown accidentally has made the startling discovery that when ice-cream sales go up, accidental drowning increases.

This reporter has found a relationship, or *correlation*, between two variables: ice-cream sales (A) and the rate of accidental drowning (B). When one value goes up (or down), so does the other.

Correlation

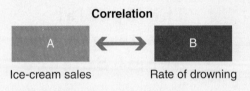

Ice-cream sales   Rate of drowning

Because ice cream isn't typically served at funerals, the reporter had no reason to believe that drowning leads to ice-cream sales. So the reporter concluded that eating ice cream (the independent variable) must somehow contribute to accidental drowning (the dependent variable). Ice cream can kill you, she reasoned.

However, this proposed *causal relationship* is *not* supported by the evidence. Instead, the reporter has stumbled upon a *spurious* relationship between A and B, a correlation that does not result from any direct relationship between the two variables but from their relationship to another variable (C).

To establish causality, three conditions must be met typically (Babbie 2013):

1. The variables must be correlated.
2. Cause must precede effect. In other words, change in the independent variable must occur before the change in the dependent variable.
3. The causal relationship must not be explainable by some third variable.

Spurious Relationship

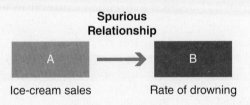

Ice-cream sales   Rate of drowning

Although a correlation exists in the case of the reporter's story, both ice-cream sales and drowning can be explained by a third variable, weather temperature. People are more likely to eat ice cream and to go swimming when the weather is warm. An increase in temperature, therefore, produces an increase in both ice-cream sales and drowning accidents.

Causal Relationship

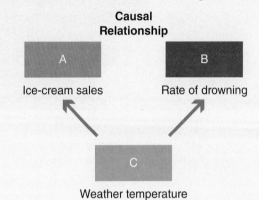

Weather temperature

This example is simple, but sociologists encounter complex questions about the relative influence of different variables all the time. Does gender, work experience, or discrimination best explain the pay gap between women and men? Is it race, class, or some other factor that influences educational attainment most? What factors are most important in explaining disparities in health? Sociological researchers use a variety of advanced statistical techniques to help sort out these sorts of questions, assess the influence of many variables, and avoid errors in logic like the one shown here.

So relax; you can eat that ice cream (in moderation) without worrying about lethal consequences.

think about it

1. *Can you think of another example that illustrates the idea of a spurious relationship?*

2. *The overall mortality rate in the United States does vary by season, with the highest rate of deaths occurring in the winter and the lowest in the summer. Why do you think this might be the case? How might you go about investigating the correlation between season and mortality?*

---

a compelling case that these personal stories can "help us understand how experiencing a lack of respect and dignity may turn individuals away from services intended to help them" (Hoffman and Coffey 2008, 219), a key lesson in helping social service agencies provide more effective and respectful services for people who are homeless.

Usually a quantitative study allows a researcher to gather information on many different cases but provides a limited amount of information on each case. In contrast, qualitative studies provide a wealth of detail on a relatively small number of cases. Sometimes a sociologist will use a combination of quantitative and qualitative data to get the best of both worlds.

When sociologists have conducted research among homeless men and women, they have helped local agencies better understand the experiences and needs of their community's homeless population and implement more effective services.

to rule out certain claims and identify explanations that are probably true.

The goal of social scientists is to reach tentative conclusions that they can act on, while remaining open to new insights that might be generated by more research. This skeptical attitude means that research findings remain subject to scrutiny and revision as more information becomes known. In this sense, social science research is an ongoing process: new studies respond to and build on prior research. Table 2.1 provides a short summary of the four key elements of social science research.

The Special Challenges of Social Science

Because social scientists study people and not the physical or natural world, they face a number of challenges that do not generally confront natural scientists:

TRANSPARENCY OF METHODS Social science depends on **transparency,** *the requirement that researchers explain how they collected and analyzed their evidence and how they reached their conclusions.* Transparency allows others to "see" how the research was done by reading a description of the process used in the study. Readers, including scholars, can then critically assess the research and its findings and replicate the study if they wish.

PROVISIONAL KNOWLEDGE Social science is based on **provisional knowledge**—*the idea that all truth claims are tentative and open to revision if new evidence is discovered.* According to this approach, we can never be 100 percent certain about our understanding of social phenomena, but we can use systematic analyses

- ■ *Social researchers are unlikely to be able to control conditions.* In a lab experiment a chemist can control the environment and manipulate a variable such as heat to study its impact on a chemical reaction. But for ethical, legal, and practical reasons, human beings cannot be manipulated at will by a sociological researcher. For example, a sociologist can't set up an experiment in which children are subject to varying levels of abuse to observe the effects. Some sociologists conduct lab experiments on small-group interactions, but the vast majority of research on large-scale social phenomena takes place through the use of other methods, such as surveys and observation.

- ■ *Social life cannot be predicted with the certainty of natural laws.* At sea level, raising the temperature of water to 212 degrees Fahrenheit causes it to boil.

TABLE 2.1	THE ELEMENTS OF SOCIAL SCIENCE RESEARCH
Identifying and understanding patterns in social life	Scientists seek to identify recurrent patterns in human thought and action.
Gathering empirical evidence	Patterns are identified based on evidence that can be observed or documented using human senses.
Using transparent methods	Researchers need to disclose how they collect and analyze their evidence.
Viewing knowledge as provisional	Social science is based on the idea that truth claims are tentative and open to revision if new evidence is discovered.

One of the ongoing challenges of sociological research is that those who participate in studies know they are being observed. This awareness can alter their behavior or responses accordingly.

In the early 1930s, researchers seeking to enhance productivity studied workers at Western Electric's Hawthorne Works Plant outside Chicago. They found that no matter what various small changes in working conditions they made, productivity at the plant improved. They concluded that workers were responding not to the changed conditions but to being the focus of attention, a phenomenon now known as the Hawthorne effect. Here, a supervisor monitors the performance of workers.

Assuming the conditions remain the same, the water responds exactly the same way every time the temperature increases. We can never be certain how different people will perceive, interpret, or react to a given situation, however. As a result, in social science there are always exceptions to any rule. We must talk in terms of *rates* of behavior, for example, or the *probability* of something happening. Still, as we have seen, sociologists can describe and explain the *patterns* of perception, behavior, and experience that characterize social life and predict the *likelihood* that certain social phenomena will occur.

■ ***Human beings are conscious of being studied, which may change their behavior.*** In a classic example, researchers in the 1930s tested various ways to improve the productivity of workers at Western Electric's Hawthorne plant outside of Chicago (Roethlisberger 1939). No matter what changes the researchers initiated— whether they increased or decreased the lighting or lengthened or shortened break times—they discovered that productivity went up. They concluded that the very fact that workers were being observed, rather than the particular changes being tested, contributed to higher productivity. *The fact that human beings will react differently because they know they are in a study has since been referred to as the* **Hawthorne effect.** Although researchers have ways of dealing with such behavior, the Hawthorne effect is a constant challenge.

The important elements and special challenges of social science research are best seen by examining the actual work of research, a subject to which we now turn.

Doing Research

Two key components, theory and data, act together in social science research. Theory helps us identify key research questions and interpret the data that are collected. Data provide the evidence that can support existing theory, lead to changes in theory, contradict a theory, or result in the development of a new theory (Merton 1968a). In this section we explore the role of theory as well as the various types of research techniques used to collect data.

The Roles of Theory

Theory plays several vital roles in social research: (1) it can highlight key questions or issues; (2) it can help explain the data collected; and (3) it can help us see the connections between phenomena that are not immediately apparent. *Deductive* reasoning occurs when a general theory informs the gathering of specific data. *Inductive* reasoning occurs when researchers develop a theory based on data they already have.

To illustrate the roles theory plays in social science research, let's consider a classic theory proposed by Arnold van Gennep ([1909] 1961) in the early twentieth century regarding *rituals*—repeated patterns of behavior performed at specific times, often involving symbols. Recall that the functionalist approach suggests that if something exists in the social world for an extended period of time it must be serving some social function. Van Gennep's more specific theory was that the function of some rituals was to mark a change of social status; he called such rituals *rites of passage*. Van Gennep's theory suggests that rites of passage help encourage or reinforce certain behavior, affirm common ties through their use of cultural symbols, serve as a communal acknowledgment of the change of status, and provide an outlet for emotions related to the status change.

HIGHLIGHTING KEY QUESTIONS A researcher can use van Gennep's theory about rites of passage to ask questions about the social world. What are the significant rites of passage today? How do these rituals mark changes in social status? The features that characterize rites of passage can be found in graduations, weddings, retirement parties, and funerals—each of which marks a significant change in status. High school graduation ceremonies mark the rite of passage from adolescence to young adulthood. They commemorate an accomplishment that society encourages and usually involve symbolic clothing such as robes, mortarboards, and tassels. These events also help channel the many mixed emotions—on the part of graduate and parents alike—that often accompany such a change in social status.

Similarly, when a family member or friend dies we typically follow culturally specific rituals as we mourn and remember. Funerals acknowledge a change of status, provide an outlet for grieving, and are laden with culturally significant symbolism, such as the color and types of clothing mourners typically wear. Whatever the specifics of the symbols involved, each rite of passage helps mark a transition. Van Gennep's theory alerts us to the significance of these rituals.

SPOTLIGHT

on social theory

Functionalism suggests that long-lasting social phenomena serve a useful purpose for society, and van Gennep's theory suggests several useful purposes for rituals. What rituals have been important in your life, and, in retrospect, what purposes did they serve?

EXPLAINING COLLECTED DATA Theory can help explain data that have been collected. When James Diego Vigil (1996) studied Chicano street gangs, he learned that a prospective gang member would routinely be attacked and beaten by several gang members at the same time. Vigil argued that this "street baptism" had the practical purpose of revealing a prospective member's fighting skills. But it was also a symbolic ritual that helped promote gang solidarity and establish an initiate's new identity and status as a member of the gang. Understanding the theory associated with rites of passage helps make sense of this apparently odd behavior.

SEEING CONNECTIONS By moving beyond description and analysis of specific phenomena to a more general or abstract level, theory can help us see patterns and connections between phenomena that are not immediately apparent. For example, through the theory of rituals as rites of passage we can see the common features of graduations, funerals, and "street baptisms." With a little sociological imagination, you can begin to recognize rites of passage in a wide range of social settings and expand your insights into the various roles they play in social life.

The Theory–Research Dynamic

We've noted that theory helps us interpret research and research helps us build theory. To better understand this interactive relationship, let's look at a hypothetical example from the world of sports.

What makes a team successful? Of course, different levels of talent and experience are important, but some sports teams seem to perform better than expected, whereas other teams that are highly talented "on paper" don't live up to expectations. Emile Durkheim's theory of *social solidarity* (see Chapter 1) could provide a starting point for an investigation into this question. Durkheim proposed that any well-functioning social group is held together by shared values. So perhaps bonding is a key to team success.

But does winning help bond the teammates to one another, or do they win because they are already bonded? Theory has helped us to identify a useful concept—social solidarity—and develop two competing hypotheses about the relationship between solidarity and success in sports. To assess our hypotheses, we need to design a study that will begin to untangle the relationship between solidarity and success. Perhaps we could survey the members of various teams about their values and level of solidarity before a season begins and again after the season concludes. Coupled with the team's performance record, a survey would give us data to assess our competing hypotheses.

We hope that our results will elaborate and clarify our theory, which will lead us (and perhaps other researchers) to conduct further research about the relationship between success and solidarity in any number of organizations, including businesses, schools, or military units. One study will not provide a final answer to the broader theoretical question about success and solidarity, but each study will provide additional insight into this relationship.

Different theoretical approaches may highlight different aspects of the same social relationship. For example, feminist theorists might suggest that we pay close attention to how gender dynamics might influence group solidarity on sports teams. Do girls or women bond differently on teams than do boys or men? What happens on co-ed teams? Considering a different theoretical approach can lead us to ask yet another set of research questions.

Theory, then, suggests areas of possible research by highlighting key questions, and it helps explain the data collected. In turn, we need data to assess the accuracy of theory. In some cases, research findings lend credence to theories; in others, the data contradict the theory. Either way, we gain a better understanding of the social world when we consider theory and data together.

One instance in which the data did not support the theory involved efforts to reduce heavy episodic drinking, also known as "binge drinking," on college campuses. To encourage students to drink moderately, about half of all four-year college campuses in the United States have adopted a program called "social norms marketing" in recent years. Researchers found that students usually overestimate how much their peers drink, and therefore they often drink more in order to "keep up" with what they perceive to be the norm of the group. Instead of telling students what they should *not* do ("You shouldn't binge drink!"), social norms marketing emphasizes the fact that most students *don't* binge drink. Using flyers, posters, ads, and other venues, college health officials let students know that, for example, "On this campus, 80% of students have fewer than five drinks when they party." By pointing out that the norm on campus is *not* to binge drink, college officials—according to this theory—can persuade more students to moderate their own drinking. However, when Wechsler and his associates (2003) gathered data from 118 college campuses over a four-year period to test this theory, they found that campuses using a social norms marketing approach had no significant reduction in student drinking. In this case, the data called into question the theory that underlay social norms marketing.

Research Methods

There is no single correct way to gather evidence for a research study. Instead, sociologists use a variety of **research methods,** *the procedures used by a researcher to collect and analyze data.* Generally they choose whatever method allows them to collect the most appropriate type of data needed to address the questions they are asking. Researchers who are interested in, say, what percentage of students at a particular school voted in the last presidential election (quantitative data) might use surveys and perhaps analysis of existing sources, such as official poll results. Those researchers who wanted to know *why* the students voted the way they did (qualitative data), though, might be more likely to conduct interviews and use focus groups. Other topics might require the researcher to do field research or conduct experiments.

SURVEY RESEARCH Probably the most commonly used technique in sociology is the **survey,** *a data collection technique that involves asking someone a series of questions.* Surveys are popular in part because they are very versatile, are useful for a wide variety of issues, and effectively describe large populations, if appropriate sampling techniques are used (Czaja and Blair 2004).

Survey researchers can use different kinds of questions. Some survey questions are constructed in a *closed-ended* or fixed-response format, which means a respondent must choose from a given set of responses. For example, the Pew Research Center for the People and the Press (2012) gathers data regularly on which media outlets people in the United States turn to for news. The center's 2012 Media Consumption Survey asked more than 3,000 adults a series of questions about how frequently they watch specific television news programs. For each program, respondents were asked to select from four possible responses: *regularly, sometimes, hardly ever,* or *never.* The advantage of closed-ended questions is that the researcher can easily code them for quantitative analysis. According to the Pew Center's 2012 report on news media audiences, 12 percent of respondents watch CNN "regularly," and 48 percent watch the local news "regularly."

However, if you have ever filled out a survey consisting of nothing but closed-ended questions, you might have noticed that sometimes the preselected answers didn't fit what you really wanted to say. Moreover, these types of answers may encourage people to respond in ways that they might not have otherwise. To address such problems, some surveys include *open-ended* questions that do not provide predetermined response categories. The Pew Center's media study also includes open-ended questions, such as "About how much time did you spend watching the news or any news programs on TV yesterday?" This type of question allows respondents to give their own estimate—say, 25 minutes or 2 hours—rather than fit their response into a preexisting category. Other news surveys might ask people *why* they watch specific news programs. Such open-ended questions allow for a wider, and perhaps more accurate, range of responses. However, the wide array of answers can be time-consuming to record and difficult to summarize and analyze.

Researchers also need to pay careful attention to the way the questions in a survey are worded because even small variations in wording can influence results significantly. The following are just a few of the many problems that can arise when researchers write survey questions:

■ *Lack of clarity.* An unclear question can produce inaccurate results. In one infamous example, the well-known Roper polling firm found that 22 percent of people in the United States believed it was possible that the Holocaust never happened, while another 12 percent said they weren't sure (Morin 1994). This startling finding was later revealed to be the result of a poorly worded question: "Does it seem possible or does it seem impossible to you that the Nazi extermination of the Jews never happened?" This awkwardly phrased question required a person affirming the existence of the Holocaust to agree with a double negative: that it was impossible it never happened. The percentage of people expressing doubt dropped to the single digits when the question was later rephrased to read, "Do you doubt that the Holocaust actually happened, or not?"

- **Different definitions.** *Validity* refers to successfully measuring what you intend to measure. For example, one study found that when the Census Bureau asked about the hours that a person worked "last week," most people thought the phrase referred to Monday through Friday. In fact, the question was supposed to include the weekend as well (Polivka and Rothgeb 1993). The researchers discovered that the wording of their question accidentally undermined its validity, since they were measuring something different than what they had intended.

- **Loaded language.** Some "hot button" words and expressions have positive or negative connotations that can influence a survey's results. One study (Rasinski 1989) found that only 23 percent of respondents said too little money was spent on "welfare," but 63 percent said too little money was spent on "assistance to the poor"—essentially the same thing. Clearly, the word *welfare* had a negative connotation.

- **Double-barreled questions.** Each question should be about one topic only. Questions that cover more than one topic are called "double-barreled." A question intended to measure trust and widely used by pollsters for decades reads, "Generally speaking, would you say that most people can be trusted or that you can't be too careful in dealing with people?" Researchers (Miller and Mitamura 2003) showed, however, that this question is really double-barreled: it asks whether or not people can be trusted *and* whether or not you should be careful. It's quite possible to trust people in general but still feel you should be careful in dealing with them. Trust and caution are not the same thing, and the question as originally worded conflates the two concepts.

When you are considering the results from survey research, examine the questions to see if their wording might have influenced the results.

When you interpret survey results, it is also important to know two factors. What is the *population*, the target group a researcher is interested in studying? And who participated in the survey? Researchers refer to this group as the **sample,** or *part of the population that represents the whole.*

Depending on what is being studied, a population might be made up of individual people, institutions, newspaper articles, or a host of other things. Let's say you want to study how students on your campus get news about current events. In this case, you would be interested in the entire student population on your campus. It would be virtually impossible for you to gather data on all the cases in that population—all the students who attend your college. Instead, to conduct high-quality research, you need a good sample that accurately represents the larger population you are studying.

There are many different types of samples. (See Table 2.2.) One way to obtain a high-quality sample is to choose it randomly. In a **random sample,** *every element of the population has an equal chance of being chosen.* To draw a random sample, you need a complete list of all the members of the population you want to study. Putting the names of all the students enrolled at your college in a (very large) hat and choosing some of the names would be a random sample, since every student from that population (your college) would have an equal chance of being chosen.

Random samples of adequate size allow researchers to accurately **generalize,** or *describe patterns of behavior of a larger population based on findings from a sample.* Pollsters, for example, are able to make good predictions about the outcome of national elections in the United States by sampling only about 1,200 people. Such polls are not perfect, but they give a close approximation of the views of the target population as a whole. (See the Sociology Works box.)

TABLE 2.2	THREE TYPES OF SAMPLES		
	Convenience Sample	**Quota Sample**	**Random Sample**
Key feature	Data are not representative, in a statistical sense, of a broader target population.	Specific groups in the broader target population are included in representative proportions.	Every element of the population has a known and equal chance of being chosen.
Strengths	Simple and often inexpensive.	Balances generalizability with practicality.	Generalizable to a broader population.
Weaknesses	Not generalizable to a broader population.	More difficult to achieve than a convenience sample.	Often not practical; most difficult and expensive to achieve.

SOCIOLOGY WORKS

Andrew Kohut and Public Opinion Research

Have you ever wondered who comes up with the polling numbers about elections? One main source of election forecasting and other types of public opinion data is the Pew Research Center, a nonpartisan "fact tank" that provides information on the issues, attitudes, and trends shaping the United States and the world. From 2004 to 2012 Andrew Kohut was president of the center. For Kohut, the study of sociology paved the way for a career spent studying American attitudes and political opinions. His academic training in research methods as a sociology major prepared him for its wider application in the public sphere.

Instead of conducting research as a university professor, Kohut worked at the Gallup Organization, one of the most prestigious polling firms in the country, where he was president for 10 years. Kohut later became founding director of the Pew Research Center, an umbrella organization that is home to seven independent research groups that examine journalism, technology, religion, global attitudes, and social and demographic trends.

Today, Kohut is a well-known commentator about American public opinion. He appears regularly on radio and television and writes essays for the op-ed page of the *New York Times*. In founding the Pew Research Center, he established one of the most reputable sources of information on public opinion in the United States.

Kohut also directs the Pew Research Center's Global Attitudes Project, which conducts public opinion surveys around the world on a wide range of subjects, from the attitudes of the Chinese about their country's economy to the extent of anti-Semitism in Europe to global attitudes about free trade, health care, and the image of the United States. By 2009 the project's survey team had completed more than 330,000

Andrew Kohut

interviews in 60 countries. Conducting public opinion research on a global scale requires researchers to address a variety of challenges: translating their questionnaires into local languages, conducting face-to-face interviews in some nations, and interviewing over both landlines and cell phones in others.

In summing up his ambitions for the projects he directs, Kohut notes: "Our greatest hope is to do a good job of informing the American public about the opinions and trends that are shaping their lives and the world—from politics to the media, to foreign policy, to the major social issues of our time. Our greatest challenge is to tell the story of public opinion fully and with nuance, and at the same time communicate it in a way that is understandable to our audiences" (Kohut n.d.).

> "Our greatest hope is to do a good job of informing the American public about the opinions and trends that are shaping their lives and the world."

think about it

1. *Have you ever responded to a survey—by mail, phone, or online? What did you think of the experience?*

2. *Do you think it is helpful to know the results of public opinion research about current events? Why or why not?*

3. *For what research project might you want to design your own short survey?*

For many research projects, however, it is not possible to gather a totally random sample. For your hypothetical study of how students on your campus get news about current events, you might decide to walk across campus and give your survey to people you meet "at random." This method will *not* yield a random sample of the students at your college, though, since your selections will be influenced by the area of campus you choose, the time of day you go out, and so forth. In other words, every student at the college will *not* have an equal chance of being chosen. This method is called a *convenience sample*, a way of choosing

study participants based simply on the fact that it is convenient for the researcher. In this case, because you do not know if your sample is representative of all students at the college, you cannot generalize your findings to the population of the campus as a whole.

In between a random sample and a convenience sample is the *quota sample*, in which the researcher tries to achieve a generalizable sample by making sure various groups within the target population are present in representative proportions. The groups typically targeted in a quota sample are those that are relevant for the research question at hand and those that have proven to be significant in other research. For example, if you were studying whether or not students at your school were satisfied with their college experience, you would want your sample to match key features of the student population as a whole, including gender and full- or part-time status. If 60 percent of the students at your college are women, and 25 percent of students attend part time, then your quota sample should match these characteristics. Even though a quota sample is not a true random sample, the more specific your quota system, the more confident you can be that the sample can be generalized to the larger population.

There is one final critical factor in using samples: research studies should report how a sample was generated so that readers can make their own assessment of how well the sample represents the population as a whole.

INTENSIVE INTERVIEWS AND FOCUS GROUPS

An **intensive interview** (sometimes known as a "qualitative interview" or "in-depth interview") is *a data-gathering technique that uses open-ended questions during somewhat lengthy face-to-face sessions.* These interviews are semi-structured, with the interviewer usually using a combination of preplanned questions along with follow-up and clarifying questions that he or she improvises as the session progresses (Rubin and Rubin 2004). Intensive interviews produce more in-depth information from a respondent than a survey provides, but they are very time consuming to conduct. As a result, intensive interview studies generally include a far smaller number of respondents than surveys, commonly fewer than 100 participants, making it more difficult to generalize a researcher's findings to larger populations. One way to expand the number of people involved is to interview them in a *focus group*, made up usually of 6 to 12 people (Stewart, Shamdasani, and Rook 2006). A moderator asks preplanned and follow-up questions, encourages participation, and helps ensure that no one participant dominates the discussion.

When sociologist Gayle Sulik (2007) set out to explore women's experiences with breast cancer, she designed a study that used intensive interviews as the primary source of data. In her interviews with 60 breast cancer survivors, Sulik asked the women to provide their "illness narratives"—accounts of the initial diagnosis and how their experience with cancer had influenced their lives; descriptions of their relationships with family members, friends, and doctors; and stories of how they managed during the most difficult times. Sulik found that women experience breast cancer—especially the medical and emotional care they receive—in ways that reflect broad expectations about women's role as caregivers. In particular, women with breast cancer were often remarkably selfless: they tended to be unwilling to ask for help and reluctant to accept help from others. They had to deal with their own fears and pain while trying to help their families cope with the disruption and fear surrounding the illness. The interview format allowed Sulik to gather information that a closed-ended set of questions would not have revealed.

FIELD RESEARCH

As the name suggests, **field research** (sometimes called *ethnography* or *field work*) is *a data collection technique in which the researcher systematically observes some aspect of social life in its natural setting.* In some cases, the researcher tries to remain separate from the activities he or she is studying. In other cases, the researcher engages in *participant observation*, a type of field research in which the researcher both observes and actively takes part in the setting or community being studied. Field researchers talk to the people they observe and develop detailed field notes about what they see and hear—notes that form the foundation of the researcher's analysis (Schatzman and Strauss 1973). One of the key challenges for observational field researchers is gaining access to the setting and being accepted by those they are studying.

As field researchers immerse themselves in the environment they are studying, they become aware of significant questions or issues that deserve closer attention. Mark Fishman worked as a newspaper reporter for seven months in his investigation of how news is made. In a now-classic study, *Manufacturing the News*, Fishman (1980) drew on his field notes from his participant observation as an apprentice reporter to explore how reporters' daily routines—where they look for news and whom they talk to each day—define the stories that become news.

More recently, researchers conducting observational research at Euronews, a multilingual news channel that broadcasts throughout Europe (Baisnee and Marchetti 2006), found that the demands of producing 24-hour news in seven different languages resulted in a kind of "sedentary journalism," in which journalists produce most of the news without ever leaving their offices. Rather than cover a story on location, the reporters—responding to the norms of round-the-clock news—rely on phone interviews, online and archival research, and the use of video images shot by other journalists.

EXISTING SOURCES

Researchers frequently rely on existing sources, making use of available data and documents rather than collecting new data and evidence.

A researcher who conducts **secondary data analysis** *uses data previously collected by other researchers*. Government and private agencies such as the U.S. Census Bureau, the National Opinion Research Center, and Statistics Canada maintain and continually update major data sets, which are made available to researchers wishing to address a variety of research questions. Since such ready-made data sets enable them to skip the time, cost, and effort of gathering original data, many researchers find them an attractive option.

For example, one researcher used data from the 1974 through 2010 General Social Survey to examine whether the level of confidence Americans have in the scientific community has changed over time (Gauchat 2012). His analysis shows that overall public confidence in science has remained rather stable over 35 years. However, political conservatives and those who frequently attend church are exceptions to the national trend; they have shown a long-term growing distrust of science. Such distrust likely has been a factor in fueling political debates about climate change, creationism, and other politically contested issues.

Researchers can also analyze various other kinds of existing sources. Historical documents found in libraries and archives are essential to a researcher who is creating a social history. Similarly, mass media content such as a TV reality series or a video game can be an important source of sociological information. **Content analysis** refers to *a variety of techniques that enable researchers to systematically summarize and analyze the content of various forms of communication—written, spoken, or pictorial* (Holsti 1968).

One recent content analysis examined gender portrayals in the world of video games (Dill and Thill 2007). Drawing on a representative sample of images from the top-selling video game magazines—a total of 479 images of game characters from *Electronic Gaming Monthly*, *PC Gamer*, *Game Informer*, *The Official Xbox Magazine*, *Computer Gaming World* and *Game-Pro*—the authors found that gender stereotypes are rampant. Sixty percent of female characters were depicted in a sexually suggestive way; almost 4 in 10 of the female characters appeared scantily clad. Less than 1 percent of male characters were depicted in this way. In addition, more than 80 percent of male characters and more than 60 percent of female characters were

portrayed as aggressive—engaged in combat, posing with weapons, wearing armor. Summarizing their findings, Dill and Thill note: "The vision of masculinity video game characters project is that men should be powerful, dominant, and aggressive. The story video game characters tell about femininity is that women should be extreme physical specimens, visions of beauty, objects of men's heterosexual fantasies, and less important than men. An emerging trend, though, is that these sexy, curvaceously thin beauties are also now typically violent" (p. 861). In this study, content analysis gives researchers quantitative data on a popular culture trend that may have broader significance for our society.

EXPERIMENTS   An **experiment** is *a data-gathering technique in which the researcher manipulates an independent variable under controlled conditions to determine if change in an independent variable produces change in a dependent variable, thereby establishing a cause-and-effect relationship* (Campbell and Stanley 1963). In an experiment a researcher compares two groups of subjects: a *control group* and a group that is exposed to some "stimulus" or "treatment." Afterward, the two groups are compared to evaluate the effects of the treatment. Since researchers need to control the experimental situation, experiments usually

A recent content analysis of popular video games revealed that they are full of gender stereotypes, with aggressive male characters and sexually suggestive female characters. But many of the female characters are both aggressive and sexualized, including the characters Skarlet and Mileena from the Mortal Kombat series. How might you go about studying gender in video games?

must take place in a laboratory setting, rather than in a natural social setting. This requirement greatly limits the types of issues that sociologists can examine using experiments and is one of the reasons experimental research is relatively uncommon in sociology. Still, some sociologists have designed innovative studies that have taken advantage of the benefits of an experimental design in a real-world setting.

For example, an experiment that sociologist Devah Pager (2007) designed to determine the impact of a criminal record on a person's job opportunities made use of actual job interviews with real-world employers. Pager hired and trained two pairs of testers—one pair was white and one pair was African American—and gave them identical backgrounds and resumes, except for one difference. In each pair, one of the testers was given a criminal record and the other was not. She sent the testers out to apply for a total of 350 jobs (the pair of African American testers applied for 200 jobs and the pair of white testers applied for 150 jobs) and waited to see who would be called back for a job interview. The study design was complex, but Pager made sure that the only difference within each pair of job applicants was the criminal record. The independent variable in each pair, then, was a job applicant's criminal record; the dependent variable was whether the applicant would be invited for a job interview. Pager's findings were stark but not unexpected: those applicants with a criminal record were far less likely to get called

back for a job interview than their counterparts with no criminal record. Pager's more significant finding was that white job applicants with a criminal record were more likely to get a callback for an interview (17 percent) than were black job applicants with *no* criminal history (14 percent). And black job applicants with a criminal record received a callback only 5 percent of the time. The study's rigorous experimental design applied in a real-world setting, rather than a laboratory, enhances the validity of Pager's research.

Table 2.3 summarizes the most common data collection methods.

Research Ethics

Regardless of which data-gathering techniques they use, sociologists are expected to adhere to ethical standards in their research activities. Some standards apply to all types of researchers in the natural and social sciences, such as those forbidding the falsification of data or the misrepresentation of findings. All researchers are also expected to take active steps to help ensure the integrity of their work—for example, by disclosing all sources of funding for the research. But other ethical standards apply to the unique situations that arise when scientists study people.

An important summary of ethical standards for social science research can be found in the professional "Code of Ethics"

TABLE 2.3	MAJOR RESEARCH METHODS		
	Features	**Strengths**	**Weaknesses**
Surveys	A series of questions is administered in writing (on paper, via Internet) or verbally (by telephone or in person).	Cost-effective way to get information on a wide range of issues. Results, especially from large random samples, can be generalized.	Closed-response options can be limiting. Data are broad but often not particularly deep.
Interviews and focus groups	Open-ended questions and improvised follow-up questions are asked in relatively lengthy face-to-face interviews that are typically recorded for later analysis.	Allows subjects the freedom to develop detailed responses in their own words; researchers can immediately ask follow-up questions.	Time and labor intensive. Data are rich and deep, but small, nonrandom sample limits generalizability.
Field research	Researchers work in natural settings observing social interactions and ongoing nature of social life.	Less intrusive than direct questioning, resulting in more natural data. Goes beyond what people say to observing what they do.	Very time and labor intensive. Data are rich and deep, but small, nonrandom sample limits generalizability. Researcher presence can affect results.
Existing sources	Quantitative data are reanalyzed or existing materials, such as media content or historical records, are used.	Convenient and cost-effective. Existing content not affected by researcher's presence.	Data specific to the researcher's question may not be available.
Experiments	Researchers use controlled manipulation of social conditions to test hypothesis.	Can isolate specific variable to study and establish causality.	Typically limited to micro-level questions. Ethical considerations restrict their applicability.

developed by the American Sociological Association (1999). The code states that the primary goal of ethical guidelines is "the welfare and protection of the individuals and groups with whom sociologists work"—in other words, to ensure that people involved in sociological studies are not harmed in any way. Studies that might be highly stressful or embarrassing, for example, are typically forbidden.

Sociologists are also expected to protect the privacy of their research subjects. In studies providing *anonymity*, subjects remain "nameless" even to the researcher, such as when surveys are returned to a researcher without identifying information. Anonymity is very difficult to achieve, however, since in most studies researchers know who the subjects are. It is more common for researchers to ensure *confidentiality*: the researcher knows each subject's identity but will not make it available to the public in any way. Some studies simply report collective data—on opinions, behavior, or demographic characteristics—and never cite any single individual. A study that quotes an individual may use a pseudonym or no name at all or may change some identifying details to ensure confidentiality.

Perhaps the single most important ethical standard in research is the principle of **informed consent,** which means that *subjects in any study must know about the nature of the research project, any potential benefits or risks that they may face, and that they have the right to stop participating at any time, for any reason.* This broad principle goes a long way in protecting human subjects. Because some populations are considered unable to provide informed consent—including those under age 18 and those who are mentally ill—special restrictions limit the sorts of research in which they can be involved.

Any college or university that receives funding from the federal government for research involving people must comply with certain rules and regulations aimed at protecting the subjects of the research. One of the most important is that schools must have an Institutional Review Board (IRB) to review proposed research projects and ensure that they comply with ethical standards, thus providing another layer of protection for research participants.

The Research Process: A Student Example

Perhaps the best way to appreciate all the steps in the research process (Figure 2.2) is to use as an example a project appropriate for a student in an introductory sociology class, like you. Even though this project is simpler in scope than the typical sociological study, the basic research process is the same:

1. *Choose and explore a general topic.* A variety of factors, including personal interest, intellectual curiosity, the availability of existing data, and political commitment, could influence the general topic you choose. Perhaps the data on age and voting presented earlier in this

chapter piqued your interest, and you find you want to learn more about the behavior of young voters. After choosing young people and voting as your general topic, you explore the existing research to find out what is already known about the voting behavior of this age group. You'll want to look at recent research on this topic so that you can begin to get a handle on the broader theories that help explain voting attitudes and patterns among young people.

2. *Identify a specific research question.* "Young people and voting" is too general a topic. You would need to narrow it down to a specific question of manageable size. For example, you may have noticed that many of your friends did not vote in the last presidential election. At the same time, in your research you may have read the theory that people who vote are also more likely to get involved in other kinds of civic activities. This connection between your own observations and your knowledge of a specific theory might spark a question: What *is* the relationship between voting and volunteer service or charitable work? In posing this research question, you may decide to hypothesize a relationship between two variables: Young people

FIGURE 2.2 | THE RESEARCH PROCESS

The research process can be thought of as a cycle because existing research is part of the scholarly literature that researchers consult when they develop and design a new study. When findings from a new study are published, they become part of the research literature that future scholars will review as they develop their own research projects.

who do service or charitable work are more likely to vote than are young people who do not do such work. This is the hypothesis you would now investigate.

3. ***Design the research study and specify the data to be collected.*** You now have a question that you must translate into a concrete study. Given your limited resources and time (issues that plague all social researchers!), you decide a survey would be the most efficient way to collect the data you need. To create your survey, you must operationalize your terms. For example, what qualifies as service or charitable work? Helping family members? Charity work completed to fulfill a requirement for a course? Do respondents have to be engaged in such work now or can they have done it in the past? You must be clear about how you will measure these and all other variables in advance of your study. Once you've clarified your key terms, you'll need to create a *questionnaire*, the specific set of questions that you will ask each person you survey.

At this stage, you must also devise your sampling strategy—that is, determine who will receive your survey. Since this is a small school project, you will likely have to limit your study to students on your own campus. The results of your survey, therefore, will not accurately reflect the voting behavior of all young people, which limits your ability to generalize your findings. Students on your campus are likely to be different from students elsewhere and will certainly be different from young people who do not attend college. But even for your small study, you need to make sampling decisions: How many students will you select for the study? How will you choose them? In addition, you will need to decide how you want to administer the survey—by mail, by phone, over the Internet, in face-to-face interviews, or any combination of these methods.

4. ***Consider ethical dimensions of your research and, if necessary, get approval from your school's Institutional Review Board, or IRB.*** You should be sensitive to any ethical issues your research raises. In addition, any research project involving people will likely have to be reviewed by your school's IRB, which will want to make sure, for example, that all participants will provide informed consent.

5. ***Collect, analyze, and interpret the data.*** Finally, you are ready to administer your survey. Afterward, you must enter the resulting data in a computer using a software package that will allow you to analyze this information. Your analysis of the data could range from simple summaries of the responses (for example, 42 percent of respondents voted in the last election) to comparisons between groups (for example, similarities and differences in the amount of charity work done by voters and nonvoters) or more complex analyses of the relationship between the variables. Once your data analysis is complete, you will need to summarize what you have

found. The conclusions to be drawn from data are not self-evident, however; data must be interpreted in light of theoretical or substantive questions. How does your evidence apply to the question you raised originally? What have you learned about the relationship between voting and service or charity work? Has your hypothesis been confirmed? Do your findings have any bearing on theories in this field?

6. ***Report the results.*** The final step involves writing a report of the study. Adhering to the norm of transparency, you will identify your initial research question, explain the process of data collection, present the results, explain what you think these results tell you about your research question, and show how these results fit with previous research and theory on these issues. You might also decide to write a summary of your findings for a broader audience and publish an article in your school's newspaper. Perhaps another researcher will take your study into account when developing his or her own related project, bringing the research process full circle.

Even a simple school project such as this one reveals the complexity of doing research. At every step of the way, you must make decisions that balance the "ideal" project with reality: the limitations under which you are working. Social scientists face similar dilemmas all the time. They do not have unlimited staff, budgets, or time. As a result, research projects always involve compromises. In the best research, though, social scientists find creative ways to gather the data they need to address the question at hand adequately. This process involves both the precision of science and the ingenuity associated with any challenging endeavor.

Now that you have a sense of the general research process, let's take a look at different types of sociological research.

Types of Research

Sociology is a "big tent" discipline that includes a diverse array of approaches to studying the social world. These research approaches can be categorized into three major types summarized in Table 2.4: *positivist*, *interpretive*, and *critical* social science (Benton 1977; Fletcher 1974; Guba and Lincoln 1994; Ritzer 1975). Because some of the assumptions of these perspectives are mutually exclusive, different researchers tend to emphasize one approach over the other two. However, during their careers, many researchers use two or even all three approaches, depending on the question at hand. Although they vary in some important ways, all three types of research share the basic elements of social science we discussed earlier: their practitioners search for patterns in social life, insist on empirical evidence to support knowledge claims, demand transparency in the methods used to gather and analyze data, and consider knowledge produced by research to be provisional.

TABLE 2.4   THREE APPROACHES TO SOCIAL SCIENCE RESEARCH

	Positivist	Interpretive	Critical
Areas of agreement	All three are based on the search for patterns in social life, require empirical evidence to support claims, demand transparency in the methods used to gather and analyze data, and consider knowledge produced by research to be provisional.		
Nature of the social world	Composed of discrete elements that interact in recurring patterns, producing usually stable social systems	Composed of evolving definitions of reality formed in the context of human interaction	Structured by power imbalances that produce conflict and result in social change
Goal of the research	Identify laws in social life to enable prediction and control	Better understand the meaning that the social world holds for others	Better understand how society works to promote social change
The role of values in research	Scientific research should be value-free; researchers should pursue objectivity by maintaining a detached distance from those being studied.	Scientific research should present an accurate portrait of the people being studied, including their values; researchers can gain insight by building relationships with those being studied.	Scientific research inevitably involves a value position that researchers should make explicit; researchers should help promote positive social change.

In the following sections, we review these three basic approaches—especially with respect to their assumptions about the nature of the social world, their goals, and their view of the role of values in research. We use studies about class and economic inequality to illustrate each type of research.

Positivist Social Science

The most commonly used approach to sociological research is positivism—a term that dates back to Auguste Comte, as you may recall from Chapter 1. **Positivist social science** is *an approach that assumes that the social world, like the natural world, is characterized by laws that can be identified through research and used to predict and control human affairs* (Hoover and Donovan 2007). Researchers using the positivist approach usually look at quantitative data and use the language of variables in their analyses. Positivist social scientists strive for **value-neutrality,** *removing any personal views from the research process.* That is, positivists tend to argue that, with the exception of choosing a topic to study, science should not involve the researcher's values, beliefs, or opinions, and, ideally, social scientists should remain disinterested parties in the research they conduct. To positivist social scientists, a sociologist's job is to study the social world, not try to change it.

One of many examples of positivist research is sociologist Miles Simpson's (1990) examination of the relationship between political democracy and economic inequality. Using existing data from 62 countries, Simpson tried to test various theories about why some countries have greater economic inequality than others. Proponents of some economic theories argue that inequality increases in the early stages of a

country's economic development, peaks, and then decreases as the country becomes more developed. These theories explain inequality by focusing on *economic* processes. However, other theories suggest that greater income inequality is the result of greater inequality in the *political* system. Simpson's examination of the data lends support to the latter theory. He finds that more democracy in a society is associated with less income inequality.

Interpretive Social Science

If positivist social science tends to encourage distance between researcher and subject, interpretive social science does just the opposite. Those using this approach suggest that the study of social life cannot be limited to features that are external to individuals, such as economic data. Instead, **interpretive social science** focuses on *an understanding of the* meaning *that people ascribe to their social world.* This focus on meaning makes interpretive social science fundamentally different from the natural sciences in the methods researchers use. In particular, interpretive researchers try to empathize with the people they study in order to understand the world from their perspective. This method requires close contact with the people in a study, an approach often traced to Max Weber, who argued for using *verstehen*—a German word that means "to understand"—in social research.

Interpretive researchers usually use qualitative data, often in the form of the words and explanations given by the people they are studying. However, interpretive researchers are not interested simply in how individuals understand social life; they seek to uncover patterns in the ways people make meaning of their social worlds and then

Research and Change

As we saw in Chapter 1, sociologists have been studying change since the discipline's beginning. In the 1960s and 1970s, researchers were examining the nature of the widespread civil rights, antiwar, women's rights, and student movements, often while being a part of those campaigns. This work helped shed light on the nature of protest actions. Rather than seeing demonstrations as made up of mobs of irrational actors, sociologists showed them to be rational responses to grievances. These responses depended on the mobilization of key resources (recruiting volunteers, raising money, choosing tactics, cultivating skills) and the development of clear messages (identify an injustice, propose an alternative inspire action) to challenge institutional power. Today, sociologists examine how such efforts are changing as activist groups adopt new technologies such as social media, address new global issues such as climate change, and work to overcome new challenges such as political cynicism and electronic surveillance. One key question for today: Can social change efforts succeed using only the Internet, or must traditional street actions ultimately be a part of a movement's tactics?

describe the form and content of such interpretive patterns. This work does not necessarily promote social change, but often it can promote empathy and understanding for the people being studied.

Interpretive studies tend to deal directly with people's values, beliefs, and opinions because those are an integral part of the social world the researcher is studying. To adhere to the requirement of transparency, interpretive researchers often include a substantive discussion in their published research reports of their relationship with their research subjects. Interpretive researchers share the social science norm that their own personal values, feelings, and opinions should not distort their research findings. However, they also believe that their close connections with the people they are studying can enhance, rather than detract from, the accuracy of a study because their rapport with their subjects means there is less chance that they will misinterpret their findings.

For example, in his pioneering study of a poor urban neighborhood, sociologist William Foote Whyte (1914–2000) spent three years living in "Cornerville" (later revealed to be Boston's North End), spending much of his time with members of a gang of young men he called "the Nortons." Whyte was particularly close with the gang's leader, Doc, and the two men regularly discussed the community, the corner gang, even the best way to meet people from different sectors of Cornerville society. Whyte's interpretive study, the now-classic *Street Corner Society* ([1943] 1993), is full of lengthy quotes from Doc, who served as an invaluable neighborhood guide, a sounding board for Whyte's still-developing understanding of the community, and a critical reader of the early drafts of what became Whyte's book.

Critical Social Science

Critical social science is *research carried out explicitly to create knowledge that can be used to bring about social change.* Critical researchers do not focus solely on understanding society; rather, they are interested in understanding society in order to *improve* it in some way. A broad range of sociologists have followed in this tradition. Some invoke a famous line from Karl Marx ([1845] 1978, 145): "The philosophers have only *interpreted* the world, in various ways; the point, however, is to *change* it."

Critical social science rejects the idea of value neutrality, for which the positivists strive. For the critical researcher, value neutrality is neither possible nor desirable because all science incorporates some value position. Even advocating value neutrality is itself a value-laden position. Critical researchers say the issue is not *whether* values will be a part of their work but rather *which* values will inform research. Critical social science is usually associated broadly with values that encourage human freedom and social equality. As a result, this approach often addresses issues of power and inequality in society. The fact that critical researchers embrace such values, they argue, does not undermine the credibility of their research. To the contrary, critical social science researchers want to better understand and reveal the dynamics of power in society in the hope of bringing about social change. If such efforts are to be successful, they must be based on an accurate picture of how society works. Thus, although values are at the core of this approach, critical social scientists seek to understand society *as it is* in order to help promote society *as it might be.*

One critical social science study involved living wage campaigns, which try to ensure that the wages paid to workers are high enough to keep them and their families out of poverty. These efforts are usually local, and local economic conditions determine the specifics of each campaign. In the early years of this movement, an activist from the Los Angeles Living Wage Coalition turned to Robert Pollin, an economist, to assess the living wage proposal being considered in that city. Pollin teamed up with Stephanie Luce (1998), a sociologist specializing in labor markets, to produce a study of the proposal. Their study concluded that the living wage ordinance would help low-wage workers and would not lead to job losses. The researchers didn't stop there, though. They presented their findings to the Los Angeles City Council and helped get the ordinance passed. The two researchers were then approached by other living wage activists from around the country. Recognizing a need, they decided to produce a book that presented their own research on the issue and also examined other existing work.

These three approaches to social science research share some common ground. At the same time, they allow for multiple approaches to a single issue.

Thinking Critically: How to Assess Research

We can't all be experts on research methodology, so it is helpful to have some authorities who monitor the quality of the research for us. The scientific community does this monitoring through the **peer-review process,** *a way in which scholars evaluate research manuscripts before they are published in order to ensure their quality.* When a research article is submitted for publication to a peer-reviewed journal, the editors send the article out to be reviewed anonymously by several other scholars in the field. These scholars provide the editors with their analysis of the strengths and weaknesses of the study. The article will be published only if the reviewers and the editors agree that the study is credible and worthy of consideration. The reviewers do not have to agree with the study's findings; they just have to attest that the question being examined is significant, that the data collected

are appropriate and adequate, and that the conclusions reached are warranted. University presses often use a similar process when publishing books.

Although far from perfect, the peer-review process does provide the reader with a certain level of confidence about the basic competence of published research. Many research databases available through libraries allow you to limit your search to works that are published in peer-reviewed journals. You need not dismiss research and evidence published elsewhere, but you may want to give such work a more skeptical look since it has not been subjected to this rigorous review process.

After having surveyed some of the basics of social research in this chapter, you too are now equipped to carry out your own review process of the research that you encounter in both scholarly and popular publications. The ability to think critically about research findings is an important skill to develop that will be relevant to whatever field of study you pursue.

To assess a social scientific study, be sure to ask at least these six questions:

1. **What is the research question?** This is a simple but fundamentally important issue. Be sure the author has clearly identified the specific research question examined in the study.

2. **What is the theory informing the research?** What concepts and perspectives is the researcher emphasizing in this study? What issues might be left out by relying on this theoretical approach?

3. *How are variables operationalized?* When different research studies about the same topic reach different conclusions, it is often because of the way variables are defined and operationalized. One study may define "political participation" as "whether or not someone has voted," whereas another study may define it as "whether or not someone has done any of the following: voted, made a campaign contribution, worked on a campaign, joined a social movement organization, volunteered for a political cause, or taken part in a protest or demonstration." Conclusions about political participation in these two studies are likely to differ considerably because their authors have defined variables differently. When you read a study, be sure you understand what the authors mean by the variables they use.

4. *What is the sample?* Research is almost always based on a sample of a larger population. Different ways of selecting samples of the same population may lead to different results. When reading research, be sure you understand the sample on which the study is based. Is the study based on a single or a few cases, or on a larger sample? Was the sample chosen randomly? Understanding the dynamics of the sample can help you understand the results of a study.

5. *What are the data?* When reading research, be sure you understand what data have been assembled and analyzed. For example, is the research based on a survey that was designed specifically for this study? When and where did the researcher conduct observational fieldwork? What specific materials are the subjects of a content analysis? It is important to ask such questions when assessing how the author reached his or her conclusions.

6. *Are the conclusions justifiable?* In the final section of most studies, researchers usually interpret their data and explain the significance of the data for the question under consideration. Be sure you understand the claims the authors are making for their work and try to assess whether these claims are justifiable given the data presented in the report.

Asking these questions can help you think critically about knowledge claims and be an informed consumer of social scientific research.

A Changing World

TECHNOLOGY AND SOCIAL RESEARCH

W. E. B. Du Bois ([1899] 1996) spent more than a year conducting his house-to-house survey of African Americans in Philadelphia's Seventh Ward in 1896 and 1897. Around the same time, Emile Durkheim ([1897] 1951) and his research assistant examined the records of 26,000 suicides to determine each person's age, sex, and marital and parental status. In both cases, the authors completed all their data analysis by hand, painstakingly classifying and calculating everything manually.

Since then, technological changes have helped transform social research. Early sociologists relied mostly on qualitative accounts of social life. After World War II, though, academics quickly adopted the first computers to help them record, store, retrieve, and analyze quantitative data. These efforts were primitive by today's standards, but as increasingly powerful computers became available, a quantitative revolution took place in the social sciences. By the 1960s, much of the best-known and most prestigious research being published in sociology journals used sophisticated quantitative data and statistical techniques that depended on computers. As researchers began to use personal computers throughout the 1980s and 1990s, software packages that can store and analyze quantitative data became a common tool even for those with modest budgets. Computers were also central to the growing popularity of survey research. Researchers use computer-assisted telephone interviewing systems to conduct surveys. A caller reads a prepared script from a computer screen and records respondents' answers directly onto the computer with specially designed software.

Another revolution came about with the development of software programs designed for qualitative data analysis. Data from qualitative interviews and other sources still had to be painstakingly transcribed onto a computer, but a new generation of software allowed researchers to code their transcripts so that they could instantly retrieve relevant portions later on. Other software gave researchers the ability to code digital images and sound recordings as well. Such technology helped raise the profile of qualitative research once again.

Today, by enabling researchers to expand the scale of their work, keep costs down, and manage time efficiently, the Internet and related technologies have transformed many aspects of social research (Sappleton 2013). For example:

- Rather than relying solely on published articles, researchers use social networks to discuss their preliminary work, get feedback from peers, and learn about the research of others, thus speeding up the process of research innovation. Investigating published research is easier than ever with searchable digital databases of published work.

- Existing data sets on a wide range of topics are publicly available on the Internet and thus more accessible than ever for secondary analyses.

- The digitization of newspapers, magazines, and other forms of media makes it easier to conduct content analyses of these traditional cultural artifacts. Meanwhile, the vast content of Twitter, blogs, YouTube, and social media offers researchers new opportunities to study current ideas, politics, and popular culture in real time.

- The digital trail we leave in our daily lives has enabled increasingly sophisticated social network analyses that map our connections to media content and one another.

- Researchers routinely use the Internet and even smartphones to collect survey data. Intensive interviews can now be conducted using Skype and other Internet-based channels. One researcher (Davis 2013) even studied the online virtual environment, Second Life, by using her avatar to interview other people through their avatars.

As sociologists look for new avenues of research in the twenty-first century, they are certain to take advantage of today's lower-cost digital video cameras and recording devices, no doubt fueling an increase in multimedia research projects. With more academic journals available on the Internet, research reports are beginning to include sound, photographs, and video along with the written word. More advanced voice-recognition software that allows digitally recorded interviews to be transcribed automatically will greatly reduce the amount of labor for qualitative researchers. As new research tools continue to develop, researchers will find ingenious and practical ways to put them to use as they investigate the social world.

thinking sociologically about
The Research Process

■ Sociology is an activity that uses the framework of science to ask questions, gather data, and seek answers about the phenomena of the social world.

■ There are four key elements of social science research: (1) identifying and understanding patterns in social life; (2) gathering empirical evidence; (3) explaining how the evidence was collected and analyzed; and (4) viewing research claims as provisional knowledge, subject to revision.

■ Theory and data act together in social science research. Theory helps us identify key research questions and interpret the data that are collected. Data provide the evidence that can support existing theory, lead to changes in theory, contradict a theory, or result in the development of a new theory.

■ Sociology includes a diverse array of approaches to studying the social world. These research approaches can be categorized into three major types: *positivist, interpretive,* and *critical* social science.

■ Given that we are not all experts on research methodology, it is helpful to have some authorities who monitor the quality of the research, which the scientific community accomplishes through the peer-review process. The ability to think critically about research findings is an important skill to develop that is relevant in a variety of professional fields.

Looking Back

1. Conclusions based solely on a belief in authority, common sense, tradition, personal experience, or selective observation risk being inaccurate.

2. In addition to being a perspective and a discipline, sociology is an activity that involves basic research aimed at a scholarly audience, applied research often directed to some problem or need, as well as public sociology that tries to communicate the findings of both basic and applied research to a general nonacademic audience.

3. Social science research seeks to investigate patterns in social life systematically through the collection of empirical evidence. In doing their research, social scientists are committed to making their methods transparent, and they recognize that their truth claims are provisional.

4. Social science presents special challenges since the subjects being studied—people—are conscious of being studied and may change their behavior in response. In addition, it is difficult to control social life for experimentation or make predictions with certainty because different people can perceive, interpret, and react to a situation differently.

5. Research involves both theory and data. Theory helps us define research projects and interpret the data we collect. Data provide the evidence that helps us evaluate and build theory.

6. Research methods are the techniques researchers use to systematically collect and analyze data about the social world. The major methods of data collection are surveys, intensive interviews, field research, and experiments. Some research is based on secondary analysis of already-collected data.

7. Especially because people are involved, social scientists must adhere to basic research ethics that protect subjects from any harm caused by a study.

8. Sociological research generally follows a series of steps that includes exploring a general topic, identifying a specific research question, designing a study, considering the ethical dimensions of the study, collecting and analyzing data, and reporting results.

9. The three approaches to sociological research—positivist, interpretive, and critical—each carry distinct assumptions about the nature of social reality, the goals of research, and the role of values in research.

10. Knowledge of research methods helps us critically evaluate sociological research.

11. Rapidly changing technology in the past few decades has enabled researchers to collect and analyze ever-increasing amounts of data.

Critical Thinking: Questions and Activities

1. A friend who is a senior in high school tells you, "I'm not going to college. It doesn't make any sense to start off life by taking on all that debt. I saw some financial expert on TV saying you're better off today skipping college and starting a job right away. Look at my uncle; he never went to college and he manages a hotel and does well. Besides, if I don't go to college I won't have to study for SATs, figure out financial aid, or fill out those applications." Has your friend committed any of the errors in everyday thinking described in this chapter? Which ones? Explain.

2. Sometimes two research studies come to different conclusions about the same question. Knowing what you now know about the research process, identify three factors that might explain why two studies of the same issue lead to varying conclusions.

3. Suppose you have agreed to participate in a study of how college students meet potential romantic partners. Would you rather fill out a survey on this topic or participate in an intensive interview? Why? From the perspective of someone participating in a study, what are the advantages and disadvantages of each of these data-gathering techniques?

4. Identify a specific research question having to do with a topic of interest to students at your school. Your question might involve, for example, their satisfaction with their educational experience, their future career plans, their use of media, or their favorite classes. Create a short, 8- to 12-item questionnaire designed to help you better understand that topic. Remember, all the questions should be related to your specific research topic. Make sure to include both closed-ended and open-ended questions. You'll need to be careful and creative as you consider how to ask questions about your topic. Be as clear as you can in writing the questions and choosing the appropriate response categories for the closed-ended questions. Now give the questionnaire to three students and ask them to fill it out. When they are done, ask them if they were confused by any of the questions or if they have any other feedback on the questionnaire. Have the respondents brought up issues you didn't anticipate? How would you revise your questionnaire based on their feedback?

5. Advertisements frequently refer to research to demonstrate that a product is popular or effective or recommended by experts. Choose a popular magazine and look through the ads for any research-based claims (for example, "Studies show . . ."). When you have found one, evaluate the claim from a social science perspective. Are data presented to back up any claims? What kind of sample, if any, was used? Is the sample representative of a larger population? Do you agree with the conclusion about the research that the advertisement offers? Can you even evaluate the claim, given the limited information in the ad?

Key Terms

applied research (p. 33) the primary goal of this type of research is to directly address some social problem or need.

basic research (p. 33) the primary goal of this type of research is to describe some aspect of society and advance our understanding of it.

content analysis (p. 45) a variety of techniques that enable researchers to systematically summarize and analyze the content of various forms of communication—written, spoken, or pictorial.

correlation (p. 36) a relationship in which change in one variable is connected to change in another variable.

critical social science (p. 50) research carried out explicitly to create knowledge that can be used to bring about social change.

dependent variable (p. 36) the entity that changes in response to the independent variable.

empirical evidence (p. 36) data that can be observed or documented using the human senses.

experiment (p. 45) a data-gathering technique in which the researcher manipulates an independent variable under controlled conditions to determine if change in an independent variable produces change in a dependent variable, thereby establishing a cause-and-effect relationship.

field research (p. 44) a data collection technique in which the researcher systematically observes some aspect of social life in its natural setting.

generalize (p. 42) the ability to describe patterns of behavior of a larger population based on findings from a sample.

Hawthorne effect (p. 39) the fact that human beings will react differently because they know they are in a study.

hypothesis (p. 36) a statement about the relationship between variables that is to be investigated.

independent variable (p. 36) the entity that is associated with and/or causes change in the value of the dependent variable.

informed consent (p. 47) the principle that subjects in any study must know about the nature of the research project, any potential benefits or risks that they may face, and that they have the right to stop participating at any time, for any reason.

intensive interview (p. 44) a data-gathering technique that uses open-ended questions during somewhat lengthy face-to-face sessions.

interpretive social science (p. 49) an approach that focuses on understanding the meaning that people ascribe to their social world.

operationalize (p. 36) to clearly define the variables to be studied.

peer-review process (p. 51) a way in which scholars evaluate research manuscripts before they are published in order to ensure their quality.

positivist social science (p. 49) an approach that assumes that the social world, like the natural world, is characterized by laws that can be identified through research and used to predict and control human affairs.

provisional knowledge (p. 38) the idea that all truth claims are tentative and open to revision if new evidence is discovered.

public sociology (p. 33) the effort to bring the findings of both basic and applied sociological research to a broader nonacademic audience.

qualitative data (p. 36) any kind of evidence that is not numerical in nature, including evidence gathered from interviews, direct observation, and written or visual documents.

quantitative data (p. 36) evidence that can be summarized numerically.

random sample (p. 42) a sample in which every element of the population has an equal chance of being chosen.

research methods (p. 41) the procedures used by a researcher to collect and analyze data.

sample (p. 42) part of the population a researcher is studying that represents the whole.

secondary data analysis (p. 45) a type of research using data previously collected by other researchers.

survey (p. 41) a data collection technique that involves asking someone a series of questions.

transparency (p. 38) the requirement that researchers explain how they collected and analyzed their evidence and how they reached their conclusions.

value-neutrality (p. 49) the goal of removing any personal views from the research process; part of positivist social science.

variables (p. 36) measures that can change (or vary) and thus have different values.

3

Culture

looking AHEAD

What is **culture**, and how can you use the sociological perspective to understand its impact on your life?

How can **culture** both promote consensus and create conflict?

Why is **cultural** diversity increasing today?

When writer John Wray visited his cousin, an aid worker among the Amazonian Shuar community in a part of Ecuador accessible only by canoe or small plane, he was greeted as an honored guest. His hosts in the village of Pampansa invited Wray to the home of a local community leader, where they would share a bowl of *chicha,* an alcoholic beverage traditionally offered as a friendly greeting to visitors (Wray 2010).

While Wray was honored by the warm welcome and knew that his hosts were offering him a traditional drink as a gesture of friendship, he reports that he would "have given almost anything to escape." That's because in Pampansa, women prepare *chicha* by chewing on fermented yucca root and spitting into a large barrel, where the beverage accumulates before being transferred into a ceramic bowl for drinking.

After Wray's cousin Martin downed his bowlful of *chicha,* which their hosts described proudly as the best in the region, a newly refilled bowl was placed in front of Wray, who paused, wondering how he had ended up in this situation. After all, a year earlier he had visited Martin in a neighboring village and had managed to take only a sip of ceremonial *chicha.* This time, Wray found the *chicha*'s odor overpowering, likening the smell to "an old man's false teeth." Now, out of respect for his hosts, he was faced with guzzling the entire bowl.

In search of a way forward in this unfamiliar—and, for Wray, very unappetizing—situation, Wray recalled something that made the idea of drinking *chicha* more familiar and eased his sense of anxiety. He thought of all the times he had tasted someone else's saliva: "Hadn't I tasted spit countless times before? What was *chicha* drinking, after all, but French kissing once removed?" With the inspiration of this familiar activity in mind, Wray quietly gulped down his portion of *chicha,* paying respect to his host's generosity.

What we drink and eat, and how we prepare our food, is a familiar—and often vivid—illustration of how culture works. When we are part of a culture, our way of life seems natural, and we take it as a given; we are like fish in water. However, a cultural practice taken for granted by insiders may appear to outside observers as interesting, odd, curious, disturbing, or even threatening.

This chapter explores the central role of culture in social life and its pervasive influence on who we are as human beings. It considers some of the opportunities and challenges posed by our contemporary world, as people of many different cultures interact with increasing frequency and cultural diversity becomes a fact of daily life. As we gain a better understanding of the meaning of culture, we are able not only to analyze its impact on our own lives but also to prepare for a lifetime of interactions with people from cultures other than our own.

Defining Culture

Culture is one of sociology's core concepts. Indeed it is an essential part of the very definition of **society**—*a group of people who live together in a specific territory and share a culture.* Many people associate the word *culture* with museums and symphonies, a connection that is understandable because one definition of the term does involve the "cultivation" of the mind by studying the "best" a society has to offer. In the West, *culture* in this sense generally refers to such attributes as education and refinement in the arts and such artifacts as great works of literature and classical music. For sociologists and anthropologists, however, culture has a much broader, more inclusive meaning. **Culture** is *the collection of values, beliefs, knowledge, norms, language, behaviors, and material objects shared by a people and socially transmitted from generation to generation.* Sometimes culture is simply referred to as a way of life.

Culture must be learned; it is not biologically based. In fact, we can think of culture as all aspects of society that are transmitted socially rather than biologically. That you may be tall is a biological reality. That you use your height to advantage when you play basketball is a result of cultural influences. The process through which people learn about their culture is called *socialization*, a topic we explore in Chapter 6.

Culture operates at multiple levels, from everyday actions by individuals (micro level), to the norms that operate within an organization such as a school or business (meso level), to the beliefs and practices associated with very large groups of people, including entire societies (macro level). At each level, the elements of culture influence how people live.

At any level, culture can serve as a source of both consensus and conflict in society. Regardless of the size of a particular group, its culture serves as a common ground connecting group members to one another. As we see later in this chapter,

however, cultural differences can also contribute to tension and cause clashes among groups within a society and between different societies.

The Elements of Culture

Cultures consist of both material and nonmaterial elements. **Material culture** refers to *the physical objects produced by people in a particular culture, including tools, clothing, toys, works of art, and housing.* **Nonmaterial culture** refers to *the ideas of a culture, including values and beliefs, accumulated knowledge about how to understand and navigate the world, and standards or "norms" about appropriate behavior.* Nonmaterial culture exists in the world of thoughts and ideas; by contrast, material culture is physically real—it can be observed or touched. Collectively, the ideas and practices of a culture make up an entire way of life, affecting how people eat, work, love, think, worship, dress, learn, play, and live.

Because material objects can have symbolic (nonmaterial) meaning, the material and nonmaterial aspects of culture are often interconnected. For example, at the heart of many religions are sacred texts, such as Judaism's Torah, Christianity's Bible, and Islam's Qur'an (or Koran). These writings relate the central beliefs of each faith, thus comprising an essential part of the faith's nonmaterial culture. At the same time, the books themselves are often considered sacred as physical objects, to be treated with great respect as a part of the material culture. The books (Bibles, Qur'ans) are physical objects (material culture), but they also have symbolic (nonmaterial) significance. Thus Islamic detainees at the infamous Guantánamo Bay detention facility have alleged that U.S. interrogators exerted psychological pressure on them by desecrating the Qur'an, stepping on it and even putting it in a toilet, actions that are a grave violation of Islamic cultural norms (Lewis 2004).

Let's consider how the various aspects of culture work together by looking at a much less serious topic: the everyday activity of grooming hair. Most people put at least some thought into what their hair looks like. Whether unkempt or coolly styled, our hair often expresses who we are. Hairstyles also reflect cultural values; we learn what is considered attractive and what meaning different hairstyles convey. We may think we are making purely individual statements when we style our hair, but in fact, as the photographs on page 60 show, we are likely to be influenced heavily by the ideas and practices of our culture.

Often, we are so familiar with our own culture that we have a hard time recognizing its various elements or their significance. If we take a sociological perspective, however, we can see the often hidden ways that cultural ideas and practices help define our identities and our relationship to various communities. The elements of culture—to which we now turn—are summarized in Table 3.1.

Cultures develop different ideas about what constitutes a desirable appearance. These seem perfectly "normal" from the perspective of those inside a culture but can seem odd from the outside. Which hairstyles appear strange to you? Are there appearance norms in your culture that might seem unusual to outsiders?

TABLE 3.1	ELEMENTS OF CULTURE

Values: Deeply held principles or standards by which people make judgments about the world, especially in terms of what is desirable or worthwhile (for example, wealth equals success, family is important)

Beliefs: Convictions or opinions that people accept as true (for example, my country is good, God exists, the gods exist)

Knowledge: Information, awareness, and understanding that helps people navigate the world (for example, language, mathematics, sociological insight)

Norms: Rules and expectations for "appropriate" behavior (for example, how to dress, what standards of hygiene to maintain)

Behaviors: The actions associated with a group that help reproduce a distinct way of life (for example, "appropriate" sexual practices, the pursuit of formal education)

Objects and artifacts: The physical items that are created and associated with a culture (for example, food, clothing, music)

Symbols: Anything—a sound, a gesture, an image, an object—that represents something else (for example, a handshake, a corporate logo)

Language: An elaborate system of symbols that allows people to communicate with one another in complex ways (for example, English, Spanish, Chinese, American Sign Language)

Culture in Our Heads: Values, Beliefs, Knowledge, and Norms

Let's look more closely at the ideas of culture—the particular values, beliefs, knowledge, and norms that lend a culture its unique character. Together, they shape how people think, behave, and view their world.

VALUES: WHAT IS DESIRABLE? A **value** is *a deeply held principle or standard that people use to make judgments about the world, especially in deciding what is desirable or worthwhile.* For example, U.S. culture is highly individualistic. That is, people in the United States generally value individual freedom and autonomy above collective responsibility and commitment to community (Bellah et al. 2007). In contrast, some cultures place much more value on family well-being or some broader collective good than on individual achievement. The Japanese, for instance, emphasize group solidarity and loyalty, and this kind of collective orientation shapes ideas about what it means to be successful (Hofstede 1980; Silver 2002). China, too, has had a strong collective tradition, but recent research shows its values in the twenty-first century to be shifting. The Chinese now have a more favorable view of competition than do the Japanese and even, according to the World Values Survey, than do people in the United States (Marsh 2009; World Values Survey 2005–2008).

FIGURE 3.1 | RATES OF TAXATION AND POVERTY RATES AMONG INDUSTRIALIZED COUNTRIES

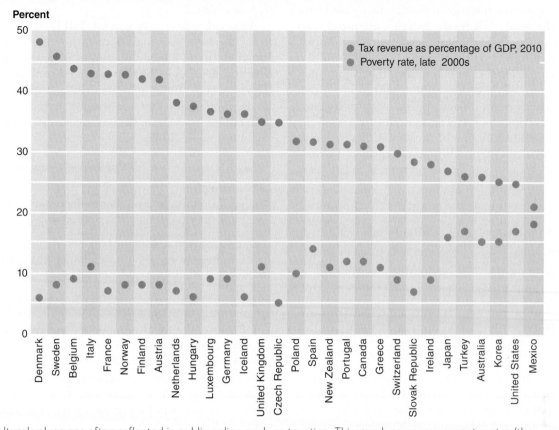

Cultural values are often reflected in public policy, such as taxation. This graph compares poverty rates (the percentage of the population living in poverty, defined as those in households earning less than half the median household income) with taxation rates (as measured by tax revenues as a percentage of gross domestic product, or GDP, which represents the value of all the goods and services produced in a country) for most of the world's industrialized economies. In general, the lower the tax rate, the higher the poverty rate. The United States, with among the lowest tax rates, has one of the highest poverty rates. In contrast, Denmark, with nearly double the tax rate of the United States, has one of the lowest poverty rates. What might account for the apparent, significant differences in Danish and U.S. cultural attitudes toward taxation and poverty? *Source:* Organization for Economic Cooperation and Development Factbook 2013.

Values can translate into public policy. For example, the relatively low rate of taxation in the United States reflects more than an aversion to taxes; it reflects popular support for the principle of small government (though major social programs such as Medicare and Social Security have widespread support). However, the relatively low tax rates in the United States also correlate with a relatively high rate of poverty. In contrast, in most other industrialized nations, individualism is less valued, tax rates are much higher, and the poverty rate is far lower. Figure 3.1 shows the relationship between tax rates and poverty rates for 30 industrialized countries.

The link between cultural values and public policy can sometimes have dramatic—even deadly—consequences, as illustrated by the recent experience of Niger, a poor African country beset by periodic food shortages. Niger has long relied on a culture of generosity based on Muslim traditions of charity and communal support to provide for the poor during these shortages (Timberg 2005). Building on this

tradition, the government had made a policy of keeping the price of basic food items affordable to help ensure their widespread availability.

In recent years, however, Niger, like many other developing nations, has absorbed Western cultural values emphasizing individualism and deregulated free markets. This cultural change was partly a response to requirements by international institutions, such as the World Bank, that governments eliminate price controls and other market interventions in order to qualify for loans. In Niger, the government abandoned its commitment to price controls. At the same time, the traditional commitment to charity weakened. As Malan Hassane, a local religious leader, commented at the time, "There is nothing like generosity now. Selfishness is gaining ground" (Timberg 2005). When the country suffered a food shortage in 2005, this shift in values from an emphasis on collective responsibility and mutual aid to an emphasis on individual economic success in competitive markets proved disastrous for Niger's poor. Without price controls and without the support of traditional charity, many could not afford even the most basic foods. Facing widespread starvation, the country had to call on international aid organizations for help.

Sociologists are often reluctant to label the major values of a given society because they do not want to imply that values are unchanging or universal. The most widely cited sociological description of American values appears in the classic book *American Society: A Sociological Interpretation* by Robin Williams (1970). Williams identified 15 basic value orientations as central to post–World War II society in the United States:

Achievement and success	Freedom
Activity and work	Conformity
Moral orientation	Science and secular rationality
Humanitarian mores	Nationalism-patriotism
Efficiency and practicality	Democracy
Progress	Individual personality
Material comfort	Racism and related-group
Equality	superiority

Williams described these value orientations as tendencies and suggested a series of questions to help understand their depth and meaning. For each value on his list—and, we would add, for each value you would include in an updated, twenty-first-century list of American values—Williams (1970, 453) would ask a series of questions: "Is it actually an important value in American society? How do we know whether it is or not? Where does it stand in relation to other values? [W]hat groups or subcultures are the main bearers of the value, and what groups or subcultures are indifferent or opposed?" Finally, Williams asks how do the various value systems "work towards or against the integration of the culture as a whole?"

In contrast to Williams, contemporary American sociologists have rarely sought to articulate a list of major American values, but they continue to ask versions of Williams's probing questions about the sociological significance of values. Summarizing recent research on values, sociologist Robert Wuthnow (2008) recognizes that they explain only partially individuals' choices, but he notes that "the influence of values on behavior remained evident in study after study; people with conservative values voted Republican, people with religious values attended religious services, people with altruistic values did volunteer work, and so on" (p. 337). In addition, values change over time, especially during times of broad social change. For example, we may ask how, if at all, changes in contemporary society, including globalization and the development of new technologies, are influencing our basic values (Gecas 2008).

Although values vary a great deal from culture to culture, research shows that certain values are common across cultures. A series of studies in dozens of countries over two decades by Shalom Schwartz and his colleagues (Davidov et al. 2008; Schwartz 1992, 1994) has identified 10 distinct values that are widely shared and generally understood to have a similar meaning across cultures (Schwartz et al. 2001):

Power	Universalism (appreciation of and concern for all humanity)
Achievement	
Hedonism (the seeking of personal pleasure)	Benevolence (generosity and compassion)
Stimulation (the seeking of excitement and personal challenge)	Tradition
	Conformity (the desire to blend in)
Self-direction	Security

Of course, the relative importance of each value on this list differs from culture to culture, and the values do not always coexist easily. It may be difficult, for example, to value power and benevolence or security and stimulation equally. Thus different cultures prioritize values differently, and these differences can be a major source of conflict between cultures. For example, theocratic societies such as Iran or Saudi Arabia, which are ruled or dominated by religious authorities, value tradition and conformity. They often dislike what they perceive to be the values of secular Western democracies, such as self-direction, stimulation, and relative hedonism as exemplified by popular notions of "rugged individualism," the widespread promotion of consumption, and the prevalence of sexualized media content.

That some people place a higher priority on one set of values over another can also be a source of conflict *within* a particular society. Sociologist James Davison Hunter (1991, 1994) has argued that the United States is in the midst of an ongoing **culture war,** *an intense disagreement about core values and moral positions.* According to Hunter, the fault lines of this conflict are readily apparent in venues such as the family, schools, and the arts. For example, debates about same-sex marriage are fundamentally conflicts over the definition of marriage and family. In schools, debates about how to teach American history and sex education are part of broader conflicts about patriotism and sexuality. The arts have long been an arena in which the values of free expression and respect for tradition clash. In 2010, for example, the National Portrait Gallery in Washington, D.C., removed a video from an exhibit of work on sexual differences after a Catholic organization complained that the

MAP 3.1 | THE 2012 ELECTION: RED AND BLUE OR PURPLE?

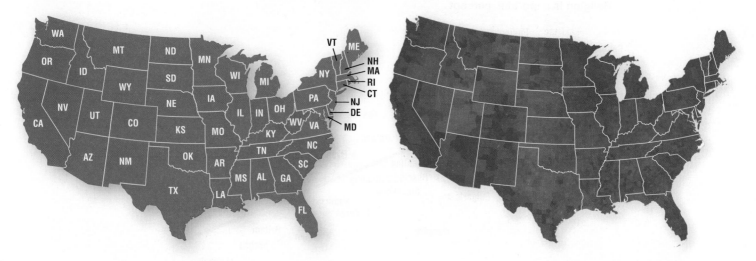

The map on the left (*A*) shows the results of the 2012 presidential election by state; Mitt Romney won the red states and Barack Obama won the blue states. The map on the right (*B*) represents the results of the 2012 election by county and uses red, blue, and shades of purple to indicate percentages of voters for each candidate. *Source:* Newman (2012).

CORE CONCEPTS CHALLENGE

Which of these maps do you think is a better representation of the election? What do these maps suggest about how divided the political **culture** *really is in the United States? Did the media's coverage of the 2012 election suggest a country that was more like the map on the left or the right?*

video's depiction of a crucifix covered with ants was "hate speech" (Trescott 2010). In all such cases, debates can become extraordinarily heated because they are rooted in profound differences in values, and these differences often arouse intense reactions. This culture war is waged primarily at the level of ideas, but occasionally it erupts into acts of violence. For example, gays and lesbians have been targeted for harassment and assault and, in a few cases, extremist antiabortion activists have killed doctors who perform abortions.

Are the differences in how various groups prioritize values in the United States so profound, however, that they truly warrant the label *culture war*? This question has been the subject of much debate among sociologists and other scholars (see, for example, Fiorina 2011; Hunter and Wolfe 2006; McConkey 2001; Thomson 2010). Certainly you will find people with different positions on just about any current social or political issue—from same-sex marriage and immigration policy to health care reform and the war on terrorism—depending on the values they think are most important. Though people differ in the values they consider most essential, however, they are not necessarily intolerant of other views. Some scholars argue that it is the political elites—politicians seeking to mobilize voters and raise money and political commentators trying to attract audiences and sell books—who highlight differences in values and encourage polarization and extremism. Ordinary citizens are actually far more ambivalent about their own views and more

tolerant of others (Baker 2005; Fiorina 2011; Koch and Steelman 2009).

Journalists who use the familiar shorthand "red state" and "blue state" to describe differences between conservative and liberal regions of the United States encourage the notion of a culture war. Identifying each state as simply red or blue implies that each state is fundamentally conservative or liberal and that the two types of states have little in common with each other. In reality, however, each state includes communities with differing views and values that reflect varying degrees of conservatism and liberalism. A map reflecting the complexity of value preferences in the United States would consist of various shades of purple rather than stark reds and blues (see Map 3.1).

BELIEFS: WHAT IS TRUE? Whereas a culture's values are usually a set of broad principles, its **beliefs** are *the specific convictions or opinions that its people generally accept as being true.* Our cultural beliefs encourage us to understand fundamental issues in the world in a particular way. Is democracy the best form of government? Should marriage be based on love, or is it primarily an economic arrangement? What constitutes "success" in life? Is violence justifiable in pursuing an important goal? Are all people created equal? Does God exist? The way people answer these questions depends, in part, on their cultural beliefs. What people believe is, in turn, deeply influenced by the culture of which they are a part.

The Elements of Culture

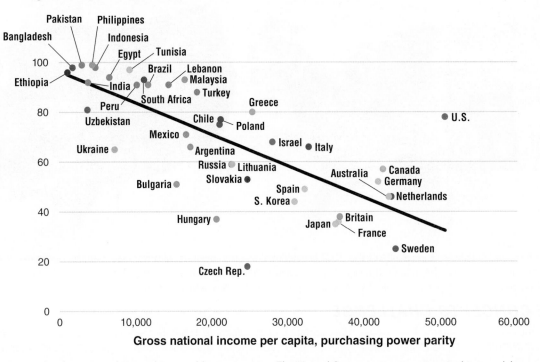

Poorer countries tend to be more religious than wealthier countries. The United States is an exception to this trend, however. Although it is a very wealthy nation, it is far more religious than its comparative wealth would suggest. In a Pew survey, 78 percent of U.S. respondents said religion was "very" or "somewhat" important to them, far higher than in the other wealthy countries in the survey but lower than in many poorer countries. *Sources:* Survey data are most recent for each country from the Pew Global Attitudes Project (2013) database. Gross national income (GNI) purchasing power parity (PPP) data are for 2012 from the World Bank database (2013). (GNI per capita is the total value of goods and services produced within a country, plus the balance of income received from, or payments made to, other countries, divided by the population. PPP adjusts this value for the actual price of goods and services in different countries.)

Belief in a god and concern for religion are widespread but more so in some societies than in others. In general, the importance of religion in a culture declines as people become more educated and affluent. As Figure 3.2 shows, however, there is one major exception to this trend: the United States. In a survey of people in 23 countries, 78 percent of people in the United States said religion was "important" in their lives, about double the figure for Britain (38 percent) and France (37 percent), and triple the number for Sweden (25 percent) (Pew Global Attitudes Project 2013). Such a relatively high level of religiosity helps explain why debates about abortion, stem cell research, teaching evolution, and gay rights are often more vocal and intense in the United States than in many other industrialized societies. A higher percentage of people in the United States tend to believe in God than in other developed countries, and these religious beliefs influence political debates.

In poor countries, though, religion plays an even more important role in people's lives than it does in the United States. An overwhelming percentage of respondents said religion was "important" in their lives in countries such as Bangladesh (100 percent), Tanzania (99 percent), Philippines (99 percent), and Pakistan (99 percent). Beliefs about God and the importance of religion are central to the culture of these societies.

KNOWLEDGE: HOW DO I GET THINGS DONE?

In the context of culture, **knowledge** is *the range of information, awareness, and understanding that helps us navigate our world.* Sociologists sometimes refer to such knowledge as *cultural capital*, an idea we explore in more detail in Chapter 9, where we consider class-based cultures. People often take for granted the knowledge they have internalized about their own culture. They learn how to speak, read, and write the language; how to dress appropriately for work; and how to behave properly in different situations. To navigate U.S. culture, for example, you have very likely learned how to read a map, how to use a credit card, how to apply to college, how to select items and pay for them in a supermarket, how to practice safe sex, and how to drive a car. In short, you have learned about the sorts of behavior that are rewarded and necessary for success in this culture.

Culture shock is *the experience of being disoriented because of a lack of knowledge about an unfamiliar social situation.* You are most likely to experience culture shock when you are traveling outside your own country, as John Wray did in the Shuar community in our opening example. In describing a research trip to Kenya, Rachel Irwin (2007) told of her anxiety about riding in a *matatus*—a minibus typically filled well beyond capacity with people and sometimes goats, driving at "breakneck speeds" on poorly maintained roads. Culture shock can also occur within your own country. When someone raised in a small town visits a big city for the first time, or when a person who is not religious spends time in the home of a devoutly religious family, the visitor may suddenly feel out of place.

Cultural knowledge is essential for survival. People from the United States who are traveling in Australia had better know that motorists in that society drive on the left side of the road—otherwise, they are in for an abrupt case of culture shock! Of course, most cultural knowledge is subtler, involving how to act in order to get something done. When you entered college, you probably had to learn about what makes the culture of higher education different from that of high school.

NORMS: WHAT IS APPROPRIATE? **Norms**

are *a culture's rules and expectations for "appropriate" behavior.* (Behavior that violates the norms of a culture is often labeled as *deviant,* a topic we explore in Chapter 8.) In a sense, norms serve as a bridge between a culture's ideas and its practices since they suggest which practices are appropriate. Norms can tell people what they *should* do as well as what they should *not* do. However, norms are not fixed or rigid. For example, smoking in public places—once a practice taken for granted in our culture—now increasingly violates informal norms and local laws. People are now expected (or required) to buckle their seat belts when they are driving or riding in an automobile. As recently as the 1960s, however, many automobiles did not even have seat belts.

As society changes, culture evolves to address new situations. Nowhere is this process more apparent today than in cyberspace. Norms for those who participate in its various venues—sometimes referred to as "netiquette"—developed rapidly, contributing to an emergent culture among Internet users. Different parts of the Internet each have their own norms. E-mail users learn to use "bcc" (blind carbon copy) when they send out a group e-mail so that they do not reveal the e-mail addresses of their friends or colleagues. At online discussion groups, new users learn to read the FAQs ("frequently asked questions") page before asking questions. Social networking sites such as Facebook strongly discourage "flaming"—posts that attack, insult, or ridicule other users. If you are a regular Internet user, such norms may seem obvious to you now, but they had to be created over time. Like all new users, you had to learn them at some point.

Social norms do not always keep up with technological change, however. In the 1920s, sociologist William Ogburn (1922) coined the term **cultural lag** to describe *the ways that new technological developments often outpace the norms that govern our collective experiences with these new technologies.* For instance, recent developments in digital photography and the proliferation of high-speed Internet access have made it extremely easy for many people to post photos and videos online for wide public viewing. However, the norms that define what is appropriate to make public, how to distribute such images, and what privacy means in this context are still

FAST-FORWARD

Social Change and Norms

Through most of the twentieth century, cigarette smoking was a widespread and socially respectable activity, well within acceptable norms. Tobacco companies marketed their product aggressively, associating it, as in the Camels ad above, with both sex appeal and, ironically, health. Since confirmation of the health dangers of smoking, an antismoking movement, using public service ads like the one here that parodies cigarette ads, has gradually but effectively succeeded in changing the norms regarding smoking, making it an activity that now receives widespread social disapproval.

catching up to the technology. Perhaps this concept helps explain the posting of photos of alcohol-fueled high school parties on Facebook or the "sexting" of nude photos among teenagers. As these examples suggest, cultural definitions of what is—or should be—public and private information are lagging behind the development of the Internet. New norms and behaviors will undoubtedly emerge and solidify as we advance further into the digital age.

Cultural norms for social interaction vary depending on whether the interaction is face-to-face, over the telephone, via e-mail, on social networking sites such as Facebook, through text messaging, or on Twitter. When we interact face-to-face, we use more than words to communicate; we use our tone of voice, hand gestures, and facial expressions, as well. When we send e-mail and text messages, we do not have these additional means of expression, which is why emoticons—symbols such as ;o) or :o(created by text characters—or abbreviations like LOL are so useful in online communication. Also, some topics are not appropriate for certain types of communication. Would e-mailing a friend to ask him to go out for pizza be appropriate, or not? How about breaking off a romantic relationship with a text message?

Society enforces most norms informally. If your cell phone rings during a movie, for example, be prepared for dirty looks from those sitting near you. However, more formal regulations, like a university's code of ethics or the legal system, serve to reinforce particularly significant norms. The study of deviance and crime is linked closely to the study of culture since both are largely about violations of a culture's norms.

Norms that are strictly enforced, with potentially severe penalties for violating them, are called **mores** (pronounced MORE-ays). Contemporary mores in the United States forbid physical or psychological abuse of one's children, for example. Those who violate such mores face public shame, potential loss of their children, and the possibility of a prison sentence. *Taboos* are things that carry the most severe prohibition or restriction. For example, the incest taboo restricts sexual activity between certain family members. Cannibalism, too, is a widespread taboo and is considered repugnant in nearly all circumstances.

In contrast, the term **folkways** describes *group habits or customs that are common in a given culture*. Those who violate folkways are not likely to be subject to punishment (Sumner 1906). It may be customary to wear a bathing suit to swim, for example, but those who go swimming in jeans are likely to face only some surprised glances.

Taken together, values, knowledge, beliefs, and norms—the ideas of a culture—help shape people's orientation toward the world, providing an unwritten guidebook on what to think and how to behave. By studying the ideas of a culture, we focus our attention on how people make sense of their experiences. Understanding what people value, believe, and know and what people define as appropriate and deviant reveals a great deal about the complex workings of society—your own, as well as those of other societies. To communicate the ideas of our culture to one another, however, we need symbols and, in particular, language.

The flags of Indonesia (*left*) and Poland (*right*) are both horizontal blocks of red and white, the same shapes and colors. But they are distinct flags, with specific meanings to their citizens.

CORE CONCEPTS CHALLENGE

*Can you think of other **culturally** specific symbols that look very similar but have different meanings? Or one symbol that has different meanings to different people?*

Communicating Culture: Symbols and Language

A **symbol** is *anything—a sound, a gesture, an image, an object—that represents something else.* An image of five interlocking rings represents the Olympic Games. A red light means "stop." An upraised forefinger placed on the lips means "quiet." The letters d-o-g together represent the sound "dog," which in English represents a domesticated four-legged creature (which, in turn, represents faithful companionship to many Americans).

The association between a symbol and the thing it represents is arbitrary and culturally defined. The people of Indonesia recognize a banner with a band of red over a band of white as their national flag; turn that banner upside down, however, and you have instead the Polish national flag. In most languages other than English, "dog" is a meaningless sound (and in some cultures the animal itself might more likely represent dinner than companionship). Similarly the same symbol can have different meanings in different cultures. In Mexico, raising your hand with a circle formed by the thumb and forefinger is an obscene gesture; in the United States it represents "OK." A "thumbs-up" gesture has a positive connotation in some societies but is an insult ("Up yours!") in Australia, Russia, Greece, Iraq, and much of Western Africa. In many societies, nodding your head up and down means yes, whereas turning it from left to right means no, but in Bulgaria the opposite is true.

Culture is fundamentally symbolic, and it is through symbols that we communicate and reinforce the elements of our culture to one another and pass them on to our children. As the Through a Sociological Lens box makes clear, cultural symbols in many forms can evoke emotionally powerful associations. However, one form of symbolic communication, language, is our primary vehicle for cultural transmission.

thinking about culture

Can you think of an example of a formal code or system of regulations that governs your life? In Chapter 8 we consider systems of social control, as well as the people who deviate from such systems.

How We See Powerful Symbols

Symbols can be a powerful means of representing cultural beliefs, especially in the areas of religion and politics. The meaning we give a particular symbol can vary by culture, however. When the symbol is a potent one, the various meanings can be a source of confusion and sometimes conflict.

One of the most controversial symbols in recent American history has been the "Southern Cross." This flag (left) was never

the official flag of the Confederacy but rather was one of a number of battle flags used by Confederate forces during the Civil War. In the 1940s the Ku Klux Klan adopted the flag, and in the 1950s supporters of racial segregation used the flag as a prominent symbol of their cause. Today, various white supremacist groups still use the flag as their emblem. As a result, for many in the United States the flag symbolizes the fight to maintain slavery as well as recent and contemporary racist movements. For some Southerners, however, the contemporary use of the flag is not racist. To them it represents "heritage not hate."

Sociologist Lori Holyfield and her colleagues (Holyfield Moltz, and Bradley 2009) sought to untangle the complex meanings of the Confederate flag. They conducted focus group discussions with white college students at a large southern university. After reading aloud a news article about a controversy involving the Confederate flag in Leesburg, Virginia, groups discussed their views of the controversy and opinions of the flag.

The authors heard only rare instances of overt racism in these focus groups. Instead, they found that white students typically sought to downplay the racial meanings associated with the Confederate flag or became defensive and diverted the discussion away from racial issues. In fact, faced with a highly charged symbol, most of these white students had difficulty explaining their own understanding of southern heritage or the meaning of the flag, even as they refused the implication that the flag is a racist symbol. In analyzing the ways these focus groups largely ignored history and disregarded persistent differences in power and privilege, Holyfield and her colleagues (2009) suggest that, even if unintended, the use of such symbols can convey racist messages. They write, "participants need not approve of uses of the Confederate Flag or racism in order to participate in and perpetuate racist discourses" (p. 525).

The controversy over the Confederate flag is part of a long history of symbols carrying multiple—and sometimes conflicting—

meanings. For example, many Christians use the cross, symbolizing the crucifixion of Jesus (below left), as a sign of their faith. But the cross has been used by other, non-Christian cultures as well. In ancient Egypt the cross (above) was a sign of life. The ancient Greek cross (left)—with vertical and horizontal arms of equal length—represented the four elements: earth, air, fire, and water.

Perhaps the most reviled symbol of the past century is the swastika (right), now forever linked with Nazism. But the swastika is an ancient symbol used in many different cultures. For example, it was a variation on the Christian cross; a Hindu symbol associated with the ferocious goddess Kali; and a Navajo symbol related to healing rituals.

think about it

1. *What symbols do you encounter in daily life? In what other contexts are they used?*

2. *There has been a great deal of debate in recent years about whether statehouses in the South should fly the flag associated with the Confederacy. Where do you stand on this issue? Do you think the flag is simply a symbol of the South's heritage, or do you see it as a symbol of hate?*

LANGUAGE A **language** is *an elaborate system of symbols that allows people to communicate with one another in complex ways.* Other animals have call systems that allow them to alert each other about their immediate environment—the presence of predators, for example. Human language, in contrast, is unique in its ability to convey information about objects and situations that are not immediately present. With language we can converse about events that happened in the past and plans we are making for the future, and we can even relate stories about imaginary people and occurrences. Language allows us to accumulate and store information, pass it on to one another, and forge a shared history. It is no wonder, then, that efforts to maintain marginalized cultures threatened with extinction often focus on preserving those cultures' languages. Sometimes groups try to revive dying or extinct languages as a form of cultural preservation. For example, members of two Indian nations in Long Island, New York—Shinnecock and Unkechaug—are working with linguists at a local university to document and teach languages last spoken 200 years ago (Cohen 2010).

Sharing a language, however, does not necessarily mean sharing a culture. English, for example, is spoken in many countries worldwide, in some as a first language and in many others as a nearly universal second language, but the people of these countries do not all share a common culture. They usually do, however, speak a particular **dialect** of English. A dialect is *a variant of a language with its own distinctive accent, vocabulary, and in some cases grammatical characteristics.* For example, what Americans call a "stove," the English call a "cooker." Further, a "truck" and an "elevator" in the United States would be called a "lorry" and a "lift" in England.

THE SAPIR-WHORF HYPOTHESIS The principle of *linguistic relativity*, developed by Edward Sapir and Benjamin Whorf and popularly known as the **Sapir-Whorf hypothesis,** *suggests that because of their different cultural content and structure, languages affect how their speakers think and behave.* For example, researchers have found that people more easily identify color differences when they have a language to describe different shades of similar colors (Kay and Kempton 1984). That is, having words to differentiate distinct colors in the red spectrum (including scarlet, crimson, rose, magenta, and maroon) helps us see those different colors.

This hypothesis is controversial, however. Many scholars believe it overstates the influence of language on thought (Pinker 2007). They point out that, like other aspects of culture, languages adapt to changing circumstances and that speakers absorb or invent new vocabulary for things as they become culturally important.

Nonetheless, language reflects the broader cultural contexts in which it evolved. As a result, every culture tends to develop unique words, phrases, and expressions that are difficult, if not impossible, to translate into another language. In that sense, language helps shape how we see the world. For example, the Mandarin word *guanxi* (pronounced "gwan-shee") translates literally as something like "connection," but it refers to a sort of social currency in traditional Chinese society. People can accumulate *guanxi* by doing good deeds for others or by giving them gifts, and they can "spend" their *guanxi* by asking for favors owed. In a society in which bonds of obligation form a crucial part of social life, such a word has a significant cultural meaning that cannot be translated easily into English (Moore 2004).

LANGUAGE AND SOCIAL INTERACTION As we saw in Chapter 1, the *symbolic interactionist perspective* emphasizes micro-level interactions—people's everyday behaviors—as the building blocks of society. Rather than focusing on large-scale institutions and processes, symbolic interactionists look at how people make sense of the world through the meanings they attach to their own and others' actions. As a result, sociologists working in this tradition are particularly attuned to the importance of the role of symbols and language in human interaction.

For example, through intensive interviews with clinically depressed adults, sociologist David Karp (1996) found that the specific language that they use helps define their reality. This self-definition in turn shapes the actions people with depression can envision, and ultimately, initiate. Early in their experiences, respondents often did not have an adequate vocabulary for naming their trouble.

By eventually coming to name their condition as "depression," they began to see it in a new light. In naming their experience depression, Karp's respondents developed a new sense of self, which shaped their response to their pain. Their illness identity also influenced how they interacted with family and friends, and helped break the social isolation that is at the center of the depression experience. They also had to grapple with the exact meaning of this new label, however. One of Karp's interviewees says: "I think of it less as an illness and more something that society defines. That's part of it, but then, it *is* physical. Doesn't that make it an illness? That's a question I ask myself a lot. Depression is a special case because everyone gets depressed. . . . I think that I define it as not an illness. It's a condition. . . . It's something that I can deal with. It's something that I can live with. I don't have to define it as a problem" (Karp 1996, 53). In contrast, other interviewees were comfortable with the definition of depression as "mental illness" and worked to find a "cure"—both distinctly medical ways to define and interpret the situation.

Karp alludes repeatedly to the importance of language throughout his study. He points out that the ideas of "anxiety" and "depression" do not exist in many languages and, therefore, that people who speak those languages cannot use them to define their reality. Even the title of Karp's study—*Speaking of Sadness*—alludes to the importance of language.

SPOTLIGHT

on social theory

Consider the experience of the people Karp interviewed. How have you reached a greater understanding of some situation by finding the right name for it, or finding the best way to describe it? How does this relate to the role of language as emphasized by **symbolic interactionists?**

Reproducing Culture: Behavior

In the context of culture, **behaviors** are *the actions associated with a group that help reproduce a distinct way of life.* When parents remind their children to tuck in their shirt, greet people with a firm handshake, and say "thank you" in response to a gift or an act of kindness, they are helping encourage a particular set of behaviors considered worthwhile in U.S. culture. These are small matters, but the accumulation of people's many small, everyday actions—at home, at work, at play, at worship—helps distinguish one culture from another.

Behavior also calls attention to the difference between **ideal culture,** *what the members of a culture report to be their*

The Super Bowl is a cultural phenomenon that has as much to do with the extravaganza as it does with football. Major corporations unveil new advertising campaigns during the broadcast, international pop stars perform in choreographed halftime shows, and the U.S. Air Force stages a high-profile flyover just before kick-off each year. Watching the Super Bowl has become an annual ritual for millions of Americans—even those who don't necessarily like football very much.

CORE CONCEPTS CHALLENGE

Put yourself in the shoes of someone from a different **culture** *who watches a football game in the United States for the first time. What would that person make of the game? Might it seem violent, for example? Now, think of how you might react if you were to watch a game you are unfamiliar with, like cricket, a wildly popular sport in much of the rest of the world.*

values, beliefs, and norms, and **real culture,** *what they actually do, which may or may not reflect the ideal.* For example, gender equality is an increasingly professed cultural value in American society, but in most two-career households, women do more housework than men (Hook 2010).

Although culture is a social phenomenon, it also permeates the most private and intimate parts of our lives. Take the case of body hair. Do you shave your legs? Your underarms? Your pubic hair? Your head? Your face? In most cases, your answers to those questions are influenced heavily by cultural norms. Since World War I, for example, most women in the United States have shaved their legs and underarms, a behavior that seems "normal" to them. Yet this practice is less common in many European nations (where in some cases it is associated with prostitution), and it is

unheard of in other parts of the world. Similarly, men's shaving their faces (but not their underarms or legs) is the norm in much of contemporary U.S. society but was much less common before the twentieth century.

Even sexual practices—perhaps the most intimate of all human activity—vary significantly from culture to culture. Cultures differ in their attitudes toward masturbation, premarital sex, homosexuality and bisexuality, prostitution, and other forms of sexual behavior. Even feeling discomfort, awkwardness, or titillation at reading about topics like body hair and sexual practices reflects a culture-laden response. Although advertisers routinely appeal to cultural norms about hair removal to sell products, and sexual imagery permeates the popular media, most people in the United States rarely engage in frank discussion about such topics.

The Elements of Culture

Cultural behavior also encompasses larger scale, organized phenomena such as religious and political rituals (the president's annual state of the union speech), theatrical entertainment (rock concerts), and sports spectaculars (Super Bowl). Indeed, the widespread popularity of the Super Bowl—and the behaviors surrounding it, including those of viewers as well as the athletes and other participants—likely reflects some unique features of U.S. culture that Americans may take for granted but that may well appear odd to someone from a different culture. Thinking sociologically, what is the meaning of such an event for viewers? What might the popularity of the Super Bowl—even among people who don't like football—tell us about the ideas and values of U.S. culture? In short, understanding culture requires us to examine the complex ways people derive meaning from the cultural behaviors of everyday life. People both create culture and are shaped by it.

Objects: The Artifacts of Culture

Sociologists often refer to the principal elements of material culture as **cultural objects** (also sometimes called "cultural artifacts"), which are *the physical items that are created by and associated with people who share a culture.* Cultural objects are often variations on basic items found in daily life. Consider the many varieties of bread, for instance. Tortillas, baguettes, bagels, and puri bread are cultural objects commonly associated with Mexican, French, Jewish, and Indian cultures, respectively. We live in a culture in which electronic devices of all sorts—such as computers, cell phones, and digital music players—are significant cultural objects.

Cultural objects are found not only in your home, however. Highly prized creations such as works of art or religious icons are also cultural objects. Museums are filled with both ordinary and extraordinary objects that help tell the story of a particular culture. And the museums themselves, as well as other public buildings, people's homes, the streets and highways that connect them, gas stations, water reservoirs, and indeed any aspect of the landscape used or modified by humans—are also cultural objects.

Popular media products—such as books and magazines, films and television programs, songs and photographs—are also cultural objects. Analyzing popular media content often reveals a good deal of information about the culture that produced it at a particular moment in history. At the same time, it can be difficult to see the underlying assumptions embedded in the popular media of one's own culture.

Culture, Ideology, and Power

We have seen how culture helps define our world, providing models for appropriate attitudes and behavior. How we dress and speak, whom we admire and despise, and how we mourn and mark holidays are all shaped by our immersion in a particular culture. Since people are typically deeply embedded within their own culture, they usually find it difficult to see its underlying ideas. Sociologists have long paid attention to the assumptions built into any culture, arguing that what people take for granted is one of the keys to recognizing how culture and power are intertwined. One way to understand the meeting of culture and power is to understand ideology.

Ideology is a tricky term that is used in a variety of ways. Sociologists typically define **ideology** as *a system of meaning that helps define and explain the world and that makes value judgments about that world.* Simply put, an ideology is a comprehensive worldview. When we think sociologically about a culture's ideology, we inevitably pay close attention to the most basic assumptions the people living within that culture make, and the consequences of those assumptions.

Within each culture, there is a **dominant ideology,** *a widely held and regularly reinforced set of assumptions that generally support the current social system and serve the interests of authorities.* Even when most people within a culture agree about how the world works, though, most scholars concur that a dominant ideology cannot prevent the emergence of alternative worldviews. Instead, different ideological perspectives, representing different interests with unequal power, engage in a kind of cultural contest.

In considering how culture works through ideology, we need to remember that our commonsense assumptions, the things we take for granted, suggest a particular understanding of the social world, and such assumptions have consequences. In the United States, for example, many people believe that it is simply a matter of common sense that women are better nurturers than men, that education is a route to economic success, and that the United States promotes democracy around the world—each of which ideas is debatable. When people adopt such commonsense assumptions—as they do with a wide range of ideas—they are also accepting a certain set of beliefs, or an ideology, about the social world.

Similarly, ideology shapes what we define as "natural." We generally think that what is natural is more enduring and stable than what is created by humans. As a result, the structures we define as natural come to be seen as permanent and

thinking about culture

What is the meaning of World Cup Soccer in U.S. culture, and what do you think its prospects are for becoming a media event comparable to the Super Bowl? Explain.

70

therefore difficult to challenge. Consider some examples of social relationships that are often seen as natural. Is it natural that some people are rich and others are poor, that most citizens are disconnected from politics, or that people prefer to live in neighborhoods with others of the same racial or ethnic background? If all these situations are simply natural, then we have little reason to be concerned about economic inequality, political apathy, or residential segregation because they are not social problems but the natural order of things. What people think of as natural and normal, then, is fundamentally about ideology.

To effectively wield power, those with power within a culture must continually reinforce the idea that certain assumptions are simply "common sense" and "natural" because people's life experiences are likely to lead them to question these assumptions. (In Chapter 5 we explore this link between culture and power, especially as it relates to justifying inequality.) In recent years, for example, widespread cultural assumptions about the definition of marriage have changed. Gay and lesbian activists demanding the right to same-sex marriage have challenged, sometimes successfully, the long-standing belief that marriage is restricted to a relationship between a man and a woman. Now, the growing belief is that recognizing same-sex marriage is an equal rights issue.

In addition, even in the most repressive societies, some people will not accept the dominant ideology, some people may resist it, and changing historical conditions will undermine certain aspects of it. Ultimately, when we look at ideology from a sociological point of view, we can see the ways that culture is a contested arena that defines our underlying, and often changing, conceptions of the world.

Cultural Diversity

Consider the case of "Billy," described in a manual used to train volunteers with CASA (Court Appointed Special Advocates), a nonprofit network of advocates for abused and neglected children. After making a visit to observe his home environment, a social worker recommended that Billy be kept in foster care (National CASA 2005). She cited the following reasons in her report:

- Billy did not have a space of his own and had to sleep in a room with several other people.
- Billy's mother did not seem to be his primary caregiver, instead letting his grandmother take on that responsibility.
- Billy did not appear to be affectionate with his grandmother; indeed, he seemed intimidated by or even scared of her since he would not look at her directly but instead averted his eyes.

Billy, however, was Native American, and the cultural practices of his tribe explained these supposedly problematic behaviors. In some Native American tribes, for example—as well as in Japanese, Hawaiian, and other cultures—leaving a child alone in his or her own room is considered a form of neglect. Instead, people in these cultures maintain close and continuous contact between a child and other family members, which they see as essential to healthy and loving development. In addition, in some Native American cultures it is perfectly normal for a parent to defer to a grandparent when it comes to childrearing decisions. Leaving children in the care of grandparents is not considered neglect but a sign of respect for elders in the family. Finally, in averting his eyes, Billy was not showing fear but rather a traditional sign of respect for his grandmother, with whom he in fact had a close and loving relationship. If the social worker had had a better understanding of Billy's culture, she could have avoided the inappropriate recommendation.

Social tasks—preparing food, creating shelter, raising children, entertaining, governing—are universal in all cultures, but the methods people use to accomplish these tasks vary dramatically. Thus culture is highly diverse, varying not only across time, but also among different societies as well as within a single society. This variation is one of the reasons why "cultural awareness" training is an important part of many professions. Billy's social worker could have benefited from more cultural awareness. For a tragic example of the need for cultural awareness training, see the Sociology in Action box.

Understanding the diversity across cultures in different societies is more important now than ever before. For much of human history, only a few travelers interacted with people from cultures other than their own. Travel was difficult, expensive, and often dangerous. Today, widespread mobility, a global economy, and technological advances have brought people from many distinct cultures into more frequent and ongoing contact. Movies, television, music, and the Internet have introduced people to the ideas, images, sounds, and practices of different cultures, even if they don't know the languages people within them speak.

To understand the impact of cultural diversity, it is essential to grasp the various types of cultures within our own and other societies, their positions in relation to one another, and how they interact in what has become an increasingly multicultural world.

Dominant Culture, Subcultures, and Countercultures

When we talk about societies—our own or those of other countries—it is common to speak about them as sharing a single culture (for example, "U.S. culture" or "Afghan culture"). To a degree, this is true; societies share basic cultural features. However, societies are large-scale, complex arrangements that inevitably contain internal differences, as well. Competing cultural systems exist even in what appear to be homogeneous societies.

Rather than consisting of a single culture, most societies contain a **dominant culture,** *a culture that permeates the society and that represents the ideas and practices of those in positions of*

SOCIOLOGY in ACTION

Cultural Competence and Health Care

Lia Lee was a Hmong child living in California. The Hmong are an ethnic group from the Southeast Asian country of Laos whose culture is rooted in a rural way of life. When Lia was born in a California county hospital, her mother spoke no English, and the medical staff spoke no Hmong. At just three months old, Lia experienced fainting episodes, which doctors attributed to epileptic seizures. Over the next four years, Lia's doctors struggled to control her symptoms by prescribing a dozen different drugs in dosages and combinations that changed more than twenty times.

This dizzying array of treatments would have been confusing to anyone, but Lia's family was especially ill-prepared to understand the process. Illiterate even in their own Hmong language, they were able to follow their doctor's advice only intermittently. Instead, they turned for relief to their culture's familiar religious beliefs about illness. According to that tradition, Lia's fainting spells were caused by the temporary departure of her soul from her body, a condition whose name roughly translates as "the spirit catches you and you fall down." Lia's parents sent away to Thailand for sacred charms to protect her and changed the child's name to fool the evil spirits (Underwood and Adler 2005).

As U.S. society becomes ever more culturally diverse, health care workers are increasingly treating people like Lia and her family, whose beliefs about sickness and health differ dramatically from those of mainstream Western medicine. To treat these patients effectively, health care workers need to pay close attention to their cultural beliefs and traditions. Unfortunately, the Western doctors did not understand the Hmong culture, and Lia's family did not understand the doctors' efforts. As a result, the medical treatment was ineffective. Four years after her initial symptoms, Lia experienced a massive seizure that left her in a vegetative state for decades. She died in 2012 at the age of 30.

Lia's story is perhaps an extreme example, but dealing with gaps in communication between patients and health care workers caused by cultural differences is a very real and growing challenge. The federal government, along with several universities, private foundations, and organizations representing health care providers, has launched a variety of public and private initiatives to promote and ensure *cultural competence*—the ability to understand and address the needs of people from different cultures (Rees and Ruiz 2003). For example, some states have enacted regulations that require medical facilities to provide culturally competent care to groups that make up a certain percentage of the community's population. As one key element of this care, facilities are required to make interpreters available who are fluent in the language and cultural traditions of different groups. Organizations such as Resources for Cross Cultural Health Care (diversityrx.org) have stepped up to the challenge. One recent study found that medical interpreters, those who facilitate bilingual communication in hospitals, often act as an essential part of a medical team, becoming informal co-diagnosticians, even though these interpreters lack formal medical training (Hsieh 2007).

As part of their training, medical students are also learning about the important role of culture in their patients' lives. One book has become required reading in more than 100 medical schools. Titled *The Spirit Catches You and You Fall Down*, it's the tragic story of Lia Lee (Fadiman 2012).

think about it

1. *Have you or your family ever had trouble communicating with a doctor or been uncertain about what is happening at a hospital? If so, do you think cultural differences help explain why?*

2. *How might cultural differences cause problems with communication in school or at work?*

---

power, as well as a number of **subcultures,** *cultures associated with smaller groups in the society that have distinct norms, values, and lifestyles that set them apart from the dominant culture.*

Political and educational institutions, major businesses, the mass media, and educational institutions, among others, mostly reflect the dominant culture. For example, until quite recently (and some would argue, still today) the dominant culture in the United States was associated with the images, ideas, and values of white, often male, professional middle-class culture. Those in positions of power were disproportionately white, professional men. The cultures of other segments of society were usually not entirely excluded, but they did tend to be marginalized.

White, professional middle-class culture was often the norm from which other cultures deviated. We can see this dominance in action in commonly used phrases such as "the black community" or "working-class literature" or "women's history," each of which signals a deviation from the standard of white, professional men. Rarely, if ever, do we use terms such as "the white community," "middle-class literature," or "men's history" because these are already the unspoken norm in the dominant culture.

---

thinking about culture

Do you belong to a particular subculture or know someone who does? What features of this subculture set it apart from the dominant **culture**? Do you think aspects of this subculture are likely to be incorporated into mainstream culture in your lifetime? Explain.

Alongside the dominant culture, societies include a number of smaller subcultures with their own distinct cultural traits. For example, Americans in general are enthusiastic about technological advancements, but the Amish—an orthodox Protestant sect living primarily in Pennsylvania and Ohio—reject the use of most modern technology, resulting in a distinct way of life. Skateboarders also form a subculture. They define and use public spaces in innovative ways, turning roads and sidewalks, steps and hand railings, into a skating space, while developing a distinctive attitude about risk-taking and authority. Since subcultures often highlight their differences from the mainstream, their members often accept, even celebrate, their nonconformist beliefs or behaviors (Gelder 2005).

Members of a subculture, then, share a common identity, whether they are extreme-sports enthusiasts, science fiction fans, or Civil War reenactors. Although subcultures typically do not have a formal membership structure, they usually develop a specialized language or style and specific behaviors and objects relevant to their culture. Trekkers—a subculture consisting of fans of the television and movie franchise *Star Trek*—share a language about the fictional Starfleet and a science-fiction version of future space exploration, and they know the various *Star Trek* heroes and villains and the lessons of their multigenerational adventures in great detail. Attending *Star Trek* fan conventions, dressing up as specific *Star Trek* characters, and collecting *Star Trek* memorabilia—even if some of your friends and coworkers think such behavior is a bit wacky—signals your subcultural connections to other Trekkers.

Work and school organizations can develop their own cultural traits, too. Thus we might speak about the corporate culture at Walmart or the organizational culture at a governmental agency such as NASA. If your school has a significant sports program, take a look around you at the next big game you attend. College athletics—complete with school colors, uniforms, mascots, cheers, and rituals—are part of the distinct cultures of many schools. Special moments in the school's sports history—winning a championship, pulling off a huge upset, a star athlete's choking in a key game—all become part of the lore of that school's culture.

At the micro level, even groups of close friends who live in the same neighborhood can develop a subculture. As they grow up, their common experiences foster similar values and beliefs. They may like the same style of clothing, music, and leisure activities. Over time their shared adventures give them a common history, filled with incidents, terminology, and characters that have little meaning for people outside the group. "Inside" jokes and references help build a sense of solidarity and belonging.

A subculture that organizes itself in opposition to the dominant culture may be categorized as a **counterculture,** which *champions values and lifestyles distinctly opposed to those of the dominant culture.* Members of countercultures challenge widely held values and attitudes and reject mainstream cultural norms.

In the past half century, a series of youth-based countercultures have challenged aspects of the dominant culture in U.S. society. For example, young hippies in the 1960s had a distinctive lifestyle and language. They challenged traditional authority by experimenting with recreational drugs, practicing communal living, rejecting materialism, espousing "free love," and protesting against the Vietnam War. Punks in the 1970s developed their own particular style, including then-atypical piercings and provocative hairstyles, along with a defiant attitude. In turn, hip-hop introduced new music, language, dance, and fashion while some within hip-hop culture advanced a powerful critique of racism and racial discrimination.

Subcultures—including countercultures—often introduce innovation and change to mainstream culture. Features of a subculture that might appear radical or threatening may over time be incorporated into the dominant culture. For example, in U.S. society, tattoos were once found exclusively among various subcultures such as sailors and bikers but have long since moved into the mainstream. Access to birth control, racial intermarriage, equal rights for women, and a host of other social reforms began their life as part of the beliefs and values of political subcultures, only to achieve broad mainstream acceptance eventually.

One way people express their connection to a subculture is by wearing distinctive clothing or costumes. Here, Trekkers—fans of the *Star Trek* television and movie franchise—are dressed as their favorite characters at a Comic Con convention that celebrates comics and related art forms.

High Culture and Popular Culture

Societies contain not only a dominant culture and various subcultures, but also different cultural expressions that are related to people's position in society. Sociologists have in fact long recognized the relationship between culture and economic inequality. **High culture** refers to *cultural forms associated with—and especially valued by—elites.* Examples of high culture include art galleries, the opera, classical music, and literature. Historically, high culture has been the domain of the wealthy and highly educated. Although others may not be formally excluded from these activities, their expense and the specialized knowledge that is often needed to understand and enjoy them can serve to restrict access to those who are able to afford them.

Proponents of high culture may define these cultural forms as the best and most enduring representations of a nation's culture. After all, disciplines that study high culture such as art history and music education are typically part of the high school and college curriculum, and many people associate the very idea of becoming "cultured" with visiting museums or attending the symphony. In contrast, **popular culture** refers to *cultural forms that are widespread and commonly embraced within a society.* Popular culture includes such widely accessible forms as television programs, Hollywood films, rock concerts, spectator sports, and amusement parks. To enjoy popular culture, a person generally does not need a substantial amount of money or specialized knowledge.

The distinction between high and popular culture suggests a fundamental conflict. As sociologist Herbert Gans (1999) maintains, "advocates of high culture attack popular culture as a mass culture that has harmful effects on both individuals consuming it and on society as a whole. The users of popular culture fight back mostly by ignoring the critique and rejecting high culture" (pp. 3–4). In the early-twenty-first century, however, the distinction between high and popular culture has become blurry. More people, including elites, now consume a diverse mixture of high and popular culture. Various hybrid cultural forms—such as graffiti art exhibited in museums or the pop musician Sting's performing his songs with the Royal Philharmonic Concert Orchestra—mix elements from both types; and many forms of popular culture, including highly rated television programs and best-selling novels, are widely enjoyed by elites as well as other demographic groups. Nevertheless, as Gans points out, the distinction between high and popular culture remains helpful since the cultural choices people make are still influenced significantly by their social standing.

Culture can also be influenced by people's physical location. The term *folk culture* indicates traditional practices, often passed on orally from generation to generation, that reflect lifestyles in specific—often rural—areas. Unlike pop culture that is widely communicated and easily available in a diverse society, folk culture is produced and consumed locally, often by working-class and poor people. In music, for example, Mississippi Delta blues and the early country and bluegrass of the rural South were distinct folk cultures closely associated with the places and people that produced them. As those examples illustrate, too, folk culture often goes on to influence popular culture.

Battani, Hall, and Neitz (2003, 91) note that, while still vibrant in some isolated rural parts of the world, "in a pluralistic world where every corner has been subjected to the gaze of the mass media and everything has its price, folk culture acquires a narrow meaning. . . . [In the contemporary United States] it is almost a genre of arts and crafts, defined by cultural transmission and learning outside of schools or books." The Smithsonian Institution operates the American Folklife Center (2013), which collects and documents traditional folk culture examples of the "everyday and intimate creativity that all of us share and pass on to the next generation," including recipes, music, stories, ways of speaking, games, crafts, and work traditions. The fact that American folk culture is now showcased in a museum reflects the dominant role that commercial popular culture now holds.

The Commercialization of Culture

Hector is driving to school with the radio playing when one of his favorite songs comes on. He turns up the volume and sings along as the artist praises a certain line of designer clothes. The lyrics are a result of work by Maven Strategies, a company that negotiates deals between major corporate advertisers and hip-hop artists. A corporation will pay the artists to mention its product in their songs. The result? Many rap songs mention brand names of sneakers, watches, vodka, and other products. Although most songs do not include paid advertisements, in 2004—the year Maven Strategies began cutting such deals—product brand names were mentioned almost 1,000 times in the top 20 singles on the *Billboard* charts (Williams 2005). This type of product placement, which continues today, is just one of many ways that *commercialism*—the marketing and sale of products—has become entrenched in contemporary popular culture.

Today, many cultural objects are commodities—products to be bought and sold—and these objects are increasingly

CHAPTER 3 Culture

74

produced by corporate conglomerates (Mosco 2009; Schiller 1989; Schor 2004). The stories children learn and the music people listen to are produced and marketed by multinational corporations like Disney and Sony. Corporations now sponsor a broad range of cultural creations, from rock concerts to museum exhibits (Rectanus 2002). From expensive tickets to major events to one-dollar DVD rentals from a kiosk, we spend much of our lives—and many of our dollars—buying cultural products.

This focus on commerce has meant that the language and images of advertising have increasingly entered public and private space, surrounding us with pictures and symbols whose primary purpose is to get us to buy something. Some communities see this as a problem and are fighting back, however. In 2007, new "Clean City" laws went into effect in São Paulo, Brazil—a city of 11 million people—that essentially banned all outdoor advertising. As the president of the city council noted, "What we are aiming for is a complete change of culture [. . .] things were out of hand and the population has made it clear it wants this" (Rohter 2006). Since then, the law has been widely seen as a positive development that has helped beautify the city and encouraged flourishing mural and graffiti art communities.

With the ever-growing influence of commercialism, people increasingly tend to measure the value of most cultural objects by their profitability. How many copies of that book or this CD were sold? What was the highest rated television program last week? What were the box office standings for movies released this past weekend? Such concerns reflect a culture in which the dollar sign increasingly denotes "success." As we see throughout this book, especially in Chapter 14, the commercialization of cultural and social life—its packaging, promotion, and sale by major corporations—is an important feature of our changing world, both in the United States and globally.

Multiculturalism

Because so many societies today contain many subcultures and cultural diversity, there is an increasing emphasis on **multiculturalism,** *the recognition, valuing, and protection of the distinct cultures that make up a society.* Rather than assume that all people will adopt the ideas and practices of the dominant culture—a process known as *assimilation*—multicultural societies accept, accommodate, and even celebrate differences in language, religion, customs, dress, traditions, and beliefs. Institutions that acknowledge and accommodate different cultures, such as certain businesses and universities, can also be considered multicultural. As the Sociology Works box illustrates, understanding cultural diversity is crucial in today's business world.

Because they live in a multicultural society, many people in the United States are exposed regularly to a number of

A multicultural society accommodates various cultural groups. One way such societies cope is by making voting materials, health care information, signs in public places, and other important information available in the languages spoken in the local community.

different cultures. Consider the variety of ethnic foods that you can choose from. Major U.S. cities today are likely to have restaurants featuring the food of many different cultures, including Italian, Mexican, Greek, Thai, Chinese, Ethiopian, and Indian cuisine, among others. Fairs and festivals celebrate the food, dress, music, and dances of various cultures. More significantly, in communities that are home to a variety of cultural groups, you are also likely to find institutions associated with these groups, such as temples, mosques, churches, and other places of worship. Businesses such as sari shops and halal butchers sell products not available in mainstream dress shops and grocery stores. Of course, the presence of different cultural groups often means a variety of languages, as well. Today's major cities are often home to people who speak dozens of different languages—and their school systems must cope with this linguistic diversity.

Because of the nature of a multicultural society, a significant number of people within it grow up and live their lives defined by more than one culture. If a student speaks English at school but a different language at home, that bilingual capability is a sure sign that he or she lives in two different cultures at the same time. Some immigrant families straddle the society and culture into which they were born and where they now live (Smith and Gurnizo 1998). Some travel back and forth to their countries of origin; others send money to aid relatives there. Some are even involved in the political affairs of their native countries (Levitt 2004). Television and the Internet help people stay in touch with the news and entertainment culture of their native countries, even while they live in their newly adopted homes. For example, the satellite service Dish Network offers a variety of packages with channels based on countries and regions such as Africa, China, South Asia, and Israel,

thinking about culture

Which policies does your college have that promote multiculturalism? In Chapter 10, **culture** helps us understand how various racial and ethnic groups have interacted in the United States throughout its history.

SOCIOLOGY WORKS

Dean Foster and the Business of Cultural Diversity

As an undergraduate, Dean Foster didn't have a clue what he would do with sociology, but he thought the subject was fascinating. He found especially appealing the basic premise that "we can understand how we work as cultural and social beings and use this understanding to improve our collective lives." When he looks back today and considers the benefits he gained from sociology, his list is extensive: "My professional career, cross-cultural friendships, life goals, and purpose."

Foster is the founder and president of DFA (Dean Foster Associates) Intercultural Global Solutions. DFA helps organizations and businesses working with other cultures around the globe develop intercultural competencies. Foster spends much of his time traveling to present intercultural seminars, give speeches, and conduct interviews around the world. Describing his work as the "perfect job," Foster notes that "I meet wonderful people from places I only could have dreamed I would visit and work in as a child. I help deal with important cross-cultural challenges in ways that I like to believe change people's lives."

When working internationally, businesses must anticipate and address some common differences among cultures. For example, different cultures have various ideas about time. Some value punctuality; in Germany, Austria, and Switzerland being late is considered a sign of disrespect and incompetence. In the countries of Latin America, by contrast, there is more latitude when it comes to meeting times and deadlines.

In addition, norms governing appropriate relationships between employers and their employees can vary a great deal from one culture to another. In some countries, employees are expected to be deferential to their bosses, avoiding eye contact with them and obeying instructions without comment. In other countries, employees are expected to be candid with, although still respectful of, their bosses, giving their input on the task at hand. In all these cases, global businesses must understand the cultural norms within a given society—and convey that understanding to their employees—if they are to communicate and work successfully in international settings.

Dean Foster

A cottage industry of diversity training specialists such as Dean Foster—often with backgrounds in sociology, anthropology, and psychology—has emerged in response to businesses' need for cultural awareness in today's global economy. Foster notes, however, that when he was a student, "there was no such field as intercultural training, so there were no internships, mentors, or courses of study." In fact, he first earned a living as a songwriter and folksinger, playing in clubs in New York's Greenwich Village. By the mid-1980s, though, he had used his sociological knowledge to start one of the first intercultural training consultancies.

Foster's work, he says, forces him "to constantly expect that which cannot be imagined, a testament to the power of culture, and the limits it places on us as cultural beings. I find this is the same kind of challenge that sociology places on us when we try to imagine how is it that we are who we are and behave as we behave. I deal with this question professionally every day."

> "I work with cross-cultural challenges in ways that I like to believe change people's lives."

think about it

1. *What do international businesspeople who come to the United States need to know about culturally specific work routines that people in this country are likely to take for granted?*

2. *In your travels, have you experienced uncertainty about basic cultural norms? What happened? What did you learn as a result?*

---

and programming in languages such as French, German, Spanish, Italian, Polish, Portuguese, Russian, Japanese, Filipino, Korean, Farsi, Arabic, and Urdo.

People who live in a multicultural society have an extraordinary opportunity to learn about and appreciate the rich diversity of human cultures. Diversity also brings with it challenges and problems, however, as people with different ways of life attempt to coexist. Unfortunately, cultural difference often leads to inequality and conflict as groups with more power oppress, exploit, or otherwise discriminate against those who are different and who have less power. The long, ugly history of religious conflict, ethnic clashes, racist violence, and warfare between nations is one result of this tendency. Therefore, to understand culture more fully, we must inevitably study conflict, relations of power (a topic explored in Chapter 5), and the domination of some groups by others.

CULTURE: CONSENSUS AND CONFLICT People from the same culture may share the same language, religion, worldview, history, and traditions. When this happens, cultures nurture and promote consensus, cohesiveness, and solidarity through a shared collective identity. However, just as the common bond of culture creates a sense of "us," it can also create a sense of "them"—those outside the culture who are different in some way. Perhaps the outsiders speak a different language, practice a different religion, dress differently, or are from a different social class. Whatever the distinction, as those who share a culture increase the sense that they have a common bond, they often have a tendency to marginalize, belittle, or even demonize "outsiders" who have a different culture.

Cultural conflict is most likely to emerge when values and beliefs differ among different cultures. Contrasting beliefs about religion and clashes over core values have been the source of or justification for many conflicts over the centuries. Unlike questions that can be answered with scientific evidence, disputes about values and beliefs cannot be resolved by appeals to reason. The cultural conflicts that result from these disputes can be intense and ongoing.

One source of cultural conflict is **ethnocentrism,** *the judging of other cultures by the standards of one's own on the assumption that one's own is superior.* Out of ignorance, the social worker mentioned earlier in this chapter was being ethnocentric in judging the Native American family's childrearing practices through the lens of her own culture. Had she known more about how children are brought up in that society, she would have understood that the family had a different approach that could also achieve the goal of raising a healthy child. This family's experience is a relatively mild example, but ethnocentrism can have harsh and even violent consequences if members of one culture act upon a conviction that their ideas, values, and way of life are superior to those of another culture. An ethnocentric worldview can be the source of **xenophobia,** *the unreasonable fear and hatred of foreigners or people from other cultures,* which, at its extreme, can result in *genocide*—the deliberate and systematic destruction of a cultural, racial, or political group.

Much of the history of colonialism, in which one country conquers or dominates others, is the story of ethnocentrism in action. The Europeans who conquered much of the world from the sixteenth century into the twentieth were confident that their way of life was superior to that of the people whose lands they colonized. They often sought to "civilize" the native peoples, teaching them their language, and converting them to Christianity. As the native peoples resisted to protect their way of life, the result was centuries of conflict.

In contrast to ethnocentrism, **cultural relativism** is *the practice of understanding a culture by its own standards.* Cultural relativism does not require adopting or agreeing with the ideas and practices of another culture, but rather making the effort to understand the culture on its own terms and with a willingness to acknowledge it as a viable alternative to one's own. In other words, to practice cultural relativism we need to *understand* a culture, not *judge* it, as, for example, when we seek to learn about religious rituals or family traditions in a different culture.

Studying cultures other than their own (an especially important task in this era of globalization) often requires sociologists to practice cultural relativism so that they can focus their attention on a group's unique values, beliefs, and practices. Such cross-cultural understanding is difficult to achieve; it is hard for any of us to operate outside of the

The infamously xenophobic Ku Klux Klan, which had several million members during its heyday in the 1920s, appropriated Christian symbolism to promote a white supremacist agenda that asserted the superiority of white Protestants and attacked the supposedly alien influence of black people and most immigrants, including non-Protestant whites. Today, some Muslim extremists similarly invoke religious symbolism in calling for attacks against perceived threats from the alien cultural influence of nonbelievers. Just as most Christians rejected the Klan, most Muslims reject these extremist views.

logic of our own culture. At the same time, once we are able to recognize our own values and beliefs—key dimensions of our own culture—we have taken an important first step toward understanding the experiences of people who live in very different societies.

THE CRITICS OF MULTICULTURALISM Less than two weeks after the attacks on the World Trade Center and the Pentagon on September 11, 2001, President George W. Bush framed the assault in cultural terms by telling Congress and the people of the United States that the members of Al-Qaeda, the Islamic fundamentalist group that had claimed responsibility, had attacked because "They hate our freedoms: our freedom of religion, our freedom of speech, our freedom to vote and assemble and disagree with each other" (Bush 2001). That quotation came to symbolize one way of thinking about the ongoing conflict between Western secular societies and Islamic societies. It suggested the conflict was based on fundamentally incompatible cultures.

One of the best-known discussions of this concept of a "culture clash" came from political scientist Samuel Huntington (1993, 1998), who argued that after the end of the Cold War between the United States and the Soviet Union, most new global conflicts would now take place between cultures rather than countries. He went on to describe what he saw as eight basic cultures (which he termed "civilizations") in the world: Western (United States, Australia, and Western Europe), Eastern Orthodox (Russia), Latin American, Islamic, Japanese, Chinese, Hindu (India), and African. These civilizations, he contended, are based on fundamentally different religious and other cultural beliefs. The Islamic world, for example, has few democratic institutions because it does not have a cultural history of separating religious and secular authority, of valuing social pluralism, and of protecting individual rights and civil liberties from the power of the state. In this way, it differs fundamentally from Western civilization. Huntington maintained that as long as globalization results in more frequent contacts between people living in these civilizations, we are doomed to experience more frequent cultural conflict.

There is no doubt that increased contact between vastly different cultures can result in conflict. However, if we analyze Huntington's thesis from a sociological perspective, we can quickly expose some of its shortcomings. For one thing, it oversimplifies the complex mix of cultures around the world and glosses over the enormous variation *within* each of these cultures (Arnason 2001). None of the so-called civilizations Huntington identifies has a single unified culture. As globalization advances and more people, products, and ideas flow across national borders, cultures continue to blend. Also, by focusing exclusively on culture, Huntington's theory ignores the ways that longstanding inequalities in the distribution of privilege and power have helped fuel global conflict (Evans 1997).

In addition, many different cultures *do* share common values. President Bush recognized these shared values when he told a graduating class at West Point, "The peoples of the Islamic nations want and deserve the same freedoms and

opportunities as people in every nation." His earlier quotation about hating freedom targeted the Al-Qaeda extremists who attacked the United States. However, violent Islamic extremists do not represent the broader Islamic culture, which encompasses a range of beliefs and values. Indeed, intense debates within Muslim societies regarding democracy, the role of women, and other cultural matters take place every day.

The results of global public opinion surveys show that democracy is widely popular in both Western and Islamic cultures—even though it has yet to flourish in Muslim countries despite 2011's Arab Spring uprisings. However, those same surveys show significant differences in the degree of support for gender equality, social tolerance, and freedom of speech (Inglehart and Norris 2003; Welzel and Inglehart 2010), indicating that the reality is complicated, not just a matter of a simple clash of civilizations or an idealized belief that all societies share a unified set of cultural values.

As we have seen, different cultures within a society can also encounter the problem of incompatible values or beliefs. Feminist political philosopher Susan Okin (1999, 117) argues that "many cultures oppress some of their members, in particular women, and . . . they are often able to socialize these oppressed members so that they accept, without question, their designated cultural status." For example, clitoridectomy (the removal of the clitoris) and other forms of genital cutting, and the prearranged marriage of children are accepted practices within some cultures. What, if anything, should be done when people from such cultures move to Western societies, where those practices are considered violations of individual rights? Should their adoptive countries accept these practices out of respect for different cultural traditions? Or do Western notions of individual freedom, human rights, and gender equality trump these traditional customs? Such questions have been on the front pages of newspapers in Europe. For example, in 2010 the French parliament enacted legislation that prohibits Muslim women from wearing face-covering veils in public places, on the grounds that such clothing conflicts with the values of French secular society (Crumley 2009; Erlanger 2010). This issue raises complex questions about incompatible cultural values and practices and challenges us to consider whether it is legitimate to condemn cultural practices we find offensive and whether we can articulate a universal standard of human rights.

Some U.S. critics of multiculturalism are not concerned with such questions because they reject its value entirely. Instead of encouraging people from diverse cultural traditions to coexist peacefully, these critics argue that new immigrants must assimilate into the dominant culture of their adoptive country; otherwise, they maintain, the common ground that is essential to unite a nation will be lost (Huntington 2005; Schmidt 1997). Some of these critics call

SPOTLIGHT

on social theory

Emile Durkheim, whose work was influential for the proponents of **functionalism**, focused on social solidarity—on how cultural values serve to unite people. How do you see this process working today in multicultural societies like that of the United States?

In 2010 the French parliament began to enforce legislation that banned women from wearing face-covering veils in public. Supporters of the legislation argue that traditional religious garb like the face-concealing veil violates the norms of secular culture in France and is a sign of the oppression of women. Opponents of the legislation contend that it violates the rights of women to express their religious faith.

CORE CONCEPTS CHALLENGE

Do you think it is appropriate for the French government to ban the veil? Would you be in favor of such a ban in your community? If you were a woman raised in a **culture** *in which wearing a veil is the norm, how would you react to an attempt to force you not to wear it? What reasons might members of a dominant culture use to justify imposing a ban on such clothing?*

for teaching Christian values in schools, the adoption of "English-only" laws, an end to bilingual education, and strict limits on immigration, among other measures, to shore up the dominant culture. As we will explore in Chapter 10, these arguments are similar to those made a century ago when new Irish, Russian, Italian, Polish, and other European immigrants arrived in the United States in great numbers. Back then these ethnic cultures were seen as a threat to American values.

Societies do need common ground—supplied by their cultures—to function successfully, and sociologists since Emile Durkheim have recognized this need. Nevertheless, cultures are also evolving constantly. Think about how global travel, electronic communications, the global economy,

and widespread immigration have changed contemporary society. Already contemporary U.S. society has found many ways to accommodate the peaceful coexistence of diverse cultural traditions.

In fact, culture can also be a basis for connection and exchange in ways that help prevent, or even heal, conflicts. Cross-cultural experiences—from reading the novels, studying the art, or learning about the cuisine of another culture to traveling to other countries, studying new languages, or hosting foreign visitors in your home or school—may provide a bridge that promotes greater understanding and improved relationships across national boundaries. Indeed, throughout history the trend has been in the direction of increased tolerance, accommodation, and appreciation among different cultures.

Cultural Activism

Many people are understandably passionate about cultural issues, which often reflect their deepest concerns. As a result, people from across the political spectrum participate in a wide range of public activities aimed at promoting or contesting culturally specific ideas and practices. In this section, we briefly review three contemporary forms of cultural activism: organizations that promote cultural pride, religious fundamentalism, and anticorporate activism.

CULTURAL PRIDE ORGANIZATIONS In communities throughout the United States, a variety of civic organizations maintain and promote particular cultures. They provide children with classes about their cultural heritage and sponsor festivals and other events celebrating their traditions. Because New York City is so ethnically diverse, activities celebrating cultural pride take place throughout the city all year long, including the St. Patrick's Day Parade in March, celebrating the experiences of the Irish and Irish Americans; the Puerto Rican Day Parade in June; the West Indian Carnival in September, which celebrates Caribbean cultures and histories; and the Chinese New Year Parade in January or February. The idea of embracing and celebrating one's cultural heritage has become firmly embedded in U.S. society as well as in many other countries.

RELIGIOUS FUNDAMENTALISM A worldwide resurgence of religious belief among fundamentalists, who believe in the literal interpretation of sacred texts such as the Bible and the Qur'an, represents another form of cultural activism. Whether at home or abroad, religious fundamentalists are using their faith as the basis for their activism. They criticize the cultural values and practices of Western secular society and develop ways to preserve and promote their own cultural values.

Islamic fundamentalists have challenged the export of Western culture to traditionally Muslim societies. They condemn what they perceive as the hedonism and decadent lifestyles promoted in such cultural products, themes that they say contradict Islamic teachings. They are especially

In the past several decades, Christian conservatives played a significant role in U.S. politics, often applying their interpretation of biblical teaching to contemporary social issues, such as abortion, and insisting that the United States should be considered a Christian nation. What are some of the potentially positive and negative consequences of intermingling religious faith with political activity?

angered by what they see as anti-Islamic media content. Pakistan, for example, ordered Internet providers to block Facebook in 2010 because one of its pages promoted "Everybody Draw Mohammed Day"—an action that violates Islamic beliefs. The ban was lifted once the page was removed. Islamic fundamentalists have turned to strict religious schooling and mass media, especially the Internet, to promote more traditional values and defend them against the onslaught of Western media.

Similarly, in the United States, Christian fundamentalists have fought—unsuccessfully—to eliminate from the mainstream media sexual imagery, violence, positive portrayals of homosexuality, and other content they find objectionable and contrary to their religious teachings. At the same time, these activists promote their religious beliefs through home-schooling, religiously based private schools, religious radio and television broadcasting, and religious books, movies, pop music, and other media content. These efforts have had a significant impact on the political culture

of the United States, where religious conservatives have been a significant political and cultural force.

ANTICORPORATE ACTIVISM The role corporations play in shaping culture is a source of contention in many countries. Critics of corporate power in the United States and elsewhere, especially on the political left, engage in yet another form of cultural activism, protesting concentrated media ownership and an unregulated global economy. In the United States, anticorporate cultural activists have established small but vibrant independent media outlets for music, art, news, and other cultural products outside of the mainstream commercial corporate system. Groups such as the Media Foundation, with its signature magazine *Adbusters*, promote a form of activism called "culture jamming," which refashions popular brand images to express a critical message about commercial culture, as in the example shown below.

Culture jamming is a form of activism that attaches new and subversive meanings to well-known corporate brands, often rewriting popular advertising campaigns. This example was produced by Adbusters. Complete with the Nike swoosh, it associates the Nike brand with slave labor—a powerful critique of Nike's labor practices.

Whether they are motivated by pride in a culture, by religious belief, or by opposition to corporate power, campaigns by cultural activists often lead to passionate public expression and debate. Although many of the issues taken on by cultural activists receive scant attention in mainstream public policy arenas, this form of activism often produces broad public discussion, testifying to the significance of culture in our everyday lives.

A Changing World

CULTURE AND GLOBALIZATION

Over 170 million people live in Africa's most populous country, Nigeria, where the largest ethnic groups are the Hausa and Fulani, Yoruba, Igbo, and Ijaw. But in the country's most successful movies, those cultures have been invisible. Indeed, in 2013, the biggest box office hit of the year was the Hollywood film *White House Down*. The previous year, it had been the James Bond film *Skyfall*. In 2011 it was the Angelina Jolie and Johnny Depp action-romance *The Tourist*. Year after year, imported Western—usually U.S.—films have dominated the Nigerian box office. Television, too, is full of Western programs, because importing these shows is cheaper than making TV programs at home.

Much of the rest of the world has been experiencing a similar media-driven globalization of culture (Crothers 2009). As in Nigeria, media globalization has primarily meant a massive export of Western television, film, music, and other cultural products to poorer nations that lack the resources or technological infrastructure to support a large media industry of their own. While often popular, these Western products also generate resentment as a kind of foreign invasion that is displacing local cultural practices and challenging traditional values and lifeways. As David Makali, director of the Media Institute in Nairobi, put it, "In Kenya, TV has become a major avenue of cultural promotion, and it is really terrible the way Western culture has taken over. The people are being brainwashed, and we are losing out culturally" (Miranda 2003).

The flood of U.S. media inundating foreign markets may have crested, however (Akpabio and Mustapha-Lambe 2008; Flew 2007). As new technologies have reduced the cost of media production, local media industries have begun competing for local audiences, though their products are almost never seen in Western cinemas or television. Locally produced programs, finely attuned to local cultures—and now distributed through new digital media platforms—are very popular, offering viewers alternatives to homogenized global content.

In Nigeria, the film industry has exploded, coming to be known as Nollywood. Nigeria is now the world's second-largest movie producer, just behind India and just ahead of the United States. Such projects, often produced on a shoestring budget, are unable to match the slick production values of expensive Western fare, but they are finding an audience. The country's few cinemas are dominated by Western films, so local movies are often shown informally in home theaters and community spaces. In 2011, iROKOtv.com—sometimes referred to as the "Netflix of Africa"—launched, offering a wide variety of African-made films on-demand for home viewing. The project suggests the potential appeal of African films elsewhere: the largest numbers of subscribers come from the United States, the United Kingdom, the Caribbean, and Australia.

The opportunities for communication among cultures are greater than ever before. However, because of the imbalance between wealthy and poor parts of the globe, affluent countries have been doing most of the talking, overwhelming the cultures of other parts of the world. Armed with today's technologies, though, artists in poor countries can feasibly begin to make themselves heard.

The on-demand Internet streaming service iROKOtv.com is the "Netflix of Africa," highlighting the work of Nigerian filmmakers and offering viewers around the world an alternative to typical Western fare.

thinking sociologically about
Culture

- Culture must be learned and can be thought of as all aspects of society that are transmitted socially rather than biologically. Culture consists of both nonmaterial and material elements: values, beliefs, knowledge, and norms; symbols and language; behavior and objects.

- Our own culture can be so familiar to us that we often fail to recognize its various elements or even why it matters. A sociological approach illuminates the often hidden ways that culture helps define our identities and our relationship to our broader communities.

- Sociologists have long paid attention to the assumptions built into any culture, arguing that what we take for granted is one of the keys to recognizing how culture and power are intertwined.

- Culture is highly diverse, varying across time and among different societies as well as within a single society. Unlike other animals whose social organization is instinctual, and therefore virtually identical wherever they are found, humans meet their basic needs by adopting a variety of culture-specific behaviors.

- Most societies contain a dominant culture, as well as a number of subcultures. These subcultures—including countercultures—often introduce innovation and change to mainstream culture.

- Living in a multicultural society gives us an opportunity to learn about and appreciate the rich diversity of human cultures. But diversity also brings challenges and problems; cultural differences are often the basis for inequality and conflict.

REVIEW, REFLECT, AND APPLY

Looking Back

1. Culture is an essential part of social life. It must be taught and learned and exists only in the context of groups.

2. The elements of culture include values, beliefs, knowledge, and norms (the ideas of culture); language and other forms of symbolic communication (for transmitting culture); and behaviors and material objects.

3. Within each culture, there is a dominant ideology that generally supports the current social system and serves the interests of authorities.

4. Most societies contain a dominant culture as well as a number of subcultures and countercultures.

5. Multiculturalism refers to the willingness to recognize, value, and protect the distinct cultures that make up a society.

6. Ethnocentrism is the practice of judging another culture by the standards of one's own. In contrast, cultural relativism is the practice of understanding a culture by its own standards.

7. Examples of cultural activism include cultural pride organizations, religious fundamentalism, and anticorporate activism.

8. Media globalization has primarily taken the form of the massive export of Western—primarily U.S.—media products to poorer nations. The flood of U.S. media may have crested, however, as local media industries have begun to take advantage of new digital technologies to compete for local audiences.

Critical Thinking: Questions and Activities

1. Why is "culture" a core concept in sociology? How can the concept of culture help us understand social life?

2. Why do changes in today's world make it especially important to understand the concept of culture?

3. Imagine that, because of your sociological training, you have been chosen to select the items to be included in a time capsule for your community that will be opened 100 years from now. Assuming the time capsule is about the size of a large suitcase, what cultural artifacts would you choose to represent your "way of life"? Explain why you believe these items are the most important.

4. Suppose you live in a foreign country and know little about the United States. Watch an hour of prime-time television and take careful notes about what you have learned about U.S. society. Were the media images you saw an accurate representation of U.S. society? Why or why not? What lessons about the United States might the export of such cultural products be teaching people in other societies?

Key Terms

behaviors (p. 68) the actions associated with a group that help reproduce a distinct way of life.

beliefs (p. 63) the specific convictions or opinions that people generally accept as being true.

counterculture (p. 73) a subculture that champions values and lifestyles distinctly opposed to those of the dominant culture.

cultural lag (p. 65) the ways that new technological developments often outpace the norms that govern our collective experiences with these new technologies.

cultural object (p. 70) a physical item that is created by and associated with people who share a culture.

cultural relativism (p. 77) the practice of understanding a culture by its own standards.

culture (p. 59) the collection of values, beliefs, knowledge, norms, language, behaviors, and material objects shared by a people and socially transmitted from generation to generation.

culture shock (p. 64) the experience of being disoriented because of a lack of knowledge about an unfamiliar social situation.

culture war (p. 62) an intense disagreement about core values and moral positions.

dialect (p. 68) a variant of a language with its own distinctive accent, vocabulary, and in some cases grammatical characteristics.

dominant culture (p. 71) a culture that permeates a society and that represents the ideas and practices of those in positions of power.

dominant ideology (p. 70) a widely held and regularly reinforced set of assumptions that generally support the current social system and serve the interests of authorities.

ethnocentrism (p. 77) the practice of judging another culture by the standards of one's own.

folkways (p. 66) group habits or customs that are common in a given culture.

high culture (p. 74) cultural forms associated with—and especially valued by—elites.

ideal culture (p. 68) what the members of a culture report to be their values, beliefs, and norms.

ideology (p. 70) a system of meaning that helps define and explain the world and that makes value judgments about that world.

knowledge (cultural) (p. 64) the range of information, awareness, and understanding that helps us navigate our world.

language (p. 67) an elaborate system of symbols that allows people to communicate with one another in complex ways.

material culture (p. 59) the physical objects produced by people in a particular culture, including tools, clothing, toys, works of art, and housing.

mores (p. 66) norms that are strictly enforced, with potentially severe penalties for violating them.

multiculturalism (p. 75) the recognition, valuing, and protection of the distinct cultures that make up a society.

nonmaterial culture (p. 59) the ideas of a culture, including values and beliefs, accumulated knowledge about how to understand and navigate the world, and standards or "norms" about appropriate behavior.

norms (p. 65) a culture's rules and expectations for "appropriate" behavior.

popular culture (p. 74) cultural forms that are widespread and commonly embraced within a society.

real culture (p. 69) what members of a culture actually do, which may or may not reflect the ideal.

Sapir-Whorf hypothesis (p. 68) the idea that because of their different cultural content and structure, languages affect how their speakers think and behave.

society (p. 59) a group of people who live together in a specific territory and share a culture.

subculture (p. 72) cultures associated with smaller groups in society that have distinct norms, values, and lifestyles setting them apart from the dominant culture.

symbol (p. 65) anything—a sound, a gesture, an image, an object—that represents something else.

value (p. 60) a deeply held principle or standard that people use to make judgments about the world, especially in deciding what is desirable or worthwhile.

xenophobia (p. 77) an unreasonable fear or hatred of foreigners or people of a different culture.

4

Social Structure

looking AHEAD

How can learning about social **structure** help you see how it operates in your life?

How can your actions and those of others change social **structure**?

As you send a text message on your cell phone or sign an online petition, how does your behavior illustrate the dynamic interplay between **structure** and action?

SOCIOLOGY in ACTION

Working to Eliminate Sweatshop Labor

Clark University sociologist Bob Ross began studying sweatshop labor in the early 1980s, and he published one of the first articles about the reemergence of sweatshop conditions in the garment industry in the United States. In his research, Ross highlighted the growth in New York City sweatshops, in which people worked long hours making clothing for extremely low wages, often in unsafe conditions (Ross and Trachte 1983). But Ross's research was not widely read outside of academic circles.

Fast-forward to the 2000s. Bob Ross's research, especially his book *Slaves to Fashion* (2004), is now required reading for a growing student movement concerned about the rise of sweatshop labor. Led by United Students Against Sweatshops (USAS), the anti-sweatshop movement is best known for its "sweat-free campus" campaign, active on more than 200 college campuses, which demands that apparel bearing a college logo (for example, T-shirts, sweatshirts, baseball caps) be produced in factories that pay their workers a living wage. As we saw in Chapter 2, a living wage is typically one that pays enough to keep a worker and her or his family out of poverty.

USAS has partnered with the Workers Rights Consortium to develop tools aimed at encouraging colleges and universities to purchase apparel from manufacturers that respect the rights of their workers. In response to USAS organizing, a wide range of colleges and universities have signed on to the Designated Suppliers Program (DSP), which articulates three key principles for the production of apparel bearing college logos: factories producing the clothing must (1) comply with internationally recognized labor standards, (2) pay workers a living wage, and (3) permit workers to organize a labor union or other employee association. By 2013, USAS had 180 affiliated colleges and universities, including large state universities such as the University of Maryland, Michigan State University, and the University of Texas and small liberal arts colleges such as Carleton College, Occidental College, and Skidmore College.

USAS works to pressure more schools to make public commitments to sweatshop-free college apparel and to monitor the compliance of those schools that have already pledged to steer clear of producers that operate sweatshops. In 2010 USAS launched a new campaign—Nike: Just Pay It—that is mobilizing colleges and universities to demand that Nike disburse more than $2 million in severance pay owed to Honduran workers at factories closed abruptly by Nike subcontractors in that country. In response to the USAS campaign, both the University of Wisconsin and Cornell University announced in 2010 that they planned to stop purchasing licensed apparel from Nike.

Sweatshops are not a problem just for workers outside the United States. More than 400,000 people in the United States worked under sweatshop conditions in the 1990s; this number dropped to about 250,000 by 2004, as the apparel industry moved more and more jobs offshore. The reason that sweatshops reemerged in the United States in the 1980s, after more than 40 years of decline, can be traced to the changing structure of work in the global economy. As unregulated international trade grew, labor unions weakened, and large chain stores in the United States became more prevalent and powerful, sweatshops returned to the United States as a viable way of structuring work.

Sociologist Ross is a frequent speaker at meetings and organizing events for anti-sweatshop groups. Student activists know his talk as a compelling "Sweatshop 101," a sociological perspective that gives his audience a clear introduction to the causes and consequences of contemporary sweatshops.

think about it

1. *Do you know where the apparel that bears your college's or university's logo is made and under what conditions the clothing is produced?*

2. *Would you participate in, or support, the anti-sweatshop movement if you learned that your school sold products made in sweatshops? Why or why not?*

How Structures Change: Action

So far in this chapter, we have considered the ways in which social structure operates at every level of our social world and how it shapes our social lives at the micro, meso, and macro levels. However, human beings are not simply products of structure. We think, choose, and act, and even if social structure imposes limits, we always have some capacity for action, as the example of the student anti-sweatshop movement makes clear. Structure and action are in fact two sides of the same coin. As we consider how structure is affected by human action, we need to understand the broader social context as well.

Types of Action

Max Weber, the pioneering German sociologist whom we met in Chapter 1, defined sociology as the science concerned with understanding social action, that is, human action in social context. Weber was particularly interested in understanding what motivates our actions, and he showed that the goals of human action change across time and culture.

Weber identified three basic types of human action:

- **Traditional action** is *motivated by custom*. Guided by the past, traditional action is anchored by a sense that things have always been done in the same way. Perhaps you have family practices that have been passed on for generations, such as how you celebrate a particular holiday.

- **Affective action** is *guided by emotions and feelings*. When fans tear down the goalposts after their team wins a big college football game, they are guided by their feelings.

- **Rational action** is *motivated by calculations of efficiency*. When people determine their goals and decide how to achieve them, their analysis is a form of rational action. Employees who attempt to act efficiently to help achieve a company's financial goals are guided by this type of action.

Of course, as Weber well knew, human action is complex and is often guided by a combination of these different motivations. But Weber's study of human history led him to believe that modern industrial society is increasingly shaped by rational action. Weber recognized the central role of rational action in the development of modern societies and industrial economies. At the same time, he was concerned that rational action had a tendency to squeeze out other ways of living. A society thoroughly saturated by rational action might be very efficient and highly productive, but Weber worried that it would also be cold and impersonal.

Traditional and rational action are examples of two very different, and sometimes conflicting, understandings of authority. Many people contend that it is appropriate to display representations of the tablet containing the Ten Commandments of the Judeo-Christian tradition, which invokes religion as a traditional authority, near government offices or courthouses. Others believe that courthouses should emphasize rational authority through the rule of law, rather than religion.

Rational Action: McDonaldization

More recently, the sociologist George Ritzer (2013) has argued that a form of rational action he calls McDonaldization is increasingly organizing our everyday lives (see Table 4.1). According to Ritzer, the effect is to impose the standardized, efficient structure of a fast-food restaurant on all aspects of our lives, including school, work, travel, and leisure. For Ritzer, McDonaldization represents an extreme form of rational action. Just as workers respond to the various timed buzzers and "beeps" in a fast-food kitchen, more and more aspects of our lives are organized by the quest for efficiency. For example, grocery shopping now requires no contact with other people. You can use a handheld device to scan each item as you put it in the cart, swipe your customer card, place your deli order with a few keystrokes, and pay with your credit card in the self-

TABLE 4.1	RITZER'S FOUR DIMENSIONS OF McDONALDIZATION
Efficiency	Seeking the best possible method for completing tasks, often by following a series of highly specified, predesigned steps.
Calculability	Emphasizing the quantitative aspects of products and services (focusing on, for example, product size, cost, and time), often characterized by the notion that "more is better."
Predictability	Striving to make products and services the same, regardless of place or time. This process of standardization can be comforting to customers, who know what to expect, but may produce jobs that offer little room for creative thought.
Control	Exercising control over employees and customers by enforcing rigid rules, limiting options, and using new technologies that monitor and regulate behavior.

Source: Ritzer 2013.

FAST-FORWARD

Technology and Change

As customers started to use the telephone more and more for socializing, telephone companies changed their marketing approach. They stopped emphasizing the practical and emergency uses of the telephone, as in this ad from the 1930s (*top*) which says: "Remember—a telephone in your home saves you time, money, and worry, and minimizes inconvenience, anxiety, and loneliness. It places you within a few seconds' talking distance of all the other people who are already 'on the phone,' while, in cases of emergency, you can summon the doctor, or call the police in a few moments." By the 1970s, ads were stressing the ways talking on the phone can be fun. Contemporary ad campaigns for mobile phones (*bottom*) highlight the cell phone as a tool for connecting with family and friends, near and far, from just about anywhere.

With phones having become far more than devices for talk, how do you think smartphones will continue to develop, and be marketed, as tools that are practical and fun, productive and sociable?

---

serve checkout aisle. You can prepare meals by simply pressing a few buttons on your microwave oven. Or you can preplan just about every minute of your vacation, scheduling each activity, tour, meal, and night's sleep as part of a package tour aimed at guaranteeing that you make the most of your time off.

This intense focus on efficiency, however, may lead to unintended consequences. For example, in the name of efficiency we do an increasing amount of unpaid labor—becoming, in effect, our own checkout clerks, bank tellers, gas station attendants, and insurance claims representatives, to name just a few of the tasks we do for ourselves. Simply put, the purpose of a fast-food restaurant is to serve inexpensive, great-tasting food quickly. People who eat in fast-food restaurants, however, sometimes have to wait in long lines, pay more money than they anticipate, and find the food to be unappetizing and unhealthful. Workers in fast-food restaurants do jobs that are so routinized and standardized that they have almost no room for independent action. For Ritzer, this disconnect between the allure and experience of the fast-food restaurant is the puzzle of McDonaldization: how and why can highly rational action produce outcomes that, as Ritzer (1993) puts it, "limit, ultimately compromise, and perhaps even undermine their rationality" (p. 121). Put another way, rational action aims to enhance human experience through a commitment to efficiency and progress. Ritzer suggests that the extreme rational action he calls McDonaldization may be both inefficient and, ultimately, dehumanizing.

McDonaldization is an example of the way human action is shaped by the broader structural patterns of society, in this case the commitment to efficiency in business. The history of phone communication, which we look at next, provides another example of this relationship between action and structure.

Technology and Action: Telephone to Smartphone

The history of phone communication, from the earliest landline devices to today's smartphones, provides a good example of the way human action interacts with evolving technologies to determine the impact of those technologies on social structures. Whatever potential a new technology has, human action—how people use it—is the key to understanding its social significance.

According to Claude Fischer's study *America Calling* (1992), when telephones first became widely available in the early twentieth century, the leaders of the industry marketed them primarily to businesses and stressed their business uses. When phone companies turned their attention to residential users in the 1920s, they marketed the telephone as a practical tool for managing household affairs and for obtaining help in emergencies. The way people used the home telephone, however, was mostly for regular, informal conversations with family and friends. Nonetheless, until some 40 years after the introduction of the telephone, marketers continued to stress its practical uses, not its social uses.

thinking about structure

Can you think of other examples in which human *action* determined the purpose of a technological advance?

Some observers feared that the telephone might undermine local communities, since people could ignore their neighbors and instead build relationships with people who lived far away. This and similar concerns reflect an underlying question: did people use the telephone in ways that changed how they related to their existing friendship structure? The answer, according to Fischer, is no. Instead, people mostly used the telephone in ways that reinforced their existing connections. Telephones made it easier to plan social engagements, though the neighborly practice of "dropping in" unannounced became less common. In addition, telephones certainly made it possible for people to stay in closer contact with their out-of-town relatives.

Cell phones and smartphones have seen a similar evolution. We tend to forget that the mobile phone today, like the telephone in the early twentieth century, is a relatively new technology. In 1990, only 5 million Americans had cell phones; by 2010 the number of users exceeded 302 million (U.S. Census Bureau 2012e). During that period, the cell phone changed from an upscale luxury item to a common accessory. As with early landline telephones, the way people use cell phones has changed over time. Like telephones, mobile phones were initially promoted as business tools and as useful in case of emergencies. Over time, however, people began using cell phones for other purposes (and cell phone technology evolved so that the phones could be used for an increasingly broad array of purposes): to talk with friends, send text messages, check sports scores, access the Internet, take pictures, respond to e-mail, listen to music, get driving directions, read the daily newspaper, play games, or watch movies or live sporting events. The list of uses continues to grow.

Cell phones make all of us more accessible to one another. If you keep a cell phone on you, your friends and family can reach you just about anytime and anywhere. As a result, frequent cell phone users probably communicate more regularly with others in their social networks than do those who do not rely on cell phones for everyday communication (Ling 2008, Ling and Campbell 2012). Cell phones also make people more available to bosses and coworkers, blurring the distinction between work time and time off (Wajcman 2008).

Cell phones have also severed the connection between person and place. When you call a person who has a landline, you are calling a particular place. When you call a cell phone, however, you are calling a specific person, but you have no idea where that person might be. In fact, it is common for an initial cell phone greeting to include the question "Where are you?"

Cell phones, therefore, may be contributing to the loss of private time and space in contemporary society, as well as to the loss of a rooted connection to place. Phones ring all around us, wherever we are, and people carry on conversations on public transportation, in cars, on the street, and in other public settings (Freedman 2009). We communicate on the go, and the boundaries between our jobs and our personal lives are increasingly permeable. How we choose to use cell phones contributes to these changes.

At the same time, people use cell phones to help arrange traditional face-to-face contact. You can find friends at a crowded concert or make last-minute dinner plans. With networking software, you can use your cell phone to find out if any of your friends are nearby and leave electronic messages at restaurants or stores that your friends can later retrieve.

Many people, especially teenagers and young adults, communicate by text message more often than they speak on the phone. People rarely send text messages to strangers; instead, most text messages are directed to friends, family, or others on a person's contact list. New communication patterns associated with texting may be different from those typically facilitated by phone conversations.

CORE CONCEPTS CHALLENGE

Consider **structure** *and action in regard to the social dynamics of text messaging. Is texting a substitute for the phone? Does texting make communication with friends and family easier, or is it a way of making new social contacts? Are people using text messaging in new or surprising ways?*

GPS-based software like Facebook's location-sharing Nearby Friends feature allows friends to map one another's movements on their cell phone. With this software, you can determine when out-of-town friends are nearby or which local friends are in your neighborhood. As this kind of software becomes more refined, you'll be able to check your cell phone or your Facebook page to see if any of your friends are at the local coffee shop.

Even as people with cell phones use them to talk casually with their friends and family on a regular basis, the social consequences for those without a cell phone may be increasing. If you don't have a cell phone, you are not always accessible, you cannot check in with people on the fly, and you will have a hard time connecting with friends who are delayed by traffic. As cell phones have proliferated, public pay phones have largely disappeared, so people without cell phones have an increasingly difficult time staying in touch. Perhaps two separate forms of social structure are evolving, one based on electronic forms of interaction (e-mail, cell phones, handheld web access) and one that is largely out of the electronic loop.

These two forms of social structure are a global phenomenon, but you may be surprised to learn that Africa is the world's fastest growing cell phone market. By contrast, landline telephones remain comparatively rare throughout Africa, with only one phone line for every 33 people on the continent (in contrast, there are more telephone lines than people in the United States). By 2013, Africa had more than 775 million mobile phone subscriptions, the equivalent of more than 70 percent of the continent's population (Ericsson 2013). In many African countries, there are more than 40 cell phone users for every 1 landline subscriber. (See Map 4.1.)

The explosion of cell phone use in Africa surprised the leaders of the telecommunications industry. Since landline telephones were so rare in Africa, industry leaders expected that there would be little interest in, or few resources to pay for, cell phones. But it turns out that demand for the cell phone, even in remote areas, is extraordinary. For most users in Africa, a cell phone is their first telephone, and people are using this technology in new and unexpected ways. For example, farmers in South Africa use their cell phones to learn the current price of fruits and vegetables in the major urban areas, which helps them negotiate with wholesalers. A fisherwoman living on the Congo River tells customers to call her cell phone when they want to buy fresh fish. She keeps the fish alive on a string in the river and prepares them for sale only after receiving a call. Health care workers in rural areas can use their cell phones to call for an ambulance, providing remote health clinics with a real-time connection to more advanced hospitals. Wildlife researchers in Kenya use cell phones to track elephants by placing a cell phone in a waterproof pouch and strapping it around an elephant's neck (LaFraniere 2005; Ngowi 2005). Community health workers in Ghana send regular text messages to expectant parents in remote areas, helping guide women through their pregnancies by providing advice on prenatal care and nutrition. Innovative electronic banking programs in Kenya, Cameroon, and Tanzania allow people who live in remote areas, far from any bank, to open and manage savings accounts via text message (Kang 2010).

Surely, Africans also use the cell phone to talk with friends and family. As these examples suggest, however, cell phone use is, in many ways, quite different in Africa than it is in the United States.

MAP 4.1 | RATIO OF MOBILE PHONE SUBSCRIBERS TO TELEPHONE LANDLINES IN AFRICA

Ratio of mobile phones to landlines

- 1–25 mobile phones for every landline
- 26–50 mobile phones for every landline
- 51–100 mobile phones for every landline
- More than 100 mobile phones per landline

Cell phones have proliferated in Africa in the 2000s, and mobile phones are far more common than landlines throughout the continent. In Liberia, for example, there are more than 400 mobile phone subscribers for every landline. *Source:* Central Intelligence Agency, *The World Factbook;* calculations by author.

Cell phone use in the United States and in other countries, like telephone use before it, shows how actions can lead people to interact with their friends in new ways and to try out new patterns of behavior, which may contribute to the development of new structures. In subsequent chapters, we look at new forms of interaction made possible by recent communication technologies such as peer-to-peer networks, blogs, and virtual reality environments. We turn next, however, to a change on a larger scale: a transformation in the structure of the workplace.

Workers Respond to Globalization

We have seen how the changing structure of work affects employees in the United States, particularly those who work in manufacturing. And as we have learned from studying the dynamic relationship between structure and action, an analysis of structural change reveals only part of the picture.

The proliferation of cell phones in Africa has been a boon for farmers and small-business people, like this market woman in Nairobi, Kenya, allowing them to keep up-to-date with one another and with wholesalers about market prices.

retired earlier than they had anticipated. Facing similar structural conditions, different people made different choices.

In the early twenty-first century, new work patterns are emerging as people negotiate the challenges and opportunities of the global economy. With continuing high levels of long-term unemployment in the United States in the wake of the 2008–2009 recession, and a steep decline in the value of many people's pensions or retirement funds, today's workers are likely to have fewer options than their counterparts did only a decade earlier. The dynamic of structure and action helps us see the magnitude of the changes, how these changes shape people's opportunities, and how people respond to these changes. One area in which new work patterns are emerging is the news industry.

A Changing World

THE EVOLVING STRUCTURE OF NEWS PRODUCTION

How do you learn about important events in your community, the nation, or the world? Although word of mouth—conversations with friends and family—is a common source of information, the foundation for much of what we know beyond our immediate experience is the news media. Whether it is an ongoing global story like the latest war, a major national development like the implementation of health care reform, or a local development like the introduction of new municipal zoning policies, the news media often serve as one of our primary sources of information. News reports inform our individual decision making and provide a common framework for public discussion about current events and issues. From local newspapers and blogs to national network television and international news websites, news media give citizens information they need to be active participants in civic life.

In the digital age, where, when, and how citizens get their news is undergoing significant change. The younger you are, the less likely you are to rely on the morning newspaper or the evening newscast on television. Instead, you may get your news anytime on your computer screen or smartphone and, with a little effort, you can access news from around the globe instantly. News consumption is in the midst of an important transition, but what about the production and reporting of news? As we will see, the organization of news production is also undergoing a major transformation.

How do news organizations decide what is news? The structure of news gathering—that is, the regular routines

We also need to pay attention to how people respond to structural change, even when their choices are limited.

As the number of manufacturing jobs in the United States declined during the late twentieth century, what choices or opportunities opened up for displaced workers? The lost industrial jobs should not be romanticized. Factory work was often monotonous, difficult, and dangerous. In a 10-year study, Ruth Milkman (1997) examined a General Motors assembly plant in Linden, New Jersey, where, as part of an effort to compete in the new global economy, the company reorganized work and introduced robots and other technological innovations. The union negotiated a buyout package for workers who wanted to leave. According to Milkman, workers who left, it turned out, were happier than those who stayed. Despite their unstable economic future, most were glad to escape the dreary, demanding work of the assembly line. With the exception of skilled workers who learned how to maintain the new robots, most workers who stayed found that new technologies and management programs made life worse for them. Their jobs became even more monotonous. Their relationships with their supervisors grew worse. Despite some economic uncertainty, most of the workers who left were ultimately able to construct better futures for themselves.

Throughout the United States, as workers lost their manufacturing jobs, some fought plant closings and layoffs, working with labor unions and community groups to try to retain jobs, find new factory owners, or buy the factory themselves. Others returned to school to learn new skills or new careers. Still others sought opportunities by moving away. Some tried to start their own businesses. Others

that editors and journalists follow as they produce the news each day—shapes, to a large degree, what becomes news. Several pioneering sociological studies of daily newsroom activities (Gans 2005; Tuchman 1978) provide insight into the structure of news reporting, the kinds of stories that are most likely to appear in the news, and the kinds that will be largely ignored. At the same time, understanding the structure of news gathering within the traditional news media—television networks, major daily newspapers, and news weeklies—helps us understand how news and the broader media environment are changing in the era of online journalism, YouTube, Facebook, Twitter, and blogging.

Among a news organization's first decisions must be where to look for news. Although some news seems to find reporters—for example, stories that go viral online and cannot be ignored—news organizations need a steady supply of suitable news to fill each day's newspaper or program. Of course, where you look has a significant impact on what you find. Reporters don't just roam the streets, hoping to run across interesting events. Major news outlets have well-developed routines that determine where reporters seek the news. Sociologist Gaye Tuchman (1978) refers to these routines as the "news net." The news net includes full-time reporters, freelance reporters and writers, wire services like the Associated Press and Reuters that provide news stories to many different news outlets, and stringers who help the organization find news in remote locations (a stringer for a local newspaper may be located on your campus). But the net cannot catch every event that happens: like a fishing net, the news net holds only the bigger stories and lets the smaller ones slip away.

To continue the fishing metaphor, we know that to gather information, news organizations send reporters to strategic locations, just as a fishing boat travels to waters where fish are plentiful. Most major news outlets in the United States maintain bureaus in New York and Washington but not in midsized cities like St. Louis and Minneapolis. As for international news, U.S. news outlets are likely to have a news bureau in London or Tokyo but not in Bangkok or Madrid. As a result, events in and around these predefined important places are more likely to be treated as news. From the outset, then, the way news gathering is organized—where news outlets station their reporters—has a powerful impact on news coverage, just as where the boat travels determines which and how many fish are caught.

In addition, journalists are assigned to look regularly for news at news beats, which include such official locations as the White House, Capitol Hill, the Supreme Court, city hall, the statehouse, and local police stations. Reporters cover these beats to generate a steady stream of news, and they do so by developing routines that help them identify the events that are newsworthy.

Like other structures, the organizational structure of the news media is subject to change. For example, 50 years ago many major newspapers assigned reporters to a labor beat, regularly writing about the activities of labor unions and the world of work from the perspective of workers. Today, few papers have a reporter assigned to cover labor. Instead, economic coverage, or business news, focuses on issues of interest to investors and executives. On the other hand, many papers today have an environmental beat, an area unheard of a half century ago.

In the digital era, the structure of the news media is in the midst of much more profound changes. For example, the reporting cycle of the traditional news—with daily deadlines for newspapers and network television and weekly deadlines for the major news magazines—is now outmoded. As cable news channels (CNN, Fox News, MSNBC) and a wide range of online media—including the websites of traditional news outlets—report and comment on news around the clock, news has moved to a nonstop, 24-hour cycle.

As traditional news media struggle to survive in this fast-paced, information-rich environment, the structure of news gathering and reporting is changing rapidly. In an effort to cut costs and speed up production, news outlets require reporters to write, conduct interviews, take photographs or shoot video, and edit all of this content to facilitate distribution across various media platforms (Klinenberg 2005). For years, including during the recession of 2008–2009, news organizations cut their staffs significantly. With fewer journalists remaining to produce the news each day, reporters faced even more pressure to do more with less. In this climate, reporters are developing new routines and practices, emphasizing speed and flexibility,

Most news organizations follow a standard set of daily routines as they identify, gather, and report the news. That's one reason why so many news outlets typically cover the same major stories each day.

consistent with the new economic and technological context (Cottle 2007; Pavlik 2008).

Most news organizations post a steady stream of news-brief updates on breaking news throughout the day on Twitter. An increasing number of journalists are exploiting Twitter as more than a tool to promote their newspapers or television programs; they are tweeting the news. For example, *The New York Times* reporter Brian Stelter used Twitter to report on the aftermath of a devastating 2011 tornado in Joplin, Missouri. And during the Arab Spring of 2011, NPR's Andy Carvin reported remotely via Twitter about events all over the region, showcasing the experiences and perspectives of many online volunteers who told their own stories and described happenings from the frontlines of the ongoing revolutions (Carvin, 2013).

In addition, traditional news now competes with new forms of citizen journalism—news and commentary produced outside the context of a professional news organization. Citizen journalism appears in a variety of media: independent websites, YouTube and other video-sharing sites, blogs, and social networking sites.

Some of the traditional media have made efforts to incorporate citizen journalism into their own news net. CNN.com's iReport section is full of videos uploaded by users with reports that "are not edited, fact-checked or screened before they post." CNN reporters monitor the iReport site, and some of the user-posted videos ultimately make their way onto CNN.

Citizen journalism represents a potentially significant change in how news is reported and in how consumers relate to the news. One scholar of online journalism argues that new forms of digital journalism position citizens as "produsers" (Bruns 2005)—part producer and part user of the news—who have a very different relationship to news than do audiences for traditional media. As the structure of news evolves in the digital age, our very definition of "what's news" may also be changing.

thinking sociologically about
Social Structure

- Social **structure** refers to recurring patterns of behavior that make social life possible. Understanding social structure helps us see connections between these patterns and people's actions and beliefs.

- We can see social structure at the micro level (for example, in the structure of talk), the meso level (for example, in organizational structure), or the macro level (for example, in the structure of work).

- Structure constrains behavior by putting limits on it, but it can also enable behavior by providing a context for smooth interaction.

- Even when we are limited by social structure, we always have at least some capacity for *action*. Structure and action are two sides of the same coin; we always need to consider the two in relation to each other.

Looking Back

1. The sociological perspective helps us see social structure, the recurring patterns of behavior in social life. Understanding social structure enables us to see the patterns and regularities in social life.

2. People always have the capacity for action, even when their choices are severely limited. Sociology encourages us to examine the dynamic relationship between structure and action by recognizing how social structure shapes, but does not fully determine, our behavior, expectations, and beliefs.

3. We can explore social structure at different levels. At the micro level, we might analyze the structure of daily interactions. For example, our everyday talk and interaction has a structure. We often take for granted our knowledge of this structure of interaction because it seems so natural to us.

4. At the meso level, we might analyze organizational structure. For example, examining organizational structure helps us understand the complex dynamics involved in the space shuttle *Challenger* and *Columbia* disasters.

5. At the macro level, we focus on broad patterns of behavior, especially the interrelationships of various institutions. For example, sociologists using functional analysis seek to understand how various parts of a society work together and the roles that different institutions and cultural components play in maintaining social order.

6. With the growth of the global economy, stable patterns of work in the United States changed for many Americans at the end of the twentieth century. The dynamic of structure and action helps us understand the significance of these changes, how globalization shaped workers' opportunities, and how people responded to these changes.

7. The evolution of phone communication, from the telephone to the smartphone, illustrates people's capacity for action. When the telephone first became available in the United States, it was marketed primarily as a business device. However, most people used the phone for conversation with friends and relatives. Today, the ways in which people choose to use cell phones and smartphones are once again changing some aspects of social life.

8. The organization of news production is changing. News reporters follow a set of daily routines when they gather the news. Analyzing the structure of news gathering helps us better understand which stories are covered on the evening news and how the news media are changing in the digital age.

Critical Thinking: Questions and Activities

1. How can the concept of structure and its mirror image, action, help us gain a deeper understanding of social life?

2. Think about the structure of your college classroom. In what ways are the patterns and routines of your classroom similar to those of your high school classes? In what ways are they different? How do the expectations associated with the student or teacher role differ from those you encountered in high school?

3. Identify some of the ways that fast-food restaurants emphasize efficiency, predictability, and an extreme form of rational action. Do you agree with Ritzer's theory of the McDonaldization of society?

4. Various efforts to introduce a videophone—long a standard in science fiction films and television—have been largely unsuccessful. Can structure and action help you explain why the videophone has never really caught on? Do you think new forms of video chat—including Skype and iChat—will be successful forms of video communication? Why or why not?

5. What are the functions of work? Earning a paycheck may be the most obvious answer, but do our jobs serve other functions as well? To answer this question, do some research by conducting short interviews with your family and friends about what they get from their jobs. Did the people you interviewed talk about more than their paychecks? If so, what did they say? Try to interview people who have different kinds of jobs or who are in different age groups. Talk with one or two retired people and ask them what they miss—and don't miss—about their jobs.

6. According to popular wisdom, there is no "I" in "team." Using your knowledge of structure and action, think about the differences between an individual sport like tennis, golf, or high jumping, and a team sport like basketball or soccer. How are the patterns of interaction different? How does the structure of the game shape how participants play, or what they are expected to do, or how fans respond to different sports?

Key Terms

achieved status (p. 90) a position in a social system that a person attains voluntarily, to a considerable degree, as the result of his or her own efforts.

action (p. 87) the ability to behave independent of social constraints.

affective action (p. 99) behavior guided by emotions and feelings.

ascribed status (p. 90) a position in a social system, assigned to a person from birth, regardless of his or her wishes.

breaching experiments (p. 91) social situations that intentionally break social rules, violating basic norms and patterns of behavior.

convention (p. 93) a practice or technique that is widely used in a particular social setting.

conversation analysis (p. 92) a method of analyzing the patterns in face-to-face conversation that produce the smooth, back-and-forth turn-taking of such exchanges.

ethnomethodology (p. 91) an approach that examines the methods people use to make sense of their daily activities, emphasizing the ways in which we collectively create social structure in our everyday activities.

organizational structure (p. 93) the rules and routines, both formal and informal, that shape daily activity within organizations.

rational action (p. 99) behavior motivated by calculations of efficiency.

roles (p. 90) the sets of expected behaviors associated with particular statuses.

social institutions (p. 87) the major arenas of social life in which durable routines and patterns of behavior take place.

social integration (p. 96) the social structures that bind people together and the values that link people to the broader society.

social structure (p. 87) recurring patterns of behavior.

status (p. 90) a position in a social system that can be occupied by an individual.

traditional action (p. 99) behavior motivated by custom.

5

Power

looking AHEAD

What is **power** and how does it affect your life?

Why do you have more **power** than you might realize?

How is understanding **power** essential for understanding inequality?

Two decades ago, Munni Akter could barely afford enough food to survive. "I was lost and had no skill to earn," Munni recalls. That's when she managed to get a microloan—just $40—from the Bangladesh Rural Advancement Committee (BRAC). The loan enabled her to begin selling food on the street at a profit. Over the years her business grew. Today Munni runs a small food factory that employs 26 workers. She is out of poverty and proudly independent.

Munni Akter is just one of millions of Bangladeshis who have benefited from microloans, and BRAC is the world's largest nongovernmental organization working to reduce poverty. But BRAC is much more than a microlender. It organizes recipients of microloans into small groups of 20 to 30 people. Group members guarantee one another's loans, provide mutual assistance, and often operate as a springboard for other improvements in their lives. BRAC also operates health care and education programs and teaches women about gender equality and the law so that they can speak up for their rights and resist exploitation.

To spread the message of empowerment, BRAC trains some women as paralegals, or *shebikas* ("helpers" in Sanskrit). These women learn how to handle crises such as rape and domestic abuse as well as to provide other legal services. Over 11,000 *shebikas* now share their knowledge and support with others.

By helping individual women become empowered and by developing a long-term organizational structure to train a growing number of educators and advocates, the women in these various programs have increased their collective power. That has always been the goal of BRAC's founder and chairperson, Fazle Hasan Abed, who observes, "Poor people are poor because they are powerless. We must organise people for power" (BRAC 2010a, 2010b; Changemakers 2009; Haq 2011).

Power is a fundamental sociological concept, affecting every level of society and influencing our daily lives in countless ways. Because power pervades social life, to understand how society works we must consider its role in various social contexts. As noted political philosopher and social critic Bertrand Russell (2004, 4) put it, "the fundamental concept in social science is Power, in the same way in which Energy is the fundamental concept in physics." Power, like energy, takes many forms and is essential in understanding why things happen as they do in society.

The amount of power that we have heavily influences what we can accomplish in life, whether at home, at work, or in our community. People with more resources typically have more power, and those with power can use it to obtain more resources. Power, therefore, is closely linked to social inequality, another fundamental feature of society. Inequality can be based on many different characteristics, including class, race, gender, ethnicity, nationality, sexual orientation, and religious affiliation. But these different forms of inequality have something in common: power and its influence.

In this chapter, we define and examine power and its various characteristics. We look at examples of power in daily life as well as how differences in power affect inequality, and we explore how different types of inequality interact. We conclude by noting how economic power is increasingly translated into political influence through campaign contributions.

Understanding Forms of Power

You know that the United States is a powerful nation and that your boss has more power than you do. But what is "power," exactly? And how can this concept be applied to such different settings as international relations and the workplace? Different approaches to understanding power highlight different aspects of this important concept (Blalock 1989; Gaventa 1982; Lukes 2005; Mann 2012; Poggi 2001; Sharp 1973; Smith 1990; Wartenberg 1990; Wrong 1979).

Defining Power

The word *power* is derived from a Latin word, *potere*, which means "to be able." Max Weber ([1922] 1978, 926) viewed **power** as *the ability to bring about an intended outcome, even when opposed by others.* Two key components of this definition are the basis for an important distinction: Some sociologists focus on the "ability to bring about an intended outcome," or the "power to" approach, so called because it highlights the capacity to accomplish something. Others focus on the ability to overcome opposition, or the "power over" approach, so called because it highlights the capacity to dominate others (Ng and Bradac 1993). These two aspects of power are not mutually exclusive, and feminist scholars, especially, have

worked to integrate both approaches into a comprehensive analysis of power (Allen 2008). Let's consider these aspects of power more closely.

Empowerment: "Power To"

As noted, the "power to" approach emphasizes *the ability to bring about an intended outcome,* highlighting the positive and constructive aspects of power. **Empowerment,** which *increases people's capacity to bring about an intended outcome,* is the focus of much feminist scholarship on power. Social philosopher Virginia Held (1993), for example, argues that power is the capacity to change and empower oneself and others. According to political scientist Nancy Hartsock (1983, 226), the "feminist theory of power" views power as a competence and ability, rather than a form of dominance. Sociologist Patricia Hill Collins (2000) highlights the use of power to resist oppression.

People often discuss power and empowerment in terms of individual effort and achievement. If your goal is to find an interesting, decent-paying job, then acquiring appropriate education and experience can help give you the "power to" accomplish your objective. Empowerment often involves individual enhancement and self-improvement. Individual self-empowerment is the theme of popular self-help books with titles such as *Empowerment: The Art of Creating Your Life as You Want It.*

SPOTLIGHT
on social theory

Feminist theories point out that power can involve competence and empowerment, rather than just the domination of others. Have you experienced empowerment in your own life in some way without diminishing the power of others?

Empowerment can also involve organizations, communities, and entire categories of people. International development agencies, for example, try to empower poor people by increasing their capacity to care for themselves and their families (Alsop and Heinsohn 2005). The Bangladesh Rural Advancement Committee mentioned at the beginning of this chapter seeks to empower an oppressed group through a combination of economic assistance and educational programs. Other programs and organizations have also used this combination to produce promising results worldwide. A program in South Africa, for instance, has empowered women to reduce by half the incidence of physical and sexual violence in their community (Kim et al. 2007). Similarly, the women's movement in the United States has helped empower women, enabling them to gain greater equality in the workplace, more options in their roles at home, better medical care, more equitable access to education, and greater participation in sports. As women have become empowered, they have accomplished these gains without dominating men, making their achievements examples of the "power to" act rather than "power over" others.

The "power to" approach can also apply to social systems such as schools, governments, or even entire societies. American sociologist Talcott Parsons (1960) saw power as the capacity of a social system to achieve collective goals. In the tradition of structural functionalism, Parsons was most interested in the overall operation of societies as social systems. According to his framework, a society is powerful to the extent that it can accomplish its goals. Doing so requires access to resources, among them money and knowledge. Wealthy societies have more resources—and thus are more powerful—than poorer societies (one way that power and inequality are often connected). Powerful societies can maintain a high standard of living for their citizens, ensure self-defense, advance scientific and technological frontiers, and achieve other collective goals. By all these measures, the United States and other wealthy nations are powerful societies, whereas impoverished countries are much less powerful.

on social theory

Functionalist theories of power focus on the capacity of social systems to achieve collective goals. What is an example of a social system that you are a part of, and what collective goals does it attempt to achieve?

Strategies of Empowerment: Educate, Organize, Network

The old saying "Give a man a fish and you feed him for a day; teach a man to fish and you feed him for a lifetime" expresses the difference between charity and empowerment. A gift provides only temporary relief and fosters a relationship of dependency; a person who is empowered develops an enduring capacity and independence. Whether adopted by an individual, a small group, or a national or an international organization, strategies to increase empowerment generally involve a combination of education, organization, and networking (Dugan 2003).

- **Education** is probably the best-known approach to empowerment. Some teaching philosophies, for example, focus heavily on empowering students rather than simply transmitting facts (Freire 1970). To achieve their goal, people or groups must understand their situation, have a vision of what needs to be done, and obtain the training and skills they need to reach their goal. For some people, a college education can be an important means of learning about their situation and developing the skills necessary for rewarding employment and a more fulfilling life.

- **Organization** involves bringing people together to identify common goals and work to achieve them. Smoothly operating workplaces are well organized, for example, with employees and management cooperating to achieve organizational goals. When communities of disempowered people organize, the neighborhood associations, labor unions, and advocacy groups that result can serve as megaphones to amplify the concerns of group members and help them stand up more powerfully to adversaries. The *shebikas* organized through BRAC's Human Rights and Legal Education program, discussed in our chapter

opening, show how organization can empower people. As one guide to community organizing notes, "Building a strong, lasting, and staffed organization alters the relations of power. . . . When the organization is strong enough, it will have to be consulted about decisions that affect its members" (Bobo, Kendall, and Max 2010, 12).

- **Networking** involves reaching outside your immediate circle of contacts to find allies. Professional associations in many fields hold conferences and social events to facilitate networking to search for employment or to advance careers. Organizations also network by forming coalitions and other collaborative efforts. In this way, they pool their resources to achieve goals they would be unlikely to accomplish on their own.

Domination: "Power Over"

At all levels of social life, people disagree. For example, a parent grounds a teenager but the teenager resists; a corporation wants to build a toxic waste incinerator near a neighborhood, but the residents object; or one political party proposes legislation that another party opposes. In all these cases, the effort to accomplish something meets opposition and produces conflict. That's why the second part of our definition of power includes the idea of conflict: "the ability to bring about an intended outcome, *even when opposed by others.*" This emphasis is called the "power over" approach, since it focuses on overcoming opposition or dominating others. In one classic definition from political scientist Robert Dahl (1957), power

This classic graphic illustrates the idea that through organization weaker parties can join forces to take on a more powerful adversary.

is seen exclusively in terms of domination: "A has power over B to the extent that he can get B to do something that B would not otherwise do" (p. 202).

Domination can occur at any level of society. Forcing children to be brides, as is done in some cultures, reflects both domination at the individual level (the future of a specific young woman is determined by her extended family) as well as inequalities at the societal level (women in such societies lack power in social life). Often macro-level inequalities in power trickle down to affect people's daily lives. At the same time, the personal choices people make have a cumulative impact on broader dynamics of social power, a process captured neatly by the feminist slogan "The personal is political" (Hanisch 1970).

The most obvious use of power as a means of domination is in political and economic conflicts, as powerful elites attempt to maintain their advantages over others. We examine such situations more closely later in the chapter, when we explore systems of social inequality.

PLS DNT TXT + DRIVE

A Public Service Announcement
brought to you by your school + other drivers

Designed and distributed by AlphabeticaDesign.com

Public service announcements, such as this one discouraging texting while driving, are an example of trying to persuade people to act—or not act—in a certain way.

achieve its goals—to the extent that it can reach and influence people through education. However, this type of power is limited, since it usually cannot overcome stubborn opposition. Also, the use of persuasion is not always forthright or honest. Some actors manipulate, distort, or withhold information to convince others to act in a desired way, such as authoritarian governments that control the media. Citizens in such societies may voluntarily comply with the government's wishes, but the rulers have obtained this compliance by using false, incomplete, or misleading information. Even in open societies, misleading propaganda efforts by governments and powerful corporations can shape the terms of debate about many issues, thereby achieving compliance under false pretenses (Chomsky 1989).

Strategies to Overcome Opposition: Persuade, Reward, Coerce

Imagine that someone you live with—your roommate, partner, or spouse—has a much lower standard of cleanliness than you do. He or she leaves the sink full of dirty dishes and leaves clothes, papers, and half-eaten food lying around. If you want this person to be neater, you have three options. First, you could try persuasion, which would involve convincing the person to clean up out of fairness, because of health concerns, or to eliminate the growing stench that is putting a damper on your social life. If persuasion didn't work, you could try offering a reward: "If you do your share of the cleaning for a month, I'll pay for us to go out to see a movie." Finally, if all else fails, you could try a threat: "If you don't keep up with your share of the cleaning, you can't live here anymore."

Participants in any conflict, whether minor or serious, have these same three basic options: persuade, reward, or coerce others to get them to comply (Kriesberg 1982, 115).

■ To **persuade** is *to get people's compliance by convincing them of the correctness of your position and goals.* An organization dedicated to combating sexually transmitted diseases, for example, might launch a campaign to educate people about the importance of condoms. Over time, as people hear this message repeatedly, some might begin to alter their behavior. The group has power—it is able to

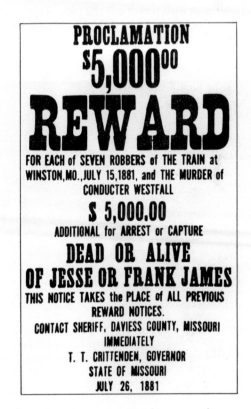

PROCLAMATION
$5,000.00
REWARD
FOR EACH of SEVEN ROBBERS of THE TRAIN at WINSTON, MO., JULY 15, 1881, and THE MURDER of CONDUCTER WESTFALL
$ 5,000.00
ADDITIONAL for ARREST or CAPTURE
DEAD OR ALIVE
OF JESSE OR FRANK JAMES
THIS NOTICE TAKES the PLACE of ALL PREVIOUS REWARD NOTICES.
CONTACT SHERIFF, DAVIESS COUNTY, MISSOURI IMMEDIATELY
T. T. CRITTENDEN, GOVERNOR
STATE OF MISSOURI
JULY 26, 1881

Rewarding others is one way to achieve compliance. Why are rewards often used to capture criminals? What rewards—other than cash—can be useful in daily life?

A second strategy to overcome opposition is to offer a reward. To **reward** is *to encourage people's compliance by offering a positive incentive.* Rewarding a child with words of praise, an athlete with a trophy, or a country with economic or military assistance are all ways to encourage or reinforce desirable behavior.

To **coerce** is *to force compliance by threatening, intimidating, pressuring, or harming someone.* Drivers generally obey the speed limit (or something close to it) because they know a speeding ticket can be very expensive. Therefore, the threat of possible punishment has a coercive effect on their behavior. In this case, compliance is a result of *systemic* coercion in which social structures—not just individuals—are in place to deliver a threat.

Reward and coercion are sometimes two sides of the same coin. As a student you may work hard in school, even when you do not enjoy it, because you have been taught that your chances for good employment—with all the accompanying rewards—will be improved significantly if you have a college degree. You also know that receiving failing grades is likely to harm your prospects for graduation and employment—an implicit coercion.

In many cases, coercion is much more sinister, involving threats to people's livelihood, freedom, or physical well-being. In some repressive societies, people who fail to comply with authority can lose their jobs, while those who obey are allowed to pursue successful careers. In the most authoritarian societies, those with power use the most sinister forms of coercion: imprisoning, beating, or killing people who refuse

Power operates in all levels of social life. Many everyday interactions involve power. In this soccer match, a referee uses his authority to intervene in a dispute.

to comply. Because these techniques are inefficient, they are typically used as a last resort. However, through the force of their example, they can have a coercive effect on large numbers of citizens. (Nations, too, use such coercion against their enemies.) Ultimately, though, because force is expensive and can create opposition, people in power cannot rely for long on coercion alone. It is more efficient to have people control their own behavior.

Physical force is typically the last resort in obtaining compliance. As a type of coercion, it is expensive, inefficient, and often ineffective in the long run because it generates anger and resentment.

Power in Everyday Life

Power is an essential part of social relationships at every level of social life, including your relationships with your family and friends, your professor, your boss, the police, and the government. Many sociologists, including Max Weber and Karl Marx, focused much of their attention on the operation of power at the macro level of society, examining governmental and economic power. We explore these ideas in more detail later in the chapter.

However, power is also involved in social interactions at the micro level. For example, intimate partner violence is a serious social issue, and rates of physical and sexual abuse are especially high among high school and college students (Straus 2004). Women, in particular, suffer the consequences of this abuse. Intimate partner violence produces a sense of powerlessness in the victim, often leading to depression. A survey of undergraduate women found that the more violence they experience in their relationships, the less powerful and the more depressed they feel (Filson et al. 2010). Perpetrators use violence to assert control and gain power over their partners.

thinking about power

How do those who have **power** over your actions and decisions maintain their control?

In between macro- and micro-level interactions are the meso-level organizations to which we all belong. Studying power can also help us understand how such organizations operate.

Power in Small Groups and Organizations

Sociologists who study power in small groups and organizations examine how such groups operate and what roles their leaders play. Many of their insights can be applied to friendship circles, families, and clubs as well as to more formal settings such as schools and workplaces.

In one classic formulation, John French and Bertram Raven identified six bases of power in small groups and organizations (French and Raven [1959] 2001; Raven 1965). Notice how these power bases overlap with the broader strategies for overcoming opposition we discussed earlier:

- **Reward power** is the control one party has over valued resources that can be used to provide positive incentives. By offering children a weekly allowance, parents can gain power over their behavior.

- **Coercive power** is the ability to punish—for example, by withholding valued resources or by inflicting verbal or physical harm. Police officers can usually generate compliance because they can issue citations, arrest people, or even shoot them if necessary.

- **Legitimate power** is exercised by those who invoke a feeling of obligation; one "ought" to obey, perhaps as a result of shared cultural values or out of respect for someone's formal rank or position in the social structure. You are likely to carry out a boss's order to do a routine task at work; you would ignore a similar order about your private home life.

- **Referent power** is based on feelings of identification, affection, and respect for another person, even if that person does not seek influence over others. A popular colleague in a workplace might have referent power because others look up to her and view her as a model.

- **Expert power** arises from the perception that a person has superior knowledge in a particular area. A lawyer has expert power in legal matters in relation to a client. Expert power is about the perception of knowledge, not necessarily actual knowledge. Someone seen as an authority carries expert power whether or not he has actual expertise. Conversely, a real authority on some topic may not have expert power if others do not recognize that expertise.

- **Informational power** is based on a person's use of facts, data, or other evidence to argue rationally or persuade. A project manager has informational power when she convinces her boss to approve a new product. Those with information can increase their influence by sharing it, withholding it, organizing it effectively, or even manipulating or falsifying it.

These categories can overlap—a leader can withhold a reward as a type of coercion—but the distinctions help us recognize different sources of power. Also, a person's use of one type of power can affect another. For example, when a manager gives an employee a bad evaluation—a use of coercive power—that action is likely to undermine his or her referent power with that person.

Sociologists and social psychologists have done a great deal of research on the dynamics of small groups, including those associated with power (Forsythe 2013). Researchers have shown that when authorities rely on reward or coercive power, their influence weakens if the amount of resources they control is reduced. However, authorities who have earned respect and are seen as legitimate enjoy group members' loyalty regardless of their ability to reward or coerce. Such loyalty can evaporate, however, if the person in authority acts in ways that group members consider unfair, unethical, or disrespectful (Lammers et al. 2008; Tyler 2005; Tyler and Blader 2003).

Compared to powerful people, those who feel relatively powerless are more likely to use coercion because they think they have no other means of achieving their aims. Some parents and teachers feel relatively powerless when children seem out of control. These adults are more likely to use coercive threats and punishment than are parents and teachers who feel empowered (Bugental and Lewis 1999).

Authorities generally prefer rewards over coercion because they worry about retaliation (Molm 1997). However, group members often tolerate a coercive leader if the group is successful in achieving its goals (Michener and Lawler 1975), or if they trust the leader (Friedland 1976). If a leader lacks referent power, uses coercion, and asks group members to carry out unpleasant tasks, though, group members are more likely to resist his or her authority (Yukl, Kim, and Falbe 1996). People are also more likely to oppose authorities if they perceive their actions as unjust, view fellow group members as comrades, learn to act together as a group, and believe they have group support when speaking out (Gamson, Fireman, and Rytina 1982).

Power Tactics

How do you try to get your way when dealing with your friends or your boss? **Power tactics** are *the specific strategies people use to influence others in everyday life.* These familiar strategies involve power, though we often do not think of them in those terms. (See Table 5.1.) A child who persists in yelling "I want it! I want it!" in a store is using a power tactic.

Tactic	Examples
Appeal	Beg for help; plead with someone to play fair
Bully	Yell; push someone around
Collaborate	Invite someone to help; provide assistance as needed
Complain	Protest to a store manager about poor service; grumble to a professor about an assignment
Criticize	Point out the limitations in a plan; find fault with someone's work
Demand	Ask for a refund; insist on speaking to a supervisor
Discuss	Talk over a situation in a group; come up with a plan of action
Disengage	Walk out in the middle of the argument; give someone the cold shoulder
Evade	Change the subject; don't return phone calls
Inform	Point out the advantages of a plan; note the personal benefits someone will receive
Ingratiate	Flatter; compliment
Inspire	Appeal to a person's loyalty; cheer someone on
Join forces	Find allies to help fight an opponent; agree to approach the boss as a group
Joke	Use humor to help others relax; ridicule opponents
Manipulate	Lie; leave out important details in a report
Negotiate	Offer a deal; offer to compromise
Persist	Refuse to take no for an answer; keep trying
Persuade	Convince someone of the wisdom of a position
Promise	Assure someone that you will follow through with a plan
Punish	Fire someone; ground a child for the week
Put down	Insult someone; disparage a person's abilities
Request	Ask for a favor
Reward	Take someone to lunch as thanks; give someone a promotion
Socialize	Ask about the family; make small talk
Threaten	Warn about taking legal action; warn that you will divulge embarrassing information

Source: Adapted from Forsythe (2013).

A worker who ridicules his or her colleague is using a power tactic. Power tactics vary along three key dimensions (Forsythe 2013, 228):

- *Hard and soft.* Hard tactics are forceful, direct, or harsh. People employing them use economic rewards and other tangible outcomes, and even threats. A cash rebate or a threat to repossess your car is a hard tactic. Soft tactics focus on relationships. People employing soft tactics make use of collaboration and friendship to achieve an aim. A friendly reminder that you need to do some task is a soft tactic.

- *Rational and nonrational.* Rational tactics appeal to logic and include bargaining and rational persuasion.

Many newspaper editorials use rational tactics. Nonrational tactics include emotional appeals, such as when television commercials imply that driving a particular type of car will make you sexy.

- *Unilateral and bilateral.* Unilateral tactics do not require cooperation to initiate; they include demands, orders, or disengagement. Military leaders employ unilateral tactics when they issue orders. Bilateral tactics involve give-and-take, as in negotiations and discussions. When a homeowner and a prospective buyer negotiate a sale price for a house, they use bilateral tactics.

The way power and inequality operate within broader society can influence the dynamics of small groups. For

Foucault's Distinctive View of Power

Did you ever think school was like a prison? If so, French sociologist Michel Foucault (1926–1984) would have agreed with you. In *Discipline and Punish* (1995) Foucault explained how modern prisons emerged in the eighteenth century as a humane alternative to torturing or killing criminals. Advocates of prison reform argued that prisons would deter crime by more effectively controlling criminals. As it turns out, prisons didn't deter crime, but they did demonstrate a new form of power and social control that involved detailed time schedules, restricting prisoners' physical movement, and observing and evaluating their behavior. These features of prisons were adapted and applied to other new social institutions, including factories, psychiatric hospitals, and modern schools. (We revisit these developments in Chapter 8, on social control.)

Foucault's study of prisons made use of his unique view of power, which has influenced many scholars. Foucault argued that though power can be oppressive and dominating, it can have a positive effect. He wrote, "We must cease once and for all to describe the effects of power in negative terms: it 'excludes,' it 'represses,' it 'censors,' it 'abstracts,' it 'masks,' it 'conceals.' In fact power produces; it produces reality" (Foucault 1995, 194).

For Foucault, power "produces reality" because it is made up of systems of knowledge that organize, label, and measure the world in distinct ways. For example, science, religion, and business each have an internal logic, unique assumptions, distinct vocabulary, and central ideas. Because a minister or priest views the world in terms of "grace," a scientist in terms of "empirical evidence," or an executive in terms of "profit," each understands the world differently. Each person's ideas and beliefs influence his or her behavior by encouraging some actions and discouraging others.

As knowledge systems—faith in a God, science, or capitalism—become accepted, they become taken-for-granted assumptions about the world and therefore assume enormous power and influence. Those who question or challenge such dominant systems of knowledge are marginalized, ostracized, and even punished. In the end, such systems of knowledge help control behavior and are therefore forms of power in themselves.

Foucault coined the term *power/knowledge* to show that how we understand and interpret the world both enlightens and restricts us. That's because systems of knowledge order, rank, and make visible various aspects of the world, enabling it to be controlled more effectively. When applied to people, such systems of knowledge serve as mechanisms of social control. New ways of thinking—like the idea for creating the modern prison—are developed into real-world social institutions in which certain types of actions are allowed and encouraged and others are prohibited and discouraged, though resistance is always possible.

Although some people benefit from certain forms of knowledge—clergy have considerable legal power in religiously based societies whereas psychiatrists are influential within our own society—they don't necessarily control the use of that knowledge. That is, individuals don't wield power; instead they navigate through a system of knowledge. In fact, Foucault argued that rather than people using power, we are the product of power. That is, power helps form our sense of self.

Foucault saw power as dispersed throughout society rather than centralized in the hands of small groups or individuals. "Power is everywhere," he wrote (Foucault 1980, 93), "not because it embraces everything but because it comes from everywhere." Power relationships play out in countless local "fields," such as the family, the prison, the workplace, a doctor's office, a classroom, and a place of worship. As a consequence, power is fragmented into many different forms. This is why much of Foucault's work was organized around particular subjects, such as prison, sexuality, and madness. Each of these fields has its own power dynamics.

Most powerful of all are the systems of knowledge that cause people to change their behavior willingly by monitoring their own actions to conform to expectations. Susan Bartky (1990) argues that because of such self-surveillance, many women closely regulate their own bodies through constant dieting, "proper" hair removal, and wearing make-up and fashionable clothing. When carried to extremes, the impact of such disciplinary power can produce eating disorders and other unhealthy behaviors—another form of prison.

think about it

1. *Do you agree with Foucault that power/knowledge helps to control people's behavior? Why or why not?*
2. *Can you think of examples to illustrate Foucault's idea that we regulate ourselves by conforming to social expectations?*

example, women have higher levels of referent power than men do; people typically evaluate women more favorably than men and like them more (Carli 1999). But women who use a direct leadership style are judged more harshly than men, and they have to outperform men to be seen as equally competent. Men have more expert power, and because people generally believe men are more competent than women, men can draw upon this perception as a source of influence. Gender differences are affected by a person's position within the social structure, however; people who are relatively powerful—women or men—report using more direct strategies to influence others than do less powerful individuals. (For a very different take on power, read the Through a Sociological Lens box.)

PEASANT WOMAN: Well, how did you become king then?

ARTHUR: The Lady of the Lake . . . held aloft [the sword] Excalibur from the bosom of the water signifying by Divine Providence that I, Arthur, was to carry Excalibur. That is why I am your king!

PEASANT MAN: Listen—strange women lying in ponds distributing swords is no basis for a system of government. Supreme executive power derives from a mandate from the masses, not from some farcical aquatic ceremony.

ARTHUR: Be quiet!

As these peasants recognize, a rational-legal process requires some transparency and logical justification, whereas tradition is, in effect, self-justifying. Weber argued that with the rise of science, industrialization, and democratic processes, rational-legal forms of authority rapidly replaced traditional ones. The contemporary spread of democratic forms of government around the world continues this trend.

Weber also described a third form of legitimate power. **Charismatic authority** is *power whose legitimacy is derived from the extraordinary personal characteristics of an individual leader, which inspire loyalty and devotion.* Charismatic leadership is usually not transferable. Therefore, this form of authority is typically short lived and episodic. Charismatic leaders can inspire groups of people to act, even though such leaders may possess no formal institutional power. Examples of charismatic leaders include compelling politicians, a motivating team coach or captain, a dynamic celebrity activist, or an inspirational spiritual leader.

The Role of Compliance

Weber based his distinctions between legitimate and illegitimate power on the perceptions of the people obeying the orders, but he did not address *how* those perceptions are created and, therefore, how different types of leaders sustain their power by maintaining their followers' compliance. To take an extreme example, long-term hostages sometimes identify with their captors and voluntarily follow their wishes, an effect called the *Stockholm Syndrome*. This phenomenon, however, does not transform the abductor's power from illegitimate to legitimate. Instead, it shows compliance is more complicated than it may at first appear.

Power is limited by the social relationships on which it is based. The president of the United States, for example, is powerful only as long as others agree to carry out his commands. If the president orders a military attack or initiates a relief effort, many other people must carry out the commands for these goals to be accomplished. Authoritarian regimes can collapse when a large enough number of citizens refuse to obey their leaders and demonstrate for change—a situation that has occurred many times in history.

On a more mundane level, those with power in everyday life also depend on compliance to maintain their position. Students must agree to complete the paper assigned by their teacher, workers usually comply with the boss's rules, and children consent to their parent's request to finish their chores. In other words, people are not passive objects of the demands of those in power; they can react in a variety of ways, from complying voluntarily to resisting and thereby undermining authority.

The degree of compliance in a social situation is often not apparent at first glance. It takes a sociological understanding of power to see that simmering conflict can lurk just beneath the apparently calm, orderly surface of societies. When compliance is withdrawn, conflict may seem to erupt suddenly and dramatically. For example, in 2011 a series of revolutions and uprisings swept northern Africa and the Middle East in what became known as the Arab Spring. Protests, riots, strikes, and other disruptions can start small and spread rapidly as people decide that they will no longer comply. This type of rebellion is itself another form of power: the power of disobedience.

The three types of authority outlined by Weber can be found in contemporary life. The pope relies on traditional authority to gain the allegiance of the world's Catholics. A police officer relies on rational-legal authority to carry out her duties. Although he no longer holds public office, former president Bill Clinton has had a significant impact on U.S. politics through his charismatic authority. What other examples of each type of authority can you think of?

SOCIOLOGY in ACTION

Promoting the Power of Nonviolence

One of the core sociological insights about power is that it depends on compliance. Consequently, those with little apparent power can use noncompliance, or disobedience, to great effect in bringing about social change. Since this insight comes from sociology, it is no surprise that three of the people most closely associated with the power of disobedience studied sociology in college.

Martin Luther King Jr. (1929–1968) was a sociology major as an undergraduate. His later activism showed his understanding of how power operates in social relationships and how those who appear powerless can organize to effect change. King's well-known role as a charismatic leader in the civil rights movement began during the bus boycott in Montgomery, Alabama, in 1955–1956, a campaign that relied on disobedience. By refusing to ride the city's buses for over a year and setting up an alternative system of transportation, thousands of African Americans helped end segregation on public transportation. King went on to aid other rights campaigns that relied heavily on *civil disobedience:* nonviolent direct action that violates unjust laws. Using this strategy, activists successfully challenged segregation at lunch counters, department stores, public swimming pools, and many other facilities, and their efforts helped achieve access to voting rights that had previously been denied to African Americans throughout the South.

Although not as well known as Dr. King, Saul Alinsky (1909–1972), who studied sociology as a graduate student, was also highly influential. Alinsky transformed his sociological understanding of power into practical applications on behalf of low-income citizens. In "Alinsky-style" community organizing, trained organizers identify and coordinate the efforts of existing neighborhood leaders, who in turn mobilize fellow residents to work on issues they identify as priorities, such as better housing, safer neighborhoods, and stronger schools. In addition to emphasizing the importance of building strong organizations, Alinsky advocated the use of creative confrontational tactics that rely on disobedience to apply pressure on those in power. He emphasized the importance of operating outside of the experience of your opponent: for example, he organized fun public demonstrations, street theater, and other actions in which community residents could participate, rather than closed-door meetings that those in authority could

dominate. In 2008, Alinsky-style community organizing received unusual popular attention when one-time community organizer Barack Obama was elected president.

King and Alinksy focused on developing tactics for civil disobedience in the United States, whereas Gene Sharp (b. 1928) studies and writes about the power of nonviolent social action to bring about change in the face of dictatorship, war, and oppression around the world. Sharp's academic training includes a master's degree in sociology. His classic three-volume work, *The Politics of Nonviolent Action,* sketches out a theory of power based on sociological principles and describes the strategic uses of disobedience. Volume Two chronicles hundreds of nonviolent protest actions, including many forms of communication (petitions, marches, teach-ins), noncooperation (boycotts and strikes), and nonviolent interventions (sit-ins, land seizures, and disclosure of secret information). One little-known action: in 1942, when the German army occupying Poland posted "For Germans Only" signs at cafes and hotels in Warsaw, Polish youth stole the signs and defiantly placed them on the lampposts and trees where Germans had hanged Polish patriots. Sharp's work, now outlined in *From Dictatorship to Democracy* (2010) and the subject of the 2012 documentary film *How to Start a Revolution,* has been translated into more than 30 languages and made available for free download on the Internet.

Sharp has irritated authoritarian regimes and influenced activists around the globe. As part of an effort to counter calls for more liberal reform and democracy, the Iranian Information Ministry in 2008 began airing a television propaganda message that condemned Sharp as a "theoretician of civil disobedience and velvet revolutions." That was a reference to the fact that many democracy movements in Eastern Europe during the 1980s and 1990s used ideas and tactics found in Sharp's work. The young people who led the Egyptian revolution in 2011 were also influenced by his work, leading the *New York Times* to comment, "For the world's despots, [Sharp's] ideas can be fatal" (Stohlberg 2011).

think about it

1. *How does the concept of power relate to the work of the three people featured in this box?*

2. *In what other situations might disobedience be a source of power? If disobedience is so powerful, why isn't it used more often?*

The Power of Disobedience

Since power operates within social relationships, one of the great ironies of social life is that those who think they are powerless often have a great deal of power. History is filled with examples of ordinary people who united and toppled powerful opponents. (The Sociology in Action box discusses several key figures associated with the strategic application of disobedience.)

Workers have united to gain concessions from employers, and women have united to achieve changes in the law and in male-dominated institutions. The nonviolent strategies of the U.S. civil rights movement during the 1950s and 1960s inspired many social movements to fight for the rights of other oppressed groups. The people behind all these movements started out with little or no apparent power to effect change. In the end, however, their collective efforts generated enough power to overcome their oppressors.

Everyone has some power. At a minimum, you always have power over your own actions. James Scott (1987) found that peasants in a Malaysian community could exert some influence over public policies by using "weapons of the weak," including gossip about those in authority, foot-dragging, noncompliance, pilfering, and sabotage. None of these were organized or formal protests, but they enabled relatively powerless peasants to resist domination.

Though it may appear that college students are another group with little power within the institutions they attend, successful student activism has led to changes in college policies and regulations and created new academic programs. During the 1980s, for example, student activism caused many institutions to withdraw their investments in apartheid South Africa. Later, student efforts on behalf of living-wage and anti-sweatshop campaigns led to policy changes regarding pay for campus staff and the way in which schools license and acquire athletic wear. In recent years, students have protested tuition hikes and cuts in funding for education. The success of these efforts demonstrates that students have more power than they often realize.

The success of efforts on behalf of oppressed groups, as well as student activism, demonstrates two simple truths about power. First, when people work together, they increase their own power as individuals to effect change. Second, disobedience is a powerful weapon for those who struggle to effect change. Since power is a social relationship, people ultimately have the power to refuse to comply. They rarely use this power, often out of fear of coercion or force. But when people unite in an act of civil disobedience, they can instigate enormous change. This insight has been a powerful tool for many social movements, which we explore in Chapter 17. Those in power typically resist change promoted by oppressed groups because it threatens the privileges they hold, a topic we turn to now.

In recent years, a variety of "Tea Party" efforts have protested health care reform and what they see as high taxes and excessive government spending. What issues related to power are likely to produce national protests in the coming years?

Power and Privilege

As we cautioned in Chapter 1, viewing the world from a sociological perspective can sometimes make people uncomfortable. Nowhere is that more true than in dealing with the issues of power and privilege, topics that cut across race, class, gender, and other social differences (Johnson 2005). Our interests and perspectives—our existing power relations—affect how we think about power (Lukes 2005). When we learn about the unequal power various groups possess, we realize that, compared to many other people in the world, we enjoy a considerable amount of power and privilege. **Privilege** is *a special advantage or benefit that not everyone enjoys*. The fact that most people go about their daily lives unaware of the privileges they enjoy is, in itself, an indicator of that power.

For example, heterosexuals need not concern themselves with their sexual orientation, since our society's norms, laws, and institutional practices have long been organized to accommodate them. Straight people can get married, obtain employment benefits for their spouses, adopt children, talk openly about their relationships without fear of negative consequences—they can go about their daily lives without thinking about being heterosexual. These are privileges that gays and lesbians often do not have. At the same time, a gay man might be acutely aware of discrimination based on sexual orientation while being unaware of his position of privilege as a white, upper-middle-class male. It is easier to recognize disadvantage than privilege.

The point of recognizing privilege is not to make people feel guilty. Rather, doing so allows us to understand society more accurately by removing the blinders that block our ability to see how power operates. In one way or another, we are all involved in power relations. In our society "race," "gender," "class," and "sexuality" tend to conjure up images of blacks and Latinos, women, working-class and poor people, and lesbians and gays. But studying these topics is not just about studying those with less power. Instead, we study such subjects to determine how *everyone* in a society is connected through relations of power. In addition, understanding privilege can help us identify the resources we have available to empower ourselves, assist others, and perhaps reduce inequality.

To understand dynamics of power and privilege, it is often useful to consider the situation of those with less power. Dorothy Smith (1987, 1990) developed **standpoint theory,** which *questions taken-for-granted assumptions about society by looking at it from multiple viewpoints, especially from the perspective of people in subordinate positions.* A "standpoint" is the place from which a person views the world. A person's standpoint is structured by his or her social location, which includes race, class, gender, and sexual orientation.

People with different standpoints see and understand the world differently. For example, in 2013, when a white Latino Florida neighborhood watch volunteer, George Zimmerman, was acquitted of murder after he shot and killed unarmed black teenager Trayvon Martin, public opinion about the verdict varied starkly by race. One poll found that 49 percent of whites were satisfied with the verdict, 30 percent were dissatisfied, and 21 percent did not know. Among blacks, only 5 percent were satisfied, 86 percent were dissatisfied, and 9 percent did not know. A full 78 percent of blacks said they thought the case raised important issues about race that needed to be discussed; only 28 percent of whites agreed. Instead, 60 percent of whites thought race was getting more attention in this case than it deserved; only 13 percent of blacks agreed (Pew Research Center 2013). To varying degrees, we can find similar differences in the perspectives of different groups (men and women, members of different classes) on a variety of issues.

In societies with deep inequalities, groups have differing perspectives. Each of these perspectives is necessarily partial. As a result, considering multiple standpoints, especially of those who have less power, is crucial to gaining a more complete understanding of social life.

Power and Inequality

As we have seen, different groups have varying degrees of power within a society, a situation that inevitably produces **inequality,** *the unequal distribution of resources among groups of people.* All societies have some form of inequality, but its nature and extent vary significantly because patterns of unequal distribution are not natural, inevitable, or the product of chance. Instead, inequality is socially constructed; it varies according to the culture and social structure of a society.

Social inequality is multidimensional: in other words, different forms of inequality coexist within a society. Max Weber ([1915] 1946b) argued that society is stratified in terms of class, status, and political power.

Class: Economic Conditions

Everyone has dreamed of winning the lottery at some point because we all know that obtaining a large amount of money can transform a person's life. With it you can buy a beautiful home, a fancy car, premium health care, travel, and other luxury items. You might also use your winnings to buy leisure time, quitting your job and hiring others to cook your meals, clean your home, handle your finances, and so on. Some people have, in effect, already won the lottery simply by being born into wealth. Clearly, one major type of inequality in society is the uneven distribution of money and other economic resources.

A **class** is *a group of people who share a roughly similar economic position and lifestyle.* Karl Marx's analysis of the importance of class was especially influential. As we discussed in Chapter 1, Marx focused on economic inequality and considered how the different classes in capitalist societies relate to each other as they participate in the process of economic production. Marx highlighted the world of work and analyzed classes as groups of people who share a common relationship to the means of production.

In many ways, Max Weber—whose ideas are also discussed in Chapter 1—agreed with Marx that economics is a key to understanding inequality. However, whereas Marx

Housing is one of the clearest examples of economic inequality in the United States. Neighborhoods tend to be segregated based on income levels. As children grow up, they tend to accept the economic standards of their neighborhood as the norm.

CORE CONCEPTS CHALLENGE

What did your neighborhood look like when you were growing up? What would pictures of your street suggest about the class composition of your neighborhood and the relative **power** *of the members of your community?*

examined the concept of class in terms of work, Weber looked at class in terms of **life chances,** *the opportunities offered by a person's economic position.* For Weber, a class is a group of people who have a similar capacity to earn money, and who consequently share a similar lifestyle. We consider class-based systems of inequality later in this chapter. In Chapter 9, we explore the importance of class in more detail and examine further the differences between Marx's and Weber's approach to this topic. For now, it is enough to know that class is one major type of inequality.

Status: Prestige

Although Weber and Marx agreed on the importance of class, Weber differed from Marx by arguing that status and political power—two noneconomic factors—were also key to understanding inequality. To Weber, both status and political power could be sources of power independent of a person's class.

Adherents of traditional Marxist thought treated class as the single most important source of inequality, supported by other types of inequality such as those based on race and gender. Weber, though, argued that a person's status—based on his or her social characteristics, such as race, ethnicity, or gender—could have an impact independent of class and therefore should be considered as a distinct form of inequality, not merely a secondary feature of economic inequality.

As we noted in Chapter 4, *status* is a person's position in a social system; it is also the prestige attributed to that individual. Depending on the context, then, status can have two meanings—the position itself or the prestige associated with it. People in their fourth year of high school have the status of a senior, a social position. In addition, seniors enjoy the prestige afforded that social position. A person has a given status because he or she belongs to a community of people who have the same lifestyle, ethnicity, race, ancestry, gender, sexual orientation, education, or occupation. Membership in a status group is usually not formal. Instead, members define some shared feature as important or valuable. Status is, in effect, self-perpetuating. Status groups develop formal and informal rules that designate who belongs. Those who belong may socialize with one another, live in the same neighborhoods, join the same organizations, send their children to the same schools, and marry others within the group.

The members of a status group can sometimes use their membership to gain power over nonmembers. **Social closure** is *the process whereby a status group maximizes its own advantages by restricting access to rewards only to members of the group.* This process can involve subtle or blatant **discrimination,** *treating others unequally based on their background or other personal characteristics.* The white populations in the southern states of the United States before the civil rights era and in South Africa before the 1990s both engaged in social closure to exclude other racial groups from access to voting, education, and other rights and opportunities.

In our society, status and class are often linked; people who belong to higher classes disproportionately come from groups with higher status. However, sometimes people of relatively modest means—respected religious leaders, influential politicians, or admired artists—gain access to high-status communities, even though they have relatively modest incomes. Conversely, people with considerable economic resources sometimes face discrimination and other hurdles because of their status. Middle-class African Americans can face both subtle and blatant harassment and discrimination because of their race (Cose 1995; Feagin and Sikes 1994). This situation has improved significantly in recent years, but in many racially diverse communities, high-status organizations and social circles still tend to be all, or nearly all, white.

Ethnicity and religion, too, have long divided status groups in the United States. At one time, people of Irish ancestry, Jews, and Catholics faced discrimination and were excluded, by rule or by custom, from some neighborhoods, jobs, social clubs, civic associations, and schools. In the nineteenth century, for example, employment ads sometimes specified, "No Irish need apply." For the most part, these groups no longer face such discrimination, but Latinos, Muslims, and other ethnic and religious groups continue to experience discrimination today. Gender and sexual orientation, too, continue to present powerful barriers.

Political Power: Strength Through Organization

In addition to class and status, Weber argued that society is stratified in terms of political power. Weber saw that by creating organizations to advance particular goals, people working together could influence society. He referred to these organizations as "parties," meaning a broad range of political groups, including what we would today call social movements, advocacy groups, and citizens' organizations, as well as traditional political parties. As we saw earlier, organizing such groups is one form of empowerment.

Weber saw political power as potentially independent of class and status. For example, lesbian and gay people in the United States who faced status-based discrimination due to their sexual orientation have been able to organize themselves into an influential political force over the past few decades. Although not particularly rich and subject to intense social discrimination, this group has been able to develop political power to improve policies and laws affecting its members' lives. Political organization, then, can serve as a

thinking about power

What status groups do you belong to? Do the members of those groups use power to maximize their advantages over others?

source of power independent of class or status and, as we have seen, can accomplish social change through collective action. But like class and status, political power is distributed unequally in society.

The Intersections of Race, Class, and Gender

As we have considered, Weber argued that social inequality involves class, status, and political power. Similarly, in his work analyzing the black community, sociologist W.E.B. Du Bois, writing early in the twentieth century, highlighted issues of race, class, and nationality. These early works suggested that we should consider many aspects of social life when examining power and inequality.

More recently, some feminist scholars, including Patricia Hill Collins (2000), have built on this tradition through **intersectionality theory,** which *highlights the connections and interactions between various forms of inequality, especially race, class, and gender.* These theorists recognize the different dimensions of inequality and highlight the interactions that take place between these dimensions. For example, white people as a group enjoy privileges in our society because of their race, but white families trapped in poverty face hurdles because of their class. Meanwhile, within the context of poor white families, men are likely to enjoy privileges not afforded to women.

Focusing on the interaction between power and inequality can help us gain a deeper understanding of social life in several ways:

- It gives us a more accurate reflection of how we experience the social world. Any person's identity is multifaceted, including his or her race, class, gender, ethnicity, sexual orientation, and nationality. Taking into account all these aspects of identity gives us a better understanding of our own social location.

- Once we recognize that these factors intersect, we can acknowledge that the relative importance of different types of inequality varies depending on the social context and circumstances. Although a Latino man living in poverty may enjoy privileges within his family because of traditional gender inequality, he also faces many disadvantages because he occupies a low position on the class hierarchy and belongs to an ethnic minority.

- We can also see that intersections involve more than simply "adding up" different identities. One aspect of identity can change another. Being wealthy or poor, for example, can change the social significance of being male or female.

- When we recognize that race, class, and gender interact, we are better able to avoid overgeneralizing about any one group of people. Patricia Hill Collins (2000, 5–6) notes, "Theories advanced as being universally applicable to women as a group upon closer examination appear greatly limited by the white, middle-class and Western origins of their proponents." For example, the idea

A woman points approvingly to a racist sign in this photograph from the early 1920s. Although this woman faced the disadvantages of gender inequality, her status as a white person afforded privileges not available to Japanese Americans of either gender.

CORE CONCEPTS CHALLENGE

How does this photograph illustrate the fact that inequality is multidimensional? How does a person's **culture** *teach the kind of attitudes shown in this photo?*

that the women's movement of the 1960s and 1970s opened the way for women's participation in the paid workforce needs to be qualified, because significant percentages of poor and working-class women in the United States—especially women of color—were already part of the workforce. By viewing women's increased participation in the paid labor force solely through the lens of gender, we miss the important impact of class and race.

Collins (2000) coined the phrase **matrix of domination** to indicate *the interlocking systems of oppression associated with race, class, and gender.* The metaphor of a matrix suggests more than one dimension and allows for the idea that people can be privileged in some ways and oppressed in others. When one group believes it is superior to another, has the right to dominate the other, and is able to do so, oppression results. Her framework highlights the active domination of weaker groups by those with more power at the individual, group, and institutional levels. Reflecting the core concept of structure, as well as the capacity people have for action, Collins recognizes that these various levels of oppression are also sites for resistance as people use their collective power to achieve autonomy and promote equality.

Collins's matrix approach shows that there are few pure oppressors or victims in society. Most people are privileged on some dimension of inequality and disadvantaged on some other. This is true across different types of stratification systems, which we consider next.

Structured Inequality: Stratification Systems

Societies formalize and institutionalize inequality—including the unequal distribution of power—by developing social structures that perpetuate stratification. **Stratification systems** are made up of *social structures and cultural norms that create and maintain inequality by ranking people into a hierarchy of groups that receive unequal resources.* Over the centuries, various societies have created different types of stratification systems. All stratification systems, however, share three key elements:

1. The unequal distribution of valued *resources*
2. Distinct *groups* that make up society's strata (layers)
3. An *ideology* that explains and justifies inequality

The particular form these elements take in any given society determines the dominant type of stratification system and the distribution of power within the society. We will take a closer look at the elements shared by all stratification systems before we consider some examples.

Unequal Resources

The first element of all stratification systems is the unequal distribution of valued resources. These may include (Grusky and Ku 2008, 6):

- *Economic* resources, including money, property, and land
- *Human* resources, such as education, training, and specialized skills
- *Cultural* resources that aid in achieving success, such as knowledge and skills learned through socialization
- *Social* resources, including access to important networks of people
- *Honorific* resources, involving the acquisition of prestige and status
- *Civil* resources, including legal rights involving property, contracts, voting, and speech
- *Political* resources, involving authority in the home, workplace, political arena, or social life

In any stratification system, some resources are distributed more evenly than others. For example, in the United States all citizens have similar legal rights based on the principle of equality under the law, but there are stark differences between rich and poor in terms of economic and human resources. In addition, if a resource is available more readily to one group than to another, that discrepancy can have an impact on another resource. Because the affluent can afford better legal counsel than the poor, the apparent equality of the legal system can be compromised.

Stratified Groups

The second element of all stratification systems is the groups that make up the various strata in society. Stratification based on class, race, and gender is especially widespread and significant, which is why sociologists pay especially close attention to them. However, stratification can also be based on ethnicity, age, religious affiliation, sexual orientation, and disability, among other factors.

The groups within systems of stratification can be based on either an ascribed or an achieved status. As noted in Chapter 4, an *ascribed status* is a position an individual has been assigned in life, regardless of his or her wishes or abilities. Race and sex are examples of ascribed statuses. Stratification systems based primarily on ascribed statuses are said to be closed: they are rigid and impermeable, making it virtually impossible for an individual to move from one stratum to another.

An *achieved status* is a position an individual attains voluntarily, to a considerable degree, as the result of his or her own effort and abilities. College graduates, for example, attain their status due largely to their own efforts. Stratification systems based primarily on achieved statuses are said to be open: it is possible for an individual within such a system to achieve **social mobility,** *movement from one stratum of a stratification system to another.* In systems of class stratification, for example, a person's class status can change as a result of structural changes in the economy, individual ability, education, effort, luck, or other factors. However, a person's achieved statuses are still influenced to varying degrees by social factors beyond his or her control. For example, the family into which you are born can significantly influence your class status.

The various social categories associated with inequality—such as races, ethnicities, classes, and genders—are not natural, inevitable, or biologically based. Instead, the meaning and significance of each category is determined by its cultural context and the social structure—in other words, these categories are socially constructed. They change over time, and they are continually contested, revised, and reinvented. We learn the meaning and significance of these categories for our time and our culture through the socialization process, which we discuss in Chapter 6.

Ideologies That Justify Inequality

The third element of all stratification systems is a related *ideology,* a system of beliefs that helps define and explain the world and justifies the existence of inequality. Those in power produce and promote these ideas to maintain the stratification system, but others sometimes internalize them as well. In fact, the most efficient way to maintain a system of inequality is to convince most people that the system is fair, inevitable, or both. If the groups within a society believe in the ideology that justifies a stratification system, or if they are cynical about any possibility of changing the system, they are unlikely to challenge it. Consequently, those who struggle to reduce inequality must often debate the ideology that supports it. For example, women's rights advocates have long had to debunk myths about women's biological inferiority.

The three key elements that all stratification systems have in common—unequal resources, distinct groups, and a justifying ideology—vary within different stratification systems. We now take a brief look at several examples of such systems.

Caste Systems: India, Feudal Estates, and Racial Segregation

A **caste system** features *stratification based on various ascribed characteristics determined at birth.* The social stratum—or caste—into which people are born largely determines their life chances, typically affecting their access to education, their work options, where they can live, and whom they can marry. Many agrarian societies have some type of closed caste system, but the best known, by far, is the one found in India, which was outlawed in 1952 but which continues to be practiced informally.

INDIA'S CASTE SYSTEM

India's stratification system is traditionally based on the unequal distribution of social honor or respect associated with four major castes, known as *varnas:*

- **Brahmins,** the highest caste, are priests, scholars, and teachers.
- **Kshatriyas,** the second caste, are kings, warriors, and political leaders.
- **Vaisyas,** the third caste, constitute a broad group that includes landowners, merchants, and skilled craftspeople.
- **Sudras,** the fourth caste, includes peasants, servants, and laborers.

Rounding out this complex system are hundreds of sub-caste groups, or *jatis,* typically organized around a single occupation, such as carpenters or barbers and often situated in a particular village or region.

At the lowest stratum of Indian society is a group that exists outside of the *varna* system. Physical contact with members of this lowest grouping is thought to pollute anyone of higher status, so they are often referred to as "Untouchables," but they call themselves *Dalits* ("downtrodden"). *Dalits* are often uneducated and typically perform the lowest and least desirable types of labor, such as cleaning public toilets. In addition, *Dalits* are social outcasts who are banned from worshiping with members of the four *varnas.* Consequently, *Dalits* have little power in society.

Membership in a particular caste is determined at birth and cannot be changed. The justifying ideology, derived from both tradition and Hindu religious doctrine, emphasizes the maintenance of caste purity by restricting social contact to members of one's own caste. People are expected to marry within their own caste.

Throughout India's history, the caste system helped maintain social order by clearly defining the rights and responsibilities of those who belonged to various castes. However, resistance and opposition to this system date back thousands of years. After India gained independence from British rule in the mid-twentieth century, it adopted a constitution that eventually outlawed discrimination based on caste. Today the caste system plays only a limited role in India's modern urban life. However, in the country's more traditional rural areas and small towns, the influence of castes remains significant.

FEUDAL ESTATE SYSTEMS

During the Middle Ages, European societies were stratified into a castelike system that regulated economic, political, and social life based primarily on the unequal distribution of land. Feudalism, as this system is now known, varied but commonly featured three *estates* that comprised a society's major strata:

- **The nobility.** The nobility, the dominant estate, owned the vast tracts of land upon which the agricultural economy—and their power—was based. Wealthy and powerful nobles lived lives of relative luxury, reaping the benefits of others' labor. An elaborate system of honorific titles, such as *king, queen, duke, earl,* and *baron,* indicated the relative rank and power of each individual within this estate. A person's rank was inherited, and marriage was typically restricted to other members of the nobility. Typically, only the eldest son of a noble could inherit land, so other male children served as military officers, judges, government administrators, or high-ranking members of the Church.
- **The Christian clergy.** As the second estate, the clergy largely served the nobles but had some independence due to their claim of religious authority. They were generally well educated and were themselves divided into an elaborate hierarchy made up of the pope, cardinals, bishops, priests, and other positions. An important role of the clergy was to articulate and enforce the ideology that justified the feudal system. The Church taught that inequality

Because of the family into which she was born, this Indian woman is a *Dalit,* or "Untouchable." The man in the portrait behind her is Bhimrao Ramiji Amdedkar, a scholar and activist who founded the movement for civil rights for Untouchables, which challenges the ideology underlying this caste system.

FAST-FORWARD

Social Change and Class Segregation

Many forms of public accommodation and transportation are segregated by class. In an earlier era, luxury ocean liners, such as the one whose accommodations are illustrated here (*top*), served a wealthy clientele. In today's faster-paced society, first-class luxury is more likely to be found on private jets, such as the one shown (*bottom*). Most Americans today are appalled by the racial segregation that once existed in public facilities. Why then is class-based segregation still taken for granted?

was the will of God and that the poor would receive their reward in heaven rather than on earth. To question inequality, therefore, was to question God's will.

■ *Commoners.* The commoners made up the bulk of the population. Typically illiterate, they did not own land but instead lived on and worked the land owned by the nobles. The commoners' labor enriched the nobles but left them living in poor and difficult conditions.

Commoners repeatedly challenged the harsh conditions of the estate system by staging peasant uprisings. Eventually, the

power of nobles was curbed with the advent of more democratic political systems and less-rigid class-based economic systems in the eighteenth and nineteenth centuries, as we saw in Chapter 1.

RACIAL SEGREGATION IN THE UNITED STATES The system of racial segregation in the United States, which evolved between the Civil War and the 1960s, can be considered a caste-based stratification system. (It influenced South Africa's apartheid, another caste-based stratification system, beginning in 1948.) The division between blacks and whites was based on birth and could not be changed. The ideology that justified racial segregation was racism, which those in power supported by invoking tradition, Christian teachings, and pseudo-science. Racial inequality was said to be the foundation of the traditional "southern way of life." Bible stories and passages were used selectively to justify slavery, including the tale that descendants of Noah's son, Ham, were cursed to be slaves (Genesis 9:18–27) and St. Paul's advice that servants accept their lot and obey their masters (Ephesians 6:5–9). So-called scientific classifications of races, based on racist assumptions, also justified racial inequality, as we examine in Chapter 10.

Though it is primarily associated with the southern states, where it was most comprehensive and brutally enforced, racial segregation existed throughout the United States. Blacks faced the most formal and broadest oppression, dating back to a race-based system of slavery. However, other races, ethnicities, and nationalities—notably Mexican and Chinese Americans—also faced segregation. Whites excluded minorities from many types of employment, and laws restricted their access to education, public transportation, theaters, restaurants, voting, and seats in public office. The legal system supported this unequal treatment. For example, in many communities, deeds to white-owned homes stipulated that they could not be sold to blacks.

Blacks and other minorities long resisted racial discrimination. The civil rights movement of the 1950s and 1960s successfully challenged the legal foundation for racial segregation. Since then, advocates for social justice have reduced the economic and social impact of racial discrimination, though its impact continues, and informal segregation is still a social reality. We examine various aspects of race and ethnicity in more detail in Chapter 10.

Class Systems: Capitalist and Socialist

Unlike a caste system, in which a person's position is determined by birth, a **class system** features *stratification determined by economic position, which results from a combination of individual achievement and family of birth.* Class systems are more flexible than caste systems and offer more opportunities for social mobility. They are still stratification systems, however; they organize the unequal distribution of resources among distinct groups and are supported by a justifying ideology. We examine classes more closely in Chapter 9. This brief preview sketches out some of the features of class systems in the two major types of economies, capitalist and socialist.

Whites used their power in the United States to create caste-like divisions between whites and blacks. Such inequality was challenged successfully when blacks organized in the civil rights movement to maximize their power.

CLASS IN CAPITALIST SYSTEMS

In the United States and other contemporary capitalist societies, considerable affluence is accompanied by significant class inequality. Economic resources such as income, stocks, real estate, and other forms of property are distributed unevenly, as are education and training. A small upper class of capitalist investors owns a substantial amount of the wealth and thereby wields enormous power. A broad middle class of relatively well-educated workers is employed in jobs that require considerable knowledge and skill and that pay well enough to afford a comfortable existence. A large working class is employed in modest-to-low-paying jobs that require less training and formal education. Those working for low wages and those unable to secure steady employment often live in poverty.

In capitalist class systems, the ideology emphasizes individualism—the idea that success is based on merit, not inherited advantage. The popular idea that "With hard work and determination, you can accomplish whatever you want" is an implicit explanation for inequality: those at the bottom do not work hard, while those at the top do. Inequality is seen as good because it motivates people to work hard to achieve economic success, thereby contributing to the overall affluence of society. As we see in Chapter 9, however, structural factors and barriers beyond an individual's control have a considerable impact on economic success or failure.

Throughout modern history, those below the capitalist class have often resisted inequality; in particular, workers in various countries have organized themselves into labor unions to gain more power and improve their working conditions. As a result, today's capitalist societies vary substantially in the degree to which they are unequal.

CLASS IN SOCIALIST SYSTEMS

The major difference between capitalist and socialist class systems is the nature and degree of government intervention in the economy, a topic we examine in Chapter 16. Capitalist ideology suggests that people should compete in the marketplace free of government interference. In contrast, socialist ideology emphasizes the collective good and economic equality as coordinated by the government. In a socialist system, the government typically owns major industries and taxes wealthy citizens heavily to pay for free or subsidized social programs such as education, health care, housing, and day care.

Because the state plays such a central role, economic stratification varies across socialist societies, depending on the type of government. State socialism—as found most notably in the former Soviet Union and other communist countries of Eastern Europe before 1991—is characterized by totalitarian governments that typically downplay the existence of inequality. In such systems, political dissent was not tolerated, and those who had access to political positions and resources—especially membership in the Communist Party and authority in the workplace—were at the highest levels of the stratification system. Thus Communist Party officials had the most power. The key divisions in society were between party leaders, workplace managers, and ordinary workers.

The politically oppressive nature of state socialism, coupled with its inefficiency as an economic system, helped lead to its demise. Today's major socialist societies are quite different. In China, for example, the Communist Party has adopted flexible economic policies, but the central authority still rigidly controls the government-owned companies that carry them out. The party also controls government bodies at all levels of society, including the military, the courts, the media, universities, and religious organizations (McGregor 2010). As a result, China continues to suppress political freedom while incorporating aspects of capitalism into its economy and harboring stark inequalities.

In contrast to state socialism, democratic socialism combines a government accountable to the electorate with an economy that includes considerable state intervention. Found most notably in some Scandinavian countries today, democratic socialism has produced some of the world's most affluent and least unequal countries. These societies tend to cultivate an ideology that values equality and the common good, even if it means putting strict limits on the income and wealth of the country's richest citizens.

Patriarchy

Another type of systemic stratification is based on gender. Women have long been subjected to **patriarchy,** *male domination*

SOCIOLOGY WORKS

Kiya Stokes and the Service Workers' Union

When Kiya Stokes enrolled in a sociology course on class and inequality, he had no idea that a few years later he would be on the frontlines of the struggle for economic justice. As he studied the sociological perspective, learned about stratification, and read about the contemporary labor movement, he started thinking that maybe he could become a part of the effort to improve workers' lives.

"As an African-American man, I was well aware of the various forms of racial discrimination and oppression that I witnessed and endured," Stokes notes. "Sociology helped broaden my perspectives and showed me in a scientific way that there were other groups within our society that were also victims of various forms of oppression." Learning about the intersections of inequality was not always easy. Stokes admits, "The process was slightly traumatic as I learned not only that there were other oppressed people here but that in different ways I had benefited and participated in their oppression. After I moved past the shame, and empathy, I decided that I needed to do something to make the world a better place."

At the suggestion of his sociology professor, Stokes enrolled in a short training program run by a labor union, and he was hooked. He went on to earn a master's degree in labor studies and then took a job with the Service Employees International Union (SEIU), the nation's largest labor union. After working in Atlanta and Washington, D.C., Stokes is now a research analyst for the union in Los Angeles. He says, "The work that I do helps support campaigns that are designed to increase worker wages, to improve safety standards, and to eventually stamp out poverty."

Reflecting back, Stokes says, "In sociology class I learned a new way to view the world. I learned that we were not just one big happy family here with a predestined lot in life. I saw that many people *do* work hard and do *not* get adequately compensated for that labor. Others do not do a bit of work but have wealth beyond our wildest imagination. I started questioning other premises and assumptions about the state of the world that most people take for granted. In the end I am certain that without the critical thinking and analytical skills that I learned in sociology class I would not be fighting for working people today."

Through his work, Stokes has seen firsthand that when people organize and work together for collective change, they can realize their own power and help promote economic justice. This approach is neatly summed up in the two-word motto of his union: "Stronger Together."

> "Sociology helped broaden my perspectives and showed me in a scientific way that there were other groups within our society that were also victims of various forms of oppression."

think about it

1. *How are the sociological concepts and ideas introduced in this chapter reflected in Kiya Stokes's story?*

2. *What did Stokes mean by saying that seriously considering inequality was "a slightly traumatic experience" for him? Do you feel the same way about your study of power and social inequality? Why or why not?*

---

through social institutions and cultural practices. Patriarchy can be thought of as a system of stratification since it emphasizes separate and unequal groups (men and women), distributes resources unequally, and justifies this inequality with an ideology that assumes the superiority of men.

Patriarchal arrangements of power are built into many aspects of social life, including the cultural norm that a man should be the "head of household," the idea in some religions that women should play secondary roles, and the continuing underrepresentation of women in positions of political and economic power. Many feminist sociologists focus on understanding women's oppression, how sexism operates, and how women's subordination intersects with other forms of inequality. Consequently, power is an important concept in feminist theory and research (Allen 2000, 2005, 2008; Hartsock 1996; Yeatmann 1997; Young 1992).

As we explore further in Chapter 11, feminist scholars have developed a variety of approaches to understanding the relationships among gender, inequality, and power (Connell 1987; Davis, Leijenaar, and Oldersma 1991; Radtke and Stam 1994). Some argue that women's oppression resulted from the power men had over them and that the liberation of women will challenge and break this power. Socialist-feminists argue that women's oppression was a result of capitalism; women were exploited as cheap labor in the paid labor force and as unpaid labor at home, helping sustain male workers. This argument links class and gender inequality.

These examples of stratification systems illustrate some of the many ways that inequality is structured. Although each form of stratification has distinct features, by viewing all of them through the lens of power, we can see many similarities.

Can Inequality Be Reduced?

If all societies have inequality, can it be reduced? The simple answer is yes, although some forms of inequality are easier to combat than others. Interestingly, equality is a fairly new value in human history. Only since the Enlightenment of the eighteenth century has inequality been seen as undesirable. Before that time, it was considered inevitable and often a part of God's will. However, sociology teaches us that inequality is socially constructed and, thus, its nature and extent are neither inevitable nor foreordained. Human action produces inequality, and people can organize to empower themselves and reduce inequality. (The profile in the Sociology Works box illustrates how sociological insights helped shape one person's decision to fight against economic inequality.)

A Changing World

MONEY, POWER, AND POLITICS

Supreme Court Justice Louis Brandeis famously commented, "We may have democracy, or we may have wealth concentrated in the hands of a few, but we can't have both" (in Lonergan 1941, 42). Brandeis's concern that concentrated economic power can be converted unfairly into political power has resurfaced in recent years as economic inequality has grown (a topic we explore in Chapter 9) and as money has come to play an increasing role in politics. These concerns cut across party lines. As former senators Bob Kerrey (a Nebraska Democrat) and Larry Pressler (a South Dakota Republican) argue, in this age of "wealthy interests" and "big money givers," "confidence in Congress has reached an all-time low in part because Americans perceive that their representatives are primarily accountable to those who fund their campaigns" (Kerrey and Pressler 2010).

Political participation in the United States is unequal and influenced heavily by class, with those at the top having the greatest voice and influence (Schlozman et al. 2005). This disparity is especially true of campaign contributions, which have always played a role in politics. But because of two recent developments, wealthy people have more ability than ever before to translate their economic power into political power, renewing concerns about the danger of which Justice Brandeis warned.

First, the amount of money involved in political campaigns has grown dramatically, making wealthy donors all the more important. For example, after holding steady for decades in the $400 to $600 million range, candidates' spending on presidential campaigns increased from $705 million in 2000 to over $1.3 billion in 2012 (in 2012 dollars) (Center for Responsive Politics 2013c). Most of this growth was due to more spending on media advertising, which accounted for 59 percent of expenditures in the 2012 election (Center for Responsive Politics 2013b). These increasingly expensive campaigns are funded by a remarkably small number of people. Just 0.53 percent of adult Americans accounted for 63.5 percent of all contributions to federal candidates, political action committees, and political parties in the 2012 election cycle (Figure 5.1) (Center for Responsive Politics 2013a). Despite garnering wide praise for cultivating small donors, the 2012 Obama campaign received only 28 percent of its funds from people giving less than $200. Mitt Romney's campaign drew an even smaller portion of its funds—just 12 percent—from small donor contributions. Meanwhile, contributors giving $1000 or more made up 39 percent of the Obama contributions and 66 percent of the Romney contributions (Campaign Finance Institute 2013).

Second, much of the money that influences elections does not go directly to campaigns but is instead raised and spent by political action committees (PACs). In a controversial 5–4 decision in 2010, *Citizens United v. the Federal Election Commission*, a divided Supreme Court swept away limitations on the amount of money that corporations, unions, and other associations can spend to influence voters. The ruling opened the door for the

FIGURE 5.1 | CAMPAIGN CONTRIBUTORS IN THE 2012 FEDERAL ELECTIONS

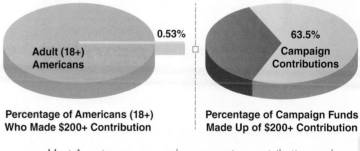

Percentage of Americans (18+) Who Made $200+ Contribution

Percentage of Campaign Funds Made Up of $200+ Contribution

Most Americans never make a campaign contribution, and most of those who do donate contribute a small amount—less than $200. During the 2012 federal elections (for Congress and the president), a tiny 0.53 percent of adult Americans gave $200 or more (some gave *much* more) and accounted for nearly two-thirds (63.5 percent) of all contributions to federal candidates, political action committees, and political parties. This group exerts a vastly disproportionate influence on the political process.

Source: Center for Responsive Politics (opensecrets.org).

creation of so-called Super PACs, political action committees that can raise and spend unlimited amounts of money to support or oppose candidates. Previous limitations on campaign contributions forced candidates to appeal to a larger number of people to raise funds. Removing these limits has allowed a tiny number of very wealthy donors to flood the political arena with their cash. The Super PACs are not required to disclose the names of donors if contributions are routed through intermediary nonprofit "social welfare" groups or "trade associations." As a result, while the bulk of this money comes from corporations and their wealthy allies, the specific source of these "dark money" contributions remains hidden from public view. After *Citizens United*, spending by outside groups more than doubled in the 2012 presidential election, compared to 2008. Spending by outside groups nearly matched the entire amount spent by the Romney campaign (Figure 5.2). Thus, although more money is flowing into the electoral process, transparency regarding the source of these funds has declined.

Will citizens organize to curb the power of money in politics? Or, as Justice Brandeis warned, will concentrated economic power erode the health of our democracy? Those questions remain to be answered.

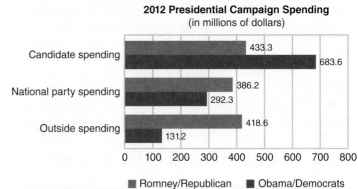

FIGURE 5.2 | TYPES OF CAMPAIGN-RELATED SPENDING

2012 Presidential Campaign Spending
(in millions of dollars)

Candidate spending: 433.3 / 683.6
National party spending: 386.2 / 292.3
Outside spending: 418.6 / 131.2

■ Romney/Republican ■ Obama/Democrats

Presidential candidates rely not only on money raised and spent by their campaigns but also on money spent by their party (Democratic or Republican) and, increasingly, on money raised by outside interest groups. Since the 2010 *Citizens United* Supreme Court ruling, outside groups can spend an unlimited amount, and such spending has exploded. In the 2012 Romney campaign, outside spending nearly equaled candidate spending.
Source: Center for Responsive Politics (opensecrets.org).

thinking sociologically about
Power

- **Power** is the capacity to bring about a desired outcome as well as to overcome resistance by others. It operates at all levels of society.

- **Power** can be used to allocate resources (economic), make rules and decisions (political), and help define reality (cultural).

- **Power** is based on social relationships and requires compliance. Disobedience can be a form of power, since it denies the compliance being sought.

REVIEW, REFLECT, AND APPLY

Looking Back

1. Power includes the ability to bring about a desired outcome ("power to"), as well as the capacity to overcome resistance ("power over"). Education, organization, and networking contribute to empowerment. Compliance may be obtained by persuasion, reward, or coercion.

2. Power operates at all levels of society and can be seen in both everyday situations as well as at the macro level. Power is commonly used to allocate resources (economic), make rules and decisions (political), and help define reality (cultural)—and thus is closely tied to inequality.

3. Power can be legitimate, accepted voluntarily by those who are affected by it; or illegitimate, relying on coercion to generate obedience. Legitimate power can be based on traditional, rational-legal, or charismatic authority.

4. Power is based on social relationships and requires compliance from others. Disobedience, or noncompliance, can be a form of power, especially for those without access to other forms of power.

5. Considering power and inequality alerts us to the issue of privilege. Understanding relations of power involves

understanding various perspectives, including those of people with little power.

6. Inequality is multidimensional and includes stratification based on class (economic conditions), status (prestige), and power (political organization). Intersectionality theory suggests that to understand inequality, we need to consider the ways in which race, class, and gender interact and form what is sometimes referred to as a matrix of domination.

7. All societies have some system of stratification, featuring unequally distributed resources, distinct groups that make up the strata, and an ideology that explains and justifies inequality. Major types of stratification systems include caste systems, class systems, and patriarchy.

8. Economic power can be translated into political power through financial contributions to election campaigns and related advertising efforts.

Critical Thinking: Questions and Activities

1. What are power and inequality, and how are these two concepts related?

2. Do you consider yourself powerful? If you answer yes, what is the source of your power? If your answer is no, what would have to change to increase your power?

3. Identify and describe a common situation in your daily life where you comply with power. Is this a case of legitimate or illegitimate power? Explain.

4. How do various types of inequality intersect in your life? In what ways are you relatively privileged? In what ways do you face disadvantages?

5. Make a list of three people or organizations that you consider to be powerful. Using what you have learned in this chapter, explain what makes each of them powerful. For each, explain how power is rooted in social relationships. Now do the same with three people or organizations that you think are relatively powerless.

Key Terms

caste system (p. 127) stratification based on various ascribed characteristics determined at birth.

charismatic authority (p. 120) power whose legitimacy is derived from the extraordinary personal characteristics of an individual leader, which inspire loyalty and devotion.

class (p. 123) a group of people who share a roughly similar economic position and lifestyle.

class system (p. 128) stratification determined by economic position, which results from a combination of individual achievement and family of birth.

coerce (p. 114) to force people's compliance by threatening, intimidating, pressuring, or harming them.

discrimination (p. 124) treating others unequally based on their background or other personal characteristics.

empowerment (p. 111) an increase in the capacity of people to bring about an intended outcome.

hegemony (p. 119) a condition that exists when those in power have successfully spread their ideas—and marginalized alternative viewpoints—so that their perspectives and interests are accepted widely as being universal and true.

illegitimate power (p. 119) a form of authority that relies on force or coercion to generate obedience.

inequality (p. 123) the unequal distribution of resources among groups of people.

intersectionality theory (p. 125) a perspective that highlights the connections and interactions between various forms of inequality, especially race, class, and gender.

legitimate power (p. 119) authority that is voluntarily accepted by those who are affected.

life chances (p. 124) the opportunities offered by a person's economic position.

matrix of domination (p. 125) the interlocking systems of oppression associated with race, class, and gender.

patriarchy (p. 129) male domination through social institutions and cultural practices.

persuade (p. 113) to obtain people's compliance by convincing them of the correctness of your position and goals.

power (p. 111) the ability to bring about an intended outcome, even when opposed by others.

power tactics (p. 115) the specific strategies people use to influence others in everyday life.

privilege (p. 122) a special advantage or benefit that is not enjoyed by everyone.

rational-legal authority (p. 119) power that has legitimacy because it is based on established laws, rules, and procedures.

reward (p. 114) to encourage people's compliance by offering some compensation as a positive incentive.

social closure (p. 124) the process whereby a status group maximizes its own advantages by restricting access to rewards only to members of the group.

social mobility (p. 126) movement from one stratum of a stratification system to another.

standpoint theory (p. 122) a theory that questions taken-for-granted assumptions about society by looking at it from multiple viewpoints, especially from the perspective of people in subordinate positions.

stratification systems (p. 126) social structures and cultural norms that create and maintain inequality by ranking people into a hierarchy of groups that receive unequal resources.

traditional authority (p. 119) power that has legitimacy because of compliance with well-established cultural practices.

6

Socialization

looking AHEAD

How were you socialized into your society's **culture**?

How do agents of socialization reproduce social **structure**?

How does **power** shape your daily life and your sense of self?

In 1998, 16-year-old Melanie Matchett Wood became the first American woman to make the U.S. International Mathematical Olympiad Team. Wood won a silver medal, went on to earn a Ph.D. in math, and is now a leading scholar in her field. Commenting on her Olympiad victory, Wood recalls, "I thought, 'Why am I so surprised?' And then I realized that it was just that I had this image of the people who won this competition—and that image was of boys." The math world included few, if any, female role models (Scharf 2003).

Wood had to overcome cultural norms and expectations that often discourage girls from pursuing high-level math, but she had plenty of support along her way to prominence. Her father, who died when she was just six weeks old, had been a middle school math teacher, and her mother helped keep his memory alive by teaching Melanie math from early childhood. Later, a seventh-grade teacher encouraged Wood's interest in math, inviting her to join the school's MathCounts team. She also found a role model in Zvezdelina Stankova, a woman mathematician with a Harvard Ph.D., who had also been an International Mathematical Olympiad medal winner. Wood notes, "Having a role model like that was a big deal in my life. Previously, I never knew a mathematician that I could look at and think 'in ten years I want to be like that person'" (Gallian 2004). Wood, in her turn, now mentors and supports aspiring women mathematicians.

As Wood understands, the gap between men and women in math achievement in the United States is not a result of innate differences in ability but rather of the powerful cultural lessons boys and girls learn in childhood about gender-appropriate interests and careers. When Wood began mentoring a Princeton undergraduate from Bulgaria, she learned that other cultures teach different lessons. "In her culture, there wasn't an idea that women weren't as good, or even weren't as numerous in math. She hadn't grown up with that" (C. Johnson 2008, A4).

ood's story illustrates the profound power that the cultural messages we absorb from infancy and throughout our lives have to shape what we believe, how we behave, and how we live. But it also illustrates how those messages—in this case, messages about gender, aspirations, and achievement—are subject to challenge and change.

Socialization is *the process through which people learn their culture's basic norms, values, beliefs, and appropriate behaviors.* Through socialization we learn who we are, what is expected of us, how society operates, and where we stand within our social world. As children we learn the language and symbols of our culture and our social roles as child and sibling. As we grow, we learn new roles, such as friend, student, teammate, employee, lover, spouse, parent, grandparent, and retiree. We also learn and internalize the structure and expectations of the various groups, organizations, and institutions in which we may participate, including families, schools, religious institutions, clubs, sports teams, friendship networks, and workplaces. Through socialization we also forge a sense of self—a sense of who we are as individuals in relation to the people with whom we interact personally as well as to society as a whole. Like Melanie Wood, we can even challenge traditional socialization messages and, in the process, become role models who help open new possibilities for the next generation.

important values such as the difference between right and wrong and the proper way to treat other people. "Say 'thank you'." "Respect your elders." "Don't hit your brother." "Always tell the truth." These kinds of instruction teach children the most basic norms, values, beliefs, expectations, and behaviors of their culture.

Families play a crucial role in the early development of a child's sense of identity. Whether or not children learn to see themselves as loved, smart, creative, and strong depends largely on how their families treat them in their early years. Families also influence what nation, ethnicity, race, religion, and class children identify with as they mature. Families are a child's first teachers about appropriate gender roles, which they often signal by the toys and clothing they choose and the chores they assign. As we see in Chapter 11, the process of gender socialization begins at a very young age. Messages full of gender-specific expectations for children about, for example, how to dress and behave are part of a broader process through which girls and boys learn how to act in ways that are promoted as gender appropriate.

Reproducing Structure: Agents of Socialization

In transmitting fundamental social norms and role expectations from one generation to another, socialization helps reproduce social structure and is a key to social stability. Socialization is a dynamic process, however. As social structure changes, the messages imparted through socialization also change.

Because socialization occurs throughout life, it takes place in different ways and in different social contexts, guided by many different **agents of socialization,** or *people and groups who teach us about our culture.* For children, the family is usually far and away the most important agent of socialization. But as children grow up and are exposed to different people and groups, other socializing agents take on increasingly important roles, including school, media, peer groups, the workplace, religion, and what are known as total institutions.

Family

Families are the primary agent of early socialization. Within the family most individuals learn basic skills such as how to talk and how to maintain personal hygiene, and they learn

In all cultures, families play a key role in socializing children, especially during the early years. Hygiene, as in this photo of a Nepalese mother washing her child, is only one of the many practices parents teach their children.

CORE CONCEPTS CHALLENGE

What other aspects of their **culture** *do parents in all societies teach their children?*

Examining Teenagers' Changing Motivations for Civic Engagement

Why do teens volunteer? When they do, what do they learn about civic involvement? Looking sociologically at how and why teenagers come to join community organizations, do volunteer work, or participate in other community service can provide insight into the process of political socialization, especially the cultural values students associate with community activities.

In a study of civic engagement among high school students in Madison, Wisconsin, sociologists Lewis Friedland and Shauna Morimoto (2005) found that young people from a variety of backgrounds are deeply involved in community service activities, even though civic engagement among Americans in general has been declining (Putnam 2000; Skocpol 2003). The sociologists also found that students' motivations for engaging in community service have changed in recent decades.

Students used to see service as a value in itself, whereas they now see service primarily as something they must do to enhance their chances of college admission. According to Friedland and Morimoto, this shift occurred because young people experience greater uncertainty than previous generations due to growing income inequality, rising part-time employment, and an increase in long-term unemployment.

Amidst this uncertainty, Friedland and Morimoto (2005) noted there is "a general awareness among most of the young people we interviewed that their life chances are directly tied to education. Almost all of the young people we interviewed expected (or at least hoped) to better their lives and linked these expectations to college education. And a majority linked their hopes for college admission to service" (p. 7).

Students see a college education as a requirement for a good-paying job and see engaging in community service as one way to improve their chances of being admitted to a good college. This phenomenon, which students refer to as "resume padding," is not confined only to teens at private schools or those seeking admission to elite colleges and universities. Young people of all social classes take this approach to service, regardless of what college they hope to attend.

Teens do not participate in civic life for purely cynical reasons, however. Friedland and Morimoto argue that resume padding is only one motivation for doing volunteer or service work. Other motivations include "altruism, religious belief, and love of politics or volunteerism" (p. 3). Students know that doing community service can make an important contribution, even if they are motivated largely by personal gain. In addition, community service seems likely to teach young people valuable skills that may translate into civic participation later in life.

Friedland and Morimoto's study highlights the complex reasons why young people get involved in civic life. It shows how a change in the economic climate has resulted in increased uncertainty about college and jobs that, in turn, has changed the meaning of political socialization for many young people.

think about it

1. *Have you ever participated in volunteer or service work in your community? If so, why? If not, why not?*

2. *Do you think the self-interest associated with resume building is inconsistent with the ethic of community service? Why or why not?*

Childrearing practices can vary by culture within a society in ways that help reproduce social structure. For example, sociologist Melvin Kohn (1977) found that in the United States, working-class parents tend to teach their children to value obedience, the expected attitude for most working-class jobs, whereas middle-class parents encourage their children to value self-direction, the attitude required for the kind of independent thinking expected in many middle-class occupations. These different values, in turn, increase the likelihood that children will end up with the same educational opportunities and in the same kind of work as their parents, thus reproducing the existing structural inequality from one generation to the next. Kohn and his colleagues (1986) found a similar dynamic among families in Poland.

Cross-national research indicates that cultural differences can lead to significantly different parenting styles. For example, family socialization in Malaysia emphasizes obedience and cooperation, values that are consistent with the society's collectivist culture (Keshavarz and Baharudin 2009). This stands in sharp contrast to the emphasis on personal happiness and achievement that is far more common in the United States, particularly in middle-class families. Similarly, Korean American parents focus far more on controlling the behavior of their children than European American parents do. Korean American children see behavioral control efforts as a sign of parental engagement and support, whereas their European American peers have a negative view of this parenting style (Kim 2005).

School

Day care, preschool, or kindergarten is many children's first extended experience with people and the world outside their home. In these settings children learn to interact with other people and adjust to being part of a group. As the agents of socialization most explicitly focused on teaching cultural knowledge, schools prepare children for their later roles in society, providing instruction in a variety of fields, including advanced language skills, mathematics, history, and science. Schools can also socialize students into the politics of getting ahead in life, as the Through a Sociological Lens box explores.

In addition to their formal academic curriculum, schools also convey a **hidden curriculum** consisting of *implicit lessons about how children should behave* (Jackson 1968). These lessons vary depending on the school and often change as children advance in grade levels. However, most U.S. schools teach children to be quiet and attentive, to obey authority, to follow rules, to be respectful of others, and to take pride in their country. Schools in the United States also tend to encourage competition and individual achievement by promoting sports, spelling bees, and honor rolls, among other activities. Schools are also the site for lessons about class and gender, topics we explore in Chapters 9 and 11.

Media

Today's children and teens sometimes have been called "Generation M" because of their heavy use of media (Rideout, Foehr, and Roberts 2010). Media play an increasingly significant role in the lives of many young people, especially in industrialized nations. On average, U.S. children between the ages of 8 and 18 spend more than seven and a half hours each day with media outside school. This is more time than they spend in the classroom and much more time than they spend interacting with their parents. More than 70 percent of U.S. youth now have a television set in their bedrooms, half have a video game console, and one-third have a computer with Internet access in their bedrooms, allowing them to watch TV, play video games, and surf the web without any parental supervision. As a result, media— television, Internet, video games, recorded music, and magazines, for example—are arguably the most influential agents of socialization in contemporary society, a situation that is relatively new.

For most of human history, children learned morals and values from the myths and other stories they heard from their families. Today, children in developed nations receive these lessons from commercial media companies whose primary interest is selling products and socializing young people to be avid consumers. Thus companies such as Disney and Viacom (which owns both Nickelodeon and MTV) now play a central part in introducing children to a set of values, beliefs, norms, and behaviors that promote a consumer lifestyle (Pugh 2009; Schor 2004). Through ads and programming, youth-oriented

FAST-FORWARD

Social Change and Socialization

Television became a fixture in U.S. households in the 1950s and emerged quickly as a powerful, and sometimes controversial, agent of socialization. Today, online media are increasingly present in the daily lives of children in the United States and around the world. With the continuing rapid development of new handheld devices, what kinds of media will the next generation of children experience?

media help define popular tastes and desires. For example, MTV's *My Super Sweet 16*, a reality-style television series, turned the Sweet 16 parties of wealthy young women into a celebration of high-end teenage consumption, with a companion website full of ideas and advice for what to wear and how to organize your own Sweet 16 party.

Media have altered the socialization of children in another important way. With television, especially, children for the first time in history have had ready access to the world of adult ideas and situations, even if they cannot read at an adult level. Of particular concern to many parents is the sexually explicit and graphically violent content of some media. Access to media also erodes the significance of physical place: it allows children to "see" the battlefields of foreign wars from their living rooms and increases their access to the intimate lives of adults. In this way the modern boundary between childhood and adulthood that was a staple of the socialization process in the United States has been blurred (Meyrowitz 1985).

The global distribution of U.S. media has increased in recent years, raising important questions about the socializing influence of media. In some countries, media imported from the United States are more popular than locally produced fare. For example, U.S. movies accounted for 61.4 percent of the film audience in Europe in 2011, more than twice the audience share of European films (28.5 percent) (European Audiovisual Observatory 2012).

Some critics argue that American values are embedded in the media products sold by U.S. corporations. Norms of individualism and consumerism, for example, saturate media exported by the United States and may conflict with traditional values in the nations where such products are consumed. From this perspective, the heavy flow of media from the United States to the rest of the world can erode local cultures and values (Tomlinson 2008). As noted in the discussion of the globalization of culture at the end of Chapter 3, however, the threat may be exaggerated. Some observers argue that the global circulation of U.S.-produced media products does not seem, as some had feared, to be Americanizing global culture.

Nor do globally distributed entertainment products seem to be creating a distinctive global consciousness. Even though hundreds of millions of children and teenagers around the world listen to the same music, play the same games, and watch the same movies, they do not appear to be losing their sense of who they are or where they belong (Ugochukwu 2008).

As a powerful socializing agent, media can make positive contributions to society. At their best, children's media can promote positive values such as honesty, compassion, responsibility, self-respect, and standing up for what you believe in. Media also give people access to a much broader range of news, images, and stories than was available in the past. Media thus allow people to learn more about their society and about the cultures of other people.

Peer Groups

Parents often worry about their children's friends, their **peer group,** *a group of people, usually of comparable age, who share similar interests and social status.* Peer groups can significantly influence people's development and behavior. This is especially true of children and adolescents, whose sense of self is not yet firmly developed and is therefore susceptible to influence by others. As they approach adulthood, adolescents usually become increasingly independent of their families, and during this period peer groups can act as a surrogate family. Peer groups provide

Peer groups can be an important socializing influence on individuals. Members of street gangs, like those pictured on the left, display all the accessories of the subculture they have been taught. They use specialized language, communicate with unique hand gestures, adorn their bodies with gang-related tattoos, often wear special gang colors, and adopt a worldview that places high value on gang membership and loyalty. College fraternities and sororities have similar characteristics. They, too, share special signals and insignia—the Greek letters that identify particular fraternities and sororities—and they encourage group loyalty and mutual assistance.

CORE CONCEPTS CHALLENGE

Peer groups can be powerful socializing agents, strongly influencing the behavior of their members. What is the nature of their **power,** *and how is it exercised?*

young people with the opportunity to experiment with values, beliefs, and behaviors that differ from their parents'. To separate themselves from their families and fit in with peer groups, adolescents commonly change the way they talk, dress, and act, as well as the interests they pursue. This process is not unique to adolescence, however. When adults embark on new jobs and careers or move to new cities or neighborhoods, they often look to members of their new peer groups for clues about social norms and appropriate behaviors. A young couple that moves from the city to the suburbs will have to adopt new norms for social interaction and will probably learn those new norms from a peer group.

There are many different kinds of peer groups. Some are informal, as with groups of friends who choose to spend leisure time together. For teenagers, peer group activities can involve going to the mall or the movies; playing sports or video games; experimenting with cigarettes, alcohol, drug use, and sex; driving around together; or just "hanging out" or texting. Other peer groups exist in more structured environments, as is the case with classmates, teammates, and colleagues at work.

The Workplace

The workplace is one of the most important social settings in which we experience socialization. **Occupational socialization** is *the process of learning the informal norms associated with a type of employment.* As you study, train, or apprentice in a given job category, you are picking up all sorts of cues, large and small, about how to be successful in a given job. For example, skilled tradespeople such as carpenters, plumbers, and electricians not only have to know the technical details of their craft, but they also typically learn the informal rules about how to work with customers, suppliers, and workers from other trades who share the job site. Understanding the expected norms, values, and behaviors of their position can be vital to success in their field.

Socialization into professional occupations—such as medicine and law—is one of the most significant, if often unrecognized, functions of graduate and professional schools. Of course, these schools provide subject-specific information: medical students study anatomy and law students study contracts. But aspiring professionals also learn the often informal, unstated norms of their profession: how to behave as a doctor or lawyer. Doctors, for example, must learn how to wield authority, dress appropriately, and talk with patients. Similarly, lawyers learn how to talk to judges, relate to clients, and deal with conflicts between their clients' interests and their own beliefs. Although some of this material may be touched upon in formal classroom discussions, students pick up most of it informally through socialization.

A classic study of students at Harvard Law School illustrates the powerful effects of occupational socialization into a profession (Granfield 1992; Granfield and Koenig 1990). The researchers found that many of these elite students entered law school intending to practice public interest law, such as by advocating for nonprofit organizations, representing poor clients, and working to prevent government and corporate fraud and abuse. However, during their three years of professional training at Harvard, they switched course. As they became socialized into their profession, many abandoned their commitment to public interest law and embraced the idea of entering a prestigious, high-paying corporate law firm. There, if their senior partners permitted, they might be able to do some *pro bono* (free-of-charge) work for needy clients.

This kind of professional socialization continues over the course of one's career. As people gain experience in a given field, they learn how to relate to younger or less experienced coworkers. If you are promoted, for example, you will have to learn the norms and expectations of your new position, which may include supervising other employees, attending meetings with senior managers, and participating in long-range planning. Your new position may also require you to dress differently, learn a new style of communication, and perhaps change your own family schedule.

Religion

Religion is the socializing agent most explicitly focused on the teaching of values and beliefs. Religious institutions in the past had enormous influence on all aspects of social life, offering social and educational opportunities as well as indoctrination in morality and values. Overall, that influence declined during the twentieth century, but religion still plays a significant role in many people's lives and the U.S. population is far more involved with religion than are residents of most European countries (Putnam and Campbell 2010). In addition, many parents who are not believers or who do not observe their religion often insist that their children obtain religious instruction.

For believers, religion can be an especially potent socializing agent because it often bases its prescriptions on texts such as the Christian Bible or the Muslim Qur'an that most believers consider sacred and some consider infallible. For people who believe that a divinity advocates or forbids certain values, beliefs, and behaviors, religion can supersede other socializing influences. In a society in which material well-being and consumerism are hallmarks of mainstream culture, religious institutions are among the few that promote the serious discussion of nonmaterial values. For example, in 2013 Pope Francis criticized "big business' idolatry of money over man," arguing instead that "we want a just system, a system that lets all of us get ahead. We don't want this globalized economic system that does us so much harm" (Zaimov 2013).

In contemporary life, efforts to promote religious culture have reached beyond traditional services in places of worship to include outreach with social media and the blending of religion with contemporary marketing. This rabbi gives seminars for others on how congregations can use social media to keep members connected.

In recent decades, religious organizations, especially in the United States, have dramatically expanded their use of mass media, spreading their message through religious-themed news, commentary, and entertainment as well as through the more traditional broadcast of religious services. In the United States, evangelical Christian groups have been particularly adept at using books, television, and radio to bring together the socializing influences of religion and media (Blake 2005).

Total Institutions

One unique group of socializing agents are what sociologist Erving Goffman (1961) called **total institutions,** *confining social settings in which an authority regulates all aspects of a person's life.* Goffman identifies five general types of total institutions:

1. Institutions that care for people who are defined as incapable and harmless—for example, orphanages and nursing homes.

2. Institutions set up to care for people who cannot care for themselves but who may represent an unintentional threat to the community—for example, psychiatric hospitals.

3. Institutions set up to protect a community from those whom authorities define as posing a significant danger—for example, prisons and jails, and prisoner-of-war camps.

4. Institutions established to pursue a specific task requiring the total commitment of participants—for example, military barracks and boarding schools.

5. Institutions intended as escapes or retreats from the world—for example, monasteries, convents, and some communes.

Total institutions typically share several key features. All aspects of daily life take place in the same setting under the guidance of the same authority. Members live in groups, and all group members are treated the same and complete the same tasks. Authorities impose a specific schedule, monitoring it through the application of formal rules and regimenting all the activities within the institution.

The closed world of a total institution provides an extreme example of **resocialization,** *the process by which individuals replace old norms and behaviors with new ones as they move from one role or life stage to another.* In total institutions people must submit to a strictly controlled regimen and live in a group with other people in the same condition. Such controlled institutions attempt to reprogram people to avoid past problems (substance abuse, for example), accept current realities (as with seniors adapting to residential elder care facilities), or prepare for future commitments. The U.S. Army, for example, requires new recruits to participate in a 10-week Basic Combat Training course that is intended to socialize civilians into soldiers. At their best, as with high-quality mental health facilities, such institutions can be benevolent means of providing care and helping people prepare for new roles in society. At their worst, as with political concentration camps, they can be coercive and oppressive, designed to destroy the individual will and obtain submission. (The Sociology Works box discusses one example of a total institution.)

Total institutions are not always successful at resocializing all their members. For example, although prisons and psychiatric hospitals control the daily lives of their inmates and can compel inmates to behave in specific ways, the inmates don't always internalize the norms and attitudes being promoted and may not behave in ways consistent with these norms when they are released. This is a matter of concern for those who work in fields such as mental health, substance abuse, and juvenile delinquency.

Socialization Through the Life Course

Although socialization is most intense in a person's early years, the agents of socialization discussed in the previous section are active throughout a person's entire life span. The **life-course perspective** on socialization *looks at how age, time, and place shape social identities and experiences over a lifetime.* Each stage of life is associated with particular experiences that influence our identity and that require

thinking about power
Total institutions resocialize people subject to their authority. How does the nature of the power they use to do this vary in different kinds of total institutions—for example, military "boot camps" as opposed to prisons?

142

SOCIOLOGY WORKS

Kate Corrigan, Teaching at a School for Blind Children and Young Adults

When Kate Corrigan graduated from The College of the Holy Cross in 2009, she had a B.A. in sociology, was fluent in American Sign Language, and was looking for a job that would allow her to combine those two qualifications. She landed a job as a teaching assistant in the Deafblind Program at a school for blind children and young adults, where her sociological background was a valuable asset.

Corrigan worked with 12- to 18-year-olds at the residential school, spending much of her time with students in the cottages where they live, rather than in a traditional classroom. Her teaching stressed developing students' communication proficiency, as well as their social and daily living skills. As part of the program's focus on negotiating everyday life interactions, Corrigan took her students on trips to the local community where they could practice communication in public settings, such as stores and restaurants. Community field trips help students learn independence and how to advocate for themselves in a range of social settings.

Residential schools of this kind have many of the features of a benevolent total institution. As a former sociology student, Corrigan understood the importance of the program's role in the socialization process. At a residential school, Corrigan has noted, "The roles, tasks, and environment typically associated with the home become part of the educational setting." Corrigan found that she often drew upon what she learned in her "Children and Society" class at Holy Cross for insight into the importance of family and school in the lives of children.

Corrigan applied the sociological perspective to the school's sometimes challenging relationship with local residents. She discovered that community expectations about people with special needs, even when well intentioned, could often impose severe limitations on students. Corrigan has noted, however, that in student-community interactions, "we like to pleasantly surprise people." Still, Corrigan recognized that the norms within the school community might not always fit smoothly with

the norms of the broader community. This sociological understanding of the complexity of the school-community relationship helped Corrigan navigate her interactions with the school's neighbors.

Corrigan, who now works at a school for deaf and blind teenagers, also appreciates how transferable to everyday life are the skills she learned in her sociology classes. Sociology gave her valuable research tools, for example, that she has brought to bear in studying the impact of assistive devices on communication among the

Kate Corrigan

deaf, the benefits of bilingual education for deaf students, and responses to disabilities among athletes in professional sports.

In reflecting on her experience as a sociology student, Corrigan offers some helpful advice. "To anyone taking a sociology course for the first time, let the subject inspire you. There are so many avenues with which the subject can be appreciated and applied. Make it your own."

> "Sociology expanded my educational horizons while also giving me the freedom to narrow my focus to exactly what I wanted."

think about it

1. *Why does a residential school qualify as a kind of total institution?*

2. *What "expectations" do you think the public has about blind and deaf students, and how do you think the students "pleasantly surprise" people? Does your local community have expectations about how students at your school should look or behave?*

---

resocialization. Although everyone progresses through various stages of life, those stages and what they mean can differ based on the historical period and culture in which a person lives, as well as on the person's gender, class, and other aspects of personal identity.

The process of change from one life stage to another can involve a shift in a person's responsibilities, living situation, or standing within their community. Moments of transition often involve initiation ceremonies or **rites of**

passage, *activities that mark and celebrate a change in a person's social status* (van Gennep [1909] 1961). Some of these ceremonies are rooted in religion, such as a confirmation or bar mitzvah, and follow traditions handed down from generation to generation. In the United States, weddings, graduation ceremonies, quinceañeras, and the Marine Corps' final training exercise known as "the Crucible," all mark the entrance into a new stage of life. Different societies have their own culturally specific rites of passage, and outsiders are likely to find some of these unfamiliar. Among the Venda in South Africa, for example, teenage boys and girls go off to separate traditional initiation schools, where older men and women prepare them for sexual relationships with their future spouses.

on social theory

As part of a broader **symbolic interactionist** approach, Arnold van Gennep theorized that **rites of passage** are a feature of the socialization process in all societies. What events in your own life would you describe as rites of passage? Did your position in your community change after those events? Did you feel different? Did people treat you differently?

The boys spend up to three months away from their families and undergo male circumcision as the central component of their transition from childhood to adulthood (Lutendo, Maharaj, and Rogan 2008).

Socialization is a never-ending process because people continually adopt new roles and identities. Some of these roles involve advanced preparation. **Anticipatory socialization** is *the process by which individuals practice for a future social role by adopting the norms or behaviors associated with a position they have not yet achieved.* For example, children are engaging in anticipatory socialization when they imitate and practice adult roles, playing with dolls to simulate being parents, or playing school to anticipate becoming students or teachers. In later life, young adults might take on internships to see if they want to pursue employment in a certain field, and couples might live together to find out if they are compatible for marriage.

Childhood

The early stages of life, which we label childhood and adolescence, correspond to the period during which infants gradually mature biologically into adults. Interestingly, however, childhood and adolescence are also social constructs; what it means to be a child or teenager varies radically over time and from culture to culture. As a result, the way young people experience this particularly intense period of socialization also varies over time and from culture to culture (Fass and Mason 2000).

Contemporary Western societies tend to view childhood as a natural condition linked to children's physical immaturity. Children are considered innocent, with limited capacities, and in need of intensive care and protection by adults. However,

according to Philippe Aries's classic study of the history of family life in Europe, *Centuries of Childhood* (1965), the idea of a distinct childhood period is really a social construction invented in Western society during the sixteenth and seventeenth centuries. Before then, childhood was not distinguished so clearly from adulthood. European paintings of the fifteenth and early sixteenth centuries, for example, often portray children as miniature adults, complete with adult clothing and adult body proportions. Parents introduced their children to the adult world early and abruptly. Given the cramped living quarters of the day, by necessity parents routinely exposed their children to the full range of adult activity; children were served alcohol and sometimes shared the same room as adults having sex. It was common for parents to apprentice their six-year-old children, sending them away from home to live and work. (This practice was imported to colonial America as well.) Peasant parents might exploit their children as a potentially valuable family resource by renting them out as servants in wealthy homes. Children unable to secure such positions would often roam the streets picking through garbage and searching for anything useful to their families. Few ever attended school.

Several historians have challenged Aries's contention that medieval people had no conception of childhood as a separate stage of life. One, for example, points out that,

This 1626 painting shows a Scottish countess and her two young daughters, both dressed as miniature adults with elaborate clothing similar to their mother's dress.

like children today, medieval children played with toys and engaged in games specifically intended for children (Orme 2003). Another suggests that parents who apprenticed their young children were helping ensure that they would have the means to support themselves as adults (Ozment 2001). But scholars agree that the social perception and treatment of children—the meaning of childhood—has evolved over time, just as the expectations of children vary among cultures today.

By the eighteenth century, children in Western society were increasingly seen as innocent, weak, and in need of protection rather than as hardy "little adults." Parents socialized their children to behave differently than adults and often punished transgressions with severe beatings. But children's participation in the adult world continued. Child labor—a term that would not have been used at the time—was common throughout the eighteenth century. Children could fit into tight spaces, so they were favored workers for picking coal in tight mine shafts or cleaning the insides of chimneys. As late as 1890 in the United States, about 1.5 million children between the ages of 10 and 15 were working, many in the nation's bustling factories (American Social History Project 2007).

Only in the early nineteenth century did reformers begin to challenge the idea that children should be employed as laborers. This was part of a broader cultural transformation as, increasingly, Western society defined childhood as a period of life distinct from adulthood. The importance of schooling grew, and the modern-day connection between children and schools was cemented. As a result, children were transformed from being an economic asset—either on the farm or through paid employment in a growing industrial economy—to being an economic burden for whom parents were expected to sacrifice.

In some of the world's poorest nations today, children sometimes continue to live as "little adults." They receive little or no schooling and, by working, begging, or other means, are expected to help support their families.

Adolescence

Adolescence—when youth are nearing physical maturity and are no longer considered children but have not yet taken on the rights or responsibilities of adulthood—was not seen as a distinct period of life until the early twentieth century. Scholars typically tie the rise of adolescence in Western societies to several social developments in the late nineteenth and early twentieth centuries (Chinn 2008; see Figure 6.1):

- Industrialization produced affluence that created a new middle class and enabled middle-class young people to stay out of the full-time workforce, separating them from adult workers.

- Because schooling became an increasingly important requirement for employment, middle-class young people continued their education, completing high school and sometimes even going to college.

- Because they were not working full time, young people had more leisure time and began to be consumers of youth-oriented products, eventually resulting in the formation of a distinct youth subculture.

- The massive increase in immigration created what we might now call a "generation gap" between young people who were socialized into the culture and customs of the new country and their older immigrant parents who had grown up in the old country.

All these factors helped separate young people from adults and helped make adolescence a distinct period of life.

Much of the turbulence we now associate with adolescence results from the contradiction that exists between culture and biology. Adolescence as a social construction is locked in a battle with puberty as a biological reality. Adolescents are capable of sexual activity and of having children—as they did through most of history—but social norms now typically discourage such behavior. Adolescents are maturing physically and mentally and are capable of working in many different jobs—as they did through most of history—but they are now expected to stay in school and delay their entry into the workforce. Cultural inconsistencies exist as well. Sex is glorified in media but discouraged by parents and other authorities. Many of the soldiers who serve in the U.S. military are too young to drink alcohol legally. Adolescence, in short, is a period of vexing inconsistencies.

The class differences that played a role in the creation of adolescence continue to play a role in how adolescence unfolds today. Many poor and working-class youth enter the workforce, marry, and start a family at an earlier age than many of their middle-class counterparts. In effect, adolescence is a shorter period for them than it is for middle-class youth. In contrast, middle-class youth are more likely to extend adolescence into their twenties by attending college and then returning home and remaining financially dependent on their parents after college. They may delay starting families or experiment with various types of employment before settling down into a more traditional pattern of adult responsibilities. Some researchers suggest that the result is a new life stage in the United States—emerging adulthood—during which people in their twenties experience greater uncertainty and instability in the development of careers and relationships on the road to adulthood than did previous generations (Henig 2010).

thinking about structure

A change in social **structure**—the rise of a new middle class—played a role in the emergence of the currently prevalent view of adolescence as a distinct life stage. How do class differences affect the way different individuals experience adolescence?

FIGURE 6.1 | THE EMERGENCE OF ADOLESCENCE

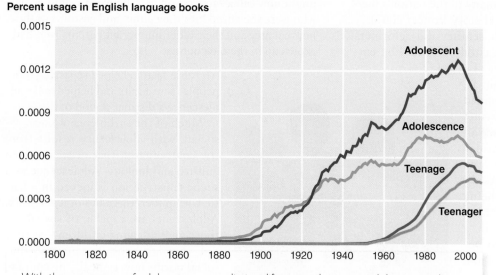

Percent usage in English language books

With the emergence of adolescence as a distinct life stage, the terms *adolescent* and *adolescence* became increasingly common in the early twentieth century. As youth subcultures rose in the 1950s and 1960s, the terms *teenage* and *teenager* came into popular use for the first time. This line graph illustrates the dramatic growth in the use of these terms in American books during the twentieth century. The graph was created by a Google tool that calculates the frequency with which any word or phrase appears in the books that have been scanned into the Google Books database so far.

Adulthood

As adults enter different stages of life, they take on new roles and responsibilities for which they learn to adopt appropriate ideas and practices (Elder 2006; Settersten 2002). For many people, adulthood is marked by a variety of milestones that require resocialization. For example, starting your first full-time job means having to adopt a largely new set of attitudes and responsibilities. Similarly, getting married or living with a romantic partner full time requires taking on the role of spouse or partner, requiring further socialization to a new set of challenges. In these and many other cases, we adjust to new roles and relationships as we accumulate experience.

Adult life-course trajectories in the United States became increasingly standardized in the twentieth century, but they varied by gender (MacMillan 2005; Shanahan 2000). A classic study of men born in the United States between 1907 and 1952 identified a sequence of transitions experienced by roughly half to three-quarters of them—completion of high school, entry into first job, marriage, and parenthood (Hogan 1978; Hogan and Astone 1986). However, this typical sequence could be interrupted by various factors, including military service and college. This life course—finish school, get a job, get married, have children—was never a universal experience, but it became a broad cultural ideal and a widespread aspiration among boys and young men of the twentieth century. The life-course sequence for women of the same generation differed from that of their male counterparts. For example, women in the mid to late twentieth century were far more likely than men to marry before starting their first job (Marini 1984).

Research suggests that the stages of the life course for men and women in recent years are more diverse than they were in previous generations. Still, the most common life-course pattern for men remains work-marriage-parenthood, which may be followed by divorce or unemployment. Women's life-course trajectories are more varied: although many follow the same stages as men, many others experience a gender-specific trajectory of work-marriage-unemployment-parenthood. That period of unemployment reflects the different impact that having children can have on women than men (Jackson and Berkowitz 2005).

Becoming a parent, however, is for many adults—men and women alike—one of the most significant life changes they will experience. Our culture encourages new parents to reorient their lives around the socialization of their children, making a priority of their children's needs and taking on the full burden of responsibility for their care and upbringing. As we saw earlier, this expectation is relatively new in Western society. People learn the dominant parenting norms of their culture through socialization. Most new parents have observed friends or family members with their children, they may have cared for younger siblings or babysat their neighbors' children while growing up, and they may have read advice books. A great deal of what new parents know results from their own childhood socialization, when they absorbed parenting lessons from their own parents—knowledge of which they are not always consciously aware. Many parents are surprised to catch themselves talking to their children with the same tone and language their parents had used with them. As this illustrates, one remarkable feature of the socialization process is that it is often invisible to us.

Aging and Retirement

As people move through the stages of adulthood, they experience a continuing set of transitions, including changing or losing a job, getting divorced or remarried, seeing children leave home, caring for an elderly parent, becoming a grandparent, surviving the death of a spouse, and

In 2003, at the age of 72, Canadian runner Ed Whitlock became the first person aged 70 years or older to run a marathon (26.2 miles) in under three hours—an impressive accomplishment at any age. In 2011, at age 80, he set a new marathon world record for his age group with a time of 3:15:51, and in 2013 he achieved a new age-82 world record at the Toronto marathon. His case may be extreme, but as millions of older citizens are living longer and remaining active, they are challenging cultural expectations about "appropriate" behavior for seniors and establishing new norms for living.

age at which Americans retire has been declining, that trend has reversed (see Figure 6.2). A restructured Social Security program delays full benefits for those born in 1960 or later until they are 67. Among the other reasons Americans are retiring at a later age are increasing life expectancy, inadequate pensions, the need to accumulate more savings for longer retirement periods, emotional and psychological ties to work, and the social integration and support provided by regular employment.

In a society in which much of our identity comes from what we *do*, leaving the workforce can be traumatic. Some retirees who have waited years to enjoy their leisure time quickly become bored and fall prey to a sense of isolation (M. Goldsmith 2004).

Increasingly, retirement is also a financial challenge as people spend more years outside paid employment because of both longer life spans and the premature loss of employment. Recent practices at many large corporations mean that long-time employees typically have far less job security than did workers in previous generations (Sennett 2007). Employees experiencing debilitating mental or physical limitations brought on by aging. As people live through these transitions, they learn the norms and expectations of the new roles they take on.

In the United States, the widespread cultural emphasis on youth can make the social experience of aging a challenge. Although there is no way to stop the aging process, many middle-aged men and women pursue a range of strategies to stay healthy and active as long as possible, including exercising regularly and following a healthy diet. Some pursue the image of youth through cosmetic surgery or other efforts to stave off the effects of aging. In this context, as people continue to grow older, part of the process of aging is negotiating an evolving social identity as someone who is no longer young (Karp 2000; Moody 2010).

Retirement is a significant life stage, and those who retire need to learn a whole new set of norms and behaviors. Like other life stages, retirement is socially constructed. Until the creation of Social Security in the 1940s, most people in the United States simply worked as long as they were able. Social Security benefits, Medicare health coverage, and Medicaid long-term care assistance enabled a much broader group of Americans to stop working when they reached the age of 65, which became the standard retirement age. Now, after decades in which the average

FIGURE 6.2 | LABOR FORCE PARTICIPATION RATE OF WORKERS AGED 65 AND OVER, 1948–2012

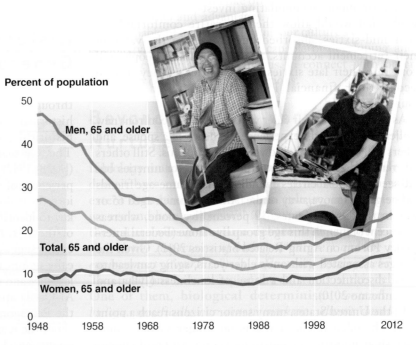

From 1948 until 1985, the percentage of men aged 65 or over who worked dropped significantly; during this period men were retiring at an earlier age. The percentage of women of that age who worked during this period stayed about the same. However, since 1985 an increasing percentage of both women and men have delayed retirement and continued to work past the age of 65.
Source: U.S. Bureau of Labor Statistics, Current Population Survey, 2012.

CORE CONCEPTS CHALLENGE

What does this graph suggest about age, gender, and changes in the **structure** *of the American workforce since 1948?*

7

Interaction, Groups, and Organizations

looking AHEAD

How does the **culture** you have been raised in affect your interactions with your friends and family?

How do your everyday activities and those of your friends help create and sustain complex, large-scale social **structures**?

How are your relationships on campus, at work, or in your family affected by who has and who lacks **power**?

In 2013, not long after leaving Google to become Yahoo!'s CEO, Marissa Mayer stirred up a debate when she ended the company's popular work-from-home policy. Rather than telecommuting, as many of the Yahoo! employees had been doing, they would now be required to travel to their offices to work (Miller and Perlroth 2013).

In a memo to employees (Swisher 2013), the head of the company's human resources office explained:

> To become the absolute best place to work, communication and collaboration will be important, so we need to be working side-by-side. That is why it is critical that we are all present in our offices. Some of the best decisions and insights come from hallway and cafeteria discussions, meeting new people, and impromptu team meetings. Speed and quality are often sacrificed when we work from home. We need to be one Yahoo!, and that starts with physically being together.

Some observers were perplexed at the idea that a leading technology company seemed to be taking a step backward by abandoning telecommuting. Some employees were disappointed, arguing that they were more productive when they worked at home and happier with the flexibility afforded by telecommuting. But as Mayer later summarized, "People are more productive when they're alone . . . they're more collaborative and innovative when they're together" (Tkaczyk 2013).

Yahoo! is not unique in its approach (McBride 2013). It turns out that while Internet companies use technology to communicate around the globe when needed, they all place a premium on face-to-face collaboration when feasible. Apple employees have been known to put cots in their offices to accommodate their long hours at work. Twitter has regular mandatory employee meetings that are called "tea time," while many other firms refer to similar meetings as "all hands" events. These practices enable highly valued face-to-face interaction, communication, and collaboration.

Consequently, it is no surprise that when Google's chief financial officer, Patrick Pichette, was asked how many people telecommute at his company, his answer was "As few as possible." Says Pichette, "There is something magical about spending the time together, about noodling on ideas. . . . These are [the] magical moments that we think at Google are immensely important in the development of your company, of your own personal development and [of] building much stronger communities" (Grubb 2013).

The example of telecommuting versus in-person collaboration illustrates the importance of social interaction. Marissa Mayer used her power as CEO to help change her company's structure in the hope of spurring a culture of innovation. In doing so, she was acting on an understanding that the nature of our interactions influences what we are likely to accomplish.

What is true in the workplace is also true in social life more broadly. Our daily interactions with others form the basis for our social lives, the topic of this chapter.

We begin at the micro level by examining face-to-face interaction and our shared understanding of social reality (culture) and then by looking more closely at how statuses and roles connect people to one another and to the patterns and routines that are the foundations of social structure. Next we look at networks, groups, and organizations, the specific social ties that form social institutions and the sites where relations of power occur. Finally, we look at the changes in social interaction and organization brought on by the expansion of the Internet.

Culture and Social Interaction

Social life begins with face-to-face interaction. Guided by cultural norms and expectations, we negotiate these micro-level encounters with family members, friends, coworkers, and strangers that are the building blocks of social life. The theoretical tradition of *symbolic interactionism*, introduced in Chapter 1, emphasizes how we make sense of the world by focusing on just these kinds of encounters. Two early-twentieth-century sociological thinkers, Charles Horton Cooley and George Herbert Mead, argued that social interactions were crucial in the development of our sense of self.

Through socialization, we become adept at taking the perspectives of others and determining the intent and meaning of their actions, making this process so much a part of our social interaction that we often forget we are engaged in it. Because it is essential to successful social interaction and to the construction of larger social groups, it is worth taking a closer look at how this process works.

Interaction: Arriving at Common Understandings

As humans, we spend our lives producing symbols. Humans have created languages, such as English or Spanish; we constantly make images, such as the pictures attached to e-mails we send to friends; and we use gestures, such as shaking our heads to mean "no." To interact successfully with others, we need to agree with them about the meaning of these symbols. As we communicate, we rely on the language and knowledge that we share with others to get our meaning across (Blumer 1986).

SHARED LANGUAGE Imagine that you are traveling in a foreign country where you do not speak the local language and the locals don't speak yours. You are separated from your travel group and suddenly find yourself lost in an unfamiliar city. You stop strangers, try to explain that you are lost, and ask for directions. Your efforts are met with quizzical looks as people try to understand what you are asking, and their attempts to help bewilder you. Maybe for the first time, you realize how valuable language is. Without the common ground of shared meaning, social interaction becomes confusing, frustrating, inefficient, even frightening.

Even among those who share a language, however, there are always words or expressions that not everyone will understand, depending on the historical period, the country, or the group or subculture using the word or phrase. If you asked an American youngster to "hop the wag," you would likely get a puzzled look, whereas many British teenagers would immediately recognize this slang phrase as an invitation to skip school. Slang is a common part of subcultures, and slang terms such as *cool*, *groovy*, or *sweet* often evolve rapidly, fall in and out of favor over a short time, and thus lose their ability—across time or even across groups in the same society—to make interactions meaningful.

When we communicate with people we know, our conversation is often rooted in common references and shared understandings, allowing us to rely on unspoken, taken-for-granted assumptions. In the United States, you might greet a friend by saying, "Hey, what's up?" This vague question is understood to mean something like, "Hello, what are you doing now?" Because you understand the slang, you know how to respond.

SHARED KNOWLEDGE Language is just one example of how shared understanding facilitates social interaction. The smooth functioning of everyday life depends on what sociologists refer to as **intersubjectivity,** *a common understanding between people about knowledge, reality, or an experience.* Successful interaction requires each person to take the perspective of the other to achieve some common understanding. In this way, social interaction constantly constructs our social world.

People within a society share knowledge not just of their common language but also of norms and customs, historical references, and other socially useful information that they have learned through socialization (Schutz 1962). In other words, they have a common perspective that enables them to understand how others see the world and allows society to function smoothly. Daily life is full of unspoken, taken-for-granted, and shared interpretations of reality. For example, you have no doubt learned cultural norms for how to conduct yourself in face-to-face interactions, including whether and when to make eye contact, how much personal space to allow, and if and how to greet a person. Do you use a formal greeting? A casual "Hi"? A handshake? A hug? A kiss? All these cultural norms are part of our routine social interactions.

The smooth functioning of everyday life, therefore, is based partially on people's shared understanding of the nature of reality. For example, when you ride public transportation in your home city, you share a common understanding with your fellow passengers and the conductors or drivers

While trying to capture our attention, advertisements must also convey meaning. By drawing on a common understanding of social reality, ads can leave many things unstated. Recognizing the way this Eurostar high-speed train ad references both Queen Elizabeth II and Marilyn Monroe is what makes this advertisement work.

CORE CONCEPTS CHALLENGE

For this advertisement to make sense, what does the reader need to know that is not explained? Do you think this ad would be effective in all **cultures**? *Why or why not?*

about where and how to board, how to pay your fare, and how and where to get off. In a different city or in a foreign country, you would have to figure out all those things, because you would not share a common framework.

Similarly, your enjoyment of any form of entertainment depends on a shared knowledge base. Television comedies like *Family Guy* or *The Colbert Report* assume their audiences will understand their writers' irreverent references to celebrities and politicians, other television programs, and current events. When you "get"—and laugh at—a joke, your enjoyment is rooted in the unspoken assumptions that you share with others. Advertisers, too, often rely on shared views of what is attractive and desirable. That's why logos and slogans

can communicate so much about the meaning and identity of specific brands or products.

When you meet and interact with strangers, shared elements of culture form a common ground that facilitates routine interactions. For example, imagine you are purchasing a computer cable at an office products store. As you interact with the check-out clerk, your facial expression, tone of voice, words, and body language all contribute to the brief interaction, during which you and the clerk share basic assumptions about how to proceed (greet each other, exchange money). You don't try to haggle about the price; the clerk doesn't try to give you a hug.

Suppose, however, that you know very little about computer hardware and are trying to find the cable you need to make your printer work. You ask a clerk about the difference between the various cables for sale and—to your shock—she replies by telling you about the differences between ATA, USB, DVI, and an alphabet soup of cables. The clerk's enthusiasm is blinding her to your perspective—you just want her to pick out an inexpensive cable for you. Exasperated, you leave abruptly without buying anything. In this case, you and the clerk failed to achieve intersubjectivity: you never fully agreed on what was needed for this interaction to be successful.

Some failed social interactions can have far more serious consequences than a frustrating trip to the computer store. For example, in 2006 the U.S. commander in charge of day-to-day military operations in Iraq, Lieutenant General Peter Chiarelli, found that some American troops had been their "own worst enemy" because they didn't understand fundamental aspects of Iraqi culture (Rainey 2006). Chiarelli told the story of how U.S. soldiers arrested a Sunni Arab insurgent in his home. In keeping with the emphasis in Iraqi culture on maintaining a man's honor, the suspect asked to be handcuffed outside, out of view of his family. Instead, U.S. troops forced the man to the floor, handcuffed him, and jerked him out the door—in full view of his family and neighbors. General Chiarelli summed up the incident's consequences in this way: "Every single person in the room, because of this whole concept of honor in this culture, has said, 'To hell with the Americans.'" In this case, an interaction based on fundamental cultural misunderstanding had potentially serious consequences.

People who occupy different social positions often see the world from different perspectives. African Americans living

thinking about culture

How would an understanding of local **culture** help American soldiers in their interactions with citizens abroad? What examples of cultural misunderstandings can you think of?

Having a common culture facilitates ordinary social interactions. In the text we describe a routine interaction with a computer store clerk. Now imagine purchasing food from this street vendor in Egypt. How might the two interactions differ? How might they be similar? What explains these similarities and differences?

relative sizes of the continents more accurately, though it distorts their shapes. Finally, although we typically (and arbitrarily) represent the North Pole as the top and the South Pole as the bottom on maps and globes, the earth has no top or bottom, so the "inverted" presentation of the Peters projection is just as accurate as the "right side up" Mercator projection.

The early-twentieth-century American sociologist W. I. Thomas (1863–1947) helped develop our thinking about the need for people to interpret a social situation before they act. During this process, which Thomas (1923) called "the definition of the situation," we consider both our spontaneous interpretation of the circumstances at hand as well as what society has taught us about those circumstances. Our interpretation then influences how we act. Thomas stated his insight, now known as the **Thomas theorem,** this way: *"If men define situations as real, they are real in their consequences"* (Thomas and Thomas 1928, 572). In other words, subjective interpretations of reality have objective effects. If we are to understand how and why human beings act the way they do, we need to pay attention to how they define reality and how that definition, in turn, influences their behavior.

The Thomas theorem helps us understand how interpretations of a situation shape social interaction on various levels. For example, on the micro level, if a stranger asks for a handout, your definition of the situation is likely to influence whether you give money (see Figure 7.1). Your interpretation may depend on the way you answer some questions: Is this person down on his or her luck? A victim of a weak economy? A veteran? A substance abuser? Someone who is too lazy to hold a job? Or someone with mental illness? The theorem applies to large institutions as well. If the government of one nation sees a neighboring country as a military threat, that government may be more likely to invest substantially in weapons. The neighboring country may then misinterpret this investment as a threat instead of a defensive strategy and increase its own investment in weapons, thereby triggering a dangerous arms race. Whether or not these assessments of threat were accurate, the initial definition of reality can have consequences and shape interpretations of future events.

The Thomas theorem can also help us understand stereotypes, which define individuals as typical examples of whole groups of people. **Stereotypes** are *exaggerated, distorted, or untrue generalizations about categories of people that do not*

in a city center likely see the world differently not only from their white urban neighbors but also very likely from African Americans who live in affluent suburbs. The same dynamics operate on a global scale as well: people in France or China often have a different vantage point on world events than do residents of the United States. Each group draws upon different stocks of knowledge and experience to understand the social world.

Defining Situations as "Real": The Thomas Theorem

By being socialized in a particular culture we learn to see our world from a particular perspective, and that viewpoint becomes our reality. Sociologists maintain that what we experience as "reality" is what we learn from our society; in other words, it is socially constructed. Not only do we take our definitions of reality for granted so that we resist seeing society in all of its complexity, but these definitions can also have very real consequences in action. For example, Maps 7.1 and 7.2 show two ways of seeing the world—ideas about geography that have affected the way we view the significance and size of various regions and nations. The traditional Mercator projection (Map 7.1), developed in the 1500s, badly distorts the relative sizes of the continents. Also, the orientation of the map—with South America and Africa on the bottom—is completely arbitrary. The Peters projection (Map 7.2), developed by cartographer Arno Peters in the 1970s, represents the

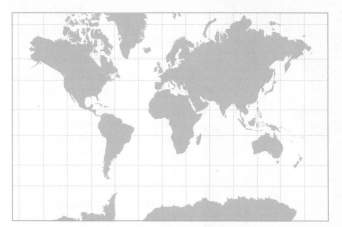

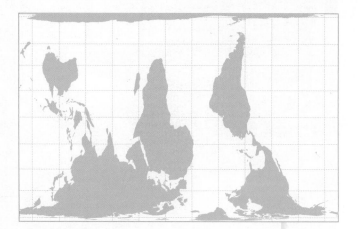

The Mercator projection (Map 7.1, left) and the Peters projection (Map 7.2, right) are two-dimensional representations of the three-dimensional globe, though both maps contain distortions. For example, North America appears to be larger than Africa in Map 7.1. Also, the orientation of the map is completely arbitrary. The Peters projection represents the relative sizes of the continents more accurately. For example, it shows Africa (11.7 million square miles) as being larger than North America (9.4 million square miles), and the inverted presentation is actually as accurate as the Mercator projection. However, the Peters map distorts the shapes of the continents, making them appear stretched out. *Source:* radicalcartography.net.

CORE CONCEPTS CHALLENGE

Which of these maps appears "right" to you? What role do you think **culture** *played in your choice?*

acknowledge individual variation. Stereotypes are often negative; we have all heard stories and jokes that belittle various ethnic groups. Indeed, stereotypes typically perpetuate unfair negative images of people and have little relationship to who they are, as individuals or as a group. (Some of the possible interpretations noted earlier for the stranger asking for money—especially that the person is a substance abuser or too lazy to work—are common stereotypes about homeless people.) At the same time, however, you may also be able to think of some "positive" stereotypes, such as the false belief that "All Kenyans are fast runners." Such positive stereo-

FIGURE 7.1 | **THOMAS THEOREM**

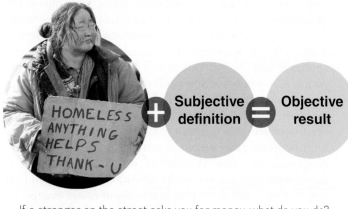

If a stranger on the street asks you for money, what do you do? Whether accurate or not, your subjective definition of this situation will likely determine whether you give this person any money.

types also fail to take into account individual variation. Some of the world's best runners are Kenyans, but the vast majority of Kenyans are no more skilled at running than are people from any other society, and top runners come from many parts of the world.

Because they are shared definitions, all stereotypes create a sense of reality, and they can therefore have serious consequences. Television, for example, is full of stereotypes of working-class people, depicting them as unintelligent, lazy, and crude—think of Homer Simpson. Such stereotypes help to justify economic inequality by implying that highly educated professionals are somehow better than working-class folks. The Sociology in Action box examines how using a sociological perspective can challenge stereotypes based on social class and promote social change.

Social scientists often generalize about groups, of course, but their generalizations are usually carefully qualified and based on data. The statement "On average, U.S. citizens have among the highest annual incomes in the world" is not a stereotype because it is qualified appropriately (that is, with the phrases "on average" and "among the highest annual incomes"), and it can be backed up with data about income levels in different countries. By contrast, the statement "All Americans are rich" is a stereotype because it paints with an overly broad brush ("All Americans") and ignores the wide variation in income that exists in the United States. It also employs an undefined term, "rich," which people interpret in a variety of ways.

SOCIOLOGY in ACTION

Overcoming Class Stereotypes

▶ Jenny was having lunch with a friend. When the server made an error with their order, Jenny's friend commented, "Well, if she was smart, she wouldn't be a waitress."

▶ Terry received an invitation to attend an annual conference of progressive political activists that cost $100 per day, a significant sum for many working people. The invitation noted, "Anybody who does not feel committed enough to pay is not committed enough to participate."

▶ Gilda was a community organizer. A colleague told Gilda that if she would mobilize working-class residents for a meeting on a local issue, he would then step in and negotiate on their behalf. Gilda noted, "He thought of working-class people as props and their voices as sound bites."

These real examples, from readers of a website called Class Matters, illustrate some of the many ways that poor and working-class people can be stereotyped as unintelligent, uncommitted, or unable to stand up for themselves. The pervasiveness of such stereotypes—sometimes even among middle-class activists who are advocating on behalf of poor and working-class people—makes it difficult for individuals from different classes to work together to accomplish common goals. Sociological insights can be useful in helping people understand and overcome such stereotypes.

"I think the sociological imagination is really essential to making social change happen," says Betsy Leondar-Wright, a sociologist who grew up in a comfortable upper-middle-class family. Leondar-Wright (2005) has spent years working for a variety of organizations that address issues involving poverty and economic equality. She held jobs as an organizer in low-income communities and as a coalition builder, working across class, race, and ethnic lines. Her work often involved bringing together people from different backgrounds to address pressing needs such as affordable housing and neighborhood safety. In doing so, she discovered that people had to get past their stereotypes to collaborate successfully.

For example, community organizations based in low-income neighborhoods were frequently staffed by middle-class activists. Too often, activists did not think local residents were capable of leading their own campaigns for neighborhood improvement. "It's easy to fall into stereotypes about people with a particular amount of money or a type of occupation or neighborhood," she writes: "easy and dangerous." Such stereotypes blind people to the complex realities that exist within any group and choke off potentially creative ideas from local residents.

Leondar-Wright argues that what keeps people from being active in their communities is not a stereotypical lack of intelligence or commitment but rather a lack of hope. She notes that "most people can't imagine institutional arrangements" that differ from the ones they know. "[A]t one point my job was to knock on doors of low-income tenants to tell them that their housing was in danger of becoming unaffordable after a certain date [because of changes in ownership]. I saw firsthand how most people in their fear jumped immediately to individual solutions: 'My sister is in Tennessee. Maybe she could take us in for a while if we moved there.' The most valuable thing I brought to them was the information that other tenants in other towns had organized and bought their properties and turned them into permanently affordable housing. Three tenant groups I organized now own and run their apartment complexes. My main contribution to their victories was a sense of informed hope. If we want more people to get active, we need to recognize the critical shortage of hope."

Successful community-based organizing efforts like the one in which Leondar-Wright has been involved directly contradict the stereotypes that poor and working-class people cannot make a difference in their communities. In turn, Leondar-Wright believes that the insights of sociology can themselves be a valuable resource in making a difference.

Source: Opening examples copyright © 2011 Betsy Leondar-Wright. www.classmatters.org. Affiliated with Class Action, www.classism.org.

think about it

1. *Do you ever see stereotypes of poor or working-class people on television or in movies? Explain.*

2. *Have you ever been involved in a group or an organization that included people from different class backgrounds? How do you think class stereotypes influenced the group's dynamics?*

Three Steps to Constructing Social Reality

In their classic work, *The Social Construction of Reality*, Peter Berger and Thomas Luckmann (1966) summarize the process by which people construct reality. As they put it, "Society is a human product. Society is an objective reality. Man is a social product" (p. 61). They label the steps of constructing social reality as externalization, objectivation, and internalization:

1. *Externalization.* People create society through an ongoing process of physical and mental activity. This complex process helps ensure a stable environment within which we can live. For example, you become friends with another person, spending time together and interacting in ways that create a special relationship.

2. *Objectivation.* Through this process, social arrangements come to seem objectively real; society appears separate from human creation and instead seems "natural," inevitable,

and out of people's control. To continue the example of friendship, your newly formed relationship becomes part of your reality. You call each other "friend" and others recognize your relationship as real.

3. *Internalization.* This is the complex process through which we learn our society's culture and establish our view of the world. Through this process humans come to be influenced by their own creations; they are social products. For example, your friendship influences you: you comply with specific expectations associated with this relationship (such as helping your friend move into a new apartment).

The same three-step process occurs with larger social structures as with micro-level social interactions. People create various structures and social institutions such as families, schools, and governments. They then treat those socially constructed entities as objectively real. Finally, people are influenced by the society they create. With large social structures, which often take decades to develop and solidify, the influence is often felt by later generations. We didn't create our form of government, but it certainly influences our lives. However, the government—like all social institutions—is continually maintained and reproduced through the actions of participants. Political candidates run for office; citizens vote for their preferred candidates (or choose not to vote); and the winning candidate goes to Washington (or the state capital or city hall) to represent his or her constituents. Social order emerges from human action, and it continues to exist only when humans reproduce it through their participation.

Because people are continually constructing society and are, in turn, affected by it, the social world in which we live is always in flux. Anything that humans create they can also change. Thus our definition and understanding of work, families, schooling, and other aspects of society is open to change and evolution.

Social Statuses and Roles

As we have seen, successful social interaction requires some shared understanding through which to create our social reality. But interaction is also shaped by statuses and roles, which provide some of the glue that connects individuals to one another and to the behavioral patterns that constitute social structure. We touched on these ideas in Chapter 4 and examine them in more detail here.

STATUSES   A **status,** as we saw in Chapter 4, is *a position in a social system that can be occupied by an individual.* (In a different context, the word *status* is used to indicate honor or prestige associated with a position.) A **status set** is *the collection of statuses that an individual holds.* For example, you might be a student, an employee, a parent, a neighbor, a brother or sister, an immigrant, a band member, and a Christian. Each of these positions is a status, and collectively they are your status set. A **status category** refers to *a status that people can hold in common,* such as nurse, father, or New Englander.

Some statuses apply automatically. **Ascribed statuses** are *those that are assigned to us from birth or that we assume later in life regardless of our wishes or abilities.* Your nationality, your sex, your race or ethnicity, and your status as someone's cousin are among the ascribed statuses you might have had at birth. Other ascribed statuses may be assigned later in life, such as teenager, person with mental illness, or widow. In most cases, we cannot change an ascribed status, since it is determined by others.

Achieved statuses, in contrast, are *those that we voluntarily attain, to a considerable degree, as the result of our own efforts.* A person might be the mayor of a city, a doctor, a professional athlete, a criminal, or a spouse—all examples of achieved statuses. You must work, in some way, to acquire an achieved status.

The line between these two types of status is not always clear-cut. Your family may have influenced some of your achieved statuses, such as your choice of religious affiliation or your decision about whether to attend college. You inherited your class status from your parents as an ascribed status, but that status may change in your adult life. You are assigned a nationality at birth, but you might achieve another nationality by becoming a citizen of a second country.

Some statuses can be achieved only by working through formal structures and meeting certain criteria, whereas other statuses are fairly easy to achieve and are open to most people. Lawyers achieve their status through an arduous process that involves completing college, attending and completing law school, and passing a rigorous bar exam. In contrast, basketball fans can achieve that particular status just by regularly watching games on television.

In addition, not all statuses are equally important. In U.S. society, the status of cousin, say, has much less significance for most people than the status of college graduate. For many Americans, a cousin is often a relatively distant relative they see once a year at holiday gatherings, whereas being a college graduate can be a requirement for a desirable job. In some cultures, though, kinship—even within an extended family— may be an essential status. Extended family ties are typically

Achieved status

thinking about structure
Humans create, sustain, and change social **structure.** How do your everyday actions and interactions help maintain or change the structure of your community? Of your college?

very strong in Native American communities, for example. In these families, relatives such as cousins often interact on a regular basis and have a sense of mutual obligation to provide economic and social support (Cheshire 2006).

Because statuses are social positions, they exist within hierarchies; as a result, some statuses provide more or less social prestige than others. A **status hierarchy** is *a ranking of social positions according to their perceived prestige or honor.* You can probably recognize the status hierarchy within your college: the president and senior administrators hold the positions with the highest prestige, whereas custodial, food service, and clerical workers—all essential for the smooth operation of the school—occupy less prestigious positions. Status is linked to social inequality because different positions often receive different levels of prestige, power, and, in this case, income. At many college campuses, custodial workers begin their workday before sunrise, receive low pay, and are invisible to many students and faculty. In contrast, college presidents are highly paid and likely to have a formidable presence on campus, with the power to make decisions about college operations.

Many people, regardless of their place in a status hierarchy, have one status that overrides all others. A **master status** is *a social position that is overwhelmingly significant, powerfully influences a person's social experience, and typically overshadows all the other social positions that person may occupy.* Sociologists coined this term to describe the significance of race in the United States in the first half of the twentieth century (Hughes 1945). In the segregated South at that time, race was a master status: it overpowered the importance of other statuses such as education level, religious affiliation, class, gender, and occupation. For example, in the pre–civil rights era, and to a lesser degree today, highly educated African American men were identified primarily by their race, despite their status as skilled professionals or community leaders. For white shopkeepers, police officers, and other people in largely segregated cities, a person's status as a black man was so prominent that it made his other statuses nearly invisible. Even today, as we explore in Chapters 10 and 11, race and gender are among the most visible and most important statuses in U.S. society.

ROLES Whereas statuses are positions in a social system, **roles** are *the sets of expected behaviors that are associated with particular statuses.* As a student, you are expected to go to class, turn in assignments on time, and take part in college activities; at the same time, you have the right to choose your own major

and courses and to fair treatment from professors, among others. Those general expectations regarding behavior, duties, and rights that are associated with that role were defined by our culture before you became a student. You can be somewhat creative in how you carry out a role, but the general rules are well established.

Similarly, the general expectations associated with the parent role in our society are fairly clear. Parents raise their children, are responsible for providing for their basic physical needs, and are expected to give social and emotional support—at least until children leave home as adults. Some parents are unable to fulfill the parent role and are negligent, risking a loss of custody. But there is no single way to fulfill this role effectively, and parents accomplish it in a variety of ways. Some are strict, whereas others emphasize open discussion rather than discipline. Still others try to be friends with their children (and their children's friends) and are a constant presence in their lives. And some parents are so "hands-off" that their children rarely see them.

The roles associated with many statuses are even less formal than that of student or parent. Yet the sets of expectations that come with the role of friend or good neighbor, for example, are still widely recognized. Other roles, such as the one taken on by a person who is ill, are generally understood as well. In a classic essay, Talcott Parsons (1951) argued that physical illness (the "sick role") has a social side that involves four particular expectations. First, being sick exempts an individual from other role expectations, especially if a doctor has certified the illness. Second, people with an illness are

SPOTLIGHT
on social theory

Talcott Parsons was the leading proponent of the **functionalist perspective,** which stresses how the various elements of society work together. How might playing the sick role, in the way Parsons described, help reinforce social stability?

Talcott Parsons revealed the widely recognized expectations associated with the "sick role." Like the sick role, other informal roles also involve sets of unstated expectations. Consider, for example, what we might call the "winner role." What expectations exist for this role?

FIGURE 7.2 | ROLE CONFLICT AND ROLE STRAIN

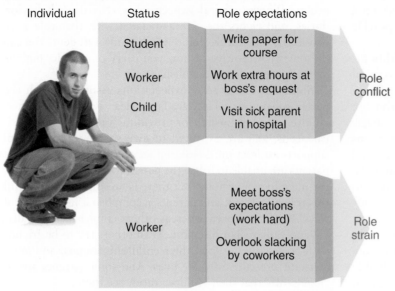

Individual	Status	Role expectations	
	Student	Write paper for course	
	Worker	Work extra hours at boss's request	Role conflict
	Child	Visit sick parent in hospital	
	Worker	Meet boss's expectations (work hard)	Role strain
		Overlook slacking by coworkers	

Because individuals hold many statuses simultaneously, they often have trouble meeting associated role expectations successfully. Role conflict occurs when two different roles have incompatible expectations. Role strain occurs when a single role has competing expectations. Have you experienced either role conflict or role strain?

often not held responsible for taking care of themselves; a spouse, parent, or health care professional is likely to provide the necessary attention. Third, because illness is socially undesirable, we expect that sick people will want to get better. Fourth, sick people are also expected to make an effort to recover, especially by seeking competent professional help. Sick people who fail to fulfill their role thwart the expectations of others around them. If, for example, you refused to see a doctor after a lengthy ongoing illness, your parents and friends would probably become increasingly frustrated with you and might even attempt to force you to seek medical help.

We are all constantly juggling the many roles associated with the various statuses we occupy. **Role conflict** occurs *when the expectations associated with different roles clash.* For example, your boss asks you to work extra hours at the café during a particularly busy period, but at the same time, you need to finish a major project for one of your courses. Because there are only so many hours in the day, you must make a choice, and one of your roles—student or worker—is likely to suffer. Parents who must juggle the care of children with the demands of their work are especially prone to such role conflicts. **Role strain,** in contrast, occurs *when the expectations associated with a single role compete with each other.* Teachers experience role strain from the dual responsibility they have both to help and support their students and to evaluate the same students, sometimes with a failing grade (see Figure 7.2).

Roles are crucial in the construction of our everyday lives because they link us to other people. Roles link parents and children, teachers and students, employers and workers,

friends, and a host of other statuses. These interconnecting roles form a network of social relationships that are the basis of social structure.

Dramaturgy: Playing at Social Life

If the idea of people playing roles reminds you of actors performing in a film or play, you are not the first to see this analogy. Shakespeare wrote over 400 years ago "All the world's a stage, and all the men and women merely players." Sociologists use this idea as well. **Dramaturgy,** *an approach to the study of social interaction that uses the metaphor of social life as a theater,* is most closely associated with Canadian-born sociologist Erving Goffman. In his well-known work *The Presentation of Self in Everyday Life,* Goffman (1959) drew on some of the elements that make up a theatrical performance to illuminate the nature of social interaction.

ROLE EXPECTATIONS In a play, the playwright largely determines the actor's role. In real life, cultural expectations establish the content of a social role. For example, imagine a lawyer walking into a courtroom dressed in basketball shorts and a T-shirt and greeting the judge by saying, "Hey, buddy." He pulls his papers out of a knapsack and, as the case proceeds, giggles out loud at the opposing attorney's questions and the witnesses' testimony. Such behavior would be absurd, of course, precisely because it violates our expectations about a lawyer's proper "costume" (formal business attire), "props" (briefcase), language (a respectful "your honor"), and emotion (serious). We often take for granted such expectations, but their significance becomes obvious when they are violated.

Appropriate costumes, props, language, and emotions are among the resources actors use to achieve a convincing performance. But an actor must still interpret a role, and there is considerable room for creativity. The same is true with social roles. The expectations associated with any role are socially defined, but individuals who occupy a particular status must actively "play" the role. A lawyer might be folksy and warm in his summation to the jury, for example, or he might be outraged and impassioned. Either behavior could be appropriate to the role.

on social theory

Dramaturgy is an approach that uses the idea of social life as a kind of theater. Consider a particular role that you play in that theater. What costume, props, language, and emotions are associated with that role? Do you ever feel the need to separate yourself from the role? Why?

IMPRESSION MANAGEMENT Role playing occurs in the presence of an audience. Actors try to convince the audience that they are "real," that their interpretation of

THROUGH A SOCIOLOGICAL LENS

Focusing on Emotions and the Employee Role

"Thank you for choosing our airline!" "Can I help you find something?" "Would you like to hear our specials for today?" "How may I direct your call?" "I hope your stay with us was a pleasant one!" Health care workers, salespeople, flight attendants, waitstaff, customer service representatives, and workers in many other fields are often required to project an emotion to their customers or clients. Usually these jobs require workers to be exceptionally nice; that is, friendly and helpful. They are expected to greet people with a big smile and cheerful small talk, so that the customer or client will feel welcome and relaxed. Bill collectors, on the other hand, need to make people who are delinquent in paying their bills feel uncomfortable; therefore, they are often nastier than natural. Either way, these employees need to express a particular emotion in order to play their role successfully.

Sociologist Arlie Hochschild (1983) developed the idea that certain interactions require us to project an emotion we may not feel—to be nicer or nastier than natural. Viewing these interactions through a sociological lens, she called the effort involved *emotion work*, which, in a classic article (Hochschild 1979), she defined as "the act of trying to change in degree or quality an emotion or feeling" (p. 561). We often engage in emotion work, according to Hochschild, because of *emotion rules,* the "social guidelines that direct how we want to try to feel" (p. 563). When people tell you that you "shouldn't feel guilty," or that you "have the right" to feel angry, they are alerting you to these commonly accepted rules. When emotion rules are applied to a workplace, they amount to what Hochschild has called the "commercialization of human feeling."

As Hochschild's (1983) research shows, however, emotion work can be stressful. Employees who identify strongly with

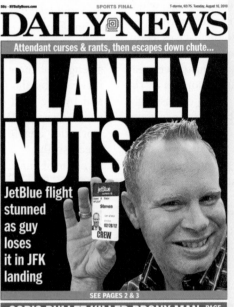

Jet Blue flight attendant Steven Slater, tired of smiling and acting friendly to rude passengers, quit his job with a dramatic flourish in 2010 by leaving the plane he was working on through the emergency exit and slide after the plane had landed—becoming a media sensation in the process.

their jobs, such as social workers, teachers, and nurses, may pour their emotional energy into their work only to experience burnout after a few years. Employees who maintain some distance from their employee role may become exhausted by the constant need to express cheerfulness or enthusiasm, even in the face of rudeness or hostility from customers. Employees who succeed in acting the part may feel like frauds for not genuinely experiencing the emotions they are expected to feel.

Demands to display specific emotions are most common in service jobs, especially in settings that involve frequent contact with customers. Retail sales clerks, food servers, flight attendants, and child care workers are all required to show deference to customers.

Hochschild's influential work called attention to the role of emotion in the workplace and elsewhere. She identified the complex and sometimes negative dynamics involved in emotional labor and spawned two decades of research on the subject (see Wharton 2009). This research now extends well beyond sociology to fields such as management (Anderson, Provis, and Chappel 2003), criminal justice (Tewksbury and Higgins 2006), and applied psychology (Rupp and Spencer 2006).

think about it

1. *Do any of the jobs that you have held involve emotional labor? What was expected of you? Were you comfortable with these expectations?*

2. *Did your emotional labor involve any stress? If so, how did you manage that stress?*

a character is authentic. As social actors, we too engage in *impression management:* we try to control the image others have of us through our performance. (This effort can involve projecting emotion and be done for pay, as the Through a Sociological Lens box explores.) Sometimes people fully embrace a role and see its performance as an integral part of

themselves. An aspiring concert pianist might enthusiastically immerse herself in her role, wearing a certain type of clothing and hair style and using body language that communicates to her audience that she is already a professional musician. In other situations, though, people attempt to maintain "role distance" by separating themselves from a role as they carry it out. These people want their audience to see the difference between the role they are playing and their "real" selves. A manager who is self-conscious about enforcing discipline, for example, may say, "Look, I hate to do this 'boss' stuff but . . ."

THE FRONT STAGE AND THE BACK STAGE

All actors are familiar with the distinction between the front stage, which the audience can see, and the back stage, which is hidden from view. Actors perform their roles on the front stage, but on the back stage they become themselves again. Social actors also behave differently depending on where they are. The waiter smiling pleasantly at customers may complain bitterly about poor tips among coworkers in the kitchen. The student feigning interest when discussing a course with a professor may later grumble to friends about how boring the class is.

As we have seen, our social ties are formed through our common culture, our shared interpretation of reality, and the statuses and the roles that we assume as we interact with one another. Our ongoing social interaction results in social networks, groups, and more formal organizations that are the backbone of social structure, to which we now turn.

Social Networks

Social networks are *the collections of social ties that connect individuals to one another.* Today, the term conjures up images of social media and the web, but people have always formed networks, and sociologists have been studying them since long before the rise of the Internet. As we will see, however, the emergence of digital networks has brought about some unique changes to social networks.

As mentioned in Chapter 4, pioneering German sociologist Georg Simmel (1858–1918) argued that the structure of social life was composed of regular, patterned interactions among individuals. Simmel ([1903] 1950) observed that in the emerging cities of his day, people gained more freedom and formed more fleeting connections to others than was common in rural village life. Elsewhere he referred to a "network" or "web of group affiliations" ([1922] 1955) that makes up modern life. Simmel, then, was the first sociologist to think systematically about social structure in terms of social networks.

The Nature of Networks and Ties

Who would be willing to lend you a little money in an emergency? Whom would you ask to be a personal reference on a job application? Whom would you invite to your graduation party? These people are part of your social network. Networks connect you to people and resources. Different social networks provide different resources (Rainie and Wellman 2012, 19), including:

- *Havens* that promote a sense of belonging and fellowship
- *Bandages* that provide emotional and other assistance to cope with stress and troubles
- *Safety nets* that lessen the impact of acute crises and chronic troubles
- *Social capital* that helps people find jobs, houses, spouses, and more

Networks come in different sizes, and they vary by the strength of their links, by the characteristics of the people involved, by the physical distance between their members, and by the kind of interaction within them, among other characteristics. Whatever their benefit or form, robust network ties enable us to navigate through social life more successfully.

Some of our networks are made up of close friends, family, or others with whom we have strong ties and intimate relationships. Typically, we want to spend time with these people, and the feeling is usually mutual. The stronger our ties are with people, the more likely they are to provide a broad range of support.

Most of our social support comes from a relatively small number of such strong ties (Wellman and Wortley 1990). These close ties can be critical during times of crisis (Hurlbert, Haines, and Beggs 2000). For example, as Hurricane Katrina approached New Orleans in August 2005, residents with strong social networks outside New Orleans were the first to leave the city, relying on family and close friends for food, shelter, and other assistance. In contrast, people without strong ties to such networks had a more difficult time leaving the city and were typically among the last to evacuate. In the absence of social networks to help with basic necessities such as clothing, food, housing, and transportation, these residents were far more dependent on federal, state, and local government for assistance than were those with strong ties outside the city (Fussell 2006).

Other networks consist of people who have relatively weak ties with one another: coworkers, neighbors, and casual acquaintances. Though they are made up of weak ties, these networks can be helpful, too, since they connect us to a broader set of social contacts, information, and resources than might otherwise be available to us. In a classic phrase, Granovetter (1973, 1974) argued for "the strength of weak ties." In his review of existing research and in his own study of men in management and the professions, he found that many men were able to obtain better jobs by using their "weak ties" to connect to new opportunities.

Alumni who help college students from their alma mater obtain internships or jobs upon graduation are a good example of this type of "weak tie" network in action. Such contacts are often stratified by class; students from more prestigious schools enjoy the privilege of alumni contacts who wield considerably more power and influence than do alumni from less prestigious colleges. On the other hand, those with less power in society—who are likely to be at less prestigious schools, if they attend college at all—are at a disadvantage because they are largely excluded from powerful social networks. This, too, is a part of the social network phenomenon: access to networks often varies based on how much power a person has; in turn, "who you know" can influence what you can or cannot do in life.

In addition, the more connections a member of a social network has, the more additional connections that individual is likely to develop over time (Barabási 2002). This is an example of what Merton (1968) called the *Matthew effect*, by which the network-rich get richer and the network-poor get poorer. (The name comes from the biblical verse in Matthew 25:29: "For to all those who have, more will be given . . . but from those who have nothing, even what they have will be taken away.") Those without strong social ties have fewer network resources and are less able to generate social support to meet life's challenges.

Social Network Analysis

The study of social networks tells us a great deal about patterns of social interaction (Scott 2000; Wasserman, Faust, and Iacobucci 1994). Sociologists analyze networks for a number of purposes: to study the social dynamics of a neighborhood, to gain insight into communication in a workplace, to analyze how HIV/AIDS is spread, and to better understand online social connections.

Such analysis can reveal that networks matter in unexpected ways. For example, Christakis and Fowler (2007) have shown that people's social network influences the likelihood that they will be overweight (2007) or that they will smoke (2008). These findings hold even when controlled for self-selection (socializing with similar people) and social environment (being influenced by common environmental factors). In another example (Fowler and Christakis 2008), happy people tend to be connected to other happy people, and people at the core of their local networks are happier than those on the periphery. Happiness is "contagious" up to three degrees of separation (to a friend of a friend of a friend), and the characteristics of a person's network can help predict independently which individuals will be happy over time.

Researchers use specialized software to map the linkages among the members of a network and to conduct complex network analyses (Watts 2004). Network diagrams such as the one shown in Figure 7.3 illustrate the connections among members and their pattern of interaction. In this way, they help reveal the hidden ties (indirect connections) that link people to one another and that illuminate some of the structure of social life. Other types of network analysis map

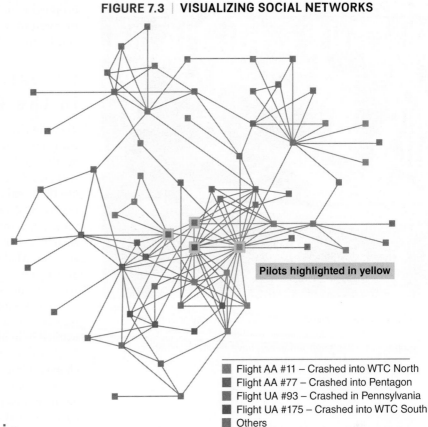

FIGURE 7.3 | VISUALIZING SOCIAL NETWORKS

Pilots highlighted in yellow

■ Flight AA #11 – Crashed into WTC North
■ Flight AA #77 – Crashed into Pentagon
■ Flight UA #93 – Crashed in Pennsylvania
■ Flight UA #175 – Crashed into WTC South
■ Others

"Small world" social networks that consist of a small number of people (for example, a family, a workplace, a terrorist network, a board of directors) can be mapped out in a simple diagram like this one, which shows the social network connecting the 9/11 hijackers, who are represented by the color-coded nodes indicating the flight they were on. The dark gray nodes are other people who had direct, or indirect, contact with the hijackers, and the gray lines show reported connections. *Source*: Krebs (2008).

interactions among thousands or even millions of people, searching for patterns that can shed light on social life.

Social network analysis reveals that our networks are more likely to include people who are like us. According to the principle of **homophily,** *social contact occurs at a higher rate among people who are similar than among those who are different* (McPherson, Smith-Lovin, and Cook 2001). Race, age, religion, and class (including education and occupation) are important characteristics that connect or separate people. As a result, most social networks are much more homogeneous than the population as a whole. Homophily influences what we know about our society, since we are apt to share and reinforce our worldview with others who are like us (Smith-Lovin and McPherson 1993).

For example, friendship networks in the United States are typically characterized by racial homophily (Mouw and Entwisle 2006; Quillian and Campbell 2003). However, students on college campuses may cultivate more robust

Many students inhabit a more racially diverse friendship network during their college years than they did in high school, and this experience can have a significant influence on the diversity of their subsequent networks as adults.

proportion of friends of different races increases during the first year of college (Boisjoly et al. 2006; Stearns, Buchmann, and Bonneau 2009).

Social Networks in the Digital Age

Teens in the United States between the ages of 12 and 17 are connected. In 2012, 95 percent of them used the Internet, nearly half had their own smartphone, and those who texted sent an average of 60 texts a day. Ninety-two percent of teens use their real name online, 91 percent have posted photos of themselves, nearly a quarter have posted videos of themselves, and they have a median of 300 Facebook friends in their network (Lenhart 2012; Madden, Lenhart, Cortesi et al. 2013; Madden, Lenhart, Duggan et al. 2013). Such connection and communication through online social networks are only one sign that social networking has exploded.

Some sociologists argue that the digital age is characterized by a new social order that is based primarily on networked individuals rather than groups (Rainie and Wellman 2012; see Table 7.1). Three revolutions have propelled this change. First, in a process that has continued since Simmel observed it a century ago, the significance of social networks has increased in modern life. Small, densely knit groups that characterized social organization in the past—such as families, villages, and small organizations—have been supplanted by networks. The social networks that characterize contemporary life are more diverse and less constraining than the social organization of the past, even those during Simmel's time. Through networking, we have more leeway in choosing who we want to be, what we want to do, and with whom we want to interact. We have broad opportunities to move well beyond our family and place of birth to explore other places, lifestyles, occupations, and values.

Second, the creation of the Internet has given people an unprecedented global communications and information-gathering platform to use in developing their social networks.

multiracial and multiethnic friendship networks than is typical off-campus. Given the degree to which schools and neighborhoods are segregated by race in the United States, college may be the first opportunity many students have for regular interaction with people of various races. White, non-Hispanic college students who have a black, a Latino, or an Asian roommate are more comfortable interacting in racially diverse settings and are more likely to have interracial friendships than are white students who have white roommates. And although white, non-Hispanic college students have far fewer interracial friendships than do black, Latino, or Asian students during their high school years, their

TABLE 7.1	GROUPS VERSUS NETWORKS: SOME DIFFERENCES
Groups	**Networks**
1. Contact is within and between groups	1. Contact is between individuals.
2. Ties are local.	2. Ties are local and distant.
3. Ties are largely homogeneous.	3. Ties are diverse.
4. Most ties are involuntary (kin, neighbors).	4. Most ties are voluntary.
5. Groups exert strong social control over the individual.	5. Networks exert weak social control over the individual.
6. Groups provide a broad range of resources.	6. Networks provide specialized resources.
7. Groups have tight boundaries.	7. Networks often have permeable boundaries.

Source: Adapted from Rainie and Wellman (2012).

The introduction of this new technology is what has enabled networks to expand and thrive as never before.

Third, the mobile revolution in communication devices, especially the smartphone, means that people can access their friendship and professional networks whenever and wherever they want. Physical locations that often were the genesis of traditional groups—home/family, neighborhood/neighbors, workplace/coworkers—are less important in contemporary life. Instead, the social and professional circles in which we travel exist increasingly in cyberspace, supplemented by "real-world" interactions.

Together, Rainie and Wellman (2012, 6) argue, these three revolutions have enabled a major shift in social life: "We have become increasingly networked as individuals, rather than embedded in groups." This does not mean that people are less social or more individualistic. Rather, the nature of our interdependence and the characteristics of our reliance on others have changed. Compared with groups in the past:

- We meet a growing portion of our social, emotional, and economic needs by connecting to broad, loosely organized and diverse networks of associates rather than to a small number of tightly knit groups.

- Our work and leisure lives are more intertwined, since the boundaries that used to separate family and friends from work have blurred.

- Similarly, our public and private lives have blurred in a network society.

While networks offer some distinct advantages, they also require individuals to take the initiative in making connections and constructing support networks. The days of automatically being part of a kinship group, community, or other older, group-based social life are past. Consequently, Rainie and Wellman (2012, 9) note, "Networked individualism is both socially liberating and socially taxing." For example, the expansion of the Internet enables people to reach out and find social contacts relatively easily. However, the Internet "also made relationships harder to sustain because it brought so many distractions and fleeting interactions." In addition, the digital divide means that differences in the level of Internet access and knowledge about how to use it effectively can make social inequalities worse.

Despite the growing influence of social networks, groups and organizations are still central elements of social life. We turn now to those types of social structures.

FAST-FORWARD

Social Change and Networks

In the Internet era, social networks are changing. Until recently, our primary social networks were rooted in a specific place and were based largely on face-to-face interaction. However, online social interaction means that geographic distance is becoming far less significant; people who regularly interact online are building strong friendship networks with people who may live across the country or on the other side of the globe and whom they may never meet face-to-face.

Social Groups

Social life involves more than interactions among individuals. Throughout society, people interact in patterns that form the basis of small groups, such as families. **Social groups** are *collections of people who interact regularly with one another and who are aware of their status as a group.* A *crowd* that happens to be in the same place at the same time, such as passengers waiting to board an airplane, is not a group in the sociological sense, since the people are gathered for a onetime event and do not think of themselves as part of some collective entity. Similarly a *category* of people, such as apartment dwellers or people with blue eyes, also are not social groups in the sociological sense. Some groups can be quite informal and can be created, changed, or dissolved with relatively little fanfare. Nevertheless, unlike a crowd or category of people, members of a group often share common interests, values, norms, and expectations.

Primary and Secondary Social Groups

Sociologists often classify groups according to the nature and intensity of their interaction. **Primary groups** are *made up of people who have regular contact, enduring relationships, and a significant emotional attachment to each other.* A family is one example of a primary group; a collection of close friends who regularly hang out together is another. In both cases group members interact regularly, often spending a great deal of time together, and their connection to the primary group endures over time. Primary group members share a sense of both caring and obligation, even if the relationships among them are not equal (for example, parent and child). Primary groups are especially influential agents of socialization and can have a major impact on a person's life, shaping values and priorities. They often provide important social support.

Secondary groups are *made up of people who interact in a relatively impersonal way, usually to carry out some specific task.* Coworkers at your job or members of a neighborhood watch group are examples of secondary groups. Typically, these groups represent shorter-term or temporary associations, without a significant emotional bond between members. Over time, you will probably join and leave many different secondary groups, and the group will usually emphasize a common task or goal—fighting neighborhood crime, for example—over connections among group members. As a result, secondary groups are not nearly as influential in our lives as primary groups.

It is not always easy to distinguish between primary and secondary groups. Is a high school soccer team, whose members train together year-round and see one another more often than their families during the soccer season, a primary group? Sometimes a primary group can form within a larger secondary group, as when a small group of coworkers develops close relationships. The best way to distinguish between primary and secondary groups is to think about the basis and depth of members' attachment to the group, the sense of mutual obligation, and the amount of influence the group has on members' lives.

Reference Groups

We saw in Chapter 6 that we derive our sense of self in part from taking into account how others likely see and judge us—the "looking glass self." **Reference groups** are *the groups against which we choose to measure ourselves.* A reference group can be a family, a circle of friends, an occupational group, or a community of worship—just about any primary or secondary group.

Reference groups matter because they can influence the choices we make. They are the social groups we take into account as we plan and assess our actions. For example, as you were deciding whether to attend college, you may have considered the following questions: "What will my friends think? Will my family be disappointed if I don't go to college? Will future employers look at my application more positively if I have a degree?" If the answers were contradictory, you needed to decide which reference group was most important to you.

Reference groups can influence our choices even if we do not yet belong to them. Graduate and professional schools, for example, socialize students about the expectations of their chosen profession. Students who have doctors or businesspeople as their reference group will often adopt new habits, ways of thinking, language, behavior, and dress to conform to that group's likely expectations.

Group Size and Social Relationships: Dyads, Triads, and Beyond

According to sociologist Georg Simmel (1964), the size of a group has important effects on internal group dynamics. (Similar observations apply to social networks.) Consider the characteristics of a *dyad*, a group consisting of just two people (Figure 7.4). Because a dyad can continue to exist only if both participants are committed to it, it is very unstable. Dyads are also the most intense type of social relationships because interaction in a dyad is always between two people. Committed

FIGURE 7.4 | GROUP SIZE AND SOCIAL RELATIONSHIPS

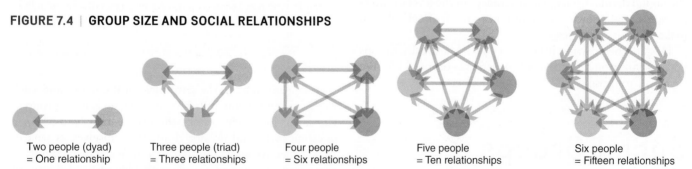

Two people (dyad) = One relationship

Three people (triad) = Three relationships

Four people = Six relationships

Five people = Ten relationships

Six people = Fifteen relationships

The size of a group affects the social relationships within it. In small groups, members are likely to interact directly with one another and to see themselves as integral members of the group. As groups become larger, there are many more potential relationships, and the connections among group members tend to be less intense. Think of both a small and a large group to which you belong. Do they fit this general pattern?

sexual relationships and marriages are classic examples of dyads, but best friends or business partners can also exhibit these characteristics.

Group dynamics fundamentally change when a third person is added, creating a *triad*. In a triad, members' attention is divided, since the number of possible interactions increases. As a couple adjusts to a first child or a new friend joins a previously existing dyad, difficulties typically emerge. One parent may feel jealous of the bond between the other parent and a new infant, for example. Two members of the triad may form an alliance in opposition to the third person, sparking tension. When a pair of friends becomes a triad, conflict may arise as two members outvote the third when deciding what to do or where to eat.

Industrial production required the coordination of huge factories, often employing thousands of workers. In this postcard image, taken around 1916, tens of thousands of workers gather in front of a Ford Motor factory in Detroit, Michigan.

Group size also influences social interaction within larger groups. Groups generally become more stable as they get larger because the group can withstand the loss of individual members. However, relationships also become less intense as a group gets larger. Because there is less focus and attention on any one person, members of a larger group typically feel less emotional commitment to one another. Therefore, small groups tend to be intense but unstable, whereas larger groups tend to be more stable but less intense.

Large and small groups also differ in the nature of the social interaction among members. To take a familiar example, the size of a class influences the social interaction within the classroom: how the instructor interacts with each student and with the group as a whole, how students interact with each other, and what kinds of in-class activities work best. You can be anonymous and passive in a lecture hall with 200 students. In a seminar with 6 students, however, you must participate actively in the discussion.

Organizations and Bureaucracy

More complex and more formal than most groups, **organizations** are *secondary groups that have a degree of formal structure and are formed to accomplish particular tasks*. This broad definition applies to organizations as diverse as your local chess club, the National Rifle Association, Microsoft Corporation, and the United Nations. Although these examples obviously vary enormously in scale, configuration, and purpose, we can learn a great deal about how they operate, and how people behave within them, by studying the structure and culture of organizations, as well as the environments in which they operate.

Organizational Structure

As with any group, the size of an organization can have a major influence on its structure and operation. Very small organizations can operate with few formal rules, straddling the line between an informal group and a formal organization. But even the smallest organizations require a process for making basic decisions. A small organization such as a neighborhood association may use consensus to reach decisions: all members' views are solicited and every effort is made to reach a general agreement. Such an organization may not need any formal leaders, such as a president or treasurer, but may instead use rotating coordinators to ensure that business gets done.

As organizations grow, however, an informal structure usually proves to be inadequate. A larger organization typically develops a more formal decision-making process and a more elaborate division of labor. As we saw in Chapter 1, Max Weber noted that a shift from traditional to rational action (the *rationalization of society*) was a characteristic of the rise of industrialized society in the nineteenth century. Early industrialists needed to manage ever-larger organizations. Businesses needed to operate factories that employed hundreds or even thousands of workers, producing goods in large quantities that were distributed through a complex transportation network. Paying workers, purchasing raw materials, and shipping goods from the factory—all required the development of complex systems. As new structures and ways of accomplishing tasks became necessary, bureaucracy developed into the dominant organizational structure of the industrial age.

Bureaucracy

A **bureaucracy** is *a hierarchical administrative system with formal rules and procedures used to manage organizations.* Bureaucracies commonly share key features (Weber 1946):

1. *A division of labor.* Because of their size, bureaucracies need specialization; not everyone can do everything. In bureaucracies, people are responsible for narrowly defined tasks.

2. *A hierarchy of authority and accountability.* Bureaucracies have a pyramidal structure (see Figure 7.5). With power concentrated at the top of the hierarchy and many bureaucrats at the bottom dividing what little influence they have, authority is highly fragmented, and managers' primary job is to enforce rules and monitor other workers.

3. *Impersonality.* Power is located within an office, not in the person who happens to hold that position. People are hired, promoted, fired, or retired, but the bureaucratic structure remains.

4. *Written rules and records.* The tasks and duties to be carried out within a bureaucracy are usually written out in formal rules and procedures. Written forms for communicating information and for record-keeping help ensure consistency.

These four features allow bureaucracies to coordinate the diverse activities of many people. Without them,

FIGURE 7.5 | FORMAL BUREAUCRATIC STRUCTURE

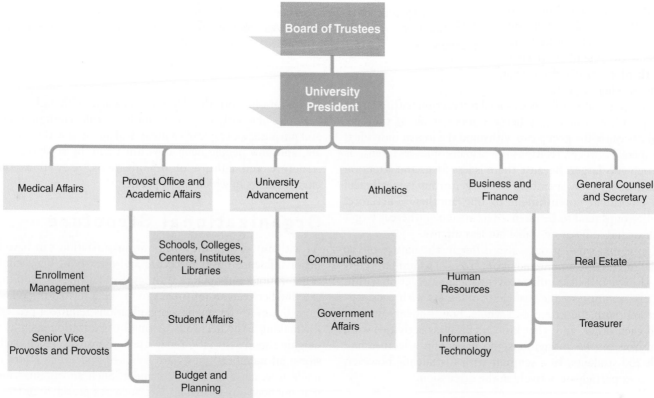

Like all large organizations, the University of Miami has a formal bureaucratic structure, summarized in this chart. Occupying the positions within its bureaucracy (represented by boxes) are particular individuals who can leave the organization without affecting its structure. Positions in such structures usually carry different amounts of power and prestige and command unequal amounts of resources, with those toward the top having more of all three than those toward the bottom. *Source*: University of Miami website.

CORE CONCEPTS CHALLENGE

Locate a copy of your school's organizational **structure,** *which may be available on its website. How does your school's structure compare with this one? What does this structure tell you about power at your school?*

organizations, especially large ones—from the national government to your favorite retail outlet—would stop functioning. Your college, for example, undoubtedly has a bureaucracy to schedule classes, coordinate student records, manage housing, pay employees, and keep buildings clean.

As you have probably experienced, however, bureaucracies can have a negative side. If you have ever gotten the "run-around" while trying to figure out who in an organization is responsible for a problem, you have encountered the sometimes maddening results of the division of labor and fragmented authority that characterize most bureaucracies. And, of course, we have all been buried in the avalanche of paperwork that can be required to accomplish a common task such as visiting a doctor, enrolling in college, applying for financial aid, or opening a bank account. All organizations have some degree of bureaucratization, but too much can be counterproductive, frustrating both employees and the people they are supposed to serve. In addition, because authority is so fragmented in a bureaucracy, these types of organizations tend to be very resistant to change.

Since bureaucracies are governed by rules and regulations that apply to everyone, they can be very impersonal, and it can be difficult to make exceptions to accommodate an individual's specific needs. For example, if the workday at your company begins at 9:00 a.m., you may not be allowed to arrive at 9:15 a.m. so that you can drop your child off at school, even if you would be willing to work an extra 15 minutes at the end of the day. Rules and regulations tend to multiply and become more refined within bureaucracies as new situations arise. As a result, bureaucratic organizations typically have detailed policies that specify not only how to enforce the rules but also how to modify them.

Even though bureaucracies are designed to coordinate activities smoothly, they can be remarkably inefficient, and efforts to maximize efficiency often seem to have the opposite effect. For example, automated customer service phone lines are designed to manage large volumes of calls. Yet customers complain so frequently about not being able to talk to a live human being that a website has been created that provides frustrated customers of hundreds of companies with guidance on how to get to a live person more immediately (www.gethuman.com).

Although large organizations rely on bureaucratic measures to run smoothly, as the layers of bureaucracy multiply, they often make organizations increasingly unwieldy. Sociologists seek to understand this complexity, recognizing both the mechanisms designed to coordinate large organizations and the dynamics that can make bureaucracies feel like an exasperating maze. Two factors they look at are an organization's culture and its operating environment.

Organizational Culture

Organizations can have distinct cultures that influence how they are organized, the values they espouse, and the way they operate. (For an example of a sociologist who works with different organizational cultures, see the Sociology Works box.) Even organizations involved in very similar activities can have different cultures. For example, the merger between America Online (AOL) and Time Warner in 2000 revealed an enormous culture clash between the two companies (Klein 2003). AOL, an Internet service provider, had a brash, aggressive approach to the business that made it a success story in the dot-com boom years of the 1990s. Its executives were often young, with an informal style, and they viewed their company as the future of the media industry. Time Warner, on the other hand, was the product of an earlier merger between two old-media giants: Time Inc., which had been involved in traditional print media, and Warner Communications Inc., which had been involved in film and television. Time Warner's leaders had a reputation for being conservative and strait-laced. The cultural differences between AOL and Time Warner reflected these different assumptions about the future of media and different experiences in the media industry and found expression in many areas, including perspectives on time. At Time Warner, workers saw themselves as potential "lifers" at a stable company with a good retirement plan. In contrast, AOL employees had made quick money in the 1990s and expected that their big payoff would come from selling what they hoped would become valuable AOL stock. Such differences were only the tip of the iceberg; employees at AOL and Time Warner didn't understand and, in some cases, didn't like each other. As a result, combining the two companies proved far more difficult than expected, and the culture clash contributed to the eventual failure of the merger in 2009.

Organizational Environment

All organizations, whatever their culture may be, operate in a larger environment, which includes other organizations as well as a variety of conditions that are part of the broader context of a society (Hall and Tolbert 2004). Collectively, *factors that exist outside of the organization but that potentially affect its operation* constitute the **organizational environment.**

SOCIOLOGY WORKS

Mindy Fried and Organizational Change

For more than two decades, sociology has informed Mindy Fried's work as a family policy analyst in state government, a lobbyist for early childhood services, and most recently as an organizational change consultant. Fried was drawn to sociology because it connected her long-standing interest in people to what she calls the "big picture." In sociology, Fried "discovered kindred spirits who asked the same kinds of questions that I had about people and their worlds—questions about how people's experiences are framed by their race, gender, age, and ethnicity, questions about how social structures in our society provide answers to how people behave, the opportunities they have, the barriers they encounter."

Describing herself as an "applied sociologist," Fried works as a consultant specializing in organizational change, drawing upon her sociological perspective to help organizations navigate changing contexts. She works with organizations to solve problems, negotiate conflicts, and respond to new challenges and opportunities, using her sociological understanding of interaction and organizational culture (Fried 2008).

Fried's main clients are nonprofit organizations. In a recent project, Fried and her colleagues at Arbor Consulting Partners worked with a university-community partnership focused on improving the health of local residents in a low-income neighborhood. Communication problems—the result of two very different organizational cultures—were hampering the partnership. Fried conducted interviews, held focus groups with members of both groups, and used participant observation—research methods that allowed her to help "key players develop a deeper understanding of how power, diversity, and agency affected their organizational dynamic."

This shared understanding helped produce more effective communication and a stronger working relationship between the two groups.

As an organizational change consultant, Fried takes the distinctly sociological approach of an "outsider within," someone who is not emotionally involved with the organization but who makes a commitment to observe, listen, and learn about the various experiences of those who are. Fried explains: "Our status as outsiders within ultimately allows us to interpret multiple perspectives, untangle conflict, and think creatively about how to maximize positive outcomes for an organization." Reflecting on her sociological approach, Fried says sociology gives her both a rich understanding of organizational dynamics and the research skills to help her clients build on their strengths and respond to new challenges.

Mindy Fried

> "Our status as outsiders within ultimately allows us to interpret multiple perspectives, untangle conflict, and think creatively about how to maximize positive outcomes for an organization."

think about it

1. How might an organizational consultant assist one of the organizations (school, community group, extracurricular club) in which you participate?

2. How do you think the perspective of an "outsider within" differs from that of either an insider or an outsider?

The strength of the economy, the stability of political rule, demographic factors, other organizations, the legal context, technology, and the cultural environment can all influence the way organizations operate.

Much like individuals, organizations link to other organizations in a network structure in the course of their normal operations. Your school, for example, interacts with a variety of other organizations. Government agencies and private corporations provide research grants, businesses sell goods and services on campus, and

graduate schools and potential employers receive student transcripts.

The organizational environment also includes the legal context within which organizations operate (Edelman and Suchman 1997). Laws define the nature of some organizations, such as corporations and nonprofit groups. Laws and law enforcement also provide a stable environment within which organizations can operate. Courts enforce contracts and settle disputes. Legal regulations may also restrict organizational behavior. For example, environmental laws limit pollution and antitrust laws help ensure that companies compete fairly.

Technology is another element of the organizational environment. Computers and the Internet have dramatically changed how large organizations function, enabling them to accumulate more data, communicate faster across long distances, and distribute information broadly both internally and externally.

The broader cultural environment also influences how organizations operate. Social norms and role expectations vary across cultures. For example, Chinese managers place a premium on relationships and loyalty, protecting the honor of all members in an organization, and solving problems privately to avoid embarrassing their workers. In addition, Chinese organizations typically feature highly centralized authority, with limited participation in decision making (Nyberg and Jensen 2009). Practicing respect in an organization in the United States might mean treating all organization members equally, whereas in China respect may mean deferring to authority within the organization. Organizations that cross cultural boundaries must accommodate to these differing cultural environments, and they must often adapt to the way power is distributed within an organization.

Power in Groups and Organizations

As we have seen, people in groups and organizations have different amounts of power, and this difference both reflects and reinforces inequality. In addition, groups can exert considerable influence over the actions of individual members, gaining obedience or compliance through various means.

In-Groups and Out-Groups

One way that groups exert control is by including or excluding members through the existence of in- and out-groups. An **in-group** is *a social group with which a person identifies and toward which he or she has positive feelings.* Members of an in-group have a collective sense of "us." An **out-group** is *a social group toward which a person has negative feelings, considering its members to be inferiors, or "them."* We feel a sense of loyalty to other members of our in-group, whether they are fellow environmentalists, soccer fans, or Methodists, and this sense of solidarity is essential to the functioning of society. But camaraderie can easily turn into a sense of superiority over those who are not part of the in-group. For example, people with high-status jobs often build social connections in wealthy neighborhoods and exclusive country clubs. Solidarity within this in-group of the wealthy may be accompanied by negative attitudes toward those less well-off ("they" don't work hard; "they" are not as smart or talented), and may lead the wealthy to exclude others from their neighborhoods and social circles. In- and out-groups cause tension, rivalry, and even overt conflict between social groups, which often struggle for power as in-groups seek to maintain their perceived superiority.

Conformity: The Asch Experiments

Sociologists have long been interested in how groups promote conformity and elicit obedience from members. Social psychologists have done important studies that reveal the formidable, and often underappreciated, power dynamics that operate within groups.

Imagine, for example, that you have signed up to take a vision test as part of an experiment. The experimenter introduces himself and explains to you and seven other participants that your task is simple. You will be shown pairs of cards, one with three vertical lines of different lengths on it and the other with a single vertical line (see Figure 7.6). You are to identify which of the three lines is the same length as the line on the comparison card and state your response out loud.

The experimenter shows the first and second pairs of cards, and each participant in turn gives the choice that is obviously correct. When your turn comes, you add your response. With the third set, though, you're surprised to hear all the respondents choose what is obviously the wrong answer. When it's your turn to respond, you wonder if they can all be so obviously wrong. Do you stick with your initial answer, or do you change it to conform to what everyone else has said?

Just such a dilemma faced subjects in the classic experiments carried out by Solomon Asch (1952, 1955). What study

FIGURE 7.6 | ASCH EXPERIMENTS

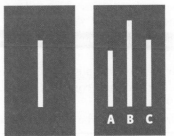

The Asch experiments suggested that group pressure can generate conformity. Experimental subjects were asked which of the three lines on the right was the same length as the comparison line on the left. When group members who had been prompted beforehand by the experimenter gave wrong answers, some subjects agreed with the obviously incorrect response.

participants didn't know was that the other "subjects" in the group were confederates (people working with the experimenter). After providing correct answers for the first two rounds, confederates provided incorrect answers for 12 of the next 18 rounds. Would the "majority effect," as Asch called it, lead the test subject to conform to the group and provide an obviously incorrect response?

Asch found that only a quarter of the respondents gave the correct answer all the time. Three-quarters agreed with at least one wrong answer, though only 5 percent agreed with every incorrect answer. On average, subjects provided an incorrect response about 37 percent of the time. (Subjects in control groups without confederates easily identified the correct answers.) Asch also found that subjects were more likely to give incorrect answers if the confederates were unanimous in their answers and that the size of the group affected the result. Having only one confederate eliminated the "majority effect," and having three or more produced the full effect.

Asch's experiments included only male college students in an artificial setting and involved only a brief, inconsequential activity. Subsequent research, however, has confirmed the findings: the actions of others often promote conformist behavior. For example, eyewitnesses in criminal cases sometimes change their account of what they saw to conform to contrary information about the crime that they receive later (Wright, Self, and Justice 2000). People seek social approval by going along with the group, and conforming is often part of a broader effort to build and maintain social connections (Cialdini and Goldstein 2004).

Some cultures are more conformist than others. People in the United States and other countries with predominantly individualistic cultures are less inclined to conform than are residents of countries whose cultures are collectivistically oriented (Bond and Smith 1996). East Asian cultures, such as in Japan and China, typically define nonconformity in negative terms, whereas Western cultures are more likely to see it in a positive light, viewing nonconformists as unique and their contributions as valuable (Kim and Markus 1999).

Social conditions can also be conducive to conformist behavior, especially in situations characterized by widespread anxiety. In particular, fear about personal safety encourages conformity (Renkema, Stapel, and Van Yperen 2008). The 9/11 attacks produced broad public anxiety in the United States. In the immediate post-9/11 period, fear bred political conformity; citizens proclaimed their national allegiance through public displays of patriotic symbols, and public approval for President George W. Bush's leadership rose sharply.

Groups vary considerably in the amount of influence they have over individual behavior. It may be that people in the United States have become more individualistic and more willing to question authority since Asch conducted his studies in the 1950s. Advertisements routinely encourage people to express themselves and stand out from the crowd. In addition, despite often-powerful group influences, individuals still have the capacity to pursue independent action, whether they are operating within an informal group or a more formal organization.

Obedience: The Milgram Experiments

In 2010, 80 contestants were recruited for the pilot of a new French reality television game show called *Zone Xtreme*. Contestants signed a contract saying they were willing to administer electrical shocks as part of the game. Each contestant was then paired with another contestant named Jean-Paul, who would be challenged with a series of questions while strapped in an electrically wired chair, which was placed in an isolation booth. If Jean-Paul answered a question incorrectly, his partner was told to push a lever to administer an electric shock. As Jean-Paul continued to answer incorrectly, the voltage increased from 20 to 460 volts—a potentially life-threatening jolt. At the lower levels, Jean-Paul was plainly startled by the mild jolts. As the shocks increased in severity, his cries of pain escalated, and he eventually pleaded, "Get me out of here, please! I don't want to play anymore!" But the game show host—a well-known French television personality—encouraged the contestants to continue administering the shocks, and the studio audience goaded them on. After a series of painful cries, Jean-Paul eventually became silent and stopped responding to the highest shock levels, presumably because he was unconscious or dead. Of the 80 contestants, 64 played the game all the way to the end, administering the highest voltages despite the pain they were clearly causing (Chazan 2010; Keaten 2010).

As you might have guessed, the "game show" was not real; it was staged as part of a documentary called *The Game of Death*. "Jean-Paul" was an actor, but the 80 contestants and the audience believed the situation was real. This demonstration was modeled loosely on experiments conducted in the United States by Stanley Milgram (a former student of Solomon Asch) in the early 1960s. Milgram's experiments took place in a research lab, where scientists in white lab coats encouraged participants to administer apparently

An overhead shot (*left*) shows the "game show" control panel used in *The Game of Death*. Contestants sat in front of the semicircular panel and were told by the celebrity host to push levers that administered increasingly powerful shocks to a contestant-partner seated in an isolation booth (*right*). Much like the Milgram experiments upon which this demonstration was modeled, most participants followed orders and administered what they believed to be painful—and potentially deadly—shocks.

CORE CONCEPTS CHALLENGE

What gave the game show host the **power** *to get contestants to continue administering the shocks, even when they clearly did not want to do so? What are some real-world situations in which similar power dynamics might operate?*

painful—and potentially lethal—electrical shocks, supposedly as part of a study on how punishment affects learning (Milgram 1963, 1965, 1969).

As Milgram's experiments—and the French game show—demonstrate, many of us are socialized to obey authority figures and to comply with social expectations, even when we know such actions are wrong. Although some people in Milgram's experiments did refuse to participate, many others set aside their better judgment and followed orders, ceding power to those in authority. Only when they saw others refusing to take part in the experiment did an overwhelming majority say no—compliance plummeted to just 5 percent when participants were teamed with someone who refused to administer the shocks.

Milgram's experiments were conducted, in part, to better understand why people would go along with atrocities such as the Holocaust, the systematic mass killing of Jews and other people by Nazi Germany during World War II. In the lab, participants often felt uncomfortable, apprehensive, and guilty about the pain they were causing, yet many voluntarily submitted to the man in the white lab coat, whose only power was the perception that he was a legitimate authority figure. A psychologist involved in the updated game show version of the Milgram experiments suggested that they reveal the "terrifying power of TV" (Chazan 2010).

Because of the potential trauma to participants, Milgram's experiments would not be allowed today. Even the French documentary was highly controversial, with some observers suggesting it manipulated people simply to produce dramatic television—even while it cautioned against the power of television.

Groupthink

Conformity can endanger designated targets of persecution; it can also endanger groups of people working together to achieve a goal. **Groupthink** is *a form of uncritical thinking in which people reinforce a consensus rather than ask serious questions or thoroughly analyze the issue at hand.* The studies that established the importance of groupthink originally focused on elite groups that operated in secrecy as they formulated U.S. foreign policy during the middle of the twentieth century (Janis 1972, 1989). Such groups sometimes produced policy disasters, including the failure to anticipate the Japanese attack on Pearl Harbor at the start of World War II, the failed Bay of Pigs invasion of Cuba in 1961, and the failure to appreciate the capabilities of the North Vietnamese forces during the Vietnam War. In all these cases, U.S. officials made false assumptions about the situation at hand that were reinforced in group discussions until they were eventually exposed as untrue.

People who engage in groupthink ignore evidence or ideas that contradict what they and fellow group members believe. The more group members are alike—the more they share key characteristics such as education, social background, and values—the more likely they are to accept common assumptions about the world rather than ask critical questions about these assumptions. The advisors who developed the Bay of Pigs invasion plan, for example, were the same experts President John F. Kennedy enlisted to assess its likely success. Staunchly opposed to Fidel Castro, Cuba's revolutionary leader, these policymakers ignored his widespread popularity among Cubans and suggested that he could be overthrown by a small army of lightly supplied Cuban exiles who, with limited air cover from the United States could invade Cuba and trigger a spontaneous uprising. The ill-prepared exiles failed quickly, and the successful Cuban defense against the U.S.-backed invasion became a rallying point for Castro supporters, reinforcing his hold on power. Groupthink likely played a role again in 2003 when U.S. leaders used military forces to invade Iraq in response to a perceived threat of weapons of mass destruction (WMDs), a threat that never existed.

Since they define situations similarly, groupthink participants are more likely to agree on a solution to a problem than to entertain other options that contradict their assumptions. Because they are homogeneous and self-reinforcing, such groups also tend to be shut off from dissenting views and the outside world, making them even more dysfunctional.

Groups that are prone to groupthink minimize internal conflict by encouraging all members to be team players. Group members may conform to steer clear of conflict or avoid appearing foolish, or simply because conforming is easier than challenging the group's assumptions. The result of this conformity, however, can be hasty or irrational decisions.

Leadership, Oligarchy, and Power

As we saw in Chapter 5, power shapes how we allocate resources, make rules and decisions, and define reality. In most organizations, especially workplaces, people struggle constantly over power (Edwards 1982). One important characteristic of any organization, therefore, is its power structure.

In formal bureaucracies, people at each level of the organizational structure have power over those below and are subject to the authority of those above. As bureaucratic organizations expanded in the early twentieth century, sociologists raised questions about their potentially undemocratic impact. German sociologist Robert Michels (1876–1936), a student of Max Weber, coined the term **iron law of oligarchy** to describe what he saw as *the eventual and inevitable consolidation of power at the top of bureaucratic organizations.* (*Oligarchy* is rule by a powerful few.)

Michels argued that bureaucracies place too much power in the hands of those at the top. Inevitably, these select few misuse their power, which they consolidate through their unique access to information and resources. Once firmly entrenched in power, leaders are cut off from meaningful contact with others in the organization or the general public, rendering them unaccountable for their actions. Meanwhile, those lower down the bureaucratic hierarchy usually feel powerless to challenge the oligarchic leaders, though they may disapprove of them; as a result, they tend to be passive.

Despite Michels's fatalistic assessment, bureaucratic inequality can be contested through covert political conflict within organizations, including subtle forms of noncooperation and even sabotage (Morrill, Zald, and Rao 2003). For example, employees sometimes "work to rule," completing only the minimum work required by company regulations, as a way of exercising power from below, a strategy that can dramatically undermine an organization. Sometimes subordinates react so slowly that they effectively prevent the implementation of policies they oppose. The inequality that is typical of hierarchical organizations can also lead workers to engage in overt efforts to change the balance of power—for example, by forming a labor union to protect their interests.

Although most traditional bureaucratic organizations do not operate on democratic principles, some bureaucratic organizations allocate positions in the hierarchy through democratic processes. Civic groups, for example, often elect officials. However, power is still likely to be distributed unequally, since election results place power in the hands of a few members—at least until the next election. More radical ways of distributing power within an organization involve consensus building and collective governance, which can dramatically reduce inequality (Schneiberg, King, and Smith 2008). Collective communities (sometimes referred to as communes), in which all members have an equal voice and all decisions are made through deliberative collective discussion, are a familiar example of such organizations. Worker-owned businesses are another example.

thinking about power

In bureaucratic organizations, power is concentrated in the upper ranks of an organization. In what ways can the "rank and file" members of an organization exert power? What hurdles do they face in doing so?

Scientific Management and Workplace Control

As we have seen, industrialization led to the first large corporations with bureaucratic organizations in the late nineteenth and early twentieth centuries. There was no illusion of democracy in these bureaucratic workplaces. Owners wanted to control the workplace and limit workers' power to demand better wages or working conditions. A number of industries relied on skilled craft workers, however, many of whom were organized into trade unions. Their knowledge was central to successful production, and therefore they wielded considerable influence over the organization of the workplace and the conditions of their labor.

To consolidate power in the workplace, owners needed to transfer knowledge about the production process from these skilled workers to a small group of managers, while reducing complex jobs to simple tasks that could be done by easily replaceable unskilled and lower paid workers. For employers, such top-down planning and control of production had the added benefit of being extremely efficient, increasing profits (Braverman 1998).

The process of deskilling ordinary workers and increasing workplace efficiency through calculated study became known as **scientific management.** Frederick Taylor (1911) was the leading proponent of scientific management, and the approach is often referred to as Taylorism. Managers would carefully observe workers doing their jobs, noting all the individual steps and measuring the time each step took. Analysts would then examine the collected information to find ways of doing the work more quickly and efficiently. By breaking down complex and highly skilled work into simple components, managers could assign each element of the task to a different worker, who would need to know only one simple step.

The classic application of Taylorism was the assembly line. Although famous for its use in the auto industry, assembly line work was first used in Chicago's meatpacking industry. Skilled employees once worked on an entire animal carcass, chopping and slicing the meat into the various cuts. With the application of Taylor's principles, the work was broken down into individual steps, each of which was performed by a separate worker, who could be hired at a lower wage and quickly trained for the monotonous and repetitive job.

Scientific management is not limited to the industrial context within which it was first applied. Today's high-tech workplaces often incorporate many of the Taylorist principles developed a century ago. Management control of the work process is almost universal in today's workplaces. Telemarketers at a call center, for example, typically use a prepared script and follow routine procedures when making phone calls. Managers monitor productivity by using software that records keystrokes on workers' computer keyboards and by occasionally listening in on calls—tactics that recall an earlier era of Taylorism.

Scientific management has its limits today, however. Professional jobs tend to be knowledge based, and workers need

Early assembly lines, like this one from a nineteenth-century meatpacking plant, broke down work into small tasks, such as splitting the backbone. An individual worker would complete his or her assigned task over and over. Each pig or cow, for example, would be worked on by as many as 300 different workers who each had a specific task to perform in transforming the animal carcass into steak or sausage.

to use creativity, collaborate, and respond to rapidly changing markets. The result is a two-tier system of employment, reflecting the class system, in which knowledge workers enjoy considerable autonomy and flexibility, along with high pay, while most other workers are monitored closely, performing routine, repetitive tasks and receiving low pay. We examine the nature of work and the workplace more closely in Chapter 13.

A Changing World

SOCIAL STRUCTURE AND PRIVACY

The nature of our social structure affects our expectations of privacy. Google failed to understand this sociological insight in 2010 when it launched Buzz, a new service that combined Facebook-like social networking with Twitter-like microblogging. When Buzz was rolled out to users of Gmail (Google's popular e-mail service), it automatically set up users with "followers" and people to "follow," based on whom the user had most frequently e-mailed or chatted with. Problematically, the default setting made these contacts public, enabling anyone to see the individuals with whom a user had been communicating (Carlson 2010; Helft 2010).

Tech reporters called it a "privacy nightmare" (Wood 2010), and users were outraged. The potential consequences were staggering. People cheating on their spouses and romantic partners could be exposed; patients' connections to psychiatrists, abortion clinics, or other personal medical contacts could be revealed. A boss could see that an employee looking for a new job had been contacting a rival company. One woman actually found that her abusive ex-husband was now "following" her on Buzz (Saint 2010). As the uproar grew, Google quickly backed down, changing the default settings and making it easier for users to limit who was in their public networks. But Buzz never fully recovered from the bad publicity, and the short-lived service was replaced by Google+, which allows users to create separate "circles" of contacts and more easily to control who sees them. Google also paid $8.5 million to settle a class action lawsuit for invasion of privacy, but the Buzz incident reflected the tone-deaf attitude of CEO Eric Schmidt, who once said, "If you have something that you don't want anyone to know, maybe you shouldn't be doing it in the first place" (Bartiromo 2009).

What Schmidt and Google apparently failed to understand is that despite the rumored "death of privacy" in the Internet age, most of us still live segmented lives that shield certain aspects of our lives from the gaze of others. This fact reflects how our lives are structured by different networks and groups in the contemporary world. In traditional villages and small towns, privacy was very limited. Residents knew almost everything there was to know about one another because they tended to dwell in the same community for a lifetime, lived in close proximity to neighbors, interacted daily with a small group of contacts, and were rooted in stable kinship groups that spanned generations.

Modern life changed all that as people moved away from extended family to cities, created a variety of distinct social networks, and experienced considerable anonymity and privacy in crowded urban settings. Today's fast-paced and ever-changing social life continues this trend. People often live their lives in a somewhat segmented fashion, separating work, family, friends, and community life. They have come to expect a certain level of privacy by maintaining these separate social networks and group memberships.

Google's Buzz disaster, though, is just one example of how companies using new digital technologies are challenging long-standing social norms about privacy. In responding to privacy problems at Facebook just a month before the Buzz incident, CEO Mark Zuckerberg argued that privacy is outdated as social norms have evolved. "People have really gotten comfortable not only sharing more information and different kinds, but more openly and with more people," he said (Bobbie Johnson 2010).

That is probably true, but the public blowback about Buzz suggests that privacy is not quite dead yet. Despite Eric Schmidt's implications, we don't have to be engaged in illegal or immoral conduct to want to keep some parts of our lives from being scrutinized by others.

thinking **sociologically** about
Interaction, Groups, and Organizations

culture

- We are socialized in a particular culture, and we learn to see our world from that culture's perspective. That socially constructed viewpoint becomes reality for us.

- Cultures inform the nature of social roles and the expectations associated with them.

- Organizations often have distinct cultures that influence how they are structured, the values they espouse, and the way they operate.

structure

- Statuses and roles provide some of the glue that connects individuals to one another and to the behavioral patterns that constitute social structure.

- People create groups and organizations, which in turn become more formal social structures.

- After creating these social structures, people treat those socially constructed entities as objectively real, and structures in turn are influenced by the society they create.

power

- People with different statuses often receive differing levels of honor, prestige, power, and income, resulting in inequality.

- Even in small, informal groups, individuals tend to conform to the views of the majority and to obey authority figures.

- In bureaucracies, power is organized hierarchically. People at each level in a hierarchy have power over those below and are subject to the authority of those above. Positions in bureaucracies are starkly unequal.

Looking Back

1. Face-to-face encounters, influenced by cultural norms, are the building blocks of social life. Through our social interactions we come to mutual understandings about reality. How we define reality can have real consequences.

2. People are involved collectively in the social construction of reality. Humans create society, treat it as an objective reality, and then are influenced by the social forces they have created.

3. A particularly important element in social life is social status, the position an individual occupies in the social system; social roles are the cultural expectations associated with a status. Statuses and roles link individuals to larger groups and institutions, helping create social structure.

4. In sociology, dramaturgy uses the metaphor of a theatrical performance to analyze roles and social interaction.

5. Society consists of links, groupings, and organizations. These include social networks that are formed out of our social ties as well as small-scale primary groups and large formal organizations.

6. The dynamics of groups, large and small, can be analyzed sociologically. For example, in small groups, conformity is an important social dynamic. People who engage in groupthink ignore evidence or ideas that contradict group beliefs.

7. Large organizations rely on bureaucratic structure to operate efficiently, but as the layers of bureaucracy multiply, they make organizations unwieldy and inefficient. The iron law of oligarchy holds that bureaucracies concentrate power in the hands of those at the top.

8. Contemporary developments, especially in technology, have affected how we interact with one another and have led to new types of social networks and to innovative forms of organizational structure.

Critical Thinking: Questions and Activities

1. Write a brief, realistic telephone exchange between two college-age friends. Now rewrite that same exchange, making explicit all the taken-for-granted information that the two speakers share. What type of information was left out of the original version?

2. List all the statuses you currently occupy. Write a brief description of the role expectations associated with three of your statuses. How did you learn about these role expectations? What consequences, if any, are there for deviating from these expectations?

3. Using elements of dramaturgical theory, describe an example of role playing from your own life. Were you successful in your performance? Why or why not?

4. Draw a diagram of the structure of a bureaucratic organization with which you are familiar—for example, a school, workplace, or community group—mapping the lines of authority. Can you explain the logic of the specific organizational structure? Does the organization operate effectively and efficiently? Can you imagine an alternative organizational structure?

5. How has the Internet influenced your social networks? Do you think communication via the Internet is replacing other forms of communication? Why or why not?

Key Terms

achieved status (p. 168) a social position that we voluntarily attain, to a considerable degree, as the result of our own efforts.

ascribed status (p. 168) a social position that is assigned to us from birth or that we assume later in life, regardless of our wishes or abilities.

bureaucracy (p. 178) a hierarchical administrative system with formal rules and procedures used to manage organizations.

dramaturgy (p. 170) an approach to the study of social interaction that uses the metaphor of social life as a theater.

groupthink (p. 183) a form of uncritical thinking in which people reinforce a consensus rather than ask serious questions or thoroughly analyze the issue at hand.

homophily (p. 173) social contact occurs at a higher rate among those who are similar than it does among those who are different.

in-group (p. 181) a social group with which a person identifies and toward which he or she feels positively; members have a collective sense of "us."

intersubjectivity (p. 163) a common understanding between people about knowledge, reality, or an experience.

iron law of oligarchy (p. 184) the eventual and inevitable consolidation of power at the top of bureaucratic organizations.

master status (p. 159) a social position that is overwhelmingly significant, powerfully influences a person's social experience, and typically overshadows all the other social positions that person may occupy.

organizational environment (p. 179) factors that exist outside the organization but that potentially affect its operation.

organizations (p. 177) secondary groups that have a degree of formal structure and are formed to accomplish particular tasks.

out-group (p. 181) a social group toward which a person feels negatively, considering its members to be inferiors, or "them."

primary groups (p. 176) people who have regular contact, enduring relationships, and a significant emotional attachment to each other.

reference groups (p. 176) the groups against which we choose to measure ourselves.

role conflict (p. 170) the problem that occurs when the expectations associated with different roles clash.

role strain (p. 170) the problem that occurs when the expectations associated with a single role compete with each other.

roles (p. 169) the sets of expected behaviors that are associated with particular statuses.

scientific management (p. 185) the process of deskilling ordinary workers and increasing workplace efficiency through calculated study.

secondary groups (p. 176) people who interact in a relatively impersonal way, usually to carry out some specific task.

social groups (p. 175) collections of people who interact regularly with one another and who are aware of their status as a group.

social networks (p. 172) the collection of social ties that connect individuals to each other.

status (p. 168) a position in a social system that can be occupied by an individual.

status category (p. 168) a status that people can hold in common.

status hierarchy (p. 169) a ranking of social positions according to their perceived prestige or honor.

status set (p. 168) the collection of statuses that an individual holds.

stereotypes (p. 165) exaggerated, distorted, or untrue generalizations about categories of people that do not acknowledge individual variation.

Thomas theorem (p. 165) the idea that if people define situations as real, they are real in their consequences.

8

Deviance and Social Control

looking AHEAD

How does deviance reinforce the **structure** of your community or college?

How can we use our bodies to express deviance, in defiance of **cultural** norms?

How do your family, your teachers, and other agents of social control use **power** to promote conformity?

Josh Corlew, a 20-something manager at a Nashville nonprofit, does not spend money on food, nor did he pay for any of the furniture in his apartment. Instead, Corlew acquires his food and other household necessities from what others throw away. He is part of a movement of Freegans or Freecyclers who try to minimize, or sometimes completely reject, the routine buying of goods and services that underpins consumer society.

Instead of buying things, Freegans seek to "reclaim" other people's waste in a process they call "urban foraging": finding clothing, household goods, books and games, artwork—just about anything you can imagine—in the trash. That also means dumpster diving outside restaurants, supermarkets, and other food stores that routinely discard fresh fruits and vegetables that may be bruised or a bit overripe, day-old bread, canned goods that have expired recently, and prepared food, including sandwiches, salads, and even sushi (Conlin 2008; Kurutz 2007; Persson 2011).

Whereas millions of poor people around the world scavenge to survive, urban foraging is not common in affluent societies like that of the United States, and Freegans do it as a matter of choice, not necessity. Most people probably react negatively to the idea of eating trash, and in many places, dumpster diving is illegal. Freegans like Corlew, however, are not desperate, and they pay careful attention to food safety. They are also aware that the way they live is nonconformist. They believe, however, that by living as much as possible a life based on reusing, recycling, and reclaiming, they can drastically reduce their impact on the environment and oppose what they see as the wasteful "throwaway" mentality of a deeply entrenched consumer society.

By refusing to conform to the cultural norms that distinguish between trash and "acceptable" items, Freegans have crossed a line from normal to deviant behavior, and they risk becoming the target of criticism, even moral condemnation. Some will want to reform them, others will question their motives—are they sick, crazy, foolish, immoral, or just plain lazy?—and still others will have the power to punish them. By foraging for their food in this way, however, Freegans hope to call attention to the environmental challenge they believe consumer society poses and to encourage social change.

What is normal behavior, and how do we recognize it? Is normal what's most common? What's most desirable? What's healthiest? Who or what has the power to enforce normal behavior? We rarely think about these questions as we go about our daily lives. When you buy food in a supermarket or order a pizza in a restaurant, you're unlikely to think, "I'm behaving normally now." We have been socialized so effectively to accept our culture's norms that we rarely recognize them.

We begin to think about these questions, however, when we confront behaviors or beliefs that challenge, or deviate, from our expectations—when we react with disgust, for example, to the idea of eating a pizza pulled out of a garbage bin. In other words, nonconformity helps us clarify the boundary between normal and abnormal.

As we've seen in previous chapters, people develop their sense of self and identity through social interaction. Interactions in small groups form the basis for social structure, and social structure provides people with norms and expectations about appropriate behavior. But how do norms get established in the first place? Why do some people violate those norms? And how is this kind of norm-violating behavior related to the nonconformist's sense of self?

This chapter focuses on **deviance,** *behavior that does not conform to basic cultural norms and expectations,* and its relationship to these questions of self and identity. As we will see, the lines between normal and abnormal, moral and immoral, appropriate and inappropriate, healthy and sick, and sane and crazy are flexible, even if most people within a society share an understanding of the distinction between normal and deviant. We also explore the consequences of violating norms, from subtle forms of social isolation to imprisonment or even execution. And we examine the various agents that encourage conformity.

Defining Deviance

Boundaries between normal and deviant are rarely clear-cut because people often disagree about where the line should be drawn. Ultimately what is defined as deviant depends on the particular social context in which the behavior occurs or a person lives and on the power of those who label it. For those defined as deviant, the negative effects can be long lasting, even devastating.

Deviance and Social Context

As Emile Durkheim established more than 100 years ago, a sociological perspective on deviance requires looking beyond particular behaviors to the connections between those behaviors and social norms. Durkheim argued that crime (and deviant behavior, more generally) could be defined only in relation to the social norms a criminal act violates. As Durkheim explained, we often misunderstand the relationship between crime and social norms. We are not offended by an action because it is a crime; rather, we define an act as criminal because it offends basic social norms. These basic norms contribute to what Durkheim called the **collective conscience,** *the shared norms, beliefs, and values in a community* (Durkheim [1893] 1997).

What is considered normal or deviant varies over time and across cultures, and definitions of normal often shift in response to social change. When we talk about deviance, then, we must bear in mind the social context in which it occurs, and we should remember that different communities may have different responses to the same behavior. For example, when women in the United States demanded the right to vote in the late nineteenth and early twentieth centuries, they were widely considered deviant, but these suffragists mobilized to gain power and change that label. Some people at the time no doubt continued to consider politics an inappropriate activity for women, but they no longer had the power to enforce such a judgment. Over time, our society's view of women as political actors changed. In some cultures today, however, women are still forbidden or highly discouraged from participating in politics—their participation is still considered deviant.

Midday naps are another example of varying definitions of deviance. An employee in the United States who went home for a rest at lunchtime would likely be branded as lazy or a slacker. However, in some places outside the United States, taking an extended midday break is standard procedure. In Spain, for example, shops and offices typically close for an hour or two after lunch to allow employees to go home for *siesta*—a short rest or cat nap—before returning to work in the midafternoon. In contrast to the U.S. standard of 9:00 a.m. to 5:00 p.m., the traditional workday in Spain includes a midday siesta and lasts until 8:00 p.m.

In recent years, the Spanish government has taken steps to abandon siesta. In 2006 it enacted regulations that require all federal agencies to limit the lunch break to 45 minutes and send employees home by 6:00 p.m. The long-standing tradition of siesta is not likely to disappear entirely, but pressure to conform to the workplace norms of the European Union is affecting work schedules in Spain.

Labeling Theory: Defining Deviant Behavior

Some acts of deviance generate widespread, perhaps even universal, condemnation. Almost every society considers child molestation and unprovoked murder as deviant behavior. With other acts, however, the boundary between normal and deviant often depends on the specific social context (Downes and Rock 2011). Is it deviant for men to pierce their ears or for women to shave their heads? What about wearing a baseball cap in a restaurant or taking a break from work for afternoon prayers? How about killing animals for sport? Having a sex-change operation? Or torturing suspected terrorists for information?

FAST-FORWARD

Change and Beach Attire

Norms about what to wear to the beach have changed dramatically over the past 100 years. Women's bathing suits introduced in the late nineteenth century (*top*) were an innovation—and some would have considered them deviant—since they revealed more of a woman's body than had been shown previously. Men's swimsuits from the same period covered most of the body. The swimwear that we now define as normal (*bottom*) would have been viewed as shockingly deviant in an earlier era. How would you explain this change in the definition of deviant behavior?

You may have a strong opinion about each of these examples, but your individual response is not what marks an action as deviant. A behavior is defined as deviant when it is marked publicly as deviant by those with enough power to enforce that designation. This is the core insight of **labeling theory,** which *argues that deviance is the result of how others interpret a behavior and that individuals who are labeled deviant often internalize this judgment as part of their self-identity.*

Sociologist Kai Erickson (1966) explains: "Deviance is not a property *inherent* in any particular kind of behavior; it is a property *conferred* upon that behavior by the people who come into direct or indirect contact with it," because they consider the behavior so dangerous or embarrassing that it requires special sanctions (p. 6). Labeling theory highlights the interactive aspects of deviance—the interplay between behavior and the response to that behavior (Becker 1973). From this perspective, behavior is deviant only when it is labeled as such.

on social theory

Labeling theory, associated with the **symbolic interactionist approach,** emphasizes the power of groups within society to designate a given behavior as deviant. Can you think of an example of behavior that is labeled deviant in U.S. society and normal in another society?

The Effects of Deviant Labels

People who are labeled deviant are likely to face negative consequences and limited options in life. Indeed, those labeled criminal or otherwise dangerous may be locked up. But labeling may have other, less dramatic consequences. For example, people who are labeled mentally ill often have a difficult time finding employment because their deviant identity becomes a kind of *master status* that overshadows all other components of their identity. In this case, education, skills, and diligence all give way to a person's status as mentally ill so that potential employers or neighbors may perceive *only* the mental illness.

More generally, those who are labeled deviant must deal with the stigma or shame associated with their deviant label. **Stigma** refers to *the shame attached to a behavior or status that is considered socially unacceptable or discrediting.* Stigma can be a source of inequality because those who are stigmatized often experience isolation or discrimination that can reduce their social, economic, or political standing (see Figure 8.1).

The threat of stigmatization can be a powerful form of social control (Goffman 1963). For example, people who live on the street, regardless of the reasons, face tremendous uncertainty about food, health, and safety. But it is the stigma of their status as homeless that has perhaps the most profound social consequences. It may prevent them from making the kinds of social connections—getting a job interview, securing a loan, finding a friend to lend a hand—that can help homeless individuals cross back into a "normal" life.

Labeling people as deviant may lead them into **secondary deviance,** *deviant behavior that is a response to the negative consequences of labeling* (Lemert 1951). In other words, labeling creates a kind of self-fulfilling prophecy. A child who is labeled as a troublemaker and treated as such by adults may adopt the role of troublemaker, become hostile

FIGURE 8.1 | COMPONENTS OF STIGMA

| Human differences are distinguished and labeled. | Labeled persons are connected to undesirable characteristics via dominant cultural beliefs. | Labeled persons are categorized, accomplishing a separation between "us" and "them." | Labeled persons experience discrimination and suffer status loss. | Stigma occurs when labeling, separation, and discrimination are linked to inequality in social, economic, or political power. |

Source: Link and Phelan (2001).

to authorities, and join with other so-called misfits in new forms of deviance. When parents label their children as rule violators, that label affects the children's own self-appraisals and identity, leading to increased deviance (Matsueda 1992).

Using the National Longitudinal Survey of Youth, Davies and Tanner (2003) found that young people who had been labeled disciplinary problems at school or who had come into contact with the criminal justice system as teenagers and young adults had significantly reduced employment prospects and income potential later in life. The effect was especially significant among women. Even girls who had returned to school or completed high school after being suspended or expelled had problems finding jobs later in life. The stigma of their deviant status, it seems, stuck with them, leading employers to steer clear of them.

Labeling marks social boundaries between the normal and the deviant, between a socially defined "us" and "them." For those labeled deviant, the consequences may be diminished life chances, economic inequality, further deviance, and long-lasting stigma.

The Role of Deviance within Social Structures

In his treatise titled *The Rules of Sociological Method*, Emile Durkheim ([1895] 1982) pointed out that deviant behavior is a feature of all human societies. But Durkheim went further, arguing that deviance can be functional, playing a positive social role and reinforcing social structures. It does this in three specific ways:

- Deviance helps define group boundaries.
- Deviance helps create social solidarity.
- Deviance is a source of innovation.

Let's look in more detail at these three functions of deviance.

Defining Group Boundaries

Deviant behavior helps clarify the boundaries of acceptable behavior within a given society. Especially because the line dividing deviant from nondeviant behavior is often subtle and hard to define, deviant behavior constantly reminds us of how to live within the boundaries of "normal"—and shows us the consequences of stepping outside those boundaries. In formal organizations, written rules and policies clearly define what behavior is and isn't tolerated. These rules reflect the identity and values of the organization. For example, cheating and plagiarism strike at the heart of academic integrity. As a result, colleges and universities have a formal system for punishing violators; suspension or even expulsion are common penalties. But not all rule violations are defined as serious enough to warrant suspension or expulsion. Although smoking indoors, for example, may violate a college's official rules, it is sometimes tolerated grudgingly.

Much of social life, however, is not governed by formal rules and policies. We don't get a handbook that tells us all the rules of our neighborhood, but that doesn't mean the rules don't exist. The boundaries between normal and deviant, acceptable and unacceptable, often remain implicit.

How do you decide who is inside or outside your closest group of friends? Presumably you don't have written rules about who can and cannot belong to this group. However,

How do you respond when people ignore no smoking signs? Your response is likely to depend on the situation. How we respond to rule violations—whether we define them as minor transgressions or serious offenses—is a result, in part, of the specific social context.

behavior, provides a powerful source of social connection among conformists.

A classic sociological illustration of this point is Kai Erickson's (1966) study of deviance within the seventeenth century Massachusetts Bay Colony. Erickson explains how the hysteria about witchcraft in Salem resulted from change within the Puritan community. In 1672 in Salem accusations of witchcraft were not taken seriously, and those who confessed to dealing with the devil were dismissed as liars. But just 20 years later the Puritans sensed that religious zeal was waning and members were turning against one another, an unsettling change for this deeply religious and insular community. In response to this threat, the community turned on presumed witches as a common enemy to all. For a brief period, lasting less than a year, the Salem Puritans united to root out the "witches," and 19 women and men were hanged. This case shows how a focus on deviance can bring together a community—and how collective hysteria about deviance can direct public vengeance at those labeled as deviant.

Even in complex, modern societies, deviance can help unite people. In the wake of the terrorist attacks of September 11, 2001, the mourning and fear helped, at least temporarily, to strengthen a sense of national unity in the United States. The shared sense of victimization, along with fear of additional attacks, produced a heightened sense that people in the United States, despite their differences, stood together. "United We Stand" bumper stickers and other public displays of patriotism were common sights at the time.

The way people respond to deviance can produce group solidarity. By highlighting group boundaries and giving sometimes diverse citizens an opportunity to express their shared distaste for behavior defined as immoral, criminal, or pathological, deviance brings people together.

your network of friends almost certainly has basic values and norms that are enforced implicitly—and perhaps explicitly. Deciding whether someone fits in or does not belong, is accepted or rejected—these are the informal means groups use to maintain internal cohesion and label certain behaviors and attitudes as deviant.

More generally, think about how individuals in the various groups to which you belong respond to specific kinds of people—for example, atheists, gun enthusiasts, gays and lesbians, vegetarians, evangelicals, or teenage parents—and you'll begin to see the ways that community definitions of normal and deviant help establish, and sometimes change, social boundaries.

Creating Social Solidarity

In addition to defining boundaries, deviance helps build group solidarity by uniting people in opposition to, or disapproval of, a shared enemy. Deviant behavior reinforces conformity within a social structure; it also strengthens the bonds among those who feel outrage at displays of deviance. The threat of nonconformity, especially when people mobilize actively to stamp out nonconformist

Providing a Source of Innovation

Durkheim also argued that deviance provides a source of creativity and innovation in social life. In fact, Durkheim believed that healthy societies *need* deviance, since societies that

After the September 11, 2001, terrorist attacks, Americans expressed their sense of national solidarity through patriotic displays. Sales of American flags skyrocketed, and "United We Stand" bumper stickers appeared on cars and trucks throughout the United States. Violent acts that caused enormous pain and suffering—in this case, acts that violated the norms of the international community and, in the perpetrators' targeting of civilians, even the norms of war—can produce a sense of social solidarity and national pride.

are totally conformist are repressive and limit human possibility. Deviant people push boundaries and, as a result, can facilitate growth and change in social structures.

Many ideas and behaviors that we take for granted today were once considered deviant. Democracy is an example. Historically, democracy is a relatively new idea, having been implemented widely only within the past 200 years. Early advocates of democracy were generally considered to be radicals and irresponsible idealists.

on social theory

The **functionalist approach** emphasizes consensus in social life and looks at the ways in which deviant behavior may benefit society. How might adherents of this approach view people or behaviors that many people currently consider deviant, such as the freegans described at the beginning of this chapter?

Other "deviant" ideas have also proven to be powerful innovations. As recently as the early 1970s, women in the United States who put their children in full-time day care risked being labeled as neglectful mothers. Now, however, this practice is common and widely accepted and, further, it is thought to provide children with an important educational and social experience. Many once-deviant notions have injected vibrant innovations into our culture and society. Public education, religious freedom, racial equality, and even rock and roll and hip-hop were all considered deviant at one time.

Explaining Deviance

Deviance is a product of the social relationship between those who affirm the boundaries of "normal" and those who cross such boundaries. What makes some people cross those lines? How can we explain deviant behavior, and what do these explanations suggest about the proper way of controlling or preventing deviance? Not surprisingly, given the wide range of deviant behaviors, sociologists and others have proposed a variety of answers to these questions (Pfohl 2009).

Some explanations focus on *individual* sources of deviance, emphasizing the flaws or weaknesses of people who are considered deviant. Such explanations, which circulate in popular discourse but are generally rejected by sociologists, describe deviance in terms of immorality or as a symptom of an illness. A more sociological set of explanations emphasizes the *social* dynamics surrounding deviance, explaining it as a rational choice, the result of inadequate or improper socialization, or the product of mismatch between social norms and economic opportunities.

Deviance as Immorality

One way to explain deviance is as the consequence of *individual immorality.* The boundary between normal and deviant, from this perspective, is roughly the same as the line between good and evil. Some fundamentalist religions tend to see the world

in these terms. More broadly, when people cannot understand or explain particularly horrendous deviant behavior—for example, the Holocaust during World War II, the genocide in Rwanda in the 1990s, or the actions of a ruthless serial killer—they sometimes simply label it as evil.

Although this approach may resonate emotionally, it does not help us uncover the actual nature of deviance. From a sociological standpoint, then, to explain deviance as the consequence of immorality does little to help us identify the social conditions that produce it or understand the ways people respond to it.

Deviance as Illness: Medicalization

A second approach based on individual behavior finds the sources of deviance in *pathology,* or *illness.* From this perspective, individuals who engage in deviant behavior are sick, suffering from a psychological or biological disorder. Here the boundary between normal and deviant coincides with the line between healthy and sick, sane and crazy. The roots of deviance as individual sickness are clearest in cases of mental illness, such as schizophrenia. But doctors now recognize an expanding list of deviant behaviors that result at least partially from underlying biological disorders and that they think will benefit from appropriate medical intervention. This process—*the designation of a deviant behavior as an illness that can be treated by medical professionals*—is what sociologists refer to as the **medicalization of deviance** (Conrad 2007; Conrad and Schneider 1980).

In some cases, specific deviant behaviors formerly identified as immoral have become reclassified as medical problems. A classic example is alcoholism (Gusfield 1996; Schneider 1978). In the early twentieth century, excessive drinking was considered a moral failure. Since the 1960s and 1970s, the public understanding of alcoholism shifted, and people began to focus on disease as its underlying cause. Recent research suggests that alcoholism has a genetic component. As alcoholism was medicalized, the solution to alcoholism also shifted from moral rehabilitation to medical treatments and psychological therapies that might control the symptoms of the disease.

Treating a deviant behavior as a disorder can alter the stigma associated with it. People who drink too much, are addicted to gambling, or suffer from extreme anxiety may be considered deviant, but designating their behavior as a medical condition insulates them from some of the hostility that deviant groups have traditionally experienced. People with a medicalized deviance are more likely to be pitied than scorned. On the other hand, if the deviance is identified as the result of an inherited disease, it may still attract a lifelong stigma (see the Through a Sociological Lens box).

Sociologists have identified the growing power of the medical profession as a primary reason for the medicalization of deviance. As the authority of doctors, especially psychiatrists and pediatricians, expands, an ever-greater realm of social life is defined in medical terms. Just think about the range of issues for which we now seek medical advice and treatment: how to

When Deviance Is Inherited: Genetic Explanations and Stigma

Journalist Clea Simon knows all too well how severe mental illness can shatter a family. Her memoir *Mad House* describes her experiences growing up with both a brother and a sister who suffered the pain and turmoil of schizophrenia (Simon 1998). Her brother Daniel, a Harvard undergraduate, ultimately committed suicide. Her sister Katherine refused help from her family, bouncing from one institution to another. Simon struggled with the knowledge that her children would "have an increased risk of developing the illness that destroyed my siblings' lives" (Simon 1997, C1).

As a result of the medicalization of deviance, researchers have increasingly focused on the genetic basis of deviant behavior. When the underlying cause of deviance is not an acquired illness but an inherited disease such as schizophrenia, is the stigma associated with deviant behavior reduced?

Sociologist Jo Phelan (2005) studied the impact of genetic explanations on the stigma associated with mental illness. Phelan focused on the degree of "social distance" caused by stigma. For example, when Phelan compared how people respond to mental illness with how they respond to physical injuries, her results indicated that they are less willing to become friends or coworkers with those who are mentally ill, and they are far more negative about the prospect of having their own child date, marry, or have a child with a person who is mentally ill. Do genetic explanations reduce the stigma that produces this desire for social distance from people with mental illness?

Phelan found that genetic explanations do not make people more sympathetic to those with mental illness. Instead, genetic

Mental illness can carry a social stigma, regardless of what people believe about its origins.

explanations tend to increase their belief in the seriousness and persistence of mental illness without decreasing the stigma or social distance experienced by individuals with the disorder. However, people are less inclined to punish individuals with mental illness when they are believed to have inherited their illness.

Genetic explanations of mental illness appear to taint the siblings and children of people with mental illness, such as Clea Simon, even as they help absolve parents of blame for their children's behavior. After all, if the roots of mental illness are genetic, parents cannot be blamed for bad parenting. But when mental illness is attributed to genetics, siblings and children of those with the illness, despite never showing signs of mental illness, may face unanticipated social isolation. They may feel reluctant to discuss their relative's condition or face social pressure to avoid having children.

In this era of genetic research, as scientists confirm that some forms of mental illness are inherited, the suspicion that children or siblings of those who are mentally ill will turn out to have the same condition has produced a new form of stigma.

think about it

1. *Do you think the siblings of people with alcoholism or cancer patients are subject to the same kind of stigma as are the siblings of those with mental illness? Why or why not?*

2. *In what ways might future genetic research remove the stigma associated with inherited illness?*

---

deal with hyperactive children, how to handle profound stress, and how to deal with trauma, to name just a few examples. The power of doctors to define issues in medical terms is only part of the picture. The pharmaceutical industry has also become a powerful engine of medicalization. Since 1997, when the U.S. Food and Drug Administration began permitting direct-to-consumer broadcast advertising of pharmaceutical products, drug companies have aggressively sought to medically define problems for which they have already developed new drug therapies. Viagra is a classic case. By actively promoting a sexual problem as a medical issue—erectile dysfunction—and identifying Viagra as the solution, pharmaceutical companies

built remarkable public demand for Viagra and other drugs (Conrad 2005b).

There are five key stages in the medicalization of deviance (Conrad and Schneider 1980):

- **Stage one.** A behavior or activity is defined as deviant.

- **Stage two.** Medical conception of this deviant behavior is "discovered."

- **Stage three.** Organized interests—medical researchers, physicians, health care organizations, pharmaceutical companies—advance claims for a medical designation for the deviant behavior.

In 2009 the FDA approved a new drug for the treatment of hypotrichosis, the medical term for a condition marked by inadequate eyelashes.

- **Stage four.** Those who advance medical claims appeal to government officials to legitimize the medical definition of deviance.
- **Stage five.** Medical definition of deviance is institutionalized, becoming an accepted part of the medical and legal classification system.

Medicalization can sometimes be successfully blocked or reversed, a process sociologists refer to as *demedicalization.* The most prominent example is homosexuality. In the late 1960s, gay and lesbian activists, newly visible with the emergence of the gay rights movement, pressured the American Psychiatric Association to change its classification of homosexuality as a "sexual deviation" in the 1968 edition of the *Diagnostic and Statistical Manual of Mental Disorders* (DSM-II). They argued that the classification was demeaning to gay men and women and had no scientific basis. In 1974 the American Psychiatric Association removed the "illness" label from homosexuality, classifying it as a disorder only for those who are unhappy about their sexuality.

Deviance as Rational Choice

Other explanations for deviance move beyond the individual level to include social factors. According to one such approach, deviance results from rational decision making; people are inclined to behave in deviant ways when deviance has significant rewards and limited costs. In many parts of the country, for example, you can drive well above the speed limit with little risk of being stopped by the police. Although individuals make strategic calculations about how to behave, the structure of incentives and penalties for deviance underlies their calculations. (Seeing more police officers stationed along your route would reduce the likelihood of your speeding.) When deviance does little harm, it may not be worth controlling. But when deviance is destructive, one way to control it is by increasing the penalties. This basic analysis underlies much of the "get tough on crime" rhetoric common in American politics.

Deviance and Socialization: Differential Association Theory

Two other social approaches explain deviance by focusing on socialization. One of these focuses on *inadequate* socialization. From this perspective, people engaged in deviant behavior have failed to internalize social norms and so are not regulated adequately by the moral framework of society. The root cause of this deviance is the inability of basic socializing agents, including family and schools, to transmit core values. When politicians or police argue that teenagers are getting in trouble because they haven't learned to respect authority, they are drawing from this perspective.

An alternative approach focusing on socialization views deviance as a result of social connections. Perhaps the most well-known articulation of this approach is Edwin Sutherland's (1893–1950) **differential association theory,** which suggests that *deviance is learned through interaction with other people involved in deviant behavior* (Sutherland 1947; Sutherland, Cressey, and Luckenbill 1992). Your parents' warning to be careful about whom you hang out with is a simple, common-sense version of this explanation. This perspective views people as socialized into a deviant subculture. By associating with other nonconformists, they learn how to be deviant and critical of social conventions, and they may be pressured into behaving in a deviant way or joining in deviant activities.

When deviant behavior becomes part of a group's collective identity, it creates strong social bonds among its members. From this perspective, the most effective way to control deviant social groups is to limit interaction among group members, thus breaking the social connections that lead people to violate social norms. As we will see,

on social theory

Differential association theory explains deviance as a learned behavior. Can you think of a time when you or someone you knew felt pressured to engage in deviant behavior?

thinking about culture

How can the concept of **culture** help you analyze the meaning and significance of deviant subcultures, including any to which you belong?

however, some subcultures are strong enough to withstand attempts to control them or break them up.

DEVIANT SUBCULTURES We all face social pressures to conform. In most cases—at home, school, or work—parents, teachers, and supervisors reward us for conformity and punish us for nonconformity. Over time, we internalize many of these prescriptions. Long-term deviance is likely to require the social support of a **deviant subculture,** *a group in which membership is based on a shared commitment to specific nonconformist beliefs or behaviors.*

Sometimes deviant subcultures promote behaviors and attitudes that challenge mainstream social norms. For example, members of white supremacist organizations often belong to a subculture that actively opposes racial equality. Before the civil rights movement, white supremacist attitudes were consistent with social norms within many white communities and were reflected in widespread racial segregation backed in many places by the force of law. The civil rights movement eliminated legal segregation and stigmatized overt racism, but white supremacists continue to promote white power and advocate the separation of people by race.

The persistence of white power political activism in the Ku Klux Klan and Aryan Nations and various skinhead groups is rooted in a subculture that transmits white supremacist attitudes from one generation to the next, building a sense of shared identity (Futrell and Simi 2004). Through family gatherings, Bible study groups, informal parties, and other spaces hidden from public view, such groups "encourage members to safely and openly express their radical racist ideologies" (p. 23). These local spaces are supported by conferences such as the World Aryan Congress and white power music festivals. In all these settings, members of the subculture share stories, listen to speeches, or wear clothing that reaffirms their commitment to white power, thus emphasizing the boundaries between their group and outsiders.

Music-based youth subcultures are familiar examples of deviant subcultures. They can provide valuable social support for alienated young people (Heckert, Heckert, and Heckert 2005). Members participate in a community that gives them an opportunity to express themselves and connect with others who feel as they do. In her exploration of suburban heavy metal culture, Donna Gaines (1991) found that deviant subcultures could help teenagers survive in difficult circumstances. The suburban teenagers that Gaines studied performed poorly in school, regularly smoked pot and drank alcohol, and had their share of encounters with local police. These teens knew they'd been labeled as

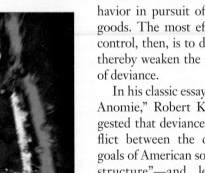

losers, and the bonds they formed within their music subculture gave them a sense of self-worth, providing them with an identity that was more than that of troubled kid or loser (see the Sociology Works box).

LONER DEVIANCE Deviance is not always connected to a subculture. In some cases, deviant behavior is intensely private, with little or no connection among those who engage in similar behaviors. Sociologists describe this behavior as **loner deviance,** *the activities of individuals who commit deviant acts without the social support of other participants* (Best and Luckenbill 1982). One study of self-injurers, or cutters—people who intentionally cut, burn, or otherwise mutilate their bodies—found that they have little contact with one another (Adler and Adler 2005). Cutters rarely share information about their activities and generally try to hide their self-induced injuries.

Without the support system of a subculture, most self-injurers ultimately stop injuring themselves on their own. The instability of loner deviance highlights an important sociological point: deviant behavior occurs within a specific social context. The growth of the Internet and the proliferation of online communities, however, may provide new opportunities for loner deviants to interconnect. A virtual community can provide the kind of social support that is generally associated with deviant subcultures.

Deviance and Structure: Merton's Strain Theory

Yet another social explanation of deviance emphasizes how underlying contradictions in the social or economic environment can drive people to deviance. From this perspective, nonconformity is caused primarily by inequality, which is embedded in social structure. Unequal access to money, power, education, or leisure leads some people to deviant behavior in pursuit of these socially valued goods. The most effective form of social control, then, is to decrease inequality and thereby weaken the structural foundations of deviance.

In his classic essay "Social Structure and Anomie," Robert K. Merton (1938) suggested that deviance results from the conflict between the dominant norms and goals of American society—the "normative structure"—and legitimate means of achieving these goals. Merton's approach was the basis of **strain theory,** which *emphasizes that strain or pressure on those who lack the means to achieve culturally defined goals leads them to pursue deviant routes to success.*

What are some contemporary examples of the connection between deviance and a lack of legitimate access to resources? How might the structural inequality that causes this behavior be addressed?

SOCIOLOGY WORKS

Donna Gaines and the World of Rock Music

Sociologist Donna Gaines always struggled to fit in—as she describes her life in her memoir *A Misfit's Manifesto: The Spiritual Journey of a Rock-and-Roll Heart* (2003)—but she has found that a sociological imagination is a valuable skill for a misfit to possess. She's been a social worker, consultant, journalist, culture critic, and rock critic. As a regular contributor to the *Village Voice*, *Spin*, and *Rolling Stone*, Gaines has drawn upon her sociological training to explore youth culture, focusing primarily on youth-based music subcultures. Her 1987 *Voice* article "Teenage Wasteland" described the group suicide of four teenagers in Bergenfield, New Jersey. Gaines wrote sympathetically of the "rock and roll kids" who died of carbon monoxide poisoning in a car parked in an abandoned garage, noting that the kids were heavy-metal fans who were labeled as "burnouts" by their peers in the local high school. Later, when Gaines returned to Bergenfield to talk with friends of the suicide victims, she learned about how they dealt with their experiences as so-called deviants and how they built a rich subculture that gave them a sense of community. She subsequently published a book on youth subcultures called *Teenage Wasteland* (1991).

As a journalist and critic, Gaines has reported on the world of punk music in New York City. All her stories share an interest in the music subcultures of kids who feel alienated from mainstream culture. She notes, "I have never thought of my work as a job, or of sociology as a profession, rather as a passion, a calling. I was very blessed to be at the right time and place to do what I love and also make a living. Formal training in sociology opened my mind and my heart, and gave me a wide range of skills to draw from."

Over the years, Gaines developed a close connection with the pioneering punk band The Ramones, first as a fan and later as a close friend of the band's lead singer, Joey Ramone. Gaines wrote the liner notes for the 2001 reissue of their first album, "Ramones," and she wrote a tribute to Joey Ramone in *Spin* magazine shortly after his death from cancer in 2001. When The Ramones were inducted into the Rock and Roll Hall of Fame in 2002, Gaines wrote an essay that is full of sociological insight about the importance of music subcultures in the lives of disaffected young people. As she reflects on her own connection to The Ramones, Gaines sums up her admiration for Joey Ramone: "Today the former high school reject is a personal hero. By just being himself, 'the King of Punk' gave teenage outcasts everywhere something to believe in, an alternative to killing themselves or blowing up the high school."

Donna Gaines with Joey Ramone

> "I have never thought of my work as a job, or of sociology as a profession, rather as a passion, a calling. . . . Formal training in sociology opened my mind and my heart, and gave me a wide range of skills to draw from."

think about it

1. *How do subcultures help build community among alienated youth?*
2. *Thinking sociologically, explain why music is so often the focal point of youth subcultures.*

For example, most people in American society share the goal of financial success. Parents, schools, and the media all promote the importance of having a good job, as well as the satisfaction, status, comfort, and security that accompany financial success. But although many people share this goal, legitimate opportunities to achieve financial success are limited and unevenly distributed.

What happens when the goal of financial success is widely accepted but only some members of a society have the resources to achieve it? Most people will conform: they play by the rules and use socially acceptable means to try to achieve that goal. They will seek additional education, attempt to start businesses, or try to work their way up the company ladder. Others will find conventional avenues to

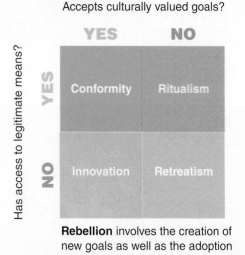

FIGURE 8.2 | MERTON'S STRAIN THEORY OF DEVIANCE

Accepts culturally valued goals?

	YES	NO
YES — Has access to legitimate means?	Conformity	Ritualism
NO	Innovation	Retreatism

Rebellion involves the creation of new goals as well as the adoption of new means.

success blocked off to them because of limited access to higher education, racial or gender discrimination in hiring, or a scarcity of good jobs in a particular area.

When conventional opportunities are blocked, people will find various ways to adapt to the disparity between goals and the legitimate means to achieve them, and some ways may lead them to nonconformist behavior (see Figure 8.2). One common deviant response is what Merton termed *innovation*—socially unacceptable (deviant) routes to success such as embezzling, drug dealing, or black market schemes. Thus strain theory understands deviance as a response to contradictions in the social structure.

Merton's theory explains other forms of behavior besides conformity and innovation. Those who have access to legitimate means to achieve success but reject culturally valued goals—say, burnt-out teachers no longer excited by their jobs—engage in *ritualism*, going through the motions but no longer believing in their work. Another response, *retreatism*, occurs when a person has no access to the means and rejects the goals, often leading to social isolation and withdrawal. Finally, those who *rebel* often create new goals and adopt new means of attaining them, thereby acting as agents of social change.

Sociologist Elijah Anderson (1999) explored the development of deviant social norms in an extremely poor neighborhood in Philadelphia. He found that many young people felt alienated from mainstream American society, experienced racial discrimination, had few job prospects, and did not believe

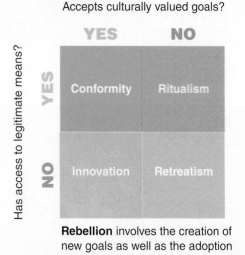

SPOTLIGHT

on social theory

The **functionalist approach** emphasizes consensus in social life and sees deviance as a means of reinforcing social structure. According to strain theory, which is associated with this approach, some people for whom conventional opportunities are blocked will use illegitimate means to achieve success. What examples of this behavior—other than street crime—can you think of?

that the police would make their neighborhoods safe. Consistent with Merton's analysis, poverty, racism, and alienation led many young people to reject mainstream norms, adhering instead to what Anderson calls the "code of the street." These street norms are the foundation of an alternative social structure, one that emphasizes respect, the ability to defend oneself, and—often—the use of violence to gain or maintain respect.

As Anderson's study shows, in poor inner-city neighborhoods two social worlds collide: the mainstream social world of what he calls "decent families" and the oppositional world of "street families." These represent distinct norms and patterns of behavior—social structures—that coexist in the same physical space. Those who follow the code of the street are likely to be involved in the underground economy, including the sale of illegal drugs, and may have enough money to show off their fancy cars, clothes, and jewelry and to host a steady stream of visitors and parties in their homes. At the same time, the code of the street represents a rejection of traditional family life, low-wage jobs, and civility. Even those who do not live by street values are still likely to know the street code, since knowing this code is often necessary to ensure one's physical safety within inner-city communities.

Much of the classic research on juvenile delinquency and youth gangs has found that youth crime emerges in response to blocked opportunities and in the context of long-term inequality, as entrepreneurial young people look for alternative ways to get ahead (Cloward and Olin 1960; Thrasher 1927). The organized drug trade is also rooted in blocked opportunities, especially for young men of color in urban areas. Terry Williams's (1990) study of young cocaine dealers portrays them as businesspeople, skilled at managing the large-scale distribution of illegal drugs. Similarly, Philippe Bourgois's (2003) study of crack dealers in New York's Puerto Rican community shows how young men and women deal with severely limited economic opportunities by working in the underground economy.

The point of these studies is not to demonize or glorify the young people who live by the code of the street or join gangs, but rather to explain the roots of such deviant behavior and the appeal of activities that are often dangerous and destructive. Such analysis tells us that any viable solution to the problems of inner-city alienation and violence must begin with an understanding of the structural roots of deviance.

Culture and Deviance: Deviant Bodies

So far we've looked primarily at questions about deviant behavior. However, we also know that powerful social norms define how our bodies should look and perform. We most intimately experience society's definitions of normal and deviant in our own bodies. In this section, we look at how ideas about body weight, physical appearance, and disability are shifting and, in the process, sometimes literally changing us.

Body Weight

Although cultural norms about appropriate body size encourage us to look as slender as a Hollywood star and as fit as an Olympic athlete, the body size of average Americans does not match this culturally approved definition. The conflict between the widely accepted norm of thin-as-attractive and the actual size of most people is a source of substantial strain, especially for women (Bordo 1993). According to a 2011 Gallup poll (Mendes 2011), two-thirds of adults in the United States are above their "ideal" weight, and most American adults—73 percent of women and 55 percent of men—have tried to lose weight. In 2011, about one-third of adult women and one-quarter of adult men in the United States reported that they were attempting to lose weight (Saad 2011).

Widespread efforts to lose weight—and the growth of a diet industry that includes weight-loss programs and best-selling diet books—are a response to the increasing body weight of the U.S. population (see Figure 8.3). Because serious health problems are associated with obesity, losing weight is often part of a broader effort to live an active and healthy life.

At the same time, the desire to be thin is rooted in cultural norms that define fat bodies as deviant (Saguy 2013). Given the pervasiveness of the thin ideal, perhaps it is not surprising that people in the United States hold negative attitudes toward obese individuals (Puhl and Brownell 2001), and the stigma associated with obesity has real consequences.

Carr and Friedman (2005) analyzed a national survey of American adults and found that overweight people are more likely than people of "normal" size to experience workplace discrimination, and the most severely overweight are more likely to face interpersonal discrimination as well as discrimination from health care providers. Further, weight-related stigma can have significant psychological consequences; very obese people have "poorer self acceptance levels" than people who are at a normal weight, which may be attributed to the experience of living with the shame of obesity (Carr and Friedman 2005). The connection between obesity and discrimination held regardless of race, gender, or age, suggesting that obesity may be a master status, surmounting other aspects of a person's identity.

If a powerful social stigma is attached to fat bodies, what about thin ones? Many young people, especially girls, desire a thinner body. Research indicates that 45 percent of teenage girls are dissatisfied with their body weight and see themselves as overweight (Boyd et al. 2011). More than half of adolescent girls (54.2 percent) and almost one-third of adolescent boys (32.1 percent) use "unhealthy weight control behaviors," such as skipping meals, fasting, taking diet pills, smoking, and inducing vomiting (Vander Wal 2012).

FIGURE 8.3 | OVERWEIGHT AND OBESITY TRENDS IN THE UNITED STATES

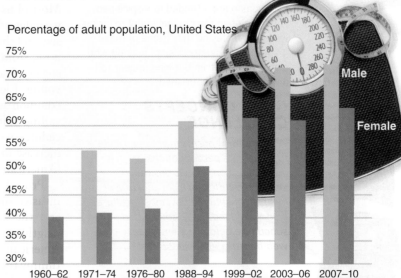

Percentage of adult population, United States

The percentage of adults in the United States who are overweight or obese has increased substantially since the early 1960s. According to data from 2007–2010, more than 73 percent of men and more than 63 percent of women were overweight or obese. Data shown here are for adults aged 20 to 74 and are age adjusted. *Source:* National Center for Health Statistics (2013b).

People sometimes challenge their classification as deviant. In response to restrictive norms about appropriate body size, some overweight men and women have organized a size acceptance movement, demanding to be treated with respect and dignity.

CORE CONCEPTS CHALLENGE

What does this kind of demonstration suggest about the **power** *of people who are considered deviant?*

sports, didn't wear traditional clothes or hairstyles, and often had a defiant attitude toward authorities. Skateboarding and other extreme sports were outsider activities in the 1970s and 1980s, but today they are popular and mainstream: top skateboarders have corporate sponsors, skateboard styles are available in suburban malls, and X Games broadcasts are highly popular on ESPN.

The world of indie music provides many similar examples, as alternative bands become popular on radio stations, on MTV, and in the major-label music business. Punk, rap, and grunge music began in deviant subcultures, and all three became commercial genres of music and fashion. The irony is that alternative music—and youth subcultures, more generally—become commercially successful *because* they have their roots in nonconformity. Deviance sells because it represents authenticity in a society full of mass-produced images (Moore 2005). Commercial success is a double-edged sword, however. As deviant activities and styles are marketed widely, they gain visibility and popularity that may undermine their initial authentic image. Once youth subcultures are absorbed into the mainstream corporate culture, these expressions of nonconformity often lose credibility.

Businesses have learned that deviance can be packaged and sold. The advertising campaigns and new product lines directed at the global youth market are saturated with images associated with individuality, authenticity, and rebellion. Advertisers and market researchers actively seek out deviant youth subcultures, trying to anticipate upcoming trends. In a type of street research known as "cool hunting," businesses search for groups of kids—often connected to deviant subcultures—who are perceived to be a window on what's likely to be popular in the near future (Gladwell 1997). In the world of the cool hunt, deviance is a potentially valuable commodity.

Many types of nonconformist behavior are not obviously harmful, even though some people consider them offensive. In some cases—such as sporting a dramatically unconventional hairstyle or cross dressing at school or work—the potential stigma associated with deviance may become a kind of badge of honor, one that people wear proudly to proclaim their independence from stifling forms of convention. It would be a mistake, however, to conclude that the growth of deviance as a leisure activity or commercial product is a sign that social control has weakened substantially. Instead, embracing deviance and transforming nonconformity into a leisure activity are becoming new mechanisms of social control. Considered in this way, deviance-as-leisure is a kind of safety valve, allowing us to blow off steam from the pressure of social conformity without threatening basic social norms. In the age of tell-all reality television, YouTube videos, and online role-playing games, we are fast becoming a society in which both performing and consuming deviance are popular forms of entertainment that may largely reinforce existing norms and social structures.

thinking sociologically about
Deviance

culture

■ Cultural norms and beliefs define what society views as normal or deviant. These norms are taught through socialization and vary over time and across cultures.

■ In some cases, deviance can result from inadequate or unsuccessful socialization. In such cases, people engaged in deviant behavior have not thoroughly internalized social norms and are not fully regulated by the moral framework of society.

■ Because it runs counter to the dominant culture, long-term deviance is likely to require the social support of a deviant subculture, which helps nurture deviant behavior.

structure

■ We learn norms and expectations about appropriate behavior through interactions in the small groups that form the basis for social structure. Through their actions, people can either reinforce or challenge norms about deviance.

■ Merton's strain theory suggests that barriers posed by social structure can result in deviance when a conflict exists between the dominant goals of a society and legitimate means of achieving these goals. Strain on those who lack the means to achieve culturally defined goals leads them to pursue deviant routes to success.

power

■ Often, powerful segments of society can promote and enforce their definition of deviance and effectively label less-powerful people as deviants. Access to power enables some privileged groups to engage in distinct forms of deviant behavior without being branded or punished as deviant.

■ Those in society with few resources—money, power, education, or leisure—sometimes engage in deviant behavior in pursuit of these socially valued goods. Those who are stigmatized as deviant often experience isolation or discrimination that can contribute further to social, economic, or political inequalities.

■ The criminal justice system, which is designed to prevent crime and apprehend and punish those who commit crimes, serves as a powerful agent of social control. It also reflects imbalances of power in society, since authorities can choose which norms to enforce and which forms of deviance to punish.

Looking Back

1. Studying deviance, or nonconformist behavior, helps us understand how definitions of "normal" are the product of social processes. Definitions of normal and deviant are context specific. Different communities may respond differently to the same behavior.

2. Labeling theory focuses on the social reaction to nonconformist behavior and suggests that behavior is deviant only when it so labeled by those in power.

3. Deviance is a feature of all human societies. Sometimes deviance that has been attributed to moral shortcomings is reclassified as a medical problem. Sociologists refer to this change as the *medicalization of deviance.*

4. Deviant subcultures provide an alternative community for people who do not fit in with, or choose not to be a part of, mainstream social groups.

5. One structural source of deviance is conflict between the dominant goals of a society and access to the means of achieving those goals. When legitimate opportunities are blocked, some people will use deviant behaviors to try to achieve these goals.

6. By focusing on body weight, cosmetic surgery, and disability, we can see how the body is a site where definitions of normal are experienced and sometimes contested.

7. Sociological approaches to deviance emphasize the relationship between deviance and social control. Socialization is a form of social control, since we often police ourselves to make sure we are conforming to social expectations. Other agents of social control, including family, school, and religion, articulate and enforce cultural norms and impose consequences for rule breaking.

8. The criminal justice system, designed to prevent crime and punish criminal offenders, is a powerful agent of social control. Sociological perspectives on punishment lead us to examine questions about the goals, forms, and consequences of punishment.

9. New cultural dynamics have made deviance a potentially marketable product. People sometimes practice deviance as a short-term leisure activity. In other cases, advertisers actively seek out deviant subcultures, trying to anticipate upcoming youth-culture trends.

Critical Thinking: Questions and Activities

1. Identify some unspoken rules or norms in your own family or friendship network. How are these rules communicated and enforced? What happens, if anything, when these rules are violated? Try to answer these questions by focusing on one specific rule or norm.

2. What is the relationship between deviance and inequality? How can persistent inequality be a source of nonconformist behavior? Would efforts to alleviate inequality lead to a decline in the frequency of deviant behavior? Why or why not?

3. Think of a specific example of how you police yourself. Make this a mini-research project, and keep a running list of moments when you encourage yourself to conform to social expectations, or when you deviate from these expectations. Looking back at your list, what does it tell you about socialization and social control?

4. Think about the five different rationales for punishment. Now apply these five rationales to the question of capital punishment. Do you believe capital punishment is justifiable? If not, why not? If you believe it is justifiable, which of the five rationales provides the strongest justification?

5. What is your "normal" body weight? Where would you look for a definition of normal body weight? How do we know the difference between normal and abnormal weight? What, if anything, happens to those who violate guidelines for normal weight?

Key Terms

agents of social control (p. 208) the authorities and social institutions that enforce norms and rules, attempt to prevent rule violations, and identify and punish rule violators.

capital punishment (p. 216) the death penalty.

collective conscience (p. 193) the shared norms, beliefs, and values in a community.

control theory (p. 208) a theory that suggests that our behavior is regulated by the strength of our connection to major social institutions, including family, school, and religion.

crime (p. 210) deviant behavior that violates a law.

crime rates (p. 211) statistics that measure the incidence of crime in relation to population size.

decriminalization (p. 210) the process of making an illegal action legal.

deviance (p. 193) behavior that does not conform to basic cultural norms and expectations.

deviant subculture (p. 200) a group in which membership is based on a shared commitment to specific nonconformist beliefs or behaviors.

differential association theory (p. 199) according to this theory, deviance is learned through interaction with other people involved in deviant behavior

labeling theory (p. 194) the theory that deviance is the result of how others interpret a behavior and that individuals who are labeled deviant often internalize this judgment as part of their self-identity.

loner deviance (p. 200) the activities of individuals who commit deviant acts without the social support of other participants.

medicalization of deviance (p. 197) the designation of a deviant behavior as an illness that can be treated by medical professionals.

normalization (p. 204) a shift in which previously deviant behaviors become accepted as conventional.

overconformity (p. 204) following cultural expectations to an excessive degree.

positive deviance (p. 204) overconformity that gets a favorable response.

recidivism (p. 214) a relapse into criminal behavior.

secondary deviance (p. 194) deviant behavior that is a response to the negative consequences of labeling.

social control (p. 207) the incentives and punishments that promote conformity in social life.

stigma (p. 194) the shame attached to a behavior or status that is considered socially unacceptable or discrediting.

strain theory (p. 200) a theory that emphasizes that the strain or pressure on those who lack the means to achieve culturally defined goals leads them to pursue deviant routes to success.

surveillance (p. 208) monitoring by authorities who police the boundaries of what is normal.

white-collar crime (p. 206) crime committed by people of high social status in the course of their occupation.

9

Class and Global Inequality

looking AHEAD

How has class structure shaped your family's experiences?

How does culture influence how you experience class?

How does economic inequality affect and reflect the **power** of different players in the global economy?

Large paper-making machines dwarf the workers tending them. With the rise of industrialism, capital—needed to finance large manufacturing facilities like this one—became the key economic resource, giving industrial capitalism its name.

the working class and the capitalists are locked in an eternal conflict that is part of the very structure of the capitalist system.

Furthermore, capitalists exploit workers, paying them less than the real value of their labor. The gap between what workers are paid and the value they bring is one of the sources of profits for owners. Eventually, according to Marx, this exploitation would result in an economic crisis, an

unsustainable gap between rich and poor, and workers would unite to overthrow the capitalist system. The result, according to Marx, would be *socialism*, an economic arrangement in which the state owns the major means of production on behalf of the workers, thereby abolishing class distinctions based on the ownership of major property.

Marx was aware of other classes, but he did not see them playing a central role in capitalist systems. Small-business owners, for example, whom Marx called the *petite bourgeoisie*, neither generate profit primarily from other people's labor nor earn wages in somebody else's enterprise. Marx argued that over time the large capitalists would swallow up small-business owners. An example today would be local merchants who go bankrupt in the face of competition from big-box chains like Walmart and Home Depot.

As capitalism evolved, scholars adjusted Marx's theories to account for new developments, especially the rising importance of the middle class (Dahrendorf 1959; Walker 1979; Wright 1985). For example, in Marx's day, much of the industrial base was owned by families or small groups of capitalists. Since that time, however, public corporations have gained enormous power and influence. Stock in publicly traded companies is owned by tens of thousands of different people and institutions, none of which has direct control over a given company. Instead, authority in the workplace is in the hands of highly paid executives and managers who are part of the upper middle class. As a result, when analyzing class, some scholars focus on the role of authority rather than ownership in the workplace.

Through the late nineteenth and early twentieth centuries, labor struggles in the United States were more violent than in any other industrialized country, with hundreds killed and thousands injured in labor disputes. (The photo on the left is from a 1926 strike at the Gera Mills in Passaic, New Jersey, where club-wielding police attacked workers and their children.) Today, such violent clashes with police and military troops are more likely to occur in developing countries, where workers struggle for better wages and working conditions. (The photo on the right shows a clash between union members and the police in South Korea.)

CORE CONCEPTS CHALLENGE

*What does the often-violent history of labor relations reveal about **power** in society?*

Weber's "Life Chances"

Max Weber ([1922] 1978), working a generation after Marx, differed from him in two major ways. First, rather than focusing exclusively on class inequality and the economy, Weber emphasized the interaction of three dimensions of inequality: class, social status, and political power. For example, political power can limit economic power. Governments can tax corporations and regulate their actions through laws governing environmental standards, minimum wage requirements, and rules governing package labeling and other aspects of doing business.

Second, Weber differed from Marx in the way he conceptualized class. Whereas Marx saw class in terms of the organization of work, Weber looked at class in terms of **life chances,** *the likelihood a person has of obtaining valued economic and cultural resources.* Essentially, for Weber, a class is a group of people who share a common market situation—that is, they have a similar capacity to earn money and they pursue a similar lifestyle.

Weber's approach to class solves a problem with Marx's analysis. For Marx, a member of the working class is essentially anyone who earns a wage in a workplace that he or she doesn't own. By that definition, a corporate lawyer who earns $200,000 per year and a minimum-wage fast-food worker earning just over $15,000 per year are both members of the working class. Yet the life of a high-paid professional

and that of a low-paid service worker are fundamentally different. Weber's focus on life chances allowed him to introduce the idea of a middle class. The members of this class are primarily wage earners and are not capitalists. Their formal education and training, however, provide them with a scarce resource, enabling them to obtain a higher standard of living, with different life chances, than most members of the working class. People in the middle class and those in the working class often differ in everything from the leisure activities they enjoy to their preferences in music and food. In effect, different classes have different cultures.

Is Class Stratification Functional?

For Marx and Weber, class inequality was intertwined with struggles for power in society. In contrast, American functionalists in the mid-twentieth century analyzed economic inequality in terms of the positive good it contributes to society as a whole (Alexander 1985; Merton 1968c). In this view, as expressed in a classic article by Kingsley Davis and Wilbert Moore (1945), economic stratification helps ensure "that the most important positions are conscientiously filled by the most qualified persons."

To Weber and Marx, class competition produces winners and losers, in part based on how much power each competitor has. In contrast, to functionalists, free competition among individuals for lucrative positions produces a win-win benefit for society. Functionalists argue that for society to survive, well-qualified people must fill important positions. These positions tend to require higher levels of training and often scarce talent. The higher rewards associated with these positions motivate people to train and compete to fill them. Who would undergo the expense and years of education and training required to become a doctor, for example, if a career in medicine provided no greater rewards than a job that required only a high school education? Instead of conflicting classes, then, functionalists see a continuum of occupations offering a variety of rewards and contributing to the survival and smooth functioning of society.

Critics of the functionalist perspective, however, point out that the real world doesn't operate this way (Tumin 1953). Instead, preexisting inequality affects how competitive a person can be, and barriers to mobility often prevent deserving individuals from advancing. In any society that produces more material goods than are necessary for basic survival, conflict inevitably emerges over how to distribute

To order a bottle of fine wine in a gourmet restaurant, a diner not only needs to be able to afford the wine, which can easily cost over $100 a bottle, but also must have some knowledge of grape vintages, the varieties of international cuisine that the wine might accompany, and perhaps even the foreign languages in which the names of wines and their labels are written. All of these reflect cultural aspects of class distinctions.

CORE CONCEPTS CHALLENGE

What other common social interactions reflect aspects of class **culture***?*

that surplus (Lenski 1966). Those who win the conflict can consolidate their power, alter a society's rules and laws, and pass on their advantages to their children. Critics argue that the functionalist analysis fails to account for this kind of enduring inequality and instead rationalizes and legitimizes existing inequality. Indeed, in the mid-twentieth century, when functionalists were formulating their approach to stratification, many social groups, including women and African Americans, were effectively barred from competing for society's best-rewarded positions.

Another problem with the functionalist approach to stratification is that it fails to define what is meant by "the most important positions." Who decides what they are? A top movie star can command tens of millions of dollars for a single film, while a teacher may earn a modest salary. Which job is more "important" to society?

Although functionalism proved to be an inadequate explanation of class inequality, it did describe some of the important dynamics of the labor market. Some of its ideas are still popular and, as we will see, are used in promoting education as a means of improving individual life chances.

Class Inequality in the United States

The students at Grove City High School in the working-class suburbs of Columbus, Ohio, were hit hard by budget cuts in the past few years (Garcia 2009). All sports were eliminated, but the cuts didn't stop there. Now there is no marching band, no student government, and no prom. Cuts like this are a reality in poor and working-class communities across the country that can no longer afford to pay for such "luxuries" amidst a deep economic downturn. However, the business of luxuries is booming. In 2011, for example, one seller (ridetoys.com) was offering a gasoline-powered Ferrari Testarossa scale-model car for just over $97,000 for 6- to 11-year-old children of the super-rich. In 2010, popular holiday gifts at Chicago luxury stores included $20,000 men's suits, $16,000 women's crocodile handbags, and $40,000 jewel-encrusted cell phones (Sweeney 2010).

These starkly different realities reflect some of the class inequality in the United States. As we explored in Chapter 5, all stratification systems are characterized by three key elements:

1. The unequal distribution of valuable resources
2. Distinctive groups that make up the various strata in society
3. An ideology, or system of beliefs, that explains and justifies the existence of inequality

Class systems comprise all three of these key elements.

Mapping the Major Classes

The class structure of the United States can be described in various ways (Beeghley 2008; Gilbert 2011; Kerbo 2011; Marger 2013; Zweig 2011). The four-class model used here (see Table 9.1) combines Weber's recognition of people's market situation with Marx's emphasis on the importance of ownership and control. In this model, each class is identified by the primary asset that it controls and contributes to the economy. Of course, the lines between classes are not hard and fast; people move up and down between them and the characteristics of individual members in each class can vary considerably. Nonetheless, the broadly defined class distinctions illustrated in Figure 9.1 and summarized in Table 9.1 can give us insight into the dynamics of inequality in American society.

THE CAPITALIST CLASS: INVESTMENTS AND INHERITED WEALTH **Wealth** refers to *the value of financial assets such as savings, real estate, stocks, and bonds, minus any outstanding debts.* **Income** is *money received from*

FIGURE 9.1 | A MODEL OF THE U.S. CLASS SYSTEM

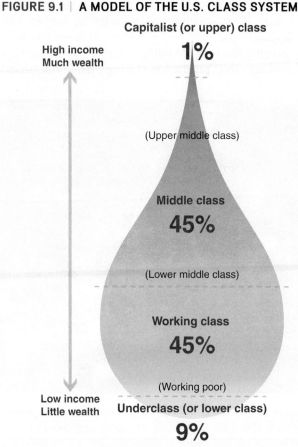

High income
Much wealth

Capitalist (or upper) class
1%

(Upper middle class)

Middle class
45%

(Lower middle class)

Working class
45%

(Working poor)

Low income
Little wealth

Underclass (or lower class)
9%

The bulk of the U.S. population is about evenly divided between the middle and the working classes. However, a broader range of incomes is found among the middle class, contributing to the elongated shape of this model. The highest incomes in the capitalist class extend far beyond what can be represented here.

TABLE 9.1   MAJOR U.S. SOCIAL CLASSES

	Major Economic Asset	Occupations	Education	Income Level	Wealth
Capitalist (or Upper) Class	Investment capital	The wealthiest often do not work at a job. Some oversee the management of their investments. Some are top corporate executives.	Often college educated, but not necessarily, especially when wealth is inherited.	Top 1 percent of household income (about $394,000 or more). Higher end makes many times more.	Wealth is central. Major holdings in stocks, bonds, real estate, and other investments.
Middle Class Upper ("professional") middle class Lower middle class	Knowledge, expertise	Professionals: engineers, scientists, lawyers, doctors, etc. Other occupations requiring a college degree, such as schoolteacher.	College education is essential to success in this class.	55th–99th percentile (about $57,000–$394,000).	Ranges from limited assets such as a small home and savings to an expensive home, significant savings, and stock and other investments.
Working Class (including the working poor)	Skilled and unskilled labor, including service work	Wide variety, including office workers, factory workers, sales clerks, home health aides, customer service reps, etc.	High school diploma is the norm; technical school common; some college possible—especially when vocationally oriented.	10th–55th percentile (about $12,000–$57,000).	Usually little or no wealth; home is key investment; often in debt.
Underclass (or Lower Class)	None—chronically unemployed	Typically none; sometimes informal economy; public assistance.	Less than a high school diploma is common.	Bottom 9 percent or less (less than $12,000).	No assets; often in debt.

Sources: Estimate for income of top 1 percent is based on Saez (2013). Other income ranges are authors' estimates based on 2012 Current Population Survey household income data, retrieved from https://www.census.gov/hhes/www/cpstables/032013/hhinc/toc.htm.

sources such as wages and salaries as well as from the interest, dividends, and rent generated by wealth. Most people derive their income primarily from wages and salaries. In contrast, the defining characteristic of the *capitalist class* (or "upper" class) is that its members often generate income primarily through their wealth rather than through employment.

Some wealthy people have jobs that pay high salaries and bonuses, but generally speaking, the richer people are, the smaller the percentage of their income that comes from employment. Instead, businesses they own generate income for them, stocks produce dividends (profits distributed to shareholders), and real estate yields rental income. For some, management of these investments is their only "job," whereas others hire advisors to manage their wealth and live a life of leisure. The number of families in the United States that are true capitalists is small, perhaps as little as 1 percent of all households. These families have average incomes of about $1.1 million dollars a year—a few make hundreds of millions—and possess enormous wealth (Piketty and Saez 2010).

Unlike income, wealth accumulates over time and can be passed on from generation to generation. As a result, the concentration of wealth in the United States is much greater than the concentration of income (as we will see), and much of the wealth of the upper class is inherited. In the 2013 *Forbes* magazine list of the nation's wealthiest people, four of the ten richest Americans (who are also among the 20 wealthiest people on the planet) were siblings who inherited their money from their father—Walmart founder Sam Walton. Even after an economic downturn, each was worth over $33 billion. Using a baseball analogy, a study found that one out of five people on the 2012 *Forbes* 400 list (21 percent) were "born on home plate"; they inherited enough money to make the list automatically. In addition, over 40 percent received varying amounts of inherited wealth and assistance—sometimes tens of millions of dollars—thus enjoying major advantages. Only 35 percent began "in the batter's box," from middle- or lower-class families (United for a Fair Economy 2012). Your best chance of being part of this class is to be born into it.

THE MIDDLE CLASS: PURSUING THE BENEFITS OF EDUCATION

The **middle class** is *a group that contributes specialized knowledge and expertise to the economy.* To members of the middle class, education and training—usually obtained at college and professional schools—are essential resources. Encompassing roughly 45 percent of the population, the middle class is often subdivided informally into the upper middle class and the lower middle class. Those at the higher end have powerful jobs—often with considerable autonomy—that generate large salaries. Unlike capitalists, members of the upper middle class rely primarily on their salaries for their income, though they may also accumulate stocks and other investments and own expensive homes. Most lawyers, doctors, scientists, engineers, and other professionals fall into this category, as do most business executives.

Lower-middle-class occupations, such as schoolteacher, low-level manager, and social worker, generally offer lower income, fewer benefits, and less autonomy than upper-middle-class jobs. Members of the lower middle class may own their homes and have modest personal savings or retirement accounts but little else. Some lower-middle-class workers—such as teachers and government employees—are heavily unionized, which can help them improve their pay, benefits, and working conditions.

Although upper-class families can ensure their children's financial success by handing down wealth, education cannot be inherited; each generation must learn anew. As a result, middle-class parents are often especially concerned about obtaining the best education for their children so that they can maintain or improve upon their middle-class status.

THE WORKING CLASS: LABOR AND SERVICE

Like the middle class, the working class is broad and diverse, encompassing roughly 45 percent of the population. Whereas members of the middle class are generally engaged in knowledge work and earn a weekly or annual salary, members of the *working class* usually make a product or provide a service and earn hourly wages. The income range for the working class is considerably narrower than the range for the middle class.

All working-class jobs require some skill and knowledge (Rose 2004). However, these jobs can be placed on a continuum, with well-paid skilled trade workers such as mechanics, electricians, and technicians at one end and low-paid, relatively unskilled workers such as home health aides, garment workers, and food service employees at the other end. Skilled trade workers generally need specialized knowledge, but they also work with their hands. Some belong to trade unions that help them get better wages and benefits than their nonunion counterparts. Unskilled workers may be able to find only part time or seasonal employment and—even if they work full time—earn low wages that may not keep a family above the poverty line. These working poor include farmworkers, hotel housekeeping staff, home health aides, garment workers, and food service employees. Union members in these occupations tend to enjoy modestly better wages and benefits than their nonunion counterparts, but they still struggle financially.

Historically the term "working class" has evoked images of blue-collar workers in factories and building construction. Although manufacturing jobs are still important, today working-class jobs in the United States—such as day care provider, food service worker, customer service representative, and retail sales clerk—are increasingly service oriented. Because members of the working class generally earn relatively modest paychecks, working-class families typically have only some savings, and they may own a modest home. Many families have no assets at all, living paycheck to paycheck or struggling with persistent debt. (The Sociology Works box looks at how one sociologist examines issues in the changing workplace.)

THE UNDERCLASS: CHRONIC UNEMPLOYMENT

Sociologists often use the term **underclass** (or *lower class*) to refer to *chronically unemployed people who have no ongoing relationship to the mainstream economy.* Members of the underclass include those only sporadically and briefly employed, those dependent on long-term public assistance, and those who earn money from the informal economy (off-the-books transactions that are not taxed or monitored by the government and can include everything from child care services and auto repair to begging and drug dealing). A variety of reasons can prevent members of the underclass from finding or retaining regular employment. Their employer may have closed, they may have family responsibilities that prevent them from working,

SOCIOLOGY WORKS

Russ Eckel and the New Workplace

In the 1980s, sociologist Russ Eckel could see that work and the workplace in the United States were in flux. At the same time, Eckel, who had received a Ph.D. in sociology, recognized that employees were rarely included in company discussions about workplace change. Drawing upon his training as a sociologist and his research on automobile workers in the 1980s, Eckel started a consulting group, Nommos, to work with companies and labor unions. The goal was to help employers and employees better understand and manage change in the work setting.

Since founding Nommos, Eckel has worked primarily with major automobile companies—including Ford and General Motors—as they have negotiated a changing global auto industry. In all its consulting projects, Nommos emphasizes the importance of three interrelated elements: (1) bringing employees into the center of the picture so that change is not something "done to" them; (2) listening to and understanding the employee experience; and (3) educating and training workers and giving them meaningful work that allows them to use their skills.

Eckel's newest endeavor, the Millennial Work Project, aims to help organizations understand the skills and expectations of a new generation of workers—young people who have come of age in the era of the global economy and the Internet and who bring a new style and new set of attitudes to work. As part of the Millennial Work Project, Eckel found that young workers differ from their counterparts of previous generations in three important respects:

▶ Young workers do not want work to take over their lives. They have a strong sense of the value of maintaining a life outside of work.

▶ Unlike previous generations, young workers not only want but fully *expect* to have meaningful jobs.

Russ Eckel

▶ Employee benefits—including health insurance, vacation time, and, perhaps most important, educational opportunities—are an essential component of job satisfaction for young workers. They are especially concerned about opportunities for continuing education and training throughout their work lives.

Eckel views the Millennial Work Project as a long-term endeavor that will become more important as older workers retire and young workers move up through the ranks. For Nommos, sociology continues to provide valuable tools for helping companies and employees navigate the churning waters and shifting tides of the new economy.

> **Sociology provides valuable tools for helping companies and employees navigate the churning waters and shifting tides of the new economy.**

think about it

1. *How does Eckel's effort to include employees so that workplace change is not simply "done to" them run counter to the usual class-based power differences in the workplace?*

2. *Do Eckel's findings about younger workers resonate with you (if you are in this group) or with your perception of young workers (if you are not)? Explain.*

---

they may lack the skills and education for jobs that are available, or they may have physical disabilities or suffer from mental illnesses or substance abuse. Because they are either unable or unwilling to participate regularly in the mainstream economy, the members of this group typically live in poverty.

Income and Wealth Inequality

The differences among classes reflect substantial inequality in the distribution of income and wealth in the United States.

Income and wealth levels are usually measured by household rather than individual, because counting the income of multiple wage earners and the collective wealth of a household more accurately reflects people's standard of living. In Figure 9.2, the first bar divides U.S. households into five groups (known as *quintiles*), each of which makes up 20 percent of the population. The income bar shows the disproportionate distribution of income among these groups, with the highest-earning 20 percent of American households in 2012 receiving 51 percent of all household income. In contrast, households in the bottom 20 percent received only 3.2 percent

FIGURE 9.2 | THE DISTRIBUTION OF U.S. HOUSEHOLD INCOME AND WEALTH (BY QUINTILES)

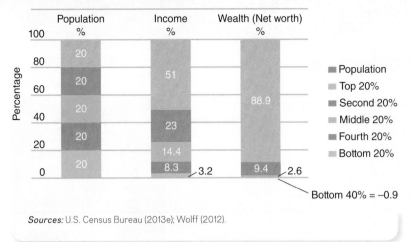

Sources: U.S. Census Bureau (2013e); Wolff (2012).

households has 22.3 percent of income and 63.1 percent of wealth. In fact, 35.1 percent of all wealth is owned by just the top 1 percent of households.

Both income and wealth inequality in the United States have grown significantly. Using 2012 dollars (adjusted for inflation), Figure 9.3 shows that the average household income for most quintiles has remained stagnant, while the top quintile—and especially the top 5 percent—has seen major increases, resulting in a much larger gap between those at the top and the rest of society. In 2012, the average household income for the top 5 percent of households was $318,052, the middle quintile was $51,179, and the bottom quintile was $11,490.

of all income—barely visible on the chart. Income inequality is actually greater than suggested here, because the Census Bureau figures on which this graph is based do not include *capital gains* (money earned from stock and other investments), most of which flow to the richest households.

The wealth bar illustrates *net worth* (the value of assets minus debt) and shows that wealth is even more unequally distributed than income. The wealthiest 20 percent of households, with an average net worth of about $2.1 million in 2010, owns 88.9 percent of the nation's total wealth. The bottom 40 percent has a negative net worth—these households are in debt and therefore are not shown on the wealth bar. Both income and wealth in the top quintile are skewed toward the very top. The top 5 percent of

Class Mobility and Class Barriers

Because hierarchical class systems have fewer positions at the top, relatively few people can move up to the highest positions, regardless of talent, dedication, and hard work. As sociologist Jay MacLeod (1995) puts it, "Our society is *structured* to create poverty and extreme economic inequality. . . . This roughly pyramidal structure ensures that even if everyone excels in school and strives ceaselessly for the top, the great majority are automatically bound to be disappointed" (p. 239). Class structure, then, ultimately limits upward mobility and ensures inequality.

Still, class systems are less rigid than caste or feudal systems (see Chapter 5). In a caste system, the caste into which people are born almost completely determines their life chances. In contrast, class systems permit some **class mobility**, *the ability to move from one social class to another*. There are two general types of class mobility: structural and individual. **Structural mobility** occurs because *a shift in available occupations changes the class system as a whole*. For example, in the past several decades the number of relatively high-paying manufacturing jobs has declined, forcing people to find other types of work. Since the fastest-growing occupations have been those with low wages (see Table 9.2), many people experienced downward mobility. Workers laid off from an automobile factory that provided good wages and benefits, for example, might have found themselves working instead at big-box stores or fast-food restaurants for much less.

Individual mobility occurs *when a person's class position changes without any change in the larger class structure*. Alfred Lubrano's entry into the middle class, discussed in the chapter opening, is an example of this sort of mobility. Despite the popularity of rags-to-riches stories, however, most

FIGURE 9.3 | AVERAGE U.S. HOUSEHOLD INCOME, 1967–2012 (BY QUINTILES AND TOP 5%)

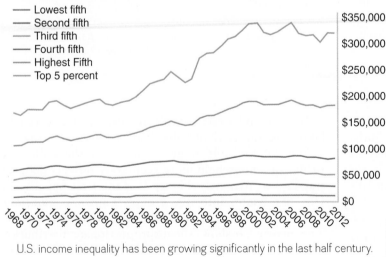

U.S. income inequality has been growing significantly in the last half century.

Numbers are in constant 2012 dollars.

Source: U.S. Census Bureau (2013d).

Examining the Intersection of Race and Class: Growing Income Inequality Among African Americans

Over 100 years ago, sociologist W. E. B. Du Bois ([1903] 2005) famously wrote, "The problem of the twentieth century is the problem of the color-line" (p. vii). In the ensuing years, activists targeted segregation and the legal barriers that prevented African Americans and other racial minorities from participating fully in social, economic, and political life. By the latter half of the twentieth century, the strict color line that Du Bois had written about was crumbling, but deeply entrenched class divisions remained.

This shift is embodied in the career of Martin Luther King Jr. During the often-overlooked last five years of his life, King focused less on racial injustice and more on what he saw as the new social divide in the United States that cut across all races: class. As Michael Eric Dyson (2000) puts it, "King sensed the raging of a more powerful force than he had confronted in all the years of his civil rights struggles: structural economic inequality. . . . King saw that in the struggle to free Northern blacks, race mattered, but class mattered more" (pp. 82–83).

By 1980, sociologist William Julius Wilson confirmed that the life chances of individual blacks now were influenced more by their class position than by their interaction with whites. Race was still significant, Wilson (1980) argued, but "in the economic sphere, class has become more important than race in determining black access to privilege and power" (p. 2). Because of class divisions within the black community, he argued, black people no longer share a uniform experience. A more complex social reality has replaced Du Bois's idea of a single "color line," requiring sociologists to examine the interaction of race and class.

Race continues to contribute to social inequality. For example, median family income for whites in the United States remains about a third higher than it is for blacks. However, income disparities among black households have grown significantly.

As racial barriers fall and new opportunities arise, growing black middle and upper middle classes have emerged. After adjusting for inflation, the number of black households with incomes in the $50,000–$100,000 range has increased by almost 50 percent since 1970, while the number of black households earning more than $100,000 has increased by more than 400 percent (U.S. Census Bureau 2010b).

Not surprisingly, as class differences have increased within the black community, significant cultural differences in corresponding attitudes and values have appeared. In one survey, nearly a third of African Americans said that poor and middle-class blacks share "only a little" or "no" values in common (Pew Research Center 2007a). Over 60 percent of blacks felt these values were becoming more different over time. At the same time, over 50 percent of African Americans felt that overall, the values held by blacks and whites were becoming more similar. Nearly 4 out of 10 African Americans in the survey agreed with the statement "Blacks today can no longer be thought of as a single race because the black community is so diverse" (Pew Research Center 2007a, 4).

think about it

1. *How does increasing income disparity among African Americans illustrate why it is useful to consider the intersection of different types of inequality when examining a person's life chances?*

2. *Growing class differences among African Americans have been accompanied by growing cultural differences. How would you explain this relationship between social structure and culture?*

---

children end up with income levels similar to those of their parents (see Table 9.3), and studies suggest that the influence of parents' class on children's futures may be even greater than once thought (Bowles, Gintis, and Groves 2005; Morgan, Grusky, and Fields 2006).

The best way to ensure economic success is to choose your parents wisely. Individual decisions, actions, effort, and ability are not irrelevant, but they always exist within a structural context that shapes the options available. This interplay between individual action and social structure, of course, is precisely the focus of sociological study.

The Impact of Class Inequality on Social Life

Class has a concrete impact on daily life. People who share a common class position often share conditions and experiences, such as their state of health, the quality of their education, the type of work they do, their level of political participation, and their lifestyle.

HEALTH   The impact of class on health lasts a lifetime (Chandola, Brunner, and Marmot 2006; Lethbridge-Cejku,

---

thinking about structure

How have the **structural** conditions into which you were born helped shape your life options? How have your own choices and actions been influenced by these options?

TABLE 9.2 **OCCUPATIONS WITH THE LARGEST JOB GROWTH, 2010—2020**

	Change, 2010–2020		Median Annual Wage, 2010
	Number	Percentage	
Registered nurses	711.9	26.0%	$64,690
Retail salespersons	706.8	16.6	20,670
Home health aides	706.3	69.4	20,560
Personal care aides	607.0	70.5	19,640
Office clerks, general	489.5	16.6	26,610
Combined food preparation and serving workers, including fast food	398.0	14.8	17,950
Customer service representatives	338.4	15.5	30,460
Heavy and tractor-trailer truck drivers	330.1	20.6	37,770
Laborers and freight, stock, and material movers, hand	319.1	15.4	23,460
Postsecondary teachers	305.7	17.4	45,690

Seven of the 10 occupations that the U.S. Labor Department projects to grow the most between 2010 and 2020 have median annual wages below $31,000, while only 1 has wages over $50,000. What might these data suggest for the future of economic inequality in the United States? *Source:* U.S. Bureau of Labor Statistics (2012).

TABLE 9.3 **MOBILITY AND FAMILY INCOME**

Parents' Family Income	Child's Family Income				
	Bottom 20%	Fourth 20%	Middle 20%	Second 20%	Top 20%
Top 20%	7.3%	11%	18.4%	26%	37.3%
Second 20%	10.7	19.5	19.6	22.9	27.2
Middle 20%	15.3	19.2	25	23.3	17.3
Fourth 20%	24.5	26.2	20.6	16.9	11.8
Bottom 20%	42.3	24.1	16.5	10.8	6.3

Class systems allow for some mobility. However, parents' income level is strongly correlated with the eventual income level of their children—especially at the top and bottom of the income hierarchy. More than a third (37.3 percent) of children whose parents' income level was in the top 20 percent stayed there, six times the rate at which children with parents in the bottom 20 percent rose into the top 20 percent. *Source:* Adapted from Hertz 2005.

CORE CONCEPTS CHALLENGE

Most of us would like to think that where we end up in life is the result of our own effort and ability. But the table suggests that social **structure** *is a major influence as well. What factors might be contributing to the patterns shown in this table? What does the table suggest about the extent of intergenerational mobility?*

Schiller, and Bernadel 2004; Schulz and Mullings 2005). Compared to the poor, wealthier people in the United States eat better, enjoy better health care, experience less stress, reside in safer neighborhoods, and live an average of seven years longer. The more education and income you have, the less likely you are to develop—or die from—heart disease, diabetes, strokes, and many forms of cancer.

Your health is partly a result of your individual behavior, but your behavior is also influenced by the structural aspects of class. For example, people with lower incomes are less likely to learn about and adopt healthy eating habits, in part because they are less likely to live near grocery stores that offer fresh fruits and vegetables. Poor and working-class people are also more likely to have highly stressful and insecure jobs over which they have little or no control. Work stress is a major contributing factor to physical illness, including heart disease and diabetes, and also to mental illness, such as depression. People in higher-paying jobs with a great deal of responsibility may also experience considerable stress, but they generally have more personal control over their work and are more likely to have access to high-quality health care.

EDUCATION   Education is part of what determines your class, but the class into which you are born affects the type of education you are likely to receive. The more money your family has, the better your education is likely to be.

The class gap in education begins with the way public schools in the United States are funded (Kozol 2005). Because school funding is based largely on local property taxes, schools in affluent communities are likely to be better funded than those in poorer communities and better able to provide children with early educational advantages. Affluent families are also better able to afford advantages outside the public school system, including private schools, tutors, and test-preparation courses. Affluent parents who once provided weekly tutoring (for as much as $795 for a single 50-minute session and up to tens of thousands of dollars a year) primarily to help their children prepare for SAT and other standardized tests now increasingly do so to ensure their children get A's in regular high school courses (Anderson 2011).

The class into which you are born also influences whether or not you pursue higher education as well as the type of higher education you receive. The families of students attending four-year colleges have always been more affluent than the population as a whole. By 2005, this gap reached the highest level ever recorded. In addition, families of students at private colleges and universities have higher incomes than those at public colleges (Pryor et al. 2007). Also, families with a history of college attendance have role models who can encourage and mentor younger family members to strive for and succeed in college; working-class first-generation college students typically do not enjoy such resources.

Higher education is also highly stratified along class lines (Karabel 2005; Stevens 2007). At the 146 most selective schools in the United States, 74 percent of students come from families in the richest 25 percent of the population, whereas only 3 percent come from the poorest 25 percent (Carnvale and Rose 2004). Despite increased attention to this issue, the nation's top schools have become even less economically diverse in recent years (Kahlenberg 2010b).

There are several reasons for this stratification. First, the cost of selective elite universities can be more than $50,000 a year, making them far out of reach for most students, discouraging those with more modest means from even applying. Second, even when such schools offer substantial financial assistance, their admissions processes favor better-prepared students who have had the early educational advantages that a higher class position offers. Third, elite schools often give preference to legacy admissions—children of alumni—thereby helping perpetuate class inequality across generations. Such preferences are estimated to be worth the equivalent of 160 SAT points and increase the chance of admission for legacy children by 20 percent (Espenshade, Chung, and Walling 2004).

Less selective schools are more accessible to those of more modest means, often because of both a lower price tag and looser admissions standards, although students from more affluent families are still overrepresented at these schools. The most diverse schools are two-year community colleges, which come the closest to drawing evenly from across class categories. These schools typically have open enrollment and lower costs. They serve students looking for a two-year degree, students planning on transferring to four-year institutions, and working adults looking to improve their job skills. Many community college students are adults who live at home and work full or part time while they commute to campus. Their college experience differs from that of students at a four-year residential college, an essential life experience for most people in the upper middle class (Leondar-Wright 2005).

In recent years, a growing number of for-profit private education companies such as the University of Phoenix have tailored college degrees to the needs of working adults by emphasizing flexible online classes that focus on job skills. Some of these schools have generated controversy, however, for being exceptionally expensive, failing to deliver marketable skills, and engaging in unethical recruitment practices (Field 2010).

WORK Your class also affects the experiences you will likely have at work. Working-class jobs tend to be regimented and closely supervised. Working-class employees often must punch a time clock, take breaks and lunch at specific times, and even ask for permission to use the bathroom. Their work is likely to be closely monitored electronically and by supervisors. Overall, they tend to have little or no control over their work, and the work tends to be relatively low paying with limited or no benefits.

By contrast, middle-class workers often enjoy a high degree of autonomy, looser work rules, less supervision, more flexible work hours, and their own office space, and they are sometimes allowed to work from home. Often, middle-class workers supervise working-class employees.

Middle-class employees tend to work at desk jobs in quiet offices with climate-controlled environments on a regular weekday schedule. In contrast, many working-class employees toil in extremes of heat or cold and in exceptionally loud, stressful, and sometimes dirty and dangerous environments. Working-class occupations, such as truck driving, logging, fishing, farming, and ranching, have the highest rates of death and injury on the job. Working-class jobs often involve night shifts or rotating between shifts—all of which can disrupt family life.

Many middle-class jobs—especially upper-middle-class positions—come with much better benefits than most working-class jobs, including private pension plans, medical insurance, generous sick leave, paid vacation, and paid educational leave. Top-level benefits can include expense accounts, company cars, membership in private clubs, company stock options, and tickets to sporting events.

POLITICS Political participation varies according to class in the United States, leaving those with the highest rates of participation with the most power. There are bigger class differences between voters and nonvoters than there are between Republicans and Democrats; the higher a person's income, the more likely that person is to vote (Figure 9.4). The upper middle class and affluent are also most likely to fund political campaigns, either directly or through donations to political action committees (PACs), political parties, and other intermediaries. For example, almost half of the campaign contributions to members of Congress in 2008

FIGURE 9.4 | REPORTED VOTING BY FAMILY INCOME, 2012

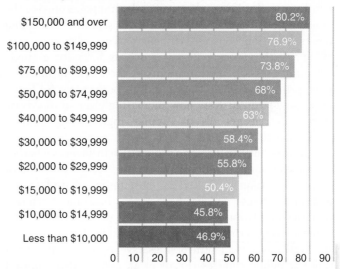

Percentage of citizens voting by family income

Family income	Percentage
$150,000 and over	80.2%
$100,000 to $149,999	76.9%
$75,000 to $99,999	73.8%
$50,000 to $74,999	68%
$40,000 to $49,999	63%
$30,000 to $39,999	58.4%
$20,000 to $29,999	55.8%
$15,000 to $19,999	50.4%
$10,000 to $14,999	45.8%
Less than $10,000	46.9%

Those with higher incomes are more likely to vote (as shown here), volunteer for a campaign, and make a campaign contribution, skewing political participation by class.
Source: U.S. Census Bureau (2013f).

FAST-FORWARD

Change and Conspicuous Consumption

In the last half of the nineteenth century, industrialization produced a "Gilded Age" dominated by so-called robber barons who controlled key industries. These newly wealthy industrialists often engaged in conspicuous consumption, as in the case of the castle-like Biltmore Estate in Asheville, North Carolina (*top*), which was completed in 1895 for one of the sons of Cornelius Vanderbilt, a shipping and railroad tycoon. Today, some members of the upper middle class have embraced a more modest version of conspicuous consumption, expressed through the "McMansions" (*bottom*) that helped fuel the housing boom—and bust—of the 2000s.

came from people with family incomes of at least $250,000 (American National Election Studies 2007). Early donors get a chance to influence which candidates are viable long before a single vote is cast.

LIFESTYLE When you were growing up, did your family have *dinner* or *supper*? Was flying fairly routine for

you or did you rarely, if ever, travel by air? Was it taken for granted that you would attend college, or was going to college an unusual accomplishment? Did your parents have an accountant, or did they make use of storefront check-cashing establishments? Such questions have to do with lifestyles, and lifestyles vary by class.

In an early work on class and lifestyles, sociologist Thorstein Veblen ([1899] 1973) coined the term **conspicuous consumption** to refer to *lavish spending, done to compete for status*. Veblen associated conspicuous consumption with the *nouveau riche* (French for "new rich"); in his day, these were mostly industrialists who had recently acquired their fortunes and often spent lavishly on mansions and other luxury items. Their lifestyle contrasted starkly with that of people who had so-called old money, wealth that had existed for generations. The old-money wealthy generally frowned upon ostentatious displays.

Many class-based status groups recognize members not merely by the amount of money they have but by social factors such as family heritage, race and ethnicity, educational background, and personal behavior. Such groups often develop formal or informal rules that identify who belongs and who does not. Joining an exclusive country club not only may cost thousands of dollars just to apply and thousands more for membership fees, but it also typically requires sponsorship from an existing member, ensuring that only the "right" people are allowed in. More informally, class-based status groups often share a lifestyle because they

thinking about culture
How did the **culture** you experienced growing up reflect your family's class status?

socialize together, send their children to the same schools, join the same organizations, and marry within exclusive social networks. These behaviors erect barriers of inclusion and exclusion that sometimes involve **classism,** *prejudice or discrimination based on social class.* Membership in a high-status group or low-status group can significantly affect an individual's life chances, including access to education, friendship networks, marriage opportunities, job opportunities, and business and professional contacts.

Poverty

In 2007, 12-year-old Deamonte Driver died when an infection from an abscessed tooth spread to his brain (Otto 2007). The Maryland boy, who lived in poverty, had no access to dental care, despite being eligible for Medicaid assistance. The newspaper story about his death noted that more than two-thirds of the children on Medicaid in Maryland receive no dental care whatsoever—and the situation is worse in other states. Lack of access to dental care, however, is just one of the countless hurdles that poor people face every day (Tyron 2007). Perhaps no group in U.S. society feels the impact of class inequality more acutely than those who live in poverty.

Absolute poverty refers to *a scarcity of resources so severe that it is life-threatening.* Nearly 20 percent of the world's population lives on less than a dollar a day, one indicator of absolute poverty. **Relative poverty** refers to *a lack of the basic resources needed to maintain a standard of living considered acceptable in a particular society.* This form of poverty varies in different societies. Being forced to live without indoor plumbing or running water would certainly be seen as a sign of poverty in U.S. society today, but in some developing nations such conditions are common and do not by themselves necessarily distinguish people as poor.

Poverty is not "natural" or "inevitable." Poverty levels result, at least in part, from government decisions about the allocation of resources. For example, one reason the United States launched the Social Security system in the 1930s was to reduce the high level of poverty among those over age 65. Today this age group has the nation's lowest poverty rate. Similarly, new social programs introduced during the 1960s helped cut the poverty rate in half between 1960 and 1970 (U.S. Census Bureau 2010b). Nations with similar degrees of wealth have significantly different poverty rates. The poverty rate in the United States is one of the highest among industrialized nations. In 2013 the United States ranked 31st among the 34 member nations of the Organization for Economic Cooperation and Development; only Chile, Israel, and Mexico had higher rates. The U.S. poverty rate is more than three times that of the Czech Republic, the country with the lowest poverty rate (OECD 2013). Also, many of the other nations provide more noncash benefits (such as housing, health care, and food), making the impact of poverty less onerous than it is in the United States.

U.S. POVERTY RATES
How do we determine who is poor and calculate the number of poor people? The federal government adopted the method used to determine an acceptable standard of living in the 1960s, when policymakers estimated that poor people spent about one-third of their income on food. Since then, the U.S. **poverty line** has been *a measure of scarcity determined by figuring the cost of a minimal food budget and multiplying it by three.* Each year, the government adjusts poverty thresholds by recalculating the cost of food.

The official measure of poverty now significantly undercounts the poor, in part because people today typically spend one-fifth of their budget on food instead of one-third. Adjusting the poverty calculation by multiplying the cost of food by five would place many more people below the poverty line. In 2011 the Census Bureau began producing a Supplemental Poverty Measure as an alternative to the older model. This supplemental measure reflects real-world conditions more accurately by factoring in expenses such as housing, child care, and medical treatment. In 2011, this estimate showed poverty to be about one percentage point higher than the official measure.

Until then, the government continues to use the outdated measure as the basis for determining the official U.S. **poverty rate,** *the percentage of the population that falls below the poverty line.* In 2012 this rate was 15 percent, meaning that more than one out of seven Americans—46.5 million people—lived in poverty (Figure 9.5).

Poverty threshold figures take into account family size, the age of family members, and the number of children in the household. The government counts as income not only wages but also child support and certain public assistance payments, but it excludes noncash benefits such as food stamps and housing subsidies. In 2012 a single parent with one child had to earn $15,825 to stay above the poverty line. However, if that parent worked full time at a job paying the federal minimum wage ($7.25 an hour in 2012), he or she would earn $14,500 and thus remain under the official poverty line.

MISCONCEPTIONS ABOUT POVERTY
The characteristics of the poor are often misunderstood. Two-thirds of poor people in 2012 were white (66.3 percent) and fewer than a quarter were black (23.5 percent). Children are more likely to be poor than people in any other age group, and more poor people live in rural or suburban areas than in urban areas. In the last half of the twentieth century, class and gender intersected in a **feminization of poverty,** *a trend in which women made up an increasingly large share of the poor.* Subsequently, by 2012, just over half of all poor families were headed by a single woman, about double the rate in 1960 (U.S. Census Bureau 2013e). Other characteristics of the poor are outlined in Table 9.4.

Another myth is that most of the poor remain in poverty for a long time. In fact, however, families and individuals move in or out of poverty from year to year, sometimes repeatedly. From 2009 through 2011, approximately 31.6 percent of the population fell below the poverty line for at least 2 months, but only 3.5 percent of the population lived in poverty for all 36 months (U.S. Census Bureau 2013e).

FIGURE 9.5 | NUMBER IN POVERTY AND POVERTY RATE, 1959–2012

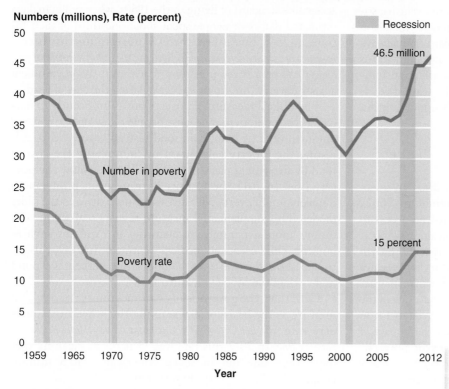

Numbers (millions), Rate (percent)

After dropping by nearly one-half in the 1960s, the poverty rate in the United States has hovered between 11 percent and 15 percent since the early 1980s. *Source:* U.S. Census Bureau (2013e).

CORE CONCEPTS CHALLENGE

The poverty rate increases during periods of recession (shaded), as it did in 2008–2009. How are such data an illustration of the role of social **structure**?

Perhaps the biggest misconception about poverty is that people are poor because they are unwilling to work. In fact, 43 percent of the poor are either too old (over 65) or too young (under 18) to work (U.S. Census Bureau 2013e). In addition, the poverty rate increases during periods of recession (when economic activity slows down) and declines when the economy improves, indicating that structural factors beyond individuals' control are a major cause of poverty. In reality, people live in poverty for many reasons. Some are born into it; others become poor as a result of job loss, divorce, the cost of a debilitating illness, or the addition of a child. People of sound mind rarely choose voluntarily to live in poverty. One reason for misconceptions about the causes and prevalence of poverty is ideology.

Ideology: Justifying Inequality

Growing up, were you told that you could be whatever you wanted to be? That with hard work and perseverance you could accomplish whatever you set your mind to? If so, you were learning an early lesson about ideology.

As we saw in Chapter 5, in the context of stratification, an *ideology* is a system of beliefs that explains and justifies the existence of inequality. An effective ideology helps legitimize inequality by making it appear natural, inevitable, and acceptable. In the past, belief in "God's will" justified strict systems of inequality. However, in modern societies other ideologies have emerged. If you were raised in the United States, you are probably familiar with these common ideas:

- Everyone has an equal opportunity to succeed (but is not guaranteed success).
- Success is based on merit (not on wealth, family ties, or other special statuses).
- People can achieve success through individual ability and hard work.

Together, these beliefs suggest that class stratification is the outcome of individual characteristics, unimpeded by structural constraints and unaided by group privilege. In other words, success comes from talent and effort; failure results from individual shortcomings. The message of such an ideology is clear: because everyone has an equal chance to succeed, society is basically fair.

To state these ideas more precisely, the dominant ideology in the United States generally includes the intertwined notions of equal opportunity, meritocracy, and individualism. **Equal opportunity** is *the idea that all people should have the same chance to achieve success.* **Meritocracy** is *a system in which people are rewarded and are able to advance because of their abilities.* These ideas suggest that our stratification system is open and fair. Finally, **individualism** is *a system of beliefs that highlights the importance of the single person over any social group.* Individualism is associated with personal rights and freedoms as well as personal responsibility and self-reliance. The idea of pulling yourself up by your bootstraps and the notion of the self-made man are popular expressions of individualism.

Ideologies help justify the advantages of those in power, and they are also crucial for maintaining social control; otherwise, subordinate groups would more readily challenge structural inequality. People who suffer the consequences of economic inequality sometimes believe the dominant ideology and blame themselves for their predicament. Many, however, see through these ideological myths but do not have the power to challenge or change the system of inequality. Although few people actually believe that class inequality results from merit and individual effort alone (McCall 2013; Smith and Kluegel 1986), holding on to the promises offered by the dominant ideology can be a source of hope that things will one day improve.

TABLE 9.4

THE POOR IN THE UNITED STATES, 2012

RACE AND ETHNICITY

Most poor people are white. Of the 46.5 million poor:

- 66.3% are white (including white Hispanics)
- 40.7% are white non-Hispanics
- 23.5% are black
- 29.3% are Hispanic (of any race)
- 4.1% are Asian

The poverty rate is highest among blacks and Hispanics.

- Black, 27.2%
- Hispanic (of any race), 25.6%
- Asian, 11.7%
- White, 12.7%
- White (non-Hispanic), 9.7%

AGE

The poor are disproportionately children. Of the 46.5 million poor:

- Over one-third (34.6%) are children under the age of 18 (16.1 million)
- 8.4% are at least 65 years old (3.9 million)

One out of five children live in poverty (21.8%)—the highest poverty rate; the lowest poverty rate is found among the elderly (9.1%); for adults aged 18 to 64, the rate is 13.7%.

FAMILY AND GENDER

Half of poor families are headed by single mothers. Of the 9.5 million poor families:

- 51.3% (4.8 million) have a single female householder
- 38.9% (3.7 million) have a married couple
- 10.7% (1 million) have a single male householder

WORK

Many poor adults work. Of the 26.5 million poor people aged 18–64 years:

- 10.8% work full time, year-round
- 29.5% work less than full time, year-round
- 59.7% did not work at least one week during the year

LOCATION

Poor people are found in both urban and suburban areas in similar numbers. Of the 46.5 million poor people:

- 19.9 million (42.9%) are in urban areas
- 18.1 million (38.9%) are in suburban areas
- 8.5 million (18.2%) are in rural areas

The poverty rate in rural and urban areas is similar:

- 19.7% in urban areas
- 11.2% in suburban areas
- 17.7% in rural areas

Source: U.S. Census Bureau (2013e).

Instead of relying on ideological myths, sociologists have studied how economic inequality really works and found that factors other than merit and individual effort heavily influence the likelihood of our success or failure.

Culture, Structure, and Class Reproduction

Why does class inequality persist? To begin with, families and schools socialize people to adopt beliefs, behaviors, and outlooks consistent with their class, thus reproducing the culture of that class. Public policy also helps reinforce class inequality.

Cultural Capital

To explain the reproduction of classes, French sociologist Pierre Bourdieu (1930–2002) built upon Weber's attention to culture and lifestyles. For Bourdieu, people reproduce classes across generations by passing on to young people not only money but also cultural assets. To describe these assets, Bourdieu coined the term **cultural capital,** which *consists of various types of knowledge, skills, and other cultural resources.* Different forms of cultural capital are valuable within different social contexts. Bourdieu contended that young people are socialized differently depending on their family's class and that they learn class-based tastes, behaviors, and attitudes that distinguish them from people in other classes. As in other examples of socialization, people internalize these lessons, and the associated tastes, behaviors, and attitudes come to seem natural to them. These internalized lessons can help steer young people toward class positions similar to those of their parents. Bourdieu was especially interested in how everyday consumption—our choice of food, music, fashion, and leisure—marked class-based differences.

on social theory

Symbolic interactionism stresses the role of interpersonal interactions in reproducing culture and social structure. Have you ever been in a situation in which you felt at a disadvantage because you lacked the cultural capital to know what behavior was expected of you?

Bourdieu (1986) notes that cultural capital interacts with economic capital and with **social capital,** *relationships that are potentially economically valuable resulting from membership in a group.* For example, it is not enough to want to sail as a pastime; you need to have the economic capital to pursue such an expensive leisure activity. Similarly, knowing powerful, wealthy, or influential people—having social capital—can assist you in getting into high-status schools, companies, and professions.

Families: Training Children

Applying Bourdieu's framework to the contemporary United States, Annette Lareau (2011) studied the socialization of children in black and white middle-class and working-class families. She found that children of the same social class—regardless of race—have much more in common than children of the same race who belong to different social classes. Lareau speculates that as the children she studied grow up, race is likely to become a more significant factor.

In her study, Lareau distinguished between two types of childrearing. Parents who practice *concerted cultivation* actively assess their children's skills, interests, and behaviors. They arrange play dates; organize sports; provide music lessons, tutoring, and museum visits; engage children somewhat like "little adults"; and ask their children about their opinions, feelings, and thoughts. This approach to childrearing is especially prominent in middle-class families, regardless of race.

In contrast, working-class families tend to rely on what Lareau calls the *accomplishment of natural growth*. They focus on providing basic necessities and on creating opportunities for children to spend time at home, playing informally with peers, siblings, and other relatives. These parents also maintain a clear distinction between adults and children and are more inclined to tell their children what to do than to reason with them.

Each approach to childrearing offers advantages and disadvantages that in the end help reproduce class inequality. The constant challenges middle-class children face, and the frequent social interactions they encounter with a variety of people, socialize them to interact effectively with people in many different middle-class settings. However, their hectic schedules leave them little time to simply enjoy being with their families. By contrast, working-class children develop more independence and self-reliance, but they participate in a more limited range of activities. Consequently, they grow up to be less familiar and less comfortable with different social settings than are middle-class kids.

Schools: Individual Mobility and Class Reproduction

One purpose of schools, and higher education in particular, is preparing people for employment. In doing so, schools can provide individuals with a chance at social mobility while, paradoxically, helping reproduce class inequality for society as whole.

EDUCATION PAYS   The role of education in helping individuals compete for good-paying jobs is well known and well documented. Figure 9.6 shows that higher educational attainment is associated with lower unemployment and higher wages. More variation exists within each category of educational attainment than these average numbers suggest, however. For example, income levels for people with a bachelor's degree vary significantly depending on their major and the type of school from which they graduated. Still, on the whole, the more education you have, the more likely you are to be employed and well paid.

Education can help individuals compete, but it does not change the class structure. As we saw earlier in the chapter, structural factors—including the way public schools are funded and the high cost of higher education—create barriers to quality education that contribute to unequal educational outcomes. In addition, schools sort students by class. In high school, middle-class students are steered into college-prep courses emphasizing independent thinking and self-direction, which prepare them to move on to higher education and middle-class life. Working-class students are more likely to be channeled into classes that emphasize the importance of following rules and obeying authorities, thereby preparing them for working-class jobs that have similar expectations. In this way, although schools serve employers and the capitalist system by providing appropriately trained workers, they help reproduce class distinctions in society (Bowles and Gintis 1976).

REWARDING CULTURAL CAPITAL   Culture also plays a role in how schools reproduce inequality. Schools are generally organized to value the cultural

SPOTLIGHT
on social theory

How would **functionalist theory** explain the relationship between education and earnings? Do you think this theory adequately explains the levels of income of different people you know?

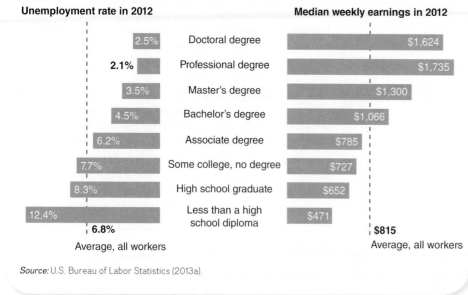

FIGURE 9.6 | UNEMPLOYMENT AND EARNINGS BY EDUCATIONAL ATTAINMENT

Unemployment rate in 2012

2.5%	Doctoral degree
2.1%	Professional degree
3.5%	Master's degree
4.5%	Bachelor's degree
6.2%	Associate degree
7.7%	Some college, no degree
8.3%	High school graduate
12.4%	Less than a high school diploma

6.8%
Average, all workers

Median weekly earnings in 2012

Doctoral degree	$1,624
Professional degree	$1,735
Master's degree	$1,300
Bachelor's degree	$1,066
Associate degree	$785
Some college, no degree	$727
High school graduate	$652
Less than a high school diploma	$471

$815
Average, all workers

Source: U.S. Bureau of Labor Statistics (2013a).

capital of the higher classes and reward students accordingly. Since more affluent students already possess that sort of cultural capital, the academic playing field is tilted in their favor, increasing the odds they will achieve academic success. Working-class students are at a disadvantage when trying to meet the middle-class expectations of the school environment and often feel alienated. As a result, they can rebel, refuse to conform to academic expectations, and inadvertently help recreate their status in the working class (Willis 1977).

Jay MacLeod (2008) studied young, low-income black and white men in Boston, focusing specifically on the role of aspiration in their lives. The youth MacLeod studied related to their schoolwork quite differently based on their differing aspirations. MacLeod found that the young white men he studied had a fairly pessimistic outlook on their future. They saw their schooling as irrelevant and their prospects as lower than those of their parents because of the loss of good-paying working-class jobs. On the other hand, the young black men he studied were more optimistic, because they measured their prospects against the more repressive history of discrimination faced by African Americans in the past. They hoped their efforts in school would pay off, and they expected diligence in the workplace to be rewarded with increased responsibilities, promotions, and pay raises. However, aspiration by itself cannot overcome structural barriers. When MacLeod followed up with these black men seven years later, he found most ended up in dead-end jobs, like their white peers. Most now tempered their belief in the openness of American society but often blamed themselves for their failure.

SCHOOLS AND IDEOLOGY
When the students MacLeod studied blamed themselves for their failure, they were reflecting another influential role that schools play in reproducing class: ideology. Schools can strengthen class inequality by helping justify it and by reinforcing the idea that failure results from individual shortcomings, not structural biases.

We are so accustomed to accepting the connection between education and unequal rewards that we rarely see data such as those in Figure 9.6 as unfair. Instead, we usually understand them as a reflection of a generally fair system of meritocracy that rewards those who have ability, work hard, and make smart choices about their chosen field of study. In such an analysis, we tend to ignore the structural and cultural forces that work in favor of students from affluent backgrounds and against students from more modest backgrounds.

Public Policy and Inequality

Beyond the role of culture, economic inequality is caused in part by—and can be reduced through—government social policies. These policies tend to follow two different approaches.

One approach aims to create more *equal outcomes* by reducing the gap between the rich and poor. One way of accomplishing this is to provide everyone with some basic public goods, such as health care and free education, which reduces the impact of income differences. Another way is to raise the floor (raise wages for those in low-income positions) and lower the ceiling (increase taxes on the highest income-earners). This ensures a living wage for those doing necessary but lower-paying work while limiting inequality that results from extremely high incomes. Government intervention of this sort produces less inequality.

The second approach focuses on encouraging *equal opportunity* by creating a more level playing field on which people compete for scarce good jobs. This is usually done by supporting more education as the means to individual mobility, thereby promoting fairer competition. This limits government intervention but results in more inequality.

U.S. society and government policy have mostly favored the equal opportunity approach over the equal outcomes approach, encouraging more education while accepting higher levels of inequality. As a result, the percentage of Americans over age 25 with at least a four-year college degree nearly tripled between 1970 and 2012, from about 11 percent to 31 percent (U.S. Census Bureau 2013c), but during the same period economic inequality *increased* significantly. More education for more people did not reduce inequality because it did not change the overall class structure nor did it change the rewards associated with different types of employment. Instead, the United States has more economic inequality than is found in other industrialized nations. Those countries, in contrast, have placed higher value on reducing economic inequality and enacted different economic policies.

To give one example, the United States is the only advanced economy in the world that does not guarantee workers any paid vacation, whereas some countries mandate over 30 days of paid vacation annually (Figure 9.7). Without the protection of federal mandates, U.S. workers in the private sector must rely on individual employers to provide paid vacations and holidays. As a result, nearly one out of four workers gets no paid vacation time at all. Private-sector employees get an average of nine paid vacation days a year—less than half the number mandated in most other wealthy countries—and six paid holidays, also less than in most other wealthy countries (Ray and Schmitt 2007).

WAGES AND LABOR LAWS
Raising the wage floor helps reduce inequality, and the most direct way to raise low-income wages is to legislate a minimum wage. Because the federal minimum wage is not adjusted for inflation, its real value has fluctuated since it was first implemented in 1938. It peaked at $10.77 in 1968 (in 2013 dollars), was allowed to reach a nearly 60-year low by 2007, and was

Number of days

Country	Paid annual leave	Paid holidays
France	30	1
Finland	25	9
Denmark	25	9
Norway	25	2
Sweden	25	
Germany	24	10
Austria	22	13
Portugal	22	13
Spain	22	12
Italy	20	13
Belgium	20	10
Ireland	20	9
Australia	20	7
New Zealand	20	7
Greece	20	6
Netherlands	20	
Switzerland	20	
United Kingdom	20	
Canada	10	8
Japan	10	
United States	0	

■ Paid annual leave   ■ Paid holidays

The United States is the only developed country that does not mandate a minimum number of paid vacation days and holidays for its workers. *Source:* Ray and Schmitt (2007).

increased to $7.25 an hour in 2009 (Elwell 2013). Given the relatively low federal minimum wage, some states implement their own, higher, minimum.

Labor laws that enable workers to form unions without fear of being fired can also help ensure higher wages and better benefits. Union members in the United States earn, on average, about 14 percent more in wages than nonunion workers (after controlling for experience, education, region, industry, occupation, and marital status). Measured against comparable nonunion workers, the rate of union members with health insurance is 28 percent higher; the rate with pensions is 54 percent higher; and union members enjoy 26 percent more vacation time (Mishel 2012).

Current labor laws make it very difficult for workers to join a union, while making it relatively safe for private employers to try to get rid of unions ("union busting") or to prevent workers from forming them (Compa 2004; Levitt 1993; Logan 2006; Mehta and Theodore 2005). In 2012, only 6.6 percent of private-sector workers belonged to a union. Public-sector (government) employees have been less likely to face union-busting tactics and are five times as likely (35.9 percent) as private-sector workers to belong to a union (U.S. Bureau of Labor Statistics 2013d). In recent years, though, some state legislatures—typically citing budgetary concerns—have curtailed or eliminated the rights of public-sector unions to bargain collectively. Partly as a consequence of the low rate of unionization in the United States, many U.S. workers have relatively low wages and benefits compared to workers in other industrialized countries. (The Sociology in Action box examines how sociologists have studied the challenges facing workers' organizing efforts.)

TAXES   If the minimum wage raises the floor to reduce inequality, then imposing higher taxes on the wealthy lowers the ceiling. But compared to a half century ago, the wealthy today enjoy substantially lower taxes whereas taxes on middle-income families are higher than they were (Johnston 2003, 2007). In a system of **progressive taxation,** *those with higher incomes pay a higher tax rate.* Throughout the 1950s the U.S. federal tax rate on personal income beyond the first $400,000 for married couples filing jointly was more than 90 percent—a highly progressive rate aimed at limiting the extremes of income inequality. However, that rate was slashed in the 1980s and was 39.6 percent in 2013. The tax rate on capital gains—income earned from investments mainly by those in the highest income brackets—has similarly been cut by more than half since the mid-1970s and ranges from 15 to 20 percent in 2013. In contrast, the top tax rate for median family incomes rose substantially in the late 1960s and 1970s, and although it dropped again in the 1980s, it remains higher today than it was in 1955 (Tax Policy Center 2011a).

Well-known billionaire investor Warren Buffett has criticized this system, noting that because capital gains are taxed at a lower rate than wages, the tax rate on his income is nearly half that of his secretary (Bawden 2007). In late 2010, he argued that taxes should be cut for most Americans, "But I think that people at the high end—people like myself—should be paying a lot more in taxes. We have it better than we've ever had it" (Ovide 2010).

American workers pay more in taxes than they used to in part because corporations pay less. One congressional study found that by taking advantage of tax loopholes, nearly two-thirds of U.S. companies and 68 percent of foreign companies pay no income tax at all (Government Accountability Office 2008). For example, 46 of the biggest U.S. corporations paid no income tax in 2003, including Walt Disney, Reebok, Time Warner, Marriott International, AT&T, and Boeing (McIntyre and Nguyen 2004). The government has made up the difference by increasing the payroll taxes on

SOCIOLOGY in ACTION

Why David Sometimes Wins: Organizing Workers

Workers in the United States face an uphill battle in organizing. On paper, they have the right to join a labor union to pursue good wages, benefits, and working conditions. In reality, though, labor laws are stacked against them while giving employers an unfair advantage, according to the international human rights group Human Rights Watch (Compa 2004). For example, employers can legally launch aggressive pressure campaigns against employees attempting to organize, including holding mandatory meetings at which workers are often threatened with dire consequences if they join a union. Employers are even allowed to permanently replace workers who strike over wages and working conditions. Employers also often illegally fire workers who try to organize a union, exploiting a slow and ineffectual legal process that can tie up worker complaints about labor law violations for months or years and bring resolutions long after a union election is held (Compa 2004).

Such laws and procedures contribute to a relatively weak labor union movement in the United States compared to many other industrialized countries. Union weakness contributes to higher poverty rates and greater economic inequality and is one of the key reasons why many U.S. workers do not have the sorts of wages and benefits that workers in other nations enjoy.

Sociologists have been studying the organizing efforts of workers and identifying their most effective organizing strategies. For example, Jennifer Chun (2009) showed how low-wage service workers in both the United States and Korea have gained wide community support by focusing on broad and culturally resonant issues of social justice rather than on narrow workplace disputes. After studying California organizing campaigns in the janitorial services, residential construction, railroad transportation, and apparel industries, Ruth Milkman (2006) found that organizing campaigns were more likely to fail from inadequate funds than from employer opposition and were more likely to succeed if run in a "top-down" fashion by labor leaders (rather than from below by rank-and-file workers). She also found that immigrant workers were sometimes more effective at organizing than native workers because they have a stronger sense of group solidarity resulting in part from their experience with labor and political struggles in their native countries. Moon-Kie Jung (2006), who analyzed the efforts of Hawaii's agricultural workers to organize over a 50-year period, found that by

explicitly embracing diversity—even reserving certain union positions for representatives from different racial and ethnic groups—workers successfully countered employers' efforts to keep them divided along ethnic lines by repeatedly bringing in new workers from different countries.

Sociologist Marshall Ganz draws on his own experience as a labor organizer in his work in labor studies. In the 1960s, Ganz dropped out of college to work with the United Farm Workers, best known for its charismatic leader Cesar Chavez. Ganz eventually became the union's head of organizing, helping direct one of the most famous labor struggles in U.S. history. He later returned to school, got a Ph.D. in sociology, and began teaching at Harvard University about organizing and leadership strategies. In 2008, Barack Obama's presidential campaign made him a key advisor for the training of the campaign's field organizers.

In 2009, Ganz wrote *Why David Sometimes Wins*, a sociological analysis of his experiences with the United Farm Workers whose title invokes the biblical struggle of an underdog against a giant. Ganz (2009) argues that the success of the farmworkers developed from diverse leadership teams—in terms of factors such as ethnicity and gender—with ties to different social networks. They built the union's strategic capacity—doing the most with what resources they had—through an ongoing process of experimentation, learning, and adaptation that involved taking risks, evaluating results, and implementing changes in strategy. In this way, ordinary workers built an organizational structure that had the power to influence employers with much greater resources. When such strategies were later abandoned, Ganz argues, the union's effectiveness declined.

Such nuanced sociological studies have provided organizers with a range of insights to improve the effectiveness of their work. Some sociologists argue that a revitalized and more effective labor movement is essential to reducing economic inequality (Clawson 2003).

think about it

1. *What role do culture, structure, and power play in these sociological analyses of union organizing?*

2. *How might a stronger labor movement in the United States affect political decision making, as well as the conditions of workers?*

workers (also known as FICA—Federal Insurance Contributions Act), which pay for Medicare and Social Security. Payroll taxes are a form of **regressive taxation** since they *disproportionately affect those with lower incomes.* For example, as of 2013, federal law exempted income above $113,700 per year from the Social Security payroll tax.

Taxing the inheritance of large estates has traditionally been another way to help reduce the concentration of wealth. When the first-ever U.S. billionaire, oil tycoon John D. Rockefeller, died in 1937, his children paid a 70 percent estate tax on most of his fortune they inherited, leaving them and their offspring with enough money to remain among the nation's wealthiest people to this day. The situation was different when oil industry billionaire Dan Duncan died in 2010. This time, because of dramatic changes in U.S. tax policy, Duncan's four children inherited his $9 billion fortune tax-free, making Duncan the first billionaire ever to pass on his estate without paying a single dollar in estate taxes (Collins and Pizzigati 2010). Since then, the estate tax has been reinstated. As of 2013, the first $5,250,000 is exempt from taxation and the highest tax rate is 40 percent.

PUBLIC ASSISTANCE Public policy also affects economic inequality through the administration of public assistance programs. **Public assistance** *includes either tax credits or actual payments and benefits provided to citizens by the government.* Welfare for the poor is the best-known form of public assistance. It includes cash payments, food stamps, child care, and housing subsidies. Since major welfare reform took effect in the mid-1990s, the focus of welfare benefits has shifted from direct cash payments to programs that promote work, such as job training and child care.

Contrary to popular perception, however, most public assistance goes to people in the middle and working classes—not the poor. If you are attending a state college or university, for example, you are benefiting from public assistance because the cost of your education is subsidized by taxpayers. Perhaps the most important form of middle-class public assistance is the home mortgage tax deduction, which allows homeowners to deduct the interest on a loan of up to $1 million used to purchase or improve a home; the larger the price tag on the home, the larger the government tax break. Consequently, about 80 percent of home mortgage tax benefits go to the top 20 percent of households in terms of income. In 2008 the mortgage interest tax deduction program cost the federal government about $100 billion, three times the amount spent on all public housing and low-income housing subsidies combined (Blau and Abramowitz 2007; Timiraos 2009).

The public assistance provided to corporations, sometimes referred to as "corporate welfare," is also many times more generous than the assistance given to the poor. Corporations—and indirectly the shareholders who own them—receive billions in this kind of assistance in the form of direct subsidies and tax breaks and the free or low-cost use of public resources such as forests. For example, in 2006 the federal government paid $21 billion in direct subsidies to agricultural concerns—many of which are large, profitable agribusiness corporations. Of that money, 66 percent went to the richest 10 percent of recipients (Slivinski 2007). States and localities, too, often compete to attract businesses by slashing taxes, paying for infrastructure, subsidizing utilities, and providing other incentives, all at taxpayer expense.

In 2008 and 2009 the federal government spent over $600 billion to stabilize the economy, including nearly $250 billion to bail out large banks after they teetered on the brink of collapse, largely due to irresponsible lending practices. Though some of these loans were repaid by 2013, the bailouts had still cost taxpayers over $50 billion and were the biggest example of corporate welfare in U.S. history (Kiel and Nguyen 2013).

The use of public resources to aid the middle and upper classes is the outcome of a political process. Those with the most political power write the rules, and they tend to write them for their own benefit. As we will see, political power also plays a role in global inequality.

Power and Global Inequality

In 2010, as its stock price surged, Apple surpassed Microsoft for the first time as the world's most valuable high-tech company, likely bringing smiles to the faces of its investors (Helft and Vance 2010). But in China, workers who assemble many Apple products, including the popular iPhone and iPad, were not celebrating the good news. Instead, 10 of them committed suicide in the first five months of the year, most by jumping off the balconies of company-built dormitories next to their massive factory complex in Shenzhen (BBC 2010a, 2010b). The workers were employed by Taiwan-based Foxconn Technology, the world's largest assembler of computers and handheld electronic devices, which contracts with Apple and other high-tech companies. Foxconn employees work six days a week for entry-level pay of $132 a month. They typically put in 10- to 12-hour workdays and are routinely expected to work overtime. They are forbidden to talk during their shifts and are subjected to what workers refer to as military-style discipline, leading one worker to tell reporters, "It's like a prison." Yet Foxconn is considered to be one of the better places to work. Conditions in many other Chinese factories are much worse.

The rash of suicides attracted embarrassing media coverage until government authorities ordered the Chinese press to tone down its coverage. After the Western media picked up the story and companies that contract with Foxconn expressed concern, the company instituted a 20 percent pay raise to improve morale and installed nets around its dormitories to foil suicide attempts.

Similar tales of bleak working conditions lurk behind many of the consumer electronics and other brand-name goods that dominate today's global economy. The economic inequality that we have explored in the United States has parallels in other countries, and inequality *within* individual countries exists side-by-side with **global inequality,**

thinking about power

How do the social policies that the government enacts, such as tax policy, reflect the relative **power** of different segments of society?

MAP 9.1 | A GLOBAL VIEW OF PER-CAPITA INCOME LEVELS

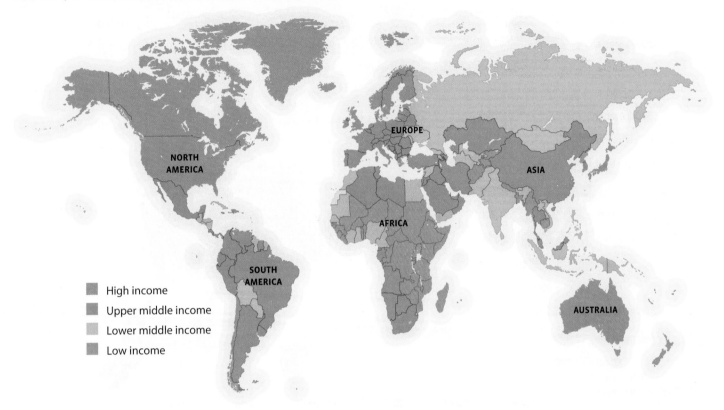

High income

Upper middle income

Lower middle income

Low income

This map is based on 2012 per-capita income (average income per person). Per-capita income in low-income countries is $1,035 per year or less; in lower-middle-income countries, $1,036–$4,085; in upper-middle-income countries, $4,086–$12,615; and in high-income countries, $12,616 or more. *Source:* The World Bank.

CORE CONCEPTS CHALLENGE

What does this map suggest about the relationship between a nation's wealth and its global political **power***? How might a nation's wealth influence its power? How might its political and military power influence its wealth?*

the differences in wealth and power among the countries of the world. The economic systems of individual countries are increasingly interconnected, and to understand economic inequality in any one country, including the United States, we must consider that country's place in the global economic structure.

Categorizing National Economies

Researchers and others commonly use the terms *developed*, *developing*, and *underdeveloped* to summarize a country's level of industrial and technological development. A country at a higher level of development generally produces more goods. As a result, its people have a higher material standard of living than those in less-developed countries.

Analysts sometimes use more nuanced categorizations of national economies. For example, Map 9.1 sorts the world's countries into four income levels, according to an analysis by the World Bank. Widespread poverty in much of Africa

and southern Asia make these among the poorest places on earth, whereas the United States, Canada, the nations of Europe, Japan, and Australia are among the world's wealthiest countries.

We can get a more concrete idea of what high and low incomes mean on a global scale by considering *purchasing power,* the average value of the goods and services people in a country can purchase in a year. As Figure 9.8 shows, purchasing power ranges from nearly $67,000 per person per year in Norway to just $370 in the Democratic Republic of Congo.

The global distribution of income is extremely unequal (see Figure 9.9):

- The average income of the top 20 percent of the world's population—which includes nearly all U.S. citizens— is about *50 times* the average income of the bottom 20 percent.

- More than 50 percent of the world's income goes to the richest 10 percent of the world's population, and nearly 75 percent goes to the richest 20 percent.

Power and Global Inequality

FIGURE 9.8 | PER-CAPITA PURCHASING POWER IN U.S. DOLLARS FOR SELECTED COUNTRIES, 2012

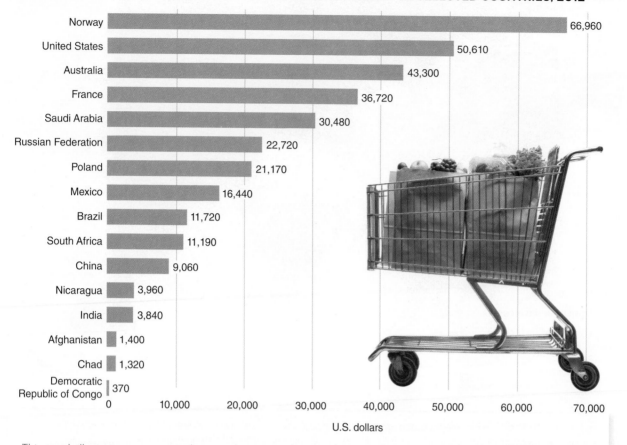

Country	U.S. dollars
Norway	66,960
United States	50,610
Australia	43,300
France	36,720
Saudi Arabia	30,480
Russian Federation	22,720
Poland	21,170
Mexico	16,440
Brazil	11,720
South Africa	11,190
China	9,060
Nicaragua	3,960
India	3,840
Afghanistan	1,400
Chad	1,320
Democratic Republic of Congo	370

This graph illustrates, on average, how much a person from each country could purchase in a year in 2012. Data are in 2013 U.S. dollars and take into account the relative cost of goods and services in different countries.
Source: The World Bank, World Development Indicators.

- Just 1.5 percent of the world's income goes to the poorest 20 percent of the population, and only 5 percent goes to the poorest 40 percent—roughly 2.5 billion people—who live on less than $2 a day.
- The world's 500 richest *individuals* have a combined income greater than the world's poorest 416 *million* people (UN Development Programme 2005).

The Impact of Global Inequality

As we saw earlier in this chapter, your class status within the United States has implications for your health, education, and lifestyle. Similarly, a country's income level typically corresponds to a variety of social indicators, resulting in starkly unequal social conditions around the world:

- *Life expectancy and health.* Poverty kills. On average, life expectancy for people in the world's poorest nations is about 30 years less than it is

FIGURE 9.9 | GLOBAL INCOME DISTRIBUTION

World income distributed by population quintiles, 2007

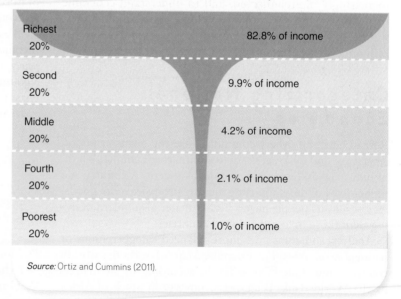

Richest 20%	82.8% of income
Second 20%	9.9% of income
Middle 20%	4.2% of income
Fourth 20%	2.1% of income
Poorest 20%	1.0% of income

Source: Ortiz and Cummins (2011).

MAP 9.2 | WITHIN-COUNTRY INCOME INEQUALITY

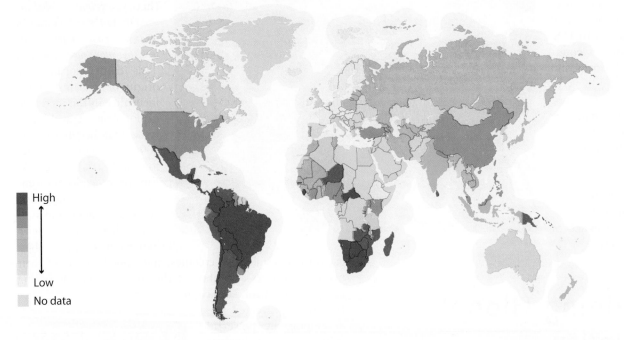

High

Low

No data

This map shows the degree of economic inequality within each country, based on family income. *Source:* www.siteatlas.com.

for people in wealthy nations. Poor countries have high rates of infant mortality, and people die at an early age from malnourishment, pneumonia, malaria, diarrhea, and HIV/AIDS. Around 10 million children under age five die each year of undernutrition and related causes; these comprise 30 percent of all childhood deaths (Commission on Social Determinants of Health 2008; World Health Organization 2004).

■ *Housing.* About a third of the world's urban population—more than a billion people—live in slums—housing that lacks durability, sufficient living area, access to clean water and sanitation, and secure occupancy rights (UN Human Settlements Programme 2003a, 2003b). The rural poor in developing nations migrate to urban areas for jobs and schooling, often only to find grinding poverty and disease amidst vast city slums.

■ *Education.* Most people in many poor countries are illiterate. Adult literacy rates in Afghanistan (18 percent), Mali (26 percent), and Niger (29 percent)—among the world's lowest—reflect the deep poverty of such countries, where schooling is often not free and children must work from a very early age (World Bank 2011).

Over the past half century the number of people living in absolute poverty has decreased, largely due to the dramatic economic growth in China and India, which together account for about 40 percent of the world's population. However, in other parts of the world, particularly sub-Saharan Africa, poverty persists, and the number of people living in poverty has increased significantly (United Nations 2005).

These global changes have had a direct impact on the United States. Because China and other countries with growing economies use more resources, oil and food prices have increased worldwide. The shift of manufacturing to developing nations has reduced employment in U.S. factories, while contributing to a massive trade deficit as the United States imports more foreign goods. In addition, poverty, despair, and inequality contribute to instability and conflict in various parts of the world, situations that have in some cases led to the involvement of U.S. military troops.

Inequality within Countries

Inequality exists in every country, produced in part by the kinds of public policy decisions we disc____ ___ ____ _____ chapter. Map 9.2 illustrates the varying ____ __ ____ equality around the world. The highest ____ ___ ___ Central and South America and southern____ ___ ___ eas, a small elite controls limited resource ____ ____ live in poverty. In many highly unequal ____ ____ ___ and business elites use agreements with ____ ___ and governments to maintain their weal____ __ ___ expense of the nation's poor and working ____ ___ inequality within nations is connected to ___ ____ ___

Wealthy nations such as France and Sweden generally have comparatively low levels of economic inequality because of high taxes on the wealthy, generous minimum wages, and other policies that reduce inequality. The exception is the United States, the most unequal wealthy country in the world. In societies with the least amount of inequality, moderate and

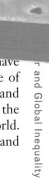

r and Global Inequality

low-income groups tend to have much more power than they do in the United States. Compared to U.S. citizens, people in countries such as Norway and Canada are more likely to be organized into labor unions, to vote, and to have the option of voting for a political party that represents labor or the working class. In many respects, therefore, the nature and extent of inequality depends on the balance of power in a society.

Explaining Global Inequality

Global inequality has many causes. For example, different countries have different climates and different amounts of natural resources, both of which undoubtedly contribute to their degree of affluence or poverty. In addition, most sociologists acknowledge two major *social* causes of global inequality: culture and power.

Culture and Global Inequality: Modernization Theory

Through most of human history, people possessed relatively few material goods, so economic inequality was limited. However, as we saw in Chapter 1, industrialization transformed northern European societies by destroying traditional ways of life and creating unprecedented material abundance. But not all countries experienced this change.

Modernization theory *attributes global inequality to cultural differences among countries.* According to this theory, some societies resisted industrialization, preferring to retain traditional ways of life rather than adopt disruptive new technologies. Maintaining family and community relationships, the agricultural economy, and traditional religious beliefs were more important than adopting new means to produce greater material abundance. These differing cultural traditions helped open up an economic gap between industrialized nations and the developing world.

Power and Global Inequality: Dependency Theory

Many sociologists argue that today's global inequality is rooted in a much less benign process than cultural differences. Their alternative, **dependency theory,** *attributes global inequality to the exploitation of weaker, poor nations by wealthy, more powerful ones.* This theory locates the origin of growing global inequality in the increased exploration, travel, and trade that began roughly 500 years ago—long before industrialization. As European explorers ventured to Africa, the Western Hemisphere, and East Asia, they clashed with indigenous peoples, subjugated them, established colonies, and gained control of their natural resources and labor. Rather than voluntarily opting out of development, poor countries were prevented from developing by powerful colonizers who became wealthy by exploiting their natural resources and cheap labor. Typically, colonial powers would import raw materials from colonies and turn them into valuable manufactured goods. With slavery, colonial powers took West Africans to labor in American plantations, enriching the colonial nations while impoverishing the colonies.

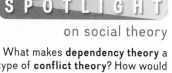

SPOTLIGHT
on social theory

What makes **dependency theory** a type of **conflict theory**? How would dependency theory apply to countries you may have visited or to the countries in which you or your ancestors were born? How does it apply to the United States?

Colonialism and Neocolonialism

In the modern era, roughly since 1500, nations have struggled fiercely over resources. The most obvious type of global struggle was **colonialism,** *the use of military, political, and economic power by one society to dominate the people of another society, usually for economic benefit.* From the 1500s through the 1900s, European powers used their military might to subjugate other peoples across the globe. According to a famous saying, the sun never set on the British Empire because its colonial holdings were spread out across the world. The use of the English language in many regions of the world today is in part a legacy of this colonial subjugation. Africa, India, North America, much of South America, and other areas of the world were all conquered by colonial powers.

Colonial powers typically exerted direct political control over their colonies or established puppet governments (controlled by the outside colonial power) while engaging in military occupation and establishing cultural dominance.

Most important, colonial powers usually sought to extract the natural resources from their colonies and exploit the labor available there.

Most colonies resisted their colonial occupiers. By the latter half of the twentieth century, independence movements had successfully brought an end to colonial rule. However, these new nations often struggled to overcome their colonial past, which had stripped them of vast resources, left them ill prepared to develop modern economic systems, and often institutionalized a culture of political corruption. Some observers argue that colonialism has been replaced by **neocolonialism**, *a system of economic domination of poorer nations by wealthier ones without formal political control or military occupation.*

In a neocolonial situation, former colonies continue to depend on wealthier nations for capital investment and technical expertise, giving these wealthier countries enormous influence over their development. In addition, former colonies often experience civil wars and political infighting as different factions struggle for control of resources, adding yet another hurdle to economic development (United Nations 2005).

World Systems Analysis

Another approach to global inequality, **world systems analysis** *focuses on the interdependence among the countries in a single global economic system.* Sociologist Immanuel Wallerstein (1974, 1979) sees the poverty of some countries as connected directly to the wealth of others. He sorts countries into one of three primary groups, depending on their relationship to the global economy:

- *Core nations* include the United States, Canada, Japan, and the European countries. These, the world's wealthiest countries, are at the center of the global economy. Most core nations benefited from colonialism and continue to dominate the global economy through multinational corporations and global financial institutions.

- *Periphery nations* include many countries in Africa, Latin America, and parts of Asia. These are the world's poorest and least powerful countries, at the fringe of the global economy. They participate in the global economy by providing natural resources and cheap labor for the transnational corporations while also serving as markets for some goods.

- *Semi-periphery nations* include China, India, Mexico, and Pakistan. These middle-income nations are better integrated with the economies of core countries than are the periphery nations and often have a stronger domestic industrial base.

With modern communications and transportation, capital from core nations can move easily around the globe. Poorer countries are often dependent on this foreign investment to fund their economic development. They frequently compete against one another to attract foreign investment by offering low or no taxes, minimal environmental regulations, and a low-cost, nonunion labor force.

Typically based in core nations, multinational corporations look to cut costs and boost profits by shifting production to semi-periphery nations. This allows them to take advantage of low-wage labor and lax environmental regulation and to avoid paying some taxes in core nations. In doing so, they create jobs and stimulate the local economies in these poor countries.

This local economic development is often temporary, however. For example, in the 1990s—especially after the passage of the North American Free Trade Agreement (NAFTA)—some U.S. corporations moved manufacturing jobs to Mexico, which helped devastate some "rust belt" communities in the United States but helped Mexican workers, whose average manufacturing wage rose to $2.08 an hour. But these gains were short lived: many companies soon began the process over again by moving production to China, where manufacturing workers were earning an average of just 61 cents an hour (Ferriss 2003).

This is an example of the *race to the bottom*, the process of poorer nations competing for foreign investment by sacrificing wages, tax revenue, worker safety, and environmental standards. The race to the bottom can keep periphery and semi-periphery nations poor while channeling profits back to investors in core countries. If workers in these poor countries organize into unions to improve their conditions—as workers once did in wealthier nations—or if national governments insist on high-quality environmental standards, corporate investors can simply move to a new country that offers more favorable incentives. The existing rules for the global economy—rules that favor the free flow of capital—are coordinated through the world's global financial institutions.

Global Financial Institutions

In recent decades, global financial organizations have had an enormous influence on the economic and social policies of poor countries (Kaplinsky 2007). The three major players in global finance are the World Bank, which provides poor countries with investments and loans for development; the International Monetary Fund (IMF), which provides financial and technical assistance to promote economic growth; and the World Trade Organization, which administers trade practices between countries. Although all three organizations ostensibly aim to promote development in and provide aid to poorer nations, many critics contend that they are key vehicles through which core nations and multinational corporations dominate poorer countries.

For example, critics contend that the conditions the World Bank sets for loans—known as *structural adjustment programs*—actually benefit foreign investors rather than the poor countries and in fact lead to increased poverty. In some cases, to receive assistance from the World Bank and IMF, countries have been required to shift from producing essential food crops for domestic use, such as corn and beans, to cash crops intended for export, such as coffee and cotton, thereby worsening hunger locally. These organizations have also insisted that governments slash vital social service spending in order to repay foreign loans, sometimes with disastrous results for the health and education of the local population.

In recent years, activists from around the world have organized to promote basic labor and environmental standards and to advocate debt forgiveness. Activists have used education, the promotion of "fair trade" goods whose production meets basic labor and environmental standards, and street protests at the meetings of global financial institutions to advance their cause. Their advocacy has led to more public scrutiny of these institutions as well as some reforms (Stiglitz and Charlton 2007).

A Changing World

U.S. INEQUALITY IN GLOBAL CONTEXT

Economic inequality in the United States has long been closely connected to the global economy, and this close relationship has produced starkly different results in two recent periods. From 1945 to the 1970s, the U.S. economy experienced enormous growth. The economic infrastructure of most industrialized countries had been damaged or destroyed by World War II. With virtually no competition, U.S. manufacturers dominated much of the global marketplace. Plenty of well-paid working-class jobs were available in automobile plants, the steel industry, and other types of manufacturing. Strong labor unions fought for better working conditions and wages, and the benefits of this economic growth were spread across all income levels (see Figure 9.10).

By the 1970s, global economic conditions had changed. U.S. companies failed to invest adequately in newer technologies such as smaller, more fuel-efficient automobiles and were caught off-guard by newly emerging global competition. To stay competitive, corporations based in the United States began exporting many of the high-paying manufacturing jobs that had provided economic security for working- and middle-class Americans to poor nations that offered lower wages, fewer labor and environmental regulations, and, often, repressive governments that maintained political stability and made labor organizing difficult or impossible. The result was **deindustrialization,** *the process by which investment in the nation's manufacturing capacity decreased*, devastating the economies of many communities, especially in the Midwest and Northeast. The export of good-paying working-class jobs often left middle-income workers scrambling for jobs with lower wages, while increased corporate profits translated into higher incomes for affluent stockholders. The result was increased inequality.

The economy continued to grow, but now, as Figure 9.10 shows, the benefits went disproportionately to those already making higher incomes. From 1979 to 2012, the income growth of the richest people remained high, while people at

FIGURE 9.10 | **CHANGE IN REAL FAMILY INCOME, 1947–1979 AND 1979–2012**

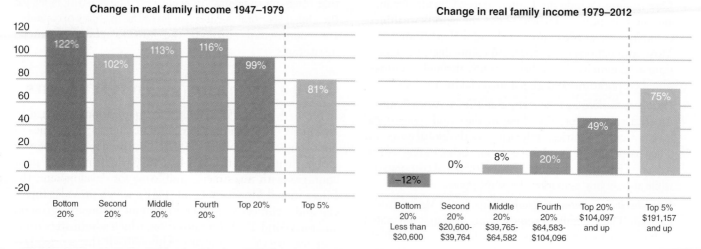

In the decades after World War II, the benefits of economic growth were spread evenly, and families at all income levels enjoyed significant increases in their income. In recent decades, however, those with already high incomes have seen the biggest gains; most people have experienced more modest gains or no gains at all. *Sources:* Gordon (2013); U.S. Census Bureau, (2013e).

lower income levels had much lower growth or none at all. Working-class and lower-middle-class workers have actually fared worse than Figure 9.10 suggests, because in the past few decades more families have become two-income households. In a historic shift in family structure, both husband and wife in most families today work outside the home to improve or just maintain their standard of living (Levy 1998). In the future—especially in the wake of the most recent financial crisis—many families will probably see their incomes decrease.

What all this means is that the gap between rich and poor has expanded significantly, and income inequality in the United States today is greater than at any time since the Great Depression of the 1930s. This growing inequality has profoundly affected both family structure and social structure as a whole. For example, because of stagnant wages, parents in many families work longer hours or take on a second job; as a result, they have less time to care for their children, volunteer, or become politically active. As employer-provided benefits have declined, millions of Americans have found themselves without health insurance, leading to some reform of the system in 2010, popularly known as Obamacare, aimed at reducing the ranks of the uninsured. Many families have also taken on a growing amount of personal debt. This trend, as well as a decline in personal savings, contributed to the economic crisis that began in 2008. This crisis is still reverberating around the world, and its impact on the global economy will influence both U.S. and global inequality for years to come.

thinking sociologically about
Class and Global Inequality

culture

- Class is not just about money: it includes a major cultural component that is passed on through socialization, especially through the family and schools.

- Different societies have different cultural values that place more or less emphasis on limiting economic inequality.

structure

- Individual action is important in determining your class position, but it always takes place within a structural context that shapes the options available to you.

- The structure of the global economy helps shape the opportunities and living conditions of people around the globe.

power

- Because of their different levels of material and cultural resources, people from different classes have different levels of power in society.

- Wealthy, industrialized nations have considerably more power than poor or developing countries. Multinational corporations based in wealthy countries, along with global financial institutions, have considerable power to influence the global economy.

10

Race and Ethnicity

looking AHEAD

How does **culture** define your race?

How do individuals and institutional **structures** perpetuate racial and ethnic inequality?

How do majority and minority groups reflect inequalities in **power**?

People make racial distinctions in part by paying attention selectively to some physical variations while largely ignoring others. Why are the different skin tones in these men more socially significant than their different hair color? What does this selective attention suggest about the arbitrary nature of race?

increased probability of having a child with birth defects for women and reduced fertility for men. Melanin—and the dark skin associated with it—protects against these adverse effects, but it also reduces the skin's ability to produce the essential nutrient vitamin D from sunlight. As a result, dark skin provides an evolutionary advantage in sunlight-intense tropical environments, whereas lighter skin provides an evolutionary advantage in regions of less intense sunlight (Jablonski and Chaplin 2002). As humans across many generations migrated and adapted to different geographic regions, they developed a range of skin tones that vary more or less continuously from dark to light between regions of intense sunlight and those of less intense sunlight (Map 10.1) (Jablonski and Chaplin 2002).

In addition, skin tone is not consistently connected to other physical features such as hair type or nose shape. Dark- or light-skinned people can have all types of hair, noses, and other physical attributes. Skin tone, in other words, is not a fixed biological attribute of any one race. To understand how it became

Human physical variation is too subtle and diverse to be captured accurately by a handful of racial or ethnic classifications.

MAP 10.1 | **GLOBAL DISTRIBUTION OF SKIN TONE**

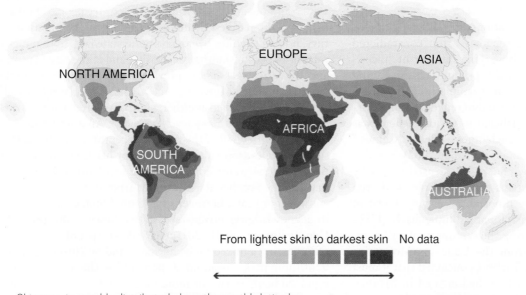

From lightest skin to darkest skin   No data

Skin tone is roughly distributed along the earth's latitudes so that, for example, people in parts of Mexico, northern Africa, and portions of China all share similar skin tones, even though they are commonly classified as belonging to different racial groups. *Source:* Jablonski and Chaplin (2002).

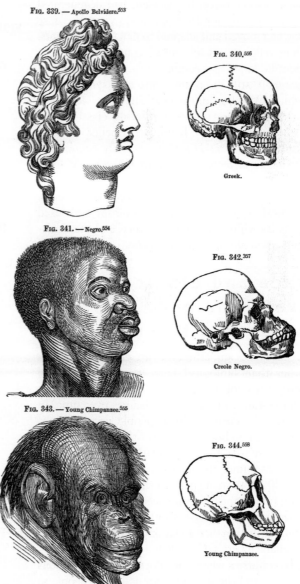

Fig. 339. — Apollo Belvidere.553

Fig. 340.555

Greek.

Fig. 341. — Negro.554

Fig. 342.357

Creole Negro.

Fig. 343. — Young Chimpanzee.565

Fig. 344.556

Young Chimpanzee.

linked with race in the popular imagination, we have to look to social factors—cultural beliefs, social structures, and power relationships—not to biology.

Pseudo-Science and Race

The term *race* took on its popular contemporary connotations in the eighteenth century, when European scientists began systematically to name and classify the plants and animals of the natural world. When they turned their attention to humanity, however, ethnocentric assumptions of European superiority reduced their efforts to pseudoscience (Smedley 2007).

For example, the Swedish naturalist Carolus Linnaeus (1707–1778), who laid the foundation for the biological classification system still in use today, invented four subspecies of *Homo sapiens*, attributing to each not only physical traits but also judgmental character traits. White-skinned *Europeanus*, described as creative and governed by laws, was at the top. The other three were copper-skinned *Americanus*, described as stubborn, easily angered, and governed by customs; sallow-skinned (yellowish) *Asiaticus*, described as greedy and governed by opinions; and dark-skinned *Africanus*, described as lazy, negligent, and

Early pseudo-scientific classification schemes perpetuated racist beliefs. This image is from an 1857 book titled *Indigenous Races of the Earth* by physician Josiah Nott and Egyptologist George Gliddon. It suggests white biological superiority, with blacks somewhere in between whites and chimpanzees.

The Role of Culture: Inventing Ethnicity and Race

governed only by impulse (Smedley 2007). This classification laid the groundwork for "scientific" justifications of **racism,** *the belief that one race is inherently superior to another.*

Later writers developed variations on this sort of racist classification system. These schemes often contradicted each other, proposing a widely varying number of "races," each based on different physical types and accompanying social characteristics. Whites, for example, were often divided into subgroups that purported to reflect the superiority of northern Europeans—labeled in various schemes as "Teutonic" or "Nordic"—over such other whites as "Celtics," "Semitics," and "Mediterraneans" (Smedley 2007).

From today's perspective, the rationale used to justify these racial classification systems seems arbitrary and even bizarre. For example, in the nineteenth century, German anatomist and anthropologist Johann Blumenbach (1752–1840), apparently after admiring the symmetry of a particularly well-preserved skull from the Caucasus Mountains (located between Russia and Turkey), concluded that it must have been Caucasians whom God had created in his own image. Other races, he decided, had degenerated physically and morally from God's vision because they had moved and adapted to new environments. Thus, religion and folk belief, couched in pseudo-scientific language, combined to give us the term *Caucasian,* still in common use as a synonym for "white" (Mukhopadhyay et al. 2007).

These arbitrary and conflicting classification systems went hand in hand with a belief in **racial essentialism**—*the idea that supposedly natural and immutable differences separated the races.* Whites who created the classification systems lived in societies with the power to enforce these ideas. Cultural notions of racial essentialism were used to justify white supremacy, slavery, and the European colonial domination of other peoples.

Race and Ethnicity over Time and Across Cultures

Because races and ethnicities are cultural creations rather than biological facts, the definition and significance of racial and ethnic groups varies from culture to culture and changes over time. In nineteenth-century China, people drew distinctions based on body hair rather than skin tone. To them, extensive facial hair marked European missionaries as uncivilized barbarians (Mukhopadhyay et al. 2007). In many parts of the world, ethnicity is more important than race; people are much more concerned about one another's tribe, clan, or ethnic affiliation than about skin color or other physical characteristics (Cornell and Hartmann 2007).

In countries where race does matter, definitions of race—and the standards for assigning people to one race or another—vary enormously. In the United States, sexual encounters between white owners and black slaves were common, and in the nineteenth century people of mixed race were often called "Mulattos." In the early twentieth century, however, whites began changing state laws so that racial categories became mutually exclusive, and in the case of mixed ancestry, the black status prevailed. For example, Virginia passed the "Racial Integrity Act" in 1924 mandating that all newborns be classified as either white or colored, with colored including those with *any* black or Native American ancestry. During the first half of the twentieth century, versions of this so-called one-drop rule—one drop of black blood makes a person black—were adopted by state legislatures throughout much of the South and Midwest (Murray 1997).

In recent years, however, the United States has returned to acknowledging mixed-race status. Since 2000, the U.S. Census Bureau (2011b, 2011c) has allowed people the option of indicating a mixed racial heritage, and by 2010 more than 9 million people—about 3 percent of the population—reported being of two or more races (see Figure 10.1). Some

FIGURE 10.1 | RACE, ETHNICITY, AND THE U.S. CENSUS

8. Is Person 1 of Hispanic, Latino, or Spanish origin?

☐ **No,** not of Hispanic, Latino, or Spanish origin
☐ Yes, Mexican, Mexican Am., Chicano
☐ Yes, Puerto Rican
☐ Yes, Cuban
☐ Yes, another Hispanic, Latino, or Spanish origin — *Print origin, for example, Argentinean, Colombian, Dominican, Nicaraguan, Salvadoran, Spaniard, and so on.* ⤵

9. What is Person 1's race? *Mark* ☒ *one or more boxes.*

☐ White
☐ Black, African Am., or Negro
☐ American Indian or Alaska Native — *Print name of enrolled or principal tribe.* ⤵

☐ Asian Indian   ☐ Japanese   ☐ Native Hawaiian
☐ Chinese   ☐ Korean   ☐ Guamanian or Chamorro
☐ Filipino   ☐ Vietnamese   ☐ Samoan
☐ Other Asian — *Print race, for example, Hmong, Laotian, Thai, Pakistani, Cambodian, and so on.* ⤵   ☐ Other Pacific Islander — *Print race, for example, Fijian, Tongan, and so on.* ⤵

☐ Some other race — *Print race.* ⤵

The U.S. Census includes questions about race and Hispanic origin. The categories included in these questions reflect the unique social history of the United States. *Source:* U.S. Census Bureau.

people with mixed-race backgrounds, though, still choose to identify with a single race. When President Obama filled out his 2010 census form, he identified himself only as black, although his mother was white (Roberts and Baker 2010).

The countries of Latin America and the Caribbean have long had a variety of categories for people of mixed descent—including mixtures of European, African, and Indian—and physical appearance carries much less social significance in the region than it does in the United States. For example, the legacy of slavery in Brazil endured in the ranking of people by racial category. However, in Brazil these categories were never codified legally. In addition, intermarriage and sexual relations among indigenous peoples, Africans,

and Europeans were much more commonly accepted than in the United States. Brazilians now have dozens of racial categories based on differences in a variety of physical features, including hair, lips, eyes, and noses, as well as skin color. As a result, siblings from the same family can fall into different racial categories. Also, in Brazil the presence of any white ancestor helps determine a person's classification, and over half of Brazilians fall into the broad category of "white" (which is broken down into many smaller subcategories). However, many white Brazilians would be perceived as black if they traveled to the United States (Kephart 2003). For a look at various systems of racial and ethnic classification, see Figure 10.2.

FIGURE 10.2 | RACE AND ETHNICITY ACROSS CULTURES

Australia 2001 Census

Are you of Aboriginal or Torres Strait Islander origin? If you are of both Aboriginal and Torres Strait Islander origin, mark both 'Yes' boxes.

- ☐ No
- ☐ Yes, Aboriginal
- ☐ Yes, Torres Strait Islander

What is your ancestry? Provide more than one if necessary.

- ☐ English
- ☐ Irish
- ☐ Italian
- ☐ German
- ☐ Greek
- ☐ Chinese
- ☐ Australian
- ☐ Other

England 2001 Census
What is your ethnic group?

A) White
- ☐ British
- ☐ Irish
- ☐ Any other white background

B) Mixed
- ☐ White and Black Caribbean
- ☐ White and Black African
- ☐ White and Asian
- ☐ Any other Mixed background

C) Asian or Asian British
- ☐ Indian
- ☐ Pakistani
- ☐ Bangleshi
- ☐ Any other Asian background

D) Black or Black British
- ☐ Caribbean
- ☐ African
- ☐ Any other black background

E) Chinese/other ethnic group
- ☐ Chinese
- ☐ Any other

Brazil 2000 Census

Choose your race:
- ☐ White - branca
- ☐ Black - peta
- ☐ Yellow - amaréta
- ☐ Brown - parda
- ☐ Native, aboriginal - indigena
- ☐ Undeclared

Bulgaria 2001 Census

What is your ethnic group?
- ☐ Bulgarian
- ☐ Turkish
- ☐ Gypsies
- ☐ Other

Canada 2001 Census

Are you an aboriginal person, that is, North American Indian, Métis or Inuit (Eskimo)? If "Yes"; check the box(es) that describe(s) you now.

- ☐ No, > Continue with the next question
- ☐ Yes, North American Indian
- ☐ Yes, Métis
- ☐ Yes, Inuit (Eskimo)

Are you a member of an Indian Band/First Nation?
- ☐ No
- ☐ Yes, member of an Indian Band/First Nation

Are you a Treaty Indian or a Registered Indian as defined by the Indian Act of Canada?
- ☐ No
- ☐ Yes, Treaty Indian or a Registered Indian

Mexico 2000 Census

Are you Náhuatl, Mayan, Zapoteco, Mixteco or of another indigenous group?
- ☐ Yes
- ☐ No

South Africa 2001 Census

How would you describe yourself in terms of population group?

- ☐ Black African
- ☐ Coloured
- ☐ Indian or Asian
- ☐ White
- ☐ Other

Because race and ethnicity are social constructions, they vary by culture. Different countries use different classification systems in their census collection. If you moved to another country, your race or ethnicity might change. *Source:* American Anthropological Association (2011).

Minority and Majority Groups

In any given society, people often think of its members who are of different races and ethnicities in terms of majority and minority groups. A **minority group** is *a collection of people who suffer disadvantages and have less power because of identifiable physical or cultural characteristics*. In contrast, a **majority group** is *a collection of people who enjoy privileges and have more access to power because of identifiable physical or cultural characteristics*. Sociologists do not use these terms in a literal sense. A minority group need not be an actual minority of the population, and a majority group need not be an actual majority. In South Africa under the white supremacist apartheid regime, for example, the black population held the minority status even though they far outnumbered whites.

Although the status of individual members of a minority can vary widely, *as a group*, compared to the majority group, minorities tend to have lower incomes, less education, less political influence, and poorer health. Conversely, individual members of a majority group may not wield great power or have access to great resources, but, *as a group*, majorities dominate society. In addition to greater resources, the majority group also has the power to create and enforce the labels used to designate minority groups.

Members of minority groups tend to be conscious of their status and aware of the hurdles and barriers they face in society. To navigate a majority-dominated society successfully, they must learn how the majority group operates. In contrast, majority-group members often take their status for granted and are unaware of their relative privilege. They typically do not need to learn about minority cultures to be successful within a society their group dominates.

Patterns of Majority-Minority Interaction

The relationship between majority and minority groups in a society can range from benign to destructive. In some cases, members of a minority group might find acceptance and equal standing with the majority group, whereas in other situations a minority group may be subjected to widespread prejudice and discrimination. To have **prejudice** means *to "pre-judge" someone or some group negatively based on inadequate information*. These judgments are often based on **stereotypes,** *exaggerated, distorted, or untrue generalizations about categories of people that do not acknowledge individual variation*. Stereotypes can be either negative or positive; examples of positive stereotypes are the Asian math whiz and the African American sports star. Prejudice is limited to beliefs and attitudes that individuals hold but may not act on. When prejudice is joined to action, however, it leads to **discrimination,** *unequal treatment that gives advantages to one group of people over another without justifiable cause*.

The patterns of interaction among majority and minority groups can take a variety of forms, sometimes straddling more than one category. In a society that embraces **pluralism,**

FAST-FORWARD

Social Change and Race

For many years, white people were the assumed norm when manufacturers created "flesh"-colored products such as adhesive bandages. Today, reflecting changes in the culture, manufacturers are more likely to recognize a diversity of skin tones, as with these "multicultural" crayons.

Structure and Power Among Racial and Ethnic Groups

By identifying certain cultural or physical traits as socially significant, people create a social reality that influences how they behave with one another. In other words, "seeing" others in terms of race, ethnicity, and other social categories (such as religion, age, and sexual orientation) can affect how we act toward them and help legitimize social inequality based on those categories. Let's look at some of these dynamics.

distinct ethnic and racial groups coexist on equal terms and have equal social standing. Members of these groups recognize and maintain their differences, but the differences have no significant impact on anyone's political, social, or economic standing. Switzerland is a successful pluralistic society. The Swiss Confederation—Switzerland's official name—unites four cultures, each with its own regions and its own official language: German, French, Italian, or Romansch (based on Latin).

Amalgamation is *the process by which a majority and a minority group blend or mix to form a new group.* This is typically accomplished through intermarriage over the course of several generations. For example, Mexican society today is primarily an amalgamation of Indian and Spanish cultures that have blended to create what is now a distinctly Mexican identity.

Assimilation is *the process by which members of a minority group come to adopt the culture of the majority group.* As we will see, the experience of many white European ethnic groups in the United States has been one of assimilation; ethnic groups largely abandoned their distinct cultures and were absorbed into the nation's dominant culture. The assimilation experience is often partially voluntary, as minority group members emulate the dominant culture, and partially coerced as majority-group members require others to conform to their cultural expectations.

Segregation involves *keeping distinct social groups physically and socially separate and unequal.* In the United States, segregation is most associated with the oppression of African Americans, especially in the South after the Civil War and before the civil rights movement.

Genocide is *the systematic killing of a group of people, based on their race, ethnicity, nationality, or religion.* Typically, genocide involves a majority group seeking to exterminate a minority group. The deliberate killing of Jews and others by the Nazi regime in Germany and other European countries during World War II is the most infamous example of genocide, but not the first and, unfortunately, not the last (Kiernan 2007).

Minority Group Responses to Discrimination

Minority groups can respond to majority-group domination in a variety of ways:

- **Withdrawal** involves physically escaping the worst oppression. As we will see, the Great Migration of African Americans out of the South to the North and Midwest in the early and mid-twentieth century is one example of this strategy. Other examples include the formation of racial and ethnic enclaves in urban areas: places with names like Germantown, Little Italy, and Chinatown.
- **Passing** involves blending in with the dominant group. White ethnics in the United States often changed their names on arrival to better blend into the dominant Anglo-Saxon culture. Germans with the name "Schmidt" would change it to "Smith," for example. Today many recent immigrants from Vietnam, China, India, and elsewhere similarly adopt names that are more familiar to native-born Americans and easier for them to spell and pronounce. Passing can also occur when people in a minority group take advantage of physical similarities to the members of the majority group, as when light-skinned blacks conceal their race or even change their hair to appear more "white."
- **Code-switching**—a term coined by sociologist Elijah Anderson (1999)—refers to the strategy of complying with the social expectations of the majority by creating a front-stage self-presentation while maintaining a different more comfortable and authentic backstage identity. Code-switching may involve dressing "white" or using "white" English at work or school, while retaining a more comfortable mother tongue, ethnic slang, and ethnic dress at home.
- **Resistance** involves actively asserting oneself—either individually or collectively—in defiance of majority discrimination. The many civil rights struggles that have characterized U.S. history are examples of this strategy.

The Origins of Racial and Ethnic Diversity in the United States

In the United States, ideas about race and ethnicity are rooted in the country's history—the European conquest of native peoples, the immigration of Europeans, the enslavement of Africans, and the recruitment of Asian laborers.

Native Peoples

In 1492, before Europeans established their first permanent settlements in the Western Hemisphere, an estimated 50 million people lived in North and South America, about 5 million of them in what is today the United States and Canada (Taylor 2001). When Europeans arrived, the Aztec capital of Tenochtitlán had a quarter of a million inhabitants—five times the size of London at the time (Gonzalez 2000). Native peoples formed hundreds of different societies with unique languages, religions, forms of government, and cultural traditions. These ranged from the Inuit, who lived in nomadic bands in what is today the Canadian Arctic, to the powerful urban civilizations of the Aztec and Maya in what is today Mexico and the Inca in what is today Peru.

Understanding Whiteness

In a classic essay, Peggy McIntosh (1988) notes that whites are often taught to recognize the disadvantages that minorities face but not the advantages they enjoy as whites. She describes some of the dozens of ways that she benefits from white privilege in her daily life. When she shops, for example, she doesn't experience the suspicion and harassment to which minorities are often subjected. Minorities are often judged individually as if they represented their entire community: If they excel, they are a credit to the community; if they behave questionably, it's because of the deficiencies of their community. As a white person, McIntosh does not bear this burden. Cumulatively, these and similar advantages constitute an "invisible package of unearned assets," as McIntosh calls it, that reflects the dominant position of the white majority in the United States.

McIntosh's essay is one example of the study of whiteness. People often think of race in terms of minorities. But white majorities in the European colonies created the modern idea of "race" during the eighteenth century, and to understand "race" we must understand whiteness and its connection to power and inequality.

Although he is best known for writing about the condition of black Americans, African American sociologist and activist W. E. B. Du Bois ([1935] 1998) recognized the importance of whiteness a century ago. Although American society as a whole was divided by class, he noted, the working class was divided further along racial lines. White workers might be poorly paid, but they were "compensated in part by a sort of public and psychological wage. They were given public deference and titles of courtesy because they were white" (p. 700). They, like white people of all classes, could attend public functions and enjoy public parks. They were served by a white police force, by a court system staffed by white jurists, and by white elected officials, and they had access to the best schools, which were reserved for them. Ironically, however, by embracing these race-based privileges, white workers lost the opportunity to organize with black workers to improve conditions for all of them.

Sociologists today are using Du Bois's sociological insights to inform their current analysis of race, particularly on the nature of whiteness (Rothenberg 2004). Sociologists engaged in whiteness studies examine both the historical roots and the contemporary processes associated with whiteness and white privilege. The questions they explore (some of which are discussed in this chapter) include: How did diverse ethnic groups once considered fundamentally different become lumped together as whites? How have the U.S. political, legal, and economic systems been structured to give advantages to whites? Does white privilege endure, and, if so, what forms does it take? How can whites help combat racism and its legacy?

The point is not to blame today's whites for the history of racial injustice. Instead, whiteness studies help us better understand that history of injustice, to recognize its continuing legacy today, and to use those insights to work toward a more just society.

think about it

1. *Has your education about race included consideration of what it means to be white?*

2. *How does the study of whiteness illustrate the sociological insight that power is a social relationship?*

---

of this work sparked many labor disputes, which increased in the 1960s and 1970s with the rise of the United Farm Workers union led by César Chávez and Dolores Huerta.

PUERTO RICANS   Puerto Ricans, the second largest Latino group in the United States, are also linked to U.S. expansion. The United States invaded and occupied Puerto Rico during the Spanish-American War of 1898, transforming the island from a Spanish colony to a U.S. colony. In the ensuing decades, U.S. sugar companies acquired vast tracts of land on the island, displacing small growers and prompting sometimes violent labor clashes. Many agricultural workers fled to the U.S. mainland in search of better opportunities. In 1917, Puerto Ricans became U.S. citizens and, in 1947, Puerto Rico became a commonwealth with the right to elect its own governor. Although it otherwise remains subject to U.S. law, it has only a nonvoting delegate to Congress and its residents cannot vote for president. Puerto Ricans are divided about the island's future political status. Some support the current arrangement, some favor gaining U.S. statehood, and some advocate independence (Takaki 2008).

CUBAN AMERICANS   The Spanish colony of Cuba, unlike Puerto Rico, gained formal independence after the Spanish-American War. However, it remained subject to U.S. military and economic intervention and suffered from political instability. In 1959, Fidel Castro led a revolution to overthrow the Cuban dictator Fulgencio Batista and instituted radical economic reform, eventually aligning his nation with the Soviet Union and communist bloc nations. Castro's reforms were popular among many of the country's poor, but not among the more affluent middle and upper classes, many of whom fled to the United States, forming the core of today's Cuban American community.

WASPs and White Ethnic Groups

The colonies founded by Great Britain on the east coast of North America were what became the early United States, and for many years the descendants of colonial-era immigrants from Great Britain—white Anglo-Saxon Protestants, or WASPS—were the country's most powerful ethnic group. Other white ethnic groups arrived in large numbers during the nineteenth and twentieth centuries.

WHITE ANGLO-SAXON PROTESTANTS

The WASP label combines race, ethnicity, and religion. It refers mostly to people of English ancestry but also includes those of Scottish and Welsh ancestry. It excludes whites from other parts of Europe as well as Catholics and Jews. (The Through a Sociological Lens box explores the study of whiteness.)

WASPs were not a single unified group. Religious rivalries and class divisions made life better for some than for others. However, as the first immigrants to what was to become the United States, WASPs were able to develop and control the country's emerging government, business, and religious institutions. They thus amassed enormous power and avoided the sorts of discrimination that later immigrants would have to overcome. In the early years of the United States, WASPs typically believed in white racial superiority—often calling themselves the Anglo-Saxon race—and created laws to exclude nonwhites from the new nation.

The monopoly on power that WASPs maintained through much of U.S. history loosened considerably by the middle of the twentieth century. The influence of this group endures, however, on much of U.S. culture, most noticeably in the use of English as the country's dominant language and the standing of Protestant Christianity as the country's largest religious affiliation.

WHITE ETHNIC GROUPS

The first major wave of European immigrants who were not WASPs arrived in the early and mid-nineteenth century. After their English landlords evicted them to make way for more grazing lands for cattle and sheep, many impoverished Irish tenant farmers were left dependent on potatoes for survival. When blight devastated the potato crop in Ireland in 1845, hundreds of thousands of Irish tenant farmers fled to the United States. At around the same time, large numbers of Germans arrived as well.

Many WASPs at first denied these and other European newcomers equal racial standing with themselves, referring to them instead as "Celtic" (Irish, Welsh, Scots), "Alpine" (German, Norwegian, Swedish, and other central European), and "Mediterranean" (Italian, Spanish, Greek, and other southern European). But as the new groups gained some power, they rejected these separate designations and claimed the mantle of racial superiority together with WASPs as part of a broadened white race (Mukhopadhyay et al. 2007).

Along with Italians, Jews, Greeks, and others, Irish immigrants were among those not considered white in the nineteenth century and subject to discrimination. Common complaints were that new immigrants did not speak English, held unfamiliar religious beliefs, had strange cultural practices, had too many children, engaged in crime and excessive drinking, and took away jobs from established Americans. How do such criticisms compare to today's discussions about immigration?

The history of the Irish in America illustrates this process (Ignatiev 1996). The Irish had white skin, but they were Catholic, not Protestant, and many spoke Gaelic (Irish) rather than English. As a result, many WASPs considered the Irish a different race and discriminated against them as they did against black people, though never subjecting the Irish to the systematic legal discrimination blacks faced. Often poor and unskilled, the Irish commonly lived in the same neighborhoods as free blacks in northern cities and were often referred to as "white Negroes." Common stereotypes portrayed them as happy, lazy, and stupid with a penchant for drink, dance, and music—stereotypes that were also associated with blacks.

thinking about culture

In what ways has the WASP influence on culture affected you? Consider common words you use, values you have, and the history you were taught in school.

In time, the Irish learned English and took steps to differentiate themselves from black people, establishing their own churches and schools and forming their own social organizations. Although they had earlier supported the abolition of slavery, they gained political power by associating themselves with the Democratic Party, which at that time supported slavery. As a result, the Irish eventually came to be perceived as whites in American society—an option not available to darker-skinned people of African or Asian descent.

The second—and largest—wave of white ethnic immigrants arrived between 1890 and 1924. During that span, 20 million people came to the United States, most of them from southern and eastern Europe, including Italians, Poles, and Jews. Driven by poverty or political repression and drawn by the demand for labor in a rapidly industrializing United States, they were often met with resentment, prejudice, discrimination in housing and employment, and, sometimes, outright violence (Daniels 1997).

Anti-immigrant sentiment increased after World War I (1914–1918), resulting in the Immigration Act of 1924. This law slashed total immigration to 150,000 a year (excepting immigration from the Western Hemisphere) and dramatically reduced the percentage of foreign-born people in the United States for the next 40 years. The legislation effectively ended Asian immigration because it prohibited immigration by "aliens ineligible to citizenship" and naturalization was limited to whites only. It also slashed immigration from southern and eastern Europe through a severely restrictive quota system (Daniels 1997).

African Americans

Unique among the diverse racial and ethnic groups that make up the U.S. population, most African Americans are descended from people forcibly removed from their homeland, sent here against their will, and subjected to a lifetime of coerced labor. This experience is reflected in the distinctively North American idea of race that European colonists created to justify an economic system based on the slave labor of Africans. Before the American experience, slavery existed mostly independent of race. Greeks and Romans kept slaves with pale skin just like themselves, while some dark-skinned Africans captured and enslaved dark-skinned members of other African tribes. In what became the United States, however, a new notion of race was invented piecemeal, over a series of decades, and eventually used to justify a race-based slave system that was the foundation of the agricultural economy of the day, especially in the American South (Johnson and Smith 1999; Smedley 2007). This process so influenced the uniquely American notions of race—and the interaction between race and class in the United States—that it warrants close attention.

INDENTURED SERVITUDE
Race-based slavery emerged only after a labor system based on white indentured servitude failed. When English colonists settled the region that later became the United States, they needed workers to build settlements and raise crops. Especially during the early and mid-1600s, colonists relied primarily on the labor of indentured servants. These poor whites, mostly Britons and Germans, contracted to work for a period of four to seven years in exchange for trans-Atlantic passage and sometimes "freedom dues"—which might include food, clothes, a gun, and, most important, land—upon completion of their contract. Some came voluntarily; others—including homeless children, convicts, beggars, and others considered by British officials to be social undesirables—were shipped forcibly. The work was brutal and the conditions harsh, and many indentured servants died before gaining their freedom. In many ways, they were essentially slaves: they were bought and sold as property, served at the whim of their employers, and were often chained and beaten. Unlike slaves, however, they suffered only temporary servitude; slavery was lifelong (Jordan and Walsh 2008).

Indentured servitude declined eventually, however. As word of the harsh conditions spread, fewer people volunteered to indenture themselves. Unrest grew among indentured servants who had been cheated of their freedom dues, and in 1676, white and black servants joined black slaves in Bacon's Rebellion in Virginia, frightening wealthy colonial officials. To maintain their authority, powerful whites used race to keep poor whites from joining forces with poor blacks and slaves (Horton and Horton 2005; Johnson and Smith 1999).

SLAVERY AS AN ECONOMIC INSTITUTION
In the early 1600s, Africans were only a small part of the colonial workforce. At first, many were treated similarly to white indentured servants. They lived with white servants; had similar legal rights, including the right to sign contracts; and could travel to some extent. As the supply of indentured servants dwindled, however, white planters began to rely increasingly on the labor of black African slaves. The enslaved Africans were the victims of an economic system that linked England, West Africa, and England's American colonies in a three-stage pattern of trade (see Map 10.3). In

MAP 10.3 | THE TRIANGULAR TRANSATLANTIC SLAVE TRADE

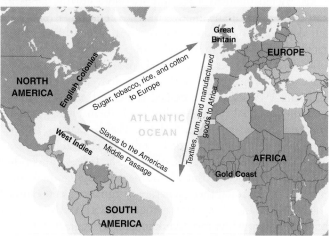

The triangular trade linked Europe, Africa, and the Americas economically.

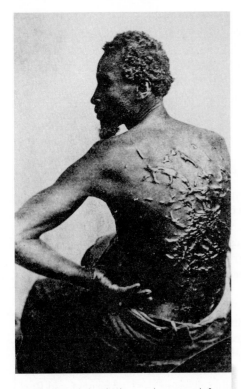

This man's back shows the scars left from brutal whippings he received as a slave in the American South.

This idealized image of George Washington, painted in 1853, shows the nation's first president on his Mount Vernon plantation among his slaves. Like other large landowners of the time, Washington depended on slave labor to run his home and to generate his wealth by working his plantation.

CORE CONCEPTS CHALLENGE

What cultural beliefs about the nature of slavery does this painting promote? Who do you think is the intended audience for a picture like this?

the first stage, English goods were shipped to West Africa and traded for Africans who had been kidnapped by fellow Africans and sold to European slavers. Packed into ships under horrific conditions, up to 20 million captives suffered the second stage, the infamous "middle passage" from Africa to the Americas that only half would survive. In the Americas, they were exchanged for raw materials such as tobacco, rice, and cotton. Finally, the raw materials were shipped to England and exchanged for finished goods, beginning the cycle again (Horton and Horton 2005; Johnson and Smith 1999).

THE RACIALIZATION OF SLAVERY As
the importance of slave labor grew, the ideology justifying it changed. At first, colonists claimed that as non-Christians, Africans were unworthy of freedom. In a few cases, African slaves successfully sued for their freedom after converting to Christianity. By the end of the 1600s, however, with slaves increasingly converting to Christianity, religious differences no longer provided a convincing rationale for enslaving Africans and their descendants (Horton and Horton 2006; Johnson and Smith 1999). Instead, whites now drew on pseudo-science and, ironically, biblical scripture to claim that black Africans were a different and inferior human subspecies fit only to serve the superior white race (Smedley 2007).

At the same time, wealthy southern landowners used their political clout to strip slaves of any legal rights and to define slave status legally in racial terms. In 1705 the Virginia Assembly for the first time passed laws designating slaves as property. Slave rebellions in the following years provoked increasingly restrictive laws, including laws making it illegal for slaves to learn to read (Horton and Horton 2005; Johnson and Smith 1999).

SLAVERY AND AFFLUENCE Race-based
slavery, justified by an ideology that viewed Africans as less than human, underlay the growing wealth of the new colonial elites and not just in the South. Members of a white planter aristocracy owned large estates and benefited directly from the labor of their many slaves. George Washington, among the wealthiest colonists of his day, owned more than 300 slaves. But even the northern colonies—not directly dependent on plantation agriculture—benefited from slavery. Merchants, shipbuilders, metal smiths, rum distillers, sawmill operators, and many others all profited directly or indirectly from the slave trade (Horton and Horton 2006; Johnson and Smith 1999).

Slaves lived under varied conditions, but their labor was always coerced, and the coercion was backed by force, often applied barbarically. White masters also often took it as

A group of white people in Indiana pose proudly for a photo after a lynching in 1930. Lynchings of this sort, often of alleged criminals, were conducted in broad daylight with the consent of local authorities. Some were treated as community events with a carnival atmosphere. Photos like this one—sometimes including children—were regularly taken to commemorate the occasion, and copies of these gruesome pictures were then sold as postcards.

their prerogative to rape their female slaves, and the off-spring of these encounters were legally slaves at birth. Slaves resisted their oppression in various ways, from avoiding work, to escaping, to joining rebellions (Horton and Horton 2006; Johnson and Smith 1999).

SLAVERY'S LEGACY While Thomas Jefferson was writing "All men are created equal" in the Declaration of Independence, a slave in the next room was on call to attend to his every need. In 1776, some whites recognized that slavery was unjust and spoke out against it, but they were few. Slavery persisted for nearly 100 years in the newly independent United States until it was outlawed by the Thirteenth Amendment to the U.S. Constitution in the wake of the Civil War (1861–1865). The legacy of slavery endured, however, with the imposition of legalized (*de jure*) racial segregation in the South and segregation in fact (*de facto*), if not by law, in much of the rest of the country. Under the South's so-called Jim Crow laws, all aspects of life, including housing, employment, education, and political participation, were structured along racial lines, ensuring that blacks and whites would remain separate and unequal.

Racial segregation was enforced through violence and terror. Between 1882 and 1968, for example, white mobs lynched and killed an estimated 4,742 blacks (and many members of other ethnic minorities, as well) (Allen et al. 2000). During the Great Migration of the early and middle twentieth century, many African Americans—some two million by 1930—fled the repressive South in search of economic opportunity in the urban North (Takaki 2008).

African Americans had long challenged their subordinate status under Jim Crow, and in the 1950s these efforts coalesced and intensified in the civil rights movement. By the mid-1960s, this landmark movement had succeeded in dismantling legal segregation and begun to significantly change the country's entrenched culture of racism.

Asian Americans

The experiences of African slaves in the plantation economy were unique. However, throughout U.S. history, race and ethnicity have been used repeatedly to divide workers for the benefit of the powerful. Early Asian Americans experienced this phenomenon as well.

CHINESE AMERICANS Early Chinese immigrants to the United States fled the violence of Britain's "Opium Wars," political turmoil resulting from peasant rebellions, and harsh economic conditions. The hope of finding possible riches in the California Gold Rush of 1849 motivated the earliest Chinese to immigrate. More came between 1863 and 1869—recruited to displace higher-paid Irish workers—to build the transcontinental railroad, a massive, sometimes brutally dangerous, labor-intensive project. After the railroad was completed, some Chinese workers moved to cities, most notably San Francisco, while others played a prominent role in California's emerging agricultural economy (Takaki 2008).

The Chinese were particularly vulnerable to discrimination because, as nonwhites, they were ineligible for U.S. citizenship. California, for example, targeted them with a special tax on foreign miners who were not going to become citizens. Over the years, white workers grew increasingly resentful of Chinese workers, often blaming them for taking their jobs and driving down wages. In the 1870s, Irish American politician Dennis Kearney rose to prominence in California with the slogan "The Chinese must go!" and led violent attacks on Chinese workers. In the early 1890s, unemployed white workers rioted throughout California, beating and sometimes shooting Chinese immigrants and shipping them out of town in freight cars in what the Chinese would come to call the "driving out" (Takaki 2008). Anti-Chinese feeling culminated in the Chinese Exclusion Act of 1882—the first U.S. law to prohibit immigration on the basis of a specific nationality—effectively ending Chinese immigration for a decade (Takaki 2008).

In the face of this hostility, Chinese immigrants already in the country often had to develop their own businesses and rely on their own community for support. Chinese laundries—which were inexpensive to start up—became a staple of many western cities, and urban "Chinatowns" emerged as the center of Chinese social and economic life.

JAPANESE, KOREAN, AND FILIPINO AMERICANS Japanese, Koreans, and Filipinos have distinct cultures and sometimes conflicting histories, but they share some common experiences in the United States. In the late nineteenth and early twentieth centuries, some 200,000 Japanese, along with others from countries including China, Korea, and the Philippines, were recruited to work on sugar-cane plantations in Hawaii, which was annexed as a U.S. territory in 1898. Plantation owners expected that this ethnic diversity would keep their workforce divided and vulnerable to exploitation. In 1919, however, the workers united in a successful strike and formed the Hawaii Laborers' Association, Hawaii's first interethnic union (Jung 2006; Takaki 2008). From Hawaii, some Japanese, Korean, and Filipino immigrants went on to the mainland, most of them to work on farms in California. The Asian Exclusion Act, part of the Immigration Act of 1924, however, brought Asian immigration to a virtual stop.

In what was perhaps the most dramatically racist act against an Asian group in the country's history, the U.S. government interned nearly 120,000 Japanese Americans—two-thirds of them U.S. born—for the duration of World War II. In the wake of Japan's attack on Pearl Harbor in December 1941, the government uprooted entire families and sent them to camps in often remote and desolate areas of the country. Although the United States was at war with Germany and Italy as well as Japan, such widespread measures were not taken against white Americans with German or Italian ancestry. In 1988 the U.S. government paid survivors of the camps $20,000 each in reparations and apologized for what it called a "grave injustice," admitting that the internments were done "without adequate security reasons" and "were motivated largely by racial prejudice, wartime hysteria, and a failure of political leadership" [Public Law 100-383 (1988)].

A group gathers behind the barbed-wire fence of an internment camp in California around 1942. Camps like this kept Japanese Americans confined for the duration of World War II.

Diversity Today

U.S. society is one of the most racially and ethnically diverse in the world. That is due to the country's past as well as more recent changes in immigration and demographic trends.

Racial and Ethnic Groups Today

Diversity in the United States varies significantly from region to region. In the Northeast, Irish ancestry is the most common (17 percent), whereas African American ancestry is most common in the South (19 percent), German in the Midwest (29.3 percent), and Mexican in the West (23.4 percent) (Census Bureau 2009).

WHITE AMERICANS At 73.9 percent of the population, white people of many different ancestries continue to be by far the largest racial group in U.S. society. However, a growing proportion of whites are now Hispanic; non-Hispanic whites account for 62.8 percent of the population (see Table 10.1). Whites are found in substantial numbers throughout the country, with especially heavy concentrations in parts of the Midwest and northern New England. In 2012, only Hawaii, California, New Mexico, and Texas (as well as the District of Columbia) were "majority minority" states with a non-Hispanic white population of less than 50 percent. In contrast, about half of the states were at least 75 percent white and non-Hispanic.

HISPANICS OR LATINOS Latinos are the largest minority group in the United States. Numbering nearly 53 million in 2012, they make up 16.9 percent of the U.S. population and are expected to be one-third of the U.S. population by 2050. Nearly 66 percent identify themselves as white only, 2.2 percent as black or African American only, and 4.5 percent as two or more races; and 26.3 percent report being of "some other race," likely treating Hispanic as a racial rather than ethnic category. Latinos are concentrated in the Southwest and West (reflecting the annexation of these

Race	% of U.S. Population
White (any ethnicity)	73.9%
White, non-Hispanic	62.8
White, Hispanic	11.1
Black or African-American	12.6
Asian	5.0
American Indian or Alaska Native	0.8
Native Hawaiian and Pacific Islander	0.2
Other	4.6
Two or more	2.9
Total	100%
Ethnicity	
Hispanic or Latino	16.9%
White alone	65.6
Other race alone	26.3
Two or more	4.5
Black alone	2.2
Indian, Alaska Native	0.9
Asian alone	0.3
Total	100%

Source: Calculated from data from U.S. Census Bureau (2013a).

areas from Mexico), in Florida (where Cuban Americans are concentrated), and in the New York metropolitan area.

AFRICAN AMERICANS African Americans number more than 39 million. At about 12.6 percent of the U.S. population, they are the nation's largest racial minority. Most African Americans live in the South, but they are also a major presence in cities of the northeast and northern Midwest. In addition, recent immigrants are diversifying the African American community, especially in major metropolitan areas. In 2012, nearly 9 percent of those who reported their race as only black were foreign born, compared with just 1 percent in 1960 (U.S. Census Bureau 2013a).

ASIAN AMERICANS Asian Americans today account for 5 percent of the population in the United States. Chinese Americans are today's largest Asian sub-group.

Those in the second largest subgroup—from India—are relatively recent arrivals. Filipinos are the third largest subgroup. In addition, many Koreans and Vietnamese immigrated to the United States in the wake of the Korean War and the Vietnam War. Asian Americans are mostly located on the West Coast, in major Hawaiian urban centers, and in the New York region (U.S. Census Bureau 2013a).

Asian Americans are found at every class level, but on average they have both higher incomes and more education than members of other racial and ethnic groups, including whites. As a result, they are often perceived to be a "model minority," a label that overlooks the diversity within the Asian community and disregards the discrimination Asians have endured during much of American history. It can also place unfair pressure on Asian youth to live up to a stereotypical ideal.

NATIVE AMERICANS In 2012, an estimated 1.7 percent of the U.S. population (over 5.2 million people) were American Indians or Alaska Natives. About half saw this as their only racial identity, while half identified as multiracial (U.S. Census Bureau 2013a). As with other groups, most native peoples identify with a particular tribal heritage—such as Cherokee, Iroquois, or Navajo—more than with such generic, outsider-imposed terms as "Indian," "Native Peoples," or "Native American."

Not until the passage of the Indian Citizenship Act of 1924 were Native Americans granted the unlimited right to American citizenship. Before then, they had only limited access to citizenship that usually required them to give up tribal membership. Citizens or not, poverty and bleak prospects drove many to move away from reservations and into the white-dominated society. In the 1960s and 1970s, though, Native Americans organized to revive their traditional cultures and gain wider recognition of the injustices committed against them. In 1976 the Supreme Court ruled that states do not have the right to regulate activities on Indian reservations, opening the way for the establishment of the casinos and other gambling operations that have provided economic opportunity for some tribes.

ARAB AMERICANS The Arab world consists of more than 20 culturally varied Arabic-speaking countries. As a result, Arab Americans are a diverse ethnic group whose members, like those of other ethnic groups, often identify more with their specific ancestral homelands than with a broader ethnic label. The three largest Arab American subgroups are those who report ancestry from Lebanon (24 percent), Egypt (14.1 percent), and Syria (8.1 percent) (U.S. Census Bureau 2013a). Often highly educated, Arab Americans hold both bachelor's and graduate degrees at nearly double the rate of Americans as a whole, and their median household income is slightly higher than the U.S. national median (Arab American Institute 2010).

In the United States, many people confuse the ethnic label "Arab" with the religious label "Muslim." In fact, more than 80 percent of the world's Muslims live *outside* the Arab world, mostly in sub-Saharan Africa, Southeast Asia, and the Far East. Furthermore, one out of ten people in the Arab world is not Muslim (Kayyali 2006). Among Arab Americans, between 50 percent and 63 percent are Christian, whereas between 24 percent and 50 percent are Muslim (Kayyali 2007). Just 0.49 percent of the U.S. population, or about 1.6 million people, claim Arab ancestry (U.S. Census Bureau 2013a). However, because many Christians with Arab ancestry do not self-identify as Arabs, the actual number of Arab Americans may be much higher, perhaps 3.6 million (Arab American Institute 2012).

The earliest Arab immigrants, mostly Lebanese Christians, began arriving in the 1880s. Among more recent immigrants, Muslims predominate. In a striking example of the social construction of race, in 1915, George Dow, a Syrian immigrant living in segregated South Carolina, successfully argued in court that Syrians were white and therefore eligible for citizenship under the existing immigration laws, which limited citizenship to "free white persons" (Naff 1985). The U.S. Census Bureau ever since has counted Arab Americans as white. However, some Arab Americans petitioned the Census Bureau, unsuccessfully, to make "Arab" a separate racial category on the 2010 census (Ashmawey 2010).

Since the September 11, 2001, attacks by Muslim extremists, many Arab Americans, particularly Muslims, have found themselves demonized and subjected to discrimination and violence. Half of American Muslims report that it was more difficult to be Muslim in the United States after the attacks (Pew Research Center 2007b).

Immigration in the Post–Civil Rights Era

One major source of diversity in the United States today is the changing nature of immigration. The sheer volume of global migration has increased dramatically in recent decades, usually as people from poorer countries seek economic opportunity in the world's wealthier countries. In the United States, this immigration has come from an increasingly diverse array of countries, because the civil rights movement of the 1950s and 1960s succeeded in dismantling legal discrimination for the first time in U.S. history, including getting Congress to change immigration laws.

The Immigration and Nationality Act of 1965, passed in the midst of the civil rights revolution, eliminated the discriminatory national quotas that had favored immigrants from northern and western Europe. Instead, the act put in

FIGURE 10.3 | FOREIGN-BORN POPULATION SINCE 1960

Percentage of foreign-born population by region of origin

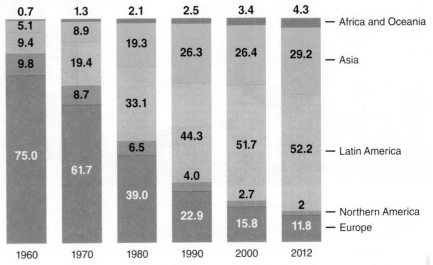

Changes in immigration law enacted in the 1960s eliminated preferences for European immigrants, contributing to a shift toward greater immigration from Latin American and Asian countries. *Sources:* U.S. Census Bureau (2010c, 2013a).

place a system that favored family members of U.S. citizens, skilled workers, and political refugees. New immigrants started arriving from more regions than before, and as a result, the percentage of foreign-born people in the United States from Latin America and Asia, especially, increased significantly, whereas the percentage of foreign-born people from Europe declined (see Figure 10.3).

Significantly, the 1965 legislation allowed naturalized immigrants to sponsor an unlimited number of family members as new immigrants. Once naturalized, these family members could in turn sponsor more family members, a process sometimes called "chain immigration." An unintended consequence of this provision was to increase overall immigration to unprecedented levels, raising the foreign born as a percentage of the country's population to levels approaching those of the 1920s (see Figure 10.4). By 2012, more than one out of eight people in the United States was born elsewhere. Because recent immigrants tend to have a higher birthrate than native-born Americans, the result will significantly affect the racial and ethnic composition of the United States in the coming decades (Lee and Bean 2004). (The Sociology Works box explores a sociology major's work with immigrant tenants.)

Transnational Migrants

Unlike earlier immigrants, who often sought to assimilate into the dominant society and typically had limited contact with their homelands, many of today's immigrants are **transnational migrants** who *retain strong personal, cultural, and economic ties to both their country of birth and their newly adopted home* (Gibson 1988; Portes and Rumbaut 2001). Many recent immigrants have access to inexpensive telephone and

The increase in unauthorized immigration has generated considerable controversy.

CORE CONCEPTS CHALLENGE

Some people advocate limiting immigration, stricter enforcement of immigration laws, and a clampdown on the borders. Others argue for continuing high levels of legal immigration and contend that unauthorized immigrants should have more access to citizenship. What role do **culture** *and* **power** *play in these conflicts?*

Internet services that can provide instantaneous communication with family at home. They can travel to their homeland more easily and can stay abreast of home country news and entertainment on satellite television and the Internet. Transnational migrants often make *remittances*—money transfers to relatives back home—which make up a significant share of the national economies of most Central American countries, the Philippines, Pakistan, Egypt, and other nations (Vertovec 2009). Recognizing these trends, some countries—such as the Philippines—make it easy for migrants to retain their citizenship even as they become citizens in their new homeland. These emerging models of citizenship are likely to become more common, promoting economic advancement and social integration without full cultural accommodation.

Unauthorized Immigration

The surge in immigration that began in the 1960s has been followed by a political backlash similar to the one that followed the earlier surge that began in the late nineteenth century. As before, critics worry that increasing the number of immigrants from different cultures will potentially "disunite" the country (Schlesinger 1998). Unlike before, however, the focus of today's backlash is unauthorized immigrants.

Because these immigrants are by definition "unauthorized" (they are also called "illegal" or "undocumented"), determining their exact number is impossible. Approximately 11.7 million unauthorized immigrants were estimated to be in the

FIGURE 10.4 | FOREIGN-BORN POPULATION WITHIN THE UNITED STATES, 1850 TO 2012

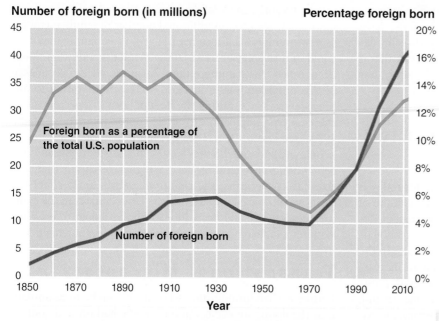

The *number* of people in the United States born elsewhere has reached unprecedented levels (purple line, left axis), but the *percentage* of the U.S. population that is foreign born is still less today than it was in the late 1800s and early 1900s. *Sources:* U.S. Census Bureau (2010c, 2013a).

SOCIOLOGY WORKS

Mikey Velarde and Community Organizing

When Mikey Velarde began college, he intended to study cognitive science. He had no idea that a few years later he would be helping organize a tenants' meeting in New York City's East Harlem as part of his new job as a community organizer. But, motivated by a growing desire to understand—and challenge—racial and ethnic inequalities, Velarde switched from cognitive science to a major in sociology. He graduated with a bachelor's degree and now works primarily with immigrant tenants to help them secure dignified housing in the face of plans for urban development that threaten to displace low-income residents. Velarde has learned a broad array of skills as he works to support local community activists in myriad ways. He knocks on doors to build support networks and to staff meetings of the local tenant association; he organizes community protests; he corresponds with journalists; and he conducts research on housing code violations.

Velarde helps organize local tenants' associations and support the development of local leaders within these organizations. He sees the formation of these community-based organizations as serving a dual purpose: they contribute to a broader social justice movement and help deliver specific, immediate benefits to local tenants.

As an undergraduate, Velarde took a range of sociology courses that emphasized questions about the relationship between power and inequality with a specific focus on the experiences and perspectives of oppressed groups. These classes deepened and broadened his knowledge of the dynamic intersection of race, class, gender, sexuality, and nationality in contemporary U.S. society.

Just about every day Velarde is reminded of the relevance of sociology to his work and the lives of the people he serves. He recalls, for example, how, during a discussion at a community meeting, tenants began to grasp the connections among racial inequality, poor housing conditions, and city policies.

The fragile housing situation in their neighborhood, they concluded, was more than an isolated phenomenon; it was an expression of structural relationships that kept them disadvantaged.

Overall, Velarde concludes, "The best and most basic tool sociology has given me is, as Mills put it, a 'sociological imagination.'" Ultimately, he says, sociology "has given me a language to critique and contest unjust social arrangements. I am reminded even in the most difficult times that these very arrangements are within the reach of social actors." For community organizer Mikey Velarde, sociology encourages hope in the capacity of human beings to recognize—and challenge—injustice.

Velarde has combined his personal experience as a Chicano from El Paso, Texas, with the insights he gained from sociology to cultivate a sociological imagination that he brings to bear on his efforts to help the residents of East Harlem improve their lives. He urges others to similarly bring the sociological imagination to bear on their own goals and circumstances. His advice? "Connect to the material from your own social location and life experience."

Mikey Velarde

> "Ultimately, he says, sociology 'has given me a language to critique and contest unjust social arrangements.'"

think about it

1. *What relationship does Mikey Velarde see between sociology and his work in East Harlem?*

2. *How does the sociological perspective encourage Velarde's optimism about our capacity to challenge injustice?*

United States in 2012. About 60 percent of these immigrants live in just six states: California, Florida, Illinois, New Jersey, New York, and Texas (Passel, Cohn, and Gonzalez-Barrera 2013). They are employed mostly in agriculture, construction, and service occupations.

Several factors have contributed to the increase in undocumented immigrants. First, many Mexicans were recruited as legal temporary workers under the *bracero* program that began in the 1940s. When the program ended in 1964, many stayed in the United States without documentation (Durand, Massey, and Zenteno 2001). Second,

the North American Free Trade Agreement (NAFTA) took effect in 1994, eliminating barriers to cross-border trade and investment and undermining broad sectors of the Mexican economy. In particular, many small-scale Mexican farms failed in the face of competition from government-subsidized U.S. agricultural products. As a result, displaced Mexican workers sought opportunities in the United States (Portes 2002). Finally, U.S. employers play a significant role in recruiting immigrant laborers, including undocumented workers, especially in agricultural and meat processing facilities (Rodriguez 2004).

Changing Population Trends

The saying "Children are our future" is certainly true when it comes to U.S. racial and ethnic diversity. All signs point to significantly increasing diversity in the coming years. In 2011, for the first time ever, most infants (50.4 percent) under 1 year of age were members of minority groups; non-Hispanic whites constituted less than half of this population (U.S. Census Bureau 2012d). A factor in this shift is that recent immigrants tend to be young compared to white residents and are more likely to be of childbearing age. Also, white women tend to have fewer children than black or Hispanic women but more than Asian women (National Center for Health Statistics 2013a). In part as a result of this low birthrate, fewer non-Hispanic whites were born in the United States in 2012 than died—another first in U.S. history. This white population in the United States is considerably older than other racial and ethnic groups, so the trend is expected to continue as white "baby boomers" born in the 1940s and 1950s begin dying in large numbers (Morello and Melnick 2013).

Culture, Structure, and Power: The Nature of Racial and Ethnic Inequality Today

Clearly, blatant racism fueled the nation's past. But you might be thinking, "Things are different now. Overt racism is ancient history, and while there are still some racists at the fringes of society, the United States has moved on, outlawing racial discrimination, electing a black president, and broadly embracing racial and ethnic diversity."

All of that is true to a degree. But sociological research suggests that to understand racial and ethnic conditions today, we need to recognize more complex dynamics, including four seemingly contradictory developments that we sketch out in the remainder of the chapter:

1. *"Old Racism" is largely dead.* As is widely understood, the racist beliefs and practices of the past have largely been eliminated in mainstream society. The civil rights struggle made a difference, paving the way for changes in the U.S. legal and political systems and helping drive a major cultural shift in racial attitudes toward more tolerance and an embrace of diversity.

2. *Inequality persists.* Despite the undeniable changes that occurred to restrict old-style racism, deep and profound racial and ethnic inequalities persist in all aspects of social life—sometimes virtually unchanged in the last half century.

3. *"Old racism" left an influential legacy.* Part of the explanation for persistent inequality is the powerful legacy of old-style racism, the effects of which continue to be felt today.

4. *"New racism" has emerged.* As old forms of racism have been overcome, new beliefs and practices have emerged that explicitly reject blatant racism but actually help perpetuate racial and ethnic inequality.

These four developments reflect aspects of changing culture, structure, and power in society. Before we explore them, we review the nature of discrimination at both the individual and institutional levels and consider some theories of prejudice and discrimination to inform our later discussion.

Prejudice and Discrimination: Individual and Institutional

Sociologists make an important distinction between the behaviors of individuals and the dynamics associated with social institutions.

INDIVIDUAL ATTITUDES AND BEHAVIORS: PREJUDICE AND DISCRIMINATION

While the legacy of the past continues to affect racial disparities today, many types of prejudice and discrimination are fresh creations of contemporary social life. Social-psychological theories that focus on individual attitudes and behaviors can help us understand how people come to adopt their views about inequality. As we noted in Chapter 7, people often define themselves as a member of an *in-group* and feel negatively toward members of an *out-group*. Racism creates an in-out group distinction based on a usually negative stereotype. According to the Thomas theorem (also discussed in Chapter 7), social characteristics that are defined as real have real consequences. Thus a widely accepted stereotype can become the basis for prejudicial attitudes toward the members of an out group.

Stereotypes and prejudice are limited to beliefs and attitudes, but discrimination, as we have seen, involves actions and behaviors (Pettigrew and Taylor 2000). Racial discrimination, for example, involves actions that help maintain the domination of one race over others based on the dominant group's belief in the subordinate group's inferiority (Wilson 1973). As such, discrimination is generally limited to those who have the power to act in ways that hinder others. Those who are relatively powerless may have prejudices of their own, but they generally lack the resources or ability to turn those prejudices into effective discriminatory action. In this sense, discrimination can be thought of as prejudice plus power.

INSTITUTIONAL DISCRIMINATION: STRUCTURAL BARRIERS TO EQUALITY

Individuals can discriminate—for example, a small-business owner might refuse to hire members of a different racial or ethnic group. However, racial and ethnic inequality is typically produced and reinforced through institutional discrimination, not just individual action. **Institutional discrimination** *results from the structural organization, policies, and procedures of social institutions such as the government, businesses, and schools.* Institutional discrimination is especially powerful, since it affects large numbers of people. It is especially difficult to change, since it is not associated with any one individual but rather is a generalized feature of an institutional bureaucracy.

In some cases, institutional discrimination is intentional, as with Jim Crow laws in the pre–civil rights era South. In many cases, though, policies and practices that are not themselves overtly or intentionally discriminatory can have a discriminatory impact. For example, the hiring practices of many workplaces rely heavily on informal word-of-mouth communication. When those workplaces are nearly all white, the result can be institutional discrimination toward racial and ethnic minorities who do not have access to these informal channels of communication. Long-standing "redlining" practices by banks and real estate agencies that make it more difficult for minorities to finance or acquire a house in certain areas are also examples of institutional racism that have been particularly significant.

Theories of Prejudice and Discrimination: Culture and Group Interests

Sociological explanations for prejudice and discrimination tend to fall into one of two theoretical traditions, those emphasizing culture and those emphasizing group interests. Much sociological work on the subject, however, combines elements of each approach.

LEARNING PREJUDICE THROUGH CULTURE

Cultural explanations focus on the way familiarity breeds comfort whereas unfamiliarity often produces anxiety or fear. Our socialization has made it easy for us to interact with people who look and behave like us because they are familiar and predictable. By contrast, interacting with people who look different or whose behavior is unfamiliar and therefore unpredictable, can make us uncomfortable.

As children grow up, their socialization often encourages them to form attachments with those in their own group, people like themselves, while often learning negative stereotypes about out-group members, people less like themselves. Some research suggests that youngsters learn stereotypes and develop prejudices as early as age three, often before fully comprehending their meaning or significance (Aboud 1988). Later in life, the mass media can perpetuate negative stereotypes with entertainment that presents such stock characters as the Asian martial-arts expert, the black criminal, the Arab terrorist, or the exotic Asian sex symbol (Wilson et al. 2003).

According to Gordon Allport's (1954) *contact hypothesis,* contact between members of different groups will reduce prejudice *if* the contact is sustained, involves groups with equal status who share common goals, and is sanctioned by authorities. Those are difficult conditions to meet, but college campuses often qualify. For example, one study found that white students randomly assigned a minority roommate had more contact and were more comfortable with members of other races than white students who were assigned a white roommate (Boisjoly et al. 2006). However, without a structure to encourage interaction, diversity on campus does not necessarily translate into increased interracial or interethnic contact.

DISCRIMINATING TO GAIN ADVANTAGE

Group-interest explanations of prejudice and discrimination focus on the way groups compete with one another for scarce and valuable resources such as jobs or desirable housing. Such competition can lead to conflict and to discrimination by one group against another as a means of gaining an advantage over them. As we saw, discrimination often seems to increase in difficult economic periods as competition for scarce resources increases.

Split labor market theory *argues that ethnic and racial conflicts often emerge when two racial or ethnic groups compete for the same jobs.* According to this theory, employers, higher-paid workers, and lower-paid workers form three groups with separate and competing interests (Bonacich 1972, 1976; Gordon, Edwards, and Reich 1982). Employers recruit lower-paid workers to maximize their profits, thereby creating conflict between higher-paid workers and the lower-paid workers who are replacing them. As we have seen, employers often encouraged immigration as a source of inexpensive labor, sometimes stoking racial and ethnic divisions among workers to prevent them from organizing for better wages and working conditions. In the short term, discrimination against minorities also served the interest of higher-paid workers—often whites, in the context of American history—because it prevented minorities from competing with them for desirable jobs. In the long term, however, these divisions weakened the negotiating power of all workers.

SPOTLIGHT
on social theory

Split labor market theory is in the tradition of *conflict theory.* Have you worked in or seen a workplace in which higher-paid workers and lower-paid workers were divided along ethnic or racial lines?

thinking about structure

The **structure** of an organization can contribute to institutional discrimination. How can an institution's structure help prevent discrimination?

More generally, members of one group can see those of another as a threat, especially when facing difficult circumstances. A **scapegoat** is *an individual or a group of people falsely blamed for a negative situation*. When people are frustrated by their inability to overcome difficulties, they sometimes seek simplistic explanations for their troubles in the form of a scapegoat. In the wake of World War I, for example, Germany faced enormously complex economic and political difficulties, but the Nazis scapegoated Jews and other minorities, blaming them for all the nation's problems. In the United States, blacks, Irish, Jews, communists, immigrants, and Muslims, among many others, have all been targeted as scapegoats at different times (Hardisty 1999).

The Death of "Old Racism": Changing Practices and Attitudes

Barack Obama's election as the nation's first black—or, more accurately, multiracial—president undoubtedly symbolized the changing nature of racial and ethnic conditions in the United States. In the past, blatant voter discrimination suppressed the black vote and made voting rights a central demand of the civil rights era. In a striking reversal, when Obama was elected president in 2008 and 2012, the rate of black voter turnout surpassed that of whites (Weiner 2013). More broadly, racial discrimination of the sort that marked Jim Crow has long been prohibited. Civil rights legislation bans racial segregation and makes discrimination in employment, housing, and other arenas illegal. These developments mark a stark contrast to the nation's long history of legal and overt discrimination based on race and ethnicity.

At the same time, individual attitudes about race have dramatically changed as well. For example, whereas only 4 percent of Americans approved of interracial marriage in 1958, 87 percent approved in 2013 (Newport 2013b). A majority of Americans embrace growing racial and ethnic diversity, with 70 percent agreeing that we will learn more and be enriched by exposure to many different cultures and 65 percent agreeing that as diversity increases, people will become more accepting and willing to find common ground (Teixeira and Halpin 2013).

These and other changes are real and significant. They confirm that old-style racial discrimination, while never eliminated entirely, is greatly marginalized and largely a relic of the past.

Enduring Inequality

Even as practices and attitudes have changed, a huge volume of research has found that racial and ethnic inequality persists in virtually all aspects of social life, including the following:

In 2012, George Zimmerman, a white and Hispanic neighborhood watch coordinator for a gated community, shot and killed Trayvon Martin, an unarmed 17-year-old African American. After a public outcry, Zimmerman was tried but found not guilty of second-degree murder. Some observers, including this media outlet, linked the controversial event to the long history of race-related lynchings and police shootings of black men.

- *Economics.* Blacks and Hispanics are about two-and-a-half times more likely to be poor than are non-Hispanic whites. The median income for non-Hispanic white households is nearly 40 percent greater than it is for black households and nearly 30 percent greater than for Hispanic households. Blacks have only about one-tenth the wealth of whites (Oliver and Shapiro 2006; U.S. Census Bureau 2013e).

- *Housing.* Numerous studies show that racial discrimination is a significant factor in the continuing stark racial and ethnic segregation of the nation's neighborhoods (Logan 2011; Squires, Friedman, and Saidat 2002; U.S. Department of Housing and Urban Development 2005).

- *Education.* Although their achievement is comparable in the early school years, black students lag behind white students on many education measures by the time they reach middle school. Teachers in black-majority districts have less experience and are more likely to be teaching outside their area of expertise than are those in

thinking about power

People in authority have often used scapegoats as a means of gaining or maintaining their power over others. Can you think of an example of the use of this tactic, from your own life or from recent history?

white-majority districts (Jones 2007). Enormous disparities in the rate of college completion make higher education a source of continuing racial inequality as well (Carnevale and Strohl 2013).

- **Health.** Blacks in the United States can expect to live five years less than whites. Racial and ethnic disparities extend across a host of health measures, including infant mortality, causes of death, and mental health (American Sociological Association 2005). Racial minorities and Hispanics tend to receive a lower standard of health care than do non-Hispanic whites, even after controlling for key factors such as income and insurance (Institute of Medicine 2003).

- **Justice.** The United States imprisons a larger share of its population than any country in the world, and that prison population is made up disproportionately of racial and ethnic minorities. More than a third of the prison population is black, and more than a third is Hispanic, numbers that are far higher than these groups' proportion in the population as a whole (Alexander 2012).

- **Media.** Stereotypical portrayals of racial and ethnic minorities have a long history in the media and are not entirely a relic of the past (Entman and Rojecki 2001; H. Gray 2004; Wilson, Gutierrez, and Chao 2013).

- **Hate Crimes.** While nowhere near the levels of the past, assault, vandalism, and even murder continue to be a reality in the United States. Of the 6,222 hate crimes the FBI documented in 2011, nearly half (46.9 percent) were based on race, and another 11.6 percent were based on ethnicity or national origin (Federal Bureau of Investigation 2012).

In these and other ways, racial and ethnic inequality continues to beset U.S. society. Such disparities are not a thing of the past, as shown in Figure 10.5.

Perhaps most disturbingly, some measures of racial and ethnic inequality have remained almost unchanged for 50 years, since the March on Washington for Jobs and Freedom where Martin Luther King Jr. delivered his famous "I Have a Dream" speech. For example, the percentage of black students attending black-majority schools is almost unchanged since then, reflecting continued residential segregation. In 1963, the unemployment rate for blacks was 2.2 times the rate for whites; in 2013, the ratio was almost unchanged at 2.1 to 1 (Austin 2013). Such lack of progress belies claims that the inequalities of the past no longer exist.

However, polls suggest that most people do not blame discrimination alone for enduring inequality. Though blacks (and Hispanics) have worse jobs, income, and housing than whites, 83 percent of whites and 60 percent of blacks say this situation is "mostly due" to factors *other than* racial discrimination. The last 20 years have seen a slow decline in the percentages of people who see this inequality as mostly the result of discrimination, from 21 to 15 percent for whites and from 44 to 37 percent among blacks (Gallup 2013). But discrimination is more likely to be seen in the area of criminal justice, where, for at least the past 20 years, about two-thirds of African Americans have consistently said they see the U.S. justice system as biased against blacks, while the percentage of whites who agree has declined from 33 percent in 1993 to 25 percent in 2013 (Newport 2013a).

FIGURE 10.5 | RACIAL AND ETHNIC INEQUALITY, 2012

Median family income (in thousands of dollars)

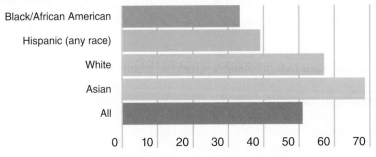

Percentage living in poverty

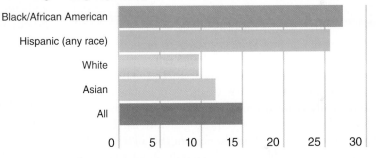

Percentage of those aged 25 or older with at least a 4-year college degree

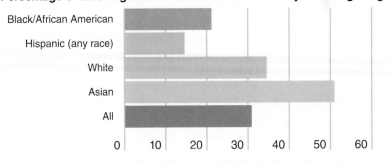

A half century after the civil rights movement, a number of measures indicate the persistence of racial and ethnic inequality in the United States today. **Sources:** U.S. Census Bureau (2013b, 2013e).

CORE CONCEPTS CHALLENGE

How do the group disparities illustrated here reflect the relationship of race and ethnicity to American social **structure**?

The Legacy of Past Discrimination: The Black-White Wealth Gap

We have devoted considerable attention to the history of race and ethnicity in the United States because rather than being separate and unconnected to today's issues, the long history of "old racism" has set the stage for conditions today.

Consider the following analogy. Imagine a long-distance foot race in which some competitors are shackled with leg irons at the start, while others can run freely. Partway through the race, a judge instructs the runners to stop where they are and orders the leg irons removed. The race then continues, but even though all competitors are now allowed to run freely, the gap between frontrunners and those who had been shackled continues to affect the outcome. This analogy reflects the dilemma facing U.S. society in dealing with the legacy of racism.

The conditions that originally created the inequalities no longer exist and the individuals who were responsible may not be around any longer, but the effects of those unequal conditions reverberate through subsequent generations. Sociological research shows that people's life chances are shaped dramatically by the families into which they are born. So, even those who have not directly experienced discriminatory practices can still indirectly inherit either the privileges or disadvantages that those practices create. One of the clearest examples of this legacy is the black-white wealth gap.

As we saw in Chapter 9, *income* refers to money a person receives over a set period of time. *Wealth* refers to what people own, including savings, real estate, stocks and bonds, and other investments. Recall that wealth is distributed much more unequally than income, because wealth can be accumulated and passed on to subsequent generations. The median income of blacks is about 60 percent that of whites, but the median wealth of blacks has been only about 10 percent that of whites. Even when we compare only college graduates, whites have four times as much wealth as blacks (Oliver and Shapiro 2006). And, as we will see, this situation has been greatly exacerbated by the "Great Recession" of 2007–2009, which increased the white-black wealth gap to record highs (Kochhar, Fry, and Taylor 2011).

The racial wealth gap reflects the multigenerational nature of wealth accumulation. That is, advantages or disadvantages from the past continue to affect later generations. The race-specific barriers of old-style racism constitute what sociologists Melvin Oliver and Thomas Shapiro (2006) call the **racialization of the state,** *the implementation of government and private-sector policies that discriminated against minorities and provided whites with numerous advantages.* These policies included:

- The legalization and enforcement of slavery.
- Laws that barred blacks and other minorities from owning property.
- Local ordinances that barred blacks from entering certain occupations.
- Regulations that prevented blacks from selling to whites, making it nearly impossible for blacks to compete with white-owned businesses.
- Segregated and unequal schooling that ensured unequal opportunities in the job market based on race.
- Biased federal home loan programs that steered money to the rapidly growing white suburbs after World War II.
- Biased bank loan practices that required black applicants to meet more stringent mortgage criteria than white applicants and continued long after legal segregation ended.

These sorts of discriminatory practices made it far more difficult for blacks than whites to accumulate wealth and pass it on to their children. The impact of this legacy continues to be felt today.

Take the example of housing discrimination, one of the most important factors contributing to the racial wealth gap today. As we examine in more detail in Chapter 15, explicit residential racial segregation, blatant discriminatory lending practices, and discriminatory government policies once limited the demand for homes in nonwhite neighborhoods, artificially depressing their value. As a result, minorities who owned homes were not able to benefit from their increased value as much as white homeowners did. Today, because of existing wealth disparities passed on through inheritance and family financial assistance, white families are able to buy homes an average of eight years earlier than black families, make larger up-front down payments, and qualify for lower interest rates, all of which widen the racial wealth gap over time. And in recent years, African Americans are more likely than whites to have been the victim of predatory high-risk mortgages, and borrowers of color are twice as likely as whites to have lost their homes to foreclosure after the 2007 housing bust. Because owning a home makes up a larger part of the wealth black and Hispanic families have, compared to whites, the housing bust affected them disproportionately. By some estimates, the housing bust and ensuing Great Recession of 2007–2009 led to black families' collective loss of fully *one-half* of their wealth and to Hispanic families' loss of *two-thirds* of their wealth; these losses further contributed to a major increase in the racial wealth gap (McKernan et al. 2013; Shapiro, Meschede, and Osoro 2013).

So, even if we optimistically note that old-style racism has largely passed, the legacy of this historical discrimination combines with more recent developments to cast its shadow on today's world. One lesson of contemporary research, then, is that racial and ethnic inequality continues today because the discrimination of the past still matters. One attempt to overcome this legacy involves **affirmative action,** *policies and programs that aim to avoid discrimination and redress past discrimination through the active recruitment of qualified minorities for jobs, promotions, and educational opportunities.* One debate over affirmative action is explored in the Sociology in Action box.

SOCIOLOGY in ACTION

Race, Class, and the Affirmative Action Debate on Campus

If education is to serve as a fair mechanism for individual social mobility, it must be equally accessible to all qualified students. Historically, college and university administrators limited or barred the admission of racial and ethnic minorities while giving wealthy white children of alumni preferential treatment (Kahlenberg 2010a; Karabel 2005; Stevens 2007). Since the 1960s, race-based affirmative action has been used to help overcome the effects of this discrimination and promote more racially diverse campuses. In recent years, however, court decisions have limited race-based affirmative action, and some states have prohibited its use altogether. Meanwhile, some scholars and policymakers have been using sociological insights to suggest new ways to maintain diversity and promote fair access to higher education.

One major sociological criticism of race-based affirmative action programs is that they are blind to the way race intersects with class to affect who benefits from them. Perhaps the most comprehensive study of the subject suggests that the greatest beneficiaries are minorities from middle- and upper-class backgrounds (Bowen and Bok 1998). The programs can also benefit the growing number of recent minority immigrants, even though they have not suffered the effects of American racism's historical legacy. Meanwhile, affirmative action provides no benefit to poor and working-class whites disadvantaged by attending weak schools in low-income school districts.

Consequently, some analysts argue for a shift from race-based to class-based affirmative action, thereby assisting students to overcome educational disadvantages, regardless of race (Kahlenberg 1997, 2010b). They argue that well-designed class-based programs will continue to benefit racial and ethnic minorities because minorities are disproportionately represented among the poor and working class. At the same time, however, class-based programs would also benefit white students of modest means, thus overcoming the political objection faced by race-based programs that they unfairly exclude disadvantaged whites.

If they are to be fair, however, class-based affirmative action programs must take into account the sociological insight that the wealth gap between races is much greater than the income gap. Relying solely on family income as a measure of class would likely harm some racial and ethnic minorities because it would mask the effect of this legacy of racial discrimination. One possible solution would be to define class broadly enough to capture factors beyond income that can influence early educational quality, such as school-district income levels, parents' education level, and family wealth.

Sociologists have also pointed out that one of the principal tools colleges use to evaluate students for admission—scores on standardized tests such as the SAT and ACT—is inherently unfair and a good example of institutional racism. The tests are supposed to be an unbiased measure of a student's individual ability, but they turn out to be weak predictors of later academic success. Competitive colleges nonetheless rely heavily on them, giving the appearance that admission decisions are based solely on merit. In fact, these tests give an advantage to affluent disproportionately white students who typically score higher than less affluent students, thanks to well-funded schools, expensive test-taking tutoring, and a home environment that promotes college-related cultural capital. In fact, some sociologists argue that overemphasis on standardized test scores, to the neglect of other indicators of ability such as class ranking, is precisely what puts both racial minorities and lower-income students of all races at a disadvantage. If such tests were a less important part of the decision, the admissions gap between the races and classes would be greatly reduced (Alon 2009; Alon and Tienda 2007).

In the coming years, sociological insights about race and class will continue to help inform the debate over affirmative action and contribute to the development of policies that try to create a fairer system of higher education.

think about it

1. *Overall, do you think affirmative action based on race has been useful? Why or why not?*

2. *Do you agree with advocates who now suggest shifting to class-based affirmative action? Why or why not?*

The Emergence of "New Racism": Hidden, Implicit, and Color-blind

While "old racism" has left a legacy that sheds light on today's enduring racial inequality, sociological research also suggests that new beliefs and practices help explain how racism operates in a society in which racial discrimination is often illegal and covert (Quillian 2006).

HIDDEN PREJUDICE Robert Merton (1949) recognized long ago that people who were not prejudiced could engage in discriminatory behaviors to conform to biased social norms. Some whites in the segregated South, for example, acquiesced to the dominant culture even though they personally rejected its racist assumptions. Similarly prejudiced people may keep silent about their attitudes when the dominant norms condemn them but still engage in discriminatory behavior. Indeed, recent research suggests that, in some cases, norms promoting racial and ethnic equality in the post–civil rights era have not eliminated racism but rather have driven it underground, transforming overt prejudices into covert ones.

For example, some people refrain from racist talk or action in public but give vent to racial or ethnic stereotypes when among friends and family. In one study, over 1,000 students from a variety of colleges and universities kept journals recording their social interactions for several weeks during the 2002–2003 academic year (Picca and Feagin 2007). The journals of the more than 600 white students in the study showed them to be nearly always polite to their black peers, avoiding racially offensive language in public "frontstage" situations. However, in "backstage," white-only settings, students reported the frequent use of the word "nigger" and other racial epithets to refer to blacks. Some students reported feeling uncomfortable about the racist language but lacked the courage to object. In their journals, the white students also commonly referred to blacks in terms of racial stereotypes, describing them as lazy, criminally inclined, and oversexed. The results suggest that, even 50 years after the civil rights movement, these stereotypes and prejudices remain deeply entrenched and widely prevalent.

on social theory

As part of the *symbolic interactionist* tradition, **dramaturgical theory** draws attention to the differences between frontstage and backstage behaviors. Are research findings that racist backstage behavior is relatively common among college students, whereas frontstage behavior is noticeably free of such actions, consistent with your own experiences?

Although marginalized racist beliefs are usually kept "backstage," the Internet offers a public stage on which racist ideas can be shared. The posting of such racist ideas highlights not only the enduring nature of racist beliefs but also their marginalization from mainstream culture. For example, in 2013, a heartwarming television ad about the health benefits of the breakfast cereal Cheerios featured a black father, a white mother, and their cute young biracial daughter. But when the ad was uploaded to YouTube, viewers' racist comments generated a vicious flame war with references to "Nazis" and "racial genocide," eventually leading to the disabling of the comments for the video. Viewers rallied, though; the ad received over 4.5 million views by the end of the year, and the Facebook page for the ad had over 1 million "likes" (Whitaker 2013).

Hidden prejudices can also lead people who deny they are motivated by any personal prejudice to engage in discriminatory practices. White employers, for example, may justify their acknowledged reluctance to hire blacks by citing the prevalence of crime in black communities. Ironically, some managers admit to steering clear of hiring blacks precisely because of the public sanctions against racial discrimination:

The multiracial daughter of a black father and white mother in a 2013 Cheerios TV ad generated a racist backlash from some YouTube commentators but, over time, elicited an overwhelmingly positive response from viewers.

CORE CONCEPTS CHALLENGE
How does such an incident reflect a **culture** *in transition?*

they fear a discrimination lawsuit if an African American employee needs to be fired (Wilson 1996).

IMPLICIT BIAS In 1926, Emory Bogardus published a study of the *social distance* between groups, based on a nationwide survey of college students. To measure social distance, he asked students how closely they were willing to interact with the members of certain other groups. Being willing to marry someone from a group, for example, indicated very little social distance, whereas wanting to bar members of a group from the country indicated great social distance. Bogardus—and later other researchers—repeated the survey over the years, refining the measures and expanding the sample to include the general population, not just college students (Bogardus 1967). The results show decreasing social distance over time, indicating a reduction in racial and ethnic prejudice. There are exceptions, though. In the wake of the September 11, 2001, terrorist attacks, for example, the acceptance of Muslims and Arabs declined (Parrillo and Donoghue 2005).

As researchers learn more about how the brain works, however, they are finding that some biases may be more implicit—existing at the subconscious level—than overt and at a conscious level where they can be measured in surveys. Recent research suggests that we learn prejudices at a deep, unconscious level and respond to people with lightning-fast assessments that are beyond rational evaluation (Vedantam 2005). In our conscious activities, we can control our behaviors and overcome implicit biases, but this restraint is cognitively challenging and requires additional effort (Richeson et al. 2003). At the unconscious level, we may be acting on well-known stereotypes and deeply held prejudices.

Social psychologist Mahzarin Banaji and her colleagues have devised a series of implicit association tests (IAT) that measure unconscious biases by tapping into fast, unexamined responses. (You can take some of these tests yourself online at https://implicit.harvard.edu.) These researchers have found that most respondents show an unconscious preference for people like themselves, regardless of their stated beliefs. Even when people who feel and say they are not biased are tested, in most cases the results indicate they actually have unconscious biases based on race, ethnicity, sexual orientation, and class as well as other categories. These tests have their critics (Blanton and Jaccard 2008), but, if confirmed by further research, they may demonstrate that implicit bias is one source of enduring prejudice and discrimination in contemporary society.

Racial discrimination persists in many areas of social life, whether because of prejudice, hidden racism, or implicit bias. One method sociologists use to measure discrimination is the *field audit* (Quillian 2006). In typical field audits, researchers pair people from different races or ethnic groups who are otherwise similar on all characteristics that might affect the study's outcome. They then send each member of the pair into social situations in which they may encounter discrimination, such as renting an apartment or applying for a job. Using this method repeatedly, researchers have documented persistent racial discrimination in housing (Turner and Ross 2005) and hiring (Altonji and Blank 1999). One study even found discrimination based on no more than the name on otherwise comparable resumes mailed in response to ads for jobs. Resumes for people with white-sounding names, such as Emily and Greg, were 50 percent more likely to get a callback than were those for people with black-sounding names, such as Lakisha and Jamal (Bertrand and Mullainathan 2004). Another study found that employers were much more likely to hire a white person with a criminal record than a black person with a criminal record (Pager 2003). Yet another study found that doctors recommended different treatments for people of different races who came to them with identical symptoms (Shulman et al. 1999).

COLOR-BLIND RACISM Sociologists often refer to today's persistent racism as *the new racism*, and they describe its dynamics with a variety of approaches that have a variety of labels, including "symbolic racism" (Kinder and Sanders 1996), "laissez-faire racism" (Bobo, Kluegel, and Smith 1997), "color-blind racism" (Bonilla Silva 2001, 2009), and "modern racism" (McConahay 1986). Although their analyses vary somewhat, these approaches agree on two points:

- Prejudice and discrimination persist in contemporary social life.

- The ways in which prejudice and discrimination manifest themselves have changed in the post–civil rights era.

For example, in a significant shift from earlier attitudes, many Americans today advocate race neutrality and a "color-blind" society. But ideas that once might have been progressive and antiracist can reinforce existing racial inequality in a different historical era. **Color-blind racism** is *the promotion of race neutrality when it actually helps maintain existing racial and ethnic inequality*. It reveals itself in the rejection of efforts to reduce racial and ethnic inequality on the grounds that those efforts violate a color-blind approach to society and may even constitute reverse racism. Research suggests that many Americans are deeply ambivalent about how to embrace an ideology of color blindness while simultaneously embracing racial diversity as a positive development (Burke 2012). How can race matter but not matter at the same time?

Some who advocate color-blind policies are likely using race neutrality as a cover for prejudiced views, understanding that overt racism is no longer acceptable in our society. However, color-blind approaches are not inherently prejudicial, and some advocates of this view genuinely believe that race neutrality is the best route to racial justice. The result is a complex mix of racial and nonracial beliefs that in combination—intentionally or not—can help perpetuate racial inequality.

How do those who believe that racism is no longer a significant hurdle in our supposedly post-racial society explain the continuing inequality among racial and ethnic groups in U.S. society? Some simply deny that inequality and discrimination exist, despite the vast body of social science research showing that it does. Some point to cultural differences to account for this variation and, in particular, to the success of Asian Americans as evidence that racial and ethnic discrimination no longer holds back social advancement. Some have argued that enduring racial inequality simply reflects the natural outcome of competition between groups with inherently different abilities. Richard Herrnstein and Charles Murray (1996), for instance, claimed that differences in scores on intelligence tests (IQ scores) reflect innate and unchangeable differences between the races. Critics have pointed out the inadequacies of such studies, which ignore the impact of environment on IQ scores (Fischer et al. 1996). They argue that efforts to measure differences in intelligence are repackaged racist ideas that hark back to the ugly history of racist pseudo-science.

Critics of color-blind policies argue that to pretend that race no longer matters is to overlook the legacy of racism and the persistence of prejudice and discrimination. As U.S. Supreme Court Justice Harry Blackmun famously said in defending the use of affirmative action, "In order to get beyond racism, we must first take account of race." In the end, Americans are divided when they assess the dream of a truly just and color-blind society. When asked if they believe that Martin Luther King's dream of racial equality has been achieved, barely half of Americans (51 percent) say yes, with African Americans slightly more optimistic (54 percent) than whites (49 percent) (Jones 2011).

In the nineteenth century, a civil war led to the end of slavery in the United States. In the twentieth century, the civil rights movement led to the end of racial segregation and legal discrimination. In both cases, social change came only after intense controversy and prolonged conflict. Just as those struggles were contentious in their day, so too are the efforts to understand inequality and advance racial and ethnic justice in a post–civil rights society.

A Changing World

MULTIRACIAL AND MULTIETHNIC IDENTITIES

As part of his stand-up act a few years ago, comedian Chris Rock would raise a question about the success of golf great Tiger Woods and popular rapper Eminem. "What's happening in America," he would ask in astonishment, "when the best golfer is black and the best rapper is white?" This line always got a laugh, but it also exposes enduring racial stereotypes. Tiger Woods's father had a mix of African American, Chinese, and Native American ancestry, and his mother had a mix of Thai, Chinese, and Dutch. Yet in the United States, Tiger Woods is still often seen simply as black.

Woods's complex ancestry highlights the growth of multiracial and multiethnic identities. As marriages across racial and ethnic lines increase, people with these new identities are likely to play a larger role in tomorrow's world. It has long been common for people to identify with multiple ethnicities, saying, for example "I'm Irish on my father's side and Russian on my mother's." Today, however, multiethnic identities include an ever-larger range of ethnicities from all parts of the world.

As immigration and intermarriage increase, so do the number of people with multiracial identities. In the 2010 census, 9 million Americans (3 percent of the population) identified themselves as being of two or more races, although this number is an undercount since those who answer "multiracial" are classified as "some other race" (U.S. Census Bureau 2011b, 2011c). In addition, cultural norms still encourage people in the United States to identify with only one race. For example, in the 2010 census, only 7.4 percent of blacks indicated they had a multiracial background, even though the U.S. Census Bureau estimates that at least 75 percent of black Americans have a multiracial ancestry. In 2012, when pop singer and actress Beyoncé did a L'Oréal advertisement that mentioned her "mosaic" racial identity of African American, Native American, and French, she was roundly criticized for supposedly distancing herself from the black community (Stodghill 2012). As multiracial identities become more socially accepted, however, we are likely to see a significant increase in the percentage of people who embrace them, the latest development in our evolving conception of race and ethnicity.

Rising intermarriage is one sign that the boundaries between some racial and ethnic groups have become less rigid. Intermarriage between members of different white ethnic groups was rare 100 years ago but is now so common that only about 20 percent of whites have a spouse with the same ethnicity, and such unions are no longer even categorized as interethnic (Lee and Bean 2004). Interracial marriage was still outlawed in fifteen states when the Supreme Court declared such statutes unconstitutional in 1967. In 2010, though, about 15 percent of marriages in the United States unites either people of different races or Hispanics and non-Hispanics, a rate that has doubled between 1980 and 2010 and increased sixfold since 1960 (Passel, Wang, and Taylor 2010; Wang 2012). (See Figure 10.6.)

FIGURE 10.6 | INTERMARRIAGE RATES OF NEWLYWEDS, 2010

Percentage

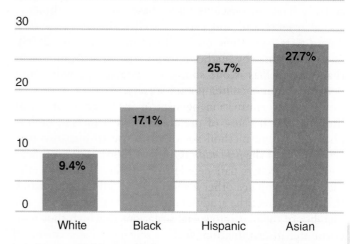

Asians are the most likely to marry someone of a different race or ethnicity. Whites are the least likely to do so.

Note: "Newlyweds" refers to people who got married in the 12 months before the survey. All groups (other than Hispanic) are non-Hispanic single races. **Source:** Wang 2012.

Keegan-Michael Key and Jordan Peele star in Comedy Central's *Key & Peele* sketch comedy show. They began their television careers by portraying black characters on Fox's *MadTV*, but on their own show, as their program's website notes, they showcase a "unique point of view, born from their shared background and experiences growing up biracial in a not quite post-racial world" (Comedy Central 2013). The number of such pop culture images is likely to increase as multiracial identities become more common.

Intermarriage by whites has doubled since 1980 and tripled for blacks but has remained fairly steady for Hispanics and Asians, probably because a growing number of Asians and Hispanics are available as potential partners as their percentages of the population increase (Wang 2012). Intermarriage rates also vary by gender within racial and ethnic groups. Among whites and Hispanics, intermarriage rates are about equal for men and women. However, the intermarriage rate for black men (23.6 percent) is more than twice as high as it is for black women (9.3 percent), whereas Asian women (36.1 percent) intermarry at twice the rate of Asian men (16.6 percent). Younger people and native-born adults are more likely to marry outside their racial or ethnic group than are older people and immigrants, suggesting intermarriage will likely increase in the coming years as the taboo against it fades and recent immigrants become more established (Passel et al. 2010).

As the trend toward intermarriage continues, it promises to alter the nature of racial and ethnic relations in the United States, making it easier for members of minority groups to cross boundaries in employment, housing, and marriage. Perhaps it will even diminish the social significance of racial and ethnic categories altogether.

thinking sociologically about
Race and Ethnicity

culture

- Race and ethnicity are social constructs whose definitions change over time and vary across cultures.
- Social norms about race and ethnicity—both racist and antiracist—are learned through the process of socialization.

structure

- Interpretations of race and ethnicity influence patterns of social interaction.
- The policies and practices of social institutions can both reflect racist beliefs and perpetuate racial and ethnic inequality.
- Groups, from slaves to the activists of the civil rights movement and later, have resisted racial discrimination, sometimes producing long-lasting changes in the social structure.

power

- Racial and ethnic inequality reflects differences in power within society.
- Powerful groups have historically justified their privileges on the basis of their supposed racial or ethnic superiority.
- The post–civil rights era has seen both enduring racial and ethnic inequality as well as new relations of power, reflecting the increasing diversity of society.

Looking Back

1. Race is not a biological reality, but rather a social construct whose origin lies in eighteenth- and nineteenth-century pseudo-science. Ethnicity is also a social construct that, like race, has been interpreted differently in different cultures and in various historical periods.

2. Grouping people into different races and ethnicities sets up majority-minority group dynamics that become a part of the social structure and reflect inequalities in power.

3. The social history of the United States resulted in unique ideas and practices concerning race and ethnicity. In particular, whites used ideas about race and racial superiority to justify slavery and adopt laws that enshrined racial inequality.

4. Native societies were decimated by the arrival of European colonizers. Spanish colonists, the ancestors of today's Hispanics, took control of what is now the southwestern United States. White Anglo-Saxon Protestants settled primarily on the east coast and rapidly expanded their landholdings westward. African slaves were imported in growing numbers as labor for an agrarian economy. In the nineteenth century, Asian laborers—especially Chinese—were recruited to work on railroads and in other industries.

5. Rising immigration from throughout Europe in the nineteenth and early twentieth centuries increased ethnic diversity. Some groups—including Jews, the Irish, and Italians—were not considered white until they gradually assimilated.

6. The civil rights movement helped transform society, making racial and ethnic discrimination illegal and promoting tolerance. One consequence was a change in immigration laws that opened the way to new diversity. Recent immigrants, who come mostly from Asia and Latin America rather than Europe, are substantially changing the racial and ethnic makeup of the country.

7. Despite the gains of the civil rights movement, racial and ethnic inequalities endure, reflecting racism's historical legacy as well as contemporary practices. Racial prejudice and discrimination operate at different levels of social life, involving individual attitudes and behaviors and the structural barriers created by institutions. Prejudice and discrimination can be fueled by cultural differences or by the pursuit of group interests. In a post–civil rights society, prejudice and discrimination can be hidden, implicit, or produced by support for color-blind policies.

8. One consequence of our increasing diversity is the growth of multiethnic and multiracial identities, in part the result of an increase in interracial marriage.

Critical Thinking: Questions and Activities

1. A friend asks, "Are you blind? Of course race exists!" Explain to your friend why race is, in fact, a social construction, rather than a biological fact.

2. How did you first learn about race and ethnicity? Did this early socialization include the perpetuation of stereotypes? Explain. What socializing forces later influenced your understanding of these issues?

3. Is the social history of race and ethnicity in the United States summarized here consistent with what you learned in high school? If not, how is it different?

4. How do you think changing demographics in the United States will influence other aspects of life 50 years from now?

5. Do you think racial attitudes today among people under age 30 differ significantly from those held by older people? Why or why not? (How could you find out for sure?) What factors do you think contributed to this situation?

Key Terms

affirmative action (p. 280) policies and programs that aim to avoid discrimination and redress past discrimination through the active recruitment of qualified minorities for jobs, promotions, and educational opportunities.

amalgamation (p. 263) the process by which a majority and a minority group blend or mix to form a new group.

assimilation (p. 263) the process by which members of a minority group come to adopt the culture of the majority group.

color-blind racism (p. 283) a form of bias in which the promotion of race neutrality helps maintain existing racial and ethnic inequality.

discrimination (p. 262) unequal treatment that gives advantages to one group of people over another without justifiable cause.

ethnicity (p. 257) shared cultural heritage often deriving from a common ancestry and homeland.

genocide (p. 263) the systematic killing of a group of people, based on their race, ethnicity, nationality, or religion.

institutional discrimination (p. 277) unequal treatment that results from the structural organization, policies, and procedures of social institutions such as the government, businesses, and schools.

majority group (p. 262) a collection of people who enjoy privileges and have more access to power because of identifiable physical or cultural characteristics.

minority group (p. 262) a collection of people who suffer disadvantages and have less power because of identifiable physical or cultural characteristics.

pluralism (p. 262) a situation in which distinct ethnic and racial groups coexist on equal terms and have equal social standing.

prejudice (p. 262) to "pre-judge" someone or some group negatively based on inadequate information.

race (p. 257) a category of people widely perceived as sharing socially significant physical characteristics such as skin color.

racial essentialism (p. 260) the idea that supposedly natural and immutable differences separate the races.

racialization of the state (p. 280) the implementation of government and private-sector policies that discriminated against minorities and provided whites with numerous advantages.

racism (p. 260) the belief that one race is inherently superior to another.

scapegoat (p. 278) an individual or a group of people falsely blamed for a negative situation.

segregation (p. 263) keeping distinct social groups physically and socially separate and unequal.

split labor market theory (p. 277) the theory that ethnic and racial conflicts often emerge when two racial or ethnic groups compete for the same jobs.

stereotypes (p. 282) exaggerated, distorted, or untrue generalizations about categories of people that do not acknowledge individual variation.

transnational migrants (p. 273) immigrants who retain strong personal, cultural, and economic ties to both their country of birth and their newly adopted home.

11

Gender and Sexuality

looking AHEAD

How has **culture** influenced your understanding of gender roles and sexuality?

How are your ideas about gender and sexuality reinforced through social **structures** such as your family and your school?

Are differences in **power** in your family or friendships the result of inequalities based on gender and sexual orientation?

On April 19, 1967, 20-year-old Kathrine Switzer was running the Boston Marathon when a truck carrying photographers and race officials drove by slowly. One of the officials, Jock Semple, was stunned when he noticed Switzer. Jumping off the vehicle and yelling, "Get the hell out of my race!" Semple lunged at the young runner and tried to rip off her official race number. He missed the number but grabbed the back of Switzer's sweatshirt, momentarily preventing her from advancing. Switzer's boyfriend, who was also running, shoved the race official, allowing Switzer to escape and finish the race.

What had Switzer done to evoke such an angry outburst? She had dared to run a marathon at a time when women were banned from competing. A year earlier, Roberta Gibb had become the first woman to finish the Boston Marathon, but she had run unofficially, and she even had to hide in the bushes near the start so that race officials would not spot her. Switzer managed to obtain an official number by registering under a gender-neutral name, K. V. Switzer (Switzer 2007).

At the time, the men who organized long-distance road races in the United States used their power to ban women from competing in marathons for what they argued were biologically obvious reasons: women were simply too frail to complete the grueling 26.2-mile event safely. Conventional wisdom held that even if some women could finish the race, doing so would likely cause physiological damage, perhaps even preventing them from having children. Women could not compete officially in U.S. marathons until 1971 or in an Olympic marathon until 1984.

Today, hundreds of thousands of women run in marathons each year. Their safe participation shows that what was widely considered biological reality just a few decades ago was, in fact, a social construction—a part of the structure of sports produced by the power of men that created needless social barriers for women.

In this chapter, we examine the idea of gender and consider how people mistake socially constructed differences as natural. We look at how cultural norms are reinforced or modified in daily life and within social structures, and how artificial distinctions between women and men contribute to gender inequality. In addition, we consider similar issues of social construction as they apply to human sexuality. We also look at how people have organized to challenge inequality based on gender and sexuality.

Biology and Culture: Sex and Gender

In everyday life, you often see the terms *sex* and *gender* treated as if they meant the same thing. For example, a questionnaire might ask for your "gender," expecting you to indicate either "male" or "female." Sociologists distinguish between sex and gender, however, to highlight the difference between biology and culture (Stoller 1968).

Sex is *the biological distinction between females and males.* In contrast, **gender** refers to *the socially constructed cultural expectations associated with women and men.* Biology makes us male or female; culture teaches us to be men or women. To take two simple examples, most females have the physical capacity to give birth to children, but males do not. This ability is a sex difference. In our culture, women are free to wear dresses in daily life, but men are generally discouraged from doing so. This restriction is a gender difference. It is based on culture and has nothing to do with biology.

The distinctions between sex and gender are not always so clear-cut. Scholars debate the influence of biologically based sex differences on social behavior. However, much of what our culture associates with *sex* differences are, in fact, socially produced *gender* differences. For example, when Kathrine Switzer ran in the 1967 Boston Marathon, the women's world record in the marathon—from competitions outside the United States—was 3:19:33, while the men's record was 2:12:00. Some men pointed to this 67-minute gap as evidence that women were biologically unfit for the difficult race. As of early 2014, however, women runners had narrowed the gap to less than 12 minutes: 2:15:25 for women and 2:03:23 for men. Clearly, social factors, not biological ones, were responsible for most of the gap between women's and men's performance in the past. In sports, as in many other areas of life, we can mistakenly attach biological explanations to what are primarily social factors. To help unravel the relationship between sex and gender, let's examine each more closely.

The Biology of Sex

A person's sex is determined at conception when the mother's ovum (or egg cell) contributes an X chromosome to the embryo and the father's sperm contributes either an X or a Y chromosome. An XX combination produces a female; an XY combination a male. Chromosomes help determine physical development, including distinctions between the sexes. *Primary sex characteristics*, including the genitals and reproductive organs, are sex differences that are directly involved in reproduction. *Secondary sex characteristics*, including wider hips and breast development in females and more extensive body hair and increased muscle mass in the upper body in males, are not directly involved in reproduction.

Sex differences can be grouped loosely into two categories: absolute differences and differences of degree. Absolute sex differences include those related to reproduction. Only females menstruate, ovulate, become pregnant, and breastfeed their babies; only males can impregnate females. Other differences, though, are of degree. Both men and women possess the same hormones, for example, but in different amounts.

Most individuals are clearly biologically female or male. But some people are **intersexual**—*individuals born with ambiguous reproductive or sexual anatomy.* Intersexual people have some ambiguity in their genitals, chromosomes, gonads (female ovaries or males testes), or hormones. Being intersexual can include conditions such as having external female genitals but internal testes, an additional chromosome (XXY), or hormonal irregularities that at puberty produce secondary sex characteristics associated with the other sex. Because of the range of conditions involved, experts disagree about who and how many people qualify as intersexual, with one study estimating between 0.2 and 1.7 percent of the population (Blackless et al. 2000).

The Limits of Biology

Imagine that researchers devise a project to investigate whether the ability to walk in high-heeled shoes is biologically based. They choose a random sample of women and men, have them strap on some heels, and record the results. Lo and behold, it turns out that, on average, women perform significantly better than men. The researchers might suggest that these results are likely due to biological differences between the sexes in body mass, balance, and coordination.

Actually, the ability they are measuring has been learned with practice—as anyone proficient in walking in heels can tell you. With some effort, it's entirely possible for men to develop this skill, but in our culture they are not encouraged to acquire it. Socialization, not biology, produced the difference.

In fact, studies show an overwhelming number of similarities in the psychology and abilities of women and men, with more variation occurring within each sex than between the two (Hyde 2005). Yet the popular media often highlight misinterpretations and pseudo-science regarding supposedly innate differences between the sexes. For example, a once-popular book touting that "men are from Mars and women from Venus" (J. Gray 2004) simply treats cultural stereotypes—such as women are passive while men are active—as innate differences, without adequately considering the role of gender socialization in producing them. We can recognize the falseness of such claims in an outrageous example such as our hypothetical study of walking with high heels, but more subtle real-world studies can be misleading.

For example, men often outperform women in tasks that require subjects to use visualization and mentally manipulate objects. Researchers sometimes attribute such superior performance to innate differences that developed during evolution and cite these results as a reason why men dominate some scientific fields such as engineering. An understanding of how gender influences human development, however, provides us with a different perspective on this research.

In one study, researchers briefly showed subjects a grid that contained two dozen identical objects and one object that was different (Feng, Spence, and Pratt 2007). The subjects had to determine the location of the odd object quickly. Consistent with the idea that they have evolved better spatial abilities, men succeeded in the task 68 percent of the time, whereas women succeeded only 55 percent of the time, a statistically significant difference. However, after some of the subjects spent 10 hours playing a video game that involved shooting at a target (a game popular with boys, less so with girls), the difference between the sexes disappeared upon retesting both at once and five months later. A difference in skill that researchers and others could have misinterpreted as the result of innate physiological differences instead turned out to be easily influenced—and erased—by environmental conditions, in this case, access to and practice with video games.

There *are* actual differences in the architecture of male and female brains. In the coming years we will likely learn more about these differences and how men and women use their brains in different ways to get the same job done. As we saw in Chapter 6, though, the human brain has a remarkable ability—known as brain plasticity—to restructure and reorganize itself in response to social experiences and learning. As we will see, expectations about gender create different social experiences for women and men from the moment of birth. Just as the gender gap in marathon performance was due largely to culture, not biology, so are many of the differences measured by today's research. If we want to understand the social life of women and men, then, we need to look beyond biology to gender and its social construction.

Gender as a Social Construction

Almost all the differences we associate with men and women are culturally produced, not biologically based. From infancy, we are taught our culture's expectations regarding gender, we develop identities that are based on those expectations, and we view the world through the lens of gender expectations that we usually take for granted. For example, if you got into a taxi cab with a female driver, you would probably take note; without even thinking about it, you most likely expect a man to drive a taxi. Similarly, you might be surprised to encounter a male dental hygienist or day care provider.

If we look at how notions of gender differ over time and across cultures, we can see the powerful influence of culture.

GENDER IN A DIFFERENT TIME Throughout the history of the United States, activists have challenged widely accepted ideas about gender and, over time, changed how people think. In 1848, participants at a ground-breaking women's rights convention in Seneca Falls, New York, pointed out some of the oppressive political, legal, educational, and economic conditions that women faced. In a document modeled after the Declaration of Independence, these activists produced an inventory of grievances that included the fact that women could not vote, had no legal or property rights and could be abused by their husbands at will, were excluded from most occupations and professions, and were prevented from obtaining a college education. "The history of mankind," they concluded, "is a history of repeated injuries and usurpations on the part of man toward woman, having in direct object the establishment of an absolute tyranny over her" (Stanton 1889, 70–71).

The activists at Seneca Falls were an important part of the women's movement that ultimately changed the way most people in our society view gender. Eventually, their efforts helped win the vote for women with the passage of the Nineteenth Amendment to the Constitution in 1920. In hindsight, we can see the biases behind the gender claims that dominated nineteenth-century America, even as we recognize their persistence in some parts of contemporary society.

GENDER IN A DIFFERENT CULTURE Blatant and comprehensive discrimination against women continues in many parts of the world, illustrating how ideas about gender vary not only across time but also across cultures. In Saudi Arabia, for example, a close ally of the United States, women play no official role in government or politics, have few social rights, and are not treated as equal members of society (U.S. Department of State 2012). Although women make up 58 percent of university students, the types of work they can perform are restricted, and they comprise only 15 percent of the workforce. They are expected to remain at home caring for husband and family. By law and custom, schools, workplaces, and transportation are segregated by sex, and women cannot attend most public events unless a close male relative accompanies them. Saudi women generally cannot drive, appear in public with their heads uncovered, travel abroad, receive an identity card, or be admitted to a hospital for treatment without permission from a male relative or guardian. A woman cannot conduct financial transactions (even if she owns a business) without deputizing a male relative as her representative. In the court system in Saudi Arabia, which is based on Islamic law, the testimony of a woman is given half the weight of the testimony of a man.

Many of these gender practices contrast sharply with contemporary Western values, but they are similar to those in the United States a century and a half ago, when the activists at Seneca Falls produced their inventory of grievances. Despite strong restrictions on political protest, some Saudi women have dared to challenge their treatment publicly; however, there are no ongoing women's rights organizations in the country.

Gender Identities and Transgender People

As these examples of difference over time and across cultures show, gender is a social construction that originates in culture but that becomes a part of a person's sense of self. **Gender identity** is *a person's identification as a woman, a man, or some combination of the two.* Most males learn to identify as men; most females learn to identify as women. (Some cultures recognize three or four genders; see the Through a Sociological Lens box.) We explore this process in more detail later in this chapter.

Gender identity is largely learned; however, it remains unclear whether, and to what degree, biology—especially prenatal hormones—might influence the development of gender identity. This is another example of the current recognition that both biology and culture play a role in human development, although much work remains to be done to specify this relationship (Fausto-Sterling 2000). Broad consensus exists among researchers that biology does not *determine* gender identity, however.

Gender expression is *the communication of a person's gender identity to others, through behavior, clothing, hairstyle, and other means.* Since gender is different from sex, gender identity and gender expression are not necessarily consistent with biology. The differentiation between sex and gender is central to the idea of transgender identity. **Transgender people** are *individuals who identify with a gender different from the one associated with their sex.* Some transgender people report that they feel trapped in a body of the opposite sex. Some wear the clothes

Colleges and universities have taken the lead in creating gender-neutral environments. Many schools have added gender identity and gender expression to their nondiscrimination policies; some have gender-neutral bathrooms that are open to both women and men; and dozens have gender-neutral housing where roommates are of the same gender but not necessarily the same sex.

thinking about culture

Ideas about gender vary by culture. Have you experienced a culture or subculture in which some gender norms differed from those commonly found in the dominant U.S. culture?

behavior, sexuality is heavily influenced by norms and expectations that vary by culture and change over time. In discussing sexuality, then, we need to consider both biology and culture.

Biology, Culture, and Sexuality

There are two basic ways to approach human sexuality. On the one hand, we can look at humans as highly evolved animals for whom sex is simply a "natural" biological activity necessary for reproduction, as it is for other animals. Hormones help fuel a sex drive that enables human beings to reproduce successfully—perhaps *too* successfully, since population growth strains the planet's resources. In this vein, some people invoke "nature" to make judgments about what is "normal" sexual activity, and some observers condemn homosexuality as "unnatural" because it cannot result in conception. However, contrary to common belief, other nonhuman primates—our closest animal cousins who are social beings and have relatively large brains and facial features similar to humans—engage in a variety of sexual activities, some of which have nothing to do with reproduction. Bonobo chimpanzees (also known as pygmy chimps), for example, use sex as play, to mark an end to an argument, to help form a friendship, to trade for food, and more. Since bonobos often engage in homosexual sex, oral sex, or sex with juveniles, their sexual behavior is not only for procreation. Therefore, even in nature, sex includes a broad range of practices with a variety of purposes.

On the other hand, human behavior is the product of culture as well as biology, and in this sense, human sexuality isn't so much "natural" as it is a set of socially regulated practices that vary across cultures and over time. Religious belief—which often includes ideas about right and wrong expressions of sexuality—has been one way of communicating cultural norms about sexuality. For example, the use of birth control was forbidden by all Protestant denominations until 1930 and is still considered sinful by the Catholic Church today. The Church also condemns masturbation and homosexuality (Jutte 2008).

Cultures typically have a variety of norms and expectations regarding sexuality. At what age is sexual activity appropriate? Is sex with a first cousin acceptable? Is sex outside of marriage acceptable? Is monogamy—commitment to a single sexual partner—necessary? Different cultures answer these questions differently. However, all cultures have some form of **incest taboo,** *a norm restricting sexual relations between certain relatives.* Since reproduction between close relatives increases the risk that offspring will be born with harmful physical or mental effects, incest taboos reduce this risk. Incest taboos also promote social integration by

encouraging people to reach beyond their immediate family for a sexual partner and reduce conflict within the family by marking boundaries that restrict competition for sexual partners. Other taboos, such as age restrictions, protect vulnerable children not yet mature enough to consent to sexual activity.

As with other aspects of human social life, sociologists understand that sexuality is the result of both nature and nurture; it has a biological basis but varies culturally. As such, it is another aspect of our lives that is socially constructed.

Sexuality as a Social Construction

The bedroom may seem like the last place that would be submitted to a sociological analysis. But sociology applies not only to our public actions but also to the most personal and private aspects of our lives. Sex reflects a culture's collective norms.

Culture heavily influences when, how often, where, with whom, and how humans have sex (Kimmel 2007). Researchers have documented a variety of sexual customs around the world. A passionate kiss on the lips frequently initiates a sexual encounter in U.S. culture. But the Thonga of Mozambique and Siriono of Bolivia, among others, find such kissing to be repulsive because of the possibility of exchanging saliva; mouths are intended to be used for food. The Zande people of central Africa typically have sex several times a night but, in contrast, the Yapese people of the Pacific Islands typically have sex only about once a month. In some cultures, sexual intercourse always occurs outside so as not to "contaminate" the living quarters; in others it always happens indoors. Oral sex is a staple of sexual encounters in some cultures but is absent from others. Men typically initiate sex in many cultures, whereas women typically do so in others.

Because all these sexual behaviors and more are considered "normal" in their cultural context, there clearly is no single understanding of human sexuality. Amid all these variations in sexual behavior, humans manage to reproduce, express love, form strong social bonds, experience pleasure, and simply have fun.

Changing Norms: The Sexual Revolution in the United States

To get a sense of the social construction of sexuality, consider how sexual attitudes, behaviors, and norms have evolved in the United States. In a major cultural shift, the past century has seen an increasing willingness to discuss sexuality openly and a greater emphasis on individual freedom and personal choice in matters of sexuality.

Through much of the twentieth century, sexuality was closely controlled by restrictive social norms. Morality and religion preached that the only appropriate use of sex was to start a family. Reflecting the inequality of the day, women were subjected to a double standard: premarital sex by men was commonly tolerated, whereas women were expected to remain virgins until marriage. Because women didn't have easy access to effective birth control or safe legal abortions, and unmarried mothers were subjected to severe social stigma, female abstinence before marriage was a practical necessity.

By the mid-twentieth century, however, a number of factors helped change sexual attitudes and behaviors in the United States, creating what came to be called the sexual revolution:

- In 1948, Alfred Kinsey and his colleagues helped spark serious public discussion of sexuality when they published the first of two books on male and female sexuality (Kinsey, Pomeroy, and Martin [1948] 1998; Kinsey et al. [1953] 1998). Though crude by today's standards, the work used a social scientific approach to explore what had largely been taboo subjects, including homosexuality. Their findings suggested that many people were more open to a variety of sexual experiences than was often acknowledged. Such work was significant, since sexuality was typically considered a private matter not to be discussed in public, and most people lacked even basic sexual information to a degree that is difficult to imagine today.

- The vibrant youth culture of the post–World War II baby boom generation during the latter 1950s and 1960s rebelled against many social conventions, including restrictive sexual norms. Students living away from home in rapidly growing residential college campuses encountered a social environment that enabled sexual experimentation. By the late 1960s, some members of this youth subculture were advocating the wholesale rejection of sexual conventions and promoting sexuality for pleasure, not just procreation.

- The introduction of the Pill in 1960 helped make such sexual freedom possible. Oral contraceptives made it easier for women to control if and when they had children.

- A broader women's movement decried the sexual double standard and affirmed the right of women to control their own bodies and enjoy their sexuality.

This new freedom was not without consequences. As people engaged in more frequent sex with a greater number of partners, the frequency of sexually transmitted diseases (STDs) and teen pregnancies rose in the 1970s, which helped spark a backlash against the sexual revolution. Social conservatives advocated a return to "family values," including a revival of earlier norms regarding sexuality and gender roles.

Debates over these cultural values continue to this day, but most aspects of the sexual revolution have long since moved into the cultural mainstream, influencing the expression of our sexual identities.

Sexual Identities

Queer theory argues that sexual identities are socially constructed, evolve, and can change during a person's life (Seidman 1996). **Sexual identity** (or sexual orientation) refers to *our sense of self as it relates to the type of sexual attraction we have for others*. In our society, there are four basic sexual identity groups (summarized in Figure 11.4):

- **Heterosexuals** are *attracted to people of a different sex*.
- **Homosexuals** are *attracted to people of the same sex*.
- **Bisexuals** are *attracted to people of both sexes*.
- **Asexual** people *experience no sexual attraction for anyone*.

Although it remains an area of debate, growing evidence suggests that sexual identity is rooted in biology but influenced by culture. The American Academy of Pediatrics offers its clinicians advice that is typical of this growing consensus: "Sexual orientation probably is not determined by any one factor but by a combination of genetic, hormonal, and environmental influences" (Frankowski 2004, 1828).

Sexuality is a sensitive and private topic, and many people are guarded about discussing it. It is therefore impossible to ascertain whether what people *say* in surveys about their sex lives is accurate. Also, given the continuum of attitudes and behaviors that marks sexuality, classifying people into distinct categories can be difficult and misleading. For example, most people who report having engaged in same-sex activities at some point in their lives do not identify as gay, lesbian, or bisexual (Herbenick et al. 2010; Laumann et al. 2000). Thus the percentage of the population that falls within each type of sexual identity is a matter of debate.

More recently, the U.S. Census Bureau has begun to collect data on same-sex couples and the gay, lesbian, and bisexual population in the United States. Based on these and other surveys, one analysis found that 9 million people—3.5 percent of the adult U.S. population—identified themselves as lesbian, gay, bisexual, or transgender (Gates 2011). In 2009, there were 581,300 same-sex couples in the United States, a number that is likely to increase as the social stigma and threat of discrimination associated with homosexuality and same-sex relationships decreases (Gates 2010).

FIGURE 11.4 | SEXUAL IDENTITIES

Degree of Same-Sex Attraction	Degree of Opposite-Sex Attraction	
	High	*Low*
High	Bisexual	Homosexual
Low	Heterosexual	Asexual

Inventing Heterosexuals and Homosexuals

Just as culture influences how people understand sexual behavior, it also influences how we understand sexual identity. In fact, the very idea of linking identity to sexuality—of identifying as "straight," "gay," or "bi"—is a relatively recent social invention.

All forms of sexual behaviors have existed throughout human history. Some forms of homosexual activity were a routine part of social life in some societies, as we saw from the example of the two-spirits earlier in this chapter. Perhaps most famously, homosexuality was prevalent in ancient Greek culture, and the word *lesbian* is derived from the island of Lesbos, home of the ancient Greek poet Sappho, who wrote her love poems for women and girls.

However, through most of human history, sexual behavior and what we now call sexual identity have been separated. In earlier times, engaging in heterosexual or homosexual activity didn't necessarily mean a person was regarded as a heterosexual or a homosexual. Not until early scientific efforts to categorize human sexual behavior in the mid-nineteenth century was the notion of "homosexuals" as a distinct category of people created to contrast with "heterosexuals."

In *The History of Sexuality*, Michel Foucault (1980) argued that in the mid-nineteenth century, in part because of the increasingly diverse and rapidly growing populations concentrated in recently industrialized cities, scientists undertook new efforts to study sexual behaviors. For the first time, sexuality—which had always been a part of daily life—was scrutinized and analyzed. In the process of studying sexual behaviors, researchers began classifying them into distinct categories—including "normal" and "deviant." Increased knowledge about sexual practices led to efforts by those in power to restrict them. Governments began trying to regulate and control these newly labeled deviant practices. For example, they enacted sodomy laws banning practices associated with homosexuality (though performed by many heterosexuals as well), such as anal intercourse and oral sex. By the end of the nineteenth century, Western societies treated someone who engaged in homosexual activity as a member of a new and distinct social category: homosexuals.

In the latter half of the twentieth century, however, skepticism about the strict separation of sexualities and efforts to enforce it increased. As early as 1948, Kinsey suggested that

rather than belonging to one of two distinct categories, men's sexuality fell along a continuum, with many men experiencing both heterosexual and homosexual feelings and behaviors to varying degrees. Many researchers have confirmed Kinsey's findings, though popular culture often still views "gay" and "straight" as sharply divided and mutually exclusive identities.

Bisexuality and Asexuality

Are you gay or straight? As noted, our culture generally insists on dichotomous—either-or—sexual identities. But what if your answer to that question is "both" or "neither"? Being *bisexual* means having a sexual identity based on attraction to both women and men. People in various cultures have long engaged in sexual activity with people of both sexes, but the notion of bisexuality as a distinct identity emerged in the nineteenth century. The term *bisexual* was not commonly used until the mid-twentieth century.

Being *asexual* means lacking sexual attraction to either gender. This identity, too, violates our culture's expected norms about sexuality. Asexual people are not celibate; they typically don't choose to refrain from sex, resist sexual urges, fail to find a sexual partner, or have moral or religious objections to sex. Instead, asexuals—who make up about 1 percent of the population, according to the limited research available on the subject—are simply not sexually attracted to anyone (Bogaert 2004).

Sexual Identities and Inequality

Cultures have widely divergent views about lesbian, gay, bisexual, and transgender (LGBT) people. **Heterosexism,** *a set of attitudes and behavior that indicates an assumption that everyone is heterosexual,* is common. Assuming a female friend is referring to a man when she mentions a date is an example of heterosexism. People with heterosexist attitudes don't necessarily have negative feelings toward LGBT people; they simply overlook their existence. In contrast, **homophobia** is *the disapproval and fear of LGBT people.* Homophobia is often the source of hostility and discrimination.

Discrimination against lesbian, gay, bisexual, and transgender people is pervasive, though movement toward more

thinking about power
Once scientists categorized people as homosexual or heterosexual, governments sought to use their **power** to control individuals with sexual identities they considered deviant. In what ways do governments still use power to control people's sexual identity?

MAP 11.1 | SAME-SEX MARRIAGE AND RELATIONSHIP RECOGNITION LAWS, 2013

States with full marriage equality
Massachusetts (2004); Connecticut (2008); Iowa (2009); Vermont (2009);
New Hampshire (2010); District of Columbia (2010); New York (2011); Maine (2012);
Maryland (2012); Washington (2012); Rhode Island (2013); Minnesota (2013); Delware (2013);
California (2013); New Jersey (2013); Hawaii (2013); New Mexico (2013); Utah (2013); Illinois (2014)

States with broad relationship recognition laws
civil unions: Colorado (2013)
domestic partnerships: Oregon (2008); Nevada (2009)

States with limited relationship recognition laws
domestic partnerships: Wisconsin (2009)

While marriage equality for gay and lesbian couples has been gaining momentum, most states continue to ban same-sex marriage. *Source:* National Gay and Lesbian Task Force (2014).

CORE CONCEPTS CHALLENGE

How does the legal **structure** *in various states create barriers for same-sex couples? Does legally recognizing same-sex marriage create barriers for heterosexual couples? Explain.*

---

in the workplace. For example, as of 2013, 88 percent of *Fortune* 500 companies prohibited discrimination on the basis of sexual orientation and 62 percent offered domestic partner health insurance benefits to LGBT employees (Human Rights Campaign 2013a).

Same-sex marriage is legal in more than a dozen countries, including Canada, the Netherlands, South Africa, France, Brazil, and Spain, whereas various forms of civil unions are legal in at least 15 other countries. In contrast, the United States passed the 1996 Defense of Marriage Act (DOMA) defining marriage as a legal union between one man and one woman. This law empowered states to refuse to recognize same-sex marriages performed in other states where they are legal. Moreover, a section of DOMA prevented the federal government from recognizing same-sex partners as spouses, thereby barring them from receiving federal marriage benefits. When this part of the law was judged unconstitutional in 2013, the door was opened for broader recognition of same-sex marriage in the United States at the federal level. Still, most states continue to bar same-sex marriages, limiting the legal rights of gay and lesbian partners (Map 11.1). As yet, LGBT parents have no consistent legal standing across the states. Child custody, visitation, and adoption rights are

equality is evident. Homophobic laws and customs have blatantly discriminated against LGBT people, often forcing them to stay "in the closet." The American Psychiatric Association labeled homosexuality a "mental disorder" until the mid-1970s. Sodomy laws were used almost exclusively to target gay men until the U.S. Supreme Court ruled them unconstitutional in 2003 (American Civil Liberties Union 2010).

Because federal legislation does not bar discrimination against LGBT people in employment, in the absence of state protections, it is legal to fire or refuse to hire people simply because they are gay, bisexual, or transgender. Some states, though, have adopted employment protection laws prohibiting such actions. In some ways, the private sector has been ahead of government in recognizing LGBT rights

just some of the issues still being debated and resolved in various legal venues.

Homosexuals were banned from military service until 1993, when a compromise "don't ask, don't tell" policy (designed by sociologist Charles Moskos) permitted gays and lesbians to serve as long as they did not openly disclose their sexual identity. In 2010, a federal court found this policy unconstitutional, prompting congressional action later that year that finally overturned the ban.

Homophobic beliefs are often rooted in religious doctrine, but there is no consensus among the world's religions regarding the status of LGBT people. Indeed, debates about homosexuality, the role of gays in each faith, and the blessing of same-sex unions have deeply divided some denominations. The Episcopal Church in the United States was deeply

Sexuality

divided in recent years over the ordination of an openly gay bishop, for example. Intolerance can be extreme. In a few Muslim countries, including Iran and Yemen, homosexuality is still punishable by death.

More informally, our culture still contains homophobia. For many young people, *gay* is a synonym for *lame* or *stupid*. "Gay bashing" ranges from well-known insulting slang terms—such as *fag* or *dyke*—to hate crimes such as harassment, assault, and even murder. Such harassment sometimes leads to suicides, especially by beleaguered gay teens (Dvorak 2010).

In one particularly horrendous period of persecution, German Nazis arrested and beat tens of thousands of gay men—sometimes castrating them—and used them as forced laborers in concentration camps. Once imprisoned, they were forced to wear pink triangles, which activists have since recast as a powerful symbol of the LGBT movement.

Sexuality and the Internet

The term *pornography* refers to material that explicitly portrays sexual acts or naked people and is primarily intended to stimulate sexual excitement. With the rise of the Internet, pornography is more easily available than ever before. Consequently, porn has increasingly drawn the attention of sociologists and others for its portrayal of human sexuality.

The porn industry is vast. Though accurate data are difficult to obtain, some estimates are that porn generates over $13 billion each year in the United States alone and that the Internet features well over 4 million websites devoted to pornography (Dines 2010). Pornography is a major part of the bottom line not only for its producers but also for mainstream corporations. For example, sexually explicit television channels are highly profitable for cable providers, and most hotels offer lucrative pay-per-view porn movies.

Pornography helped fuel many of the Internet's early innovations, including online payment systems, video streaming, and video chat, as well many of its nuisances, among them spam, malware, and pop-up ads (Tynan 2008). Owing to the Internet, porn has also become increasingly do-it-yourself, with "amateur" photos and videos commonly uploaded to porn websites. Some of these postings are malicious, as in the case of "revenge porn," which involves uploading sexually explicit photos or videos—sometimes obtained surreptitiously—without the knowledge or consent of the person in them.

One concern about the growth of pornography is that child and teen Internet users now have access to a sea of sexually explicit material. This development has toppled a traditional social barrier that once separated adults and children. Loaded with clichés that are far removed from real-world sexual practice, dominated by portrayals of women whose only role is to fulfill male fantasies, and often laced with misogynistic images of women being mistreated and humiliated, pornography, many observers argue, badly distorts young people's understanding of healthy sexuality (Dines 2010; Gallup 2011). One review of the research on pornography and young people (Horvath et al. 2013) concluded that early exposure to porn is associated with unrealistic beliefs about sex and the adoption of attitudes favoring gender inequality, such as male dominance and female submission. Boys and young men are more likely than girls and young women to seek out pornography, and they tend to have more positive views about it. The review also found that while not necessarily a causal relationship, access and exposure to pornography are associated with higher rates of risky sexual behaviors, including practicing unprotected and oral sex, combining sex with alcohol and drug use, having sex with multiple partners, and engaging in "sexting"—the sending of sexually explicit photos or messages by cell phone.

Observers have noted that, in part due to the easy availability of sexually explicit material over the Internet, pornography has moved into mainstream culture (Sarracino 2009). Music videos have adopted poses and conventions from pornographic films, often featuring submissive women. Some television programs, such as *Sex and the City*, have featured story lines celebrating porn use. The 2011 erotic novel *50 Shades of Grey*, sold mostly as an e-book, mixed a traditional romance formula with explicit sex scenes of bondage and sadomasochism to reach *The New York Times* best-seller list and sell over 70 million copies. Other self-published "erotic novels" have gained considerable popularity among e-book readers, especially women (Berlatsky 2013). Oprah Winfrey's magazine, *O*, has featured an adult film guide for women suggesting that using such material can lead to a more satisfying sex life.

As porn has gone mainstream, its content has diversified. Illegal pornography involving children or deadly violence is still rampant. Traditional "hardcore" adult pornography includes depictions that degrade women, portray humiliating sexual acts, and involve coercion, abuse, and violence. But a growing segment of pornography can be labeled *erotica*, a subjective term referring to sexually explicit material that is not violent, degrading, or exploitative and that features compassionate sexual encounters. Such material appears to be reaching new and wider audiences.

Feminist scholars and activists have long debated the nature of and appropriate response to pornography (Cornell 2000). Some critiques of pornography note the negative impact of stereotypical and violent porn on consumers and the broader society, as well as the disturbing exploitative and dangerous practices that characterize the porn industry and affect porn workers. Critics sometimes call for the censoring of pornography, considering it to be "sexual slavery" that inevitably constitutes violence against women. Groups such as Stop Porn Culture are "dedicated to challenging the pornography industry and an increasingly pornographic pop culture" (stoppornculture.org).

Other feminists condemn traditional pornography but endorse sexually explicit material produced in a noncoercive way, which treats women and men as equals and portrays healthy, caring sexual encounters in the context of larger relationships (O'Connor 2013). Further, feminist porn highlights diversity and aims to "contest and complicate dominant representations of gender, sexuality, race, ethnicity, class, ability, age, body type, and other identity markers" (Taormino 2013, 9). That is, it challenges dominant images of sexuality, many of which are the result of traditional porn.

Debates among these critics continue even as the study of pornography itself has become more mainstream. In 2014, *Porn Studies* was launched, the first academic journal devoted to the study of pornography.

Challenging Inequality Based on Gender and Sexual Identity

A half century ago, a chapter such as this one simply would not have appeared in a sociology textbook. In an example of how human action can change cultures and social structures, however, feminists and LGBT activists have helped modify political, legal, and cultural reality as well as the scholarly agenda. This section briefly explores some of these efforts.

Gender in Sociology

As we saw in Chapter 1, most early mainstream sociologists ignored issues of gender and sexuality, reflecting the sexist views of the societies in which they were working (Kandal 1988). The "founding fathers" of sociology in the nineteenth and early twentieth centuries often based their generalizations about society on the experiences of heterosexual men. Women writing sociological works at the time were mostly excluded from formal academic positions. As a result, gender played a marginal role in early conventional sociology.

One exception was a critical theory of gender stratification developed by Friedrich Engels, a close collaborator of Karl Marx. Engels ([1884] 1972) tied gender stratification to the rise of private property and class. Drawing on early anthropological research, Engels noted that in hunting and gathering societies, private property did not exist, family structure was fluid, and women's and men's labor was comparably valued because each was essential for survival. Agricultural development, however, resulted in material surpluses that enabled private property and class distinctions to emerge. Male property owners now needed to control the sexuality of women to know who their rightful heirs were. This development produced an emphasis on premarital virginity, monogamous marriage, and the rigid modern family. Later, capitalism elevated the importance of wage labor outside the home but depended upon women's devalued and unpaid labor in the home to feed and care for current and future workers. Thus, for Engels, gender stratification emerged from changes in the economy. Although he made gender secondary in importance to class, Engels at least recognized gender inequality as unjust and saw the intersection of class and gender stratification. Consistent with his work, the emancipation of women was a goal of many socialist political movements.

GENDER STRATIFICATION AS FUNCTIONAL By the middle of the twentieth century, Talcott Parsons was one of a number of sociologists who wrote about "sex roles." Parsons recognized the role strain involved in being a woman in middle-class America, especially the tension between being a mother and working in paid employment. However, reflecting his functionalist theoretical orientation, Parsons accepted uncritically the idea that the specialization of sex roles served a useful function in society.

According to Parsons, paid labor serves an *instrumental* function because it is task oriented, with short-term, impersonal interactions, while the family serves the *expressive* functions involved in stable, long-term, personal relationships. With work separated from home life, men specialized in instrumental functions, whereas women focused on the expressive tasks of nurturing children and caring for husbands. Parsons seemed to assume that women and men voluntarily accepted this state of affairs and embraced the values associated with it. For Parsons, this clear separation of sex roles reduced competition between husband and wife for status in the family. "If both were equally in competition for occupational status, there might indeed be a very serious strain on the solidarity of the family unit," Parsons wrote (1954, 79). He argued that the useful functions provided by sex role segregation helped explain why "the feminist movement has had such difficulty in breaking it down" (p. 80). In the 1960s and 1970s, the women's movement challenged these assumptions.

SPOTLIGHT
on social theory

Parsons's **functionalist** approach to gender rationalized inequality between the sexes. Do you agree that specialized roles for each sex can serve a positive function? How might such specialization be dysfunctional for society?

FEMINIST SCHOLARSHIP Objecting to the functionalists' assumptions, feminist scholars pointed out that there was no reason why individuals could not perform *both* instrumental and expressive tasks, or if these tasks were to be separated, why men had to be limited to instrumental and women to expressive. They also pointed out that functionalist arguments ignored reality: first, a significant portion of women—overwhelmingly members of the working class—were already in the labor force, and second, Parsons's model of family life was limited to a particular middle-class version that was dominant in the United States in the middle of the twentieth century. Since that time, feminist scholarship has influenced every subfield in the discipline (Chafetz 1999). This chapter reflects many insights from feminist scholars.

Women's Activism

Feminism is *a philosophy that advocates social, political, and economic equality for women and men.* Activism on behalf of women's equality has been a constant force in the modern world, but various periods of especially intense activism are commonly identified as "waves." *First-wave feminism* took place mainly in the United States and the United Kingdom during the late nineteenth and early twentieth centuries, when activists working on behalf of women's political and social rights won the right to vote for women. The Seneca Falls convention mentioned earlier in this chapter is from this era, as are such noted feminist leaders as Susan B. Anthony and Elizabeth Cady Stanton. The activists of this period had broad goals beyond winning the right to vote, including eliminating discriminatory laws, increasing access to higher education, and working to make birth control more readily available.

Second-wave feminism refers to the period of intense activism during the 1960s and 1970s, when activists tackled issues related to gender inequality, including discrimination in the workplace and in education, gender stereotypes in popular culture, restrictive gender roles, reproductive rights, and sexual freedom. During this era well-known activists such as Betty Friedan, the author of *The Feminine Mystique* (a book that helped inspire a revival of interest in women's rights), helped form the National Organization for Women (NOW), and Gloria Steinem, another important activist, founded *Ms. Magazine* as a platform for feminist ideas.

Third-wave feminism refers to activism beginning in the 1990s, though some feminist scholars and activists view this period as a continuation of second-wave feminism. Activism today promotes female self-empowerment and sexual self-esteem, gives special attention to race and class diversity within women's experiences, and often includes a playful subversion of popular culture. For example, third-wave feminists combated the patronizing use of the word *girl* to refer to women by reclaiming it as "grrl power," a confident affirmation of women's strength.

LGBT Activism

Sexual identity and gender identity are not just private issues; they are also public and political concerns. During the past half century, social activism has made the public increasingly aware of issues affecting LGBT people (Clendinen and Nagourney 1999; Miller 2006). On June 28, 1969, the New York City police raided a gay bar called the Stonewall Inn, as they had done many times before. This time, however, patrons refused to go quietly to jail, and while the police waited for patrol wagons, a crowd gathered outside the bar and began

In 1969, gays and lesbians were forced to live almost entirely "in the closet," and public gay rights activism was so rare that the clash (*left*) between police and gay men outside New York's Stonewall Inn became iconic. Today, many LGBT people live openly and LGBT activism is common, including the movement to recognize same-sex marriage. On the right, supporters of same-sex marriage march past the Stonewall Inn to celebrate the enactment of New York's same-sex marriage law in 2011.

heckling and then attacking the officers. The spontaneous demonstration that followed was repeated on subsequent nights in what has become known as the Stonewall Riots, a defining moment for the LGBT community and a symbolic turning point in the history of social movements. After years of being forced to hide from police harassment, gay people took to the streets to demand their rights.

Stonewall primarily involved white, gay men. Since then, a diverse gay rights movement has emerged, taking on a broad range of issues, including supporting LGBT people of color; combating hate crimes; supporting teens who face bullying, harassment, and estrangement from their families; mobilizing people of faith to support LGBT rights; assisting aging gay couples who face unique financial challenges as a result of their not being allowed to marry; combating discriminatory laws and practices in civilian society and the military; working for equality in the workplace; and helping same-sex parents. College campuses have been especially active in cultivating LGBT activism and developing movement leaders. Over the years, activists have shifted the nation's culture and laws toward considerably more equality for the LGBT community, though much remains to be done.

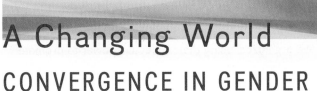

A Changing World

CONVERGENCE IN GENDER AND SEXUALITY

As we have seen, ideas about gender and sexuality are changing constantly. In recent years, one ongoing change has been that women and men have become more similar in both gender and sexuality.

Gender Convergence

Gender convergence is *a trend toward increasing similarity in how women and men live.* This convergence varies depending on social context, much like gender itself. Some women in booming developing countries, for example, are experiencing increased economic opportunities and independence for the first time, newfound freedom that is allowing them to carve out new gender roles in otherwise traditional societies. Those most affected are middle-class, educated women who have the chance to defer marriage and motherhood while pursuing careers in fields such as business and technology. In India, for example, a growing population of young, single women has chosen to live independently rather than staying at their parents' house or getting married. Although Indian women marry young compared to their Western counterparts, the average age at which they marry has risen

slightly, with college-educated women putting off marriage the longest. Although arranged marriages are still common and traditional gender roles still deeply entrenched, new economic realities are enabling some women to pursue careers and lifestyles once limited to men (Sengupta 2007).

In wealthy developed countries, traditional ways of dividing responsibility between work and family are becoming less common and gender roles less rigid (Fischer et al. 2007; Lang and Risman 2007). As we have seen, women and men participate in the labor force at rates that are converging. Consequently, they now have increasingly similar attitudes toward the best way to allocate their time: both women and men report they want to strike a balance between work and family life.

In particular, younger men and women in wealthy societies are increasingly taking on similar roles. Younger fathers spend more time doing child care than their own fathers did (Gerson 1987, 2010). College students of both sexes have similar aspirations to pursue advanced degrees and careers, have similar attitudes about the appropriate role of women in society, provide similar answers to a variety of questions about personal values (including about the desire to raise a family), and hold comparable opinions about some social and political issues (Astin 1998).

Sexual Convergence

Over the past few decades, gender convergence has gradually changed the sexual double standard between men and women, especially among younger people. Though differences remain, the age at which women and men become sexually active, their number of sexual partners, and their attitudes toward sexuality have become more similar. One phase of this convergence occurred in the wake of the sexual revolution of the 1960s and 1970s, when girls became more sexually active at an earlier age, thereby behaving more like boys. A second phase got under way in the 1990s, when boys began delaying the age of their first sexual activity, thereby behaving more like girls.

Risman and Schwartz (2002) suggest that the traditionally large gap between the rate of girls' and boys' sexual activity before the sexual revolution meant that a few sexually active girls were having relations with a larger number of boys. Gender norms of the time discouraged sexual activity on the part of "good girls," leaving boys to pursue sex with "bad girls," who were ostracized as "sluts." As gender norms changed, girls' sexual activity has become more accepted and widespread. Consequently, boys' early sexual activities are now more likely to be in the context of an ongoing relationship with a girlfriend rather than a fleeting encounter with a "bad girl." Sex in such ongoing relationships is more likely to be safe and responsible, contributing to some positive trends. In recent years, the rates of sexually transmitted diseases, teen pregnancies, and abortions have all declined, suggesting that teens are being more sexually responsible.

thinking sociologically about
Gender and Sexuality

culture

- *Gender* refers to the socially constructed cultural expectations associated with men and women. Different cultures produce different gender norms.

- From infancy, we are socialized into our culture's gender expectations, develop gendered identities, and view the world through the lens of gender expectations that we usually take for granted.

- Sexuality also varies by culture, and different cultures have different norms regarding sexual identities that must be taught through socialization.

structure

- Gender is built into social structure, as when social institutions enforce gender expectations.

- Gender must constantly be maintained and re-created—actions that sociologists call "doing gender." Gender roles and identities are fragile and may be contested and changed.

- Social structures often reflect expectations regarding sexuality, as when the legal system is tailored to heterosexual couples.

power

- In every society, differences in power between men and women have resulted in social institutions with considerable gender inequality.

- Inequality based on sexuality also reflects differences in power in society.

- Feminists and LGBT activists have organized, using their collective power to promote change.

REVIEW, REFLECT, AND APPLY

Looking Back

1. *Sex* refers to the biological characteristics that distinguish females and males. *Gender* refers to the socially constructed expectations associated with women and men. Transgender people, who identify with a gender not typically associated with their sex, illustrate the difference between sex and gender.

2. Much of what our society attributes to sex is, in fact, gender. Notions of gender vary over time and across cultures. Gender is taught through socialization, and "doing gender" refers to daily interactions in a variety of social settings that involve the reinforcement or modification of gender.

3. Gender inequality and stratification are part of the structure of society. Sex differences likely played an important role in the establishment of patriarchy, whereas cultural developments have radically reduced the importance of sex in relation to gender.

4. Gender inequality can be found in all the major social institutions, including the workplace, family, media, politics, and religion. Individual or organized violence against women is one way male power is used to dominate women.

5. Norms about sexuality and sexual identity are culturally produced, resulting in wide variations. In Western society, the invention of distinct sexual orientations is a relatively recent phenomenon. Sexual minorities are often subject to discrimination.

6. Feminist efforts have helped create more equality between women and men. Activism has also helped reduce discrimination against LGBT people. Gender and sexual convergence have occurred in many areas of social life, as standards become more similar for men and women.

Critical Thinking: Questions and Activities

1. Both gender and race have socially constructed characteristics that are mistakenly attributed to biology. Using a sociological perspective, describe how else race and gender are similar. How are they different?

2. Take note of how the words *sex* and *gender* are used to refer to women and men in popular media and other places. Can you find examples in which the word *gender* is being used to mean biological differences?

3. What do you think are the major differences, if any, between how gender affects your life and how it affected the lives of your parents?

4. Where do you see the most entrenched forms of gender inequality? Why has this particular area been so resistant to change?

5. How were you socialized to understand different sexual identities? Did this socialization include homophobic biases?

Key Terms

asexual (p. 311) people who experience no sexual attraction for anyone.

bisexual (p. 311) people who are attracted to others of both sexes.

doing gender (p. 297) creating gender through interactions in particular social settings.

domestic violence (or intimate partner violence) (p. 307) a pattern of abusive behavior in any relationship that is used by one partner to gain or maintain power and control over another intimate partner.

feminism (p. 316) a philosophy that advocates social, political, and economic equality for women and men.

gender (p. 291) the socially constructed cultural expectations associated with women and men.

gender convergence (p. 317) a trend toward increasing similarity in how women and men live.

gender expression (p. 293) the way a person communicates gender identity to others, through behavior, clothing, hairstyle, and other means.

gender identity (p. 293) a person's identification as a woman, a man, or some combination of the two.

gender role (p. 296) a set of social expectations regarding behavior and attitudes based on a person's sex.

gender stratification (p. 301) the systematic and unequal distribution of power and resources in society between women and men.

glass ceiling (p. 305) the often invisible barrier created by individual and institutional sexism that prevents qualified women from advancing to higher levels of leadership and management.

heterosexism (p. 312) attitudes and behavior that indicate an assumption that everyone is heterosexual.

heterosexual (p. 311) people who are attracted to people of a different sex.

homophobia (p. 312) the disapproval and fear of LGBT people.

homosexual (p. 311) people who are attracted to people of the same sex.

incest taboo (p. 310) a norm restricting sexual relations between certain relatives.

intersexual people (p. 291) individuals born with ambiguous reproductive or sexual anatomy.

matriarchy (p. 301) a social system dominated by women.

patriarchy (p. 301) a social system dominated by men.

second shift (p. 305) the phenomenon of employed women still having primary responsibility for housework and child care.

sex (p. 291) the biological distinction between females and males.

sexism (p. 296) the ideology that one sex is superior to the other.

sexual harassment (p. 306) unwelcome sexual advances, requests for sexual favors, and other verbal or physical harassment of a sexual nature.

sexual identity (or orientation) (p. 311) our sense of self as it relates to the type of sexual attraction we have for others.

sexuality (p. 309) a person's sexual desires, behaviors, and identity.

transgender people (p. 293) individuals who identify with a gender different from the one associated with their sex.

transsexuals (p. 295) people who have sex reassignment surgery to change their physical appearance.

12

Family and Religion

looking AHEAD

How does **culture** influence your understanding of family and religion?

How are the **structures** of family and religion that you experience today different from those of previous generations?

How does **power** operate in your family?

How much **power** does religion have in your life?

Unlike most young American women who expect to experience love and marriage in that order, 25-year-old Vibha Jasani was preparing to marry a man she hardly knew (Span 2003). To find a mate, the Virginia Tech graduate had recently traveled with her mother to India, her family's homeland. There she spent three weeks meeting at least one man a day who had been prescreened by her uncle. Jasani eventually chose Haresh Umaretiya, met with his family to get their approval (some 20 people in all), and was quickly engaged. A few months later, Jasani and her family were back in the United States preparing for her wedding and mapping out her future using a mix of religious custom and family tradition.

In India's Hindu culture, marriage is considered the union of two families, not just two individuals. To Hindus, parents have not completed their responsibilities until a child is married, so parents usually become deeply involved in helping choose mates for their children. Parents appraise the bloodlines and reputation of each candidate's family and take into account the education, class, age, and appearance of prospective spouses. Wives and husbands are expected to be reliable and dependable partners, not necessarily to fall in love or be close confidantes.

While the tradition of arranged marriages is centuries-old, contemporary Western values introduced by globalization have been transforming it. Today, "arranged introduction" might be a more accurate description since the potential bride and groom can each veto any proposed match. Reflecting her embrace of U.S. values, Jasani was clear that she was not about to give up her career to become a traditional housewife. When it came to housework, she insisted on "someone who'd be fifty-fifty with everything."

Looking back after a large successful religious wedding, Jasani is a bit surprised that she went through with the traditional process. "I never thought I'd do it this way. It's really weird how life works, y'know? But I'm happy with the way it ended up. Seriously happy."

arious types of arranged marriage—some of which incorporate considerable individual choice—are still common in many parts of the world, and new immigrants to the United States often bring these traditions with them. However, the U.S.-born children of immigrants grow up in a different society from their parents. They typically move away from arranged marriage—as well as traditional norms regarding gender roles, dating, and courtship (Dugsin 2001; Khandelwal 2002; Manohar 2008). As Jasani did, these U.S.-born children often adopt a strategy that blends parental guidance with individual choice. Others simply reject the practice outright.

They are not alone. Perhaps more than ever, attitudes about family, marriage, and religion are in transition, both in the United States and around the world, with new patterns of social life emerging as old ones are abandoned. In this chapter, we explore family and religion in a changing world, considering their variations within and across cultures, and their evolution over time.

Understanding the Family

We begin by examining the sociological definition of the family and the functions families perform in society.

The Family as a Social Institution

Sociologists define a **family** as *two or more people, related either by birth or through social commitment, who share resources, care for any dependents, and often maintain close emotional relationships.* This broad definition helps identify "Who is family?" as well as "What do families do?" With its enduring patterns of relationships and behaviors, the family is a key *social institution.* Biologically based relationships—so-called blood relations—play a role in establishing family links, but social commitment such as adoption, marriage, civil union, or a steadfast enduring relationship can also establish **kinship,** or *family bonds.*

Ultimately, the meaning of family is culturally defined. A culture's notions about family establish, for example, whose relationships are significant, what obligations individuals have to each other, and what actions are expected from each. Families vary enormously because they are social constructions that reflect the norms and beliefs of different cultures at different points in history. However, as in all social institutions, it is the actions of individuals that maintain or change family structures. Finally, the family is influenced by broader social forces, some of which help create differences in power that perpetuate inequality.

Families take many forms. Some families include caregivers with children or elders as dependents; others consist solely of an adult couple. Some families live together, but some extend well beyond a single household. Love is often central to marriage and family life, but relationships in some marriages and families are quite formal, without loving, intimate interaction. Despite these variations, all families perform at least some core social functions, as we see next.

Social Functions of the Family

Sociologically speaking, what is important about families is less the form they take than the roles they play in society. Sociologists working in the functionalist tradition have highlighted several positive social functions of families (Parsons and Bales 1955).

- **Social stability.** Families create kinship ties. On a micro level, these relationships create a social bond between individuals and their relatives. On a macro level, kinship ties can create intricate social networks that include extended family and multiple generations. In preindustrial societies, these networks were an especially important source of social stability because they promoted solidarity. The marriage of two individuals could serve as a political alliance between separate kinship networks for common defense and shared prosperity. In industrialized societies, formal governmental and economic institutions have displaced many of the functions of these extended kinship networks, but smaller kinship units—families—continue to play a significant role.

- **Material aid.** Family members typically help one another by pooling their material resources and labor. In some cases, they work together to produce their necessities of life, including food, clothing, and shelter. In wage-based economies, earnings are used for the material benefit of family members, whereas unpaid labor in the home contributes to the family's maintenance and well-being. Regardless of the model, pooling resources is a common feature of families. Power within the family often resides with those in control of these resources.

- **Descent and inheritance.** *Descent* refers to the way people trace kinship over multiple generations. *Inheritance* refers to the rules regarding the reallocation of property within a family after someone dies. In modern industrial societies, descent is commonly *bilateral,* traced through both mother and father. In many traditional, preindustrial societies, descent is *unilineal,* traced either through the father (*patrilineal descent*) or the mother (*matrilineal*

thinking about structure

The patterns of behavior found in families are a part of social **structure**. What are some of the ways that your family structures social life by enabling specific patterns of behavior?

This Christian family saying grace before a meal (*left*) is affluent by global standards and the distinct product of U.S. culture. It contrasts starkly with this Muslim family of modest means from Senegal (*right*), who are also about to share a meal. Their geography, culture, class, race, nationality, and religion may differ, yet both families perform remarkably similar social functions.

descent). Because the family serves as the primary agent for inheritance of property and other wealth, it is central to the reproduction of class in society. When inheritance favors male heirs, these practices can also help perpetuate gender inequality.

- **Care and socialization of dependents.** Families often care for a variety of dependents, especially children, family members with disabilities, and elders. In addition to teaching children practical skills, family members also socialize them in particular values and beliefs, as we saw in Chapter 6, including gender roles, morality, and religion. Caring for elders is increasingly important as more people live longer and some of them begin to experience debilitating physical and mental conditions.

- **Sexual regulation.** Cultural norms typically indicate which sexual relations are socially acceptable. As we saw in Chapter 11, incest taboos prohibit sex with certain family members. Some societies have strict prohibitions against sex between unmarried couples. Marriage simultaneously legitimates a sexual partnership while typically defining sex outside the partnership as illegitimate.

- **Emotional support.** In addition to its practical functions, the modern family is often expected to be a source of emotional comfort and intense emotional bonds. Love is expected to figure centrally in marriage, and family members are expected to assist one another out of a sense of mutual responsibility, commitment, and concern.

SPOTLIGHT

on social theory

Functionalist theories emphasize a variety of tasks that are carried out by families. How did the family you grew up in accomplish these tasks?

The family is a social institution that retains its central role throughout the life course, from infancy to old age. However, in industrialized societies today other social institutions have emerged to take on functions previously performed by the family. The education system instructs children and socializes them to be adults. The health care system cares for those who are sick and elderly. The government provides for our defense; citizenship, rather than membership in a clan, tribe, or other kin group, entitles us to protection.

Family Diversity in Global Context

Whatever type of family you belong to, it's probably very different from that of the Na, an ethnic minority at the foot of the Himalayan Mountains in southwestern China (Hua 2001). The Na are a matrilineal society, tracing descent from mothers to daughters. Until the 1990s, when the Chinese government began to pressure the Na to change their way of life, social concepts of marriage and fatherhood were irrelevant to them. Instead of getting married when they reached adulthood, Na men and women continued to live in their mothers' homes but were free to have consenting heterosexual relations with others in the village. A women and her family raised any children she bore. Because monogamy was not expected of anyone, paternity was usually uncertain and unimportant. As this example suggests, families can vary radically in form and still perform essential social functions.

A Na woman in China poses with her grandchildren. The Na's matrilineal society, using a family form quite different from our own, successfully meets the basic functions of family as a social institution.

CORE CONCEPTS CHALLENGE

*What effect do you think a family **structure** like that of the Na might have on gender relations and the relative status of women in Na society?*

Global Variations in Family and Marriage

Families vary in a variety of ways, including the following:

- *Family networks.* Families vary by size and composition. A **nuclear family** (sometimes referred to as a conjugal family) *consists of a parent or parents and their children.* An **extended family** *consists of the nuclear family plus other relatives such as grandparents.* For example, in some cases newly married adults move in with one set of parents permanently. Such arrangements provide assistance for young couples, who are expected to care for their parents as they age.

- *Marriage and cohabitation.* The nature of the social bond between couples in a nuclear family varies. **Marriage** is *a social relationship that creates family ties, typically involves sexual intimacy, and is formalized by legal contract, religious ceremony, or both.* **Cohabitation** is *a social relationship that can create family ties and typically involves sexual intimacy, in which people live together as unmarried partners.* In some cultures cohabitation carries a negative stigma, whereas other cultures accept cohabitation as either a prelude to marriage or, increasingly, a legitimate alternative to it.

- *Marriage eligibility.* Cultures vary according to how they limit eligible marriage partners. Sometimes cultures enforce **endogamy,** *the restriction of marriage either by law or custom to people within the same social category.* People might be forbidden or discouraged from marrying across caste, class, or racial lines, for example. As we saw in Chapter 5, marriage across caste lines in India was once strictly forbidden. In other cases, cultures allow or require **exogamy,** *marriage between people from different social categories.* Because of the incest taboo, many societies require marriage outside of one's immediate family. A culture might at the same time require endogamy within certain categories but exogamy between others.

- *Marriage arrangements.* In some cultures, romantic love figures prominently in marriage and people are typically responsible for choosing their own mates. But, as we saw in the chapter-opening vignette, marriages are arranged in some cultures based on economics and status rather than romantic love. In such arrangements, parents often play a significant and sometimes determining role in choosing spouses for their children. In practice, most marriages for young people have some degree of parental involvement and include practical concerns such as financial stability as well as consideration of personal compatibility, if not outright love.

- *Marriage forms.* **Monogamy** is *the practice of restricting sexual relations to one partner.* In most marriages and committed long-term relationships, expectations of monogamy are strong, and violation of this norm can break up the union. However, some cultures permit **polygamy,** *the marriage of one person to multiple spouses.* The most common form of polygamy is *polygyny,* the marriage of one man to multiple wives. *Polyandry,* the marriage of one woman to multiple husbands, is less common but is still practiced in parts of Tibet.

- *Gender roles.* Families also vary in the degree to which they are organized along gender lines. In some cultures, the roles of women and men overlap. Women often work outside the home and men often play a significant—though usually secondary—role in childrearing and housework. In other cultures, however, gender distinctions within the family are relatively rigid. Stricter gender roles often preclude women from working outside the home and assign them sole responsibility for child care and maintenance of home life. Men take on the dominant role in life outside the home and are expected to provide financially for the family. In some societies, gender stratification overtly perpetuates male domination of women—physically, legally, and culturally.

Global Trends in Family Life

Despite the diversity of family types around the world, several large-scale trends can be identified in many parts of the world in recent years, though they are by no means universal or uniform in their progress (Berardo and Shehan 2004):

- *Families are getting smaller.* In preindustrial societies, large families can be beneficial since they provide labor to work the land and otherwise contribute to the family's sustenance. As societies industrialize, however, a large family can become an economic burden, representing more mouths to feed with little economic return. Such economic incentives, coupled with greater access to contraception, have contributed to smaller families.

- **Extended families are less common.** As more of the world industrializes and as some regions become more affluent, more people can afford smaller households and the privacy they offer. As a result, the nuclear family household has been replacing extended family households.

- **Open-mate selection is growing.** Increasingly, the world's societies are moving away from arranged marriages, and some of the ethnic, racial, religious, and other boundaries that once limited mate selection are eroding. Instead, individual freedom in choosing a mate is growing.

- **Women are waiting longer to get married.** Often women postpone marriage in order to continue their education or to work outside the home. This delay contributes to smaller family size.

- **People spend fewer years of their lives being married.** Cohabitation and divorce rates are rising; as a result, people today are spending a smaller portion of their lives married than in the past.

- **More women are joining the paid labor force.** This increased economic independence for women has likely been a factor fueling some of the other changes in marriage and family life, including smaller families.

- **Families increasingly include more elderly members.** Advances in health information and medical treatment have prolonged human life, resulting in an increasingly large number of elderly people, some of whom require special care from family members.

The Social History of Family Life in the United States

Some of the broad global trends in family life are reflected in the United States, where families have been evolving and becoming more diverse than ever. These changes have been the subject of sometimes deeply divisive political debates (Benokraitis 2000). Often framed in terms of "family values," many of these debates have centered on the decline of the "traditional" two-parent, one-wage earner, nuclear family and the perceived negative social consequences of this shift.

But family diversity is not new. Different forms of family life have long coexisted, and the dominant type of family in the United States has changed with changing circumstances. Social histories of the family and marriage (Coontz 2000; Fischer and Hout 2006; Weiss 2000), along with the work of a variety of feminist scholars (Bielby 2006; Ferree 1990; Fox and Murray 2000; Thorne and Yalom 1992), suggest that what is decried today as the "decline" of the family may simply be the most recent phase in ongoing change.

The "Traditional" Family Reconsidered

The popular story often told about the traditional family goes something like this: In the 1950s, strong nuclear families headed by married heterosexual couples anchored U.S. society. The husband assumed the role of breadwinner, the wife that of homemaker. Such families represented stability, with low divorce rates and healthy, well-mannered children. Compared to those idyllic days, the story continues, today's families have fallen apart, contributing to numerous social ills. Divorce is rampant, unwed mothers are common, fathers are absent. Further, even in two-parent families, the hectic schedules of two wage earners means families rarely spend time together, undermining social bonds and proper socialization. A picture emerges of families under threat, marriages in crisis, and children left neglected, unsupervised, and out of control (Popenoe 2009; Wilson 2002).

As we will see, families in America today are, without question, different from what they were in the 1950s. There is also no doubt that recent changes in family life have created new challenges for raising healthy children. But sociological research shows that the often-told story of the traditional family is an idealized one that leaves out important aspects of a more complicated truth.

Families in Historical Context

The so-called traditional family prevailed in the United States for a relatively brief period. It was a historical anomaly of the unique post–World War II period that reflected relative economic affluence combined with limited aspirations for consumer goods. As a result, many people could live comfortably on a single income. These conditions did not exist prior to World War II and began to disappear by the 1970s.

The "traditional" nuclear family would have been almost unrecognizable at other times in U.S. history. In colonial America, parents routinely sent their children and adolescents to live in other households as servants and apprentices or simply let them be raised by other relatives. Sexual activity sometimes started at a young age—the "age of consent" in most states was twelve or younger, as late as 1896 (Coontz 2000). In the early 1900s, thousands of children worked in factories, mines, and mills, often living away from their parents. In middle-class and more affluent families, servants often handled childrearing tasks. Practices considered "traditional"—from the daily family sit-down dinner to much of what we take for granted as proper childrearing—are in reality mid-twentieth-century creations that represent just one of the many ways families have been structured at various times (Coontz 1992, 2000; Fischer and Hout 2006; Weiss 2000). (The Through a Sociological Lens box addresses other ways in which our understanding of family and life stages has changed.)

Class, Race, and Family Life

Even at its height during the 1950s, the family model based on two parents with one (male) breadwinner coexisted with other family forms. The idealized model was most prevalent among middle-class whites. Better paying unionized jobs enabled some in the working class to also adopt this family model, but class divisions left many other working-class and poor people without access to the good-paying jobs that enabled a single wage earner to support a family. Because they were subjected to the widely prevalent discrimination of the day from both employers and unions, African Americans and other racial and ethnic minorities were especially likely to be shut out of lucrative employment.

In working-class and poor families of all races, mothers were often part of the paid workforce long before the women's movement of the 1960s and 1970s opened up broader employment opportunities. In much of the South, especially, many black women had to leave their own children at home while they worked in white middle-class homes as servants, often caring for the children of their employers. In fact, just as today, the lifestyles of many middle-class and affluent families in the mid-twentieth century were made possible in part by the availability of low-wage minority workers to do household chores, cook, and care for children (Zinn and Dill 1994).

As we saw in Chapter 9, childrearing practices tend to vary by social class, and families of more modest income are more likely to need the mutual aid provided by extended families. But class also affects families today in other ways. For example,

- People with four-year college degrees get married later than those with less education, but by their forties these college-educated individuals are more likely to be married than are other Americans (S. Martin 2004).

- College-educated couples are less likely to get divorced than are other couples, probably because they have fewer financial troubles, which are a leading cause of divorce. Among women with bachelor's degrees, about 8 in 10 first marriages are still intact after 20 years, a rate that

FAST-FORWARD

Media Images of Families

Idealized images of the white, middle-class family, with its prominent patriarch, distinguished numerous television programs of the 1950s. Among them was *Beulah,* whose title character was a black servant—one of the first major television roles for an African American. Programs today are more diverse in the family types they portray. *Modern Family,* for example, includes interethnic and gay families.

is double that of women who have not completed high school, for whom only about 4 in 10 first marriages survive 20 years. The divorce gap between college-educated women and those with less education has been increasing since the 1980s (Cherlin 2010; Copen et al. 2012).

- Women without a college education are more likely to have children outside of marriage. Again, economics is key here; many of these women want to be married but cannot find a suitable, financially stable partner (Edin and Kefalas 2005).

Delaying Adulthood

"Children grow up so fast today." We've all heard this popular refrain. But as we saw in Chapter 6, the social trend has long been to *delay* entry into full adulthood, as with the creation of "adolescence." Today, many young people are delaying adulthood even further, often living with their parents well into their late twenties and even thirties. This trend has provided rich folder for popular media commentaries about "boomerang kids" and this generation's "failure to launch." Social scientists, though, see what they call *emerging adulthood* as simply another example of how life stages are based on social definitions that vary over time and are influenced by broader social developments (Arnett 2004; Henig 2010).

The transition to adulthood does not follow consistent age-specific rules. In the United States, you can join the military at 18 but can't drink alcohol legally until you are 21. You can drive at 16, but if you are a full-time student living at home, the Internal Revenue Service considers you a legal dependent until you are 24 years old, and children can be covered by their parents' health insurance plans through age 26. Emerging adulthood can be a period of creative exploration when young adults fully develop their identity, but it can also be a time of anxious instability and transitional preparation for an uncertain future.

Adulthood in the latter half of the twentieth century was often marked by the milestones of completing school, leaving home, becoming financially independent, marrying, and having a child. These milestones now commonly occur later in life. Many people are postponing marriage and parenthood and pursuing more education than in the past, delaying the completion of their schooling. A weak economy and high levels of student debt have created hurdles to financial security

for many young adults. As a result, more young people are still living at home with a parent or parents today than was the case a half century ago, a development that has changed family structures. Between 1960 and 2012, the proportion of 18- to 24-year-olds who lived at home (including students attending college) increased by 30 percent (from 43 percent to 56 percent), whereas the proportion of 25- to 34-year-olds who lived at home increased by almost 50 percent (from 9.1 percent to 13.6 percent) (U.S. Census Bureau 2012a).

One analysis that focused on 22- to 34-year-olds found that compared to those who had left home, those who still lived with their parents were more likely to be younger, enrolled in school, never married, and unemployed or disabled. African Americans, Asian Americans, and Hispanics were more likely than white non-Hispanics to live at home. Young adults with at least a bachelor's degree were half as likely to live with their parents as those with just a high school diploma. In turn, parents housing adult children were more likely than others to have higher incomes, live in a single family home, and own their home (Kreider 2007).

During the twentieth century, the idea of adolescence as a distinct life phase was identified and eventually widely accepted. It remains to be seen if the same will happen to emerging adulthood in the twenty-first century.

think about it

1. *When do you think adulthood begins? Why?*
2. *How, if at all, has your life followed the trend of emerging adulthood?*

Gender, Power, and the Family

The idealized traditional family of the mid-twentieth century was highly stratified by gender, reflecting a deep imbalance of power. Fathers supported the family financially but were largely absent from the lives of their children and often spent leisure time away from the family. Childrearing was left almost entirely to the mother.

The barriers produced by this imbalance of power left many women deeply frustrated, but divorce was not an easy option due to its deep social stigma, strict divorce laws, and the lack of economic opportunities for women. Low divorce rates could mask profoundly unhappy relationships and dysfunctional family life. During this period, deep social ills, including child and spousal abuse, went largely unacknowledged and unaddressed publicly. Finally, families of the idealized traditional type were based strictly on heterosexual couples; gay and lesbian families would have been impossible to maintain publicly in the homophobic environment of the time.

Even today, when gender relations are far more equitable, family life continues to be shaped by the same inequalities that influence the broader society. Many contemporary wedding ceremonies still carry the symbolic vestiges of patriarchy, with the father "giving away" his daughter to a new male who, in turn, bestows his name upon his bride. Growing up in a family, we learn, and often internalize, the gendered social expectations of a previous generation, as well as today's more subtle but enduring gender stratification (Macoby 2007; McHale and Crouter 2003). For example, one recent survey found that 70 percent of adults in the United States believe it is ideal for fathers of young children to work full time; in contrast, only 12 percent of adults think it is best for mothers with young children to hold full-time jobs (Pew Research Center 2013d). As we saw in Chapter 11, however, gendered social relations are complex interactions that people actively create in everyday life. Just as families can serve to perpetuate gender inequalities, they can also help create new expectations about gender equality.

Current Trends in U.S. Family Life

Although the families of the mid-twentieth century were never as homogeneous as is sometimes believed, today's families are more diverse than ever (Demo, Allen, and Fine 2000; Zinn, Eitzen, and Wells 2011). Some changes may be cause for concern; others merely represent new ways of meeting social needs. (See the Sociology Works box.)

Marriage and Cohabitation

People in the United States today are less likely to marry than at any time in the nation's history. In 1960, about 88 percent of people aged 35–44 were married; by 2011 that proportion fell to about 65 percent (Marquardt et al. 2012). Even if couples do marry, they are waiting longer to do so. As Figure 12.1 shows, in the 1950s the median age at marriage in the United States reached a modern-day historic low (another way in which this period was an anomaly), at about

age 20 for women and 23 for men. In the 1960s, age at first marriage began to rise, and by 2012 it had reached historic highs of 26.6 for women and 28.6 for men.

Marriage patterns are changing as well. In contrast to earlier years, marriage is now significantly more common among college-educated people than among others. Since people tend to marry a partner from roughly the same class background, college graduates are likely to marry other college graduates, and this pattern often results in relatively affluent two-income households. Meanwhile, poor and working-class individuals likewise look for financial stability in a partner but are less likely to find it in people from their own class, a trend contributing to lower marriage rates among these economic strata (Pew Research Center 2010a; Smock, Manning, and Porter 2005; Wilcox 2010). When affluent people marry each other, and poorer people stay single, economic inequality between households increases.

Cohabitation patterns have also changed. The legal protections provided by marriage were always less relevant for poor and working-class people with few economic assets, so they were more likely to cohabit. Because of the social stigma attached to cohabitation, relatively few affluent heterosexual couples lived together before marriage. However, cohabitation increased substantially across class lines beginning in the 1960s, a period of cultural change during which people began to question the value and necessity of marriage. Also, the introduction of the birth control pill reduced the threat that sexual relationships would result in unwanted pregnancy (Brown 2005).

In recent years, just over half of young adults live with their partner before they get married. An increasing number are choosing cohabitation as an alternative to marriage

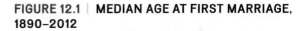

FIGURE 12.1 | MEDIAN AGE AT FIRST MARRIAGE, 1890–2012

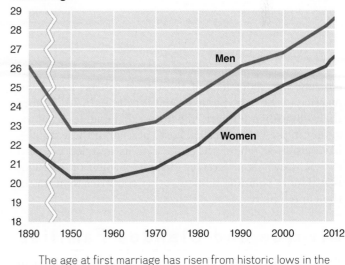

The age at first marriage has risen from historic lows in the 1950s to historic highs today. *Source:* U.S. Census Bureau (2012a).

SOCIOLOGY WORKS

April Bombai Pongtratic and Family Assistance

Many families face economic challenges in meeting basic needs and preparing for the future. Sociology major April Bombai Pongtratic helps make a difference in the lives of some low-income families in her work as an executive assistant at the Long Beach Community Action Partnership (CAP) in Long Beach, California. The agency is part of a national network of approximately 1,100 Community Action Partnerships whose mission is to empower low-income individuals and families with educational, social, or economic barriers and foster their personal development and self-sufficiency through education, training, and cultural awareness. For those who qualify, the Long Beach CAP offers a variety of free services, including youth programs, job training, energy assistance, and job development opportunities.

Pongtratic's role includes administrative duties, serving as a liaison between the agency and the community, and maintaining the agency's social networking platforms. Such work relates directly to her early interests. She notes, "I was always interested in how society works and how things like race, religion, economic status, and geographic location are factors in its operation. I felt that it was important to understand why there were certain inequalities and how some issues can be remedied. . . . I wanted to be an advocate for those who may not have an outlet to speak up for themselves."

Pongtratic cites hands-on experience as her best asset, but she's also benefited from her sociology training. "My studies in sociology have assisted me in my current job when writing grants or when dealing with clients and understanding the socioeconomic background they come from and the barriers they face," she says. And "knowing how to read statistics and apply them to reports has also been helpful."

She advises students, "If you feel passionate about what is going on in your community, stay with sociology. If you want a major that will keep your mind engaged, major in sociology because it allows you to explore a wide range of topics including health care, the justice system, economic issues, and race."

Pongtratic's work experience and preparation in sociology have put her on the front lines of efforts to help today's diverse families.

> "If you feel passionate about what is going on in your community, stay with sociology. If you want a major that will keep your mind engaged, major in sociology."

April Bombai Pongtratic

think about it

1. *Did your family or someone you know ever benefit from social services of the sort provided by the Long Beach CAP? Explain.*

2. *In what specific ways might the skills that April Pongtratic learned from her sociology training help you in your planned (or current) career?*

---

entirely, but about half of those who cohabit have been married in the past (Bumpass and Lu 2000). In 2012, more than 7.8 million unmarried heterosexual couples lived together in the United States. Forty percent of these couples have children (about the same rate as married couples) (Vespa, Lewis, and Kreider 2013). Cohabitation, though, is still more common in many other countries than it is in the United States.

Divorce and Blended Families

People in the United States marry at a higher rate than in other industrialized countries—but they get divorced at higher rates as well. Once taboo, divorce has become common and accepted in mainstream society. There is even a *Divorce Magazine* that touts itself as providing help for "Generation Ex."

A variety of legal and cultural changes contributed to the sharp increase in divorce rates in the 1960s and 1970s. Legal restrictions severely limited divorces for much of U.S. history. To qualify, an individual typically had to prove wrongdoing such as infidelity or cruelty by his or her partner. That requirement changed in the 1970s with the introduction of "no-fault" divorces in which family courts could grant a divorce based solely on the request of one of the partners. Earlier generations often regarded marriage as a practical necessity and an irrevocable commitment. People who marry today are more likely to see it as a means to achieve

FIGURE 12.2 | U.S. DIVORCE RATES, 1960–2009

Divorces per 1,000 married women aged 15 and older

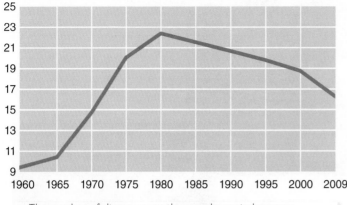

The number of divorces per thousand married women in a single year provides one measure of the annual divorce rate in the United States, which peaked in 1980.
Source: Wilcox (2011).

personal happiness and self-fulfillment. If it fails to meet these expectations, couples are more willing to dissolve the partnership and, often, try again with a new partner. Ironically, as love increasingly has become the basis for marriage, it has raised the expectations for personal satisfaction and made the institution of marriage more fragile (Coontz 2006).

Nearly 50 percent of all first marriages eventually end in divorce. The annual rate of divorce more than doubled between the mid-1960s and early 1980s (Figure 12.2). Since then it has declined significantly but has remained at higher levels than in the past. The more formal education that people have attained, the more likely they are to get married and stay that way. Among those who were married in the late 1990s, more than one-third of women without a college degree were divorced within a decade, as compared to 11 percent of college-educated women (Wilcox 2010).

Divorce can end an unhappy and damaging marriage and free children from feuding parents and a tension-filled home. However, it is stressful for everyone involved. As Cherlin (2013) summarizes, research shows the following:

■ Almost all children experience an initial period of intense emotional upset after their parents separate.

■ Most resume normal development without serious problems within about two years after the separation.

■ A minority of children experience some long-term problems that may persist into adulthood.

After a divorce, the parent who has custody of the children—usually the mother—typically sees a decline in income, often leading to stressful changes such as relocation to less expensive housing and a change of schools. The stress of divorce can make parents less available to supervise their children or to provide them with emotional support.

Long-term issues affecting children can include higher risks of dropping out of school or having a child as a teenager and greater likelihood of being divorced as an adult (Cherlin 2013; Wolfinger 2003). However, some of these effects may be due to the lingering negative impact of their parents' bad marriage rather than to the divorce. One long-term study that separated the effect of the two found that children whose parents were in marriages with high levels of conflict did better if their parents divorced than if they stayed together, whereas children of parents with low-conflict marriages did worse after divorce than those whose parents stayed together (Amato and Booth 2000).

Increased divorce and subsequent remarriage have led to the creation of more "blended" stepfamilies that include two adults and at least one child from a previous marriage or relationship. Such arrangements create new questions for children: Where will I live? Will I have to change school? Do I have to call my stepfather "Dad"? Parents, too, often face challenging and emotional issues in negotiating the new social relationships that emerge from blended families. But such arrangements can also create unique benefits. One parent reflects, "Becoming part of a blended family has certainly helped my own kids become more tolerant of the idiosyncrasies of others. . . . They've learned to compromise with their stepsiblings and to understand that there's more than one way of doing things" (quoted in Shimberg 1999, 207).

Gay and Lesbian Families

As discussed in Chapter 11, gay and lesbian relationships are increasingly being formally recognized. Countries where same-sex marriage is legal today include Canada, the Netherlands, Belgium, Spain, South Africa, Norway, Sweden, Portugal, Iceland, and Argentina (Fastenberg 2010). By late 2013, 20 U.S. states legally acknowledged same-sex relationships in some form (Human Rights Campaign 2013b):

■ Fourteen states (California, Connecticut, Delaware, Iowa, Maine, Maryland, Massachusetts, Minnesota, New Hampshire, New Jersey, New York, Rhode Island, Vermont, and Washington) and the District of Columbia issue marriage licenses for same-sex couples.

■ Six states (Colorado, Hawaii, Illinois, Nevada, Oregon, and Wisconsin) recognize civil unions or domestic partnerships that extend various legal rights within the state to unmarried couples, including same-sex couples.

In June 2013, the U.S. Supreme Court ruled that the Defense of Marriage Act (DOMA), which barred federal

Married or unmarried, with or without children, straight or gay, with one or two parents, nuclear or extended, blended, interracial; all of these and more are now part of the diverse fabric of American families.

recognition of same-sex marriage, was unconstitutional. As a result, same-sex partners who marry in states that recognize same-sex marriage now have the same federal rights and protections as all married couples. For example, they can file a joint federal tax return, can use the federally protected family medical leave to care for their spouse, and will have access to Social Security survivors' benefits and veterans' spousal benefits. Still, about half of the U.S. population lives in states that ban all same-sex unions. (See the Sociology in Action box for a discussion of sociological research and the DOMA case.)

Because data on same-sex cohabiting couples is limited, we still know relatively little about this segment of family life. Even basic estimates about the number of same-sex couples vary because of the different ways such numbers are calculated (Black et al. 2000; O'Connell et al. 2010; Patterson 2000). One U.S. Census Bureau estimate calculated just over 605,000 same-sex-partner households in 2011 (Vespa et al. 2013), but this figure is likely a significant undercount because many same-sex couples are still reluctant to acknowledge their partnerships in the face of continuing prejudice. In the coming years, same-sex couples and families are likely to be treated increasingly as equals to married heterosexuals, leading to increased numbers in the official statistics.

Falling Fertility Rates

The U.S. **fertility rate**—*the average number of births per female*—has fluctuated throughout the country's history. At the beginning of the twentieth century, it was far higher than it is today, with women averaging between four and five children (though many of the children died at birth or soon thereafter). The fertility rate hit a low of just over 2 births per woman during the Great Depression of the 1930s (likely

SOCIOLOGY in ACTION

Research, Public Policy, and the Law

Sociological research often provides information that is relevant in policymaking and judicial processes. One way sociologists participate in public life is by communicating social science research findings to public officials, including legislators and the courts. When the U.S. Supreme Court considered a 2013 legal challenge to the Defense of Marriage Act (DOMA) and California's Proposition 8—respectively, a federal and a state law banning same-sex marriage—the American Sociological Association (ASA) offered the Court a clear and compelling assessment of the conclusions of scholarly research on the key questions.

One of the foundations of laws limiting marriage to heterosexuals has long been the claim that it is harmful to children to live in a household with gay parents. In its "friend of the court" brief to the Supreme Court, the ASA tackled this claim head-on, explaining that its comprehensive review of research shows no evidence of such harmful effects on children. "The clear and consistent consensus in the social science profession is that across a wide range of indicators, children fare just as well when they are raised by same-sex parents when compared to children raised by opposite-sex parents" (ASA 2013b, 3).

The ASA's brief provided the justices with a comprehensive review of research findings on the experiences of children whose parents are same-sex couples. This review details the range of ways that children of same-sex couples and opposite-sex parents are similar: academic performance, cognitive development, social development, psychological health, teenage sexual activity, substance abuse, and delinquent behavior. Measures of each of these dimensions consistently show no significant differences in the outcomes for children raised by gay couples in comparison to those raised by straight couples. Summarizing the ASA's assessment, the brief concludes that "as the overwhelming body of social science research confirms, whether a child is raised by same-sex or opposite-sex parents has no bearing on a child's well-being. Instead, the consensus is that the key factors affecting child well-being are stable family environments and greater parental socioeconomic resources, neither of which is related to the sex or sexual orientation of a child's parents" (pp. 13–14).

Given these findings, the ASA's (2013b) brief articulated a clear position in support of marriage rights for same-sex couples. As its authors explicitly argued, research indicates that permitting same-sex couples to marry "has the potential to

The American Sociological Association (ASA) weighed in on the Supreme Court case that overturned the law limiting marriage to heterosexual couples. The ASA pointed out that research overwhelmingly shows that children fare as well when raised by same-sex parents as they do with opposite-sex parents.

improve child well-being insofar as the institution of marriage may provide social and legal support to families and enhances family stability, key drivers of positive child outcomes" (p. 31).

When the Supreme Court announced its judgment overturning the Defense of Marriage Act in June 2013, ASA president Cecilia Ridgeway praised the Court's decision. She noted, "As the court recognized, DOMA undermined the validity of state sanctioned same-sex marriages and thus diminished their stability. By removing a federal barrier to stability in state sanctioned same-sex marriages, the Court has acted to support the well-being of children" (ASA 2013a).

think about it

1. *How do you think opponents of same-sex marriage are likely to respond to this kind of presentation of a scholarly consensus?*

2. *On what other issues do you think a summary of sociological research findings could be useful to policymakers or judges?*

---

due to women deciding to defer childbearing and to the effects of poverty on women's health), before rising during the "baby boom" of the 1950s to more than 3.5 births per woman. By the mid-1970s the average fertility rate declined by nearly half to 1.8 births per woman. The rate subsequently rose slightly and leveled off at around 2.1, but it declined again during the recent recession and stood at 1.9 in 2011, the lowest total fertility rate in the United States since 1987, just about the rate needed to replace the current population (Fischer and Hout 2006; Martin et al. 2013).

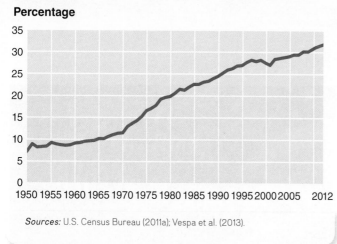

FIGURE 12.3 | PERCENTAGE OF U.S. FAMILIES WITH CHILDREN UNDER 18 HEADED BY A SINGLE PARENT, 1950–2012

Percentage

Sources: U.S. Census Bureau (2011a); Vespa et al. (2013).

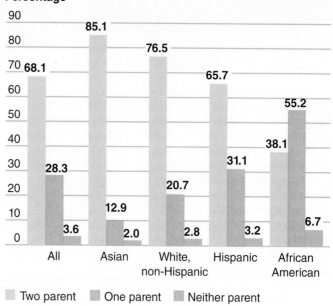

FIGURE 12.4 | U.S. CHILDREN AND FAMILY TYPE, 2012

Percentage

Two parent   One parent   Neither parent

The family structure within which children are raised varies considerably by race and ethnicity. Children with "neither parent" often live with other relatives. *Source:* U.S. Census Bureau (2012a).

The fertility rate among married women has fallen faster than it has for unmarried women. As a result, a higher proportion of children are born to unmarried parents. In 1950, only 1 out of every 25 births (4 percent) was to an unmarried woman. That figure rose consistently in subsequent decades; 2 out of every 5 births (40.7 percent) were to unmarried women by 2011 (Marquardt et al. 2012).

Single Parents

About two-thirds of children today are raised in two-parent households (U.S. Census Bureau 2012a). This figure increased in the middle of the twentieth century but is roughly the same today as a century ago. What differs now is that when children are not living in such households, they are being raised by single parents rather than by an extended family (Fischer and Hout 2006). As Figure 12.3 shows, the percentage of single-parent families with children under age 18 has quadrupled from about 7 percent in 1950 to more than 30 percent by 2012 (U.S. Census Bureau 2011a; 2012a).

Single-parent families are overwhelmingly headed by women. Asian Americans are least likely to raise children in a one-parent household, and African Americans most likely to do so (Figure 12.4). About 29 percent of births for white women occur outside of marriage, as opposed to 72 percent of births for black women (Martin et al. 2013).

The continuing increase in the prevalence of single-parent families is a cause for concern. Considerable evidence indicates that, all other things being equal, children fare better in households with two parents than they do in single-parent families (McLanahan and Sandefur 2006). It does not appear to matter whether those parents are married or cohabitating (Heiland and Lui 2006) or are a same-sex couple (Wainright, Russell, and Patterson 2004). Compared to their peers growing up in two-parent households, children from a single-parent household are twice as likely to drop out of high school, are more likely to become single parents themselves, and are one and a half times more likely to have unsteady employment as young adults (McLanahan and Sandefur 2006).

A major reason for this difference is that single-parent households are much more likely to be poor. In some cases, women are poor before they have children. In others, divorce leads to a drop in income. Either way, single-parent families generally do not have access to as many economic resources as do two-parent families. In addition, a single parent typically cannot provide the same level of supervision and social support that two parents can. Finally, divorce and limited financial resources tend to create unstable living situations for children. Divorce and poverty make it more likely that a child's family will move into a lower-income neighborhood with fewer resources, causing a loss of friends and connections to other sources of social support.

Women head more than three-quarters of single-parent households. Consequently, U.S. policymakers often try to address the challenges faced by single-parent families by focusing on finding more ways to promote marriage and better enforce the financial responsibilities of absent fathers (Marquardt et al. 2012). Alternative approaches promote a broad range of policies that assist children in low-income families of all types. For example, universal health care could help stave off many of the financial crises that contribute to divorce and poverty in the first place. Financial support, school-based social programs, and affordable housing could help low-income parents—single or married—carry the cost of childrearing while helping families of all sorts raise healthy, capable children. But the United States lags behind Europe in creating family-friendly programs like these.

The United States and the nations of Western Europe have approached family issues in starkly different ways (Vogel and Theorell 2005). The United States relies heavily on promoting marriage (and thus two incomes) to combat child poverty, whereas European nations limit income inequality (through progressive taxes) and provide more income support to single parents. The result is that the children of single mothers in the United States are more than twice as likely to be poor (55.4 percent) than their counterparts in France (27.3 percent) and four to six times as likely to be poor than single mothers in Sweden (13.5 percent), Belgium (9.3 percent), and Finland (9 percent) (Heuveline and Weinshenker 2008).

Similarly, although many people struggle to balance the need to work in order to provide for their families with the responsibility to care for dependents, the United States generally does not offer government-supported child care. In contrast, many European countries do. For example, France offers free, full-day child care for children up to two years old and provides preschool programs for children over age two on a sliding-scale fee. Other nations, too, provide free or low-cost day care to support working parents (Christopher 2002). The United States likewise differs from European and other industrialized nations on policies for paid parental leave, another major support for working parents. In the United States, companies with 50 or more employees must allow up to 24 weeks of leave to new parents (12 weeks for each parent) who have been employed at least a year, but because none of this is paid leave it is difficult for many parents to use the benefit. In contrast, most other industrialized nations provide parents with at least 18 weeks of paid leave, with the option of more unpaid leave. In Norway, a mother must take 6 weeks of paid leave and fathers must take at least 4 weeks of paid paternity leave. In addition, either the mother or father is entitled to a full year of leave at 80 percent pay or 10 months at full pay (Ray, Gornick, and Schmitt 2009).

Gender Convergence

As noted in Chapter 11, men and women play increasingly overlapping roles. Women now control if and when they have children to a greater degree than ever before, they have boosted their numbers in the paid workforce, and they have changed political and cultural norms regarding gender. As a result, more women have choices in their lives. In turn, men also have more options and are taking on more of the responsibilities at home. Over the past 50 years, men have tripled the amount of time they spend with their children, although

it is still about half the time women spend (Parker and Wang 2013). But when paid labor and unpaid work are mixed together, the share of the burden that women and men carry is virtually the same in middle-class families (Bianchi, Robinson, and Milkie 2007).

Some of these changes have produced concerns that sociological research shows to be overstated. For example, two-wage-earner families are often portrayed as stressed, leaving parents without time to spend nurturing children. But research using time diary data over four decades shows that mothers in two-earner families are spending *more* time with their children than their mothers did in the 1960s (Bianchi et al. 2007). They achieve this by cutting back on time spent on housework, as well as by juggling tasks effectively. Coupled with the increased time men spend with children, the concern that parents in two-earner families are not spending enough time with their children seems to be largely the result of rising expectations for the family.

Interracial and Interethnic Families

About 8 percent of all marriages in the United States are interracial or interethnic. But in 2010, 15.1 percent of *new* marriages were interracial or interethnic, more than double the 1980 rate of 6.7 percent, documenting a trend that is literally changing the complexion of U.S. families. Almost one-third (30 percent) of these new interracial or interethnic marriages were made up of couples in which both partners were from different racial or ethnic minorities, 43 percent involved white-Hispanic couples, 14 percent involved white-Asian couples, and 12 percent involved white-black couples. Intermarriage rates vary by group: about 28 percent of Asians, 26 percent of Hispanics, 17 percent of blacks, and 9 percent of whites married someone whose race or ethnicity was different from their own in 2010 (Wang 2012). Further, the number of people who identify as multiracial has increased. Just over 9 million Americans—about 3 percent of the population—reported more than one race in the 2010 census (U.S. Census Bureau 2011c). This figure is expected to continue rising in coming years.

Living Arrangements

One-third of U.S. households are now nonfamily households, a shift representing a marked increase in recent decades. The percentage of those who live alone has risen from 17.1 percent in 1970 to 27.5 percent in 2012, while the percentage who live with unrelated people outside of a committed relationship has increased from 1.7 to 6.1 percent (Figure 12.5). This trend, along with a drop in the fertility rate and a decrease in the number of extended families, has contributed to a drop in the size of the U.S. median household from about five people in 1900 to about three people today (Fischer and Hout 2006).

FIGURE 12.5 | U.S. FAMILIES AND LIVING ARRANGEMENTS, 1970–2012

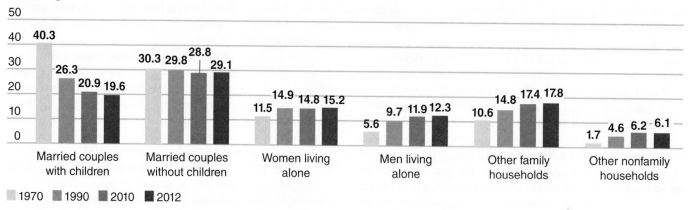

The percentage of two-parent households has declined as the percentage of other types of living arrangements has increased. *Source:* Vespa et al. (2013).

Understanding Religion

Like the family, religion is an enduring social institution that varies across cultures and is undergoing significant change. Many people are socialized into a religion at an early age in the context of the family. In this section we explore how sociologists have approached religion as a topic of sociological study, examine how it varies across cultures, and consider how it is changing in contemporary society.

The Sociology of Religion

As a social science, sociology is committed to understanding the social world—including religion—based on empirical evidence. But people experience religion typically through **faith**—*belief grounded in personal conviction or divine revelation rather than scientific evidence.* How can social science study a faith-based phenomenon? That is, how can there be a sociology of religion? Sociologists don't try to assess the conflicting truth claims of the world's many religions; they study religion to understand the role it plays in social life. As we saw in Chapter 7, the *Thomas theorem* notes that if people define situations as real, they are real in their consequences. For sociologists, the impact of religion in social life comes from some people's *believing* in the truth of their faiths and adjusting their behavior accordingly.

Religion has figured prominently throughout human history and consequently attracted the attention of some of the earliest sociologists. Here we take a look Emile Durkheim's, Karl Marx's, and Max Weber's still influential analyses of religion and then turn to Peter Berger's more recent contribution.

Durkheim on Religion: The Sacred and the Profane

In his last major work, *The Elementary Forms of Religious Life,* Emile Durkheim ([1915] 2001) focused on the most rudimentary forms of religion and their social functions. The descendant of a long line of rabbis in predominantly Christian France, who himself became agnostic, Durkheim was familiar with a variety of religious traditions. He used the religion of Australian aborigines as a key case study because he believed it embodied the simplified essential elements of religion.

Durkheim concluded that all religions share three basic elements:

- A set of core beliefs
- A set of ritual practices
- A community of adherents

In Durkheim's view, the most important belief of any religion is that the world can be divided into the "sacred" and the "profane." The **sacred** is *something extraordinary, to be treated respectfully, with reverence and awe.* Almost anything can be sacred, including objects, actions, and words. Sacred texts, idols, gods, symbols, gestures, and even animals populate various religions. In various versions of Christianity, for example, the Bible, holy water, consecrated bread and wine, and the crucifix can all be considered sacred. What makes the sacred special is that it is set apart from the **profane,** or *the ordinary world of everyday life.*

Rituals are *symbolic actions, typically performed at specified times, that help evoke an emotional bond among participants.* The sacred is embodied in ritual practices such as attending worship services, taking communion, offering sacrifices, reciting prayers or incantations (verbal charms or spells), singing, dancing, and giving blessings. These actions help create a sense of a

A Christian evangelical service and a Haitian voodoo ceremony are examples of rituals. Each is directed at something considered to be sacred, and each helps affirm a shared moral community of believers. Have you ever taken part in a religious ritual? How would you analyze it using Durkheim's concepts?

shared community that has common norms and values. With rituals, whether a believer's prayers are "answered" is less significant than the fact that praying can bring comfort and strength to the faithful, as well as a sense of social solidarity to a group that shares this practice.

Beliefs and practices are developed and passed on through communities of *adherents*—those who share a faith and join in its rituals. A community of adherents becomes a **church** when it has developed into a more *formal religious organization with broad mainstream acceptance.* Churches often have well-organized subgroups with varying interpretations of their faith, known as *denominations,* such as Baptists and Methodists among Christians and Sunni and Shiite among Muslims. A **sect** is *a small dissenting faction of a church that promotes new beliefs or practices.* Newer religious communities typically must struggle to gain acceptance as a legitimate church from mainstream society. Those with power in society—including established churches—sometimes label *small religious communities whose beliefs and practices are at odds with the dominant culture* as **cults,** often to discredit them.

SPOTLIGHT

on social theory

Symbolic interactionist theories focus on how people use shared symbols and construct society as a result of their everyday interactions. How do the religious rituals you may have observed illustrate this idea?

THE SOCIAL FUNCTIONS OF RELIGION

Durkheim's classic analysis is the basis for a sociological definition of **religion:** *a unified system of beliefs and ritual practices relating to the sacred that bond people into a moral community.* Significantly, this definition does not include a reference to **theism**—*a belief in the existence of a god or gods.* Religion needs to include an idea of the sacred but not necessarily a supernatural power or a god. Buddhism, for example, teaches followers to seek enlightenment through right conduct but does not necessarily include belief in any supernatural forces. Similarly, some new religious movements focus on the common bonds that link humanity rather than the divine or supernatural.

SPOTLIGHT

on social theory

Functionalist approaches to religion focus on its positive contributions to social life. Does religion serve some of the purposes in your life that functionalist theory suggests? Why or why not?

Regardless of its particular teachings, religion serves a variety of functions:

- *Religion promotes social solidarity.* When people of similar beliefs participate in religious activities, they develop social bonds (or "fellowship"). Because of these shared beliefs and practices, followers often consider themselves to be part of a special group (for example, "saved," "the chosen people," or "enlightened") that differentiates them from outsiders and promotes internal solidarity.

- *Religion operates as a form of social control.* By promoting values and norms, religious organizations can play an important role in socialization. Believers in a particular religion are typically expected to adhere to a code of ethics and to avoid behaviors labeled as immoral, sinful, evil, and worthy of punishment. These regulations are taught and promoted through religious activities as well as in sacred texts. The social control produced by religion is especially powerful because adherents often believe the religion's mandates emanate from the sacred. The Bible's commandments—and most other religions' teachings—would carry less moral authority if they were understood

Weber noted that every religion begins precisely with the assumption that life *has* meaning and that religion's promise is to make this meaning accessible and understandable.

By contrast, science is silent on the issue of meaning. Perhaps, as existentialist philosophy contends, life is without meaning until individuals create it (Hayim 1980). The absence of God presents the possibility of a radically free individual. But this freedom brings with it heavy responsibilities and challenges. Some people, as Weber ([1919] 1946b) put it, "cannot bear the fate of the times" and instead return to seek solace in religion, where "[t]he arms of old churches are opened widely and compassionately" for them (p. 155).

Berger on Religion: The Sacred Canopy

Because rationalization of society often has seemed to drain life of its meaning, people continue to long for the comfort of the sacred. A half century after Weber, Peter Berger (1967) emphasized that religion is primarily an effort to create a meaningful reality in which to live. Religion helps us make sense of our existence and provides order to an otherwise chaotic world. It serves as a "shield against terror," protecting humans from the "danger of meaninglessness" in which "the individual is submerged in a world of disorder, senselessness, and madness" (p. 22). Thus religion provides a "sacred canopy" under which, together, a society's members can find shelter.

However, as the metaphor suggests, religion works best when all members of a society share a single interpretation of reality—when a single canopy provides shelter. As we will see, in the contemporary world, competing and incompatible interpretations have emerged, changing the nature of religion and perhaps even helping undermine it.

Religion in Global Context

In this section we sketch briefly the distribution of religious traditions and nonbelief around the world and in the United States. We also examine the rise of secularism in Western society and the fundamentalist resistance to it.

Religion Throughout the World

About 84 percent of humanity identifies with one of the world's hundreds of religions, though not all those people are active participants in communities of worship. As shown in Figure 12.6, Christianity is the most widespread religion, with a significant presence in all areas except Asia/Pacific and the Middle East/North Africa. In contrast, Islam is relatively narrowly concentrated, with the highest percentage of Muslims in the Middle East and North Africa. About 16 percent of the world's population is nonreligious—including agnostics and atheists—who are found most commonly in Asia, Europe, and North America (Pew-Templeton Global Religious Futures Project 2013).

People in the world's wealthier, modernized nations are least likely to be religiously active, as measured, for example, by the percentage of the population who attend weekly services (Figure 12.7). Following this pattern, religious participation in the United States is lower than in most of the world's countries. However, among wealthy modernized nations, the United States has the highest rate of religious participation.

Religious Adherence in the United States

About three out of four adult Americans (73 percent) identify as Christian. Of these, Protestants (48 percent) and Catholics (22 percent) are the largest subgroups. Protestantism, though, is fragmented into hundreds of denominations. Although only 1.8 percent of the adult population, Jews make up the largest non-Christian religion in the United States. A 2012 survey found that almost one-fifth (19.6 percent) of the population consists of people unaffiliated with any religion (Pew Research Religion & Public Life Project 2012).

Religious affiliations are subject to significant shifts (Figure 12.8), and more than a quarter (28 percent) of all adults—44 percent if we include people shifting between Protestant denominations—have left the religion of their childhood (Pew Forum on Religion and Public Life 2008a). Sometimes they move to another faith; sometimes they leave religion altogether. Nearly a third of people raised Catholic have left the Church, the biggest loss of any faith, but Catholic numbers have been supplemented by recent immigrants, among whom Catholics outnumber Protestants by nearly two-to-one. Compared to the population as a whole, recent immigrants are also more likely to be Muslim, Hindu, or Buddhist, but these adherents still make up only a tiny fraction of the U.S. population. Still, as a result of declining membership and a growing unaffiliated population, Protestants now make up fewer than half of the U.S. population (Pew Research Religion & Public Life Project 2012).

The fastest-growing religious category in recent years has been the "unaffiliated" (19.6 percent in 2012) whose

FIGURE 12.6 | MAJOR RELIGIOUS TRADITIONS BY REGION, 2010

Percentage

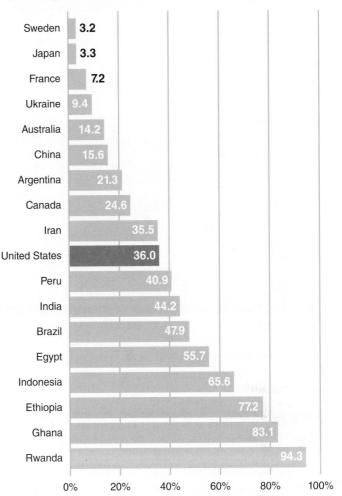

Legend:
- Christians
- Muslims
- Hindus
- Buddhists
- Folk religion
- Jewish
- Other religion
- Unaffiliated

What you believe is influenced by where you live. Two-thirds of the world's population adheres to one of the world's three largest religious traditions: Christianity (31.5%), Islam (23.2%), or Hinduism (15%). *Source:* Pew-Templeton Global Religious Futures Project (2013).

FIGURE 12.7 | GLOBAL ATTENDANCE AT WEEKLY RELIGIOUS SERVICES

Percentage who attend religious services weekly

Country	Percentage
Sweden	3.2
Japan	3.3
France	7.2
Ukraine	9.4
Australia	14.2
China	15.6
Argentina	21.3
Canada	24.6
Iran	35.5
United States	36.0
Peru	40.9
India	44.2
Brazil	47.9
Egypt	55.7
Indonesia	65.6
Ethiopia	77.2
Ghana	83.1
Rwanda	94.3

People in the United States (purple) are typically less religious than those in poorer, more traditional societies such as Indonesia and Ghana. However, Americans report the highest level of religious participation among wealthy industrialized societies, surpassing countries such as Canada, Australia, and France. *Source:* World Values Survey (2005–2008).

percentage of the overall population has doubled since the early 1990s. This category includes atheists (2.4 percent), agnostics (3.3 percent), and those who simply describe their religion as "nothing in particular" (13.9 percent). The unaffiliated do not identify with a specific religious group, but they are not uniformly secular. One-third (33 percent) of the unaffiliated say that religion is very or somewhat important in their lives, and two-thirds (68 percent) believe in God, although more than half of these are not certain about the existence of God. In addition, about one-fifth (18 percent) of the unaffiliated think of themselves as religious, and more than one-third (37 percent) describe themselves as spiritual but not religious (Pew Research Center's Religion and Public Life Project 2012).

The religious composition of the U.S. population has shifted over time, with mainline Protestant churches losing the greatest share and greatest growth occurring in the unaffiliated category.

Shopping for God in the Religious Marketplace

The relatively high level of religiosity in the United States is accompanied by a great deal of religious diversity and widespread religious tolerance (Putnam and Campbell 2010). This can likely be attributed to the country's long-standing separation of church and state. By protecting religious freedom but never having an official state religion, the United States created a vibrant climate for competition among faiths. Religion came to resemble a commodity in a marketplace—a product "sold" by competing religious organizations eager to attract adherents and "bought" (or not) by consumers who often comparison shop before making a decision (Stark and Bainbridge 1985; Warner 1993). A diverse array of religious beliefs undermines the power of any single church and results in greater tolerance and religious freedom for everyone (Heclo et al. 2007; Hutchison 2003).

FIGURE 12.8 | RELIGIOUS COMPOSITION OF THE UNITED STATES, 1972–2010

Percentage

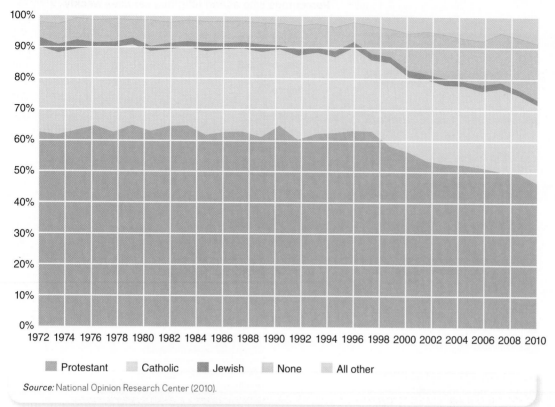

Protestant · Catholic · Jewish · None · All other

Source: National Opinion Research Center (2010).

Sociologists using this type of analysis assume that the "demand" for religion is more or less constant. However, the relative health of religion depends on how well religious organizations provide the "supply." Because traditional religious institutions often have not adapted to changing social conditions and "consumer" tastes, mainline religions in the United States—as well as European state-sponsored religions—have seen a dramatic loss of membership. In the United States, this loss is offset by innovative religions and practices that provide an almost infinite variety of choices in the religious marketplace. For individuals, having more religions to choose from makes it more likely that they can find a faith that suits their personal needs. Thus, this analysis contends, religious choice and competition is good for adherents, for religious organizations, and for religion itself.

Does all this choice make U.S. society as a whole more religious? Yes, say some researchers (Stark 1999; Stark and Bainbridge 1985). But others contend that the very idea that religion is treated as a commodity is strong evidence of religion's decline (Bruce 2002, 2011). If a multitude of religious institutions merely provides consumers in various market segments with a product they want, and "the customer is always right," then religion has lost its authority to promote a widely shared set of values or enforce a common set of social norms.

Further, Bruce (2002, 2011) argues that religion today survives in large part because it engages in activities other than connecting individuals to the supernatural—often its traditional sacred role. Contemporary religious organizations are instead involved in promoting basic moral values (often in interfaith efforts), fellowship, charitable work, and political causes.

Indeed, most Americans equate religion with personal ethics and behavior and think that more religion would help counter crime, greed, uncaring parents, and materialism. But, overwhelmingly, Americans of faith have also accepted the need to coexist with adherents of other religions and with nonbelievers, and they understand the need for pragmatic compromise (Farkas et al. 2001). For example, of those people who claim a religious affiliation in the United States, only 29 percent say their religion represents the one true faith leading to eternal life; 65 percent say that many religions—or none at all—can lead to eternal life (Pew Forum on Religion and Public Life 2008b).

Secularization

As we've seen, the fastest-growing religious category in the United States is made up of those who say they have no religious affiliation at all—now about 20 percent of the population. An even higher portion (32 percent) of young Americans

on social theory

Rational choice theories draw upon economic analyses and view people as actors rationally weighing the costs and benefits of their actions, as when they choose between competing religions. Is the idea of a religious marketplace relevant to your choice (or rejection) of religion? Why or why not?

Mega-churches like the 16,000-seat Lakewood Church in Houston adapt modern technology and marketing to compete in the religious marketplace. Modeled on the venues used for sports competition and rock concerts, these churches feature dramatic lighting, a central stage, giant video screens, and powerful sound systems in their services, which are often broadcast via radio and television and streamed on websites.

CORE CONCEPTS CHALLENGE

How would the analyses of Durkheim, Marx, Weber, and Berger apply to this type of contemporary religious **culture***?*

(aged 18–29) say they have no religious affiliation, a figure that has more than doubled in 20 years (Pew Forum on Religion and Public Life 2010a; Pew Research Religion & Public Life Project 2012; Putnam and Campbell 2010). Do such trends suggest that the influence of religion is decreasing in the United States? That question is part of a broader debate regarding **secularization,** *the decline in the social significance of religious beliefs, practices, and institutions.* There is little doubt that secularization has occurred in parts of the world during the past two centuries, but major questions and debates remain about the nature and degree of secularization.

SECULARIZATION AND MODERNITY

The founders of sociology saw that the influence of religion was diminishing due to the emergence of modernity. According to Weber, the rise of science and rationality marked a new way of thinking that emphasized the need for skepticism, questioning, and empirical evidence as the basis for knowledge and action. This was a stark alternative to the heavy reliance on faith and divine revelation found within religion. The very creation of sociology was a byproduct of this shift in thinking.

According to the **secularization thesis,** *the social significance of religion has declined in the face of modernity.* Some sociologists criticize this thesis, pointing to the relatively high levels of religious activity in the United States and to the rise of fundamentalist forms of religious belief around the world (Stark 1999)—a topic we examine later in this chapter. But most endorsers of the secularization thesis do not predict the disappearance of religion, only its declining influence on social life (Bruce 2002, 2011; Gauchet 1997; Lechner 1991; Tschannen 1991; Yamane 1997). Secularization tends to be more advanced in the wealthier societies that are more modernized, and more limited in parts of the world that are less affluent and less modernized (Karner and Aldridge 2004; Norris and Inglehart 2012).

The effect of modernity on secularization can be best understood as a multidimensional process operating at various levels of society (Dobbelaere 1999):

- **Secularization at the macro level** differentiates religion from other aspects of social life. Religion once permeated all of society, but modernization divided social life into separate spheres, such as the separation of work from home that occurred with industrialization. More broadly, public and private lives became more distinct, and religion increasingly became a matter for private life, with diminished influence in society at large. The modern world was rationalized as government and other bureaucracies operated based on policies, procedures, and rules rather than on religious tradition. Science similarly advanced learning through evidence-based analyses of the world rather than religious teaching. Once religious institutions were separated from government, the economy, schools, and the law, their influence on society declined.

- **Secularization at the meso level** is the loss of authority for the truth claims of any single religion. Urbanization and industrialization brought together people of different cultures, with different ideas about religion from which people could choose. Rather than all-encompassing divinely inspired bearers of truth, religious groups became more like other social movements or pressure groups competing for members and sometimes trying to influence political and cultural debates. This sort of secularization has often been supported by theologians and people of faith since it enabled competing belief systems to coexist peacefully (Smith 2003).

- **Secularization at the micro level** is a decline in the significance of religion for people's daily lives. Researchers often measure micro-level secularization by indicators such as whether people claim a religious affiliation and how often they attend religious services.

Collectively, secularization reflects the decline in religious authority, as seen in the decreasing influence of religious

With a huge American flag on the field, players and fans stand for the national anthem before a baseball game. Such ritualistic practices are evidence of a civil religion that promotes common values and creates emotional bonds of solidarity within a predominantly secular context. Where else have you seen evidence of civil religion in the United States?

beliefs, leaders, and institutions over individuals, other institutions, and broader social life (Chaves 1994). A secular society is radically different from one in which religious authority reigns in all sectors of society, religious adherence is nearly compulsory, and religious belief forms the basis for daily decision making in individual lives.

SECULARIZATION TODAY   Today the continued growth of individual freedoms, egalitarian democratic ideals, and respect for diversity has further challenged traditional religious authority (Bruce 2002, 2011). A rigid church hierarchy can seem out of date in an era that celebrates equality and adaptability; reliance on specially trained clergy to interpret religious doctrine can contradict a democratic spirit that emphasizes an individual's right to think freely; and a unique claim to divinely inspired truth can seem outdated when respect for the insights of differing cultural traditions increases. Further, the patriarchal nature of many religious doctrines and organizations has put them at odds with the trend toward greater gender equality.

For all these reasons, to varying degrees in different countries, religion has become a limited component of social life. The result has been a rise of **secular humanism,** *a belief system that emphasizes morality and decision making based on reason, ethics, and social justice rather than religious doctrine or the supernatural.* Instead of divinity, other values—especially democracy—have more commonly united modern societies. In effect, such societies have developed **civil religion,** *a set of common beliefs and ritual practices that bind people in a predominantly secular society.* The "sacred" symbols and rituals of democratic freedom—such as flags, the pledge of allegiance, national anthems, and military medals—serve as a secular equivalent of religious icons and rituals. Durkheim ([1922] 1956, [1925] 1961, [1938] 1977) recognized this trend and advocated using modern schools for secular moral education, another displacement of religion.

At the macro level, in modern societies, the influence of religion has declined in education (Reuben 1996), law and politics (Hamburger 2002), and science (Lindberg and Numbers 2008). Religious doctrine is not the basis for legal rulings; retail businesses remain open on religious holidays; public education is not based on religious teachings; science, not faith, informs nearly all health care decisions. People of faith weigh in on issues of the day, but religion no longer provides the primary fuel for political institutions or for cultural life.

At the meso level, as we saw earlier, a diverse array of religions compete for adherents in the religious marketplace. At the micro level, with some variation by country, church membership, religious activities, and religious belief have all declined, especially in Europe since the middle of the twentieth century (Brown 2009; Crockett and Voas 2006; Greeley 2004; McLeod

2000, 2010; McLeod and Ustorf 2011). For example, weekly religious attendance hovers around 10 percent in Britain and barely 4 percent in Scandinavian countries (Bruce 2002, 2011). Whereas nonwhite ethnic minorities who immigrate to Europe—including many Muslims—are more religious than the people already there, religiosity declines sharply in the children of immigrants (Crockett and Voas 2006).

In the United States (and Canada), respondents to surveys significantly overstate their religious attendance and activities (Brenner 2011; Hadaway, Marler, and Chaves 1993, 1998). Depending on how the question is asked, about 40 percent of Americans *say* they attend a weekly religious service, but using time diaries and other techniques, researchers suggest that the true attendance rate is only about 20 percent to 25 percent, similar to the rates found in some European countries (Brenner 2011). Also, religious attendance varies by region within the United States (Map 12.1).

However, if modernity is supposed to secularize societies, why has religious fundamentalism experienced a resurgence in recent decades? We turn now to an analysis of this development.

Fundamentalist Resistance to Change

Relying on a literal interpretation of the Bible, Kentucky's Creation Museum teaches visitors that humans and dinosaurs coexisted in the Garden of Eden, Earth is barely 6,000 years old, and evolution is a myth—but overwhelming scientific evidence contradicts all these notions. The museum's rejection of aspects of modern thought is an example of **fundamentalism,** *a religious movement that advocates strict adherence to traditional principles in all aspects of social life, usually based on literal interpretation of a religion's infallible sacred texts.*

At first glance, the resurgence in fundamentalist religions in recent decades might seem to contradict the secularization thesis. But, ironically, religious fundamentalists are perhaps the greatest advocates of the secularization thesis because they see their efforts to reinsert religious belief into all aspects of social life as a defense against secularism's rising tide.

FUNDAMENTALISM THEN AND NOW

The term *fundamentalist* comes from a series of religious manifestos first published by conservative Protestants beginning in 1910 under the title *The Fundamentals.* This original fundamentalism was more a response to other religious sects than to the secular world. After the 1925 Scopes "monkey" trial—in which a Tennessee high school teacher was prosecuted for teaching the scientific theory of human evolution instead of relying on biblical teaching—fundamentalists were marginalized from much of mainstream American society. They reemerged in the 1970s, though, resisting the social and cultural changes of the 1960s. This time they became politically active, helping drive a resurgent conservative political movement within the Republican Party that peaked in the 1980s but is still influential (Emerson and Hartman 2006; Putnam and Campbell 2010). Today's

MAP 12.1 | SELF-REPORTING OF WEEKLY ATTENDANCE AT RELIGIOUS SERVICES

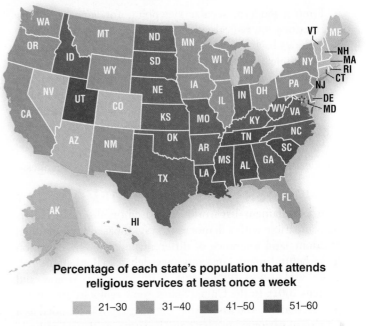

Percentage of each state's population that attends religious services at least once a week

21–30	31–40	41–50	51–60

The highest levels of religious attendance occur in the Deep South and Utah, whereas the lowest levels are in New England and some southwestern states.

Source: U.S. Religious Landscape Survey, Pew Research Center's Forum on Religion & Public Life, © 2008, Pew Research Center. http://religions.pewforum.org/.

Christian fundamentalists tend to oppose secular humanism as the framework for political life; to reject the scientific theory of evolution; to condemn practices such as abortion, homosexuality, and gender equality that they claim violate biblical injunctions; and to reject what they see as a violent, decadent, and sexualized popular culture that contradicts their interpretation of Christian values.

In 1979, at about the same time as the resurgence of Christian fundamentalism, Islamic fundamentalism hit the world stage when Iranian revolutionaries deposed the American-backed Shah of Iran and replaced a secular government with a fundamentalist Islamic state. Since then, Islamic fundamentalists in many countries have resisted Western cultural influences, especially mass media, and opposed the imposition of Western power in Muslim countries. In their place, they seek to enforce Islamic law (*sharia*) in daily life and in government (Roy 1994, 2004, 2007).

Fundamentalism today applies to many religious sects, including forms of Christianity, Islam, Judaism, and Hinduism, though some of these groups do not always accept this label. Despite important differences, the many forms of fundamentalism share a resistance to the changes in modern life, especially secularization, and seek to restore their sacred texts as absolute authority in all matters (Bruce 2000; Emerson and Hartman 2006).

The significance of fundamentalism depends on your perspective. As Emerson and Hartman (2006) summarize,

> From a modern, secular viewpoint, fundamentalists are reactionaries, radicals attempting to grab power and throw societies back into the dark ages of oppression, patriarchy, and intolerance. . . . Conversely, for fundamentalists and their sympathizers, Western versions of modernization rush over them in a tidal wave of change, ripping apart communities, values, social ties, and meaning. . . . [They] see their stand against the tidal wave of change as honorable, right, life preserving, and a life calling. (p. 131)

This clash of perspectives presents some major challenges.

FUNDAMENTALISM AND DEMOCRACY

Can a fundamentalist worldview based on absolutist beliefs be compatible with a democratic system based on individual freedoms and tolerance of different beliefs? This question lurks behind many contemporary debates (Benhabib 2002; Göle 2011; Okin 1999; Scott 2010; Shweder, Minow, and Marcus 2002). In the United States, some religious groups reject secularism and assert that the country was founded as a Christian nation whose laws and institutions should embody those Christian beliefs. This has been part of what Casanova (1994) calls the "deprivatization" of religion—moving previously private beliefs into the public sphere. For example, religious opponents of equal rights for gays and lesbians or abortion rights—including many fundamentalists—want to use their interpretation of religious teachings as the basis for laws that affect everyone.

Similarly, conflicts have erupted in Europe regarding Muslim immigrants, some of whom are fundamentalists, who advocate veiling (*hijab*), female genital cutting, arranged marriages, polygamy, and sex segregation. Especially worrisome has been the propensity for some extremist sects—claiming to be doing God's will in a cosmic war between good and evil—to endorse violence as a means to advance their cause (Juergensmeyer 2003). For these reasons, some critics contend that Islam is incompatible with modern Western secular values (Huntington 1996; Lewis 2004)—a claim once made against Catholicism in parts of Europe (Gross 2004). But in fact, Islam and Islamic movements are diverse and vary by region and context; most are not fundamentalist (Bayat 2007; Esposito and Voll 2001; Roy 2007).

In any case, violence is by no means inherent to religious fundamentalism. With the important exception of abortion clinic bombings and the assassination of doctors providing abortions, domestic Christian fundamentalism has been non-violent; its advocates organize politically to work within the electoral system. Violence by Islamic fundamentalists has captured the headlines because of its association with terrorism. Some scholars argue that this violence is more of a response to the political environment—especially Western military and economic domination—than a feature of religion itself. They point out that violence is more likely to originate in settings where a religion is repressed or a single religion is imposed by the state (Cesari 2004; Roy 2007; Schwedler 2006).

In societies with separation of religion and government, and free competition among varying religious groups, tolerance is more common and religiously based violence is rare. In addition, when Islamic fundamentalism is incorporated into democratic societies, evidence suggests that it becomes more moderate by becoming globalized (separated from the national cultures) and individualized (allowing for variation in observance and belief), much in the same way that Protestantism and Catholicism were. Even when militant religious movements take part in the political process, they tend to become more secularized and to moderate their views (Cesari 2004; Roy 2007; Schwedler 2006).

The future of fundamentalism is not clear. Some sociologists see the resurgence in fundamentalism as a relatively short-term phenomenon, the last gasp of resistance to the wave of modernization and secularism that has swept over the developed world over the past two centuries. Others see modernization and secularism as continuously creating alienating conditions that will fuel fundamentalism indefinitely (Riesebrodt 2000). This leaves still others to suggest a postsecular age, in which religious worldviews—of all sorts—will coexist and interact with secular worldviews (Habermas 2002).

A Changing World

THE FUTURE OF RELIGION

A number of religious changes in the United States give clues about where religion might be going in the future.

First, evidence indicates that religion in the United States is increasingly a source of individual emotional comfort rather than the basis of a comprehensive, collective worldview. For example, Wolfe (2005) finds that Protestants, Catholics, and Jews in the United States increasingly focus on emotional involvement with worship instead of on an intellectual engagement with a religion's history or doctrine. The result is a more personalized and individualistic approach to religion. People participate in the rituals of worship but pick and choose which doctrines to believe and, as we have seen, are more tolerant of the choices and lifestyles of others.

In stark contrast to fundamentalists' emphasis on doctrine and sacred texts, this shift to more emotional, individualized varieties of faith means less emphasis on doctrinal knowledge. Some surveys show that those most knowledgeable about the core teachings and history of major world religions are atheists and agnostics (Pew Forum on Religion and Public Life 2010b). In a society with overwhelmingly Christian adherents, surveys find that Bible-reading has declined for at least a quarter century and basic knowledge of the Bible's contents is at an all-time low (Prothero 2007). But such knowledge may not be necessary for the type of personal spiritual experience many people seek today.

In fact, a second change in recent decades has been a rise in the growing popularity of many forms of "spirituality." **Spirituality** can be thought of as *an inner sense of meaning or purpose, especially as it involves a person's relationship to something greater than the self.* As we saw in Chapter 1, some postmodern thought reacts to the central tenets of modernity, including rationalization and secularization. It rejects the idea that reality can be known only through science or any other method for achieving impartial understanding. Instead, these postmodern thinkers contend that, at best, all knowledge is partial and fragmented, and we live in a world with multiple realities from which to choose. In this context, some people embrace mystical or supernatural ways of knowing.

People can be both "spiritual" and "religious" (Marler and Hadaway 2002), but some forms of spirituality emphasize a personal relationship to a higher power without the need for a religious institution. Such practices can amount to God without religion or what one study dubbed "believing without belonging" (Davie 1994). In this situation, people continue to express belief in God but are no longer active in any religion. Some analysts see spirituality, broadly defined (including astrology, witchcraft, and paganism, for example), as likely to persist (Heelas and Woodhead 2005; Pearson 2003; Spencer 2003).

But spirituality doesn't necessarily require the supernatural or gods. Durkheim's definition of the sacred did not necessarily involve the supernatural, just the identification of something as extraordinary, to be treated respectfully, with reverence and awe. Acknowledging "a greater power" can mean simply an appreciation of the common fate of humanity, our interconnection through our natural environment, or even the sense of empowerment that comes from self-help efforts. Faiths and practices that profess such ethical and moral principles offer their adherents the chance to experience shared spiritual activity without necessarily invoking a divine being; they are religions without God. Such beliefs are often associated with "new age" religions, though they can also be found in established denominations such as the Unitarian Universalists, who note that "diverse beliefs about the existence of a higher power are welcome in Unitarian Universalism" (Unitarian Universalist Association of Congregations 2013).

The rejection of modernist rationality in favor of postmodernist spirituality can be seen throughout popular culture. Television programs, books, and movies are filled with images and stories that involve spirits, supernatural events, and mysterious beings with superpowers. Whether they are angels, vampires, alien life-forms, superheroes, or some other entity, the characters in these stories often remind humans of core values and their common destiny, as powerful religious texts have always done.

The growth of spirituality often does not include supernatural beliefs. Meditative practices, for example, can promote mental and physical health while encouraging practitioners to be mindful of the connections between people and their natural environments.

Embracing the certainty of traditional faith can offer believers comfort and reassurance in a time of change and uncertainty. But globalization has brought people, information, and competing beliefs into contact with one another as never before. The result is likely to be an increasing emphasis on the need for religious tolerance, the growth of individualized spirituality, and the declining influence—though not necessarily declining visibility—of fundamentalist religions. It is also likely to involve the continued expansion of secular humanism.

While not choosing sides in religious debates, sociologists know that if societies are to survive, they will

The broad interest in supernatural phenomena can be seen in popular culture's portrayals of vampires, ghosts, and other recurring characters.

need to identify and affirm shared values and social norms that enable them to operate peacefully in the midst of a multitude of conflicting beliefs. Perhaps this search for common ground—among nonbelievers and believers of all stripes—will be what characterizes the future the most.

thinking sociologically about
Family and Religion

culture

- Family and religion are both institutions through which culture is passed on to the next generation. Both institutions vary considerably by culture and over time, reflecting different norms and beliefs.

structure

- Families help structure daily life by performing a variety of social functions, but people can also act to change the structure of families, adapting to different circumstances and adopting new values.

- Religion has long served to provide some structure to social life by focusing on values and moral behavior and thereby serving as a mechanism of social control. The structure of religion itself has changed considerably as a large number of belief systems compete for adherents.

power

- How families are organized and operate reflects the relative levels of power held by members, sometimes contributing to gender inequality.

- Changes in religion, including the rise of various aspects of secularization, have diminished the power that religious institutions have in modern societies.

REVIEW, REFLECT, AND APPLY

Looking Back

1. The family as a social institution can perform a variety of social functions, including encouraging social stability, caring for dependents, and providing emotional comfort. But the gender roles established in families can help perpetuate inequality.

2. Families vary around the world by structure and size, marriage types, and gender roles. However, some common global trends in family life include smaller families, the growth of open-mate selection, and a delay in marriage.

3. The idealized image of the "traditional" family in the United States obscures a complicated reality that included distinct imbalances in power as well as gender, class, and racial inequalities.

4. Families in the United States today are undergoing significant changes, including fewer and later marriages, a rise in divorce rates, an increase in blended families and other family forms, an increase in single-parent families, and a reduction in the number of children born to couples.

5. Since its inception, sociology has examined religion as a social phenomenon, considering its role in social life and its functions in society. Durkheim viewed religions as a mechanism to promote the norms of society. Marx saw religion as a way for those in power to keep oppressed people submissive. Weber emphasized the displacement of religion by the rationalization of modernity.

6. Religion can promote social solidarity, exert social control, provide personal comfort, and motivate social action. But it can also be dysfunctional, contributing to social conflict and perpetuating orthodox myths.

7. Although religion has declining influence within modern industrialized societies, religiosity in the United States is relatively high. U.S. religious life in the postmodern period is characterized by a diverse spiritual marketplace, featuring many varied forms of religious and spiritual life.

8. The debate over secularization focuses on the degree to which the social significance of religion is in decline. Ironically, increasing secularism may be fueling a resurgence of fundamentalism among some religious groups that want their religious prescriptions to prevail in society.

Critical Thinking: Questions and Activities

1. How has the American family changed in the past half century? Does your family reflect some of these changes?

2. Overall, do you think the changes in marriage and the family found in the United States have been positive for society? Why or why not?

3. Growing up, were you encouraged to believe in a particular religious tradition? If not, were you encouraged to disbelieve, or was your family simply indifferent to religion? How did you learn about the different beliefs held by other people?

4. Do you think competing and contradictory claims of absolute truth, often contained within religious doctrine, pose a threat to society? Why or why not? How can such potential conflicts be avoided in a diverse society?

5. Do you think society is becoming more secularized? Less so? What is the evidence for your position?

Key Terms

church (p. 337) formal religious organization with broad mainstream acceptance.

civil religion (p. 344) a set of common beliefs and ritual practices that bind people in a predominantly secular society.

cohabitation (p. 325) a social relationship that can create family ties and typically involves sexual intimacy, in which people live together as unmarried partners.

cult (p. 337) a small religious community whose beliefs and practices are at odds with the dominant culture.

endogamy (p. 325) legal restrictions or customs that limit marriage to people within the same social category.

ethic of reciprocity (p. 338) the "golden rule" that encourages people to treat others as they would like to be treated.

exogamy (p. 325) marriage between people from different social categories.

extended family (p. 325) nuclear family plus other relatives who commonly live together.

faith (p. 336) belief grounded in personal conviction or divine revelation rather than scientific evidence.

family (p. 323) two or more people, related either by birth or through social commitment, who share resources, care for any dependents, and often maintain a close emotional relationship.

fertility rate (p. 332) the average number of births per female.

fundamentalism (p. 345) a religious movement that advocates strict adherence to traditional principles in all aspects of social life, usually based on literal interpretation of a religion's infallible sacred texts.

kinship (p. 323) the bonds of family relationships.

liberation theology (p. 339) a form of Christian belief dedicated to combating poverty and other forms of social injustice.

marriage (p. 325) a social relationship that creates family ties, typically involves sexual relations, and is formalized by legal contract, religious ceremony, or both.

monogamy (p. 325) the practice of restricting sexual relations to one partner.

nuclear (conjugal) family (p. 325) parent(s) and their children.

polygamy (p. 325) a marriage system in which an individual is allowed multiple spouses.

profane (p. 336) the ordinary world of everyday life.

religion (p. 337) a unified system of beliefs and ritual practices relating to the sacred that bond people into a moral community.

rituals (p. 336) symbolic actions, typically performed at specified times, that help evoke an emotional bond among participants.

sacred (p. 336) something extraordinary, to be treated respectfully, with reverence and awe.

sect (p. 332) a small dissenting faction of a church that promotes new beliefs or practices.

secular humanism (p. 344) a belief system that emphasizes morality and decision making based on reason, ethics, and social justice rather than religious doctrine or the supernatural.

secularization (p. 343) the decline in the social significance of religious beliefs, practices, and institutions.

secularization thesis (p. 343) the argument that, in the face of modernity, the social significance of religion has declined.

spirituality (p. 347) an inner sense of meaning or purpose, especially as it involves a person's relationship to something greater than the self.

theism (p. 337) a belief in the existence of a god or gods.

Education and Work

looking AHEAD

How—and what—have schools taught you about the social norms and values of your **culture**?

Do schools provide a **structure** that promotes social equality—or do they reinforce social inequality?

How does **power** operate in workplaces such as those where you have had experience?

W hen Claudia Crisostomo's three children—6, 9, and 10 years old—arrive home from school each day, their mother is heading out to her job at a uniform laundry. Because her shift begins at 3:00 p.m., and she returns home late in the evening, she is not able to help her children with homework or read to them before bedtime. Nor is she able to go to evening events at the school, attend after-school meetings with teachers, or take her kids to the doctor or dentist. The Crisostomos live in Newburgh, New York, a small city about 60 miles north of New York City, where public transportation is limited. Consequently, getting to important events and appointments, such as school assemblies and doctor visits, usually requires an expensive taxi ride.

Because Ms. Crisostomo, a Mexican immigrant, does not speak or read English with confidence, she feels disconnected from her kids' school experiences and has a hard time advocating for her children with school officials and medical professionals. Although educators stress that parental involvement is a key factor in helping youngsters succeed in school, Ms. Crisostomo has neither the kind of work schedule nor the facility with English needed to get involved with her children's school (Berger 2006).

n immigrant communities across the United States, the Crisostomos' experience is a familiar one. Countless immigrant parents work evening hours, and even when they can take part in school activities, they often are uncomfortable navigating the school environment. Yet the education their kids are getting in that environment is a crucial factor in helping them achieve a better quality of life than the parents themselves enjoy. Education and work are closely interconnected, as one of the aims of education is to teach individuals the knowledge and skills they will need to get jobs and lead a happy, productive life.

In this chapter we look at these two intertwined social institutions: education and work. We consider their roles and functions in society, their structure, and their relationship to social equality and inequality. We emphasize the various social and cultural factors that shape people's school and workplace experiences.

Education and Schooling

Education is a word you know well. If you are reading this book, you are probably pursuing a college education. The news is full of stories about education, politicians often talk about the importance of education, and potential employers ask job candidates about their education. Sociologists define **education** as *the social institution through which individuals acquire knowledge and skills and learn cultural norms and values.* Education is vital to the transmission of basic cultural knowledge from one generation to the next, including traditions and an understanding of history. Education also imparts knowledge and skills related to specific jobs and household management.

The learning associated with education occurs in different settings beyond schools. For example, learning takes place at home, on the playground, and at work involving parents, friends and neighbors, and employers. However, the sociological study of education focuses foremost on schools, which are the primary arena of formal education, and on **schooling,** *organized instruction by trained teachers.*

Schooling is an important part of social life throughout the world. Most countries emphasize the value of schooling and invest in organized instruction for their citizens. Three key indicators highlight the widespread belief in the importance of schooling (Brint 2006). First, young people throughout the developed world, and in much of the developing world, spend a great deal of their childhood in school (see Table 13.1). In the United States, children typically attend school six hours a day for about 180 days each year. Children in some countries go to school for more than 200 days each year; in South Korea, for example, primary school students attend school for 220 days each year, and the Indonesian primary school year is 240 days (OECD 2013).

TABLE 13.1	AGE RANGE AT WHICH 90 PERCENT OF THE POPULATION IS ENROLLED IN SCHOOL, SELECT COUNTRIES

Country	Age Range (years)
Belgium	3–18
Brazil	6–15
Chile	6–16
England	4–16
France	3–17
Germany	4–18
Israel	4–16
Italy	3–16
Japan	4–17
Korea	6–17
New Zealand	4–16
Norway	3–17
Spain	3–16
Sweden	3–18
Turkey	6–13
United States	6–16

Source: Organization for Economic Cooperation and Development (2013).

Second, most wealthy nations make a substantial investment in schooling by financing a system of formal education. A key reason is that political participation and economic growth depend, in part, on schooling to teach citizenship and job skills. Perhaps the most fundamental of these skills is **literacy,** *the ability to read and write.* As Map 13.1 illustrates, literacy rates vary throughout the world. Adult literacy is nearly universal (99 percent) in developed countries, and literacy has increased substantially in developing countries in recent decades, extending to 80 percent of adults in 2011. In Latin America and the Caribbean, adult literacy stands at 92 percent; comparable rates in the Arab states are 77 percent; in South and West Africa, 63 percent; and in Sub-Saharan Africa, 59 percent (UNESCO 2013). The overall global adult literacy rate was 84 percent in 2011, up from 76 percent in 1990. In the United States and throughout most of the developed world, government funds help finance schools from elementary schools through colleges and universities. Developing countries typically have fewer resources to invest in schools, but spending on formal education is still often a very high priority. The Education for All Global Monitoring Report (2010) cites limited financial

MAP 13.1 | LITERACY RATES AROUND THE WORLD

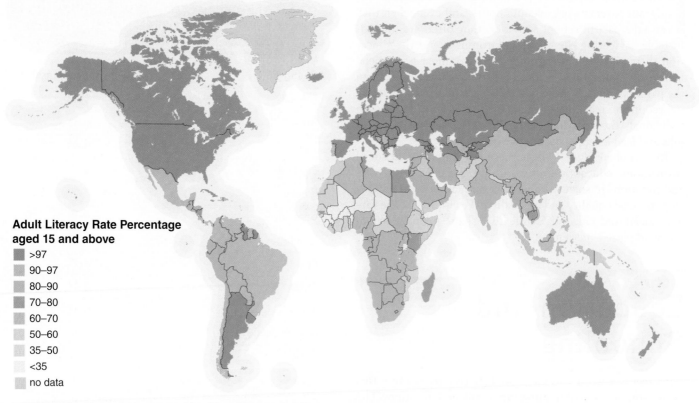

Adult Literacy Rate Percentage aged 15 and above

- >97
- 90–97
- 80–90
- 70–80
- 60–70
- 50–60
- 35–50
- <35
- no data

National literacy rates vary considerably. Literacy exceeds 97 percent in North America, Australia, and most of Europe, but literacy rates are significantly lower in most of Africa, Asia, and South America. *Source:* UN Human Development Programme (2009).

resources as one of the primary obstacles to improving education, estimating that education spending will have to double to make a basic education, including adult literacy, universally accessible in low-income countries.

Third, a large number of adults have jobs in education, working as teachers, support staff, and administrators in schools and school offices. Schools are a major employer in the United States. In 2012, there were more than 2.8 million elementary and middle school teachers, more than 1 million high school teachers, and more than 800,000 school administrators (U.S. Bureau of Labor Statistics 2013b), with hundreds of thousands of others employed in schools as teaching assistants, librarians, custodians, and food service workers, among many different occupations. Similarly, from preschools to universities, schools are a major employer throughout the world.

Education in the United States: A Brief Social History

Until the nineteenth century, most children in the United States did not attend school. Instead, children typically worked in the household, on the farm, or as wage laborers. Some children received an education in a specific trade by serving an apprenticeship. Formal education, though available, was offered almost exclusively to upper-class children, who attended private schools and private universities.

Leaders of the American Revolution, notably Thomas Jefferson, advocated the development of a public elementary school system as a way to unify the new nation and promote active citizenship and democratic self-government. Yet in the late 1700s and early 1800s, education in the United States remained a patchwork of schools with minimal government funding and limited enrollment. Women, African Americans, and Native Americans were largely excluded (Urban and Wagoner 2009).

Public schools—"common schools" at the time—did not emerge until the early 1830s, when educational reformers in the Northeast argued for the development of free taxpayer-supported schools that would be accessible to all children. With the United States amid a transformation from a rural and agrarian society to one shaped by industrialization, urbanization, and an influx of new immigrants, advocates of common schools emphasized the civic value of education. During this period of social change, according to historian William J. Reese (2005), "schools were expected to strengthen the moral character of children, reinvigorate the work ethic, spread civic and republican values, and along the way teach a common curriculum to ensure a literate and unified public" (p. 3).

After the Civil War, school enrollment increased and common schools expanded dramatically. In 1870, 57 percent of 5- to 18-year-olds were enrolled in school. By the turn of the century, there were more than 250,000 public schools in the United States, and 72 percent of children were attending school (Reese 2005). Starting with Massachusetts in 1852, states began enacting compulsory attendance laws in the middle of the nineteenth century. By 1918, all 48 states had laws requiring children to attend school, usually through eighth grade—and the foundation of our contemporary system of universal compulsory education was established.

Public education continued to expand in the first half of the twentieth century as a high school education became increasingly common. Between 1900 and 1950, the school year lengthened from an average of 144 days to 178 days, and total public school enrollment climbed from 15.5 to 25.7 million students (Reese 2005). Local governments increasingly invested in schools, which were becoming the largest public expenditure in many communities. Then, as now, schools were the focus of public scrutiny and became an arena for debate and controversy over the substance of the curriculum, teaching methods, academic standards, the goals of education, and, more generally, the place of education in society.

The Functions of Schooling

What are schools for? This question is deceptively complex and cannot be answered adequately with the obvious response, "Schools are a place to learn." A sociological perspective directs us to consider seven fundamental functions of contemporary schools:

1. *Transfer of knowledge.* Schools are a vital site where children and teenagers acquire knowledge defined as important by previous generations, including subjects from history and literature to math and science.

2. *Job preparation.* Schools play an important role in teaching job skills. Most schools help prepare future workers. Many high schools, colleges, and adult education programs emphasize specific job-related skills.

3. *Occupational sorting.* In preparing young people for future jobs, schooling helps sort people into different kinds of jobs. Not all schools are the same. Some schools emphasize specific trades, giving students skills in, say, plumbing or auto repair, whereas other schools focus on college preparation and send many graduates off to college and, subsequently, graduate school.

on social theory

A **functionalist** perspective emphasizes the role of education in society. Do you think the functions of schooling are changing in the twenty-first century?

4. *Child care.* Schools are responsible for children for the bulk of the workday and thus serve as a major source of child care for working parents. Some of the demand for a longer school day and an extended school year comes from those in need of the kind of full-time child care that schools provide.

5. *Social integration.* Schools teach common cultural traditions that help build social solidarity. Schools build community by connecting children and adults in the shared activity of teaching and learning. Schools often emphasize local and national history, helping reinforce a sense of community and national identity.

6. *Change and innovation.* In bringing students and faculty together to study and learn, schools are a site from which new ideas and practices emerge. Schools are a major source of technological innovation, and schools can be a source of ideas that stimulate economic, political, and cultural change.

7. *Socialization.* Schools serve as a powerful agent of socialization, teaching lessons that extend well beyond the subject-specific curriculum. Contemporary schools often adopt an explicit socialization role, integrating into the school day educational activities about issues such as diversity, health, sexuality, and drug and violence prevention.

In the sections that follow, we explore many of these functions of education.

Education, Culture, and Socialization

There is widespread consensus that schools should teach the "three Rs"—reading, writing, and arithmetic—but what else do schools teach? As you will see in this section, schools provide lessons that extend well beyond specific academic knowledge and skills.

The Hidden Curriculum

Much of the socialization that happens in schools takes place outside the formal subject-matter curriculum. In the early twentieth century, Emile Durkheim ([1925] 1961) coined the term **moral education** to describe *the role of schools in teaching children the central values and beliefs of their society.* For Durkheim and many later sociologists, schools play a vital part in instructing children about their culture's core values.

Schools, for example, teach children lessons about the value of hard work, discipline, obedience to authorities, being on time, following the rules, and the consequences of

thinking about culture

The ethnic diversity of the U.S. school population has increased in recent years. Did your high school stick to teaching traditional lessons about U.S. culture—or did it take into account the cultural values of recent immigrants?

355

In this classroom scene, schoolchildren are saying the Pledge of Allegiance to start the school day.

CORE CONCEPTS CHALLENGE

What are public schools teaching when the Pledge of Allegiance is a part of the school's daily routine? How are the values of U.S. **culture** *reflected in the messages conveyed in the Pledge?*

misbehaving. In addition, typical evaluation systems teach kids about inequality (some students receive higher grades than others), and the school's structure teaches about hierarchy (the chain of command in schools, leading up to the principal). Sociologists refer to these implicit teachings as the **hidden curriculum,** or *the lessons students learn simply by attending school, in contrast to the lessons from the formal subject-specific curriculum.*

In recent years, politicians and parents have increasingly demanded that schools instruct children about core values and appropriate behavior. In many communities, schools are expected to help solve social problems by educating children about violence, sex, drugs, intolerance, health, nutrition, and basic civility. As a result, a new cast of school employees—among them, student assistance counselors, violence prevention coordinators, health educators, and diversity trainers—is becoming increasingly important on the public school stage.

Students also learn a great deal about national identity during the school day. Public schools in the United States adhere to a relatively standard set of patriotic rituals that identify both the school and its population as American. For example, many public school students recite the Pledge of Allegiance each day and participate in school assemblies to recognize national holidays such as Veterans Day and Memorial Day. One study suggests that the rapid spread of American public

schools since the nineteenth century was part of a broader process of nation building in which the school became the central arena for forging national solidarity and preparing future generations to be engaged citizens (Meyer et al. 1979).

Schools also transmit fundamental social values connected to religious definitions of national identity. Consider how the Pledge of Allegiance, in referring to "one nation under God" (a phrase inserted in 1954), emphasizes a religious basis for American identity. In contrast, public schools in France present a far more secular version of national identity, and religious displays are illegal in French public schools. Consequently—and controversially—Muslim girls are not permitted to wear headscarves in France's public schools.

Socialization Messages in Schools

Schools teach about behavior and values in both formal instruction and informal interactions between students and school officials. Brint, Contreras, and Matthews (2001) identified five ways in which socialization messages are disseminated in U.S. primary schools:

1. Teacher-initiated interactions with students
2. Everyday classroom routines
3. Student participation in schoolwide activities and programs
4. Visual displays and oral rituals in public spaces
5. Subject matter in the formal curriculum

A Muslim girl in France arrives at school, where she must remove her headscarf before classes. What kinds of religious displays have you seen at schools in your community? Should they be permitted? Why or why not?

The authors found that the content of socialization messages outside the formal curriculum consists largely of traditional lessons about appropriate behavior. For example, most teacher-initiated interactions with students stress the importance of orderliness and effort, as when a teacher reminds students to "listen quietly when someone else is speaking" and to "finish on time." Broader, schoolwide activities are likely to emphasize the values of participation and respect and include conflict resolution programs and public recognition of students for positive contributions. Public spaces typically transmit messages that highlight the importance of obeying school rules and respecting authority—say, by means of a poster that reminds students to act responsibly or by requiring students' silence during the principal's morning announcements.

Brint (2006) identifies three dimensions by which schools evaluate students, producing specific language for describing students who conform to their socialization messages:

1. *Behavior conformity.* Daily life in schools is full of informal instruction on proper behavior. For example, you must raise your hand and wait to be called on before speaking, and you must request permission to use the bathroom. School authorities call students who follow these rules "well disciplined."

2. *Moral conformity.* Schools train students to internalize values about what is moral, right, or proper (see the Through a Sociological Lens box). Teachers and school officials commonly emphasize the importance of "honesty, tolerance, courage, hard work, or fairness . . . [and] may also assign reading materials that illustrate the consequences of not being guided by these moral virtues" (Brint 2006, 134). Students who appear to conform to these moral standards are generally regarded as "good" students.

3. *Cultural conformity.* Schools also instruct students on what Brint calls "approved styles and outlooks"— culturally desirable behaviors and perspectives. These are likely to vary significantly by school setting. For example, large urban public schools may teach students how to get along in complex, rule-based organizations by completing assignments precisely as instructed by the teacher. In contrast, elite private schools are far more likely to encourage students to demonstrate their creative thinking by producing quirky projects that may even question the assumptions of a given assignment. Brint notes that those who conform to cultural styles are perceived to be "well adjusted" to the cultural expectations of their specific school environment.

Mixed Messages About Socialization

The values that schools teach are a dynamic mix of old and new. They reflect both the schools' traditional interest in an orderly, achievement-oriented environment and wider, more recent social trends that encourage tolerance and respect for diversity. For example, formal instruction—including that in textbooks,

This elementary school student is learning math with the help of M&M's. Some teachers see this practice as a way to engage students in school, making math fun—and perhaps rewarding, too. When teachers use popular products like brand-name candy and pizza as rewards, what are students learning beyond addition and fractions?

assignments, and in-class lessons—now often emphasizes respect for cultural diversity and the importance of inclusiveness.

Sometimes conflicts arise within the community—or, more broadly, in the nation—about the mix of old and new messages. Educational historian Jonathan Zimmerman's *Whose America?* (2002) examines a series of long-standing conflicts over what public schools should teach about history, religion, and sexuality. Zimmerman shows that these conflicts are rooted in such deeply held beliefs that there seems to be little room for compromise or even discussion. For example, debates about prayer in school, demands to include creationist theories in science classes as an alternative to Darwin's theory of evolution, and disagreements over whether and what to teach about sex and sexuality pit different worldviews, values, and understandings of morality against one another.

The point is that socialization in schools reflects specific historical and social circumstances. Disagreements about the values children should learn have therefore made American public schools a site of ongoing political conflict.

Beyond their role as agents of socialization, schools are commonly seen as engines of social mobility and economic opportunity. In the next section, we look at how sociologists describe and interpret the relationship between education and opportunity.

Tracing the Links Between Moral Authority and School Discipline

A high school teacher before returning to graduate school to study sociology, sociologist Richard Arum was keenly aware of the complex problems facing public schools. As Arum (2003) reports in the preface to his book *Judging School Discipline,* he taught in an urban public school system where disorder and violence were common.

Arum recognized that most of the research literature and news media coverage of public schools focused on measures of educational achievement—test scores, dropout rates, college admissions statistics. For his part, Arum was concerned about the ability of a school "to foster moral development and successfully socialize youth in its charge" (p. viii). His interests were influenced by social theorist Emile Durkheim's writings on moral education, by the long-standing public concern about ineffective school discipline, and by the increasing burdens schools must bear in an age when adults spend more time at work—and less time with their children. Arum set out to explore the relationship between school discipline and what he saw as a crisis in moral authority in U.S. schools. *How* have public schools lost their moral authority, Arum wondered?

To focus his investigation, Arum turned his attention to the courts, specifically probing how court decisions might have contributed to a "decline in moral authority and the erosion of effective disciplinary practices in American public schools" (p. 4). Arum examined court data, along with data on thousands of schools from four national surveys that had studied school disciplinary practices, student and teacher perceptions of school discipline, and educational achievement. Arum and his graduate students used a computerized legal archive to identify more than 6,000 relevant state and federal court cases that involved questions of school discipline, and they employed a series of statistical techniques to analyze the patterns in these cases.

Arum's analysis showed that some states had pro-school judicial climates (in which courts were more likely to rule in favor of schools) whereas other states had pro-student court climates (in which courts were more likely to rule in favor of students). He sought to identify whether these differing court climates affected how teachers and students act in school. He found that in pro-school judicial climates, teachers felt they had more classroom control and greater support for rule enforcement from their principals. In contrast, in pro-student climates, court rulings helped undermine the legitimacy of school disciplinary practices because of the ever-present threat of lawsuits from parents and students.

Applying his sociological training, Arum relied on Durkheim's view of schools' role in moral education to interpret these

results. He noted that although pro-student court rulings were important in educating students about the core democratic rights of free expression and due process, these rulings also had significant unintended consequences. In particular, Arum argues that pro-student court decisions have been part of a broader weakening of the school as a respected institution and of the teacher as a legitimate authority—two shifts that make it much more difficult for schools and teachers to do their jobs of educating and socializing young people. Arum argues that his research suggests that courts and state legislatures need to expand the discretion and legal protections granted to teachers and school administrators so that they can develop effective disciplinary practices that will maintain order in schools—and be perceived by students and parents as legitimate.

think about it

1. *Do you think schools should focus on moral development rather than just academic achievement? Explain.*

2. *Arum argues that schools have lost their "moral authority" and have experienced a decline in "effective disciplinary practices." Do you agree? Was this your experience in high school?*

Educational Structure and Inequality

Education is the great equalizer. If you want to get ahead in the world, the best route to success is through education, right? This is the official story, and it reflects the important relationship between achievement in school and career opportunities for adults. But education is not a simple equalizer. Not all people have the same educational opportunities, and research suggests that although schools sometimes reduce inequality, they also sometimes reinforce it. In this section, we examine the ways schools sort people into different kinds of jobs, often perpetuating existing inequalities, and we probe the issue of why school structure matters for students and teachers.

Education and Income

As Figure 13.1 shows, one thing is clear: those with more education, on average, make more money. At each educational level, average income rises substantially for both men and women. In 2011, individuals with a bachelor's degree had an average income almost three times higher than those who had not completed high school, and almost double the earnings of high school graduates.

There are exceptions to this link between education and income. You may have a neighbor who never went to college but has a very high income as a building contractor. Or you may know someone who completed graduate school but struggles on the salary of a part-time teacher. Despite such examples, the education-income link is well established and quite strong. As a general rule, the more education you have, the higher your income will be as an adult.

Education and Social Mobility

Education helps an individual get a better job with greater rewards. It also substantially increases an individual's chance of upward social mobility. The benefits of schooling may affect subsequent generations as well. One recent study tracked the educational achievement of three generations over 30-year period and found that when women from disadvantaged backgrounds have the opportunity to attend college, their future children are more likely than the children of their peers who did not attend college to be successful in school and ultimately to complete college themselves (Attewell et al. 2007). However, only about one-third of adults in the United States have completed college; by 2012, 30.9 percent of U.S. adults aged 25 and over had a bachelor's or graduate degree (see Figure 13.2).

Although school achievement is a route to occupational success, the relationship among education, social mobility, and economic advancement is complex. As we saw earlier in this book, systems of stratification are made up of structural positions, the rewards associated with each position, and the people who occupy these positions. Education can help an

FIGURE 13.1 | EDUCATIONAL ATTAINMENT AND MEDIAN INCOME, MEN AND WOMEN AGED 25 AND OVER, 2011

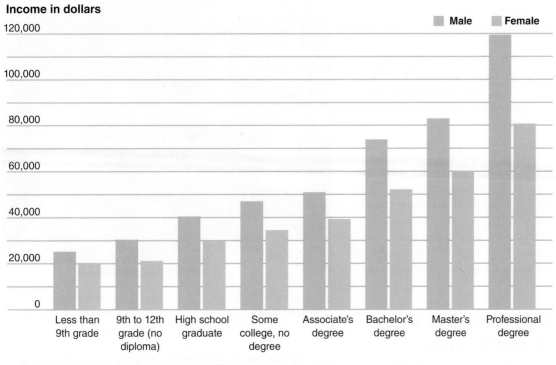

Source: National Center for Education Statistics (2012).

FIGURE 13.2 | EDUCATIONAL ATTAINMENT, U.S. ADULTS AGED 25 AND OVER, 2012

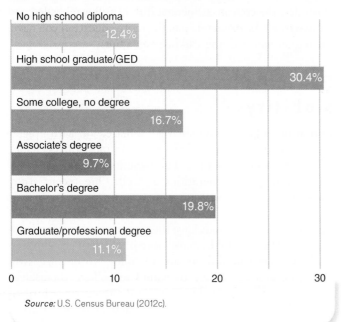

No high school diploma — 12.4%

High school graduate/GED — 30.4%

Some college, no degree — 16.7%

Associate's degree — 9.7%

Bachelor's degree — 19.8%

Graduate/professional degree — 11.1%

Source: U.S. Census Bureau (2012c).

Learning environments can vary widely from one school district to another. Some schools in well-off communities, such as Newton North High School in Newton, Massachusetts, have state-of-the-art facilities (*top*). In some poor districts, however, schooling takes place in dilapidated—and often unsafe—buildings (*bottom*). How might differences in school facilities have an impact on educational opportunities for students?

individual advance within a stratified, unequal system, but it does little or nothing reduce structural inequality itself.

Suppose, for example, that we could give every working adult in the United States a college education. Would everyone then advance to a better job? The answer is no for a couple of reasons.

First, the value of a college education would plummet, because a college degree would no longer be scarce. Indeed, consider that a college degree is valuable precisely *because* some people do not have one. As college degrees become increasingly common, graduate or specialized professional degrees become more necessary for career advancement. Second, even if everyone had a college degree, some people would still have to collect garbage, serve coffee, clean streets, and work as cashiers. There will always be a need for low-skill jobs that do not require higher education. Changing the workforce's level of education will not change this structural reality.

What *would* reduce economic inequality, though, would be to change the rewards associated with different positions, perhaps by increasing wages at the bottom and raising taxes on top income earners. In other words, to reduce economic inequality, we need to pay attention to issues such as wages and taxes, not just education. Proving the point, in the United States today, a larger percentage of the population than ever has a college degree, yet economic inequality hovers at an all-time high.

How Schools Reinforce Social and Economic Inequality

Ironically, the schools themselves—the very institutions that society counts on to pave the way to opportunity and equality—reinforce social and economic inequality. They do so through various means, some of which are unintended. **Social reproduction theory** *explores the ways that schools help reproduce systems of inequality.* Social reproduction theorists argue that social and economic inequalities are built into the experience of schooling and the curriculum and inevitably result in unequal educational opportunities.

ACCESS TO RESOURCES In August 2010, the new Newton North High School in Newton, Massachusetts, opened its doors to student and teacher raves. This state-of-the-art complex houses two theaters, a student cafe, an Olympic-size swimming pool, tennis courts, indoor and outdoor tracks, and a climbing wall, in addition to 119 gleaming instructional areas. The price tag? $197.5 million (Thomas 2010). Meanwhile, a few miles away in budget-strapped Boston, thousands of public high school students take classes in run-down old buildings. Poor sports facilities and insufficient gear put the schools' student athletes at a disadvantage on the playing field (Hohler 2009).

Perhaps the clearest reason that schools reproduce inequality is their dramatically unequal access to financial resources. Jonathan Kozol's (2005, 2012) account of daily life in public schools in poor neighborhoods features heartbreaking stories of young children trying to do their best in crumbling, unsafe school buildings with overcrowded, windowless classrooms and inadequate textbooks. Under such circumstances, academic achievement can be extremely difficult. Graduation rates in some of the nation's large urban school districts are well below the national average, including those of Detroit (46 percent), Denver (50 percent), Albuquerque (51 percent), Los Angeles (52 percent), Milwaukee (54 percent), and New York (54 percent) (EPE Research Center 2013). As Figure 13.3 shows, high school graduation rates also vary substantially by state, ranging from a 2011 graduating class low of 59 percent in Washington, DC, to a high of 88 percent in Iowa (U.S. Department of Education 2012).

The money that could improve such deplorable conditions is scarce because public schools are funded primarily from local property taxes. Therefore, poor communities have far fewer resources for their schools than wealthier communities. Given these realities, children in well-off neighborhoods (like Newton) are far more likely to attend schools that spend more money on teachers, counselors, computers, laboratories, educational materials, buildings, and playgrounds than schools in poorer districts (like many in Boston). From the starting gate, then, we have public schools that—because they reflect existing variations in the wealth of school districts—provide unequal opportunities (see the Sociology in Action box).

FIGURE 13.3 | U.S. STATES WITH THE LOWEST AND HIGHEST HIGH SCHOOL GRADUATION RATES, 2011

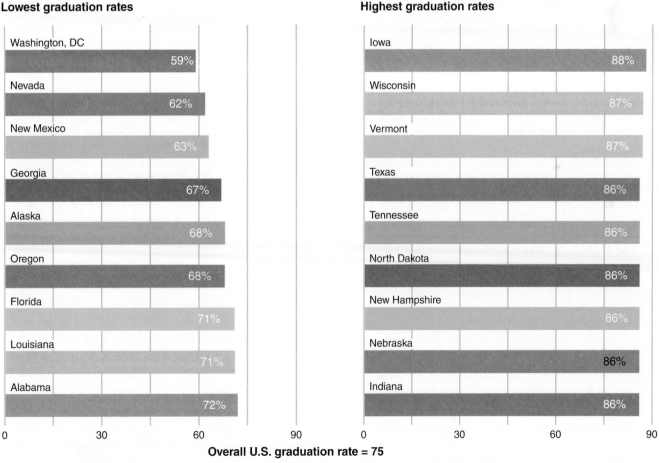

Lowest graduation rates

Washington, DC	59%
Nevada	62%
New Mexico	63%
Georgia	67%
Alaska	68%
Oregon	68%
Florida	71%
Louisiana	71%
Alabama	72%

Highest graduation rates

Iowa	88%
Wisconsin	87%
Vermont	87%
Texas	86%
Tennessee	86%
North Dakota	86%
New Hampshire	86%
Nebraska	86%
Indiana	86%

Overall U.S. graduation rate = 75

Source: U.S. Department of Education, 2012.

SOCIOLOGY in ACTION

Challenging the Structure of School Financing

The public school system in Syosset, New York, a wealthy community in Long Island, offers students an incredibly rich curriculum: courses in seven foreign languages as well as American Sign Language, almost 30 advanced placement (AP) classes, and a nationally recognized arts education program. Public school students in Ilion, New York, an economically depressed community in upstate New York, by contrast, have far fewer curricular opportunities: courses in only one foreign language (Spanish), just four AP classes, and a financial situation that makes it difficult to purchase necessary equipment for science classes (*New York Times* 2011b).

For Cassie Schwerner, program director at the Schott Foundation for Public Education, sociology provided a framework for thinking about how to challenge these educational inequities. In the 1980s and 1990s, Schwerner assisted school reform advocate Jonathan Kozol on his award-winning book *Savage Inequalities*. Kozol's book contrasts the conditions between schools in poor neighborhoods and those in more affluent areas.

Working with Kozol gave Schwerner a close-up view of what's wrong with our public education system and showed her that the structure of school financing is a primary problem. Schwerner turned to her sociology background to map a route for equalizing school financing. In graduate school she had studied a variety of organized social change efforts, looking at how advocates work with media to define social issues and how activists build coalitions. Schwerner's doctoral dissertation, "Sing a Song of Justice," examined initiatives to build multicultural organizations for social change. Schwerner paid particular attention to the complex relationships among race and class differences.

Since she joined the Schott Foundation in 1997, Schwerner has worked to organize and fund the Fair Funding Initiative, which seeks to bring racial and fiscal equity to public schools in New York State. She was a prominent participant in the Campaign for Fiscal Equity (CFE), a grassroots New York City organization dedicated to ensuring that adequate resources and opportunities are available for all schoolchildren, regardless of their place of residence or their parents' income.

The CFE went to court to challenge New York State's school financing, arguing that the current system was unfair and inadequate and led to schools that could not properly serve students in poorer communities. The problems were especially acute in New York City, where more than 85 percent of the students are African Americans, Latinos, or other racial or ethnic minorities. Schwerner guided the CFE in forging alliances among commu-

nity, school, and parent organizations and helped organize the funding community to support the reform campaign.

In 2006, after a protracted court battle, New York State agreed to a settlement of $11 billion for new school construction. Then in 2007, the state legislature voted to enact a major increase in state aid to public schools, along with other reforms, such as smaller class sizes and initiatives to improve teacher quality. Throughout this campaign, Schwerner and Schott supported the CFE financially and strategically.

The Schott Foundation continues to support efforts to promote educational opportunity for all students. Its 2012 report *A Rotting Apple: Education Redlining in New York City* points to the persistent inequality in New York's schools. The authors show that the "unequal distribution of opportunity by race and neighborhood occurs with such regularity in New York that reasonable people can no longer ignore the role that state and city policies and practices play in institutionalizing the resulting disparate outcomes, nor the role played by the lack of federal intervention requiring New York to protect students from them" (Jackson 2012, iv).

think about it

1. *In what tangible ways might the New York City public schools improve as a result of additional state funding?*
2. *What challenges and obstacles do you think are likely to remain after an increase in state funding for New York City's public schools?*

The inequality of public schools' financial resources is only the tip of the iceberg. Beyond this factor, some well-off families have the resources to send their children to elite private day schools or boarding schools. Here students not only receive educational advantages but also prepare for future power—making beneficial social connections, building up their self-esteem, and getting encouragement to see themselves as the leaders of tomorrow (Cookson and Persell

TABLE 13.2 COLLEGE COST AND STUDENT DEBT, 2001 AND 2011

Year	Average Price		Percentage of Students Who Graduated with Debt		Average Debt per Borrower Among Graduating Seniors (in 2011 Dollars)	
	2001–2002	2011–2012	2001	2011	2001	2011
Public four-year	$ 9,196	$21,000	52%	57%	$20,100	$23,800
Private, nonprofit	22,896	41,120	63	66	23,400	29,900

Sources: College Board (2012); National Center for Education Statistics (2003, 2013).

1985; Khan 2011). Untold numbers of other children, including those whose families lack the financial means for such privileged learning, do not have access to such educational opportunities.

In addition, even as access to higher education continues to expand, the high cost of college and the enormous debt incurred by many families who struggle to afford college (see Table 13.2) mean that educational inequality persists from kindergarten *through college*. And the quality of a college education can vary significant as well, with more affluent and better-prepared students benefiting disproportionately from the nation's best colleges and universities (see Figure 13.4).

SORTING BY CLASS

School districts differ in far more subtle ways than just in their monetary resources. In their classic work *Schooling in Capitalist America*, Samuel Bowles and Herbert Gintis (1976) argued that a key function of schools is to mold future workers. Thus, they said, part of schools' job is to sort students by class, preparing them for different kinds of jobs.

A primary way that schools sort by class, according to Bowles and Gintis, is by teaching students class-specific lessons about authority. For instance, students in working-class communities are more likely to be taught about the importance of obedience and following directions. This emphasis prepares them for working at the lower levels of an organization, in jobs that encourage compliance and

often permit little autonomy. In contrast, children from more privileged communities generally attend high schools (and, later, colleges) that encourage creativity, innovation, and independent-mindedness. This educational focus trains

FIGURE 13.4 | HOW EDUCATION REPRODUCES SOCIAL AND ECONOMIC INEQUALITY

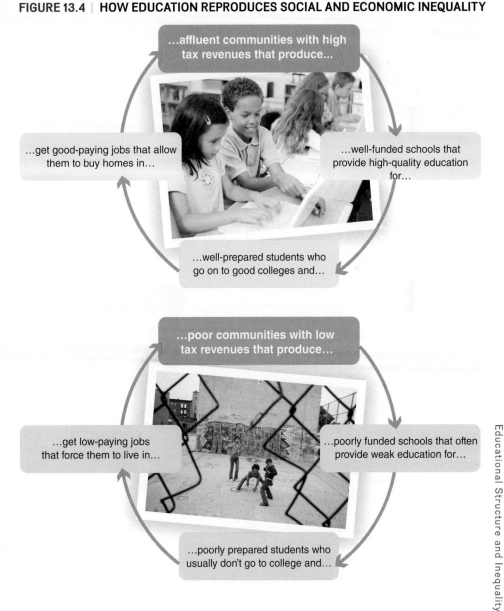

...affluent communities with high tax revenues that produce...

...well-funded schools that provide high-quality education for...

...well-prepared students who go on to good colleges and...

...get good-paying jobs that allow them to buy homes in...

...poor communities with low tax revenues that produce...

...poorly funded schools that often provide weak education for...

...poorly prepared students who usually don't go to college and...

...get low-paying jobs that force them to live in...

students to deal with authority in ways that are more suited to future managers and executives.

Teaching styles and subject-matter curricula are also likely to vary according to students' class status. Rigidly structured, discipline-oriented instructional methods—such as those featuring military-style boot-camp principles and a curriculum focused exclusively on preparation for end-of-year state tests—are increasingly common in schools that serve students from poor communities. In contrast, teaching methods that emphasize collaborative exploration and self-discovery are found far more often in wealthy public school districts and selective private schools. Furthermore, public schools in working-class and poor communities are far more likely to feature vocational and technical classes, whereas public schools in higher-income communities are more likely to include arts education, a wider range of academic subject areas beyond the state-mandated core classes, and opportunities to pursue college-level courses.

CREDENTIALING

Universities, colleges, and professional schools play a vital role in what sociologists call **credentialing,** *the process whereby individuals with advanced educational degrees and formal certificates monopolize access to the most rewarding jobs.* According to sociologist Randall Collins (1979), educational certification is so important for future career opportunities that the United States is in effect a "credential society." This state of affairs helps explain the often-intense competition for limited slots in select colleges and universities and why degree holders are quick to highlight their recognized credentials. Inequality is built into the credentialing system because the value of educational credentials stems to some degree from limited access to these credentials.

CULTURAL CAPITAL

Schools respond to—and help reproduce—people's unequal access to cultural resources. As we saw in Chapter 9, **cultural capital** refers to *various types of knowledge, skills, and other cultural resources.* Sociologists recognize that high-status groups use knowledge, taste, preferences, and styles to signal their status and to exclude others from their social circles (Bourdieu and Passeron 1977). For example, knowledge of classical music or fine art, opportunities for study abroad, and experience with diverse cuisines are forms of cultural capital. Such knowledge, experiences, and tastes provide people with advantages in high-status social networks, whether on the job, in school, or in more informal settings. Cultural capital can serve as both a ticket to enter high-status groups and a sign of one's membership.

Cultural capital gives students advantages in school. It prepares them to fit in with others, to understand what schools expect from successful students, and to use their cultural knowledge for higher grades. Furthermore, sociologists have shown that *parents'* cultural capital can have a significant impact on their children's educational opportunities and experiences. Kaufman and Gabler's (2004) study of the college admissions process in the United States found that the cultural activities of parents help explain which students ultimately attend elite colleges. Specifically, students with parents who visit art museums regularly are far more likely to attend an elite college than students whose parents do not, even when the students themselves are not regular museum-goers. Parents not only transmit their cultural capital to their daughters and sons, but also use it to help their children secure future membership in advantaged groups.

Parental cultural capital—or lack of it—can also significantly shape younger children's early educational experiences. Adrian Blackledge (2001) found that immigrant Bangladeshi mothers in England did not have the appropriate forms of cultural capital to help their children with schoolwork, even though the mothers were concerned about their children's education. These women worked hard to teach their children Bengali, the language of their home country, but did not have sufficient command of English to help with their kids' homework. As a result, the moms could not live up to teachers' expectations for appropriate parental involvement, and school officials concluded that they were not committed to their children's education. In Blackledge's view, these mothers had the "wrong" kind of cultural capital—knowledge of Bengali but not English—to the disadvantage of their children's current educational experiences and future job opportunities.

Contemporary education experts stress the importance of parents' involvement with teachers and officials at their children's schools. Lareau and Weininger (2003), for example, argue that middle-class parents have real advantages over working-class parents in fulfilling educators' expectations in this regard. Specifically, middle-class parents have forms of cultural capital that make it much easier for them to engage actively with educators and are far more likely to be comfortable with educational jargon. Further, these parents display a sense of entitlement and a confidence that they can advocate strongly for their children. Such attitudes are far less common among working-class parents.

Lareau and Weininger contrast the experiences of two families—the Marshalls, a middle-class African American family living in a wealthy suburban community, and the Carrolls, a poor African American family living in a public housing project—to highlight the significance of cultural capital in school settings. Although the parents in both families believed that they should connect with their children's schools to encourage their kids' academic success, they were not equally equipped to do so. The mother of ten-year-old Tara Carroll was not familiar with common educational jargon and was often unsure of what school officials expected of parents. When Tara's mother interacted with teachers and school administrators, she was more inclined to defer to their authority than to challenge it by actively advocating for her child. In contrast, ten-year-old Stacey Marshall's parents did not hesitate to intervene on Stacey's behalf. The Marshalls believed they had a right to advocate for their child with school officials and also trained Stacey on how best to advocate for herself. Lareau and Weininger argue that these distinctive approaches to school reflect—and help reproduce—differences in cultural capital.

RACIAL SEGREGATION In 1954 the U.S. Supreme Court ruled in *Brown v. Board of Education* that **racial school segregation,** *the separation of students into exclusively white and exclusively black public schools,* was unconstitutional. The Court declared, "In the field of public education, the doctrine of 'separate but equal' has no place. Separate educational facilities are inherently unequal."

More than a half century later, however, U.S. public schools are still remarkably segregated. After desegregation efforts during the 1960s and 1970s, a process of *resegregation* began in the late 1980s that has continued into the 2000s. A 2012 report by the Civil Rights Project at UCLA highlights the deepening segregation in U.S. schools, documenting that 74 percent of black students and 80 percent of Latino students attended schools with a student body made up primarily of minority students. Thirty-eight percent of black students and 43 percent of Latino students attended schools where 90 to 100 percent of students were racial/ethnic minorities (Orfield, Kucsera, and Siegel-Hawley 2012). As a result of resegregation, racial segregation in U.S. schools is nearly as extreme as it had been in the 1960s.

Why did resegregation happen? Research shows that racial segregation in schools results in large part from residential segregation and is associated closely with concentrations of poverty. Since neighborhoods are typically segregated by race, local schools often reflect these patterns as well. In addition, the rise of charter schools, magnet schools, and other "school choice" programs (discussed later in this chapter) appears to have magnified racial segregation because white families are far more likely to take their children out of multiracial neighborhood schools when they find other options.

The quality of education at segregated schools—and its impact on achievement—is also an issue. According to Gary Orfield, the leading scholar of contemporary school segregation, racially segregated schools "have less qualified, less experienced teachers, lower levels of peer group competition, more limited curricula taught at less challenging levels, more serious health problems, much more turnover of enrollment, and many other factors that seriously affect academic achievement" (Orfield and Lee, 2006, 29). One study of first-year college students found that even the most successful students from racially segregated schools—those who

went on to attend highly selective colleges and universities—were less prepared, both academically and socially, for college life than were similar students from racially integrated schools (Massey and Fischer 2006).

The effects of segregated schools are likely to extend beyond issues of academic achievement. For example, a recent study found that minority students in racially segregated schools are far more likely, as adults, to spend time in prison or jail than are their counterparts at integrated schools, and the incarceration rate for black students in segregated schools has increased over time (LaFree and Arum 2006).

Even so, some research suggests that under certain circumstances, there may be some benefits to racially segregated schools. One study found that in schools with predominantly minority students *and predominantly minority teachers*, students were more optimistic about their post–high school educational opportunities and future job prospects and had more positive attitudes about teachers and schools than did minority students in predominantly white schools (P. Goldsmith 2004). Although such positive attitudes do not erase the school achievement gap between minority and white students, they do promote the confidence needed for academic success.

Similarly, historically black colleges and universities—including Howard University, Morehouse College, Spelman College, and Tuskegee University, among more than 100 such schools—have served for generations as sources of educational opportunity for African Americans when they were excluded from many private and public colleges and universities. Even today, when many colleges and universities actively pursue a diverse student body, historically black colleges and universities offer African American students a learning environment that supports confidence building and academic achievement and that establishes social networks for subsequent job opportunities (Brown and Davis 2001).

Schools as Complex Organizations

Schools are complex organizations that are shaped by policies and rules, their own organizational histories, and powerful social forces. To understand what happens in schools, why, and with what consequences, we need to consider how the size and organizational structure of schools influence the educational process.

SCHOOL SIZE In one study, education scholars Valerie Lee and Julia Smith (1995) distinguished between schools organized as a bureaucracy and those organized as a community, and they show that these two structural forms are related to school size. Large schools are typically bureaucratic organizations structured along traditional, hierarchical lines, with

thinking about structure

Why might students engage more, and learn more, if they attend a school with a communal **structure**? What structure did your grade school and high school have, and how did that structure affect your learning?

teachers reporting to administrators. They usually have a uniform curriculum, and information is sent home to parents about how best to help their children. In contrast, small schools are more likely to have a communal organization that gives teachers time to plan lessons together, emphasizes curricular flexibility and cooperative learning, and actively involves parents.

Does school size affect students' level of achievement and engagement? School size *does* matter. In their study of high school sophomores, Lee and Smith (1995) found that students in smaller schools with a communal structure learn more and are more tuned in to their courses. But a communal organizational structure is far easier to implement in small schools than large ones. The lesson for school reformers might be that small schools make meaningful organizational restructuring a real possibility.

TRACKING Many schools adopt formal or informal structures of **tracking**, *placing students into different curricular paths intended to accommodate varying levels of academic work.* Tracking systems allow schools to manage students with widely varying skills and interests. Sometimes these tracks are rigid, with some students on a college-prep track and others on a vocational or jobs-skills track. In other situations, the tracks are informal and involve various courses labeled as remedial, general, advanced, AP, or honors.

Tracking was a common feature of U.S. high schools through the mid-1960s. But concerns arose that tracking was an obstacle to social mobility—that tracks locked students into a particular path from an early grade and limited future educational and work opportunities for those not on a college-prep track. Given these concerns, most U.S. high schools eliminated or substantially modified their tracking procedures between 1965 and 1975, according to Sam Lucas (1999). Lucas found, however, that even when the tracking barriers were removed and students were permitted to take a wider range of classes in high school, course placement was not based on prior achievement in a subject area. Instead, parents from economically advantaged families, who had more information about curricular choices, acted to have their children placed in more advanced courses. Thus, although in some schools formal tracking systems may be a thing of the past, informal curricular tracks, reinforced by class and educational differences among parents, remain an organizational reality.

Researchers have examined how the informal tracking structure that persists in U.S. high schools might affect academic achievement. In general, they have found that students in "higher" tracks learn more than students with similar abilities in "lower" tracks. Carbonaro (2005) examined the relationship between school structure (the learning opportunities in each curricular track) and student action (the degree of student effort) with an eye to understanding how both structure and action shape academic achievement. He found that action—in this case, student effort—matters. Those who work harder learn more and are more successful, as measured by grades and test scores.

However, the tracking structure itself remains a significant factor in shaping both effort and learning. Students in higher tracks generally put more effort into their schoolwork than do students in lower tracks. Even when students in lower-track classes apply a great deal of effort, they still learn less than comparable students in higher-track classes. In other words, effort matters, but the tracking structure exerts a powerful constraint, limiting the potential of hard work for students in lower academic tracks and rewarding those who work hard in higher tracks. The lesson from these findings: we need to pay attention to students' effort while recognizing that the action students take is shaped by a tracking structure that influences their effort, expectations, and opportunities to learn.

Contemporary Educational Issues and Trends

Shifts in the economy, advances in digital technologies, an influx of immigrants, and political change have had an impact on the U.S. educational landscape. In this section, we look briefly at some educational challenges confronting citizens and policymakers.

Accountability for Basic Skills

The No Child Left Behind Act (NCLB), passed by the U.S. Congress in 2001, aimed to make schools more accountable for student performance. NCLB's best-known provision requires schools to test all children in reading and math each year from grades three through eight. Researchers refer to these examinations as high-stakes tests because student performance on them is tied to federal school funding. Low test scores over a multiyear period can have consequences for school systems: students may be sent to other public schools, teachers and administrators may be fired, or the school might be turned over to a private company for wholesale restructuring.

The Common Core State Standards Initiative has built on NCLB. Coordinated by the National Governors Association and the Council of Chief State School Officers, the Common Core program emphasizes the development of new math and English language arts standards and assessments for K–12 students. By 2013, 45 states and Washington, D.C., had adopted the Common Core standards and were developing and implementing new curriculum and assessment tools. However, adoption of the Common Core has faced substantial opposition from parents and teachers who are concerned about the impact of new tests on the curriculum content, as well as the security of student test data that will be collected as part of the Common Core initiative.

Supporters of reforms like NCLB and the Common Core argue that this kind of testing regime will push schools with low test scores to perform better and will help address inequalities in academic achievement. Sociologists of education emphasize, however, that a successful approach to school reform must pay careful attention to outside social forces. Understanding differences in academic performance requires an examination of broader patterns of inequality affecting access to health care, housing, job opportunities, adequate income, and supportive communities (Karen 2005).

Bilingual Education

U.S. schools are home to students from diverse backgrounds, including a growing number of children for whom English is not their first language. For children in the early years of elementary school, school policies often emphasize English language acquisition with the expectation that younger students will quickly become fluent in English. However, English language instruction for new immigrant students in middle school or high school is often far more complex.

Since the 1970s, Americans have passionately debated the value of **bilingual education,** in which *students receive instruction in both their first language and English.* Although some organized immigrant groups have pressed for robust bilingual programs, opposition to bilingual education grew in the early 2000s. Voters in several states, including California, Arizona, and Massachusetts, supported ballot initiatives that largely eliminated bilingual education programs. At the same time, the number of English language learners, as students who are not proficient in English are called, was growing rapidly. The U.S. Department of Education (Aud et al. 2013) reports that today, 16 percent of kindergarten students in the United States live in households in which English is not the primary language, and 10 percent of public school students in the United States are English language learners.

Research points to the complexity of the questions raised by bilingual education advocates and critics. For example, in his study of children of immigrants in Florida and California, sociologist Alejandro Portes (2011) observed a "positive association between bilingualism and better academic performance" (p. 569). Portes also identified benefits of bilingualism beyond academic performance; bilingual high school students had higher self-esteem and higher educational aspirations than similarly situated monolingual children of immigrants. Despite these positive findings, however, other research indicates that immigrants who do not achieve English language proficiency are more likely to drop out of high school and to have lower incomes than their counterparts who learn English (Bleakley and Chin 2004; White and Kaufman 1997).

Much of the debate ultimately centers on whether bilingual programs help or hinder students' capacity to learn English and other subjects in school. One study of elementary school students in New York City (Conger 2010) found that students in bilingual programs may learn English less quickly than students in English as a second language (ESL) classes. At the same time, however, evidence indicates that non-English-speaking students learn science, math, and history more effectively in bilingual programs than in English-only classrooms. One five-year study of Spanish-speaking elementary school students in the United States found that bilingual and English-immersion classrooms were equally effective at teaching children to read English proficiently, concluding that the quality (rather than language) of instruction is what matters most (Slavin et al. 2010).

School Choice and the Debate over Charter Schools

The vast majority of U.S. elementary and secondary school students (89 percent) go to public schools. In most such cases, place of residence limits families' options about which school their children can attend.

One long-standing school reform approach revolves around the concept of **school choice,** *various policies that give families options for deciding which school their children will attend.* School choice advocates argue that granting parents the power to choose where their children are schooled will produce competition among public schools that creates incentives for positive reform. Critics of these policies argue that market-oriented school choice programs undermine the integrity of the public education system and further benefit already advantaged families who have access to better information about educational options for their children.

Perhaps the most talked-about school reform initiative in the early 2000s has been the development of **charter schools,** *public schools run by an organization independent from local school districts.* As part of their charter from state government, these schools are exempt from some rules and regulations that govern typical public schools. Charter schools have expanded dramatically since they first appeared in the 1990s. By 2013, charter schools were operating in 42 states and Washington, D.C., and there are more than 6,000 charter schools in the United States, with a total of 2.3 million students (National Alliance for Public Charter Schools 2013). In light of these schools' autonomy from state regulations and school district authorities, some reformers believe that charter schools can develop innovative approaches to

FAST-FORWARD

Education and Change

U.S. schoolchildren in the mid- and late twentieth century experienced their formal education in traditional classrooms. Students sat tall at desks arranged in neat rows and focused on the teacher at the front of the room. Today, with ongoing advances in computer and media technology, as well as in online teaching and learning resources, learners from grade-schoolers to graduate students have a world of information at their fingertips.

teaching and learning—and thus can genuinely offer families a local and public choice, especially in communities with low-performing public schools.

Large-scale research on learning outcomes of students enrolled in charter schools, however, presents a mixed picture. Some studies have found no difference in the academic performance of charter school and public school students, whereas other studies have reported that students admitted to charter schools performed better than public school students who applied to but did not attend charter schools (Renzulli and Roscigno 2011). The most comprehensive examination of charter schools, published by Stanford University's Center for Research on Education Outcomes, found that the charter school student body has become increasingly diverse. Specifically, students from poor households and African American students now represent a higher percentage of charter school students than they do overall public school students. In addition, academic performance among charter school students has improved in recent years, although reading and math scores for charter school students are similar to the corresponding scores of local public school students. Charter school reading scores, for example, are no different from local public schools' scores in 56 percent of cases. Charter schools outperform their local counterparts in 25 percent of cases, but local public schools score higher than charter schools in 19 percent of cases (National Charter School Study 2013).

The Online Classroom

Today's digital technologies mean that education no longer has to take place in the physical space of a school building. In recent years, higher education has moved online at a rapid pace. The largest private university in the United States is the University of Phoenix, a for-profit online institution with over 300,000 students. By 2011, more than 6 million college students, representing 32 percent of the total population of U.S. college students, had taken at least one online course (Allen and Seaman 2013). And millions of people from around the globe who are not enrolled in degree programs sign up for massive open online courses (MOOCs) offered by organizations such as Udacity, EdX, and Coursera (see Map 13.2).

Online education has made it easier for working adults to earn a college credential by making travel to the school site unnecessary and providing scheduling flexibility. But proponents of online courses point to more than just the flexibility they offer working adult students—who are often juggling family obligations in addition to a job and school. These supporters say that online learning makes college more accessible to students from a wider range of backgrounds, saves students and universities money, allows students to earn a degree faster, and helps universities manage demand for limited classroom space (Parry 2010). Questions abound regarding the quality and rigor of online education, the degree of student effort required for online classes, and the training of faculty to use innovative online teaching tools effectively.

Even as online learning opportunities make a college education more widely accessible, the growth in online college programs may be producing a two-tier system of higher education. To date, little comparative research has examined the learning outcomes of online versus face-to-face education. Nonetheless, one highly regarded survey of academic leaders from more than 2,800 colleges and universities found that the academic reputation of online learning is improving.

MAP 13.2 | GLOBAL PARTICIPATION IN COURSERA'S MOOCs

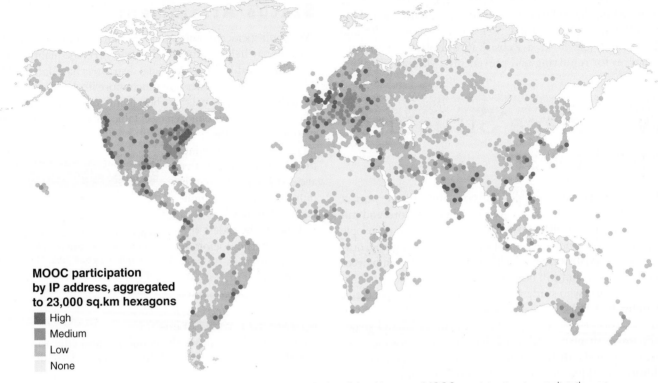

MOOC participation by IP address, aggregated to 23,000 sq.km hexagons

■ High
■ Medium
■ Low
□ None

MOOCs are worldwide phenomena, with participation spanning the globe. However, MOOC participation is not distributed equally. As this map illustrates, MOOC participation is heaviest in the United States, Europe, India, and parts of China and far more limited in Africa, central Asia, and much of South America. *Source:* Olds (2013).

By 2013, 77 percent of the academic leaders rated online education as "at least as good" as a traditional classroom, up from 57 percent in 2003. Still, about one-quarter of academic leaders judge distance learning to be inferior to face-to-face instruction. Concern about the quality of online education is far greater at schools that offer exclusively traditional classroom instruction—and these schools disproportionately are highly selective private colleges (Allen and Seaman 2013). Elite private colleges are likely to retain their focus on traditional classroom instruction, providing one-on-one mentoring and academic guidance that is largely absent from online programs.

Cyberbullying

Bullying and harassment in schools are problems with a long history and no simple solutions. Most school districts in the United States have adopted antibullying policies as part of broader efforts to maintain a safe school climate. In recent years, several high-profile cases of repeated harassment through text messages and on social networking sites, including incidents in Missouri and Massachusetts that involved teenage suicides, have helped make electronic forms of bullying, known as *cyberbullying*, an issue of national concern. What constitutes cyberbullying is still evolving, as are the legal issues associated with electronic and sometimes anonymous harassment.

Cyberbullying usually follows a pattern of repetitive actions, such as sending hostile or insulting text messages, posting inappropriate photos to embarrass someone, and rumor-mongering on social media. Two leading scholars of cyberbullying offer the following definition: "willful and repeated harm inflicted through the use of computers, cell phones, and other electronic devices" (Hinduja & Patchin 2009, 5).

The typical victims and the primary perpetrators are teenagers. Research indicates that cyberbullying "is a prevalent problem, similar to school bullying," experienced by up to one-quarter of students (Wade and Beran 2011, 45). Teachers, parents, and others who work with teenagers point to cyberbullying as a significant social problem, and news media accounts have helped focus public attention on its dangers. Research indicates that cyberbullying can lead to an array of negative consequences, including fear and embarrassment, interpersonal violence, school difficulties, substance use, low self-esteem, and suicidal thoughts (Sabella, Patchin, and Hinduja 2013).

Schools are a primary site for responding to and preventing cyberbullying. School counselors, many of whom are already well versed in the problem of bullying, can educate students and parents about the forms and impacts of cyberbullying, help build programs to offer peer support to victims, work to implement effective school policies

Contemporary Educational Issues and Trends

regarding electronic bullying and harassment, and develop clear guidelines for reporting cyberbullying (Sabella 2012). Recognizing the widespread concern about bullying and cyberbullying in schools, the U.S. Department of Health and Human Services hosts a website (StopBullying.gov) with resources for reporting and preventing cyberbullying.

Workplace Structure and Power

Work experiences are incredibly diverse. Some people work at home; others go to an office, a factory, or a retail store; and still others report to a different job site every day. Some people work for large companies with staff all around the globe, others work for small businesses with only a handful of employees in one location, and still other people are self-employed.

Sociologists who study work examine both the specificity of individual work experiences and the shared features of diverse workplaces. As we will see, broad social and structural forces shape people's work lives, and work is a source of inequality in the distribution of both status and income. In addition, workplaces teach people profound lessons about how power works (see the Sociology Works box).

Elder care is a rapidly growing field. Some elder care providers work in residential settings such as nursing homes and assisted living facilities, whereas others are home health care aides who tend to senior citizens in their own residences. What kind of pay and benefits do you think is typical of jobs in the health care sector?

Occupational Structure and Status Attainment

Work and socioeconomic status are closely connected. Differences in pay help produce, and to reinforce, inequalities of income and wealth. These financial disparities have far-reaching effects, since high earners are much more likely than low earners to live in upscale neighborhoods and to pass on the rewards of their pay to their children (see Table 13.3). As we saw earlier in this chapter, these rewards include the wider educational opportunities that are disproportionately more available to high-income families.

One of the oldest traditions in the sociology of work focuses on **status attainment**, *the process by which people come to occupy a certain level in a social hierarchy.* Status attainment research examines the economic and educational factors that shape an individual's life chances, particularly one's

on social theory

According to the **conflict approach**, groups with more power in a society have an advantage in acquiring good jobs. Think of the job you eventually hope to obtain. What factors determine that job's prestige and earnings?

TABLE 13.3	**AVERAGE HOURLY EARNINGS, U.S. PRIVATE NONFARM WORKERS, SELECT INDUSTRIES, JANUARY 2014**

Industry Sector	Average Hourly Earnings (US$)
Professional and technical services	36.98
Management of companies and enterprises	36.03
Utilities	35.48
Information	33.40
Mining and logging	30.63
Financial activities	30.43
Wholesale trade	27.95
Construction	26.40
Manufacturing	24.65
Education and health services	24.57
Transportation and warehousing	22.72
Administrative and waste services	18.61
Retail trade	16.76
Leisure and hospitality	13.68

Source: U.S. Bureau of Labor Statistics (2014).

SOCIOLOGY WORKS

Kimberly Jones and Educational Publishing

Kimberly Jones has found her sociological training and imagination to be a valuable resource in her job. The recipient of a bachelor's degree in sociology from Cornell University in 2006, Jones works in McGraw-Hill's Reading Department, where she collaborates with the editorial team that develops K–12 reading textbooks and creates online learning tools for teachers and students. Jones was unfamiliar with the sociological perspective until she took Sociology 101, through which she became intrigued by sociology's emphasis on the relationship between the individual and society.

Jones's sociology courses trained her to be a careful and critical reader, learning how to extract important information from articles and books, an essential skill in her work. However, becoming a thoughtful reader was only the first step. As Jones gained confidence in talking with classmates and instructors in the sociology classroom about their readings, she developed vital communication skills, including the ability to present her own ideas about a text and to listen attentively to and absorb different perspectives on that same text. As for the discipline itself, Jones notes that sociology helped her open her eyes and ears to different ways of thinking about issues, a vital skill in all realms of public life. These various communication and critical-thinking skills are essential components of a sociological imagination.

Sociology also gave Jones strong writing and analytical skills—key assets in *any* workplace. Jones stresses the value of writing assignments that required her to examine sociological theory critically. As a sociology major, Jones explains, "you'll learn how to compose well-written essays in which you build and defend your arguments with an engaging style. Learning

all of these skills will take you far as a student"—and in a future career.

Jones focused her study of sociology on business and organizations. Her courses taught her a great deal about what happens beneath the surface in the workplace. For example, Jones learned that there are often complex power dynamics in an office setting and that a person's official job title doesn't always align with his or her power on the job. The ability to recognize these dynamics

Kimberly Jones

and to respect the knowledge that low-ranking administrative staff often have in the day-to-day activities of the workplace has helped Jones successfully navigate a fast-paced and competitive work world. Ultimately, Jones observes, there are "endless possibilities as a sociology major."

> "With some creativity and courage, your sociology degree can take you wherever you want to go."

think about it

1. How are strong communication skills—the ability to listen, speak, and write effectively—helpful in one's work life?

2. How do you think the ability to recognize the complex workplace power dynamics that Jones describes can be helpful in navigating the work world?

---

adult occupation. The classic work in this approach is Blau and Duncan's *The American Occupational Structure* (1967), which mapped the patterns in U.S. work life. Blau and Duncan found that the circumstances that lead some people into high-status or high-paying jobs, and others into lower-status or low-paying jobs, are not based primarily on merit. Instead, the two researchers found that factors such as parents' education, race, and community of residence were major determinants of a person's adult job and earnings.

Blau and Duncan's research was part of a broader trend within American sociology to understand the roots of socioeconomic inequality and to evaluate the degree of social mobility in contemporary societies. Much of this research focuses on people's work lives because work plays such a significant role in shaping how—and often where—we live.

Occupational Prestige and Job Satisfaction

Work-related inequalities extend beyond income disparity. An individual's job is also a source of his or her social status, and some jobs are widely perceived to have higher status than others. Income and status levels of jobs do not always go together. Some jobs are high paying yet not high status; others are high status but not particularly high paying.

We are usually aware of these work-based status differences, and we may respond to people in ways that reflect their (or our) occupational status. For example, you probably are willing to wait patiently for a doctor who is running late to see you, even when you have an appointment for a specific time. But you are probably not going to be as patient if you must wait for help from a store clerk or an insurance agent. Because the profession of doctor is among the most prestigious jobs in the United States, you are more willing to wait for the doctor's attention than you are for that of people—such as store clerks and insurance agents—whose jobs do not carry the same high status.

Various surveys measure what researchers call **occupational prestige,** *collective attitudes about the status of various jobs.* The measure is based on surveys that ask people to rate their view of the prestige of different jobs. In 2009, respondents to one survey in the United States ranked firefighter, scientist, doctor, nurse, and military officer among the most prestigious jobs.

Sociologists also study what makes people happy with their work. A key assumption of their research is that **job satisfaction**—*the degree to which a person is content in his or her job*—is an integral part of one's overall happiness or well-being. Research shows a connection between occupational prestige and job satisfaction, but the link is not as strong as you might expect. One study found that about one-third of people with low-prestige jobs are "very satisfied" with their work and that more than half of those with high-status jobs are "very satisfied" (Smith 2007). However, as Table 13.4 shows, the jobs with the highest levels of satisfaction are not the same as the ones with the highest status. So holding a high-status job is no guarantee of job satisfaction. Research on job satisfaction is more focused on *levels* of satisfaction than on the reasons why people are satisfied—or not—with their work. Still, recent survey research indicates that "the most satisfying jobs are mostly professions, especially those involving caring for, teaching, and protecting others and creative pursuits" (Smith 2007, 1).

The Gender Gap at Work

A central concern for sociologists who study work is the **gender division of labor,** *differences between men and women in access to jobs.* One result of the gender division of labor is that, historically, men have monopolized higher-paying jobs and have therefore earned more money than women. Although the pay gap between men and women in the United States has closed considerably since 1980, the difference between their earnings remains significant. In 2011 the median income for women who worked full time for a full year was 77 percent of men's median income (see Figure 13.5).

As we saw in Chapter 11, sociologists seek to understand the diverse sources and the dynamics of the gender wage gap. One underlying factor is gender socialization, which likely steers girls and young women toward often lower-paying jobs such as preschool teacher and receptionist while encouraging boys and young men to enter higher-paying occupations such as engineer and architect. After marriage, moreover, women are much more likely than men to leave the workforce to care for children, a pattern again reflecting a cultural value.

Another part of the explanation for the gender division of labor is discrimination. Peterson and Saporta (2004) identify three different types of discrimination that might explain the persistent inequality in earnings between men and women:

1. *Allocative discrimination:* Patterns in processes of hiring and promotion that place women in lower-paying jobs than men.

2. *Within-job wage discrimination:* The practice of giving women lower pay than men for doing the same job at the same firm.

3. *Valuative discrimination:* The devaluation and lower compensation of occupations dominated by women in comparison to those dominated by men, even though similar skills may be required.

Peterson and Saporta report that within-job wage discrimination is not a significant contributor to the gender wage gap but that valuative discrimination is. For this reason, advocacy groups working on behalf of equal pay for women emphasize the concept of **comparable worth,** *a commitment to setting salaries for different job titles based on their value to an employer, regardless of the typical gender of those working in such jobs.* In addition, Peterson and Saporta find that allocative discrimination is also a factor; the key moment

TABLE 13.4	JOB SATISFACTION IN THE UNITED STATES

Top Occupations in Job Satisfaction	Bottom Occupations in Job Satisfaction
1. Clergy	1. Roofers
2. Physical therapists	2. Waiters/servers
3. Firefighters	3. Laborers, except in construction
4. Education administrators	4. Bartenders
5. Painters, sculptors, and related artists	5. Hand packers and packagers
6. Teachers	6. Freight, stock, and material handlers
7. Authors	7. Apparel clothing salespersons
8. Psychologists	8. Cashiers
9. Special education teachers	9. Food preparers
10. Operating engineers	10. Expediters
11. Office supervisors	11. Butchers and meat cutters
12. Security and financial services salespersons	12. Furniture/home furnishing salespersons

Source: Smith (2007).

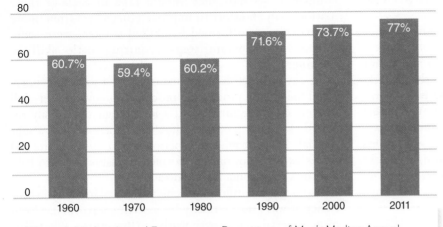

FIGURE 13.5 | THE FEMALE EARNINGS GAP

Women's earnings as a percentage of men's

Women's Median Annual Earnings as a Percentage of Men's Median Annual Earnings, Full-Time Workers, United States, 1960–2011. *Source:* Institute for Women's Policy Research (2013).

CORE CONCEPTS CHALLENGE

What traditions in U.S. **culture** *have been factors in these income differences? As more and more women attain professional jobs in which they exercise* **power,** *do you anticipate that the pay gap will close more?*

that produces lower wages is the point of initial hiring, when women are typically offered jobs that are lower in pay and status than men.

The gender wage gap is not just a problem in low-wage or low-skill jobs. Even among the most highly trained workers, earning differences persist between men and women. One study of University of Michigan Law School graduates showed that male and female lawyers earn about the same in the first year out of law school (Noonan, Corcoran, and Courant 2005). But 15 years later, the female lawyers earned far less than male lawyers with the same training—less than 65 percent of their male counterparts' earnings. The researchers noted that female lawyers work fewer hours than male lawyers and are far more likely to work part time or take time off for child care. However, the authors find little support for these as the reasons that women earn less. In fact, women *without* children earn about the same as women *with* children, and single women earn about the same as married women. Something else must explain the gender earnings gap for lawyers. Noonan and her colleagues concluded that the persistent earnings gap is a result, at least in part, of unequal treatment in the legal profession.

A subsequent study of a nationally representative sample of early career lawyers working full time in private practice (Dinovitzer, Reichman, and Sterling 2009) found evidence of a persistent gender wage gap. Even when controlling for law school credentials, size and type of law firm, areas of law practiced, and city—factors that might explain different pay levels—male lawyers still earned salaries more than 5 percent

higher than female lawyers. The authors conclude that their findings "make clear that in professional settings such as law firms, where work is defined by a complex assemblage and hierarchy of tasks, the mechanisms underlying gender inequity combine to generate a consistent devaluation of women" (p. 847).

Power on the Job

For just about all of us, work is a place where we can see and experience power in action. Let's start with a simple premise: most people who work are not their own boss. They report to, are supervised by, or are accountable to someone else. But some workers operate in the middle of a workplace hierarchy, reporting to their boss while also supervising other employees. With this kind of complexity, how can we understand power in the workplace?

One useful approach, summarized in Table 13.5, is to analyze three key assets—ownership, control, and credentials—that are distinct sources of workplace power (Wright 1985). This approach provides a valuable framework for thinking about power at work and the individual and institutional forces that wield it—owners, managers, professionals, and labor unions.

OWNERS One form of occupational power is the ability to influence broad decisions about the operation of a particular organization or company, including how the firm will operate, who will run the day-to-day operations, and what resources are invested in the company. This is the power of ownership. Owners may not be on the scene every day, but they have a distinctive form of power that is a result of their ownership status. For example, Little Caesar's Pizza founder Mike Ilitch, who owns the Detroit Tigers baseball team, does not make day-to-day decisions about Tigers

TABLE 13.5	SOURCES OF WORKPLACE POWER

Key Assets	Who Has Them
Ownership of capital	Owners of companies
Control of organizations (employees, budgets, decision making)	Managers of companies
Possession of credentials	Highly skilled professionals

games or even hire all of the team's personnel. But he establishes the budget, hires senior management, and has final say on major decisions, including those concerning large investments in players and stadium improvements.

In many instances, ownership lies in the hands of a large group of *shareholders*—individuals who own shares of stock in a company. Shareholders may not exercise power in the same way as an owner, but they can still significantly shape workplace dynamics, especially in the case of those with a large ownership stake. In the early 2000s, major newspapers throughout the United States were forced to terminate newsroom staff when shareholders demanded increased profits through cost cutting. In one notable case, the Knight-Ridder newspaper chain sold its prestigious newspapers in response to shareholders who were not satisfied with the company's financial performance.

MANAGERS

A second form of occupational power is the ability to make decisions about the day-to-day activities at a workplace. This is the domain of a company's managers. Managers have the power to direct other workers—to tell them what to do and how to do it. A given organization may have multiple layers of management, and some managers have more power and authority than others.

The source of managerial power is the organizational hierarchy. A given business or government agency will have formal guidelines that specify managers' roles within the organization and the degree of authority they have. Tigers owner Ilitch has a general manager who is responsible for acquiring players for the team, as well as a field manager who makes daily decisions about the line-up and game strategy.

The source of management's power can be very unstable. Managers, including general managers of baseball teams, are fired all the time; organizations are frequently restructured, and job titles change. That's why managers have sought a potentially more durable basis for power: credentials. Graduate schools of business—which confer the degree of MBA (master's in business administration)—provide managers with a specific credential that certifies their managerial training and differentiates those who hold a degree from those who do not.

The emergence of graduate degrees in business in the early twentieth century reflected a broader trend in U.S. business, as managers sought to develop new strategies for securing power. Many companies adopted engineer Frederick Taylor's philosophy of **scientific management** (also known as Taylorism), *the effort by trained managers to study workflow and develop precise procedures that governed the completion of work tasks.* Taylor's approach rested on time and motion studies that used a stopwatch to measure and examine the specific body motions involved in a given job. Taylor would then

reconstruct the job—identifying the precise way employees should stand and move their arms and legs, and the exact number of seconds they should take in each of these motions—in an effort to improve efficiency. Often, more complex tasks performed by skilled workers were redesigned into separate steps requiring little skill or training.

In Taylor's method, only managers, not workers, understood the overall production process. Moreover, lower-skill workers could be hired, paid a lower wage, and easily replaced. The advent of scientific management marked a substantial change from earlier periods when skilled crafts and trades workers not only performed the labor but also held the knowledge about how to do a job.

Although scientific management claimed to focus on efficiency, it was also a strategy for asserting a particular form of managerial power over workers (Braverman 1998). Today's managers may use different strategies to wield power in the workplace, often relying on the credentials of a graduate degree to legitimize their authority.

PROFESSIONALS

For some employees, workplace power derives almost entirely from having valued skills that are typically the result of a credentialing process that includes specialized training and an advanced degree. For example, physicians typically have an M.D., lawyers have a J.D., and most college professors hold a Ph.D. These are all examples of **professionals**, *a class of workers who are highly educated, hold degrees to certify their education, and have jobs that require a particular form of expertise.* Professionals make up about 15 percent of the U.S. workforce (Gilbert 2011).

Professionals typically have a great deal of control over the conditions of their own work. They are rarely subject to the kind of supervision that nonprofessional workers experience; instead, typical professionals are largely self-directed. Having control over one's own work is a significant form of workplace power.

The power of professionals is rooted in our collective belief in their expertise, which we trust because they have credentials. Perhaps that is why so many professionals—doctors, lawyers, engineers, architects, professors—display their framed diplomas on their office walls. Derber, Schwartz, and Magrass (1990) argue that professionals have learned how to "spin knowledge into gold" by turning their advanced degrees into jobs that generally pay substantial salaries and give them significant control over their own work lives.

An official-sounding credential suggests expertise, usually expertise backed by a professional association that certifies the credential-holder's training. But not all credentials are equal. For example, a financial advisor might have any of the following credentials, and it can be difficult to know what kinds of training or experience are associated with any of the specific titles:

- Certified senior advisor
- Certified retirement financial advisor
- Registered financial gerontologist
- Certified retirement counselor
- Certified financial planner
- Chartered financial analyst

The first four credentials require very little training—less than one week of classroom instruction. In contrast, the final two credentials typically require years to complete and include significant work experience as part of the certification process (Duhigg 2007).

Some professionals are certified experts in management with a graduate degree in, for example, business administration, public administration, or arts administration. Sociologists sometimes refer to these experts as the *professional managerial class*. They typically have the power to supervise and direct other workers, but their power is legitimized further by their education and certification. For *management consultants*, the high-priced experts that companies hire to help them reorganize or solve problems, power comes largely from their credentials as specialists in how to manage an organization. The recommendations of management consultants have the mark of expert objectivity because they are outsiders who have no loyalties to any specific group within an organization. These outside experts have the power and autonomy in their work that comes from their education and claims to expertise.

LABOR UNIONS Most employees do not wield a great deal of individual power in their workplaces. In contrast to professionals, the majority of employees are subject to control by superiors or by organizational rules that specify when, where, and how to work. However, far from being passive actors, employees use various strategies to cope with, oppose, evade, or otherwise act in response to workplace power.

In a widely cited study, James Scott (1992) described the diverse ways that individual employees seek to assert their power. Some arrive late to work, steal supplies or food from an employer, share information about a supervisor's whereabouts with other employees, and engage in nonwork activities during the workday. Greta Foff Paules (1992) studied how waitresses in a highway diner exercised power. Paules found that these waitresses were active agents who defined themselves as independent businesswomen trying to control the flow of people, food, and money or as soldiers fighting against both management and customers for control of the diner floor.

Individual acts of resistance often have little, if any, larger effect, however. When employees organize themselves and work together, they often have more power in the workplace than when they act alone. **Labor unions**, *associations of employees that join together for the purpose of improving their working conditions*, give workers the power to speak to their employers with a collective voice. By joining forces to address management, unions give employees power based on the group's solidarity.

The foundation for unions' power is the possibility that workers will act collectively and demand recognition for their grievances. If employers refuse to work toward a solution, unionized workers may strike to protest working conditions. A strike was the strategy adopted in May 2010 by employees at the Mott's apple juice factory in Williamson, New York. The workers had been unable to come to terms with Mott's parent company, Dr Pepper Snapple, over the company's threat of hourly pay cuts and a wage freeze. When they returned to the bargaining table in September, both sides made concessions. The president of the union local in Williamson commented, "Was it worth it? Yes, because we stood strong and the company knows we're a force to be reckoned with" (Greenhouse 2010, B6).

The basic power of union workers is that their employers need workers—perhaps not any individual worker but the group of employees as a whole. More highly skilled workers, or those in whom a company has invested by training them for specific jobs, often have more power when they organize because they may be more difficult to replace than less skilled workers.

Strikes or work slowdowns are relatively uncommon in the United States. The primary way contemporary labor unions try to exercise power is through collective bargaining. In **collective bargaining**, *unionized workers typically authorize union representatives to negotiate with their employer on questions of pay, benefits, and working conditions*. When union representatives reach an agreement with management, and union members approve the agreement, an employer and a union sign a contract that specifies the terms of the negotiated agreement. These contracts typically specify wage and benefit agreements over a multiyear period, as well as issues associated with work schedules and other working conditions.

The presence of a union generally means that workers receive higher wages and better working conditions, but employers can also benefit. Unionized workers tend to be a more stable workforce. This stability means a higher quality of work and lower employer costs for recruitment and training.

In recent years, though, employers have been exerting their own power in resisting unionization efforts, and the proportion of workers who are union members has declined (see Figure 13.6). Taking advantage of labor laws that generally favor employers, bosses at many companies have actively fought union efforts. Tactics commonly used include firing workers who lead organizing drives, intimidating workers sympathetic to unions in "one-on-one" meetings, hiring consultants from "union-busting" firms, and threatening to relocate

thinking about power

Reflect on a job you have held. Did you have **power** in this workplace? How did you know?

What were some of the consequences of your status?

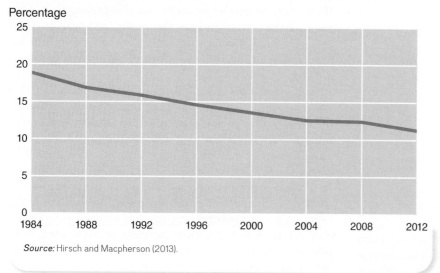

Percentage

Source: Hirsch and Macpherson (2013).

newcomers tips on how to navigate an unfamiliar shopfloor culture.

More informally, in some work settings, new employees go through an initiation process that is usually organized by fellow employees and often not officially recognized by management. The seasoned employees' intent is to teach newcomers the work group's informal rules. For example, when Major League Baseball teams travel to away games, first-year players are typically expected to carry veteran ballplayers' luggage. Experienced coal miners, according to a classic study by Charles Vaught and David Smith (2003), subject new miners to beatings and humiliation in their first days in the underground mine, as a way of "making a miner" out of the new hires. In both examples, newcomers learn

a company abroad to avoid unionization. In the past, these anti-union tactics have been used mostly against private-sector unions, but in recent years, efforts to limit or eliminate unions in the public sector—including those of teachers, police, and government workers—have increased.

Workplace Culture

In the cartoon strip *Dilbert*, frustrated, powerless employees struggle for job survival in an environment in which clueless managers create pointless rules and preside over nasty office politics. Just as workers vary in the kind of power they hold (or, as in the case of the Dilbert workers, do not hold), each workplace has what sociologist Gary Alan Fine (2006) calls a **shopfloor culture**—*a distinctive set of norms and rules that shape daily behavior and interaction on the job*. Likewise, specific occupations have their own norms and rules that help define how to be a baker, a teacher, an electrician, or an accountant.

Workplace and occupational cultures, however, are not always obvious to outsiders. When you begin a new job, you typically have to learn the ropes of the position. The task is far more complex than studying your job description and learning your specific responsibilities. In your first few weeks, you are likely to be socialized, both formally and informally, into the norms of your new work environment and new job.

Formal and Informal Socialization

Many workplaces have an orientation session for new employees to discuss the company's formal expectations. Some workplaces establish formal peer-mentoring programs that pair new employees with experienced workers who can give

Clothing styles reflect trends in the larger culture. In the first half of the twentieth century—an era when formality and tradition prevailed—professional men and women dressed in a tailored, buttoned-down manner. In today's more relaxed business culture, a looser, more individualized corporate look is in vogue. With what broader social shifts—or changes in workplace culture—might these changing norms about appropriate business clothing be connected?

that they are expected to respect old-timers and that each individual employee is subject to the work group's demands.

Much workplace socialization occurs through informal interaction with other employees, supervisors, and clients during the workday. Think for a moment about all the questions you might have on the first day of a new job. For example,

- What should I wear?
- Do I refer to my bosses by their first names or as Mr. and Ms.?
- What tools, if any, should I bring with me to work?
- Is it okay to check my personal e-mail while I'm at work? Will anyone know?
- Do I really have to work overtime if my boss asks me to stay late?

You are not likely to ask these kinds of questions in a formal orientation session. Instead, you will learn the informal rules of your workplace by interacting with others. At first, you'll probably be keenly aware that you do not know the answers to these questions. However, once you are socialized into the norms of the work group, you will know when to show up, what to wear, how to address your bosses, and when it is okay to leave at the end of the day—without having to think about these issues. If you move on to a different job within the same company, you might have to learn the norms and expectations of your new job.

Emotional Labor: Managing Feelings on the Job

When you sit down in a restaurant, you probably expect a friendly smile from your server. If you've ever worked as a babysitter, you may have recognized that your employer expected you to be warm and nurturing. These examples illustrate an aspect of workplace culture that has become increasingly important as service jobs have proliferated in the U.S. economy—specifically, the norms of jobs that involve what sociologist Arlie Hochschild (1983) has called emotional labor. **Emotional labor** describes *jobs that require employees to manage their feelings and to display specific feelings to their customers or clients.* Flight attendants, for example, are expected to smile throughout the flight and to project an attitude of calm reassurance. Those who are successful do not appear to be putting on an act. For service workers, bosses and customers typically expect their "performance of friendliness" (Simpson 2008) to seem genuine.

It is very difficult for a company to formally teach service workers how to manage their emotions in encounters with customers. One study of a chain of British pubs found that workers had little training in "customer care" and typically laughed at the idea that the company could teach them specific techniques for interacting with customers. Instead, new pub employees learned how to deal with customers and the norms of emotional labor from "observing and copying more experienced colleagues, mentoring, 'trial and error,' and other informal on-the-job training techniques" (Seymour and Sandiford 2005, 555). A key source of socialization for new pub employees was after-work conversation with other staff. Informal gatherings with coworkers provided an opportunity for pub employees to share stories and experiences and to learn from their peers about the behavior and rules for customer-oriented emotional labor.

A Changing World

UNCERTAINTY IN THE TWENTY-FIRST-CENTURY WORKPLACE

Workplace trends are tightly connected to the sweeping social, technological, and economic changes of recent years. Globalization—the ongoing worldwide integration of social life, economies, cultures, political systems, and populations—is one noteworthy factor. The development and application of new technologies, and the emergence of new industries, are also contributing to dramatic shifts in people's work experiences in the United States and around the world.

The nature of the U.S. workforce has been changing. Today only a small segment of the population works in agriculture, and the proportion of people in industrial jobs also has declined significantly. New kinds of work have emerged and grown. An increasing number of Americans work in jobs that provide services to other people and to businesses, such as health care, child care, and financial and other support services. And many new jobs are in the information sector, where workers collect, analyze, and store data about individuals and organizations. While remarkable, the changing nature of work is also a source of uncertainty.

thinking about culture

What initiation processes into a workplace **culture** have you experienced? Was there a difference between what you learned through formal and informal socialization? Why?

In today's uncertain employment climate, many jobs, such as that of a pizza delivery driver, require irregular hours, offer limited benefits, and are typically short-term positions.

characterized increasingly by "precarious work," which he defines as "employment that is uncertain, unpredictable, and risky from the point of view of the worker" (2009, 2). Kalleberg points to five components of the rise in precarious work in the United States:

1. Workers' attachment to their employers has weakened; on average, individual employees in the private sector spend fewer years with a specific employer than in years past.

2. Long-term unemployment—remaining jobless for six months or longer—has increased in the 2000s.

3. U.S. workers are more and more concerned about the security of their own jobs, according to surveys; indeed, the perception of job insecurity has risen since the 1970s.

4. A growing sector of the job market consists of jobs that diverge from the standard, full-time, full-year schedule; more jobs are now temporary or represent "contract" work.

5. Employers continue to transfer risk to workers; employee benefit plans continue to shift the burden for retirement and health insurance from employer to worker.

Pointing to the significance of the growth in precarious work, Kalleberg reminds us that "insecurity at work will have pervasive consequences for workers' health and well-being, for family-related decisions such as the timing of marriage and fertility, for decisions to invest in particular communities, and so on" (Kalleberg 2012, 445).

Many workplaces now stress teamwork and flexibility—in contrast to more rigid and hierarchical management traditions. The work-team approach emphasizes employee participation and worker "empowerment." However, researchers have long debated the merits of team-oriented workplaces, with some arguing that teamwork is liberating for workers and others insisting that it is simply a new strategy for controlling workers (Hodson 2001; Tweedie 2013).

The debate is likely to continue. It will be enriched by in-depth research in specific workplaces. Your understanding of structure and action should remind you, however, that as management imposes new work rules, employees will find ways to make sense of—and to respond to—shifting management strategies (Vallas 2007).

In recent years, U.S. corporations have increasingly relied on **outsourcing**, *moving jobs out of the country to take advantage of cheaper labor costs elsewhere*. Asia and Eastern Europe are the typical sites for outsourced U.S. jobs. A wide range of jobs—in manufacturing, information technology, telemarketing, tax preparation, market research, and pharmaceutical research, to name only a few—has migrated from U.S. to overseas factories and offices, where

You will most likely change jobs several times during your adult life and work for different organizations. You probably will even change your career at least once. This employment path will stand in sharp contrast to the experiences of people in your grandparents'—and perhaps even your parents'—generation, who were much more likely to work for one organization for many years, maybe even their entire adult lives. Today, because large employers are far less loyal to their employees than they once were, many young workers assume that they will not be able to retain the same job over the long haul. Younger workers are changing their career expectations to fit contemporary work patterns. As Richard Sennett (2007) observes, these changes pose a new challenge: "how to manage short term relationships, and oneself, while migrating from task to task, job to job, place to place" (p. 4).

Sociologist Arne Kalleberg (2009, 2011) argues that the contemporary employment climate in the United States is wages are typically far lower. Even local news reporting is now being outsourced. The company Journtent hires writers from Mexico and the Philippines to report on community meetings in the United States, which offsite reporters watch online. Journtent's founder, citing the huge volume of work necessary to do reporting on a very local level, explains, "This is how I solved the problem of time; I outsource virtually everything. I'm primarily looking for individuals who I can pay a lower rate to do a lot of work"

(Sheffield 2012). Sociologists who study work are paying careful attention to the significance of outsourcing beyond the workplace, looking at its impact on education, family life, and the changing ties that bind people together in our global economy.

The workplace of the future will surely be different from today's. However, examining the culture, structure, and power relations of tomorrow's workplaces will continue to be a useful approach to understanding these new environments.

thinking sociologically about
Education and Work

culture

- Education plays a vital part in instructing children about the core values of their culture.

- Each workplace has its own distinctive culture, which shapes people's everyday experiences at work. When people begin a new job, they typically undergo a process of socialization, learning the norms and rules of a new workplace culture.

structure

- Schools reinforce social and economic inequality through various, often unintended, means. Since existing inequalities are built in to the structure of the educational system, schools reflect and reaffirm these inequalities.

- Mapping the patterns in work life reveals the contours of the occupational structure in the United States. Research shows that the circumstances that lead some people into high-status or high-paying jobs, and others into low-status or low-paying jobs, are not based primarily on merit but on factors such as parents' education, race, and community of residence.

power

- Education helps reproduce social and economic inequality. Schooling can be a source of power for privileged students—those who have educational advantages, make beneficial social connections, build their self-esteem, and are encouraged to see themselves as future leaders.

- Workplace power is typically based on the possession of key organizational assets, which include ownership of capital (company owners), control of budgets and decision making (managers), and possession of valued credentials (professionals).

REVIEW, REFLECT, AND APPLY

Looking Back

1. Education is vital to the transmission of basic cultural knowledge from one generation to the next. The sociological study of education focuses foremost on schools—the primary arena of formal education—and on the process of schooling.

2. A sociological perspective highlights the various functions of schooling: transfer of knowledge, job preparation, occupational sorting, child care, social integration, change and innovation, and socialization.

3. Schools are among the primary agents of socialization in contemporary societies, teaching broad lessons that extend well beyond specific academic skills.

4. Schools reinforce social and economic inequality through various, often unintended, means. Because existing social and economic inequalities are built in to the educational system, schools reflect and reaffirm these inequalities.

5. Schools are complex organizations that are shaped by policies and rules, their own organizational histories, and wider social forces.

6. With today's digital technologies, education no longer has to take place in the physical space of a school building.

More and more high school and higher education classes are being held in virtual classrooms over the Internet.

7. Work and socioeconomic inequality are very closely connected because differences in work-related income help produce, and reinforce, inequalities of income and wealth.

8. To understand workplace power, we can analyze three key assets—which serve as sources of power—that people bring to their jobs. Company owners have capital assets, managers have control of organizational assets, and professionals possess credential assets. In addition, unions exercise a collective form of power that derives from their members' numbers and significance to a particular company's functioning.

9. Each workplace has its own culture—a distinctive set of norms and rules that shape daily behavior and interaction on the job. When an individual begins a new job, he or she typically has to learn the ropes of the job.

10. Globalization, the development of new technologies, and the emergence of new industries are contributing to change in and producing uncertainty about the work experiences of people in the United States and around the world.

Critical Thinking: Questions and Activities

1. Identify some socialization messages from your school experience. How have traditional and new messages coexisted in your own educational experience? Are the implicit socialization messages you are receiving in college consistent with those from high school? Explain.

2. Would making a college education available to all high school students reduce economic inequality? Why or why not? Consider what your response suggests about the relationship between education and inequality.

3. What do you think are the most important differences between online and face-to-face education? How would

you evaluate the relative effectiveness of these two learning environments?

4. Consider the occupations that are ranked highest in job satisfaction. What, if anything, do these jobs have in common? What do you think are the qualities of a satisfying work experience?

5. How does an employee learn the shopfloor culture at a new job? What are some differences between formal and informal workplace socialization?

Key Terms

bilingual education (p. 367) instruction in both a student's first language and English.

charter schools (p. 367) public schools run by an organization that is independent from local school districts.

collective bargaining (p. 375) negotiations between union representatives and an employer on questions of pay, benefits, and working conditions.

comparable worth (p. 372) a commitment to setting salaries for different job titles based on their value to an employer, regardless of the typical gender of those working in such jobs.

credentialing (p. 364) the process whereby those with advanced educational degrees and formal certificates monopolize access to the most rewarding jobs.

cultural capital (p. 364) forms of knowledge, taste, preferences, and styles that high-status groups use to signal their status and to exclude others from their social circles.

education (p. 353), the social institution through which individuals acquire knowledge and skills and learn cultural norms and values.

emotional labor (p. 377) jobs that require employees to manage their feelings and to display specific feelings to their customers or clients.

gender division of labor (p. 372) differences between men and women in access to jobs.

hidden curriculum (p. 356) the lessons students learn simply by attending school, in contrast to the lessons from the formal subject-specific curriculum.

job satisfaction (p. 372) the degree to which a person is content in his or her job.

labor unions (p. 375) associations of employees that join together for the purpose of improving their working conditions.

literacy (p. 353) the ability to read and write.

moral education (p. 355) the role of schools in teaching children the central values and beliefs of their society.

occupational prestige (p. 372) collective attitudes about the status of various jobs.

outsourcing (p. 378) moving jobs out of the country to take advantage of cheaper labor costs elsewhere.

professionals (p. 374) a class of workers who are highly educated, hold degrees to certify their education, and have jobs that require a particular form of expertise.

racial school segregation (p. 365) the separation of students into exclusively white and exclusively black public schools.

school choice (p. 367) various policies that give families options for deciding which school their children will attend.

schooling (p. 353) organized instruction by trained teachers.

scientific management (p. 374) (also known as Taylorism) the effort by trained managers to study workflow and develop precise procedures that govern the completion of work tasks.

shopfloor culture (p. 376) a distinctive set of norms and rules that shape daily behavior and interaction on the job.

social reproduction theory (p. 361) theory that explores the ways that schools help reproduce systems of inequality.

status attainment (p. 370) the process by which people come to occupy a certain level in a social hierarchy.

tracking (p. 366) placing students into different curricular paths intended to accommodate varying levels of academic work.

14

Media and Consumption

looking AHEAD

How do you experience the **power** of media in your daily life?

How might the role of media in your life be changing as the **structures** of media evolves?

How has the growth of consumer **culture** affected your social life and your community?

In 2002, a drunken Australian fell chin-first on some stairs and bit a hole through his bottom lip. He posted a picture of his injury in a chat room and referred to it as a "selfie," the first known use of the expression. From this undignified beginning, the term gradually caught on, and by 2013 the *Oxford English Dictionary* declared *selfie* its word of the year (Brumfield 2013).

Selfies—informal pictures of oneself taken either at arm's length or in a mirror—are part of a much broader phenomenon. Over half of Internet users have posted original photos to the Internet; over a quarter have posted original videos (Duggan 2013). Snapchat, Instagram, Flickr, and other services have made posting quick and easy.

While many people carefully pose their selfies to present a flattering, often sexualized image, a counterdevelopment has been the growth of unattractive selfies. On the news and entertainment website Reddit, "Pretty Girls, Ugly Faces" couples a "regular" image of a woman with intentionally unflattering selfies posted for humorous effect. But in some cases, unattractive selfies have a more serious goal: to contrast with the carefully managed—and often unrealistic—commercial air-brushed images that advertisers use to sell cosmetics and other products. "The Body Is Not an Apology," for example, is a Facebook website that promotes the posting of uncensored selfies to encourage a "positive body image" (Hills 2013).

Thus the humble selfie embodies some of the developments unique to contemporary media. For the first time, amateurs rather than professionals are producing a growing percentage of the media content we experience daily. In some cases, this self-produced content challenges the onslaught of commercial media that still dominates daily life.

Media saturate our daily lives. We learn about our world, our society, and ourselves through the media's delivery of news and information and through their fictional depiction of social life. Indisputably, media are profoundly influencing our understanding of reality and therefore are of central concern to anyone wanting to understand social life.

Much of the media content that surrounds us is produced and delivered by an enormous multifaceted industry that both sells media products to audiences and sells audiences to advertisers. Consequently, most media are inextricably linked to advertising and to promoting consumption. This connection, too, has had a deep impact on social life by influencing how we spend our time and money as well as how we see ourselves and others.

Today traditional media content produced by movie studios, television networks, music companies, and other commercial firms competes for our attention with user-generated content: the selfies, tweets, Facebook updates, blog posts, videos, and other material created by amateurs and shared with friends or the world. But while this user-generated content is often shared among social networks, it is also involved in the promotion of consumption. Indeed, commercial Internet firms create platforms to facilitate social relationships as a way to attract users that advertisers want to reach. For example, Facebook boasts to advertisers, "Over one billion people like and comment an average of 3.2 billion times every day. When you have a strong presence on Facebook, your business is part of these conversations and has access to the most powerful kind of word-of-mouth marketing— **recommendations between friends**" (Facebook 2013).

In the end, media of all types play a crucial role in socialization and are a central part of contemporary culture. The structure of the media industry, to a large degree, shapes the content of popular media. Media content also reflects broader inequalities in contemporary society. Media help promote consumerism, which reflects differences in economic power in society.

In this chapter we consider both media and consumption in contemporary society. We apply a sociological framework to understand media as a social institution, looking at the interactions among the media industry, media content, audiences, and technology within the broader social context. We then consider the role of consumption in society, examining how it is promoted and the consequences of a consumer culture.

A Sociological Approach to Media

Karl Marx, Max Weber, Emile Durkheim, and other early sociologists never saw television, imagined the Internet, or conceived of a tweet. When they were writing more than a century ago, media played a very different and much more limited role. But as the variety and significance of media have grown, media's role in society has become a central topic of sociological study (Croteau and Hoynes 2014). We begin by defining important terms and describing key characteristics of media, both old and new.

What Are Media?

Media is the plural of the word *medium*, derived from the Latin word *medius*, meaning "middle." **Media** are *the various technological processes that enable communication between (and are in the "middle" of) the sender of a message and the receiver of that message.* Radio is a medium; film is a medium; print is a medium. Collectively, we refer to these as the media. "The media" can also popularly refer to the companies that produce media content, not just to the mechanisms that deliver the content. It is important to remember that media are sociologically significant because they enable and influence communication. Some media are useful primarily for individual communication between users who know each other, such as the traditional telephone. You know specifically whom you are trying to reach; you don't typically dial a number randomly. In contrast, **mass media** *reach a relatively large and mostly anonymous audience.* Unlike personal communication, the content of mass media is publicly available. People who record music, create television programs, make films, or construct websites usually hope to reach large numbers of people without knowing specifically who they are. But, as we will see, the emergence of new forms of digital media has helped blur boundaries between mass media and interpersonal communication.

Characteristics of Mass Media and New Media

The pre-Internet years, from the invention of the printing press in the fifteenth century through the late twentieth century, can be characterized as an era of traditional mass media—including books, newspapers and magazines, radio, film, and television. Traditional mass media typically have four key features:

1. *One-to-many communication.* Mass media allow communication to be delivered from one source to a large audience; they have a *one-to-many* orientation. Television, film, magazines, newspapers, and music are centrally produced and distributed to many viewers, readers, or listeners.

2. *One-way communication.* Traditional forms of mass media are not interactive; they typically enable *one-way* communication that does not permit direct feedback from audiences. For example, when we watch television or listen to a song on a CD, we can't use those media to respond directly to their creators.

3. *Anonymous receivers.* Mass media messages generally have a known sender and are directed at a group of anonymous receivers. For example, when we read a book

or watch a television program, the names of the author or producer are displayed prominently, whereas the book readers and television viewers are anonymous.

4. ***Distinction between producers and audiences.*** In the traditional mass media landscape, a clear distinction exists between producers and audiences. Producers of mass media content are generally professionals working for commercial media companies, whereas audiences are generally individual viewers, readers, or listeners.

Although decades old, the term *new media* is still used to refer to forms of media that are a break from traditional mass media. Traditional media were stored and distributed on separate and distinct mediums such as paper, photographic film, movie film stock, vinyl, magnetic tape, and analog broadcast signals. New media, by contrast, are digital and can be stored as the 0s and 1s of computer code—a technological advance that blurs the lines between text, images, audio, and video mediums. This digital code is often easier and less expensive to copy, store, and distribute than traditional media content due to the declining cost of computers, video cameras, recording equipment, and related software.

Linking digital media to the Internet was the key to the development of the new media landscape. The Internet enables multiple models of communication. People use the Internet for one-to-one communication (e-mail), small-group communication (social networking sites), and forms of one-to-many mass communication (websites, blogs, public videos). The result is a "many-to-many" web of communication, very different from traditional media. This many-to-many model also makes the Internet potentially interactive rather than a one-way form of communication because it gives users the ability to leave comments, post reviews, rate content, register "likes," and so on.

In addition, the traditional mass media idea of known senders and anonymous receivers does not accurately describe the online media environment. Media producers may remain anonymous by using pseudonyms to post material on a blog or website. At the same time, online audiences are not always anonymous; when registration is required to post comments on a website, producers can learn specific details about individual receivers. Even if a user does not register, that individual leaves a digital trace in the form of his or her computer's IP address. As a result, online advertisers and government agencies can know far more about the identity and behavior of Internet users than they ever could in the age of traditional mass media.

Finally, new media blur the distinction between producers and audiences. More people have the capacity to create media than ever before, especially in wealthier nations. Individuals can easily build websites, write blogs, upload videos, and post pictures. Instead of being an *audience* that merely receives media, more people today are media *users*, acting

FIGURE 14.1 | SIMPLIFIED MODEL OF MEDIA AND SOCIETY

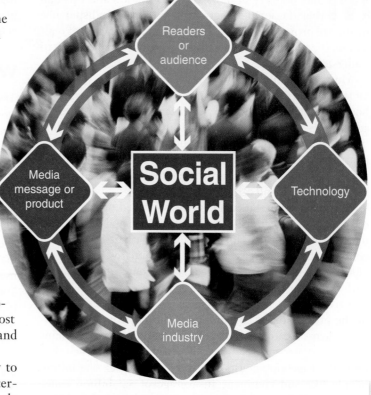

This model of media and society illustrates the complex relationships among media content, media industries, audiences, and technology. A sociological approach to media highlights the bidirectional influence shown in this graphic. For example, the specific content of media messages can influence audiences by shaping how people think; at the same time, audience preferences can have a powerful influence on media content.

simultaneously as producer and consumer of media content (Bruns 2008; Ritzer and Jurgenson 2010).

Figure 14.1 illustrates the dynamics of media (Croteau and Hoynes 2014). The model shows that the media content and the technology used to deliver it are influenced by the actions of two groups—the media industry and audiences or users. Each of these elements is influenced, in turn, by broad social forces—including cultural norms, legal standards, and regulatory practices of different societies.

The two-way arrows connecting the elements of the model indicate that interactions occur in both directions. Each element of the model exerts influence on and is affected by other elements. New technologies, for example, can influence how audiences use media, but the media industry decides how to apply new technologies and audiences ultimately choose whether or not to adopt them. We will look at each element of this media model, beginning with the media industry and the structural trends affecting it.

The Structure of Media

Why do "reality" programs and game shows dominate prime-time network television? Do portrayals of violence in media encourage real-world violence? Why does the news so often seem to focus on trivial or sensational stories? Such questions can be answered by looking at how the structure of media affects industry trends, media content, and the interaction of media with audiences.

Trends in the Media Industries

Formal organizations that make up the media industry produce and deliver the vast bulk of media products. As we saw in Chapter 4 with the case of news reporters, the structure of media organizations influences how media workers do their jobs, helping shape work routines within hierarchical media organizations.

In addition to looking at relationships within media organizations, sociologists also analyze relationships among them. Examining four significant industry trends—company growth, integration, ownership concentration, and globalization—helps us understand how the media industries operate and reveals how industry structure shapes the content of popular media and our experience of it (Croteau and Hoynes 2006).

GROWTH IN COMPANY SIZE

Along with an overall growth in the size of the media industry, media corporations have grown bigger because of mergers and acquisitions. *Advertising Age* compiles an annual list of the 100 largest U.S. media corporations based on their advertising revenue. In 1980 the magazine identified the American Broadcasting Company (ABC) as the nation's largest media company, with about $6.1 billion in revenues (when adjusted for inflation to 2012 dollars). In 2012 the largest media company was Comcast, with nearly $45 billion in revenues (Johnson 2012). The largest U.S. media company today is more than seven times the size of the largest company in 1980.

This growth in scale has significant consequences because larger companies are more influential, have more resources at their disposal, and, as we will see, own a broader range of media content, all factors that help give them considerable power in society.

Hierarchy and conflict within media organizations erupted in a dispute between television writers and the television networks in 2007. The writers wanted to be paid for the use of their work in new media contexts, such as the Internet. Media owners opposed such compensation, arguing that the financial outlook for these new uses of content was unclear. In response, the television writers' union went on strike.

INTEGRATION OF MEDIA COMPANIES

Much of this growth in scale has occurred through integration of media companies. In **vertical integration,** *a media company owns the different stages of production and distribution of a single media form.* For instance, in the book industry one company might own paper mills, printing firms, publishers, and bookstores. **Horizontal integration** occurs *when a media company owns different forms of media.* An example would be a corporation that owns television stations, radio outlets, and newspapers. Figure 14.2 illustrates these two forms of integration; many large media conglomerates are both vertically and horizontally integrated.

Large integrated media corporations have distinct advantages. Horizontally integrated companies can create and promote products that are sold in different media forms: a comic book can be transformed into a television cartoon series and then made into a movie with an accompanying video game. Each form of media helps promote the other. Consider the blockbuster film trilogy *The Hunger Games.* This story about extreme class inequality and exploitative violence for entertainment generated millions of dollars at the box office, but that was just the tip of the iceberg. DVD sales, action figures, a game app, and advertising agreements with Cover Girl makeup, Subway restaurants, and others provided a wide range of additional revenue. There was even talk of a possible Hunger Games theme park (Maloney 2013).

thinking about power

Commercial media are typically produced by hierarchical organizations, where **power** is concentrated in high-level executive positions. Decisions about what to make and how to produce media most efficiently are largely top-down processes. How do you think this top-down process influences media content?

FIGURE 14.2 | VERTICAL AND HORIZONTAL INTEGRATION OF MEDIA COMPANIES

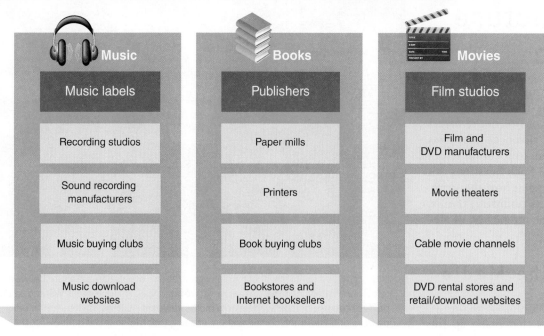

With vertical integration, illustrated in each column, a media company owns different stages of production and distribution of a single media form. Horizontal integration, illustrated by the blue boxes, occurs when one media company owns different forms of media.

CORE CONCEPTS CHALLENGE

How do media conglomerates gain forms of **power** *from having each type of integration?*

CONCENTRATION OF OWNERSHIP As the media become increasingly integrated, ownership of media is becoming increasingly concentrated. Media **ownership concentration** occurs when *more media outlets come to be owned by a diminishing number of media corporations.* Ben Bagdikian (2004) has tracked ownership patterns over the years in various editions of his book, *The Media Monopoly.* When the first edition of his book was published in 1983, Bagdikian determined that 50 media firms controlled the majority of all media products used by U.S. audiences. By the final 2004 edition of his book, he found that just 5 global conglomerates—Time Warner, Disney, News Corporation, Viacom, and Bertelsmann—"own most of the newspapers, magazines, book publishers, motion picture studios, and radio and television stations in the United States" (p. 3). These information and entertainment conglomerates produce and distribute media across a range of media platforms: print, broadcasting, film, and online.

The major media conglomerates have the potential to wield a great deal of political power. Media owners can promote a specific political agenda or support their candidacies for public office through their media holdings. Silvio Berlusconi leveraged his extensive media ownership of television and radio to become prime minister of Italy four times (1994, 2001, 2005, and 2008) before being convicted of tax fraud in 2013 (Ginsborg 2005). In the United States, media

As chair of News Corporation, Australian-born Rupert Murdoch has been known for conservative politics, daring business moves, and "tabloid journalism." Critics argue that Murdoch has used his vast media empire (see Figure 14.3) to influence elections in several countries and to produce journalism and programming that highlight sensational crime stories and endless celebrity coverage. In 2011, a phone hacking scandal at one of his British tabloids had international repercussions.

FIGURE 14.3 | NEWS CORPORATION, SELECT HOLDINGS, 2014

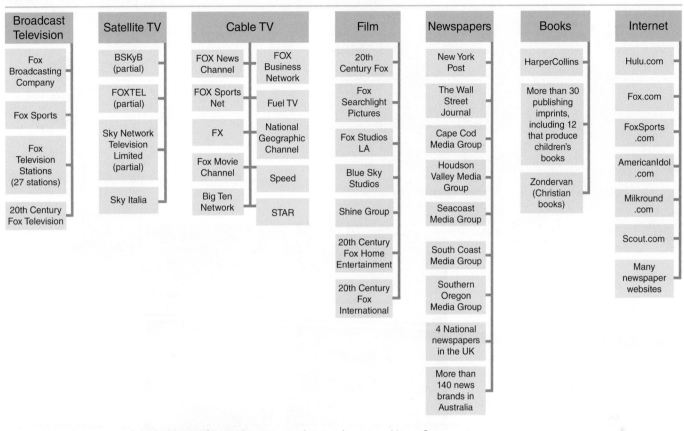

These are just some of the holdings of a single major media conglomerate, News Corporation. Sources: News Corporation and *Columbia Journalism Review.*

CORE CONCEPTS CHALLENGE

Do you think having such a vast portfolio of media holdings helps give a single company too much **power** *in contemporary society? Explain.*

entrepreneur Michael Bloomberg built on the name recognition of his Bloomberg business media products in his successful New York City mayoral campaigns in 2001, 2005, and 2009. Pointing to the vast and far-reaching media portfolios of the major media conglomerates, Bagdikian (2004) argues that the largest media companies have "more communication power than was exercised by any despot or dictatorship in history" (p. 3).

According to media scholar Herbert Schiller (1989), the major media conglomerates typically promote a "corporate voice" that is so pervasive most of us do not even think of it as a specifically corporate perspective. For example, news coverage of the 2008–2009 recession emphasized the perspectives of the business community, paying little attention to the views of everyday Americans (Project for Excellence in Journalism 2009).

GLOBALIZATION OF MEDIA CONGLOMERATES
To varying degrees, the major media conglomerates have become global entities, marketing their products worldwide. A single media conglomerate can own a vast array of media outlets that stretch around the globe. Consider News Corporation, best known for its Fox television network. News Corporation generates about half of its revenue from *outside* the United States (Wikinvest.com 2013). It owns satellite operations around the globe, as well as a variety of media that produce movies, television programs, magazines, newspapers, and books that are distributed around the world (see Figure 14.3).

The success of Hollywood movies was once measured by U.S. box office receipts alone. The *Sound of Music*, for example, was a huge hit in the 1960s, earning more than $158 million in U.S. ticket sales (the equivalent of more than $1.1 billion in 2013 dollars). With the rise of integrated and globalized media conglomerates, however, the business model that studios use to make movies has changed. For example, *Iron Man 3* (2013) made over $400 million at the U.S. box office but almost twice as much—more than $800 million—in overseas ticket sales. To maximize their profit potential in markets outside the United States, major studios tend to look for films with content that will be well-received in other cultures. They reduce risk and maximize profit by following proven blockbuster formulas.

Through a half century of television, some of the best-known white, male, working-class television characters have shared strikingly similar stereotypical characteristics. Ralph Kramden (*The Honeymooners*, above), Archie Bunker (*All in the Family*, right), and Homer Simpson (*The Simpsons*, top right) are all generally lovable but ignorant and doltish.

Media Content

The volume of media content is so vast that sociologists and other media scholars use several approaches to study it (McQuail 2005), including the following:

1. *Compare content between two or more types of media.* How does news reported on television compare with that found in newspapers?

2. *Compare media depictions to social reality.* How does the depiction of women in movies compare with their real-world roles in society?

3. *Examine media content as an expression of broader cultural values and beliefs.* How do music videos reflect contemporary values in the United States?

4. *Evaluate the quality and performance of media based on certain criteria.* How well did the news media perform in its coverage of the most recent election?

5. *Examine the potential effects of media content on audiences.* Do violent video games encourage real-world violence?

6. *Study media content as a text, with its own structure, grammar, and syntax.* How do entertainment "news" programs imitate the conventions of regular news broadcasts?

Because media play an important role in socialization, sociologists have been especially interested in how media content compares to social reality. Even content that is meant to be "just entertainment" and that does not claim to represent reality teaches us about our world. We use the example of class to illustrate this broader point.

IMAGES OF CLASS Society in the United States, as portrayed in the media, is wealthier than it is in real life. Entertainment media—especially television, films, and magazines—disproportionately feature upper- and middle-class characters and underrepresent working-class and poor people. Doctors and lawyers are common, and even shows that portray police—a working-class occupation—tend to focus on better-educated and more highly paid detectives.

The most extensive study of class representation in entertainment television remains Richard Butsch's (2005) comprehensive analysis of more than 300 domestic-based situation comedies that aired between 1946 and 2000. Butsch found that only 14 percent of such programs featured blue-collar, clerical, or service workers as heads of the household. In contrast, more than two-thirds of these programs featured middle-class families. The portrayals of working-class life that did appear were usually unflattering stereotypes, showing the blue-collar workers as bungling, incompetent buffoons.

The media also typically depict labor unions, most of which represent working-class people, in stereotyped ways. William Puette (1992) analyzed representations of labor in television, film, and newspapers and found that unions were often portrayed as protecting unproductive, lazy, and insubordinate workers and as outmoded. In general, union leaders were portrayed as more likely to be corrupted by power than the more educated or cultured business and political leaders. Christopher Martin (2004) found that news coverage of labor disputes tends to favor management. The news media often treat labor strikes as stories about inconvenience to consumers rather than as struggles over economic justice, and they rarely communicate the source and substance of the conflict, accepting often-inaccurate claims from management as fact. Meanwhile, the illegal firing of workers for supporting a union is rarely covered as a news story (Carreiro 2005).

More broadly, news organizations orient their coverage to middle- and upper-class audiences, and provide extensive economic and business news aimed at investors and managers. Other "hard news" usually focuses on people in positions of power, notably politicians, professionals, and corporate managers. Working-class and poor people tend to be featured in crime stories (Croteau, Hoynes, and Carragee 1996; Heider 2004).

CLASS, ADVERTISING, AND MEDIA CONTENT
Media content is connected to the economic aspects of the media process. Back in the 1970s, the ABC television network produced a profile of its audiences for potential advertisers that it titled, "Some People Are More Valuable Than Others" (Wilson, Gutierrez, and Chao 2013, 25). This unusually frank title summarizes a basic reality of commercial media: content is produced to attract audiences that are desirable to advertisers. This insight can help us understand the nature of much media content.

Most media firms operate in what is called a **dual product market,** in which *a company sells two completely different types of "products" to two completely different sets of buyers.* One buyer is the consumer audience, who purchase media products such as books, cable services, movies, and music CDs and downloads. The other buyer is the advertiser, who buys space or time in web and print ads, television and radio commercials, and other media platforms. Most media companies try to attract audiences so that they can sell advertising.

Dual product markets are important because the way they are structured determines who has the power to influence media content. For example, if a television program with modest ratings reaches a demographic group that advertisers want, it may be renewed, whereas a program with higher ratings but demographics less appealing to advertisers might be dropped. Higher income viewers are typically more appealing than low-income viewers because they are more likely to be able to afford many advertisers' products. In fact, for many forms of media, their customer is really the advertiser, not the audience. As a result, audiences may not get the media content they want simply because advertisers want something different.

Media content is also shaped by the desire of media companies not to offend their corporate sponsors. These sponsors have little interest in advertising in media with content critical of them (Herman and Chomsky 2002). Media without corporate sponsors, such as documentary films and books, can afford to present a broader range of critical views.

Netflix's critically acclaimed series *Orange Is the New Black* is set in a federal prison in New York. The racially diverse cast portrays complex characters who often tackle major social issues. The characters pictured here, series protagonist Piper Chapman, a middle-class bisexual woman sentenced to prison for her involvement with drug trafficking a decade earlier, and Suzanne "Crazy Eyes" Warren, a lesbian inmate with a sexual interest in Piper, add another layer of diversity.

CORE CONCEPTS CHALLENGE

What does Orange Is the New Black *suggest about the potential for media to portray diverse* **cultures***? Why do you think diverse images and characters remain rare on television?*

Media content also reflects the broader social inequality in society. Studies exploring media depictions of race, gender, and sexual orientation have found plenty of stereotypes but have also shown that the images of various groups improve as those groups gain more power in society. For example, for decades racial minorities were either excluded from mainstream media or relegated to marginal roles (Wilson et al. 2013). As racial discrimination was tempered and as people of color became a target of advertisers, racial minorities became a more regular staple of media content. The same is true for the increasing inclusion of lesbian and gay characters in television and film. For example, recent hit programs such as *Glee* and *Modern Family* have won acclaim for including diverse characters. The Sociology in Action box explores the efforts of one advocacy group to combat media stereotypes.

The Interaction of Audiences and Media

Do images of rail-thin models contribute to eating disorders? Do antismoking public service announcements have any impact? Since the advent of mass media, researchers have examined the interaction between media content and audiences, exploring how audiences use media as well as how they are influenced by them. As the findings have accumulated, researchers have come to see audiences as active participants in the media process rather than passive recipients of media messages.

SOCIOLOGY in ACTION

Combating Media Stereotypes

"Reality" shows often pander to stereotypes. MTV's *Jersey Shore* regularly used the term *Guido*—widely regarded as an ethnic slur—to describe the cast members and depicted Italian Americans as lazy, beer-guzzling, tan- and hair-obsessed beach bums. The TLC series *Here Comes Honey Boo Boo* (see photo) featured a rambunctious 6-year-old beauty pageant contestant and plenty of classist stereotypes of poor white "rednecks" in Georgia.

For decades, sociologists have been documenting how the media often stereotype groups of people, helping perpetuate racism, sexism, classism, and homophobia. Influenced by the evidence compiled by such research, numerous advocacy groups now track and combat media stereotypes, sometimes using the latest sociological studies. One such group is the Media Action Network for Asian Americans (MANAA). Among other activities, MANAA works "to advocate and provide reinforcement for fair, accurate, sensitive, and balanced depictions of persons of Asian Pacific descent in all facets of the media." As part of that effort, the group has compiled a list of common media stereotypes of Asians and the "stereotype-busters" that the media could employ to combat inaccuracies. Some of these are listed below:

Media Stereotype	Stereotype-Buster
Asian Americans as foreigners who cannot be assimilated	Portraying Asians as an integral part of the United States; more portrayals of acculturated Asian Americans speaking *without* foreign accents
Asian Americans restricted to clichéd occupations (for example, grocers, martial artists, laundry workers)	Asian Americans in diverse, mainstream occupations: doctors, lawyers, therapists, educators, U.S. soldiers, etc.
Asian racial features, names, accents, or mannerisms as inherently comic or sinister	Asian names or racial features as no more unusual than those of whites
Asians relegated to supporting roles in projects with Asian or Asian American content	More Asian and Asian American lead roles
Asian male sexuality as negative or nonexistent	More Asian men as positive romantic leads
Asian women as "China dolls"	Asian women as self-confident and self-respecting, pleasing themselves as well as their loved ones
Asian women as "dragon ladies"	Whenever villains are Asian, not attributing their villainy to their ethnicity
Asian Americans as the "model minority"	Asian characters with flaws and foibles, with whom audiences can empathize
"Asian-ness" as an explanation for the magical or supernatural	Asian cultures as no more or less magical than other cultures

Source: Media Action Network for Asian Americans.

The efforts of researchers who document media stereotyping and activists who advocate for more accurate and diverse portrayal can help make a difference. Media scholar Jack Shaheen has studied film and television images of Arabs for more than three decades. He explains the formula for successfully challenging media stereotypes: "People worked together, until finally they managed to become filmmakers themselves, producing, directing, and appearing in courageous movies that elevated their humanity" (Shaheen 2009, 6).

think about it

1. *What would you include in a list of media stereotypes about college students? What "stereotype-buster" would you suggest for each?*

2. *What TV programs have perpetuated stereotypes? What shows have "busted" them?*

ACTIVE AUDIENCES Active audiences *make choices about how they use the media and actively interpret media content.* But how audiences use and interpret media varies depending on their social position and social characteristics, such as race, class, gender, age, and nationality. In a classic study, media scholars Jhally and Lewis (1992) studied how audiences interpreted the popular 1980s situation comedy, *The Cosby Show.* They found that white and black audiences liked the show for dramatically different reasons. Blacks appreciated the references to black culture and the positive portrayal of a *black* family. Whites, though, tended to see the show as evidence that successful African Americans could be just like whites; they liked the portrayal because it was *nonracial*. In a dynamic observed in many audience studies, *Cosby* audiences were active interpreters of media content, but those interpretations were influenced by their social positions.

Media audiences are also active when they engage in various forms of audience participation, such as calling in to talk radio shows and casting a vote on *American Idol*. In addition, some members of media audiences are actively involved in fan communities where they share opinions on media personalities and media content. They may attend events with other fans or participate in online fan forums. In the digital age, new forms of audience activity have developed, as viewers, listeners, readers, and players post reviews, analysis, and criticism on their own blogs, websites, and Twitter accounts. Increasingly, audiences are active as both interpreters and producers of media in an evolving media environment (Napoli 2010).

MEDIA'S SOCIAL EFFECTS Beginning in the 1940s, studies emphasized media's power to *influence* audiences. One theory, known as the *hypodermic model* of media influence, suggested that media could inject ideas into the public mind, much like a hypodermic needle. Another approach, *mass society theory*, argued that modern society has experienced a decline in traditional social bonds, such as the family and the neighborhood, leaving audiences susceptible to the influence of mass media.

Later studies, however, incorporated an appreciation for active audiences, leading to a more nuanced view of media effects. For example, **agenda-setting theory** *holds that media may not be able to tell people what to think, but they can significantly influence what people think about.* They do so through their emphasis (or silence) on various issues. This effect is especially true for the news media, but entertainment media, too, can raise or stifle awareness of specific social and political issues.

Through constant exposure, media can influence our view of reality. **Cultivation theory** *argues that by repeated and long-term exposure to the media's portrayal of the world (especially on television), people come to accept many of these depictions as reality.* Local broadcast news programs are notorious for emphasizing crime, fires, and accidents. Such relentless media images inflame public anxiety and contribute to a "culture of fear," leading people in the United States to be "inordinately fearful of unlikely dangers" (Glassner 2009, xii). Over the long term, heavy viewers of such broadcasts are more likely than light or moderate viewers to believe that the world is dangerous, people cannot be trusted, and most people are selfishly looking out for themselves (Gerbner et al. 2008). In effect, by being exposed to constant images of danger and violence, people come to believe that this depiction accurately represents their community.

Media effects are difficult to prove definitively because we experience many influences at once in our complex social environment. Nevertheless, numerous studies using various methodologies have given us significant insight into the media's social influence.

The Explosive Growth of Media

Daneane Gallardo is located in Kitchener, Ontario, but she lives on the Internet. She coordinates website development for a living, so she is online all day long. But her media use doesn't stop there. Reading the posts in her e-mail groups, exchanging instant messages, updating her blog—these take up more hours of her day. Her life is spent in the electronic cocoon of media. As she jokes, "If I didn't have to eat, pee, and have sex, probably I'd have no need for the 3-D world" (Hof 2005).

Media have become fully integrated into most waking moments of our daily lives. People in the United States spend more time producing and consuming media than any other single activity except breathing (Ransford 2005). Arguably no other change in contemporary life has been as far reaching and influential as the explosive growth of media.

Media Growth and Saturation

This media saturation has changed not only *what* we see and hear, but also *how* we interact with our world. As in Gallardo's case, more and more of our connection to the world is filtered through media, rather than generated through face-to-face personal contact. We often interact with our family and close friends through various communication media; some parents even wake up their school-age children via text message. Most of the music we hear is recorded rather than live. Increasingly, we learn about and discuss politics online rather than in our local communities. Students may contact professors via e-mail or even take entire courses online, rather than meet face-to-face. In whatever form, we spend increasing amounts of our life with media. Just ask yourself: how much time do you spend on Facebook?

How we use media varies, depending on the social context. Sometimes we focus closely on one form of media, as when we watch a movie in a theater. Other times, media are background to other activities, as when we drive with the radio on. Often, people use multiple forms of media simultaneously, such as listening to music while surfing the Internet. This multi-tasking makes it difficult for researchers to get a precise measure of media use.

The various media devices that surround many people enable them to multitask. Fragmented attention to multiple media content has become a hallmark of contemporary life.

FIGURE 14.4 | BREAKDOWN OF AVERAGE DAILY MEDIA USE

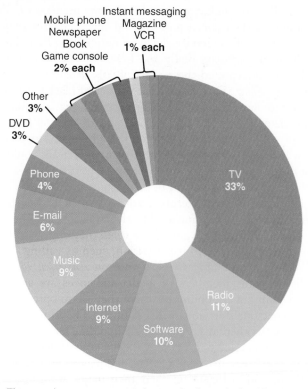

This pie chart summarizes the results from the Middletown Media Studies II project, a study that tracked the different types of media people use on a typical day. *Source:* Holmes and Bloxham (2007).

People dramatically underestimate the amount of time they spend with media (Papper, Holmes, and Popovich 2004). This tendency causes a problem for researchers who estimate media use based on surveys and individually kept records. To address this problem, some researchers followed nearly 400 individuals in Muncie, Indiana, for an entire day in 2005 to observe and record their media use at 15-second intervals. This approach enabled researchers to note whether individuals were using multiple forms of media simultaneously and whether they were carrying out other activities while they used media (Finberg 2005; Holmes and Bloxham 2007).

The study found that people used media an average of 8 hours and 41 minutes a day—about two-thirds of the time they were observed. During nearly a third of the time they spent with media, the research subjects used multiple forms of media simultaneously. Adding up the multitasking separately brought the total exposure to media to 12 hours and 2 minutes—significantly higher than the Census Bureau's estimate. As Figure 14.4 shows, television took up the largest share: just over 4 hours a day (33 percent). Overall, about 30 percent of the individuals' waking day was spent focused exclusively on using media. Another 39 percent of the time, they used media while engaged in some other activity. And there is evidence that this consumption continues to increase. A 2013 analysis of media usage—counting multitasking separately—estimated that U.S. users consume over 13 hours a day, 60 percent of which is devoted to television and radio (Short 2013).

The recent growth of media is due partly to the changing nature of media technology, which has made it possible for different forms of media to converge and has enabled the rise of portable media devices.

Media Convergence

Historically, different forms of media were marked by clear boundaries, and some still maintain distinct characteristics—for example, print newspapers do not have sound, and radio has no images. But one of the most significant developments in recent years has been media **convergence,** *the merging of different media forms.* Digital technology that makes it easy to transfer information across different media platforms has accelerated this convergence. A digital image can easily be converted to print, television, the Internet, DVD, or a host of other media formats.

Individual types of media can also deliver multiple forms of media content. The Internet can be used for personal communication (e-mail) or for mass communication (websites, e-blasts, and blogs). You can use it to send a message in the form of text, audio, or images. Even older forms of media, notably the telephone, have been reinvented as all-purpose media devices. Today's cell phones allow users to make personal calls, send text messages, listen to music, watch television, take photos and videos, and access the Internet, all while being completely portable.

User-Generated Content

Traditionally, formal organizations created mass media content. Today, however, **user-generated content** is *created by ordinary media users rather than by media organizations and is available to a potentially large audience.*

Users have always created media content. For decades, picture albums have housed family photos, home movies have starred wobbly toddlers, tapes have captured garage band performances, and yearbooks have immortalized high school seniors. Today, however, user-generated content can potentially reach a mass audience, not just family and friends. Ordinary YouTube stars, relatively unknown bands with a cult following, and podcasts aimed at a niche audience are all possible with today's media technology. More than ever, media-based information and entertainment that sidestep the media industry are available for potentially widespread distribution. Most will never develop a large audience, but some will.

Among the many forms of user-generated content are the following:

■ Personal websites created and controlled by an individual or a small group working together can serve as a platform for other media forms such as music recordings, blogs, photos, and videos.

■ Some commercial websites allow users to create or upload content. Examples include YouTube and Facebook, as well as book publishing sites such as CreateSpace and Lulu.

■ Individuals can create user-generated content by manipulating existing content (often illegally) by sampling, altering, and recombining to make mash-ups, parodies, and other hybrid creations. For example, well-known music is sometimes remixed into new forms and distributed online, a process made famous early on by Danger Mouse's *Grey Album*, combining lyrics from Jay-Z's *Black Album* with samples from the Beatles' *White Album*.

■ More broadly collaborative user-generated content, such as a *wiki*, a website, or other online resource, allows users to add and edit content. No single user is responsible for the content on such sites. Wikipedia, the collaborative online encyclopedia, is the most well-known form of wiki media.

Regardless of the type, user-generated content is an alternative to the traditional industry-generated media experience.

User-generated content is not without costs, however. This unfiltered and unregulated media environment can include disturbing material. Racist hate groups, for example, have flourished on the Internet. Their websites can help link far-flung individuals who share a racist ideology. Child pornography, bomb-making instructions, and other forms of potentially dangerous content can also flourish. Terrorists have made good use of encrypted e-mail communications, voice-over-Internet audio, and websites. Such user-generated sites can feature political analyses; instructions on how to carry out violent attacks; and videos of incendiary speeches, attacks on U.S. soldiers, and even ghastly beheadings of kidnap victims. It is possible to post this content while maintaining anonymity (*The Economist* 2007).

Functions of Media

Reading this book gives you access to information. Watching a movie or listening to the radio can entertain you. Creating a web page on a social networking site can enable you

Because the Internet is unfiltered, it can serve as a platform for user-generated content—like this white supremacist website—produced by groups that promote hate and violence.

CORE CONCEPTS CHALLENGE

*How might hate groups take advantage of the Internet to build and sustain a racist **subculture**? How might the Internet be used to combat such efforts?*

to meet people and stay in touch with friends. Clearly, the many hours we spend with media serve different functions for us personally. The media serve similarly varied functions for society as a whole.

SOURCES OF INFORMATION Media serve as the storehouse and conduit for a society's accumulated knowledge and information, from the mundane to the profound. By examining media content, we can learn everything from the latest sports scores and celebrity sightings to vital medical information and the policy positions of political candidates. In recent years, media have made information more accessible more quickly than ever before. This development has transformed human society. Whereas information once was scant and difficult to obtain, a central challenge now is to make sense of the glut of information at our fingertips.

AGENTS OF SOCIALIZATION When a man was stopped for a traffic violation in Virginia, he tossed a box from his car window. The police discovered that the box contained 60 rocks of crack cocaine. The jury at the subsequent drug possession trial found the man "not guilty," largely because the box was never tested for fingerprints. This case was one of many in which juries have acquitted suspects on charges that, in the past, would have routinely resulted in guilty verdicts. Criminal prosecutors and police believe the primary reason for the rise in acquittals is that many jurors have watched a popular television police drama, *CSI: Crime Scene Investigation*, which highlights the extensive use of forensic evidence to solve crimes. They refer to jurors' increased and unrealistic expectation that detailed forensic evidence will be collected for all crimes as the "CSI effect" (Hooper 2005; Stockwell 2005).

The "CSI effect" is one example of how media can socialize us by telling stories and informing us about our culture and its norms. Even media content that is obviously "just entertainment" can influence how we interpret the world and alter how we see reality. The same is true for thousands of other aspects of social life that we learn about through the media filter. The media even provide models of appropriate behavior for the various social roles that are part of our lived experience, such as friend, parent, and citizen.

Our steady diet of media content informs and entertains us and, over time, influences how we come to understand ourselves, our society, and our world. Indeed, most of what we know about the world has reached us through the media. Media socialization can be especially influential for children. They have limited life experience and have not yet fully developed their own identity, and yet they are increasingly barraged with media messages on TV and the Internet. Children, in fact, spend more time with media than they do in the classroom, interacting with their parents, or engaged in physical activity (Rideout et al. 2010; Roberts, Foehr, and Rideout 2005). This constant media exposure shapes their understanding of the world.

PROMOTERS OF IDEOLOGY The contest to control the media's messages—and thus its ideological influence—does not take place on an even playing field. Those with more power in society generally have greater access to the mainstream media to promote their ideas. That access is one reason why the issue of who owns and controls the media is such an important topic. User-generated content cannot compete with the deluge of media messages emanating from commercial media sources.

In discussing stratification in previous chapters, we defined ideology as a system of beliefs that justifies the existence of social inequality. But ideology also helps us define, explain, and make value judgments about the world more broadly. The dominant ideology promotes the interests and reflects the worldview of the powerful. As we will see, the media's ideological function is not carried out by a single depiction in a newspaper or movie, but through the cumulative effect of exposure to many such depictions—and to the persistent absence of other depictions.

For example, U.S. news media typically take for granted the desirability of free markets, downplaying their negative features. They raise few questions about the growing economic inequality discussed in Chapter 9 or about the exploitation of workers in a global economy. Instead, the vast bulk of economic news coverage is actually "business" news, presented from the perspective of investors and managers, not labor representatives (Kollmeyer 2004). As we will see, much media content is linked to the promotion of consumption, with little regard for the social or environmental consequences of consumer culture. Even the recent uptick in environmental news coverage is often accompanied by the call for more consumption—this time of "green" products. The end result is coverage that explains the economic world from a particular perspective and treats this perspective as if it were the only reality.

As the media carry out their various functions, they are enmeshed in a variety of social relationships that make the media a key social institution. To understand media as an institution, we need to look at how power influences the media and is used by them.

Power and Media

Some scholars have heralded the media's compression of time and space as a new stage of human history. Canadian media theorist Marshall McLuhan (1911–1980) famously argued that the "medium is the message," meaning that the most significant feature of contemporary media is their technological capabilities rather than any particular content. McLuhan (1964) wrote that, with the rise of electronic media, "We have extended our central nervous system itself in a global embrace" (p. 19). He foresaw the rise of a "global village" in which media would bring people across the planet closer together.

The Effect of Social Inequality on Media Use

In the years since McLuhan wrote, global communication has become a reality, but it is tempered sharply by social inequality. The **digital divide** refers to *the gap between those who have the knowledge and resources needed to use digital information technology*, *especially computers and the Internet*, *and those who do not*. Class is the primary determinant of this digital divide. For example, in 2013 more than 88 percent of respondents from U.S. households with incomes of at least $75,000 had a broadband (high-speed) Internet connection at home, but only 54 percent of households with an income below $30,000 had such a connection (Zickuhr and Smith 2013; see Figure 14.5).

The biggest digital divide exists between wealthy and poor nations. Comparable figures can be difficult to obtain, but as of 2012 the percentage of the population with Internet access (known as the "penetration rate") ranged from a high of 78.6 percent in North America to a low of 15.6 percent in Africa (see Map 14.1). Global media expansion has developed very unevenly, following preexisting lines of economic inequality. Rather than being a "global village," the bulk of the world is still left out of the advances in media. To a large degree, the Internet is the preserve of the world's elites.

Inequities in media access vary by medium but include all forms of media. For example, television is far more prevalent than just a decade or so ago, but it is still rare in some poor and rural parts of the globe. As access to various forms of media expands to more of the earth's population, media's influence will continue to grow, playing an increasingly important role in social life. However, social inequality in the broader society will continue to create inequities in media access and use.

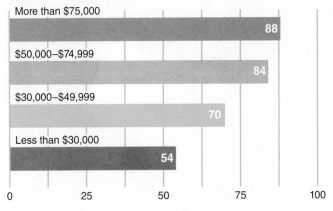

FIGURE 14.5 | THE U.S. DIGITAL DIVIDE, 2013

Household income

Percentage of U.S. households with broadband

Broadband Internet access increases with household income. Although the vast majority of higher-income households have a high-speed connection, many low-income households do not.
Source: Zickuhr and Smith (2013).

MAP 14.1 | GLOBAL DIGITAL DIVIDE: INTERNET PENETRATION RATES, JUNE 2012

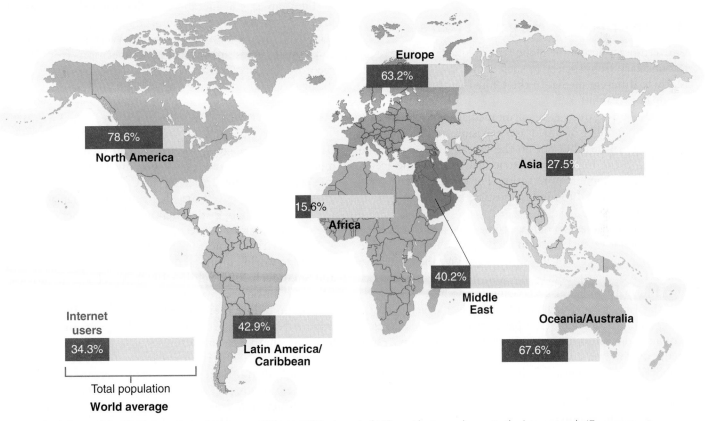

Much of the world still lacks access to the Internet. Whereas 78 percent of U.S. residents can log on to the Internet, only 15 percent of Africans are able to do so. Such dramatic discrepancies in Internet access help sustain substantial inequality in information access and communication capacity, which can have political and economic consequences. *Source:* Internet World Stats (2013).

CORE CONCEPTS CHALLENGE

In what ways can access to the Internet be a source of **power***? How might the "digital divide" help perpetuate global inequalities?*

Economic inequality across the globe locks the world's poorest out of access to media technology. However, cell phones have become the "poor person's computer" in many developing countries, providing access to the Internet, banking services in rural areas without banks, and texting services that deliver health information, weather forecasts, political news, and more. Solar-powered cell phones are popular in areas with limited or no access to electricity.

Global Media and Cultural Imperialism

In mid-November 2013, the movie *Thor: The Dark World* topped that week's U.S. box office revenue. At the same time, it was also the number one movie in 23 other countries (see boxofficemojo.com). This particular week's box office results were nothing special; it is common for U.S. movies to dominate theaters worldwide.

This U.S. domination of the global film box office is one example of **cultural imperialism**, *the tendency of media corporations from wealthier nations—especially the United States—to export so many of their media products that they come to dominate the local cultures of other, especially poorer, nations.* But films—especially big-budget Hollywood films—are somewhat unique in that they are so expensive to produce. India has a massive film industry of its own, widely known as Bollywood, and there is a large but low-budget movie industry in Nigeria, often referred to as "Nollywood," but few other countries have the scale of capital investment in facilities necessary to produce big-budget films. The introduction of digital cameras and editing programs is lowering the costs of filmmaking, but the economic gap between wealthier and poorer nations remains enormous.

The gap is considerably smaller for other forms of media. It is relatively cheap to produce high-quality music recordings, for example. As a result, Western and American music faces much more competition from local recording artists (forcing MTV to include local artists in its programming outside the United States). Still, just three conglomerates—Sony (Japan), Universal (United States), and Warner (United States)—account for nearly 90 percent of album and digital track sales (Nielsen 2013). Because of language differences, print media tend to be much more diverse and less likely to be dominated by U.S. media products. Nevertheless, the United States and other Western nations have unrivaled resources when it comes to promoting their media, making their impact on other societies a very real concern.

Some critics argue that media globalization will homogenize world culture and erode local cultures (Hamm and Smandych 2005; Schiller 1992). As television, movies, film, and music become globally mass-produced, cultures may begin to lose their distinctive elements. In response, some governments provide financial support to nurture a local alternative to imported foreign media. More than seventy countries participate in an International Network on Cultural Policy that seeks to "create an international environment that values diversity, creativity, accessibility and freedom" (International Network on Cultural Policy 2010).

Government Regulations

Governments across the globe regulate media. These regulations vary from society to society and are applied differently to different media. In the United States, for example, companies cannot advertise cigarettes on television, but they can buy cigarette ads in print media, and there are limits on the number of broadcast television stations that one company can own but not on the overall number of radio stations. Many regulations restrict activities of the media industry, but some require action. For example, drug companies are required to disclose possible side effects of their medications in ads.

Media companies typically welcome some regulations, such as copyright laws and licenses to use the public airwaves. These regulations protect their investments and give them exclusive control over their products. In some cases, media industries avoid formal regulation by policing themselves, as with the movie rating system initiated in 1968 by the movie industry.

Overall, the United States has relatively few media regulations. Some European countries have many more, especially on children's media. Some nations require that news, public affairs, religious, and children's programming run for thirty minutes before a commercial break. Others restrict the broadcast of violent programming during hours when children might be watching.

thinking about structure

Government regulations have an impact on the **structure** of media in the United States and in other countries. In what situations, if any, do you think the government has the right to regulate media structure and content? Explain.

In Singapore, a country with a large Muslim minority, a woman in a traditional headscarf walks past a Western-style advertisement featuring women in revealing bathing suits. The clash between Western media content and the different cultural values found in many societies is part of the debate regarding cultural imperialism.

The Impact of Technology on Society

What effects might the nonstop advances in media technology have on our society? New media have many widely celebrated advantages, including increased connectivity, easier access to information, and a democratization of content creation. But a variety of analysts argue that new media technologies also have negative social consequences.

Traditional print media are generally read in a linear fashion, which is ideal for contemplation and rational thought. Books store a great deal of information. But the creation of books is a slow process, and access to the information in them is limited to those who are both literate and sufficiently disciplined to stay focused on an extended linear presentation.

In contrast, media developed since the mid-twentieth century—particularly television and online media—are immediate, easy to access, and often emotionally engaging. These media lead to a preoccupation with the immediate, as with "live" news and entertainment, constantly updated websites, and instant messaging. They also use fast-changing images that evoke emotions, or hyperlinks that connect—but also fragment—bits of information.

The result of these new technologies is content that can be fast, fleeting, fragmented, and often insubstantial. Maggie Jackson (2008) argues that our embrace of new media has produced a sort of attention-deficit culture—characterized by constant stimulation, interruption, and multitasking—that provides little intellectual nutritional value. This culture undermines our ability to focus, concentrate, and attend to the deeper and more substantive issues in life that are the bedrock of intimate social relationships, wisdom, and advances in culture.

Experimental evidence from neuroscience suggests that surfing the Internet develops different neural pathways in the brain than does reading a book. The constant stimulus that characterizes the contemporary media environment contributes to a decline in people's ability to focus, concentrate, and engage in serious thought (Carr 2010).

The ability of the Internet and mobile devices to connect people is typically celebrated as one of its greatest features. William Powers (2010) agrees but argues that wisdom, insight, and perspective are gained from being *disconnected*; by creating time and space for solitude and contemplative thought. A healthy and vibrant life in the digital age, he argues, needs to involve a balance between the advantages of connectivity and the benefits of solitude.

Some critics suggest that, despite the world of knowledge at their fingertips, the generation that has grown up with new media is less informed, less literate, and more self-absorbed than any that has preceded it (Bauerlein 2008; Twenge 2006). They point to the popularity of social networking as one source of the problem. The immediacy and personalized nature of social networking, these critics argue, emphasizes the value of newness and promotes an extreme focus on the self and an immediate network of friends. Information or news that isn't about this narrow world is often of little interest. The result is a worldview that promotes entitlement and self-centeredness, what Jean Twenge (2006) dubbed "Generation Me."

This all-encompassing world of fast, fragmented, fleeting images is a part of what some observers contend makes our postmodern period of history unique. Most famously, French scholar Jean Baudrillard (1988b) argued that in many ways we experience **hyperreality,** *the condition in which media depictions of the world replace the experience of the "real" world.* Increasingly, our lives are saturated by a near constant stream of media images that can create a reality all its own. A simple

When Gannett launched *USA Today* in the early 1980s, it became the symbol of how electronic media were changing the newspaper business. The paper relied on bright, colorful graphics, kept stories very short, and highlighted entertainment topics over more substantial news. The vending machines designed to sell the papers, with rounded corners and a pedestal format, resembled television sets.

example of hyperreality is the familiar "photo opportunity"—an event created specifically for the purpose of being covered by the media. When the news becomes coverage of an event created precisely for media coverage, media reality supplants the "real" world.

As Neil Postman (2005) argues, electronic media have shifted the emphasis so dramatically from matters of substance to fleeting entertainment that we are in danger of "amusing ourselves to death." He and other observers (Downie and Kaiser 2003; Henry 2007) contend that this emphasis on immediate, engaging visuals has contributed significantly to a loss of substance in our media culture.

As media have come to permeate society, they have been accompanied by relentless messages promoting consumption. These messages have contributed to the rise of consumer culture, a defining characteristic of contemporary society.

Consumer Culture

Twenty-five-year-old Reema Patel thinks that "the first class in college should be about credit cards." That's because by the time she was 21 she had accumulated $28,000 in credit card debt and has been working hard to pay it off

ever since. Like many college students, Reema was sucked into the trap of easy credit and the allure of consumer culture, spending much more than she should have on travel, shopping, and partying. Reema's experiences occurred at the peak of easy credit on college campuses. Since then, the Great Recession has prompted belt-tightening, and passage of the Credit CARD Act of 2009 reformed industry practices and led to tighter lending standards. Consequently, the use of credit cards by college students has declined dramatically. Just 30 percents of students had a credit card in 2013—less than half of the percentage that had one a few years earlier. About a third (32 percent) pay their balance in full each month, and nearly half (46 percent) carry a balance of less than $500, a far cry from the period of easy credit (Sallie Mae 2013).

Easy credit is just one feature of a broader consumer culture that incessantly promotes **consumption,** *the process of choosing, purchasing, and using goods.* A sociological approach to consumer culture emphasizes its economic, political, cultural, and social dimensions (Zukin and Maguire 2004). To sociologists, consumption

- Is structured by the economic institutions, political regulations, and social norms that help organize the production and sale of consumer goods
- Is promoted through advertising and the media
- Involves the values, beliefs, and behaviors of consumers who, beyond meeting basic needs, use consumption to form and express their identities

Humans have consumed basic goods—such as clothing, tools, and simple household goods—for centuries. But modern technological advances—especially the rise of industrialization and capitalism—fundamentally changed the nature and significance of consumption as a social process. (The Sociology Works box explores an applied sociologist's efforts to better understand consumers.)

The Rise of Consumer Culture

Consumer culture in the United States and Europe emerged in the late nineteenth and early twentieth centuries, enabled by several key developments:

- *Industrialization made it possible to produce an unprecedented quantity of goods.* Factories could mass produce a surplus of common personal and household items.
- *Mass production greatly reduced the cost of many items, making them affordable to a much larger number of people.* More people became consumers of manufactured goods rather than producers of their own items. Fewer clothes, for example, were made in the home as more were purchased in stores.
- *The immense capital investments needed to create mass manufacturing facilities gave rise to larger, more centralized business firms.* Eventually, the production and sale of most consumer goods shifted from craftsmen and small merchants to large corporations and retail chain stores.

SOCIOLOGY WORKS

Hy Mariampolski and Consumer Research

Hy Mariampolski has been hired by the likes of Nissan, Clorox, Citibank, Microsoft, McDonald's, and dozens of other well-known corporations as well as numerous not-for-profits. With a Ph.D. in sociology, Mariampolski moved into consumer behavior studies after trying out work in an academic setting. Mariampolski and his spouse and business partner, Sharon Wolf, run a firm that specializes in qualitative data on how consumers use everyday products. Although the company, QualiData, conducts focus groups and interviews to learn about some consumer needs, it is best known for pioneering the use of ethnographic research in marketing.

Ethnographic research involves taking account of evolving cultural habits and observing consumers as they buy various brands and use products in their homes and workplaces. Mariampolski (2001, 2005) has written two books teaching these research methods and shares his tools and techniques in workshops he conducts worldwide. Firsthand observations in natural settings can shed new light on how customers use products, on their frustrations with product design, and on how they may use products in ways that manufacturers never intended. Such insights help manufacturers design better products and market more effectively to consumers.

Mariampolski likes to think of himself as representing the "voice of the consumer," providing manufacturers with feedback on what people like and don't like. For example, one of his projects highlighted how working-class men avoid many pain relievers because they cause drowsiness, which can interfere with their ability to perform their jobs. His firm was also involved in a variety of ad campaigns involving sexual health. He helped condom manufacturers find more "life-affirming" ways to advertise that encouraged consumers to integrate condoms into their "natural eroticism." "People are not necessarily motivated by ads threatening them with death," Mariampolski bserved.

Mariampolski endorses the trend among consumers that demands more socially responsible business practices, such as caring about nutrition and the environment. Nevertheless, he sometimes gets criticized for "his enthusiastic endorsement of free-market capitalism" that runs counter to sociologists whose research documents the negative effects of consumer culture and corporate advertising. Mariampolski, though, is comfortable in his alliance with corporate America. "We help corporations implement their good intentions," he says. "We're not outside throwing bricks" (Rice 2007).

> "I use my [sociology] background and knowledge every day of the week when I explain to my clients how their products may have to be adapted for new or growing demographic categories."

Hy Mariampolski

think about it

1. *Should sociologists use their knowledge and research techniques to help companies market their products effectively? What ethical issues, if any, might this form of research raise?*

2. *What insights might you gain from observational research that you might not learn from an interview or a focus group?*

■ *Over time, competition to produce and sell goods more cheaply came to dominate much of the consumer market.* As part of this process, manufacturers introduced **planned obsolescence,** *the intentional design and manufacture of consumer goods so as to ensure a loss of utility in a relatively short period of time.* Products made cheaply could sell for less but would also break or become outdated more quickly, fueling another round of profitable consumption.

■ *Excessive manufacturing capacity contributed to the rise of advertising as a way to promote more consumption.* Advertising also generated new kinds of consumer "needs" (Ewen 2001). As Stephanie Coontz (1992) notes, with the rise of consumer society, "The word consumption increasingly lost its earlier connotations of destroying, wasting, or using up, and came instead to refer in a positive way to the satisfying of human needs and desires" (p. 170).

Even when consumer culture was still in its infancy, it did not escape the notice of early sociologists. In the late nineteenth century, Karl Marx in particular considered the links between the changing methods of production and the new culture of consumption.

Alienated Labor and Commodity Fetishism

Have you ever experienced the satisfaction of doing it yourself—say, repairing a car, completing a craft project, or creating a website? For Marx, work that we engage in to meet our human needs is, ideally, creative and satisfying. Growing food, building a home, or knitting a sweater are all inherently meaningful tasks that help develop human potential. The rise of industrial capitalism, however, distorted our relationship to work so that it became separated from meeting basic needs. Rather than working for themselves to create useful things, wage laborers work at the discretion of employers for money to buy goods that will meet their needs.

This system creates a distance between what we *do* (for money) and what we *use* (as consumers). One consequence of this distance, according to Marx, is **alienation**, *the separation and isolation of workers as a result of the structure of capitalist society*. Alienation under capitalism has several dimensions:

- *Workers are separated from their natural state as creative, autonomous beings.* They become largely interchangeable cogs in a productive machine.
- *Workers are separated from one another.* Instead of working together toward a common good, workers are often pitted against one another competitively.
- *Workers are separated from what they produce.* Little or no connection exists between workers and the products of their labor, which are owned by their employers.
- *Workers are separated from the process of production.* For many, work is a meaningless, tedious activity with few, if any, intrinsic rewards.

Ironically, later researchers have found that the impersonal, isolating nature of work creates dissatisfaction and unhappiness that advertisers then exploit by encouraging consumption as a solution for this alienation. The beneficiaries of this system of production and consumption are capitalists, who gain, first, by exploiting workers—paying them less than the value of the goods they generate—and, second, by profiting from the sales of such goods back to workers.

When we no longer create or grow the goods we consume, the source of consumer products can seem obscure. Marx used the term **commodity fetishism** to describe *the failure of people to recognize the labor that created the value in the commodities they use.* In the study of primitive religions, *fetish* refers to objects that have magical powers. When we buy jeans or a T-shirt, they seem to appear magically at the local mall with a price tag, entirely separate from the workers who made them. We generally do not think about the labor process involved in an item's creation: the likely low-paid workers—perhaps even child laborers—who made the item, the extensive mark-up added to the price to create profit, or the natural resources consumed in its production and transportation. This disconnect between production of goods and their consumption has become a feature of our consumer culture.

Consumption and Identity

Your great-grandparents probably had identities that reflected where they were born and lived and worked, their religious beliefs, and their strong ties to a particular community. Your identity is no doubt still forming as a result perhaps of various moves, changing schools and peer groups, and living on your own and considering future career choices while you attend college. The nature of our identities reflects, in large part, the nature of our society.

As sociologist Peter Berger (1963) once put it, "[T]raditional societies assign definite and permanent identities to their members" (p. 48). In such societies, identity is often rooted firmly in the family and community, with rigid and permanent roles that are recognized widely. With the rise of modernity, radical economic, social, and political changes contributed to the creation of modern identities, partially freed from the influences of family and place. "In modern society," Berger notes, "identity itself is uncertain and in flux." Since our family of origin and place of birth do not necessarily determine our future, our sense of self does not develop automatically.

Today's postmodern era requires us to choose who we will become. We have more freedom to choose or construct our own social roles, decide where to live and what to do, and much more. A paramount question—one nearly unthinkable in traditional societies—becomes "Who do we want to be?"

In a highly commercial society, where nearly everything is a product for sale, what you buy and where you buy it can take on great importance as an affirmation of your identity. **Consumerism** is *an emphasis on shopping and the possession of material goods as the route to personal happiness*. Advertisers sell an identity through products, and individuals express their identity through the choices they make as consumers (or by their rejection of consumerism).

In his aptly titled book, *The Conquest of Cool*, cultural historian Thomas Frank (1997) showed how advertisers in the 1960s tapped into the popular culture of the day by promoting consumption as a type of creative self-expression. A

Regardless of the product being sold or the audience being targeted, many advertisers sell their products by associating them with a particular image and lifestyle. Are these ads really about milk, MP3 players, watches, or perfume?

variety of consumer products were touted as the choice of nonconformists, rebels, and the "hip," such as Volkswagen vans, Old Gold cigarettes, Polaroid cameras, and Suzuki motorcycles. Ads encouraged consumers to reject conformity—by following the ads' advice to buy a product. The result, of course, is conformity among all those who buy the product. The spectacle of major corporations selling mass consumption as a means of self-expression and individual rebellion—ironic though it may be—surfaces frequently in advertising campaigns. Apple Computer, for example, promoted the iPad "revolution" when it first released the new tablet computer in 2010. Its earlier "Think Different" Macintosh ad campaign featured rebels such as Mahatma Gandhi, John Lennon, and Martin Luther King Jr.

Advertisers often promote their products to particular demographic groups, sometimes reinforcing differences based on gender, race, age, and class. Products not only do something, they *say* something about who we want to be and the group to which we belong. Far removed from Marx's notion that products meet human needs, today's consumer products are often about image and identity. This phenomenon is not entirely new. As we saw in Chapter 9, Thorstein Veblen explored the "conspicuous consumption" of the leisure class a century ago. However, this kind of consumption

has expanded to include most of society. The brands we choose become infused with social meaning that go well beyond the practical use of the product. Prestigious commodities (such as cars, electronics, and clothes) are taken to be a reflection of our own social value (Baudrillard 1988a).

Promoting Consumption

Advertising is ubiquitous in contemporary society. Just think of the various places you've observed ads in the past week: on large highway billboards, on taxis and buses, at the airport, throughout your local mall, in the stalls in public restrooms, on a sticker on a piece of fruit—and in much of the media you consume. Advertising provides the primary source of revenue for most media. You don't have to pay for broadcast television and radio because advertisers foot the bill. The fees for cable television and print subscriptions are affordable because the majority of operating revenue typically comes from advertising. New media, such as Google and Facebook, have adopted the broadcast model—advertising-supported and free to users—for online sites. Most successful high-traffic websites, from news and entertainment sites to medical advice and "how to" sites, are supported by advertisers willing to pay a premium for a targeted audience.

FAST-FORWARD

Change and Sports Advertising

Until the mid-1980s, players in the National Hockey League skated on rinks with plain white ice and boards. When today's players take to the rink, they skate past countless commercial advertisements plastered on the boards and painted right into the ice on which they play. It is impossible to watch professional sports today without being forced to view the logos and other advertisements that cover and surround the playing surfaces and sometimes the players themselves. Even sports arenas and ballparks now carry the names of corporate sponsors and are designed to promote consumption.

At its most basic level, advertising provides consumers with information about specific products and services. On the whole, however, advertising promotes more than just a particular product. As sociologist Michael Schudson (1986) has noted, advertising "fosters a consumer way of life" (p. 238).

A great deal of thought, money, and effort goes into encouraging people to be consumers. Advertisers must make people unhappy with what they have and lead them to believe that a purchase will improve their condition. They cultivate dissatisfaction by encouraging consumers to feel insecure,

bored, anxious, envious, or frustrated about the life they lead and then evoke an image or a lifestyle that consumers supposedly want to emulate, a process called "emotional obsolescence." The cycles of fashion, the new car models, the constant upgrades of media devices are all techniques designed to promote dissatisfaction with the older version of a product and plant the seed of desire for the new product. This endless cycle of consumption, dissatisfaction, and consumption is an inherent part of consumer culture. Increasingly, advertisers are also exploiting the emotional vulnerabilities of children, as the Through a Sociological Lens box describes.

One problem for the advertising industry is that people generally do not like advertisements. As a result, the ad industry is constantly developing new ways to overcome audience resistance and promote consumption, including through advertising in public spaces, product integration, and stealth advertising.

PUBLIC SPACES AND CAPTIVE AUDIENCES

One way to overcome resistance to ads is simply to place them in public spaces that are difficult to avoid. In recent years, for example, ads have appeared on the exterior of airplanes, inside school classrooms, all around sports arenas, and just about everywhere on the Internet. Another strategy is to show ads in places where people are temporarily a captive audience: in elevators, taxicabs, airports, waiting rooms in doctors' offices, and rest rooms.

PRODUCT INTEGRATION

Today's television viewers can use their remote controls to change channels during commercials and to fast-forward past commercials in recorded programs. In response to such audience resistance, *advertisers make ads unavoidable by integrating the product being promoted into media content*, a technique known as **product placement.** For example, viewers of AMC's post-apocalypse zombie series *The Walking Dead* may have noticed an always-clean mint-green Hyundai Tucson SUV that reliably helps the otherwise desperate survivors get around (Steinberg 2013). And it was impossible to miss the Google promotion in *The Internship*, a 2013 summer fluff movie in which Vince Vaughn and Owen Wilson play aging interns employed by the Internet giant. The film featured mentions of Google services and products, such as Google search, Gmail, YouTube, Nexus tablets, and Google Glass, along with real Google employees as extras and free access to the corporate campus for the moviemakers (Kelly 2013). These and many more subtle efforts are product placements.

Experiments suggest that product placement is an effective strategy. For example, after a few seconds' observation of a breakfast cereal that was covertly placed in a TV sitcom, viewers were three times as likely to recall the cereal and to have a positive attitude toward the brand afterward. That influence is significantly reduced, however, if the paid product placement is disclosed to viewers (Campbell, Mohr, and Verlegh 2013).

Other media use product placement as well. In movies, the car the hero drives, the computer the police detective uses, and the wristwatch the spy consults are all likely to be products

Examining the Commercialization of Childhood

More than ever before, advertisers are using the media to target children. Today's ad campaigns are much more sophisticated than those of the past. For example, children in laboratories are studied for their reactions to various kinds of advertising; marketers even measure their eye movements and physiological responses. Children fill out marketing surveys in schools, and sponsored classroom materials sometimes include brand-name acknowledgments that serve as advertisements for youth-oriented products. Marketers also employ psychologists who help craft messages to exploit the emotional vulnerabilities of children, especially their feelings that they are "uncool," a "loser," or simply "left out" if they don't have the latest product. Children are even being hired for "stealth advertising" efforts (described later), for example, by participating in slumber parties sponsored by the research and marketing firm Girls Intelligence Agency, at which the children try to learn about and influence their friends' tastes and habits.

Once a tiny portion of the advertising industry, children's advertising has grown dramatically in recent years as corporations have found new ways to tap parents' wallets through their kids. This barrage of ad messages, says sociologist Juliet Schor, is literally making children sick, causing an array of health and psychological problems. Schor has used sociological inquiry to study the inside operations of advertising agencies that target children, and she has explored the effects of advertising on children. Her findings are alarming.

Today's children are being inundated with many more ads than any other generation has ever experienced. In the 1970s, children watched an estimated 55 television commercials a day. By the 1990s this figure had doubled to 110 (or 40,000 a year), and it continues to increase. In 2010, the American Academy of Pediatrics reaffirmed its concern about the effect of advertising. It noted that young people see ads everywhere—on television, online, in magazines, and on billboards—and that the average child in the United States views more than 3,000 advertisements per day. In recent years, ads have become increasingly prevalent in other youth-oriented media, including video games and social networking websites.

Children have a keen awareness of themselves as consumers and are often the first to try new technology. As Schor points out, "Children have become conduits from the consumer marketplace into the household, the link between advertisers and the family purse." As such, children drive many forms of household consumption, often by nagging parents until they give in or using their own allowance to purchase products. Advertisers understand this process and target children accordingly.

All this exposure to advertising, says Schor, has led to a public health crisis. An epidemic in childhood obesity can be traced in part to a sedentary lifestyle (often spent watching

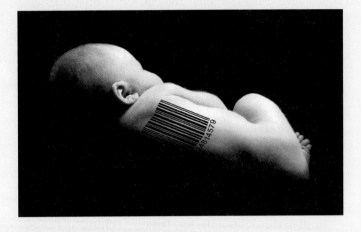

television and playing video games) coupled with a spike in the consumption of high-fat and high-sugar junk food (advertised on children's programs). Recent studies found that television commercials for fast-food restaurants routinely target children by highlighting toy giveaways and movie tie-ins (Bernhardt et al. 2013) and that ads for foods with minimal nutritional value are common in schools (Molner et al. 2013). More broadly, Schor's research suggests that the more children are caught up in the consumer culture, the more likely they are to suffer from depression, anxiety, low self-esteem, and a variety of physical complaints brought on by emotional distress. The ability of advertising to promote dissatisfaction and envy can take a toll on young psyches.

Surveys show that four out of five Americans think there should be more restrictions on children's advertising, and nearly 9 out of 10 think that our consumer culture makes it more difficult to instill positive values in children. Even many of the marketers that Schor interviewed for her study knew something was wrong; they spontaneously expressed ambivalence and guilt about what their work was doing to children.

Sources: American Academy of Pediatrics (2006); Babb (2004); Center for the New American Dream, http://newdream.org; Schor (2004); Strasburger and Wilson (2002); Strasburger, Wilson, and Jordan (2009).

think about it

1. *What sorts of regulations, if any, do you think should be placed on advertising to children? Did your parents restrict your access to media? What steps would you take as a parent to help shield your children from the effects of advertising?*

2. *List all the consequences for children who are overly commercialized. Think about the psychic as well as the economic consequences. What might these children be missing in their lives?*

provided to the movie producers and inserted into the film, sometimes for a fee. Movie producers keep costs down by using such free (or paid-for) props, advertisers get to associate their products with popular movie stars, and audiences experience a form of advertising that is woven seamlessly into the film.

Product placements show up regularly in just about every form of commercial media. Even many news programs incorporate advertising into their content. Companies distribute "video news releases" promoting their products that are broadcast by some local news programs, often without attribution. In addition, freelance "experts" appear on many local and national morning news shows offering reviews of new consumer products. Some of these experts are paid by advertisers for a positive mention of their products (Rainey 2010).

South Korean teen idol Lee Hyo Lee brought this form of advertising to its logical conclusion in her hit pop song "Anymotion." In the video for this song, Lee dances with Samsung's Anycall brand cell phone while she sings. The song, the video, even the choreographer were all paid for by Samsung, which crafted the lyrics to repeatedly include the word *any*, reminding listeners over and over again of their Anycall brand (Fowler 2005).

In all of these cases, the line between content and advertisement has been erased, a development that has angered some actors and writers. Their unions have protested these practices, saying they force actors to make product endorsements for which they are not compensated and writers to write ad copy rather than program content. They also argue that the practice is inherently deceptive (Waxman 2005).

STEALTH ADVERTISING Another increasingly common practice is stealth advertising. Sometimes called "guerilla marketing," **stealth advertising** is *the creation of*

covert advertising in everyday real-life situations. For example, many advertisers take advantage of social networking sites and consumer review features of online retail sites to plant surreptitious advertising for their products. Advertisers hire employees to pose as ordinary users of these sites and praise the attributes of their employer's products by posting enthusiastic reviews. In one high-profile 2010 case, the Federal Trade Commission (2010) charged a public relations firm with posting game reviews at the iTunes store without disclosing that the firm was hired to promote the games.

Advertisers also hire people to promote their products subtly by, for example, going to bars and ordering a particular brand of beer, in effect becoming a walking advertisement. Camera companies have hired people to pose as tourists and ask passersby to take their picture in front of a popular landmark. As this innocuous exchange takes place, the "tourists" praise the virtues of their new camera, creating another stealth ad. Such advertising techniques, which rely on people's trust and good will, are deceptive and insert commercial motivations into everyday social interactions.

The Social Impact of Consumer Culture

What happens to a culture in which consumption becomes the center of social life and citizens are subject to an endless stream of advertising? We note some of the social implications in the sections that follow.

INEQUALITY AND CONSUMPTION Social and economic inequality is important to keep in mind when considering the impact of consumer culture. The affluence necessary for consumer spending is not distributed evenly, and large segments of the world's population still endure poverty and subsistence living. The transformation to consumer culture came first to the more affluent Western societies in the nineteenth and early twentieth centuries, and only recently to parts of the developing world that are now integrated into the global economy. After the fall of communism in 1989, Eastern Europe saw a dramatic expansion in consumer culture. China, too,

American fast-food restaurants line a street in Shenzhen, China. Consumer cultures of this sort, once limited to affluent Western countries, have now expanded to some developing nations. But U.S.-style levels of consumption cannot be sustained globally; the planet simply does not contain sufficient resources.

TABLE 14.1 THE COST OF LUXURY CONSUMER PRODUCTS VERSUS HUMAN NEEDS

Luxury Consumer Products		Human Needs	
Product	Annual Expenditure	Social or Economic Goal	Annual Investment Needed to Achieve Goal
Makeup (global)	$18 billion	Reproductive health care for all women	$12 billion
Pet food in the United States and Europe	$17 billion	Elimination of hunger and malnutrition	$19 billion
Perfumes (global)	$15 billion	Universal literacy	$5 billion
Ocean cruises (global)	$14 billion	Clean drinking water for all	$10 billion
Ice cream in Europe	$11 billion	Immunizing every child	$1.3 billion

The table lists examples of the annual expenditure on luxury consumer items compared to the estimated annual expenditures needed to achieve key social and economic goals. As the authors who assembled the table note, the list debunks the idea that "many of the unmet basic needs of the world's poor are too costly to address" (Gardner, Assadourian, and Sarin 2004, 10).

CORE CONCEPTS CHALLENGE

What does the list in Table 14.1 suggest about the hidden costs of consumer **culture***?*

has recently instituted major economic changes, enabling growth in consumer spending.

Using data to measure purchasing power, a United Nations study found that 85 percent of Americans were classified as active consumers, but only 28 percent of the world's population qualified for this classification (Gardner, Assadourian, and Sarin 2004). The vast majority of the world's population is unable to participate in consumer culture because of their starkly limited resources. Those who are active consumers face some sobering choices about how they direct their wealth. Table 14.1 compares the annual expenditure on luxury items versus what might have been accomplished had those resources been allocated to more basic human needs.

DEBT AND DISSATISFACTION

As we saw in Chapter 12, Marx regarded religion as an "opiate" that gave temporary, but ultimately false, comfort to people suffering from society's injustices. Since the middle of the twentieth century, critical theorists have suggested that consumerism fills a similar role in modern society (Adorno and Horkheimer [1944] 2000). Shopping is often touted as an escape from the drudgeries of daily life. "Treating yourself," "living for the weekend," and "splurging" because "you are worth it" are all popular notions that encourage guilt-free consumption. However, the fleeting comfort of consumption

on social theory

Marx and contemporary **conflict theorists** emphasize the inability of consumption ultimately to offer satisfaction. Has consumption helped give you a sense of satisfaction? Who has benefited from your participation in consumer culture?

is often coupled with the accumulation of burdensome debt, producing more stress and anxiety in a person's life. Consumption and working to pay for it become a cyclical way of life (Schor 1999).

As far back as Durkheim, sociologists have understood that satisfaction in life comes from understanding and staying within limits and boundaries. Insofar as advertising and consumer culture encourage boundless desires that can never be satisfied, they can be a source of social instability and can undermine human happiness.

Excessive consumption cannot substitute for addressing the underlying social conditions that create unhappiness. Since the cycle of consumption is at bottom based on perpetual dissatisfaction (Ewen 2001), any comforting effects are likely to be temporary, leaving deep-seated troublesome issues unchanged. What is more likely to produce happiness and satisfaction? Scholars point to rewarding interpersonal relationships, meaningful employment, outlets for creative self-expression, and gratifying civic and community participation (Kasser 2003; Lane 1994).

COMMODIFICATION

Commodification is *the process of transforming all things into a product to be bought and sold.* Social relationships that used to be based on, and promoted by, mutual aid and trust are often just commercial transactions today. For example, a variety of goods and services that were once produced and shared among family and friends—such as yard work, pet sitting, home repairs, and child care—are now more likely to be paid services. Today we even shop for mates on the Internet.

Religious holidays and communal festivals that once promoted social solidarity are now celebrations of consumption.

Consumer Culture

407

Thanksgiving now marks the early Christmas sales. Birthdays, Mother's Day and Father's Day, Valentine's Day, and other events are marked by the obligatory mass-produced greeting card and the purchase of a consumer item. Big sales are associated with President's Day, Labor Day, and Memorial Day. The newest civic holiday, the Super Bowl, is as notable for the unveiling of new advertisements as for the game played on the field. Shopping has been transformed from a necessary chore to America's favorite pastime.

With commodification, monetary terms increasingly measure social life. If carried to an extreme, such a development can undermine the social trust necessary for a healthy society. A society in which everything—and everyone—has a price is one in which emptiness and alienation are likely to thrive (Dunn 2000; Slater 1999).

ENVIRONMENTAL DEGRADATION Finally, the spread of the culture of consumption around the globe has taken a toll on the environment. For decades, affluent nations, especially the United States, have consumed the earth's resources at a vastly disproportionate level. With about 5 percent of the earth's population, Americans consume about 25 percent of the world's resources. Now, billions of residents of developing nations are seeing improvements in their standards of living and are themselves becoming consumers. For some, consumer culture is a step up from the grinding pain of poverty. The more widespread availability of basic, affordable consumer goods has been a major positive development.

The overall expansion of consumer culture, however, has resulted in environmental destruction on a massive, unprecedented, and unsustainable scale—including slashed and burned forests, polluted air and water, toxic landfills, crippling carbon dioxide emission, holes in the atmosphere's protective ozone layer, and wholesale climate change. We explore some of these effects in Chapter 15.

A Changing World

TARGETING CONSUMERS IN THE DIGITAL AGE

The Internet has taken advertising to a whole new level because it is the only medium that allows advertisers to track the activity of potential consumers (Story 2008) and to harvest information about users' interests and habits.

In a 2010 investigative report about what it called "the business of spying on Internet users," the *Wall Street Journal* discovered that the "tracking of consumers has grown both far more pervasive and far more intrusive than is realized by all but a handful of people in the vanguard of the industry" (Angwin 2010). For example, the top 50 websites in the United States each installed, on average, 64 different pieces of tracking technology on a visitor's computer—typically without giving the user any warning. The top 50 youth sites installed a total of more than 4,000 tracking tools on users' computers. These new tracking tools are the foundation for a promotional approach known as **behavioral targeting,** *advertising sent to online users based on their earlier Internet activities.*

The best-known form of online tracking involves the installation of cookies. Cookies help websites store information such as your name, address, and payment preferences. This information can help users learn about new products that might match their interests and can make online shopping fast and easy.

In recent years, however, cookies have been installed primarily by companies that specialize in tracking and recording users' online activity and selling this information to advertisers. These companies pay websites to permit them to install tracking tools on the computers of visitors to the site. In addition, tracking tools are sometimes hidden in banner ads or free downloadable apps, games, and ring tones.

By piecing together bits of information you leave behind as you browse the Internet, advertisers can anticipate your likely interests and pitch products to you based on your past online activity. Records of your searches on Google or other sites, the products you have viewed, the articles you have read, the zip code you entered to get local weather, your Facebook likes and Instagram photos—all these pieces of information can be assembled to construct a sophisticated consumer profile that allows marketers to create a targeted online consumer experience, steering you to advertisements tailor-made to your specific interests.

The principles of behavioral targeting are also visible in political campaigns. By mining data about your online activities, campaigns can customize the information you receive about a candidate. In this way, the campaign can personalize the candidate's message and target it to you based on your demographic and consumer profile. Different citizens can literally be getting different messages from the same candidate (Howard 2005; Panagopoulos 2009).

Research suggests there is substantial public concern about online tracking (Turow et al. 2009). Public opposition to behavioral targeting is connected to broader concerns about online privacy. For example, the practice of "scraping" involves copying material from online forums, career-oriented websites, and social networking sites on which users often discuss and post information about various aspects of their lives, from school, work, and relationships to health, exercise, and

thinking about culture

As consumer **culture** spreads throughout the globe, environmental pollution is spreading as well. What aspects of U.S. consumer culture might create these problems?

At this 2012 protest in Vienna, Austria, demonstrators carry a coffin symbolizing the death of privacy amid the growth of governmental and corporate surveillance.

what people are saying about a specific topic or product. Facebook and other social networking sites, which include personal information that users post voluntarily, are particularly valuable sources for information scrapers.

In the face of the growing sophistication of behavioral targeting and other data-gathering techniques, consumer advocates have called for government regulations. The Federal Trade Commission is considering a "do not track" option that would permit users to opt out of all tracking tools. In response, online data trackers and advertisers have come up with their own proposals to head off potential regulation. A group of online tracking companies started a service called the Open Data Partnership in 2011, which allows consumers to view and edit data that have been collected on them but does not permit users to opt out of tracking altogether (Steel 2010). Google and Mozilla browsers allow users to request that they not be tracked. How many tracking companies honor the opt-out requests is still unclear (*New York Times* 2011a).

The debate about online advertising techniques is sure to continue throughout the decade, as citizens and policymakers sort through the various arguments about consumer privacy and efficient marketing. In this new era of customized consumption, sociologists are likely to pay careful attention to the power associated with information tracking and the cultural consequences of the proliferation of personalized advertising (and political) messages.

hobbies (Angwin and Stecklow 2010). In some cases, scrapers construct individual user profiles that connect people's online screen names to their real names, which they sell to advertisers, employers, and other websites. Online scrapers also sell so-called listening services, in which they report to clients

thinking sociologically about
Media and Consumption

culture

■ Media reflect and promote cultural norms.

■ Consumption has become central to our culture and is used to help form social identities.

structure

■ The structure of the media industry shapes the content of popular media.

■ Media organizations must operate within the structural constraints imposed by their legal, political, economic, and cultural environments.

■ The widespread presence of advertising helps structure consumer society.

power

■ Major media ownership is highly concentrated; those who control the media wield considerable power in society.

■ Consumerism is linked to inequality and reflects disparities in economic power in society.

Looking Back

1. As a social institution, media involve the interaction of several key elements: the media industry, media content, audiences, technology, and the broader social context.

2. The media industry has been expanding, integrating, and globalizing, while its ownership has become more concentrated.

3. Media content often reflects the broader social inequalities in society, sometimes perpetuating them through the socialization process.

4. Audiences consist of active readers, viewers, and listeners who make choices about their media use and interpret media content, often based on their social position. But extensive and long-term exposure to media does have an impact on audiences, influencing what they think about and how they view the world.

5. Converging media forms, technological advances, and the rise in user-generated content have been major contributors to the explosive growth of media.

6. Whatever their form, media act as sources of information, agents of socialization, and as a means for those in power to promote ideology.

7. The rise in electronic media technology in postmodern life is a significant change from modernity's reliance on print, introducing new ways of thinking about and seeing the world.

8. The rise of consumer culture was accompanied by an increase in advertising delivered through various media. Advertising has become a ubiquitous force, and advertisers use a variety of techniques to influence our identities and promote consumption.

9. Consumer culture has had a significant social impact on how we live, work, and value our lives. It has also been a key factor in the escalation of environmental degradation.

Critical Thinking: Questions and Activities

1. In what ways and for how long do you use media in a typical day? Keep a log for one or two days, noting every use of media. How would you summarize the role that media play in your life? How do you think your lifelong exposure to media has influenced how you understand the world? How does the influence of media extend beyond *what* you know to include *how* you relate to the social world?

2. If someone relied exclusively on popular media portrayals to understand the life of a college student today, would they get a reasonably accurate picture of your real-world experiences in college? What does this say about the role of media in teaching about aspects of the world we don't experience firsthand?

3. Note your exposure to advertising for one day. What techniques did advertisers use to get your attention? Is there any part of your life that is free from brand names, logos, and ads?

4. Would you agree to have a corporate advertiser pay for your wedding ceremony in exchange for incorporating the corporation's logo into the event (for example, printed on invitations and napkins, displayed on a banner at the reception, announced as part of the ceremony)? Why or why not? What issues does this "product placement" raise about the appropriate limits for advertising?

5. In what ways do you participate in consumer culture? Do you have any concerns about the role of consumption in your life?

Key Terms

active audiences (p. 393) audiences that make choices about how they use the media and actively interpret media content.

agenda-setting theory (p. 393) a theory that holds that media may not be able to tell people what to think but can significantly influence what people think about.

alienation (p. 402) the separation and isolation of workers as a result of the structure of capitalist society.

behavioral targeting (p. 408) advertising sent to online users based on their earlier Internet activities.

commodification (p. 407) the process of transforming all things into a product to be bought and sold.

commodity fetishism (p. 402) consumers' failure to recognize the labor that created the value in the commodities they use.

consumerism (p. 402) an emphasis on shopping and the possession of material goods as the route to personal happiness.

consumption (p. 400) the process of choosing, purchasing, and using goods.

convergence (p. 394) the merging of different media forms.

cultivation theory (p. 393) a theory that argues that, by repeated and long-term exposure to the media's portrayal of the world (especially on television), people come to accept many of these depictions as reality.

cultural imperialism (p. 398) the tendency of media corporations from wealthier nations—especially the United States—to export so many of their media products that they come to dominate the local cultures of other, especially poorer, nations.

digital divide (p. 396) the gap between those who have the knowledge and resources needed to use digital information technology, especially computers and the Internet, and those who do not.

dual product markets (p. 391) the situation that occurs when a company sells two completely different types of "products" to two completely different sets of buyers.

horizontal integration (p. 387) what occurs when a media company owns different forms of media.

hyperreality (p. 399) the condition in which media depictions of the world replace the experience of the "real" world.

mass media (p. 385) communications that reach a relatively large and mostly anonymous audience.

media (p. 385) the various technological processes that enable communication between (and are in the "middle" of) the sender of a message and the receiver of that message.

ownership concentration (p. 388) what occurs when more media outlets come to be owned by a diminishing number of media corporations.

planned obsolescence (p. 401) the intentional design and manufacture of consumer goods so as to ensure a loss of utility in a relatively short period of time.

product placement (p. 404) the integration into media content of a product that is being advertised.

stealth advertising (p. 406) the creation of covert advertising in everyday real-life situations.

user-generated content (p. 394) content that is created by ordinary media users, rather than by media organizations, and that is available to a potentially large audience.

vertical integration (p. 387) what occurs when a media company owns the different stages of production and distribution of a single media form.

15

Communities, the Environment, and Health

looking AHEAD

How does the **structure** of *where* you live—whether it's an urban, suburban, or rural community—influence *how* you live?

How does your **culture** influence your understanding of your community and the environment?

How does the amount of **power** you have affect the likelihood that you will face environmental hazards and develop health problems?

When Fan Qun moved from a rural community to the city of Beijing looking for economic opportunity, every aspect of his and his family's life changed. Unlike many others who struggled, Qun became affluent working for a consulting firm that advises Western pharmaceutical companies doing business in China.

Yet "everyone is unhappy," says Fan Hanlin, Qun's 70-year-old father. Because Qun and his wife view their marriage as their main priority, rather than their relationship with Qun's father, Hanlin has lost his traditional role as respected elder. Qun's father and mother are also upset by behaviors that contrast starkly with their lifelong frugality: Qun and his wife employ two housekeepers, frequently eat in expensive restaurants, and each own a car.

Millions have moved into China's growing cities, abandoning a centuries-old way of life and adopting the new norms of an urban, market-oriented society. Affluence has enabled many city dwellers to afford their own apartments, and some even put their elderly parents into nursing homes, a practice unheard of just a few years ago.

Perhaps the most dramatic impact of change has been on China's environment, with significant health consequences. To fuel massive growth, China's land has been overcultivated, overgrazed, and sometimes deforested, with 90 percent of trees cut in some provinces. Over a quarter of China's land mass is a desert today, contributing to massive sandstorms that sometimes halt air traffic in major cities. To attract investment, the government allowed foreign corporations to locate toxic-waste-producing factories in China, where environmental protection laws are almost nonexistent. China is the world's biggest producer of carbon dioxide emissions, opening a new coal-fired power plant every week. Researchers estimate that air pollution contributed to the premature deaths of 1.2 million Chinese people in 2010 (Wong 2013). Perhaps most amazing is that China's growth in urbanization and affluence is just beginning.

Whether changing individual families, transforming the nation, or influencing the planet, China's experience with urbanization illustrates three themes we explore in this chapter. First, *where* we live influences *how* we live. The move from traditional rural communities to the new physical and social environment of cities changes cultural norms, creates new social structures, and alters power relationships. Second, although growth creates affluence for some, it also creates environmental challenges that result in major social problems. Sociology can help us better understand the dynamics behind our environmental crises and suggest options for addressing them. Third, health is more than a medical issue; it is a social issue connected to broad social patterns, and the sociological perspective can help us understand the social dynamics that influence health-related issues.

The Structure and Evolution of Communities

Films and television have often told the tale: a small-town innocent finds his or her way to the big city and is overwhelmed. City life is so different from home! Buildings shoot up to the sky, crowds of people bustle frantically, the noise is deafening, and con artists prey on the naïvely trusting innocent. Offering a similarly comedic counterpoint to this storyline is that of the bewildered "city slicker" adrift in the foreign ways of a rural community.

Though now clichés, these tales reflect basic sociological insights. Social life *can* be vastly different in the dissimilar structures of different locations. In short, place matters (Gieryn 2000). Sociologists are well aware of "virtual communities" that exist only in cyberspace (Wellman 2001; Wellman and Haythornthwaite 2002). But these often have less influence on us than place-based communities, and virtual communities can exist only because their members occupy a physical space and use material infrastructure to access Internet experiences and cell phone communication. Even with the growth of virtual communities, place and physical environment still matter.

Community: Place, People, and Relationships

The term *community* has different meanings depending on its context (Flora and Flora 2008; Goe and Noonan 2007).

It can refer to a *place*, as in, "I just moved to this community earlier this year." It can also refer to a *group of people* who share some common characteristic or identity, such as "the Latino community." Finally, it can refer to the *social relationships* that unite people in groups, as in "College sports can promote community spirit on campus."

Here, we look at where these ideas overlap, the connection between the place where people live and work and the type of social bonds that unite them as a group. In this context, **community** is *a set of social relationships, typically arising from living in a particular place, that give people a sense of identity and belonging.* It refers simultaneously to a place, the people who share that place, and the social relationships that result.

Sociologists have long examined the relationships between *where* people live and *how* they live. To do so, they use the lenses provided by sociology's subfields, including urban sociology, rural sociology, human ecology, environmental sociology, and the sociology of community. Drawing on these perspectives, we can sketch the evolution of human communities and sample the social changes that humans created and that in turn changed their physical and social environments (Johnson and Earle 2000; Mumford 1968).

We distinguish among three kinds of environments. First, the **social environment** refers broadly to *the cultural context and patterns of relationships within which humans live,* including groups, institutions, and social positions. We have been discussing social environment throughout this book. In addition, there is a physical environment with two components. The **natural environment** is *the land, water, air, vegetation, and organisms that make up the physical world.* The **built environment** is *the physical surroundings that humans create.* These include the buildings, roads, dams, homes, and consumer products we use every day. (See Figure 15.1.)

As humans shifted from being primarily hunter-gatherers, to farmers, and then to industrial manufacturers, their relationship to the natural and built environments changed. As a result, the communities in which they lived changed as well.

Nomadic Life: Hunting and Gathering

For most of their history, humans were hunters and gatherers living in small groups and foraging their natural environment for subsistence. Rather than forming a permanent settlement, they were nomadic, following the migration of animals and the seasonal availability of plant foods around a relatively large but circumscribed territory.

Since there was so little of it, the built environment was much less significant to such communities than the natural

Even t
billions
how m
What

Prei
Prot

The cha
years. T
were tow
fewer th
their cap
larger pc

Securit
protect

TABLE 15.1	COMMUNITY TYPES AND FEATURES			
	Nomadic/ Hunter-Gatherer	Rural/Agricultural	Preindustrial Cities	Industrial and Postindustrial Cities
Key period of development	Until about 8000 B.C.E.	8000–3000 B.C.E.	3000 B.C.E.–1700 C.E.	1700s–today
Experience of natural/ built environment	Dependence on natural environment; minimum built environment	Significant dependence on natural environment; some built environment	Limited experience with natural environment; significant built environment	Pervasive built environment; little experience with natural environment
Key economic feature	Hunting and gathering	Farming (crops) and herding (animals)	Manual crafts and trades	Mass manufacturing and, later, growing information-based employment
Surplus and extent of inequality	No significant material surplus; therefore, little economic inequality	Increased material surplus and increased inequality	Significant surpluses with extensive inequality	Massive surpluses with extremes of wealth and poverty
Specialization of labor	Very limited, by gender	Limited specialization	Significant specialization	Extensive specialization

together in centralized factories, producing an explosion in urban populations. For example, in 1790, the four largest U.S. cities had a *combined* population of fewer than 100,000 people; by 1900 *each* of the four largest U.S. cities (New York, Boston, Chicago, and Philadelphia) had populations of at least 1 million (Gibson 1998). Urbanization eventually required sophisticated built environments. Electrical power plants powered factory machinery and lit homes at night. The icon of city life—the skyscraper—became possible once architects and developers introduced steel-framed buildings and electric elevators in the late nineteenth century. In this way, changes in the built environment enabled the creation of new urban communities.

The gathering of people of diverse ideas, skills, and talents provided a vibrant and stimulating intellectual and cultural environment in large cities. For those interested in new scientific ideas, the creative arts, and business opportunities, cities were the place to be. But while modern cities created enormous wealth for some, they could be places of horror for the poor. Abject squalor marked some neighborhoods. Oppressive factories or sweatshops often featured brutal 12-hour days, a hazardous environment, and dangerous machinery that could maim or kill. Overcrowded slums arose side-by-side with commercial districts and pollution-spewing workplaces, resulting in health and sanitation problems such as lung disease from air pollution and dysentery from open sewers.

Sunbelt Cities and Global Growth

In the latter half of the twentieth century, urbanization in the United States was most intense in cities such as Atlanta, Houston, and Phoenix in the U.S. South and Southwest, the area known as the Sunbelt. Most expanded rapidly by annexing adjacent lands. As a result, unlike older cities, Sunbelt cities are often decentralized environments heavily dependent on the automobile. The housing crisis that began in 2007 as part of the Great Recession hit these cities especially hard. But some analysts see this reversal as an opportunity for these now "sunburnt" cities to restore some balance to their runaway growth (Hollander 2011).

Today, industrialization and urbanization are increasingly global phenomena. In 2008, the world reached what the United Nations called "an invisible but momentous milestone" (UN Population Fund 2008, 1). For the first time in human history, a majority of people live in urban areas. By 2011, 52 percent of the world's population—3.6 billion people—called a city home, and that figure is expected to grow by 72 percent (to 6.2 billion) by 2050 (UN Department of Economic and Social Affairs 2012).

In 2025, 8 of the 10 largest metropolitan areas will be in developing nations (Table 15.2). Urbanization occurs in developing nations today for largely the same reasons it occurred in Europe and the United States in earlier periods. Cities hold out the promise of economic opportunity for people from rural areas who often suffer from grinding poverty.

Just as in earlier periods, however, cities in poorer developing nations cannot live up to the expectations of the masses of people flocking to them. Like Fan Qun, the man described in the chapter opening, some find upward mobility in cities. But many others struggle for a modest existence, and some are left destitute and without the support of the families they left in their communities of origin. In the

TABLE 15.2	TEN LARGEST METROPOLITAN AREAS, PROJECTED, 2025

City, Country	Population, in millions
1. Tokyo, Japan	38.7
2. Delhi, India	32.9
3. Shanghai, China	28.4
4. Mumbai (Bombay), India	26.6
5. Ciudad de México (Mexico City), Mexico	24.6
6. New York-Newark, USA	23.6
7. São Paulo, Brazil	23.2
8. Dhaka, Bangladesh	22.9
9. Beijing, China	22.6
10. Karachi, Pakistan	20.2

Source: UN Department of Economic and Social Affairs (2012).

miserable shantytowns that surround the more affluent cities in India, Mexico, China, Brazil, and elsewhere, a stunning inequality between rich and poor echoes what occurred in Europe in the nineteenth century.

Understanding the Culture of Urban Life

The urbanization that began in the West and continues in developing countries radically transformed rural ways of life that had existed for centuries. Early sociologists analyzed how social cohesion developed in this new urban environment.

Tönnies: Cities as a New Form of Social Organization

The most systematic early comparison of traditional rural and modern urban life came from German sociologist Ferdinand Tönnies (1855–1936). In 1887,

he published a book that used the German words *Gemeinschaft* and *Gesellschaft*—usually translated as community and society—to label two distinct ways of life, summarized in Table 15.3.

Gemeinschaft refers to *social organization in which most relationships are based upon the long-term personal ties of collective kinship, common tradition, and shared values.* Such forms of social organization are quite stable and are typically found in small rural communities where residents are very similar, often related by blood and marriage, and typically employed in similar work, often agricultural. The people usually share common religious beliefs and other cultural traditions, too. Virtually all interactions—in school, on the street, in commerce, at work—include personal relationships as well as the task at hand. For example, the merchant who sells supplies may also be a neighbor, relative, fellow church member, and former schoolmate. "In Gemeinschaft we are united from the moment of our birth with our own folk for better or for worse," Tönnies wrote ([1887] 2001, 18). As Zygmunt Bauman (2001) has further noted, the distinctiveness of a *Gemeinschaft* community provides a boundary between members of the community and outsiders, and its relative self-sufficiency makes extensive contact with outsiders unnecessary. Common life experiences produce strong, often emotionally based group norms that reinforce common identity and values, encourage conformity, and discourage deviance. The result is strong social cohesion based on commonality.

In contrast, ***Gesellschaft*** is Tönnies's term for *social organization in which most social relationships are impersonal, temporary, and based primarily on the pursuit of individual rational self-interest.* Such social organization characterizes modern city life. Urban centers attract people from various locales

The rapid growth of cities around the world has been accompanied by stark differences between newly emerging wealth and grinding poverty. Here a neighborhood of slums sits on the outskirts of bustling Buenos Aires, Argentina.

TABLE 15.3 ELEMENTS OF *GEMEINSCHAFT* AND *GESELLSCHAFT*

Gemeinschaft	*Gesellschaft*
Typified by traditional rural communities	Typified by large cities
Culture is rooted in stable tradition	Culture is newly emerging and changing
People share common life experiences	People have diverse backgrounds and experiences
Social interactions often involve multilayered personal relationships	Social interactions are often impersonal, based on a single narrowly defined role, and task specific
Little privacy and no anonymity	Considerable privacy and anonymity amid dense population
Culture tends to conformity, intolerance of difference, punishment of even mild deviance	Culture tends to tolerance of difference and some deviance
Social control is largely maintained through informal cultural norms and personal relationships	Social control is maintained through formal means (for example, police force)
Collective goals and community cooperation are common	Individual goals and pursuit of self-interest dominate

who often have little in common, who work in specialized occupations, and who remain relatively anonymous in the city's vast population. Identifying and enforcing common social norms can be difficult because people come from different places and cultures. Most social interactions in the city, therefore, are impersonal and do not extend beyond the task at hand. Tönnies argued that urban life undermines social solidarity and loosens social control mechanisms. These changes lead to more individualism and social isolation, weaker ties between people, and more deviance than in *Gemeinschaft* communities.

Tönnies insightfully argued that if people change *where* they live, they will likely change *how* they live. He suggested that something important—including a comforting sense of stable and secure community—may have been lost in the transition from rural to urban life. But today's sociologists caution against romanticizing traditional communities. Bauman (2001) notes that the restrictive homogeneity of *Gemeinschaft* can foster deep prejudice toward outsiders and anyone who dares to be different. Family duty and community responsibility override individual aspirations. So while modern urban life did represent a loss of safe and secure

tradition, it also introduced new individual freedoms. This tension between security (resulting from sameness) and freedom (resulting from diversity) has been a central one in modern social life (Bauman 2001).

Durkheim: Organic Solidarity in the City

Tönnies suggested that the individualism of urban life could undermine social solidarity. Durkheim, however, argued that a new form of collective cohesiveness emerges from the new social organization of cities (Durkheim [1893] 1997).

As we saw in Chapter 1, for Durkheim homogeneous rural communities exhibited *mechanical solidarity*—social cohesion based on shared experience, personal ties, and a limited sense of individuality. With the growth of cities, social solidarity was gradually replaced by *organic solidarity*, a new form of social cohesion based on interdependence. In modern industrial society, people are interdependent: they depend on one another precisely *because* their work and social roles are so specialized. The baker, merchant, factory worker, doctor, and teacher all need and rely upon one another. For Durkheim, the rise of specialization created interdependence, providing urban populations with a different, but effective, form of social cohesion.

Jane Addams and the "Chicago School": Community in City Life

Tönnies and Durkheim both believed the personal ties of rural life were not a common feature of urban life. However, close studies of late-nineteenth-century Chicago neighborhoods revealed a more complex reality in which immigrants and other marginalized groups maintained personal connections in urban situations.

Between 1850 and 1900, Chicago's population exploded from 30,000 people to 1.7 million, making the city the fifth largest in the world. By 1930 the population had almost doubled again to 3.3 million (Gibson 1998). This rapid growth created severe social problems including poor sanitation, crowded housing, increasing crime, and exploitation of workers. To help address some of these issues, as we saw in Chapter 1, pioneering sociologist Jane Addams cofounded Hull House in 1889, a settlement house that provided community services for ethnically diverse poor and working-class residents. (See the Sociology in Action box.) In researching Chicago's neighborhoods and their needs, Addams and her collaborators at Hull House invented a new form of urban sociology that relied on gathering detailed data and mapping the demographic characteristics of different neighborhoods (Deegan 1988).

In the 1920s and 1930s, sociologists at the University of Chicago built upon the Hull House work and began formal "community studies" of urban life that employed small-scale

SOCIOLOGY in ACTION

Jane Addams and Hull House

Sociology and social work have common roots that go back to the nation's first graduate department of sociology at the University of Chicago, which combined study and practice. Reflecting the gender inequality of the day, men dominated the main sociology department, but a strong contingent of women sociologists, most famously Jane Addams, was affiliated with it (Deegan 1988; Feagin and Vera 2001).

Beginning in the 1890s and continuing for a quarter century, many of these women worked with Hull House, a settlement house that provided community services for poor and working-class people and served as an intellectual center for residents and scholars alike. Cofounded by Jane Addams, a scholar and activist who worked for women's rights and labor reforms and was awarded the Nobel Peace Prize in 1931, Hull House grew to encompass an entire city block in one of Chicago's poorest and most ethnically diverse neighborhoods. Several thousand visitors a week came for its dormitory and bathing facilities, day care, health clinic, employment assistance, gymnasium, coffeehouse, reading room, adult evening classes, and more.

Addams and her Hull House collaborators campaigned to end child labor and improve health and working conditions, goals that helped define the liberal reform period known as the Progressive Era. To improve conditions in nearby neighborhoods, they had to understand the issues residents faced. Hull House thus served, in effect, as a center of applied sociology, where research teams gathered data, applied their findings to shape the work of the settlement house, and provided evidence used in legislative reform efforts. In doing so, Hull House workers pioneered forms of urban sociology and heavily

Jane Addams

influenced the development of community studies at the University of Chicago.

Some male sociology faculty joined Addams and her colleagues in their social reform efforts, but most focused on developing theoretical models of urbanization and its effects. They viewed the city as a "laboratory" within which to conduct their work, regarding residents more as subjects for study than as partners for change.

Over time the university institutionalized the distinction between studying urban issues and working to bring about social reform. In 1920, it transferred all the women affiliated with the sociology department to the social work department. On most U.S. campuses, sociology and social work continue to exist as separate departments, the former emphasizing the study of society, the latter focusing on providing social services.

However, Jane Addams, often referred to as a founder of social work, thought of herself as a sociologist, not a social worker. In her Hull House work she integrated study and practice, and her advocacy for social change continues today as "public sociology" and related work.

think about it

1. How does Addams's work compare to your understanding of social work today?

2. Do you think sociologists should act upon the knowledge they have to help address social problems, or should they remain detached observers, studying but not advocating for any particular change? What are the advantages and pitfalls of each approach?

---

direct observation. **Community studies** *typically look at groups of people who share some common tie and engage in social interaction within a particular geographic area.* According to these "Chicago School" studies, even in the heart of urban centers, ethnic enclaves—neighborhoods whose residents were often working-class immigrants of the same ethnic group—retained a distinct cultural identity, indicated by a distinct common language, religious practices, food, music, family relations, and other cultural traditions. Thus some of the social cohesion that marked traditional rural life survived in the new urban ethnic enclaves. Over time, though, immigrants became more fully assimilated into the dominant U.S. culture.

Some of the sociological insights gained by studying early European immigrants apply to today's city neighborhoods and communities. Like their earlier counterparts, today's immigrants often speak a language other than English, have different religious traditions, and observe distinctive norms and customs. Seeking the economic opportunities that cities offer, they form new ethnic enclaves as a means of providing mutual aid and maintaining social cohesion in a new environment (Waldinger 2001).

The Impact of Place on Social Life: Human Ecology

Early work on urbanization showed that the physical environment influences the social life that takes place within it.

This fundamental insight is the foundation of **human ecology,** *the study of the links between the physical environment—natural and built—and social life.*

The human ecology approach reveals that the physical environment is important at all levels of social life (Appold 2007). At the macro level, we can explain the location and development of cities by looking at their physical context. Major cities are usually located next to oceans, rivers, and large lakes, since these are natural resources that have facilitated travel, provided hydropower, and supplied necessary water for drinking, sanitation, and other applications. On the other hand, humans can alter the natural environment by building dams, reservoirs, and levees, actions that allow the construction of cities in the unlikeliest of places, such as the desert of Las Vegas.

Also at the macro level, the built environment of cities can reflect and reinforce broader cultural values. The tallest buildings of medieval cities were cathedrals near the city center, and towering city halls marked the rise of civil government, whereas in modern cities corporate skyscrapers dominate the skyline, reflecting a shift in power to business. In one exception, though, in 1899 Congress prohibited any building in downtown Washington, D.C., from being taller than the U.S. Capitol, symbolically asserting the power of democratic government over private commercial interests. That restriction has been challenged in recent years.

At the meso level, human ecologists note that cities are organized into distinct subsections—residential, commercial, industrial, and the like—that evolve in relationship to one another. Growth or decline of any one area can disrupt and disorganize a community, resulting in crime and neglect, but typically stability eventually returns as people establish new social norms and structures. These processes in cities resemble growth and decline in natural ecological systems. But human action can intervene, such as with modern zoning practices that define how different areas can be used (residence, industrial, and so on).

Human ecologists also point out that function, not political boundary, defines urban areas and shapes our experience of them. So to understand urban dynamics—how a city functions—we must look at the entire area, including the region beyond its formal boundaries. To help in this analysis, researchers distinguish between the various physical spaces that make up urban communities (see Figure 15.2), including

- The *inner city,* typically the most densely developed portion
- The *city proper,* a city's legal boundary
- The *suburbs,* less densely developed and populated areas that surround a city's official boundaries

FIGURE 15.2 | THE ZONES OF COMMUNITY LIFE

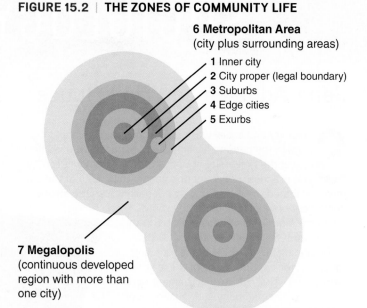

6 Metropolitan Area
(city plus surrounding areas)
1 Inner city
2 City proper (legal boundary)
3 Suburbs
4 Edge cities
5 Exurbs

7 Megalopolis
(continuous developed region with more than one city)

The different zones of a metropolitan area include (1) "inner" city, (2) city proper, (3) suburbs, (4) edge cities, (5) exurbs, (6) metropolitan area, and (7) megalopolis.

- *Edge cities,* mini-cities that develop outside the city proper and that include major business, commercial, and even industrial districts to which people travel for work, shopping, and recreation
- *Exurbs,* residential areas beyond the suburbs that have a quasi-rural atmosphere
- *Metropolitan area,* the region that encompasses a city plus the surrounding suburbs, exurbs, and edge cities
- *Megalopolis,* a continuous urban region that incorporates multiple cities

Finally, at the micro level, the physical environment within a city can also influence social life. (The Through a Sociological Lens box explores how people interpret or identify with their physical environment.) If you look around your campus to see where students like to hang out, you will probably find physical features that make these locations appealing. Benches, a wall, a green and shady lawn can all make a difference in whether and how people use a physical space. Urban planners and architects apply these social-psychological insights in designing buildings, public spaces, and neighborhoods.

Power and Inequality in City Life

What fuels urban growth? Who has the power to help determine the investment and development that will occur? How are valuable resources, including housing, transportation,

Navigating Communities

What do the design of GPS navigation systems, Internet virtual worlds, websites, and urban neighborhoods have in common? They all allow people to create a mental image of a space, and they all have been influenced by a classic piece of mid-twentieth-century sociological research.

Kevin Lynch (1960) interviewed people in Boston, Los Angeles, and Jersey City about their city, asked them for directions to a well-known landmark, and asked them to draw a map of and describe their community to see how people "read" their city. Lynch produced a map for each city from an amalgamation of these individual "mental maps" and concluded that people use five basic elements to understand their physical environment:

1. Paths—familiar routes that include streets and transit lines
2. Districts—areas perceived to be internally homogeneous, constituting a whole, like certain business districts, college campuses, and residential neighborhoods
3. Edges—dividing lines between districts
4. Landmarks—points of reference, usually simple physical objects such as a building, monument, clock tower, or sign
5. Nodes—points of reference that, unlike landmarks, can be entered, such as a square, a park, or the intersection of transit lines

The project illustrated different ways that people locate themselves in their surroundings, connect to their community, and navigate their environment. For example, since the streets of Boston are very crooked, residents rarely use them as reference points in giving directions. Instead, they use landmarks. Jersey City, though, has a rectangular grid of streets and avenues on which residents rely heavily in navigating the city. Different cities thus have different "legibility"—they can be "read" more or less easily.

The built environment of cities, therefore, results from a collaborative process. The physical landscape influences how people think about the spaces in which they live, but human actors give these physical elements meaning.

Other professionals have since expanded these basic insights to a variety of applications. Understanding how people use distances and landmarks in navigating a city can help software developers create GPS navigation systems that provide user-friendly directions, for example. People use "mental maps" to navigate websites or Internet-based virtual worlds as well, making Lynch's insights applicable to cyberspace, which did not even exist when he first conducted his research.

think about it

1. *Try drawing a map of your campus from memory, and compare it to maps by your classmates. Did you draw similar maps? Why or why not? Does your map use some of the basic elements Lynch described?*

2. *Have you ever used a poorly designed map or website? What made it difficult to use? How might Lynch's research have been applied to improve it?*

---

and city services, distributed in a city? In studying urban life, sociologists have asked such questions and documented how the powerful disproportionately influence urban development, often to the disadvantage of those with less power. An example of this research is **new urban sociology,** *an approach to studying cities that focuses on the interactions of politics and economics and locates them in the larger context of the global economy* (Gottdiener and Hutchison 2010). Here we consider examples of the insights that have emerged from this approach.

Class Inequality and the Urban "Growth Machine"

Class inequality is pervasive in urban spaces. The gap between the rich in luxurious settings and the homeless on the street is just one indicator of economic inequality. In addition to more comfortable homes, people in affluent areas typically enjoy low rates of street crime and better community services.

We also see class inequality in the attention paid to the needs of commuters. For decades, governments have built and expanded roads to accommodate mostly middle-class drivers commuting from the suburbs while often neglecting public transportation—the buses, trains, light rail, and subways relied upon by poor and working-class city residents. Stratification is emerging even among drivers, however, as some localities introduce private toll roads that allow paying drivers to bypass congestion others must endure (Layton and Hsu 2008).

Class inequality is also reflected in how cities grow. Developers, realtors, bankers, builders, and other business owners all have a stake in promoting the growth of cities because more people means more potential profits for their businesses. For politicians, growth represents grateful business owners to fund their campaigns and an expanding commercial tax base

thinking about power

How is **power**, and its distribution, reflected in the way your community is arranged? What are the desirable neighborhoods, and who lives in them? What neighborhoods are considered to have problems? Who lives in those neighborhoods?

The clashing interests of residents and developers are reflected in the conflicts that emerge over the gentrification of neighborhoods.

CORE CONCEPTS CHALLENGE

How do such clashes reflect economic inequality and differences in **power**?

to fund government budgets. Consequently, some sociologists have referred to cities as **"growth machines,"** *a label that highlights how powerful businesses and politicians work together to promote urban development, often while ignoring the interests of ordinary citizens* (Logan and Molotch 1987; Molotch 1976).

Developers pursuing profits move from project to project and do not have to live with the consequences of what they create. But for ordinary citizens, cities are not merely growth machines but the places where they live and work, communities to which they have a long-term commitment. Sometimes the growth interests of business and politicians harm the interests of ordinary citizens. For example, **gentrification** is *the process of rehabilitating older housing stock and investing in neighborhood development in a way that typically attracts new higher-income residents and displaces current middle- and low-income residents.* Because they transform relatively inexpensive properties into more desirable—and more expensive—housing, such projects can be highly profitable for investors. But gentrification often displaces middle- and low-income residents who cannot afford to buy and are unable to pay the newly increased rents. Meanwhile, investors and politicians often neglect low-income housing—a key to tackling the homelessness that exists in all urban areas—because of its relatively low profit margins.

Conflicts therefore arise between investors who pursue short-term growth and profits and residents who want to protect their quality of life. Community-based social movements often emerge to advocate for residents' interests. They typically face an interlocking concentration of power consisting of developers, realtors, and both appointed and elected officials.

In addition, because local governments play a key role in the regulation and distribution of valuable resources, such as housing, education, transportation, and social welfare benefits, they are often involved in conflict. Local disputes between government and citizen grassroots organizations represent new forms of community-based class conflict in capitalist societies that Karl Marx did not anticipate when he focused on workplace class conflict (Castells 1983).

Race and Urban Inequality

At the end of the nineteenth century, W.E.B. Du Bois, working in Philadelphia, carried out the first sociological study of African Americans. In *The Philadelphia Negro* ([1899] 1996), Du Bois used innovative methods—from mapping to personal interviews and statistics—to document employment, family composition, religion, street activity, community institutions, crime, interracial contacts, and other aspects of black urban life. His nuanced assessment of the black community included an indictment of the role white racism played in creating deplorable conditions that contrasted with white neighborhoods.

Over a century later, urban communities are still divided by race, due to the legacy of segregation (which created single-race neighborhoods), continuing economic inequality, and ongoing institutional racism (Figure 15.3). Institutional discrimination in the housing industry played a role long after the end of legal segregation in the form of **redlining,** *the use of discriminatory practices in the sale or rental of housing to minorities.* (The term comes from real estate agents' practice of marking maps with a red line indicating neighborhoods they deemed off limits to minorities.) Banks sometimes informally wrote off minority neighborhoods, denying mortgages to potential buyers and home improvement loans to owners, regardless of their financial status. Real estate agents sometimes also refused to show prospective buyers homes in these neighborhoods. These tactics contributed to the downward spiral of some minority neighborhoods. Studies show that minorities in rental and housing markets today continue to be treated differently from whites (Squires et al. 2002; Turner and Ross 2005).

In a twist on this sort of discrimination, the housing mortgage crisis of the past few years featured "reverse redlining," or predatory lending. Unscrupulous brokers and financial institutions targeted poor and working-class minorities, encouraging them to shoulder complex mortgages with high interest rates that they often did not understand and could not afford. One study found that blacks and Hispanics were twice as likely to get these high-cost "subprime" loans as whites with comparable income (Bajaj and Fessenden 2007).

The segregation picture today is mixed (Iceland et al. 2010; Logan and Stults 2011; Logan, Stults, and Farley 2004).

SPOTLIGHT

on social theory

Conflict theorists highlight the power struggles that often occur to control scarce resources. How do such struggles apply to urban development? Have you seen evidence of such conflict in your community?

FIGURE 15.3 | CONTINUING RACIAL AND ETHNIC SEGREGATION

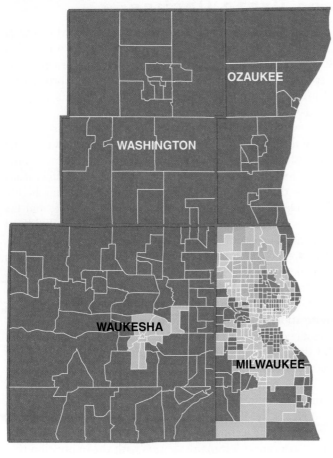

Black
	50.0% or less
	50.1 to 85.0%
	85.1% or more

Hispanic
	50.0% or less
	50.1 to 85.0%
	85.1% or more

White
	50.0% or less
	50.1 to 85.0%
	85.1% or more

Although overall segregation levels have been declining, racial and ethnic segregation remains stark in many cities. In Milwaukee, Wisconsin, and surrounding counties—the nation's most segregated urban area according to the 2010 Census—black, Hispanic, and white residents live in largely separate areas. *Source:* Denvir (2011).

Although significant racial segregation persists, fair housing legislation, the growth of the black middle class, and declining racial prejudice among individuals have enabled some desegregation to occur (Figure 15.4). However, this has largely been due to working- and middle-class minorities moving into formerly all-white areas, leaving behind neighborhoods made up predominately of poor minorities. It is far less common for whites to move into these poor minority neighborhoods, which now often feature lower-quality schools, higher crime rates, and less valuable homes (Logan and Stults 2011).

Segregation between blacks and whites peaked in the 1960s and has been declining slowly but steadily, reaching new lows in 2010. Hispanics and Asians are considerably less segregated than African Americans, and there has been little change in segregation levels for these groups in the past decade. However, the rapidly growing Hispanic population is resulting in larger homogeneous Hispanic communities.

Urbanization in a Global Economy

Just a few decades ago, local businesses and political leaders made the decisions affecting the future of a city. For example, as late as the 1960s, most hardware stores, clothing stores, restaurants, and so on were independent and owned locally or regionally. In recent decades, however, globalization has centralized much of business. Instead of hundreds of independent hardware stores scattered across the country, most communities have only a Home Depot or a Lowe's outlet. Instead of countless local restaurants, a small handful of national and international fast-food chains dominate the market. The same is true for many other industries.

This massive growth of chains has brought lower prices for consumers but has concentrated economic power in the hands of a few corporate players, against which small local businesses often cannot effectively compete.

on social theory

According to Wallerstein's **world systems theory**, a global economy links the countries of the world. How do the actions of transnational corporations within this global system affect your community?

Percentage

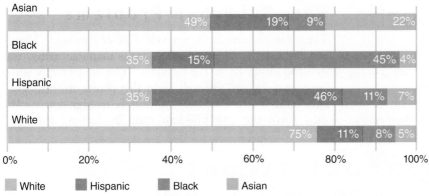

	White	Hispanic	Black	Asian

FIGURE 15.4 | AVERAGE NEIGHBORHOOD COMPOSITION BY RACE AND ETHNICITY IN U.S. URBAN AREAS, 2010

Members of each major racial and ethnic group in the nation's 367 largest urban areas tend to live in neighborhoods with very different demographics. For example, the average white person (bottom line of the graph) lives in a neighborhood that is 75 percent white and 8 percent black, but the average African American (second line) lives in a neighborhood that is 45 percent black and 35 percent white.

Source: Logan and Stults (2011).

The consolidation of economic power into the hands of large, often global, chain stores has meant that strip malls and other commercial development across the country look remarkably similar, featuring the same handful of national chains, big-box retailers, and indistinctive architecture. How are local communities affected by this sort of development?

Control over a local community's fate—its ability to attract business, promote commercial development, and so on—has often shifted to the boardrooms of major national and transnational corporations (Gottdeiner and Hutchison 2006).

An influx of investment dollars can bring jobs and prosperity, while a withdrawal of investment can lead to economic decline and urban blight. Many U.S. cities in the North and Midwest have experienced difficulties as transnational corporations pursuing higher profits moved the manufacturing jobs that provided steady employment for local residents to foreign countries with fewer regulations and lower wages (Harvey 1985, 1990). At the same time, the movement of capital abroad has helped fuel the development of cities in China, Mexico, India, and other nations. Understanding urbanization today requires understanding such global dynamics.

The Structure and Culture of the Suburbs

From 2010 to 2012, big cities grew at a faster rate than the suburbs (Frey 2013). That development could be temporary, though. The longer trend in the United States has not been urbanization but rather suburbanization. In this section we examine this development and sample some of the issues it raises.

Suburban Growth and Urban Decline

The rise of the suburbs dates to the post–World War II period. As the United States emerged from the war with a strong manufacturing infrastructure and few foreign competitors, it began a period of unprecedented prosperity. With the help of their unions, many U.S. workers acquired good-paying manufacturing jobs.

Newfound affluence among the working class allowed many to pursue a dream unthinkable before the war: home ownership. In the postwar years, federal government programs mobilized massive amounts of money to help citizens achieve this goal. The government offered veterans highly favorable terms for mortgages to purchase a home, and tax policies benefited homeowners over renters. Racially biased housing policies granted federally backed mortgages to "low-risk" areas— often interpreted as newly built (white) suburbs —while neglecting existing housing stock in central cities (Wilson 1996). Such financing, combined with mass-produced modest tract homes, made housing in the suburbs more affordable than ever. New road and highway programs facilitated transportation from central cities to the suburbs. All these structural conditions encouraged the migration of people from cities to suburbs in the 1950s and 1960s.

While public policy was making the suburbs attractive, a number of developments made cities increasingly unattractive. In the 1960s, media images of urban rioters protesting racial and economic inequality, police brutality, and other grievances left many viewers with the impression that the inner city was dangerous and crime-ridden. The export of urban manufacturing jobs overseas that began in the 1970s and 1980s undermined the economic health of many cities, deepening poverty and escalating the crime rate. With an eroded tax base, cities faced financial crises just when the need for social services had expanded. The perception of these urban problems further enhanced the appeal of the suburbs for those who could afford them, and their departure for the suburbs left the people behind with few options. Since 1950, more than 90 percent of U.S. population growth in metropolitan areas has occurred in the suburbs. In recent years, about two-thirds of the population has lived in the suburbs (Flint 2006).

New Suburban Problems

The automobile made the growth of suburbs possible. Henry Ford, the father of automobile mass-manufacturing, was sure the future lay in the suburbs. "The modern city is the most artificial and unlovely sight this planet affords," Ford once said. "The ultimate solution is to abandon it. We shall solve the city problem only by leaving the city"

thinking about structure

How does the physical **structure** of suburban communities shape social life in the suburbs and distinguish it from urban life?

(in Flint 2006, 29). The suburbs did indeed become an attractive option for many people. But rather than solving city problems, the growth of the suburbs brought unanticipated new challenges for our health, environment, and social lives.

SPRAWL The growth of the suburbs has resulted in **sprawl,** *low-density development that disperses people over a wide area, separates homes from workplaces and stores, and depends heavily on cars for transportation.* Suburban sprawl quickly consumes land that had been wildlife habitat or devoted to agriculture. As the distance between home, work, and shopping grew, sprawl also created enormous traffic congestion and long commutes to work (Figure 15.5). On average, U.S. workers spend 51 minutes a day traveling to and from work. About 8.1 percent of commuters—some 10.8 million people—have "long commutes" of two hours round-trip, and about 600,000 have "mega-commutes" in which they spend three hours or more a day going to and from work (McKenzie 2013).

Only 5 percent of people take public transportation to work. Instead, with three cars for every four people, over 86 percent get to work by car and 76 percent drive alone (see Figure 15.6). With all that driving, Americans around major cities are estimated to spend an average of 38 hours a year stuck in traffic, wasting 2.9 billion gallons of fuel (Schrank, Eisele, and Lomax 2012). Such congestion takes a toll on health: 8 percent of all heart attacks are linked to traffic congestion (Harper 2007). Driving and congestion also contribute to the degradation of our natural environment, through both air pollution and inefficient use of land. Increasingly expensive gasoline also burdens commuters with a higher cost of living.

The most common response to congestion—building more roads—usually makes the situation worse because it attracts more suburban development, which produces more traffic. In metropolitan areas with the most added road capacity in the 1990s, the hours commuters were stuck in traffic jumped by 70 percent (Flint 2006).

HIGHER TAXES Local governments lose money on suburban residential growth, making growth expensive for taxpayers (Flint 2006). In most cases, the tax revenue new residents bring in is not enough to offset the costs of infrastructure such as roads and schools and the ongoing salaries of additional teachers, firefighters, and other workers needed to serve the increased population. To pay these costs, suburban governments usually increase residential property taxes, making taxpayers subsidize the residential real estate development industry.

SOCIAL ISOLATION Unlike that of cities, the built environment of suburbs often makes social life more isolated and private. Some of this privacy is desirable and one of the reasons the suburbs are attractive to many. But such a lifestyle has social consequences. The suburbanite's need to drive almost everywhere reduces face-to-face social interaction by reducing casual encounters on neighborhood

FIGURE 15.5 | SUBURBAN SPRAWL

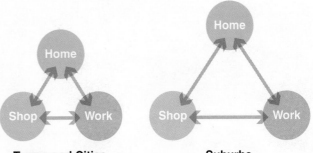

Towns and Cities   **Suburbs**

Imagine a triangle between your home, the place you work, and the key places you shop. In smaller communities or dense urban environments, the sides of the triangle typically represent relatively short distances. In suburban sprawl, though, these distances become much greater, separating various social activities so that longer car travel is required and a unifying sense of community is less likely. What are some of the other consequences of making the legs of this triangle longer?

FIGURE 15.6 | HOW U.S. WORKERS GET TO WORK

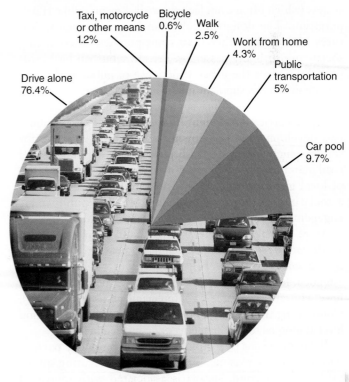

Taxi, motorcycle or other means 1.2%
Bicycle 0.6%
Walk 2.5%
Work from home 4.3%
Public transportation 5%
Drive alone 76.4%
Car pool 9.7%

The vast majority of U.S. workers commute by car, usually driving alone. *Source:* U.S. Census Bureau, 2010–2012 American Community Survey.

CORE CONCEPTS CHALLENGE

How do you get to school? How does the **structure** *of your community influence your decision to travel this way?*

As the suburbs grow, they take up land once used for agriculture and wildlife habitat, strain local water supplies, and transform the local ecosystems.

Today's Changing Suburbs

The popular image of the suburbs in the 1950s was of quiet neighborhoods, with white residents living in modest homes surrounded by picket fences. But the suburbs have changed dramatically, and today they also vary significantly from one another. Older inner suburbs have developed many social problems formerly associated with cities, such as significant crime, gang violence, poverty, pollution, and neighborhood blight. In stark contrast, other suburbs feature a relatively secure life in high-end luxury homes behind the protective walls of gated communities. Spatial development also differs greatly across suburban areas. The exurbs, for example, sometimes have no real neighborhoods at all, since homes are spread out on large multiacre lots. Some new suburbs have followed "smart-growth" principles, however, emphasizing dense development that allows residents to live, work, and shop in walkable neighborhoods—features that used to distinguish city life.

Suburbs, overall, have also become more racially and ethnically diverse. Most immigrants to the United States in the 2000s moved to small towns and suburbs rather than large urban areas (Tavernise and Gebeloff 2010). As more racial and ethnic minorities achieve middle-class status and governments and lenders eliminate overtly racist housing policies, many minorities have done exactly what an earlier generation of whites did: they have left the city and moved to the suburbs, leaving behind poorer residents in urban minority neighborhoods.

In some cases, modern technology has helped overcome the social isolation of the suburbs. Many housing developments have their own websites, forums, and e-mail lists that allow news to be shared and help organize face-to-face social and community events. Some wealthier suburban developments even hire professional activities directors to coordinate social events and community gatherings (McCrummen 2005a).

These technological and professional fixes can help people of similar incomes (who can afford to live in the subdivision) and interests make connections, but they do not promote broad civic engagement with the larger community. In fact, affluent suburban housing developments can be very homogeneous and inward looking, epitomized by gated communities that physically exclude neighbors of more modest means who often lived in the area long before the new developments were constructed (McCrummen 2005b). Such a built environment speaks volumes about the types of social connections being cultivated—and discouraged.

streets (which often even lack sidewalks) or on public transportation. The design of suburban homes frequently features back decks rather than front porches, discouraging socializing with any passersby. Private suburban backyards partially replace the urban experience of public parks; private media rooms supplant public movie theaters.

The orientation to privacy can carry over to a broader decline in civic engagement. For example, in many suburban developments, homeowner associations arrange for services such as private trash pick-up, snow removal, and road maintenance—tasks that used to be the responsibility of local governments. As a result, participation in these associations sometimes displaces broader public civic engagement.

More broadly, Robert Putnam (2000) found that "*each additional ten minutes in daily commuting time cuts involvement in community affairs by 10 percent*—fewer public meetings attended, fewer committees chaired, fewer petitions signed, fewer church services, less volunteering, and so on" (p. 213). Commuting time is second in importance only to education level among factors influencing civic involvement.

Putnam argues that commuting cuts into civic participation for three reasons. First, as noted, navigating sprawl takes time. Second, sprawl is associated with increased social segregation, reducing opportunities for connections that cross class and racial lines. Finally, sprawl disrupts community "boundedness"—the sense of living in a distinct community. People in the suburbs, whose attention is divided between where they live and where they work, have less sense of belonging to a distinct community (and thus of participating in community life) than do urban dwellers.

The Enduring Significance of Rural Life

Different government agencies use different definitions to distinguish between urban and rural. Although cities and suburbs often receive the most attention, about 72 percent of the land in the United States is classified as "nonmetropolitan" and thus rural. These rural areas are home to about 46.2 million people—15 percent of the population in 2012 (Cromartie 2013).

The overall rural population in the United States has remained relatively stable for more than 50 years but, because the urban population has increased during the same period, the rural population has declined as a percentage of the overall population. Some rural communities have shrunk in recent decades, while others have grown in population since the 1990s. So far, "rural rebound" has occurred mostly in areas that cater to tourists looking for outdoor activities such as skiing, boating, and hiking. But as more people are able to work from home over the Internet, they may begin to migrate back to smaller communities.

Regardless of their population, rural areas continue to play crucial roles in social life (Flora and Flora 2008; Lobao 2007). For one thing, cities themselves depend on rural areas for a variety of resources. The rural farmlands and ranches that are home to crops and animals feed urban populations. Rural mines generate the coal and uranium, oilfields the oil, and wind turbines the wind energy that fuel urban life. Wood, steel, and other construction materials that form the infrastructure of cities are harvested from rural forests and mines. Most of the garbage generated in urban areas ends up in rural landfills. Many tourist destinations—getaways for the mental health of urban dwellers—are also located in rural areas.

Rural communities are no longer as isolated or as homogeneous as they once were. Modern highways and road systems make traveling to them easier, while telecommuting and "extreme commuting" open up many more jobs to rural residents than just agriculture or ranching. Satellite communications bring television and the Internet to sparsely populated rural areas, connecting them to all facets of the broader culture. Local agricultural and meat processing jobs often attract new immigrants, especially from Mexico and Central America. In short, today's rural communities can increasingly include the diversity found in the broader society.

Regardless of these changes, the fields, forests, and green spaces of rural communities continue to link their residents to the natural environment. In contrast, many urban dwellers do not think about where their food is grown, where their water comes from, or where their wastes end up. For most city residents, attention to nature is largely limited to deciding whether they will need an umbrella today. But in the coming years the natural environment will demand everyone's attention because the impact of human activity has created an environmental crisis.

Environmental Sociology

On December 7, 1972, while on their way to the moon, astronauts in NASA's Apollo 17 took the first crystal-clear picture of a fully lit Earth, the "blue marble" photo, as it became known. Huge distances, vast terrains, and seemingly endless oceans confront people who travel the surface of the planet. But this single photo, taken from 18,000 miles away, shows that our tiny planet in the vast darkness of space has very real limits. Released just as concerns about environmental issues were growing, the "blue marble" photo became a symbol of our planet's limited resources and the common challenge of protecting them that we face.

Like the rest of society, sociologists have paid increasing attention to environmental issues since the days of the "blue marble" photo. As Dunlap and Marshall (2007) note, "environmental problems are fundamentally social problems: They result from human social behavior, they are viewed as problematic because of their impact on humans (as well as other species), and their solution requires societal effort" (p. 329). **Environmental sociology** *focuses on the interaction between social life, the built environment, and the natural environment.* Pellow and Brehm (2013, 232) note that environmental sociology is unique in highlighting "the inseparability of human society from nonhuman natures and the centrality of inequality and power that shape both." In examining our natural world, environmental sociologists focus on three key issues: (1) why societies are producing such daunting environmental problems, (2) how people come to recognize and understand them, and (3) how changes in social structure and behavior can help address them. We consider each of these issues, but we start with a quick reminder of the range of problems in our current environmental crisis.

NASA's "blue marble" photo, the first clear picture of a fully lit face of Earth, helped symbolize the fragile nature of Earth's environment.

2002

2011

FAST-FORWARD

Change and the Environment

One of the few ways we can see the effects of global warming is in the extensive melting of many of the world's massive glaciers. These pictures contrast a glacier in Norway photographed in 2002 (*top*) with the same glacier photographed in 2011 (*bottom*). Glacial melting has clearly accelerated in just the past few years.

Environmental Threats

In brief, the following are among the environmental challenges we face:

- **Water pollution.** Numerous pollutants threaten water quality: industrial pollutants (including industrial waste dumped in rivers and waste oil dumped into the ocean), household waste (sewage treated with chemicals and dumped in rivers, drugs flushed down the toilet), erosion from development (mud in creeks and streams), and agricultural runoff (including pesticides and fertilizers). These pollutants can create health problems and destroy habitats for microorganisms and larger water animals.

- **Air pollution.** Gases emitted by cars, trucks, and industrial processes enter the air we breathe. They can combine with water molecules in the atmosphere

and be reintroduced into the soil and water as acid rain (precipitation high in acid content). Or these toxic gases can rise and reduce the effectiveness of the ozone layer—the layer of atmosphere that protects the earth against ultraviolet radiation from the sun, a source of skin cancer and other health issues.

- **Global warming.** Air pollution in the form of excess carbon dioxide also forms a shield that prevents heat from escaping the earth's atmosphere. This process helps produce *global warming*, an increase in the average temperature of the earth's atmosphere. This climate change contributes to the melting of glaciers and may increase the frequency and severity of extreme weather, such as droughts, flooding, hurricanes, and tornadoes.

- **Solid waste.** The quantity of garbage has been exploding, and the space we have for it is limited. Nonbiodegradable trash (waste that cannot be broken down by living organisms) fills our landfills, where most garbage is buried and will remain essentially forever. Leaks and seepage of toxic wastes into the groundwater and the release of polluting gases into the air pollute areas near landfills. A fast-growing form of garbage is "e-waste"; more than 100 million computers, cell phones, and other electronic devices, many containing toxins, are discarded in the United States each year.

- **Resource depletion.** Human activity destroys, depletes, and pollutes a variety of natural resources. Logging and burning destroy rain forests, often to make room for cattle ranching or farming. But rain forests are like the earth's lungs in reverse; they absorb carbon dioxide from the atmosphere and produce oxygen. They are also home to an estimated three-quarters of the earth's plant species. Clean water is becoming a scarce commodity, and a water shortage could be one of the biggest threats in this century.

- **Energy consumption.** Energy consumption depletes natural resources (such as oil), produces toxic pollutants (such as radioactive waste from nuclear power plants), and contributes to global warming (from coal-fired electrical plants, for example). Because energy use affects the environment in so many ways, the ability to produce clean renewable energy is a huge challenge for the future of our environment.

Many of these problems have been emerging for decades. What is new is the *scale* of consumption, pollution, and resource depletion as industrialization and urbanization spread around the world.

Analyzing Environmental Problems

How can we analyze and better understand environmental problems that threaten us? One way is to draw upon the sociological perspective on environments and community life we have used throughout this chapter. The natural environment is the context within which social life occurs. The actions humans take, especially in constructing a built environment, alter that environment. The altered natural environment, in turn, influences human action.

The spectacular growth of Brazil's Rio de Janeiro has meant the destruction of the adjacent Atlantic rain forest. Urban growth around the world has put unprecedented strains on natural resources, contributing to the expanding environmental crisis.

The issue that underlies most environmental crises is a lack of sustainability. **Sustainability** refers to *a balance between resource protection and consumption that can be maintained indefinitely.* Unfortunately, humans are engaged in a number of *unsustainable* practices with enormous consequences.

Our natural environment provides essential assets that serve key functions for our survival, but their overuse results in critical environmental problems, as summarized in Figure 15.7. The three basic functions of our environmental assets are to provide a place in which to live, to provide resources needed for survival (including air, water, food, and energy), and to provide a place to dispose of wastes. Our global ecosystem has only a limited ability to serve these three functions (Dunlap and Marshall 2007). Unsustainable practices put excess demands on the environment, creating three corresponding problems. First, dramatic growth in human population is leading to overcrowding. Second, we are consuming resources at a pace that outstrips long-term supply, resulting in resource depletion. Third, pollution is overwhelming the ecosystem's ability to absorb waste products. For example, water pollution is creating dramatic "dead zones" in the world's oceans—areas so toxic that virtually nothing survives in them—whereas excess carbon dioxide is contributing to global warming.

Overuse in one area can create problems in the others. Pollution, for example, can make an area uninhabitable, while overpopulation can contribute to resource depletion. Thus the environmental problems we face are closely interrelated.

Power, Inequality, and the Environment

Who is most likely to be a source of environmental pollution and degradation, and who is most likely to be exposed to and harmed by them? In analyzing these questions, sociologists consider issues of power and inequality.

In 2000 in the Philippines, typhoons saturated a mountain of toxic garbage that had been accumulating for 30 years and had piled up at a 70-degree angle. Then the garbage came crashing down on a poor neighborhood of shanties in Quezon City, part of the megalopolis of Manila. The shanties were home to desperately poor people who scratched out a living by scavenging aluminum cans, chunks of metal, and anything else they could sell from the garbage. When the avalanche buried their neighborhood, hundreds died (Power 2006).

For decades, wealthier nations have been shipping their toxic wastes and other environmentally hazardous goods to poorer nations like the Philippines. This is one way in which power and inequality determine the impact of environmental problems. Those with more power and privilege generally reap the benefits of environmental degradation through affluent lifestyles and the ability to protect themselves from pollution. Those with less power and privilege, like the people who died in Quezon City, often bear the brunt of environmental crises.

Even in the United States, class and race play a part in disproportionately burdening poor and minority communities with environmentally hazardous materials (Bell 2012; Bullard 2000; Pellow and Brulle 2005; Walker 2012). Governments and corporations are more likely to place toxic waste dumps, chemical plants, incinerators, landfills, sewage treatment facilities, and other pollution hazards near the homes of racial minorities and people with lower incomes,

FIGURE 15.7 | FUNCTIONS OF THE ENVIRONMENT AND THE CONSEQUENCES OF OVERUSING THEM

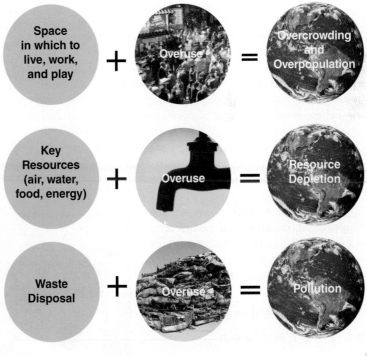

Our natural environment provides essential assets that serve a key function for our survival, but their overuse results in critical environmental problems.

Affluent nations export much of the electronic waste ("e-waste") they produce from computers, cell phones, and other electronic devices. Poor people in developing countries, such as this young Indian worker, are often employed to extract usable metals from the waste, a process that exposes them to high levels of toxins. Have you disposed of any electronic devices in recent years? Do you know where they ended up?

focus also on the effect of structural forces in creating those problems. According to one structural analysis, *capital-intensive industries and the modern state, in pursuit of continual growth as a central good, have created* a **treadmill of production** *that results in increasing resource depletion and worsening pollution* (Gould, Pellow, and Schnaiberg 2008; Schnaiberg 1980).

In a capitalist market economy, corporations increase their profits by growing bigger. For workers, economic growth provides jobs, the income from which enables them to consume more. For the state, growth represents low unemployment and an expanding tax base, as we saw with urban "growth machines." But the promotion of growth by corporations, governments, and workers produces two negative environmental consequences. First, growth contributes to resource depletion by increasing exploitation of natural resources and energy. In a world with finite resources, continuous growth that increases resource consumption is unsustainable. Second, growth creates pollution and waste, which we have seen contribute to environmental problems. As long as humanity continues to pursue an unsustainable growth strategy, we will be on this destructive treadmill.

Culture and the Social Construction of Environmental Problems

The common belief that growth is a good thing instead of a strain on our natural environment illustrates how our cultural beliefs and traditions shape our perception of the environment and the threats to it. Environmental problems have a physical reality—pollution levels, loss of animal habitat, and declining resources, for example. But sociologists have long understood that for these objective conditions to be recognized as social problems, people must frame them accordingly. This framing is the task of *sponsors*—people who work to bring these problems to the attention of the media, public officials, and the public, seeking support in addressing them (Hannigan 2006). Their work is a type of social construction of reality.

SPOTLIGHT

on social theory

Symbolic interactionists highlight how humans interpret and make meaningful the world around them.

Do you think the meaning of the natural environment is different for young people today than it was for past generations? Why or why not?

In the 1960s and 1970s, environmental activists played a pioneering role in raising the public's consciousness about environmental issues, resulting in some important legislative initiatives. Between 1970 and 1973, Congress passed the Clean Air Act, the Clean Water Act, and the Endangered Species Act.

and rarely in affluent communities, whose residents have the power to resist such threats.

Since the mid-1980s, in response to this form of inequality, activists have organized campaigns for **environmental justice,** *the prevention of harmful practices that unfairly burden low-income people and racial minorities with disproportionate exposure to environmental hazards.* In the workplace as well, class distinctions shape exposure to environmental hazards. Working-class employees are most likely to be exposed to dangerous environmental conditions that can cause disease or injury. For decades, labor unions have promoted the adoption of occupational health and safety regulations that protect workers from environmental hazards such as exposure to harmful chemicals on the job.

The "Treadmill of Production"

Environmental problems have no single source but sociologists, rather than focusing solely on the actions of individuals,

Environmental protection seemed an overwhelmingly important priority. But enforcement has been lax, and counter-efforts have chipped away at these and other environmental legislative initiatives.

In fact, as recent sociological research shows, the environmental movement has stalled, evolving from a powerful grassroots social movement into a fragmented set of Washington, D.C.–based lobbying groups and isolated local efforts. Meanwhile, conservative countermovements, think tanks, and corporations with a financial stake in growth have been promoting antienvironmental messages and attempting to discredit scientific studies that document environmental destruction. Since the 1970s, the passage of proenvironment legislation has been rare, and some indicators show a *decline* in the degree to which the public sees environmental protection as a priority (Austin 2002; Bosso 2005; McCright and Dunlap 2003).

Meanwhile, as many environmental threats have grown more serious, the United States continues to embrace a culture of consumption. With less than 5 percent of the world's population, the United States consumes about 25 percent of the world's resources and produces about 30 percent of its waste. Rapidly developing nations are emulating the U.S. record and ramping up consumption at an unprecedented pace. China, as noted in our opening vignette, has rapidly transformed many urban areas into high-consumption centers, complete with cars, consumer products, meat-filled diets, and energy-guzzling homes. But the U.S. level of consumption is impossible to reproduce on a global scale; the earth simply does not have enough resources. According to one estimate, for just India and China to consume resources and pollute at a per-capita level comparable to the United States, we would need two more planet Earths (Worldwatch Institute 2006).

Seriously addressing environmental threats requires a change in attitudes, values, and understanding—a change of culture. Environmental activists work to bring about a culture that recognizes the hazards of overconsumption, resource depletion, and pollution while prioritizing limited consumption and the reuse of goods and materials.

The U.S. culture of individualism also can handicap us. The trend seems to be away from protecting the environment toward protecting the individual (Szasz 2007). For example, many people are concerned about the contamination of their tap water with chemicals. A social response would include political action to ensure stricter water pollution measures and more funding for water treatment facilities. Instead, most people protect only themselves by purchasing bottled water and water filters. This individualized approach shields those who can afford it, while society's most vulnerable bear the brunt of environmental damage.

The use of bottled water has also increased plastic consumption, adding nonbiodegradable trash to our landfills. Individualized responses like this are expensive and often ineffective (the production of bottled water is unregulated, and some products are just tap water), and they may only hinder more effective political action to achieve real change.

Still, there are occasional signs of growing environmental awareness in the culture and its subcultures. In 2006, eighty prominent Christian evangelicals signed "Climate Change: An Evangelical Call to Action." The document used scientific research findings and relevant biblical passages to call upon Christians to make protecting the environment a major priority, noting that "the consequences of climate change will be significant and will hit the poor the hardest" (Evangelical Climate Initiative 2006). The call is part of a larger, ongoing "Green Evangelical" movement (Kearns 2014).

The Search for Solutions

Environmental sociologists have also studied how best to address environmental challenges. Buttel (2003) identifies four basic mechanisms of "environmental reform":

1. *Environmental activism and social movements,* which raise awareness of issues, promote changes in individual and institutional behavior, and advocate for legislative regulation and reforms
2. *Environmental regulation by governments,* which can promote energy efficiency, put curbs on inefficient development, and limit polluting
3. *International environmental governance,* including global treaties and intergovernmental organizations
4. *Ecological modernization,* or the use of environmentally friendly new technologies and greater technological efficiencies

Buttel argues that social movements outside the halls of power are more important in environmental reform because they are effective catalysts for other forms of action. As we saw, a vibrant grassroots environmental movement in the 1960s and 1970s helped jumpstart important environmental legislation. More recently, activists have pushed for changes in the World Bank and other international institutions that have too often promoted lucrative projects for multinational corporations that devastated the environment. Buttel argues that such action by noninstitutional players is essential to environmental reform.

Some sociologists, though, say the capitalist quest for profit can actually help the environment (Spaargaren and Mol 1992). As companies recognize that energy inefficiency represents lost profits, they will adopt energy-efficient "green" technologies. Such ideas are controversial. The cases used to illustrate success are often atypical plants, corporations, and industries that use methods others cannot adopt on a scale large enough to make a difference (Dunlap and Marshall 2007). It may be just as likely that pursuit of profit will encourage destructive practices. BP's focus on rapid growth and cost-cutting rather than employee safety

thinking about culture

How does a **culture** that values high levels of consumption and individualism help contribute to our environmental crisis? How might that culture change to encourage a more sustainable future?

and environmental protection contributed to the massive 2010 oil spill in the Gulf of Mexico, which killed 11 workers and spewed oil for three months (Chazan, Faucon, and Casselman 2010; Lustgarten 2010). Only enforcement of government regulation can protect people and the natural environment from such abuses.

Perhaps the most visible recent effort to protect the environment is the marketing of "eco-friendly" products. However, Buttel (2004) and others argue that "green" consumerism is not a viable approach. First, as we have seen, pressure toward growth originates not with individuals who are the target of green consumerism but with institutional players—corporations and governments of the "growth machine" and "treadmill of production." Second, corporate and government decisions heavily influence the choice of products available to consumers. Corporate failure to invest in more efficient cars and government failure to require higher fuel efficiency have long limited consumers' options, regardless of their preferences. Third, many products and practices promoted as environmentally friendly are of marginal benefit and may be merely "greenwashing," improving the corporation's public image. Finally, evidence suggests that many who *say* they are concerned about the environment simply do not change their consumer behavior voluntarily.

Many sociologists therefore argue that focusing on individuals rather than larger social systems is unlikely to produce change on the necessary scale. This is not to say that individual choices do not matter but that, as sociologists have long observed, human action takes place within existing social structure. Real social change requires changing those structures.

The Sociology of Health

Just as sociologists place environmental issues in a broader social context, the basic insight of the sociology of health and illness is that "both disease and medical care are related to the structure of society" (Conrad 2005a, 1). In some cases, health is linked to community as well. Our perception and understanding of health issues are also influenced by our culture, including what we learn about who is competent to treat illness. Finally, health and illness are influenced by power inequalities.

The health of a population is more than just a medical issue. Research shows that social changes are just as important as advances in medical care. For example, McKinlay and McKinlay (1977) found that the dramatic decline in U.S. death rates from specific diseases in the twentieth century stemmed only partly from improved medical services. They show that profound changes in social conditions, such as better sanitation, improved nutrition, better housing conditions, and an overall rise in the standard of living were the central reasons for declining mortality, as well as for improved health and longer life expectancy.

The sociological study of health takes us beyond questions of disease and asks us to consider the broad cultural definitions of illness—which conditions are recognized as illnesses, which illnesses are stigmatized, why some illnesses are defined as disabilities—as well as what it means to experience illness. The research tradition known as the *social construction of illness* offers powerful insight into the social processes that shape the meaning and experience of health disorders (Conrad and Barker 2010).

Culture, Structure, Power, and the Medical Profession

Today, the occupation of doctor is among the most prestigious and highly paid in the United States. But that is a relatively recent cultural development that resulted from doctors effectively organizing to institutionalize their profession and gain power over health care. Sociologist Paul Starr's classic book, *The Social Transformation of American Medicine*, traces doctors' shifting status in nineteenth- and twentieth-century U.S. society. Starr (1983) cites an 1869 medical journal that complains "medicine has ever been and is now, the most despised of all the professions" (p. 7).

Few doctors enjoyed any financial success before 1900. They lacked uniform training and universal standards of practice and were not particularly successful at diagnosis and treatment. Many people distrusted them and preferred traditional home remedies. Doctors also faced challenges from other practitioners with very different approaches to illness, including midwives, herbalists, and peddlers of "patent medicines," typically made from exotic ingredients and sold as "miraculous" cures for virtually all illnesses.

DOCTORS ORGANIZE In the early twentieth century, doctors organized into a unified group emphasizing their specialized knowledge and skills and forming what would become a powerful voice on their behalf: the American Medical Association (AMA). Its members built alliances with the growing number of hospitals in the United States and devised standards for medical training and practice. Especially important, rather than competing among themselves, doctors united around an approach to health care based on science and research, which increased their success at diagnosing and treating illness. This scientific emphasis bound the medical profession with universities, where training and ongoing research now took place.

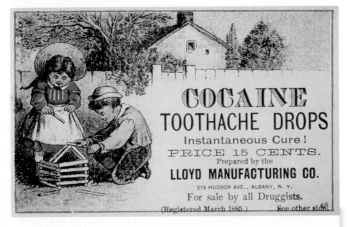

Before doctors gained the exclusive right to prescribe prescription drugs, some powerful drugs were unregulated and included in over-the-counter medicines intended for children.

CORE CONCEPTS CHALLENGE

How does this ad reflect the **culture** *of the era in which it was produced?*

By the early twentieth century, U.S. doctors had established a powerful **professional authority,** *legitimate power to define the terms of discussion within a specific field.* Citizens looked to doctors for medical advice on staying healthy and for treatment when they became ill. Mindful of the complexity of the human body and aware of doctors' distinctive knowledge, patients learned to doubt their own ability to diagnose and treat illness. A growing public trust in science, and dramatic success in reducing the incidence of dreaded diseases such as tetanus and diphtheria, elevated doctors as unparalleled authorities on health and illness. Their influence soon extended beyond medicine, as people turned to them for advice on matters from childrearing to sexual conduct.

MONOPOLIZING MEDICAL PRACTICE

Building on the high status of their powerful professional authority, doctors established an institutional monopoly on medical practice that drove out rival practitioners. They secured legislation that permitted only officially licensed doctors to practice medicine. The AMA certified medical schools, and each medical school limited enrollment, thereby controlling the supply of doctors. In this new medical system, professional authority became a means of increasing doctors' incomes to unprecedented heights.

Just as important, doctors came to act as gatekeepers, controlling access to prescription drugs and influencing policies that required people to consult them before participating in specific activities. Public schools and summer camps often won't admit children without evidence of a physical examination by a doctor. Some employers depend on company-paid doctors to screen new hires, and insurance companies require medical examinations when people make health- or injury-related insurance claims.

THE WEAKENING OF DOCTORS' AUTHORITY

Recent changes in health care in the United States have undermined the power, status, and authority of doctors. McKinlay and Marceau (2002) identify eight key factors in this shift:

1. The decline in government support for doctors in private practice

2. The bureaucratization of medical practice, as an increasing number of doctors have left private practice and gone to work for large health care corporations

3. The emerging competitive threat from other lower-cost health care workers, including nurse practitioners and physicians' assistants, who have some of the same medical privileges as doctors

4. Globalization and the information revolution, which gives patients access to international health care options and vast amounts of medical information

5. Changes in the public conception of the body, which threaten to reduce the physician from a professional who cures illness to a technician who repairs the body

6. Changes in the doctor-patient relationship and the erosion of patient trust, as doctors increasingly work in for-profit contexts and heed the demands of health insurance providers

7. Growth in the number of doctors, leading to a general oversupply

8. The weakening and fragmentation of the AMA, which has historically represented doctors' shared interests

Although some of these trends may be plusses for patients, they all threaten the authority and autonomy of doctors. More physicians are becoming employees of large organizations, including health maintenance organizations (HMOs), since it has grown increasingly difficult and expensive to enter private practice. Many work for major corporations, supervising health care and wellness programs for employees and working with policy makers on health-related workplace issues. Sociologist Elaine Draper (2003) showed how different these company doctors are from previous generations. Their employers often demand they satisfy organizational goals that clash with the professional norms of independent physicians. Employees' skepticism of doctors who are identified too closely with management intensifies this conflict.

Inequality and the Distribution of Disease

Like other patterns in social life, disease and death are not distributed equally or randomly throughout a population. Instead, social inequalities shape the likelihood that someone will be healthy or sick, die young or live a long life. In short, social inequalities are related to inequalities in health (Barr 2008). Sociologists refer to these *persistent patterns of inequality in health* as **health disparities.**

In general, social inequality works in predictable ways: people with less income and education are likely to experience more illness and to die younger. Childhood asthma is far more prevalent in low-income households than in middle- or upper-income households. The death rate associated with diabetes is also correlated with family income and is highest in the poorest households. The lowest-income adults are far more likely to experience "fair" or "poor" health whether they are male, female, white, black, or Hispanic (National Center for Health Statistics 2013). Health disparities exist on a global scale, too: wealthier nations' populations live longer, healthier lives than do those in poorer nations.

Evidence of health disparities is clear and long-standing. Syme and Berkman (1976) note that high death rates and shorter life expectancy for the lower classes have been observed since the twelfth century. Adler and Newman (2002) summarized the complex and multifaceted "pathways" that connect inequality in socioeconomic status (SES) with health disparities. They argued that each component of SES—education, income, and occupation—contributes directly to health disparities.

- **Education** shapes future job opportunities and helps determine adult income. Just as important, education gives people knowledge, confidence, and skills that increase their access to information and resources promoting health and healthy lifestyles.

- **Income** is necessary to purchase health care services or health insurance. Those who can afford high-quality health services—including preventive and specialist care—are likely to be healthier, in the long run, than those who cannot. Income is also associated with improvements in nutrition, recreation, and housing—all of which contribute to health.

- **Occupation** relates to health disparities in that people with jobs and job security have fewer health problems. However, specific jobs can contribute to health disparities. Lower-status jobs are often more dangerous, exposing workers to toxic substances and increasing the risk of on-the-job injuries. In addition, the unemployed, part timers, and those in lower-status jobs are far less likely than full-time professionals to have a high-quality employer-sponsored health insurance plan, or any health insurance at all, further increasing health disparities associated with occupation. It remains to be seen whether recent health care reform will significantly increase the availability of insurance coverage.

Adler and Newman also identified indirect ways in which inequality in SES produces health disparities, including exposure to environmental hazards in poorer-quality housing and more crowded neighborhoods.

Lower socioeconomic groups are also more likely to smoke and less likely to eat a healthy diet and get sufficient exercise—all of which contribute to health problems.

Socioeconomic differences in smoking, diet, and exercise emerged in the 1960s as new information about healthy lifestyles became available. Higher-SES individuals had the educational and income resources to change their behavior. As a result, the gap between rich and poor in the incidence of heart disease became severe in the 1960s and 1970s (Beaglehole 1990). Lower-SES individuals are also more likely to experience chronic stress and have fewer resources to treat stress-related illnesses. (The Sociology Works box examines one sociology major's work promoting community health.)

People with low SES are more likely to be socially isolated. Their isolation leaves them at far greater risk of physical illness and death, as well as of mental health problems, such as depression, which can lower energy levels and reduce motivation to seek proper medical care when needed. A tragic example of the effect of social isolation is documented in Eric Klinenberg's (2003) study of the 1995 heat wave in Chicago, which resulted in more than 700 deaths. Klinenberg found that the underlying cause of these very preventable deaths was social isolation. The victims were largely poor elderly residents who lived alone and had little access to support, resources, government assistance, or even information about how to deal with the intense heat and the power shortages that made air conditioning unavailable.

A Changing World

COMMUNITY AND ENVIRONMENTAL INFLUENCES ON HEALTH

Is new research redefining our idea of health? Although it has long been known that personal behavioral choices influence well-being, health researchers today are increasingly recognizing the many ways that place—both the built environment and the natural environment—affects our health. A large body of new research connects "neighborhood disadvantage"—high community poverty rates and accompanying unemployment, racial segregation, crime, reduced physical activity, and even traffic problems—with "a wide range of detrimental health outcomes, including low birth weight, infant mortality, asthma, tuberculosis, depression, and poor self-rated health" (Do et al. 2008, 1259).

Housing also influences health. Deteriorating lead paint poses a major health hazard to children exposed to elevated levels of lead in the air and water inside their homes. Poor ventilation, leaky pipes, and pest infestations can fill a home with allergens, a primary source of childhood asthma. Poor

SOCIOLOGY WORKS

Tristan Sanders and Healthy Communities

When students think about working in health care, they often think of medical or nursing school. But Tristan Sanders took a different route, using the B.A. in sociology he earned in 2006 from Emory University. "I always knew I wanted to work in a health-related field," he says, "and majoring in sociology allowed me to do that at a population level, which has allowed me to have far greater influence than if I were to have gone to medical school and become a doctor." Rather than treating individual sick patients, Sanders helps promote healthy living in entire communities.

He works for Kaiser Permanente in the Institute for Health Research in Denver, Colorado, where he helps evaluate a non-profit organization that Kaiser supports financially called Live-Well Colorado (livewellcolorado.org). LiveWell is a statewide organization that provides multiyear grants to local communities to implement healthy eating and active living strategies to fight obesity. These strategies include the creation of safe routes to schools (to encourage walking), farmers markets and community gardens (to improve access to healthy foods), comprehensive bicycle and pedestrian plans (to encourage healthier commuting and recreation), and school- and work-based wellness programs (to educate about and encourage healthy lifestyles).

> "Sociology opened my mind to a world of possibilities."

On any given day, Sanders may be working with technical assistance providers and local community coordinators, implementing an interactive voice response (IVR) survey to monitor behavioral and health patterns, conducting focus groups during site visits, helping write grant applications, or developing evaluation plans. To advance his career, he has completed a master's degree in public health with a focus in health systems, management, and policy.

Sanders couldn't be happier with his choice of major: "Sociology has provided me nothing but opportunities. Opportunities to thrive academically because I was studying something I was interested in. Opportunities to thrive professionally because I was able to understand and apply the many things I have learned. Even opportunities to thrive socially because of the diverse base of knowledge I gained while studying sociology." Among his most memorable sociology courses, he cites methods classes that taught him about evaluation techniques and one course called "What It Means to Be Sick," a historical look at the evolution of health and wellness and of changes in the treatment of persons who are ill over time.

Tristan Sanders

Says Sanders, "Sociology opened my mind to a world of possibilities, most specifically being able to work in the field I ultimately wanted to work in [health care and population health] without going to medical school." And he confesses, "My experience with sociology has been a bit of a love affair. The more I engage myself in the material, the more I get out of it."

think about it

1. *How does Sanders's work reflect a sociological perspective on health issues?*
2. *How might a sociology degree be a stepping-stone to a health-related career?*

---

insulation in winter and lack of ventilation in summer create health problems, too, especially for older people. Over-crowding contributes to a variety of illnesses, including infectious diseases and psychological stress.

Even the high cost of housing can add indirectly to health problems by forcing difficult trade-offs. Hefty rent or mortgage payments may be met at the expense of heat, prescription medications, or health insurance, with potentially serious health consequences (Robert Wood Johnson Foundation 2008).

The relationship between community and health is not limited to disadvantaged neighborhoods. People who live in compact cities where walking is common have lower rates of diabetes, hypertension, heart disease, and stroke than do those in suburbs where driving is the norm. Suburban dwellers are on average six pounds heavier than their counterparts in cities. In response, however, some communities are designing built environments that promote good health by encouraging physical activity, especially walking and cycling along new networks of bike and pedestrian trails (Cowley and Springen 2005; Flint 2006; Stock and Ellaway 2013).

Society is growing more aware that environmental factors also influence health. Public health officials in the United States and around the world have identified **environmental health**—*the aspects of health, illness, and disease that result from environmental factors*—as one of the keys to a healthy population. Environmental factors

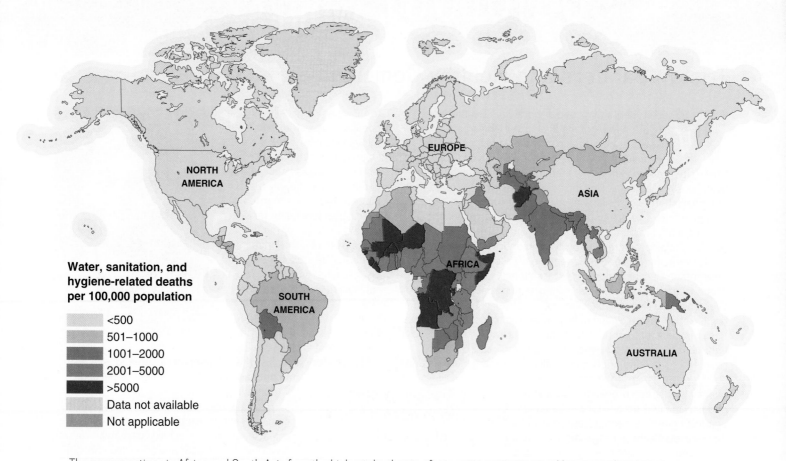

Water, sanitation, and hygiene-related deaths per 100,000 population

- <500
- 501–1000
- 1001–2000
- 2001–5000
- >5000
- Data not available
- Not applicable

The poorer nations in Africa and South Asia face the highest death rates from water, sanitation, and hygiene-related diseases. *Source:* World Health Organization (2011). Estimates based on WHO data for the year 2004. Copyright WHO 2011.

such as air, water, and soil pollution; household lead; unsanitary drinking water; and climate change can produce major health consequences. Diseases most commonly associated with environmental causes are diarrhea, respiratory infections, malaria, birth-related conditions, and certain heart diseases. The World Health Organization (2006) estimated that environmental factors account for 24 percent of the global "disease burden" (healthy life years lost to disease), and that the environment also accounts for up to 36 percent of deaths among children aged 14 or younger.

Improving and expanding access to safe water and sanitation systems can make a major contribution to global health. Deaths from diseases associated with water, sanitation, and hygiene problems are particularly high in Africa and parts of South Asia (see Map 15.1). The U.S. government's report *Healthy People 2020* identifies improvements in air and water quality and the proper use and disposal of toxic substances and hazardous waste as among the primary environmental health objectives in the twenty-first century (U.S. Department of Health and Human Services 2010).

What are the key characteristics of healthy places? A growing body of evidence shows that places that bring people into contact with the natural environment, that facilitate interaction among people, that encourage regular physical activity, and that build structures along environmentally sound principles (using nontoxic building materials and cleansers, effective ventilation, and natural lighting) promote good health among the people who live, work, and play in them (Frumkin 2003; Eriksson and Emmelin 2013; Srinivasan, O'Fallon, and Dearry 2003).

The sociology of health asks us to pay attention to the many ways in which health and illness are social issues. Understanding the community and environmental factors that influence people's physical health—both the factors that contribute to illness and disease and those that promote good health and healthy lifestyles—has emerged as a central component of the contemporary sociological analysis of health and illness.

thinking sociologically about
Communities, the Environment, and Health

culture

■ The places where we live—our communities—both reflect our culture and help promote certain types of cultural practices.

■ Our perception of and relation to the natural environment are influenced by our culture.

■ Evolving cultural norms have influenced our understanding of health and the role of health care professionals.

structure

■ The social environment that people create exists within the broader built and natural environments that help structure daily life.

■ The action of doctors in the early twentieth century helped structure the medical profession in such a way as to greatly influence the health care field.

power

■ Communities are shaped by the struggles between those with more and less power, reflecting broader class and race inequalities.

■ Natural resource consumption and environmental hazards are distributed unevenly, reflecting inequalities in power.

■ Social inequalities play a major role in shaping the likelihood that someone will have the power to remain healthy and avoid sickness.

16

Politics and the Economy

looking AHEAD

How is "security" defined in our **culture** and what is the government's role in helping achieve it?

How do politics **structure** the way our society operates?

Capitalism? Socialism? How do economies reflect different ways that **power** is distributed in society?

By 2010, the conflict in Afghanistan had become the longest war in U.S. history, and nearly 500 U.S. soldiers were killed there that year. And the fighting wasn't over; U.S. combat troops remained another four years, through 2014, with hundreds more killed. Launched by the Bush administration in the weeks following the 9/11 attacks in 2001, and significantly expanded by the Obama administration, the war in Afghanistan had begun with high hopes and broad public support. "I am convinced that our security is at stake in Afghanistan and Pakistan," asserted Obama (Obama 2009). But in an echo of public sentiment toward the Iraq War, two-thirds of Americans came to believe that the war in Afghanistan was not worth fighting (DeYoung and Clement 2013). Long before it was over, Afghanistan dropped out of daily headlines and became known as the "forgotten war" (Gaskell 2013).

Thousands of U.S. troops who had risked life and limb to fight in Afghanistan and Iraq for U.S. security were in for a major shock when they returned stateside to find that financial security at home was elusive. Unprepared for life after the military and often financially unsophisticated, many veterans tried to live on credit cards while they looked for civilian jobs—only to discover they were unemployable in a persistently tight economy. The resulting debt and despair could be a lethal combination. Christopher Fitzpatrick, the director of VeteransPlus, a nonprofit organization that helps ex-service members in financial crisis, saw it firsthand. "No one wants to talk about the fact that there are other reasons, besides PTSD, for suicide at 2 in the morning. . . . People are reaching out, literally: 'Can you please help me? I'm losing everything'" (Briggs 2013).

It's not only veterans who have been struggling with economic insecurity. The impact of the 2007–2009 Great Recession triggered by reckless—and sometimes fraudulent—corporate actions continued to be felt long afterward. The stock market recovered and more affluent Americans resumed their normal lives, but home foreclosures and lingering unemployment continued to plague millions of people. By 2012, income inequality in the United States reached its greatest level since 1928 (Desilver 2013). For many Americans, low wages, unpaid bills, and the threat of unemployment are constant reminders that security is not just a military matter.

How does a country ensure its national security while protecting its economic security? Will people be asked to put their lives in danger in a war? Will education funding be adequate to meet students' needs? Will young people be able to find jobs? Will Medicare be available for the health care of an aging population? Such questions involve both politics and the economy—the two social institutions on which we focus in this chapter. We begin by examining the role of politics and the government in society, including aspects of the military. Then we look at the structure of the economy and the government's role in relationship to it. We conclude by considering ways to define *security*.

The Structure of Politics

Politics is *the struggle over power*. As we have seen, power operates at all levels of society, so it is no surprise that power struggles occur throughout society as well. For example, we sometimes refer to "family politics" or "office politics" to indicate power struggles in these contexts.

In this chapter, though, we focus primarily on power struggles over the decisions a society makes about its priorities and policies. This type of politics often involves **government,** *the system by which authority is exercised over a specific territory*, as well as all the actors who seek to influence government decision making, including ordinary citizens, social movement organizations, businesses, and lobbyists. This is an especially important type of politics because the outcome of these power struggles can affect the way an entire society operates. Politics at this level helps answer key questions about what type of society we will have. How much freedom will we as citizens have? How will our resources be used? Will we go to war? How will we address crime and respond to our health care, energy, and transportation needs?

You've probably heard people use the term *politics* in a negative way, as in, "It's all just politics." Because so much is at stake in politics, it is an arena often full of conflict, deception, hypocrisy, and self-interest. At its worst, politics can produce murderous regimes that oppress and terrorize their own people. But at its best, politics can produce many benefits for a society, such as a well-run, responsive government that protects the quality of people's lives through regulations that minimize environmental threats, promote food safety, ensure fair treatment of workers, and guard against fire hazards. Government agencies can provide roads and public transportation; supply clean water; and offer social services, education, and health care. And through the military, police, and courts, government can help defend our physical safety and civil liberties. For better or worse, politics and governments are interwoven with the fabric of social life.

Systems of Government

German sociologist Max Weber ([1919] 1946a) recognized that politics is about power—how it is maintained, distributed, challenged, and transferred. (As we have seen, **power** is *the ability to bring about an intended outcome, even when opposed by others*.) He argued that the defining characteristic of governments (or "the state") is their successful claim of a monopoly on the legitimate use of physical force within a given territory. This distinguishes them from all other social organizations. A government can authorize military personnel to kill on its behalf in wars; its police can arrest and even shoot people in the line of duty; and its prison guards can keep people incarcerated, depriving them of their freedom.

Because political processes are socially constructed, governments around the world differ in the way they choose leaders and how politically engaged their citizens are. We can classify government structures into three basic types: monarchies, authoritarian governments, and democracies.

A **monarchy** is *a system of government headed by a single person, the monarch, who typically inherits the position as a member of a ruling family*. Monarchs' titles signify their royal status (king, queen, sultan, emir, or emperor) and are passed from one generation to the next. There are two broad types of monarchies. In *traditional* (or *absolute*) *monarchies*, a single royal leader enjoys essentially unconditional power. This form of government is very rare today, existing only in a few countries, such as Saudi Arabia (king), Qatar (emir), Oman (sultan), and Swaziland (king). Instead, most contemporary monarchies are *constitutional monarchies*, democracies that recognize a limited and often only symbolic role for the royal family. Queen Elizabeth II—the monarch of the United Kingdom of Britain and Northern Ireland—is the best-known constitutional monarch today. She plays a ceremonial role as head of state, while an elected parliament and a prime minister run the government. Upon her death, she will be succeeded by her son Charles, the Prince of Wales.

Instead of monarchies, two broad types of government now predominate: authoritarian and democratic. An **authoritarian government** *typically features self-appointed leaders who exert great control over the lives of citizens that includes severely limiting their civil liberties*. Central ruling parties or the military usually run authoritarian governments. They do not rely on popular support from citizens or tolerate meaningful political opposition, though authoritarian leaders may rig elections to try to legitimize their power. Disdainful of civil liberties, authoritarian governments often intrude in the lives of citizens, directing, for example, what people may read or publish, what religion they practice, or where they may travel. They often go to considerable expense to monitor the private lives of citizens through various forms of surveillance.

A democratic government, or **democracy**, is *a political system in which the right to vote is widespread and government leaders are selected through multiparty elections.* In its literal definition, democracy is "rule by the people." However, the specific mechanisms by which "the people" rule can vary. In a *direct democracy,* citizens themselves participate in political decision making in such venues as town hall meetings or in referendums (direct citizen votes on a possible law) to decide the fate of a proposed policy. More common is *representative democracy,* in which citizens elect delegates who carry out the policymaking processes of government. Democratic systems often include elements of both direct and representative democracy, as does the United States. Free and fair elections are a fundamental component of all representative democracies.

The widespread embrace of democracy is relatively recent in human history. Many nations have not yet adopted democracy, though some leaders use its rhetoric to help legitimize their rule. The Democracy Index, published by the *Economist*'s Economist Intelligence Unit (2013), identifies five key components of a democratic government:

- Free and fair competitive elections
- Civil liberties, including freedom of speech, expression, and the press; freedom of religion; freedom of assembly and association; and the right to due judicial process
- A functioning government that can implement democratically based decisions
- Active political participation by citizens in public life
- A democratic political culture in which supporters of losing candidates accept the judgment of voters and permit the peaceful transition of power

In 2013, Economist Intelligence Unit researchers, awarding points in each of these categories, labeled only 15 percent of the world's countries as "full democracies" (including the United States), 30.5 percent as "flawed democracies," nearly one-third (32.3 percent) as authoritarian, and the remainder (27.2 percent) as hybrids (see Map 16.1). About half the world's population (49.5 percent) lives in a democracy of some sort; the remainder does not.

MAP 16.1 | 2012 DEMOCRACY INDEX

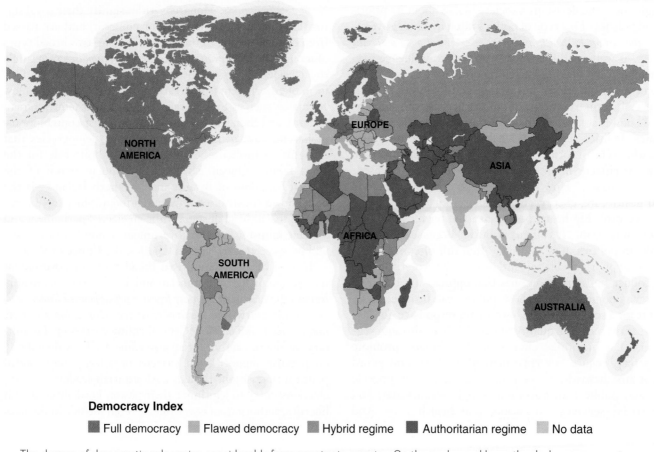

Democracy Index

■ Full democracy ■ Flawed democracy ■ Hybrid regime ■ Authoritarian regime ■ No data

The degree of democratic rule varies considerably from country to country. On the scale used here, the darker green color indicates a more democratic nation. *Source:* Economist Intelligence Unit (2013).

Political Structure and Political Action

The political structure of a society shapes the possibilities for political action, and political action can sometimes have a significant impact on the political structure.

An authoritarian society allows little opportunity for dissent, limiting the possibilities for political action. To oppose the ruling party by speaking out or joining an underground movement is to risk harsh consequences, including jail or execution. But even in an authoritarian society, actions matter. Compliance or cooperation may help reinforce the existing political structure. But with broad enough participation, as history has repeatedly shown, even small challenges can over time turn into public protests, demands for reform, or a revolution that changes the political structure.

Citizens in democracies, in contrast, have a wide range of options for political participation without fear of reprisal. In turn, how citizens use—or don't use—their rights helps determine a democracy's future.

Democracies vary. For example, voters elect the head of government in *presidential* systems, whereas members of the legislature typically elect (and dismiss) the prime minister in a *parliamentary* system. Another major distinction between democratic systems is that some offer plurality voting whereas others feature proportional representation. **Plurality voting** is *a "winner-take-all" system in which the candidate with the most votes wins the office being contested*. For example, in U.S. federal elections each House and Senate seat is awarded to the candidate receiving the most votes in that seat's district. Even if a candidate loses by a single vote, his or her party goes unrepresented in that district. In **proportional representation** systems, *parties are awarded seats in government based on the percentage of votes they receive in an election*. A party that wins 20 percent of the vote might be awarded 20 percent of the seats in the legislature. Many countries, including Japan, Ireland, Brazil, Hungary, Canada, and South Africa, have some form of proportional representation.

In the United States, plurality voting has been a major factor in the emergence of a system dominated by two parties, the Republicans and the Democrats. Although small political parties such as the Libertarian Party and the Green Party do exist (see Figure 16.1), few voters know much about them. Debate organizers typically exclude third-party candidates, and news organizations rarely cover their campaigns, helping ensure that small parties remain on the margins of political life.

Because of the structural limitations of the two-party system, major change to the system must often originate from outside the two major parties, often through social movements (see Chapter 17). In recent years, the Tea Party has received considerable media attention and influenced political debates. The Tea Party is neither a formal political party nor a social movement. It is supported by Republican Party funders, including some major corporations, and is a loosely organized collection of activists, about 80 percent of whom are from the conservative wing of the Republican Party (Mayer 2010; Newport 2010). As such, it works both inside and outside the Republican Party, pressuring the party to take more conservative positions on issues such as health care reform and government spending.

FIGURE 16.1 | MINOR POLITICAL PARTIES IN THE UNITED STATES

Green Party

Libertarian Party

Independence Party

Reform Party

Socialist Party

Plurality voting has contributed to a two-party system that helps marginalize minor parties such as the ones represented here with their logos. Do you think the United States would be better served by having more than two viable political parties? Why or why not?

thinking about structure

The **structure** of the two-party system in the United States effectively prevents most third-party candidates from winning elections. Have you voted for a third-party candidate? What was the outcome? What impact did that candidate have, regardless of the outcome?

Many countries have a more diverse multiparty system, often due to their system of proportional representation. (See Figure 16.2.) Citizens in multiparty systems are more likely to find a party that represents their views, thereby contributing to higher voter turnout than is typical in the United States. Such systems, though, can produce fragmented and unstable governments.

Political Culture

Like any social institution, politics features culturally specific norms and practices. The cultural norms we learn influence what issues we consider political and whether we speak out about them.

Political Socialization

Political socialization *teaches us basic norms and expectations about political life and attitudes toward involvement in politics.* Democratic political systems, like that of the United States, encourage citizens to participate in politics, at least to a degree. Schools typically teach students basic lessons about civics, including the significance of voting rights. (The Through a Sociological Lens box explores another way schools can promote civic engagement.) During election season, news coverage regularly stresses the importance of voting as a basic act of citizenship. Freedom and democracy are celebrated through patriotic cultural events, from schoolchildren's recitation of the Pledge of Allegiance to sports fans' singing of the national anthem at the start of sporting events.

But the U.S. political process and citizens' relationship to politics are in fact more complicated than our celebrations suggest. For most of U.S. history, the majority of citizens were denied even the basic right to vote. Scholars have documented election fraud past and present, including voting by dead people, uncounted votes, and interference with registration as well as the possibility of tampering with electronic voting machines (Alvarez, Hall, and Hyde 2008). Allegations of voter manipulation and inaccurate counting

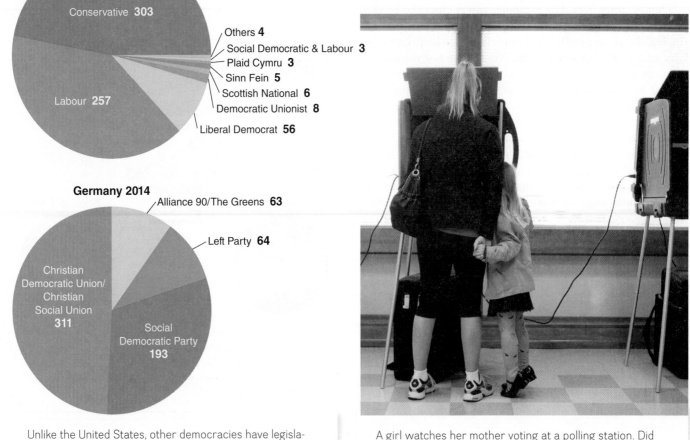

FIGURE 16.2 | MULTIPARTY LEGISLATURES: POLITICAL PARTIES IN THE UNITED KINGDOM AND GERMANY

United Kingdom 2014

Conservative **303**

Others **4**
Social Democratic & Labour **3**
Plaid Cymru **3**
Sinn Fein **5**
Scottish National **6**
Democratic Unionist **8**
Liberal Democrat **56**

Labour **257**

Germany 2014

Alliance 90/The Greens **63**

Left Party **64**

Christian Democratic Union/ Christian Social Union **311**

Social Democratic Party **193**

Unlike the United States, other democracies have legislatures with significant representation from more than two parties. *Sources:* German Bundestag (2014); U.K. Parliament (2014).

A girl watches her mother voting at a polling station. Did you receive any political socialization early in life that either encouraged or discouraged your participation in politics?

The Political Socialization of Teenagers

Sociological research on political socialization shows that schools can help connect young people with politics, activating their interest in political participation.

In one study, McFarland and Thomas (2006) examined the relationship between youth extracurricular activities and later adult political participation. Using two national surveys that followed respondents from high school through early adulthood, the authors examined the relationship between teenagers' involvement in voluntary organizations and their political participation as adults a decade later. They found that students active in specific types of voluntary organizations in high school, regardless of class background, were more likely to register to vote, to vote in an election, to participate in community service, to work on a political campaign, and to join a political party.

Not all extracurricular activities promote adult political involvement. For example, neither high school sports nor academic clubs enhance political socialization, whereas participation in student government, service organizations, debate teams, and drama and musical groups do. McFarland and Thomas (2006) explain, "Youth organizations that demand student time commitments and that concern service, political activity, and public performance have the most significant, positive relation to long-term political participation" (p. 416). These organizations encourage young people to develop valuable political knowledge, skills, and identities, including the ability to speak in public, knowledge of group processes, and a sense of community service.

think about it

1. *Have you ever engaged in voluntary activities of the sort that appear to encourage political involvement?*

2. *What other early socialization experiences do you think either encouraged or discouraged you from becoming involved in political life?*

---

periodically produce election controversies, most notably the contested 2000 presidential election settled by the intervention of the Supreme Court. Further, some observers criticize the news media for failing to adequately serve their crucial democratic functions of being a watchdog on the powerful and effectively informing citizens about politics (McChesney and Nichols 2010). Others argue that cuts in spending for public education limit the teaching of critical thinking skills necessary for a well-informed citizenry in a democracy (Nussbaum 2010). In short, although the U.S. political system and broader political culture may be preferred to many others, it is far from the ideal portrayed in children's textbooks.

As a result, many Americans are at best highly skeptical of the political process and political figures. Millions simply avoid politics and decline to vote. Ironically, the United States—which often prides itself on being a global symbol of freedom and democracy—typically has one of the lowest voter turnouts of any Western industrialized democracy (see Table 16.1).

Public Opinion and the "Spiral of Silence"

In democratic political systems, the legitimacy of government is rooted in the idea that elected governments have public support. But elections are only one measure of public support, and long periods—four years for U.S. presidential elections—often separate one election from the next. If the literal meaning of democracy is government by the people, how do the people "govern" between elections?

---

thinking about culture

In what ways might people with unpopular views become part of a subculture? Can you think of an example of such a subculture? How might this group make its views heard?

TABLE 16.1 VOTER TURNOUT IN SELECT DEMOCRATIC COUNTRIES

Country	Election Year	Voter Turnout[1] (as percentage of voting age population)
Belgium	2010	93.3%
Peru	2011	87.4
Sweden	2010	82.6
Ghana	2012	82.2
Denmark	2011	81.8
Brazil	2010	80.6
South Korea	2012	80.4
Iceland	2013	80.0
Australia	2013	79.7
Norway	2013	77.9
Argentina	2011	77.4
Israel	2012	73.2
France	2012	71.2
Netherlands	2012	71.0
Dominican Republic	2012	70.2
Finland	2011	70.1
New Zealand	2011	69.8
Greece	2012	69.4
Austria	2013	69.3
Thailand	2011	69.3
Italy	2013	68.3
Germany	2013	66.0
Philippines	2010	64.7
Mexico	2012	64.6
Ireland	2011	63.8
Spain	2011	63.3
Malaysia	2013	63.0
United Kingdom	2010	61.1
Japan	2012	59.7
Mongolia	2013	58.5
United States	**2012**	**54.6**
Poland	2010	54.5
Canada	2011	53.8
Colombia	2010	44.9
Switzerland	2011	40.0

What factors do you think contribute to the relatively low voter turnout in the United States?

[1]Voter turnout is the highest reported turnout for a presidential or parliamentary election since 2010. Data are limited to select countries classified as "full" or "flawed" democracies (see Map 16.1).

One way is by expressing their opinions about the issues of the day. But talking about politics is not always easy, especially for those with unpopular views. The **spiral of silence** is *a theory that explains how people keep quiet about controversial issues when they think their opinions are not widely shared, in order to avoid social isolation* (Noelle-Neuman, 1974, 1993).

One comprehensive review of spiral of silence theory and research summarizes the five key dynamics of this process (Scheufele and Moy 2000):

1. Societies require some degree of agreement about basic values and goals and exert social pressure on individuals to agree, including an implicit threat of isolation for those who do not.

2. As individuals develop their own opinions, they fear social isolation and seek to conform to what they see as the prevailing views in their community.

3. People monitor their environment, paying careful attention to the opinions of others as they try to decipher the most common opinions and future opinion trends.

4. People are likely to express their opinions when they believe their views are popular or rising in popularity. However, when people believe their views are unpopular or declining in popularity, they are likely to be guarded and remain silent.

5. "The tendency of the one to speak up and the other to be silent starts off a spiraling process which increasingly establishes one opinion as the prevailing one" (Noelle-Neuman 1974).

The spiral of silence narrows public discussion by squeezing out minority views and overstating the degree of political consensus. The media play an important role because people often look to media for indications of which views are currently popular. If they do not see their perspectives reflected there, they are likely to believe that their views are marginal, making it more likely they will be quiet.

Political Issues and Private Matters

If politics is the social institution whereby societies make collective decisions about priorities and policies, it matters a great deal what issues count as politics. A mixture of culture and power determines how a society defines politics. Feminist activists in the 1970s challenged traditional definitions of politics, arguing that "the personal is political" because power pervades all aspects of social life (Evans 1980). In other words, politics is not just about what happens in government but also includes many aspects of our daily and personal lives, such as the food we choose to buy

SPOTLIGHT
on social theory

Feminist theory and activism have been important in advancing the notion that the "personal is political." How might actions in your personal life have political implications?

and eat, the choices we make about the work we do, and the way we structure our personal relationships.

Social theorist Nancy Fraser (1992) points out that one consequential question that reflects our political culture is what gets defined as "private" and therefore inappropriate for public discussion. A variety of issues—including child abuse, domestic violence, sexual orientation, and mental illness—were, until quite recently, considered private matters and excluded from politics. Political and cultural changes have transformed these into political issues to which public policy is attuned and about which public discussion is permissible. On the other hand, asserting the right to have a private life—free of surveillance or intrusion—is itself a political position. Current debates about the government's right to use surveillance on citizens, conduct searches at airports, and legislate personal behavior illustrate that the relationship between public and private is always being contested and involves power struggles, to which we now turn.

A Romanian mother and her child light candles in front of cardboard women silhouettes marking the International Day for the Elimination of Violence against Women in Bucharest on November 25, 2010.

Power and Politics

By definition, politics is the struggle over power. Whoever makes the rules for a society gets to influence the direction of that society. In the United States today, do "the people" rule? Do "special interests"? Does someone else? Sociologists have long examined such issues of power, considering who takes part in politics and how government policies reflect this participation.

Theories of Political Power: Pluralism, Elites, and Class Domination

Three broad classic approaches help us understand the distribution of political power in U.S. society (Table 16.2).

Pluralist theory *argues that political power is fragmented among many different competing groups.* Business owners, labor unions, teachers, retired people, gun owners, environmentalists, antiabortion advocates, and a host of other interests are represented by organizations that try to influence public policy by educating the public, lobbying elected officials, and supporting sympathetic candidates. Developed mostly by political scientists and adopted by some functionalist sociologists, pluralism suggests that politics is a constant negotiation among these various interests and that policies change as one or another group gains more influence (Dahl 1961).

In contrast, **power elite theory** *suggests that political power is concentrated in the hands of a small dominant group of business, government, and military leaders.* Developed by sociologist C. Wright Mills (1956), power elite theory is a form of conflict theory that argues power is heavily concentrated in the hands of those who head society's major bureaucratic institutions: the very

TABLE 16.2	THEORIES OF POLITICAL POWER	
Theory	**Key Idea**	**Sociological Tradition**
Pluralist theory	Power is fragmented among many competing groups that are constantly shifting.	Functionalist
Power elite theory	Power is concentrated in the hands of a small number of elites within business, government, and the military.	Conflict
Class domination theory	Power is concentrated in the hands of a small number of wealthy people who own or control key economic resources.	Conflict (especially Marx)

wealthy who own or control big business, politicians and bureaucrats who run government, and the military brass who head the United States' military structure. Elites move back and forth among these three fields, as when a military general leaves to become an executive for a defense contractor or when a banking executive becomes secretary of the Treasury. The flow of people among the three sectors helps solidify the power these elites have over the policies and budgets of their interlocking bureaucracies. According to power elite theory, ordinary citizens' influence is minimal in the face of such concentrated power, except when elites disagree among themselves and thereby open the door to possible citizen influence.

Class domination theory *suggests that political power is concentrated in the hands of the rich who own or control a large share of the nation's economic resources.* Based on the work of Karl Marx and adapted by modern interpreters (Domhoff 2013), class domination theory is a form of conflict theory that views the economic system as the ultimate source of power. Those who control this system—especially super-wealthy owners and executives of major corporate conglomerates—use their financial clout to influence government by funding lobbyists, financially supporting political campaigns, and bankrolling "astroturf" campaigns that advance corporate goals through what appear to be grassroots citizen efforts. Corporate-owned media outlets also help limit the range of political debate on news and other programs. These uses of economic resources undermine the ability of ordinary citizens to significantly influence the political system. Although efforts to rein in the power of the rich—through higher taxes and limits on campaign contributions, for example—are sometimes criticized as promoting "class warfare," proponents of class domination theory say that it's the other way around—ordinary citizens are the real targets of class warfare.

SPOTLIGHT

on social theory

Both **power elite** and **class domination theory**—forms of **conflict theory**—argue that political power is not really in the hands of ordinary citizens, as **pluralist theory** suggests. Can you think of an example that seems to support such claims? Can you think of a situation in which ordinary citizens seem to have prevailed over powerful interests?

As investor Warren Buffett, one of the richest men in the United States, once put it, disapprovingly, "There's class warfare, all right, but it's my class—the rich class—that's making war, and we're winning" (quoted in Stein 2006).

Many sociologists would likely agree that the United States follows some aspects of the pluralist model, especially on issues that are not fundamentally economic, such as abortion, gay marriage, and gun control, where lively debates are pursued by various groups. But there is little doubt that elites wield disproportionate influence on political life, particularly economic affairs, though the precise nature and degree of this influence is a topic of ongoing study and debate.

Class Differences in Political Participation

Societies with a healthy democratic political system have broad public participation in politics, even if only in elections. But more than in many other democracies, political participation in the United States is stratified by class. Working-class and poor people are less likely to vote in the United States than are middle-class people (Verba, Schlozman, and Brady 1995). As we saw in Chapter 9, one likely reason is the absence of a strong labor or socialist party that can speak on behalf of working-class voters. All other Western democracies have such a party, and the class gap in voter turnout is considerably less in those countries. In contrast, both major parties in the United States are closely aligned with major corporate interests and depend heavily on their financial contributions.

The political socialization of young people is another important influence on political participation. Informed political discussion benefits from self-confidence, education, knowledge, and a time commitment, and these resources are not distributed equally. Although a healthy democracy requires the inclusion of diverse perspectives from all sectors of society, research suggests that higher levels of education and income contribute significantly to a sense of political competence (Jacobs and Skocpol 2007). Children from highly educated, wealthier, and higher-status families enjoy numerous advantages that encourage and enable them to become involved in politics: their parents are more likely than working-class parents to participate in politics and to talk to their children about political activity; their teachers and school officials are more likely to encourage students to become involved in school and community activities; and their peer networks are more likely to support interest and involvement in politics. People from poor or working-class backgrounds are less likely to perceive themselves as adequately prepared for political discussions and are less likely to be active in an arena that seems to reward the affluent.

Campaign Contributions, Lobbying, and Policy Outcomes

Class differences in political participation are even more pronounced in activities beyond voting. Not surprisingly, financial contributions—the lifeblood of political campaigns—come disproportionately from more affluent voters. The rich have more money to contribute. For example, the 2012 Obama and Romney campaigns received just 28 and 12 percent of their funds, respectively, from people giving less than $200. In contrast, contributors giving $1,000 or more made up 39 percent of the Obama contributions and 66 percent of the Romney contributions (Campaign Finance Institute 2013).

Once candidates are elected, money continues to be important. Officials must immediately begin fundraising for reelection while lobbyists encourage lawmakers to vote in

FIGURE 16.3 | LOBBYING EXPENDITURES BY SECTOR, 2012

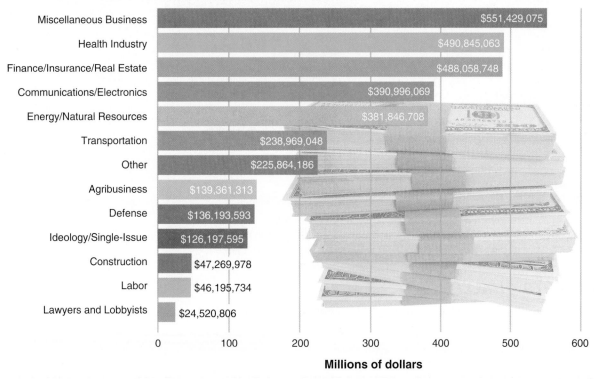

Miscellaneous Business	$551,429,075
Health Industry	$490,845,063
Finance/Insurance/Real Estate	$488,058,748
Communications/Electronics	$390,996,069
Energy/Natural Resources	$381,846,708
Transportation	$238,969,048
Other	$225,864,186
Agribusiness	$139,361,313
Defense	$136,193,593
Ideology/Single-Issue	$126,197,595
Construction	$47,269,978
Labor	$46,195,734
Lawyers and Lobbyists	$24,520,806

Millions of dollars

Business-sector spending on lobbyists far surpasses that of labor groups or single-issue organizations such as environmental, gay rights, and gun rights groups. *Source:* OpenSecrets.Org: Center for Responsive Politics.

their client's interests—often the same clients who make major campaign contributions. Although labor unions and single-issue groups engage in lobbying, the practice is dominated by the corporate sector (Figure 16.3).

Campaign donations give donors and lobbyists unique access to elected officials, which they often parlay into special assistance for projects that benefit them directly (Clawson, Neustadtl, and Weller 1998). Consider the following examples:

■ Many industries, including oil, banking, and financial services industries, lobby for reduced government regulation. Inadequate regulation and lax enforcement contributed to both the BP gulf oil spill (Levitz 2010; National Commission 2011) and the global financial crisis (Financial Crisis Inquiry Commission 2011).

■ Some observers see the taxpayer-funded bailout of big banks, financial institutions, and other companies as more evidence of the power of wealthy donors and lobbyists. Though the well-known TARP (Troubled Asset Relief Program) loans that bailed out banks were repaid, other lesser-known bailout programs will end up costing taxpayers many billions of dollars (ProPublica 2013; SourceWatch 2011).

■ In response to pressure from lobbyists representing the health care and insurance industries, the 2009 health care reform law ("Obamacare") protected the interests of the health care and insurance industries by mandating that

uninsured individuals buy insurance coverage from private companies rather than offering a government-run "public option" that advocates argued would have been more cost-effective (Eaton and Pell 2010).

In addition, wealthy corporations and individuals lobby for lower tax rates and tax loopholes (Johnston 2005, 2007). In one dramatic example, the Boeing Corporation made $10 billion in domestic pretax profits between 2008 and 2010 (and received tens of billions of dollars in government contracts) but paid no federal corporate income taxes over those three years (Citizens for Tax Justice 2011). Higher-income earners—who pay more income taxes—get the biggest piece of common tax breaks, such as deductions for mortgage payments, tax-free pension contributions, employer-sponsored health insurance, and lower tax rates on capital gains income (Congressional Budget Office 2013). (See Figure 16.4.)

Considerable research suggests that the government is most responsive to the affluent classes. In one study of public opinion and government policy between 1981 and 2002, Martin Gilens (2005) focused on issues for which the policy preferences of high-income people differed from those of middle- and low-income citizens. The inheritance tax, government-funded health care, and affirmative action are supported substantially more by those with modest incomes than by those with higher incomes. Gilens concluded that "government policy appears to be fairly responsive to the well-off and virtually unrelated to the desires of the low- and middle-income citizens" (p. 789).

FIGURE 16.4 | DISTRIBUTION OF 10 LARGEST TAX BREAKS BY INCOME GROUP

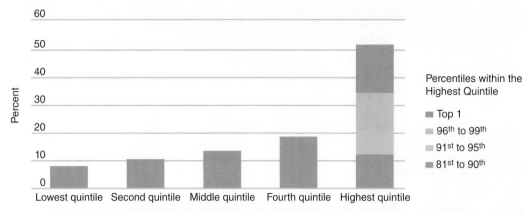

Higher-income groups pay more in income taxes, but they also enjoy major breaks that are written into the tax code. In 2013, the 10 largest tax breaks totaled over $900 billion in savings, more than half of which went to the top quintile (top 20 percent) of earners. The top 1 percent received about 17 percent of all tax break benefits. *Source:* Congressional Budget Office (2013).

CORE CONCEPTS CHALLENGE

Do you think this distribution pattern is related to the amount of **power** *various income groups have in society? Why or why not?*

Inequality, Power, and Politics

Connecting the dots between economic inequality, campaign finances, lobbying, and legislation, some critics argue that concentrated wealth is undermining democratic institutions (Collins and Yeskel 2005). (See Figure 16.5.) Those with money use their resources to influence the political system, while those struggling to earn a living have little time to take part in the political process and no money to contribute. Because political parties and politicians speak to and respond mostly to the more affluent, the less affluent often do not see political participation as a wise investment of time and

FIGURE 16.5 | INEQUALITY, POWER, AND POLITICS: A MODEL

Economic inequality can endanger the health of a democracy—and unhealthy democracy can lead to greater inequality. *Source:* Adapted from Collins and Yeskel (2005).

CORE CONCEPTS CHALLENGE

Do you think this model summarizes accurately the way political **power** *works in contemporary U.S. politics? Why or why not?*

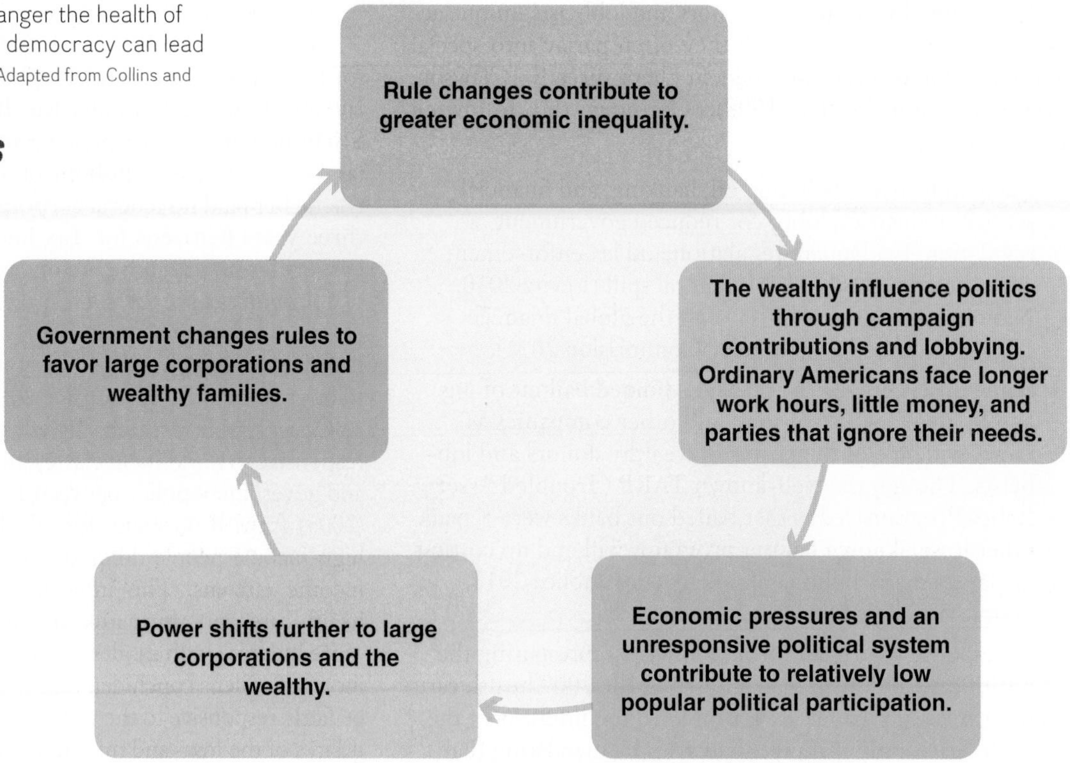

Rule changes contribute to greater economic inequality.

The wealthy influence politics through campaign contributions and lobbying. Ordinary Americans face longer work hours, little money, and parties that ignore their needs.

Economic pressures and an unresponsive political system contribute to relatively low popular political participation.

Power shifts further to large corporations and the wealthy.

Government changes rules to favor large corporations and wealthy families.

energy. However, by opting out of the political process, the less affluent virtually guarantee that politicians and the government will continue to neglect their interests. The vacuum they leave makes it easier for powerful players to shape laws, rules, and regulations to benefit their own interests, some of which increase inequality.

Democracies, however, always contain within them the possibility for reform. As long as basic civil rights, such as freedom of speech and assembly and the right to vote, remain in place, citizens can promote change through the electoral process. If that process is not working properly, then social change can occur through the efforts of social movements that challenge authority outside the electoral system (Piven 2008). It remains to be seen whether and how citizens will act to reform our democracy in the coming years.

The distinctive Pentagon building, just outside Washington, D.C., is the headquarters of the U.S. Department of Defense and the world's largest office building, with a daily workforce of 24,000 people. At the time of its construction at the start of World War II, it was widely assumed that the building would be converted after the war to some peacetime use, perhaps as an archive or a hospital. Instead, the military never left (Vogel 2007). Does the military have a visible presence in your community?

War and the Military

Mao Zedong ([1936] 2010), the leader of the Communist Revolution in China, famously justified armed insurrection with the slogan, "Political power grows out of the barrel of a gun" (p. 24). As Mao knew, **war**—*organized armed conflict among two or more specially trained military groups*—is often used to overcome opposition. Or as nineteenth-century German military theorist Carl von Clausewitz ([1832] 1976) put it, war is "the continuation of policy [or politics] by other means" (p. 87).

Some sociologists argue that war is a permanent feature of modern societies, since preparing for war is now a routine and perpetual government activity. A sociological approach to war and the military includes a consideration of the military's role in society and the socialization processes that create citizens who accept war and soldiers who fight it.

The Rise of the National Security State

During its first 125 years or so of existence—with the exception of the Civil War—the U.S. government kept a relatively small military force, even as it fought its way across the continent, acquiring new territories and subjugating indigenous peoples. At the end of the nineteenth century, when U.S. territory stretched from the Atlantic to the Pacific, some political leaders—most famously Theodore Roosevelt—wanted to continue expanding U.S. influence abroad. This goal required a much larger military, especially a modern navy that could project U.S. power overseas. The United States began building such a navy, and after its 1898 war with Spain, it quickly acquired colonies in the Philippines, Cuba, Guam, and Puerto Rico. Its time as a traditional colonial power was short, however; armed insurrections and resistance movements forced the United States to give up most of its newly acquired colonies. But the growing U.S. military continued to play an ever larger role in society, expanding dramatically during the two world wars.

After World War II ended, the United States maintained a military of unprecedented size as it engaged in the Cold War (1945–1989), an ongoing state of military tension between the United States and the Soviet Union. Although these superpowers never directly engaged in war, the United States developed a **national security state,** *a government dominated by powerful military, foreign policy, and intelligence agencies.* The key moment in the development of the national security state was the passage of the National Security Act of 1947. The act created the National Security Council to advise the president on foreign policy and the Central Intelligence Agency, which collects and analyses security information and engages in covert operations abroad. It also consolidated the military under the newly formed Department of Defense, headquartered at the recently built Pentagon (Hogan 1998).

The national security state is not monolithic. Debates often exist within its circles about the proper priorities and allocation of resources. But as a whole it wields enough power to influence major economic and political policy decisions and priorities. In the eyes of critics, the national security state has an unhealthy preoccupation with foreign and domestic enemies that distorts economic and political policy decisions and priorities. For example, military spending receives priority well beyond the amount needed to ensure territorial security (Greider 1999, 2010). Intelligence-gathering capacities have been used in ways that critics contend violate basic democratic values, since they involve secrecy, surveillance, and limits on civil liberties at home and often occur without public knowledge or review (Cole and Dempsey 2006; Greenwald 2014). The information revealed by whistleblower Edward Snowden especially has exposed some of the massive surveillance efforts of the National Security Agency (NSA), which gathers data on the e-mails, Internet activity, and cell phone communications of millions of people inside and outside the United States.

The rise of the national security state was part of a broader change in which the U.S. military grew much more powerful, enjoying unprecedented peacetime funding, and the federal government increasingly defined international affairs in military terms. In his farewell speech to the nation in 1961, outgoing Republican president (and supreme commander of the Allied Forces during World War II) Dwight D. Eisenhower warned of the growth of a military establishment and arms industry, cautioning that "in the councils of government, we must guard against the acquisition of unwarranted influence, whether sought or unsought, by the military-industrial complex. The potential for the disastrous rise of misplaced power exists and will persist."

Eisenhower's warnings were extraordinary given that they came from an army general, but they were not new. C. Wright Mills (1956), in his analysis *The Power Elite*, had already documented the rise of military influence in political life, the declining influence of civilian diplomats, the growing impact of military spending on the economy, and the influential role of military money and priorities on research on university campuses. Mills observed that "the professional military believe firmly in the military definition of world reality and . . . are genuinely frightened for their country" (p. 202). With their growing influence, military leaders were able to promote these fears and definitions of reality, thereby helping transform the United States into a more militarized society.

In recent years, the fear of terrorism served as a new catalyst for massive investments in military, intelligence-gathering, and surveillance. As a *Washington Post* investigation discovered, "The top-secret world the government created in response to the terrorist attacks of Sept. 11, 2001, has become so large, so unwieldy and so secretive that no one knows how much money it costs, how many people it employs, how many programs exist within it or exactly how many agencies do the same work" (Priest and Arkin 2010).

Military Funding

The United States is bounded by oceans on both the east and west coasts and shares its northern and southern borders with

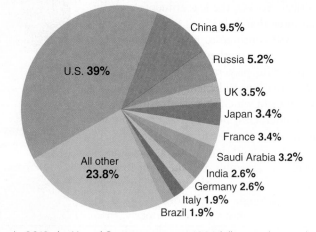

FIGURE 16.6 | GLOBAL MILITARY SPENDING, 2012

China 9.5%
Russia 5.2%
UK 3.5%
Japan 3.4%
France 3.4%
Saudi Arabia 3.2%
India 2.6%
Germany 2.6%
Italy 1.9%
Brazil 1.9%
U.S. 39%
All other 23.8%

In 2012, the United States spent over $682 billion on direct military expenditures, more than the next 10 countries combined.

Source: Stockholm International Peace Research Institute [SIPRI] (2013).

close allies, making it among the most geographically safe countries in the world. Yet, since the middle of the twentieth century, it has maintained the most powerful military in the world, on which it spends far more than any other country (see Figure 16.6.) The United States in 2012 accounted for about 39 percent of the world's $1.75 trillion in military spending (Stockholm International Peace Research Institute 2013) and in recent years has devoted about 55 percent of its federal discretionary budget to military spending (Figure 16.7).

Much of the United States' military spending is devoted to projecting power worldwide. In addition to military sites in all 50 states, the U.S. Department of Defense (2013) counts 97 sites in seven U.S. territories, and 598 sites in forty foreign countries, including Germany (179), Japan (109), and South Korea (83). No other country comes close to maintaining this type of global military presence. What's more, the U.S. military owns so much property—more than 557,000 buildings and other structures on almost 28 million acres of land across the globe—that it may be the largest property owner on the planet (U.S. Department of Defense 2013).

The Politics of Fear and Civil Liberties

Ironically, massive U.S. military spending intended to promote security has long been accompanied by a deep sense of fear and insecurity among many citizens. The postwar arms race between the United States and the former Soviet Union raised concern that nuclear annihilation could occur at any moment and that communism threatened U.S. democratic freedoms. With the collapse of the Soviet Union in 1991 and the 2001 attacks on 9/11, terrorists have replaced communists as the perceived threat to security.

Echoing some of the "spiral of silence" analysis, Altheide (2006) argues that a "politics of fear" characterizes

FIGURE 16.7 | PROPOSED U.S. DISCRETIONARY SPENDING, 2015

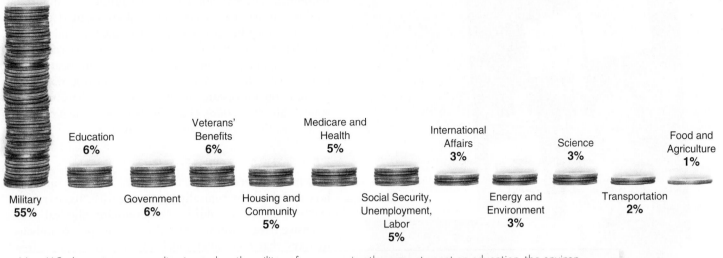

Education
6%

Veterans'
Benefits
6%

Medicare and
Health
5%

International
Affairs
3%

Science
3%

Food and
Agriculture
1%

Military
55%

Government
6%

Housing and
Community
5%

Social Security,
Unemployment,
Labor
5%

Energy and
Environment
3%

Transportation
2%

Most U.S. discretionary spending is used on the military, far surpassing the amount spent on education, the environment, and public welfare. Discretionary spending is the portion of the federal budget that must be allocated each year. It does not include dedicated trust funds, such as Social Security and Medicare, which are paid largely from payroll taxes, not income taxes. The numbers here are President Obama's proposed 2015 budget. *Source:* National Priorities Project (2014).

contemporary life. People are often afraid to disagree publicly with authorities' views and policies. Instead they remain silent to avoid being labeled naïve, foolish, or unpatriotic. Altheide suggests that news coverage defining the world as dangerous and unpredictable intensifies this politics of fear.

News and the Politics of Fear

Fear can lead people to take actions that they otherwise would not consider, including accepting policies that threaten civil liberties and jeopardize basic democratic principles in the name of security. As we saw in Chapter 10,

"WE'LL BE BACK, AFTER THIS COMMERCIAL BREAK, WITH MORE REASONS WHY IT'S NOT SAFE TO LEAVE YOUR HOUSE..."

Source: © www.cartoonstock.com

thousands of Asian Americans were sent to internment camps during World War II. During the Cold War, the FBI monitored the peaceful political activities of citizens; schools and other institutions demanded "loyalty oaths" as a condition of employment (some of which are still required today); and a congressional committee—the House Un-American Activities Committee—questioned public figures about their political views and loyalty. Many of these activities are now recognized as misguided efforts that undermined basic civil liberties.

But the 2001 USA Patriot Act, adopted after 9/11, included a range of new government policies meant to fight terrorism, including wiretapping phone lines without a warrant; collecting information about citizens' phone calls, e-mail, financial data, and health records; and detaining immigrants without criminal charges. In just a few years, these policies have been used against tens of thousands of U.S. citizens and many more foreign visitors. So far, most have accepted them as a trade-off between security and liberty.

Socialization for War

The United States has engaged in wars and major military actions for much of the past 70 years, including World War II (1941–1945), the Korean War (1951–1953), the Vietnam War (1960–1975), Panama (1989), the Persian Gulf War (1991), Bosnia-Herzegovina (1999), the Iraq War (2003–2011), and Afghanistan (2001–current). This partial list does not include countless covert CIA operations, smaller bombing runs, drone strikes, missile attacks, and other displays of military strength. U.S. citizens have grown accustomed to living in a nation that is usually at war.

War and the Military

are honored in the media and with monuments, memorials, museums, national holidays, and countless "Support our troops" car magnets. School textbooks often mark the progress of history in relationship to the start or end of a war. Socialization for war encourages citizens to accept, even actively support, military action. In many European nations, in contrast, after the devastations of two world wars fought partially on European soil, military values have much less appeal (Sheehan 2008). (For efforts to promote a culture of peace, see the Sociology in Action box.)

TRAINING SOLDIERS TO FIGHT Citizens may be socialized to support wars, but soldiers must learn how to fight them, typically beginning with "basic training" or "boot camp." In addition to developing physical fitness, intensive basic training resocializes young people to behave in ways that contradict much of what they have already learned (Dyer 2004). Raised in a culture that emphasizes freedom and individuality, recruits must learn to obey their commanding officers, follow orders unquestioningly, work as part of a unit, suppress their emotions, and kill as a normal job requirement.

To achieve this transformation, recruits, usually young, are taken away from mainstream society and kept in relative isolation for a number of weeks. Their individual identity is stripped away through the use of standardized close-cropped haircuts, identical clothing and gear, and collective barracks with no privacy. The recruits are then subjected to just enough physical and mental stress to wear them down, while—in the U.S. services—enabling about 90 percent to successfully complete basic training.

Adopting military culture can come at a cost, though. The traumatic events soldiers sometimes experience in combat, combined with the ongoing stress caused by lengthy deployments and separation from family, create enormous strains for many, resulting in mental health issues and suicides. The military lifestyle also tends to create distinct new identities for soldiers, some of whom find it difficult to reintegrate into civilian life after their service is over; substance abuse, posttraumatic stress disorders, and other psychological difficulties are persistent problems for some (Alvarez 2009b).

Social Inequality and the Military

The military is a social institution with its own traditions, values, norms and organizational structure (Siebold 2001). But it is also influenced by issues found in broader society, including social inequality.

FAST-FORWARD

Change and Politics

Despite unrivaled spending on the military, U.S. citizens have long been plagued by a sense of fear and insecurity. In the 1950s and 1960s, fear of communism led to military action abroad and a clampdown on political freedom at home. In the 2000s, terrorism became the reason for wars abroad and surveillance at home.

PREPARING CITIZENS TO ACCEPT WAR
Responding to this near-continuous engagement, U.S. culture encourages citizens to affirm their support for military actions and to revere the soldiers who fight them. Soldiers

thinking about culture
Have you or someone you know experienced military basic training? What did the experience suggest about the differences between civilian and military **culture**?

SOCIOLOGY in ACTION

Peace Studies

If peace is widely valued, then why do we so rarely study how to achieve and maintain it? That question animates peace studies, a multidisciplinary field that was founded with the significant input and insight of sociologists. Peace studies seeks alternatives to violence and promotes conflict resolution and social justice. These efforts include many campus-based programs, collaborations between activists and academics through professional associations such as the Peace and Justice Studies Association in the United States and the International Peace Research Association, and real-world implementation of the ideas developed in peace studies through the United Nations and nongovernmental organizations.

Perhaps the best-known founder of peace studies is Norwegian sociologist Johan Galtung, who has spent more than 50 years studying, teaching about, and promoting peace. Galtung is an internationally recognized advocate of innovative methods of nonviolent conflict resolution. He helped create the International Peace Research Institute in Oslo in 1959 and later started the *Journal of Peace Research,* an arena for an ongoing global conversation about the causes of war and violence, strategies of peace-building and nonviolence, and approaches to peace education.

Galtung's (1996, 2000) work reflects a sociological orientation to peace and conflict. It incorporates a structural analysis of violence, considering the forms of inequality that often underlie war and highlighting the human capacity to create a more just society. His work has included an emphasis on the importance of building a culture of peace, in which primary agents of socialization—parents, schools, media—promote values, attitudes, and behaviors that emphasize nonviolence, human rights, and social justice. Instructors in peace studies courses often teach military personnel and tackle these cultural issues, recognizing and respecting military experience but questioning the idea of "defense" and assumptions that violence is the inevitable focus of defense policies (Page 2007).

For Galtung, violence is more than just acts of physical brutality. It includes what he calls "structural violence," the underlying social conditions of inequality and injustice that prevent people from achieving their full potential and that often lead to direct physical violence. Likewise, peace is more than just the absence of overt conflict (what he dubs "negative peace"); it is the existence of social justice ("positive peace").

Galtung has been involved in over 120 mediations in dozens of countries, including Afghanistan, Colombia, Israel and the Palestinian Territories, Kashmir, Korea, Northern Ireland, Rwanda, and Sri Lanka, often with positive results. For example, his mediation was central to the resolution of a border conflict between Peru and Ecuador that had led to war three times previously. He has worked as a consultant to the United Nations on a wide range of peace-building and peace-keeping projects and since 1993 has been director of TRANSCEND, a network of like-minded colleagues from more than 80 countries who work with him to mediate conflict and provide training in conflict resolution, nonviolence, and reconciliation (transcend.org).

In a recent book, dedicated "to a country I love, the United States of America," Galtung (2009) argues that the United States as a global power (what he calls the U.S. Empire) is unraveling, like other empires before it, as its reliance on the military to achieve economic and political ends proves increasingly economically burdensome and politically ineffective. But Galtung sees this as an opportunity for the United States as a nation (what he calls the U.S. Republic) to blossom, relieved from the burdens of empire.

think about it

1. *How might U.S. culture give greater priority to promoting peace?*

2. *Do you agree with Galtung that the United States has an opportunity to blossom by refocusing from projecting power abroad toward caring for domestic needs? Why or why not?*

RACE, GENDER, AND SEXUAL ORIENTATION IN THE MILITARY The clash between the ideal of fighting for freedom and the reality of inequality in the United States has always been especially stark in the military. African American soldiers, for example, fought overseas in World War II against the ideology of racial supremacy in Nazi Germany, only to return home to racial segregation in the United States. Like other social institutions at the time, the military was a bastion of racist behaviors and policies. But the military is a unique institution in that authority within it is intensely enforced from the top down, and, as a consequence, it is able to introduce and enforce new ideas and behaviors.

In 1948—long before the peak of the civil rights movement—President Truman issued an executive order to begin a swift process of racial integration in the military. Since then, the military has often taken the lead in promoting progressive racial policies, making it a particularly attractive career choice for African Americans, Latinos, and other minorities who face continuing discrimination in civilian employment.

Women and gays and lesbians have had a more mixed experience. The military first excluded women and then grudgingly allowed them entry to an often hostile "macho" environment in which sexism and sexual violence remain major concerns to this day. The pressure to avoid being either too feminine (defined as soft and unprepared for military life) or too masculine (therefore not womanly) makes the military a site of ongoing negotiation for women (Herbert 2000).

The military has lagged behind changes in the broader society in its treatment of lesbian and gay soldiers. The military banned gays and lesbians until 1993, when it adopted a "don't ask, don't tell" policy that allowed them to serve as long as they kept their sexual orientation a secret. The policy was repealed in 2010, and gays and lesbians may now serve openly.

CLASS AND MILITARY SERVICE

Class distinctions have long marked military service in the United States. The nation's first national mandatory service (known as *conscription* or *the draft*) was instituted—and fiercely resisted—during the Civil War when both North and South allowed wealthy citizens to avoid service by hiring substitutes. In World War I substitutes were not allowed, but biased local draft boards sent a disproportionate number of poor and working-class people to war (Keith 2003). In World War II a more equitable lottery system was used, but during Vietnam class bias returned in the form of exemptions for college students, who were disproportionately middle and upper class. In 1973 the U.S. government ended required military service and instituted an all-volunteer force (Janowitz and Moskos 1979).

The military does not keep data on the family income of its recruits, but some studies suggest that the all-volunteer military draws disproportionately from working-class and lower-middle-class families; the poor (who often cannot meet the entry requirements), the upper middle class, and especially the wealthy are underrepresented (National Priorities Project 2011). To attract recruits who have limited job prospects and cannot afford a college education, the military highlights its education and training programs. Recruitment is considerably easier in periods of economic recession (Alvarez 2009a). Thus class inequality continues to mark the all-volunteer force.

An all-volunteer military provides employment opportunities, especially for working-class and lower-middle-class people who have fewer options. Given this economic bias, do you think an all-volunteer system is fair?

In its recruitment of labor, the military has also adopted a strategy from the civilian sector: outsourcing. Civilian employees of private companies are taking on an increasingly prominent role in military affairs. In 2007, for example, approximately 160,000 U.S. soldiers were in Iraq—but so were more than 180,000 civilian contractors (Miller 2007). Contractors in Iraq and Afghanistan carried out a variety of jobs, including building roads and training new Iraqi military and police forces. They were also hired to interrogate prisoners, linking them to cases of alleged torture and abuse of those prisoners, and to serve as "private security forces," protecting military installations, guarding prominent individuals, and escorting supply convoys. These contractors had immunity from Iraqi laws even when, as in one case, the Iraqi government accused a private security convoy of "deliberate murder" (Glanz and Rubin 2007). Such incidents produced considerable hostility from locals toward what were sometimes seen as mercenary troops-for-hire. Trouble continued once contractors returned home, because they were not eligible for the benefits or medical care that regular soldiers receive. As one injured contractor put it, "It's almost like we're this invisible, discardable military" (ProPublica 2010).

Some sociologists have argued that the shift to an all-volunteer military has changed military service gradually from a widely shared experience to a specialized occupation isolated from civilian society (Siebold 2001). The reliance on a small "soldier class" to carry out military duties has also had political consequences. It makes troops less likely to actively oppose a war (as draftees during the Vietnam War commonly did) and, by eliminating the risk of being drafted, may reduce civilian opposition to wars. Perhaps most important, if children of the more affluent and powerful are not a major component of the military, government officials may be less hesitant to put troops in harm's way.

Terrorism as a Political Strategy

Today, the most widely discussed threat facing the military is terrorism. There is no universally accepted definition of terrorism, in part because it encompasses a wide range of activities, organizations, circumstances, and beliefs (Tilly 2004b).

The U.S. government, for instance, defines terrorism as "politically motivated violence perpetrated against noncombatant targets by subnational groups or clandestine agents" (Perl 2006, 5). Thus it reserves the *terrorism* label for political acts (not the random violence of a psychopath, for example) that direct violence at civilian (noncombatant) targets. But the government definition makes the highly contested claim that only "subnational groups" can be terrorists; governments cannot.

In reality, however, many governments throughout history—from the Soviet government under Joseph Stalin to Saddam Hussein's regime in Iraq—have used political violence against civilians at home and abroad. Even the United States has targeted civilian populations. For example, in World War II it tried to break the enemy's will to fight by targeting

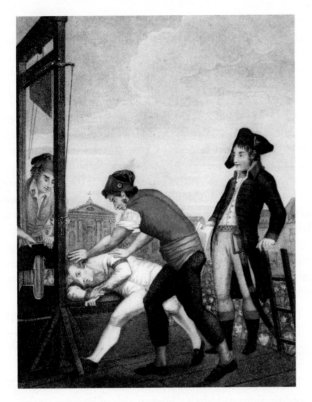

Maximilien de Robespierre (1758–1794), leading figure of the French Revolution, is guillotined in the Place de la Révolution on July 28. The revolution's "Reign of Terror" marked the first time the word *terror* was applied to political violence.

civilians in Germany (by firebombing cities) and in Japan (by dropping atomic bombs on two major cities). Indeed, political violence was first described as "terror" during the French Revolution (1789–1799), when the revolutionary government executed thousands of French civilians, often by guillotine, in what became known as the "reign of terror." **State terrorism,** then, is *political violence directed at civilians by governments.*

Sociologist Austin Turk (2004, 273) usefully defines terrorism as "the deliberate targeting of more or less randomly selected victims whose deaths and injuries are expected to weaken the opponent's will to persist in a political conflict." Combining this with the U.S. government's definition, we can say **terrorism** is *politically motivated violence that intentionally targets noncombatants.*

Labels are important. When we identify an act of violence as terrorism, we are providing a powerful interpretation of it. We typically apply the label *terrorist* to groups we oppose, while we fail to see that our allies and our own government have used strategies that could be labeled as terrorism.

Terrorism is neither new nor rare, but the technology available to inflict terrorist violence is now more readily available to more disparate parties. As a consequence, even the overwhelming conventional military might of the world's only superpower cannot guarantee the safety of its citizens. In this new era, conflict is likely to require diplomatic and political solutions rather than just military ones.

While governments are clearly concerned about their citizens' physical security, they must help ensure their economic security as well. We turn now to a consideration of the economy as a social institution and to the government's influence on economic life.

The Economy

We have already considered topics related to the economy, such as class inequality (Chapter 9), the world of work (Chapter 13), consumerism (Chapter 14), and the connection between types of communities and the economy (Chapter 15). Here we focus on the social nature of the economy and the role of government in relation to economic affairs.

The Economy as an Evolving Social Institution

The **economy** is *a social institution that includes a society's production, distribution, and consumption of goods and services.* Like other aspects of social life, economies are neither "natural" nor inevitable; they are created through human action and vary considerably over time and across cultures.

Because they are socially constructed, there are many types of economies. In Chapter 15, we traced the evolution of economies from those based on hunting and gathering to today's information-based economies. As the name suggests, *hunter-gatherer* societies obtained food and other materials by hunting animals and gathering seeds, roots, fruits, and other foodstuffs. Often these were collective efforts in which nearly the entire community took part, sharing resources and serving as a single economic unit. This arrangement was an economy, though it lacked many of the elements we associate with today's wage-based economies, such as markets, buyers, sellers, and wages. When a hunter's kill was divided among community members, or when coastal dwellers exchanged some of their fish catch for the skins of animals taken by hunters living inland, these transactions had as much to do with establishing and affirming social bonds as they did with gaining access to goods (Polyani 1977).

Later, when plants and livestock became domesticated, paving the way for agricultural and pastoral economies, the family became the primary economic unit. Family members, including children, typically worked together on land they owned, shared, or sharecropped for landowners to produce food and other goods for use, trade, or sale. The family was the center of both work and consumption, in a model that still dominates in many parts of the world today.

When industrialization expanded in the nineteenth century, economic life became increasingly separated—culturally and physically—from other aspects of social life. People left their homes and families to earn wages in workplaces where social relationships were not tied to family or personal links. Home was now associated with consumption, and work with production.

Modern economies came increasingly to rely on the **corporation,** *a business that is treated legally as an entity separate from its owners.* Corporations have many of the rights of individuals—including the right to make contracts, incur debt, and engage in political speech—but their owners are not responsible for the corporation's obligations and liabilities and so corporations are able to take more risks. This has enabled corporations to grow substantially. Today, many are huge *multinational* (or *transnational*) *corporations* with facilities spread across the globe rather than being in just one country.

The Social Economy

Regardless of the type of economy, politics and culture affect economic life just as economic conditions influence politics and culture (Holton 1992). Economic activities are inherently *social* activities requiring interaction, cooperation, coordination, and exchanges among individuals, organizations, and even governments. Max Weber ([1949] 2011) coined the term *social economics* to emphasize this connection between social and economic life, a connection we can view in relation to social cohesion, to culture, and to other social institutions.

ECONOMIES AND SOCIAL COHESION First, economic life is social because economic relationships can take place only with a level of trust. As we saw in Chapter 1, Durkheim argued that social cohesion is necessary for the maintenance of a well-functioning society, and this applies to economic life. Economic agreements—to purchase something, to provide a service, to pay for labor—will succeed only if the parties can trust each other to follow through. That is, a *social* relationship must exist prior to the economic relationship. Generalized trust—sometimes called *precontractual solidarity*—assures us that obligations will be honored and disputes resolved to allow economic life to proceed smoothly. Thus when social relationships collapse, as in war and civil unrest, economies often collapse as well.

on social theory

As Durkheim—whose ideas helped form the **structural-functionalist tradition**—saw, the trust that results from social cohesion is needed for an economy to function effectively. How is trust a part of your economic life?

ECONOMIES AND CULTURE A second reason economic life is social is that economies are embedded within and reflect the cultural values of a society (Granovetter 1985). For example, our society discourages the marketing of crack cocaine and child pornography, even though they are often profitable ventures, because cultural values outweigh the opportunity for economic gain. Different cultures also value different features of economic life. In recent years, the United States has emphasized "free trade" and "free-market" principles that encourage the relative autonomy of the economic sphere and a highly individualistic competitive economy. Other societies focus more on freedom from want, directing the economy toward meeting collective human needs such as more equal access to good schools, housing, and health care. In either case, economic priorities and policies are being filtered through broader cultural values. (A sociologist whose work focuses on freedom from want is featured in the Sociology Works box.)

ECONOMIES AND OTHER SOCIAL INSTITUTIONS A third reason economic life is social is that the economy is intertwined with other social institutions. We saw in Chapter 13 how education and work are often closely connected. Another especially important relationship exists between the government and the economy.

Here is a simple example. Imagine you and some friends start a small business making accessories for cell phones and MP3 players. Being independent-minded entrepreneurs, you want to run your business your own way, without government interference. However, ironically, the very existence of your business and its success depend on government intervention and assistance at every step of the way:

- The government produces deeds and titles certifying the ownership of your building and the land it is on. (If you rent, your lease agreement complies with government regulations protecting both landlord and tenant.)

- A police force monitors and enforces your property rights, and firefighters help lower your risk of loss due to fire.

- A legal system provides a mechanism (courts) for settling disputes and enforcing your contracts.

- The government issues and enforces trademark protection for your company's name and logo. Copyright law protects some of the designs you use on your merchandise, and patents protect your innovative products.

- Public utilities commissions manage access to rights-of-way for power lines, water pipes, and fiber optic cables through public spaces, making available the power you purchase from the electric company and other services.

- A government-financed system of roads and airports enables you to ship products anywhere.

- Government-issued currency enables you to carry out your business.

Because all contemporary economies depend on government intervention of one sort or another, the real question isn't *whether* the government will be involved in the economy but rather *how* and *to what extent*. Different societies answer these questions in ways that result in different economic systems.

Major Economic Systems

Capitalism and socialism have been the modern world's two dominant economic systems. Here we take a basic look at the idealized theory behind each system (see Table 16.3 for a summary); then, following this section, we consider the more complex economic conditions that exist in the real world.

SOCIOLOGY WORKS

Mark Nord and Food Security

As an undergraduate, Mark Nord studied electronics and aviation, topics far removed from sociology. But after being a bush pilot in Indonesia and Central America, where he observed the impact of technology on local cultures and people, he went to graduate school to study rural sociology. Nord brought his new training to the U.S. Department of Agriculture (USDA), where he and his colleagues study the degree to which households have consistent access to adequate food, the economic and social condition scholars describe as food security. The USDA defines *food insecurity* as "limited or uncertain availability of

nutritionally adequate and safe foods or limited or uncertain ability to acquire acceptable foods in socially acceptable ways."

Each year, working with data from the Census Bureau, Nord and his colleagues analyze the results of a national survey of about 50,000 households that asks a range of questions on household access to food and spending on food. Their analysis appears as an annual report, "Household Food Security in the United States." Nord and his colleagues found that in 2012, 14.5 percent of U.S. households (17.6 million) experienced food insecurity (Coleman-Jensen, Nord, and Singh 2013).

> "Watch. Listen," he advises. "You will see reality being created right before your eyes."

Mark Nord

Nord's work serves as a helpful tool for the development of social policy aimed at combating food insecurity. Nord once learned that a congressional committee working on a bill related to nutrition programs cited his new data just a few hours after they were released. As he says, "It makes a researcher want to be really sure that the numbers are right and that their meaning is correctly explained and understood!"

Although his focus is food security, Nord sees the applicability of sociology everywhere. "The sociological insight—that reality is, to a large extent, socially created—has proved useful for understanding human interactions ranging from family get-togethers to policy debates in the halls of Congress."

MAP 16.2 | FOOD INSECURITY IN THE UNITED STATES, 2010–2012

- Food insecurity below U.S. average
- Food insecurity near U.S. average
- Food insecurity above U.S. average

Source: U.S. Department of Agriculture Economic Research Service (2013). http://www.ers.usda.gov/topics/food-nutrition-assistance/food-security-in-the-us/key-statistics-graphics.aspx#.U074DPldV8E

think about it

1. *Have you or has anyone you know experienced food insecurity?*
2. *How is food insecurity related to economic security?*

Capitalism in Theory

Capitalism is *an economic system that emphasizes private ownership of the means of production, which are operated for profit.* Under capitalism, businesses and industries that produce and sell goods and services are owned privately, either directly or indirectly (through stock ownership). These businesses seek to generate profit for their owners by selling goods and services at a price higher than the cost of producing them. Profits are the incentive for companies to be innovative and efficient. By providing a product or service many consumers want and keeping costs as low as possible, owners can maximize their profit. The profit incentive drives the capitalist system; profit is the yardstick by which success is measured.

TABLE 16.3 IDEAL CHARACTERISTICS OF MAJOR ECONOMIC SYSTEMS

	Capitalism	Socialism
Major means of production	Owned privately	Owned publicly
Driving incentive	Personal profit	Public good
Economic structure	Markets	Government planning

Capitalism relies on competitive markets to operate successfully. Ideally, informed consumers get to choose between multiple providers who compete to offer the best product at the best price. Collectively, these purchasing choices decide the fate of various products and businesses. Meanwhile, workers look for jobs that offer the best wages, benefits, and conditions, and employers try to attract the talent they need at the lowest possible cost. The system as a whole emphasizes individual freedom: of owners to operate their business, consumers to make choices in purchasing, and workers to choose employment.

Socialism in Theory

Socialism is *an economic system that emphasizes public ownership of the major means of production, which are operated to meet human needs and promote social justice.* Major industries—energy production, communications, banking, health care, and the like—are publicly owned through the government. (Smaller businesses providing retail consumer goods and services may be privately owned.) Ideally, instead of focusing on generating profits for owners, these state-owned industries meet basic human needs by making essential goods and services available to all citizens. Free or subsidized public goods and services can include health care, education, housing, day care, public transportation, and other essentials. These are paid for, in part, through a system of progressive taxation (which taxes higher incomes at a higher rate), thereby limiting economic inequality.

A socialist system relies on government to coordinate key economic functions. Since they are nonprofit and able to eliminate the wasteful costs of marketplace competition (advertising, duplication of services and administrative bureaucracy, excessive executive salaries, and so on), well-functioning socialist governments can help meet basic needs efficiently. Because they make major economic decisions in the name of the public good to promote social justice, they can take into account the collective benefits of labor rights and environmental protection, for example, rather than just their costs for individual private firms. The system as a whole emphasizes the collective good by directing resources to meet basic human needs.

Often confused with socialism, *communism* can refer to both an economic and a political system. Economically, communism is an egalitarian system in which property is owned collectively and class inequality is nonexistent. Some simple hunter-gatherer societies can be considered a form of primitive communism, but no modern economies have been truly communist. Politically, communism is a system associated with Russian revolutionary Vladimir Lenin, in which an elite political party supposedly leads the nation toward an egalitarian (thus communist) future. The Soviet Union and China were communist societies in the political sense—led by a communist party—but not in the economic sense—a classless society with collective ownership of the means of production.

The reality of capitalism and socialism is more complicated than the simple economic theories we have just outlined. Neither system has worked in the way economic theory suggests, in part because economies are affected by broad social forces, especially inequalities in power.

Capitalism in Reality

Capitalism has proven very successful at unleashing productivity and innovation. A competitive marketplace motivates producers to search constantly for new goods and services to offer consumers, promoting innovation and reacting quickly to new market conditions and needs. Pursuing higher profits by lowering costs motivates producers to look constantly for ways to be more efficient and productive.

"Free-market" capitalist theory argues that governments should ensure the conditions necessary for businesses to operate and then leave them free to function as they see fit (which is why it is also called *laissez-faire* capitalism (*laissez-faire* is French for "leave alone"). Free-market adherents often oppose labor, environmental, and consumer protections, all of which add to the cost of doing business.

Nineteenth-century industrial capitalism is probably the closest we have come to a fully free-market system, and in many ways it was a disaster. One problem is that without government intervention and regulation, unfettered capitalism tends to produce a concentration of enormous wealth and power in the hands of a small elite who can then use that power to prevent others from competing fairly, thus undermining the very premise of a capitalist system. Shrewd late-nineteenth-century U.S. industrialists—"captains of industry" to their admirers—became more commonly known as "robber barons" for their unscrupulous business behavior. They used their early success to build "trusts," powerful companies that unfairly forced out competitors and monopolized key industries, including railroads (Cornelius Vanderbilt), steel making (Andrew Carnegie), and oil (John D. Rockefeller). These industrialists then used their resources to help undermine democracy by financing political campaigns and improperly influencing government decision making. As a result, government provided them with special favors and enormous giveaways of public resources such as vast tracts of land for building commercial railroads.

In recent decades, U.S. capitalism has produced enormous rewards for the affluent while millions of workers struggle just to survive. The result has been a dramatic growth in economic inequality.

While producing great wealth for a few in a period during the late nineteenth century known as the Gilded Age, this system also produced enormous hardship and poverty for many. Powerful industrialists often subjected their workers to grueling working conditions, including 12-hour workdays, six days a week, for poverty wages. Exhaustion coupled with inadequate safety equipment often made work deadly. Steel mill workers were sometimes roasted alive in spills of molten metal. Workers—sometimes children—were decapitated or had limbs torn from their bodies by rapidly moving machinery. Early reformers documented thousands of such cases (MacLaury 2011). Meanwhile, the advantages of early industrial activity were passed from generation to generation, fueling a cycle of inequality. To this day, the names Vanderbilt, Carnegie, and Rockefeller are icons of inherited wealth and power.

A variety of social movements of the late 1800s and early 1900s pressed for more government intervention in the economy. In the United States, these included the early labor movement, the Populist Movement (which included farmers and small business owners oppressed by the large business trusts), and the Progressive Movement (which advocated various economic, political, and social reforms, including workplace safety). These movements pressured federal and state governments to introduce reforms, including outlawing anticompetitive monopolies and cartels, setting wage and safety standards, and protecting the right of workers to form unions. Eventually, government intervention limited the power of industrialists, protected the basic rights of workers, and, many historians argue, helped save capitalism from itself.

Reforming Capitalism

Governments around the world have repeatedly intervened since then to address the excesses of capitalism and to shore up unstable capitalist economies subject to cycles of "boom and bust," or rapid growth followed by collapse. The second period of major government intervention in the United States took place in the wake of the Great Depression of the 1930s. A variety of causes contributed to this worst economic depression, or deep economic slump, of the twentieth century, including the 1929 stock market crash that followed a boom in speculation (high-risk investment in stocks or other ventures in the pursuit of high profits). Other factors were the collapse of thousands of U.S. banks that cost millions of workers their savings, and high levels of economic inequality that helped undermine the economy.

Elected in 1932 following this calamity, President Franklin Roosevelt did not respond by implementing socialism in the form of a government takeover of banks and major industry. Instead, the New Deal policies he introduced in 1933 were intended to revive the economy and help stabilize capitalism. Though business leaders opposed many of his reforms, they were extremely popular and included the following:

- New spending for public works programs that created jobs by building roads, dams, and national parks. (Later, massive military spending for World War II created even more jobs and an endless demand for military supplies.)
- New social programs, notably Social Security, that helped create a social safety net to protect modest- and low-income workers from economic setbacks.
- New government regulation and intervention in the financial system, such as the creation of the Federal Deposit Insurance Corporation (FDIC) that insures bank deposits.
- New worker protections through the Wagner Act, which recognized the right to form unions in the workplace and to strike for better wages and working conditions.

These reforms became a central feature of the U.S. economic system during the period of post–World War II prosperity.

By the 1980s, though, the global economy had enabled large businesses to move production to foreign countries and flee government regulation, giving them greater leverage in negotiations with government. Employers aggressively opposed labor unions, undermining their political power. In this new climate, conservatives called for the deregulation of business, financial institutions, and the economy. In the 1980s, deregulation of savings and loan institutions (S&Ls), which had been limited to providing savings accounts and mortgage loans, allowed them to operate more like banks, but without any of the regulations that governed banks. This deregulation contributed to a new financial crisis in which over 700 S&Ls failed, requiring government action to clean up the mess and stabilize the industry through new regulations. The S&L scandal costs taxpayers at least $125 billion and led to some bank executives serving time in prison (Pizzo, Fricker, and Muolo 1989).

The Housing Bubble and Global Economic Crisis

The S&L crisis was small compared to the global financial meltdown, rooted in the housing industry, that occurred in 2007–2009 with effects that continue today (Das 2010; Financial Crisis Inquiry Commission 2011; Foster and Magdoff 2009; Friedman and Posner 2009; Glass 2008; Rajan 2010; Sorkin 2010; U.S. Senate Permanent Subcommittee on Investigations 2011). A closer look at this most recent crisis illustrates the economy as an integrated social system—from micro-level consumers to macro-level global investors—that can sometimes be dysfunctional.

SOURCES OF THE CRISIS

The global economic crisis—sometimes referred to as the Great Recession—stemmed from several factors:

- Facing stagnant wages, many ordinary U.S. households relied increasingly on credit. Meanwhile the world's richest investors searched for investments that would yield steady profits, eventually buying much of this consumer debt.

- Deregulation in the financial services industry enabled commercial banks to engage in high-risk speculation, which had been prohibited before.

- The financial services industry developed new forms of complex and unregulated investment devices (known as *derivatives*) that led to massive high-risk speculation.

- Corporations engaged in misleading and fraudulent behavior. Some of the world's largest financial firms—including JP Morgan, Citibank, and Merrill Lynch—often had been caught laundering money, defrauding customers, and committing accounting fraud. In most such cases, the firms agreed to pay large fines—sometimes well over $100 million—but did not have to admit to any wrongdoing. But when fraudulent tactics were used in the housing market, the impact was much more widespread.

When these factors combined, the result was disastrous.

THE HOUSING BUBBLE AND BURST

A "bubble" occurs when the price of something is overinflated. The recent housing crisis involved social relationships between various parties in a chain that connected individual homeowners to global investors, linking micro-level economic decisions with macro-level economic forces:

- Homebuyers acquired cheap mortgages that often featured low rates in the early months that increased dramatically over the life of the loan. Some borrowers used poor judgment in entering these contracts; others were greedy and bought more expensive houses than they should have. Many, though, either did not understand the conditions of their mortgage or were defrauded by unscrupulous lenders who misled applicants and approved high-risk mortgages to clearly unqualified borrowers.

- Some lenders used deceptive or fraudulent sales tactics to entice borrowers into mortgages they could not afford. Lenders had an incentive to make as many loans as possible, regardless of people's ability to pay, because they sold these individual loans to investment banks that preferred risky subprime loans because they carried higher interest rates and, thus, the potential for more profits.

- Investment banks bought a large number of mortgages from lenders, combined these with other debt, such as student loans and credit card debt, and then sold pieces of this debt as a type of derivative called *collateralized debt obligations* (CDO). Major investment firms such as Goldman Sachs were selling CDOs to investors as a safe investment, while simultaneously betting that CDOs they didn't own would fail.

- Ratings agencies (Standard & Poor's, Moody's, Fitch)—paid by the investment banks—evaluated CDOs and often gave them the highest possible grade, AAA, obscuring their actual high-risk nature.

- Investors from around the world in search of steady profits purchased CDOs, believing them to be safe investments, thereby generating massive profits for the investment banks that sold them.

In the short term, everyone in the chain benefited. Homebuyers had a chance to

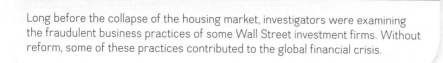
Long before the collapse of the housing market, investigators were examining the fraudulent business practices of some Wall Street investment firms. Without reform, some of these practices contributed to the global financial crisis.

experience the American Dream of homeownership. Lenders, rating agencies, investment banks, and investors made money. Wall Street executives and traders, especially, became enormously rich on bonuses they had generated from these often-tainted deals. For example, between 2000 and 2007, the CEO of the Lehman Brothers investment firm, Richard Fuld, took home about $529 million (Sterngold 2010).

Since almost anyone could get a mortgage in this system, the housing market boomed, creating an artificial bubble in which housing prices nearly doubled in less than 10 years. The FBI and some leading economists warned of massive and widespread mortgage fraud, but those warnings went unheeded and the government failed to step in to regulate the industry. In fact, many of the major government regulators and economic advisors were former finance industry executives. Henry Paulson, for example, was paid $35 million in 2005 as CEO of investment firm Goldman Sachs while it was issuing billions of dollars in high-risk CDOs, and in 2006 he was appointed secretary of the U.S. Treasury (Sloan 2007).

By 2007 the housing bubble had burst. Homebuyers could not keep up with mortgage payments and families lost their homes. Investment banks found themselves still holding tens of thousands of mortgages whose values were plummeting and that could not be sold. Investors began losing their money. The impact of these failures rippled through the economy as banks and the insurance companies that insured them teetered on the brink of bankruptcy. The stock market plunged, and everyone from major institutional investors to individuals with retirement accounts invested in stocks suffered major losses. Unemployment increased as firms facing financial trouble began laying off workers.

At the height of the crisis, the federal government responded with massive spending to bail out major commercial firms and stimulate the economy. After years of criticism that the U.S. Department of Justice had not pursued Wall Street criminals aggressively enough, the government reached an agreement with JPMorgan Chase in 2013 directing the firm to pay the largest civil fine ever: $13 billion for its role in knowingly bundling "toxic" loans and selling them to unsuspecting investors (Barrett and Fitzpatrick 2013). As of this writing, though, the government has not prosecuted any of the corporate executives who helped destroy their companies, wreck the economy, and walk away with the fortunes they accumulated carrying out these actions. After the crisis, U.S. banks are bigger, more concentrated, and more powerful than ever before. They were able to use their political clout to successfully resist any significant reform of Wall Street.

Periodic crises lead many observers to conclude that capitalist markets seem to operate best when they are well regulated to prevent fraud and abuse by powerful economic players. Canada, for example, had much stronger regulation of its banking industry and largely avoided the economic crisis that affected the U.S. banking industry. In addition, capitalism seems to require a robust social safety net to assist those left behind in the competitive marketplace. Critics of these measures, however, see such developments as an abandonment of capitalist ideals and the encroachment of socialism.

Socialism in Reality

By prioritizing social needs over personal profit, a socialist economy can effectively reduce inequality and drastically reduce or even eliminate some social problems commonly found in capitalist economies, such as homelessness, lack of health care, and lack of affordable access to higher education (Lebowitz 2010). But as the most prominent experiment with socialism—the former Soviet Union—has illustrated, this system can also lead to disaster.

SOVIET-STYLE SOCIALISM Russia was an agricultural society, lagging far behind Western industrialized nations in economic development, when the Russian Revolution of 1917 ended its monarchy and eventually brought an authoritarian communist government into power. This government began a massive transformation of the economy that introduced gigantic industrialization campaigns, dramatically raised living standards, and catapulted the newly formed Soviet Union into a global superpower in a single generation. But, especially under the leadership of Joseph Stalin, the authoritarian government used its power to ruthlessly suppress political dissent, condemning those accused of anti-Soviet or anticommunist activity to remote penal labor camps (*gulags*), where prisoners often died or disappeared. These camps played a key economic function for the then-industrializing Soviet Union, which exploited the labor of millions of imprisoned criminals and political dissidents to work in mines, on infrastructure projects like roads and bridges, and on other development efforts.

By the 1960s, the economic role of the gulags had declined dramatically. However, the government's significant expenditures on a large military to compete with its Cold War adversary, the United States, worsened the bureaucratic inefficiencies of centralized economic planning right up to the country's formal dissolution in 1991. Economic inequality in the Soviet Union and the Soviet-dominated countries of Eastern Europe was very low by Western standards, but so too was the standard of living.

Under the leadership of Mikhail Gorbachev in the late 1980s, the Soviet Union sought to simultaneously reform its economic structure (*perestroika*) while introducing more democratic freedoms (*glasnost*). The changes proved too radical, and the Soviet Union disintegrated into separate nation-states. Since the collapse of Soviet-style socialism, Russia and other Eastern European nations formerly under Soviet control have experienced widely divergent fates. With the privatization of public resources, capitalism has created enormous wealth and even some billionaires (sometimes due to rampant fraud and corruption). However, rising unemployment has pushed millions of other people into poverty and created a vast new set of social problems, including skyrocketing alcoholism and a resurgence of tuberculosis, a disease typically associated with poverty.

A basic problem with Soviet-style socialism was that it was administered by an authoritarian government with no accountability. Socialism coupled with democracy, however, has achieved greater success.

DEMOCRATIC SOCIALISM Whereas capitalism needs government intervention to curb the excesses of concentrated economic power, socialism needs a democratic political system to curb the excesses of concentrated government power. Scandinavian countries that feature both democratic political systems and socialist economies are among the most affluent and democratic countries in the world.

One example is Norway, a constitutional monarchy in which real power rests in a parliamentary system where a half-dozen major political parties regularly compete for power. In the three decades following World War II, the country developed a system that features state ownership of major industrial, financial, and communications firms and a major role for labor unions in deciding workplace issues. It also includes free universal health care, nearly free higher education, and a generous lifelong social welfare system that includes twelve months of paid leave for new parents. Combined, these programs make up about half the country's goods and services. Since the 1970s, Norway has maintained its programs in part because the government, rather than private corporations, controls its major oil and natural gas resources. But during this period it has decentralized control of its government assets, allowing local and regional authorities to adapt social and economic programs to their own particular needs. It has also introduced more market-based competition as it has become a significant participant in the global economy. While the global economic crisis has caused much of the industrialized world to stagger, close regulation of its financial sector, large public-sector employment, astute management of natural resources, and a culture of financial thrift have largely insulated Norway from the worst effects.

The Rise of Mixed Economies

Our brief survey of economies shows that four ideal types of political-economic systems exist. They differ based on the degree of government intervention in the economy and the presence or absence of a democratic political system (see Table 16.4). We have already considered capitalist democracies, state socialism, and democratic socialism. The final form of political-economic system is authoritarian capitalism.

China is an authoritarian capitalist system. Over the past several decades, China has allowed many aspects of market capitalism and encouraged foreign investment, though state-run enterprises still play a major role in the economy. However, China's leaders maintain strict political control by suppressing dissent, most famously during the 1989 uprisings in Beijing's Tiananmen Square, which unsuccessfully called for democratic reforms.

Today, the world's largest and most vibrant economies are all mixed economies to varying degrees, and the line between socialism and capitalism is becoming murkier every year. **Mixed economies** *contain elements of both market-based capitalism and the significant government intervention associated*

with socialism. Successful socialist nations have learned to harness the power of markets to spur innovation and respond to consumer needs, while still directing key industries to meet social needs, guarding public resources for the common good, and providing a broad social safety net for citizens. Successful capitalist nations have learned that reasonable government regulation of business and markets can help protect against abuses of concentrated economic power, that a social safety net blunts the excesses of capitalist inequality, and that government intervention can help limit capitalism's characteristic boom-and-bust cycles.

Convergence theory *suggests that capitalist and socialist economies are becoming increasingly similar.* Globalization appears to have accelerated the process, introducing competitive markets to economies around the world and making them more capitalistic. Globalization has also made many capitalist economies more volatile and vulnerable to the pressures of competition from other nations. This is in large part the reason for the decline of manufacturing industries in the United States and the global financial crisis. Governments in capitalist economies have responded to such economic difficulties by intervening more actively in economic affairs, a tendency typically associated with socialist economies. The result has been the global rise of mixed economies.

TABLE 16.4   BASIC POLITICAL AND ECONOMIC SYSTEMS

		Political System	
		Democratic	**Authoritarian**
Economic System	Capitalist	**Capitalist democracies** have democratic political systems and private ownership of industry with modest state intervention in the economy. Example: United States	**Authoritarian capitalism** is found in countries that have considerable private ownership of industry and market-based economies but few civil rights or political freedoms. Example: China
	Socialist	**Democratic socialism** is found in countries that have democratic political systems, public ownership of some key industries, and significant state intervention in the economy. Example: Norway	**State socialism** involves an authoritarian government that dominates a largely centralized economy. Example: North Korea

A Changing World

WHAT IS SECURITY?

As we saw in this chapter's opening vignette, military action abroad in the name of national security can seem inadequate when threats to economic security loom at home. A defeat in Vietnam, a protracted engagement in Iraq with mixed results, and the United States' longest war ever, in Afghanistan—again with mixed results—highlight the limits of both conventional military power and the traditional notion of security. While most discussions about "security" in the United States still focus on the military and "national security," the idea of what security is has been undergoing some changes.

"Economic security" is the most prominent alternative to "national security." **Economic security** is *the condition of having a stable means of financial support adequate to maintain a given standard of living.* Economic security can include a population's access to good employment and assistance during times of sickness or disability. For example, the Social Security Act of 1935 aimed to provide government support for those who are elderly, disabled, or unemployed, and mothers and children, as well as to promote public health. Although we typically think of Social Security as a benefit program for retired persons, the original act implied a government commitment to the general welfare. Other countries have an even stronger focus on economic security.

As the public has become more aware of the dangers of environmental degradation, concern has grown about **environmental security,** *the safe management of natural resources to protect social stability.* Policymakers worry that environmental problems such as drought, erosion, toxic waste, and air pollution could become a consistent source of conflict that might escalate into military confrontation.

Environmental security also takes into account how threats to the natural environment may imperil the foundations of our society. The effects of climate change, for example, can threaten people's homes and their health, uproot communities, and compromise food supplies, endangering individual and collective security. Climate change will likely increase the number of short-term refugees, as people flee worsening natural disasters, and the scale of long-term migration, as people move to where water is more plentiful and crops can be grown more easily. With the world's attention focused more intensely than ever on environmental degradation and protection, the environmental dimensions of security are becoming ever clearer (Chalecki 2013).

The United Nations has developed an even broader definition of security: **human security,** which *emphasizes the health and rights of individual human beings rather than the security of nations.* The UN Commission on Human Security, created in 2001, has worked both to clarify the concept of human security and to support projects that make a real contribution to advancing this cause. Instead of focusing exclusively on military threats, those who advance the human security concept define poverty and illiteracy, HIV and drug abuse, the displacement of populations into refugee camps, and the trafficking of women and children into forced prostitution as threats to the security and dignity of individuals and communities. The UN Commission on Human Security (2004) identifies two interrelated approaches to advancing human security: *protecting* people's basic rights and freedoms and *empowering* people to act on their own behalf.

The breadth of the human security concept makes it a challenge for advocates to define concrete goals and measure the success of human security projects (MacFarlane and Khong 2006). Still, by articulating a new nonmilitary vision of security and connecting that to the ability of ordinary people to take control of their own lives, advocates of the human security concept have challenged governments—and all of us—to address many of the threats and indignities that people experience every day.

thinking sociologically about
Politics and the Economy

culture

- Cultural values help shape both political and economic systems.
- A broad sense of insecurity and a culture of fear help support a large investment in the military.
- Differing cultural approaches to individual freedom or social justice inform capitalist and socialist economies.

structure

- The political structure of a society shapes the possibilities for political action, creating specific constraints and opportunities for individuals and groups to engage in political action.
- Similarly, economic structures help shape the opportunities people have.

power

- Politics involves the exercise of power to decide priorities and policies for society.
- The type of government helps determine who has power in society.
- The decisions governments make can have a profound impact on levels of inequality, especially since the way in which economies are organized can either increase or decrease economic inequality.
- Socialist economies make reducing inequality a priority, whereas capitalist economies accept greater levels of inequality and prioritize the free pursuit of profit.

REVIEW, REFLECT, AND APPLY

Looking Back

1. Politics is the arena in which societies make collective decisions about priorities and policies, and government is the focus of political activity. Governments claim a monopoly on the legitimate use of force in a given territory. Contemporary forms of government include democracies, authoritarian governments, and monarchies. Political culture influences whether and how we become involved in politics.

2. Pluralism, power elite theory, and class domination theory each explain power and politics in a different way. Political involvement in the United States reflects class inequality: people in the middle class are more active than those in the working class, and the political system responds most readily to concerns of the affluent.

3. As part of the national security state, the size, reach, and financial resources of the U.S. military are unrivaled. But a politics of fear continues to shape how we think about the world, leading to policies that would otherwise be unlikely to be adopted. People are socialized to accept war, and recruits are resocialized to become soldiers. The military reflects some of the social inequality that exists in society. Terrorism, which is perhaps the biggest threat faced by today's military, has no universally accepted definition.

4. The economy is a social institution that includes a society's production, distribution, and consumption of goods and services. Economies reflect the cultural values and political priorities of the societies in which they exist.

5. Capitalism and socialism have been the modern world's two dominant economic systems. The ideals of both these systems contrast with complicated realities that expose each of their shortcomings, including the periodic crisis of capitalism and the repressive nature of state socialism.

Capitalist and socialist economies have become more similar to each other, producing mixed economies that incorporate elements of each system.

6. As governments cope with providing security, new notions of security have emerged, including economic security, environmental security, and human security.

Critical Thinking: Questions and Activities

1. Do you feel prepared to participate in politics? Do you vote? How can you explain your specific engagement with—or disengagement from—the world of politics?

2. Why do you think the United States spends so much more on the military than any other country? Do you think this is a wise investment of resources for the country? Why or why not?

3. What are the basic differences between capitalist and socialist economies? Do you think the U.S. economic system is best described as capitalist, socialist, or mixed? Why?

4. What do you think is the best way to define security? What, if anything, should the government do to help achieve this security?

Key Terms

authoritarian government (p. 445) a government that typically features self-appointed leaders who exert great control over the lives of citizens, which includes severely limiting their civil liberties.

capitalism (p. 453) an economic system that emphasizes private ownership of the means of production, which are operated for profit.

class domination theory (p. 452) a theory that suggests that political power is concentrated in the hands of the rich, who own or control a large share of the nation's economic resources.

convergence theory (p. 468) a theory that suggests capitalist and socialist economies are becoming increasingly similar.

corporation (p. 462) a business that is treated legally as an entity separate from its owners.

democracy (p. 448) a political system in which the right to vote is widespread and government leaders are selected through multiparty elections.

economic security (p. 469) the condition of having a stable means of financial support adequate to maintain a given standard of living.

economy (p. 461) a social institution that includes a society's production, distribution, and consumption of goods and services.

environmental security (p. 469) the safe management of natural resources to protect social stability.

government (p. 445) the system by which authority is exercised over a specific territory.

human security (p. 469) concern for the health and rights of individual human beings rather than the security of nations.

mixed economies (p. 469) economies that combine elements of both market-based capitalism with the significant government intervention associated with socialism.

monarchy (p. 445) a system of government headed by a single person, the monarch, who typically inherits the position as a member of a ruling family.

national security state (p. 455) a government dominated by powerful military, foreign policy, and intelligence agencies.

pluralist theory (p. 451) a theory that argues that political power is fragmented among many different competing groups.

plurality voting (p. 447) a "winner-take-all" electoral system in which the candidate with the most votes wins the office being contested.

political socialization (p. 448) the inculcation of basic norms and expectations about political life and attitudes toward involvement in politics.

politics (p. 445) the struggle over power.

power (p. 445) the ability to bring about an intended outcome, even when opposed by others.

power elite theory (p. 451) a theory that suggests that political power is concentrated in the hands of a small dominant group of business, government, and military leaders.

proportional representation (p. 447) an electoral system in which parties are awarded seats in government based on the percentage of votes they receive in an election.

socialism (p. 464) an economic system that emphasizes public ownership of the major means of production, which are operated to meet human needs and promote social justice.

spiral of silence (p. 450) a theory that explains how people keep quiet about controversial issues when they think their opinions are not widely shared, in order to avoid social isolation.

state terrorism (p. 461) political violence directed at civilians by governments.

terrorism (p. 461) politically motivated violence that intentionally targets noncombatants.

war (p. 455) organized armed conflict among two or more specially trained military groups.

Social Change: Globalization, Population, and Social Movements

looking AHEAD

How has globalization affected your experience of **culture**?

How will the coming changes in the population **structure** affect social life in your lifetime?

What are the sources of **power** in the social movements that are important to you?

Twenty-three-year-old Feng Jianme had no idea that a picture of her would help reform China's one-child policy (Beech 2012). In 2012, while she was seven months pregnant with her second child, government family planning agents forcibly injected Feng with a chemical that killed the fetus and then induced her to give birth. This procedure violated Chinese law, which prohibited abortion after six months. Outraged by this abuse of power, Feng's sister posted photos on the Internet of Feng lying in her hospital bed next to her dead baby. The graphic pictures went viral on Sina Weibo, China's version of Twitter, and then circulated around the globe. Some of the officials responsible for the death were fired, and the government formally apologized. But the damage to the controversial policy's public image had been done. The incident helped galvanize a long-simmering protest movement against the policy, which ultimately was reformed, in 2013.

Implemented in 1979, the one-child policy had been one of China's responses to an internal population explosion. Officials had feared that drastic population growth would outstrip China's resources, creating economic and environmental catastrophes and derailing the government's attempts to improve people's standard of living. The family planning policy limited many women to having one child, especially in urban areas, although there were numerous exceptions. Also, families could pay a hefty fine to have a second child, an option Feng Jianme could not afford. The policy had long been opposed by people who resented the government's intrusion into the personal lives of citizens, and Feng's case—elevated by the global exposure it received via social media—was another factor that contributed to the policy's reform. But like much social change, the victory was partial and incomplete. Opponents are still waiting for the policy's complete repeal (Denyer 2013).

The case of China's one-child policy highlights three areas of contemporary social change that we examine in this chapter: globalization, population change, and social movements. These forces represent types of change, as well as being catalysts for further social change.

The theme of social change is highlighted throughout this book because change is an important aspect of social life and an essential topic of sociological inquiry. Our world is in transition, and sociology helps us understand these ongoing developments. At its best, sociology can inform our efforts to promote positive social change. In this chapter, we explore examples of contemporary change. First, however, we consider some broad features of social change itself.

The Nature of Structural and Cultural Change

Social change is *the modification of structure or cultural patterns over time.* Structural change includes shifting patterns of behavior and interaction. Cultural change involves the transformation of values, beliefs, knowledge, and norms, as well as the introduction and adoption of new cultural objects, such as new technologies.

The Continuous and Partial Nature of Change

"Nothing endures but change," observed Greek philosopher Heraclitus 2,500 years ago. Indeed, because society is not static, change is a *continuous* feature of social life and a major focus of sociology (Harper and Leicht 2007; Jordan and Pile 2002; Sztompka 1993). People must constantly reproduce social structures and cultural norms, and their actions can alter society. This is part of the interplay between structure and action that is so central to a sociological perspective.

Although change is continuous, the *pace* of change varies considerably. Sometimes change is slow and difficult to perceive as it is happening. Long periods of human history were characterized by stability and slow incremental change. Individuals could expect to live as generations of ancestors had, experiencing a similar lifestyle, employed in similar sorts of labor, and holding similar cultural values, beliefs, and norms. But other historical eras have featured a frantic pace of change. As we saw in Chapter 1, sociology first emerged in the nineteenth century as an effort to understand a period of particularly rapid and widespread change. At the time, industrialization, urbanization, and democratic movements were among other forces dramatically altering the Western social landscape. Today, we are once again living in a period when the pace of social change is swift and highly visible. (The Sociology Works box examines how sociology majors are doing in a changing job market.)

Though continuous, social change is always *partial*, and certain aspects of social life are persistent. One central reason for the existence of cultural traditions, organizations, and social institutions is to help ensure that they outlive any particular individuals and provide society with some stability and permanence. As a result, some structural patterns and cultural perspectives linger even as others change. For example, the U.S. government today is vastly different from the government in power at the nation's founding, yet key structural features such as the three separate branches of government have provided relative stability and continuity for more than two centuries. Also, the central cultural values that informed the creation of the U.S. government, such as democracy and personal freedom, continue to be important, even though citizens' interpretation of those values has changed significantly since the eighteenth century. In short, continuity coexists with social change.

LEVELS OF STRUCTURAL CHANGE One helpful way to think about various types of structural change is to consider the *level* at which a given change occurs (Harper and Leicht 2007). Changes that originate at various macro, meso, or micro levels can affect other levels. For example, free trade agreements among multiple nations occur at a transnational, or world, level. However, the impact of such changes can trickle down to individual societies and their economies, as well as to specific companies and in turn to those firms' employees. Conversely, some changes start at the micro level and eventually have worldwide implications. Whatever the direction of change, humans often initiate change unwittingly, and the change they create is frequently unintended.

UNINTENDED CHANGE A **social trend** happens *when many individuals act independently but similarly.* Often the cumulative—and unintentional—effect of such behavior is to produce social change.

An interplay between individual action and larger social forces usually propels any social trend. For example, as we saw in Chapter 15, in the post–World War II era many U.S. couples decided to move from cities to suburbs. Individual couples did not start out wanting to change society; rather, they acted for personal reasons. Collectively, though, their behavior led to social change. Importantly, people's choices

thinking about **structure**

What are some **structure**-related changes that have begun at the micro or meso level and spread over time to the macro level—thus having global significance? What impact have these changes had on you?

Sociology Majors After Graduation

The Sociology Works box in Chapter 1 explored the ways in which a degree in sociology can prepare you for a variety of jobs. But what do sociology majors do once they graduate? Here are some answers from students:

▶ "I am an ongoing caseworker for abused and neglected children."

▶ "I work in the business development of technology hardware and professional services."

▶ "I am a paralegal."

▶ "I research climate change policies in several western states."

▶ "I am a 7th and 8th grade social studies teacher in a middle school in a large urban city."

▶ "I am a police officer in a large urban city."

▶ "I am a marketing consultant for a broadcasting company."

▶ "I am a statistician in the Fertility and Family Statistics Branch of the U.S. Census Bureau."

These responses are from an American Sociological Association (ASA) study surveying 1,777 sociology majors from a variety of schools, part of the ASA's work analyzing the experiences of sociology majors both before and after graduation. These ongoing efforts have included surveys and in-depth interviews with students from the classes of 2005 and 2012 (Senter, Van Vooren, and Spalter-Roth 2013; Spalter-Roth and Van Vooren 2008, 2009, 2010).

Two years after graduation, 82 percent of students from the class of 2005 were working in jobs or paid internships, and some of them were also attending graduate school. Another 13 percent were attending graduate school but not working for pay. The most frequent job category was social

> "I am a caseworker."
> "I research climate change policies." "I am a teacher."
> "I am a police officer." "I am a marketing consultant."
> "I am a statistician."

services. Over 90 percent of students reported being "very" or "somewhat" satisfied with their jobs. Four years after graduation, many students reported having moved from entry-level positions, such as those with clerical or administration support duties, to service or management positions in their chosen fields.

Reflecting the versatility of an undergraduate sociology degree, more than half (57 percent) of sociology majors who were seniors in 2012 planned to attend graduate or professional school in a wide range of fields. The most popular fields of graduate study were sociology, social work, psychology, education, criminal justice, public policy, public health, business management, and law.

One challenge, the ASA study noted, is that few jobs are listed as "sociologist." Students therefore must identify the skills and knowledge they have developed as sociology majors (such as learning about racial and ethnic groups and understanding data in tables and charts), include them on their resume, and discuss them during job interviews. Many students in master's programs focus on honing their research skills and using statistical software packages, as competencies in these areas can increase an applicant's opportunities in many fields.

think about it

1. *What is your desired career path? How might a sociology major be an asset in helping you land a good job?*

2. *List the main knowledge and skills you are developing in your sociology course. How would you describe these on your resume? What other skills do you hope to develop before you graduate?*

during this period were significantly influenced by outside social forces, such as the prosperous postwar economy and the government's decision to use tax credits to encourage home ownership. Structural and cultural forces influenced individual actions; in turn, the cumulative effect of those actions helped create social change.

In addition to the inadvertent change caused by social trends, many human actions have **unintended consequences,** *results that are unplanned and unforeseen.* For example, the pursuit of home ownership in the suburbs produced greater reliance on the automobile for commuting, with a resulting increase in traffic and pollution, and the rise of shopping malls dominated by chain stores, with a consequent decline in the fortunes of independent local businesses.

RESISTANCE AND CONFLICT IN RESPONSE TO CHANGE Change is often resisted by one segment of society or another. Sometimes, for example, cultural change poses a challenge to deeply held values, as when growing secularization within a society threatens religious communities. Sometimes social change brings an end to meaningful ways of life, as when residential development destroys the long-standing routines and rhythms of a rural community. In other cases, people simply are comfortable with the status quo and uneasy about new ways of doing things, such as using new technologies for interpersonal communication. Often individuals resist change because it represents a shift in the balance of power between social actors—and therefore threatens them directly or indirectly.

Cell phones have increased enormously in availability and popularity and are used virtually everywhere in U.S. society, creating a new driving hazard as an unintended consequence.

CORE CONCEPTS CHALLENGE

*How has the advent of cell phones affected U.S. **culture**? What other unintended consequences for society have resulted from the widespread use of cell phones?*

Causes of Social Change

Traditionally, historical accounts have highlighted the actions and accomplishments of powerful individuals—presidents, judges, generals, business tycoons, and others who have made key and far-reaching decisions. Such actors can play an important role in social change. However, many contemporary historians examine the larger social factors that contribute to change, writing what is known as *social history.*

Similarly, various sociological theories emphasize two broad sources of change instead of focusing on the actions of particular individuals. Some theories look at change that originates because of *material factors* in the physical world, such as economic conditions and technology. Other theories are concerned with change that is driven by *ideas* from within the human mind, such as thoughts, values, and beliefs. Recall from Chapter 1 that these "objective" (material) and "subjective" (idea-based) approaches make up an important dimension of all sociological theory.

Material Factors in Change: Historical Materialism and Technology

The best-known materialist theory of social change comes from Karl Marx ([1859] 1978). The part of Marx's work now referred to as **historical materialism** *suggests that the economic base of a society is the primary force driving change in other aspects of social life.*

To survive, Marx argued, humans must work with the resources found in nature to produce the material necessities of life, among them food, shelter, and clothing. A society's economy—its *mode of production*, in Marxist terms—defines how these basic necessities are created. Humans work collectively to produce these material necessities and in so doing enter into social relationships, or what Marx called *relations of production.* These social relations involve the roles people play in the production process, as well as other factors, such as the laws and regulations that affect how businesses operate.

According to Marx, *forces of production*—primarily the type of technology that is available to produce material necessities—determine the specific relations of production in a society. For example, the advent of the plow helped make large agriculturally based societies possible; the invention of various machines, such as the mechanical loom and the steam engine, enabled the growth of industrial manufacturing; and the microchip and related developments in computers have facilitated our information-based economy. Each of these changes in the forces of production contributed to change in communities and transformed many social institutions. In other words, a change in the economic base of the society had a powerful impact on other aspects of social life. Marx's theory reminds us that understanding social change often involves attending closely to the economy.

Later materialist approaches developed more specific arguments about technology's role in social change without adopting a broader Marxist framework. Writing mostly in the 1930s, American sociologist William Ogburn identified three routes by which technology and other forces could change society: invention, discovery, and diffusion. *Invention* involves the creation of new materials, ideas, or patterns of behavior; consider, for example, how the microchip, used in computers and countless other devices, has revolutionized social life. *Discovery* entails finding something new that already exists, such as DNA or the neutron. *Diffusion* occurs when new technology or ideas spread from one society to another, as when the machinery that enabled industrialization spread around the world. Ogburn argued that material things like technological innovations generally change more rapidly than a culture's ideas, values, and beliefs. The result is *cultural lag*, a delay in a culture's adaptation to technological innovation, often resulting in social problems.

A dramatic example of cultural lag was noted by scientist Albert Einstein at the end of World War II when he warned, "The unleashed power of the atom has changed everything save our modes of thinking and we thus drift toward unparalleled catastrophe" (Einstein [1946] 1999). Though Einstein himself had played a prominent role in encouraging the development of the first atomic weapons, he concluded that people of the time did not fully grasp their destructive power—and therefore did not change their behavior accordingly. As Ogburn might have observed, society's ideas and beliefs about warfare had not yet caught up with the new technological reality that made the annihilation of humanity a real possibility.

In the end, technology has important implications for three reasons (Harper and Leicht 2007, 18):

1. It creates new alternatives for a society.
2. It alters patterns of social interaction.
3. It gives rise to new social problems that must be addressed.

One of Ogburn's examples—the introduction of the automobile into American life—illustrates all three points. With cars, individuals could travel farther in less time than ever before and could do so more comfortably. It became possible for people to live at some distance from where they worked, and this new option in turn spurred suburban growth. Cars also changed how people interacted: for example, the automobile made visits to distant relatives easier and provided young dating couples with a newfound privacy. Finally, cars contributed a host of new social problems, including road accidents, air and noise pollution, and traffic congestion.

Ideas as Factors in Change: Weber's Protestant Ethic and Ideology

The ideas, values, and beliefs that are part of a culture can also fuel social change. Whereas Marx analyzed the rise of industrial capitalism in materialist terms, Max Weber argued that religious belief also played a key role.

Weber's study, *The Protestant Ethic and the Spirit of Capitalism* ([1905] 1958), suggested that capitalism emerged first in certain areas because it was compatible with the Calvinist version of Protestantism. Calvinists saw economic success as a sign of God's blessing. Therefore, their religious values and beliefs encouraged hard work and frugality, which facilitated the accumulation of money. This money became available for investment in the new technologies and infrastructure that enabled industrial capitalism to grow. In this way, the Protestant ethic's emphasis on hard work and frugality contributed to the rise of capitalism. Weber argued that societies with different religious beliefs did not encourage the same accumulation of capital and therefore did not smooth the way for the rise of capitalism. Thus, according to Weber, a particular set of religious ideas advanced economic development.

A wide range of cultural values and beliefs can drive social change efforts. For example, the ideal of democracy in U.S. culture and elsewhere has provided a powerful spark for many social movements. In this way, ideas can encourage action that leads to social change.

Change in Context

Most sociologists today adopt **contextual analyses** that *take into account the particular historical and social environment within which change is occurring and do not assume that a single factor is the most important in all situations.* This orientation is less a consistent theory about change in particular than a general approach to studying any aspect of social life. A contextual analysis might find that in a particular situation, the adoption of new technology may be the leading factor driving change, but in another case economic conflict may play a role that is equally—or more—important. Government action, new ideas, changing population trends, and other factors can be crucial sources of change in particular situations. In short, the question, "What causes change?" can best be answered by saying, "It depends."

Globalization as Change

Apple iPods are among the most popular electronic devices ever created. Conceptualized and developed in the United States, iPods are mostly manufactured elsewhere and are sold around the world (Linden, Kraemer, and Dedrick 2007; Varian 2007). The Japan-based company Toshiba provides some components but outsources most of the manufacturing to lesser-known firms in China and other Asian nations. Meanwhile, Western companies steer the marketing and promotion of iPods.

We may not think of globalization when we see an iPod, but like many other products sold today, the tiny iPod is a global creation that transcends any individual country. It is just one example of how globalization enters our daily lives. The coffee you sip, the semester you might spend abroad, the foreign film you stream via Netflix, the price you pay for gasoline, the clothes you wear, the CNN report live from Afghanistan, the Chilean grapes you eat, the Internet, the Afro-pop tracks loaded on your MP3 player, the new immigrants in your community (and perhaps you)—all are the result of globalization trends.

Throughout this book we have traced the impact of globalization—on culture, the economy, the media, and other areas of society. In this section, we link these many different dimensions by considering globalization as a social process and by examining how it is both a type of change and a catalyst for change.

Globalization: Integrating Societies

Globalization refers to *the interaction or integration among various aspects of social life, including economies, cultures, political*

thinking about culture

Has your college's **culture** (in the form of norms and rules) lagged behind the introduction of cell phones and laptops in the classroom? Has this lag created any problems? Explain.

478

One unintended consequence of increased global travel is that communicable diseases are more easily spread worldwide. Pictured is a family wearing masks in the Taipei, Taiwan, airport after Taiwan confirmed its first case of a new deadly strain of bird flu in 2013. What other problems are created or made worse by globalization?

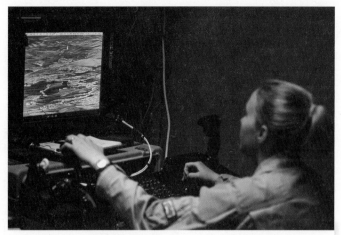

Through advances in communication technology, soldiers can operate drones for either reconnaissance or attack from command centers thousands of miles from the battlefield. This capability has decreased the significance of both distance and physical location.

systems, and populations. As such, the word is an umbrella term that highlights the links among multiple and simultaneous developments that are continually evolving (Held et al. 1999; Sassen 2007; Scholte 2005).

The most significant feature of globalization is the increasing interconnection of societies. Globalization reflects a world that is more a single, integrated place than a collection of relatively isolated and separate societies. Not only are individuals interconnected by means of instant communication, but countries are, too, by global networks of trade agreements and political treaties. This global dynamic involves increased interaction among people, companies, and countries, as well as the creation of new transnational structures and organizations, such as the World Trade Organization.

A second key feature of globalization is the decreasing significance of distance and physical location. Because of advances in communication technology and the increasing ease of travel, geographic space is less significant than it once was; the world is a "smaller" place. Think of how the Internet connects people across vast distances, allowing them to interact in cyberspace. More and more people throughout the world interact using the Internet and other technological bridges across major distances to discuss, buy, learn, organize, and have fun. Physical travel is also more accessible and commonplace, and consequently world travel, tourism, and international business have grown dramatically. People from far-flung locations now routinely come into social contact within the same physical space.

As stunning and rapid as these developments have been, you probably already take them for granted. To appreciate the significance of globalization, we must consider what came before it.

Early Globalization's Colonial Roots

Almost unimaginably, for much of human history, people lived and died in or near the communities of their birth and had little accurate knowledge of the wider world. Travel of more than just a few dozen miles was uncommon, and communication outside a person's immediate region was limited. The necessities of life were largely self-produced or acquired locally. Even well into the middle of the nineteenth century, most people did not travel beyond a few hundred miles of their home, and letters and other communications reached their destination by physical means.

Yet limited forms of what we might now call globalization did exist. For centuries, a few daring souls ventured outward over land and sea to make a living by buying and selling goods across considerable distances. Such commercial ventures increased contact between widely separated peoples and forged limited economic ties.

Most early globalization, however, came by way of empires spanning continents and featured the military domination and colonization of other societies. From roughly the 1500s through the early 1900s, European colonialism in particular expanded the reach of a few powerful countries, making events in foreign countries relevant to people in a new way (Map 17.1). Colonial populations were subjugated by governments that sometimes ruled from halfway around the globe. At the same time, individuals in the home countries of the colonial powers became linked to events that occurred in distant colonies, and in this way they began to learn about the other societies that were now a part of their empire.

MAP 17.1 | THE BRITISH EMPIRE IN THE 1920S

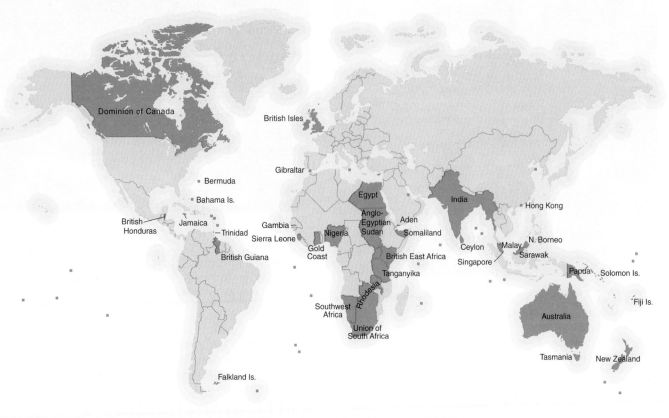

Early globalization derived primarily from the establishment of colonial empires such as Britain's. *Source:* Based on archival maps at www.probertencyclopaedia.com and www.britishempire.co.uk.

CORE CONCEPTS CHALLENGE

What forms of **power** *did colonizing nations use to build large empires and spread their influence?*

In the postcolonial era, the formal ties of colonialism have been severed as former colonies have gained their independence. However, new means of influencing national and regional politics have arisen. As we saw in Chapter 9, critics contend that *neocolonialism* (economic domination without formal political control or military occupation) is often carried out through transnational economic organizations such as the World Bank and the International Monetary Fund (Danaher and Mittal 2004; Toussaint and Millet 2010). Transnational corporations, which have no allegiance to any particular country, have also taken center stage in the global economy and have had a major impact on the economies of smaller, poorer nations, in particular. The continuing legacy of colonialism, with power imbalances and inequality among nations and regions of the world, has contributed to persistent international tensions and conflict.

Contemporary Globalization's Multiple Dimensions

Since the mid-twentieth century and especially in the past few decades, globalization has become more pervasive, far reaching, swiftly developing, and technology dependent than ever before. The very term *globalization* came into wide use only in the 1980s as these trends became more readily apparent and began to have an impact on growing numbers of people. Globalization is now one of the most important social forces affecting societies around the world.

Many issues can no longer be understood merely by looking at a single society; the dynamics involved are now global or transnational. Moreover, globalization affects a diverse array of overlapping areas of social life, including the following:

- *Economy.* Globalization has meant an increased flow of goods (trade), capital (investment), and people (migration) across national boundaries.

- *Culture.* Globalization has powered a surge of ideas, beliefs, and lifestyles across national boundaries—everything from democratic movements, media products, religious proselytizing, and travel and tourism to sporting events such as World Cup soccer and the Olympic Games.

- *Communications technology.* More than 900 communication satellites orbit Earth, an ever-growing number that facilitates the flow of communications on a vast scale

Typically carried out behind closed doors, global economic meetings such as the 2013 G20 Summit in Russia bring together leaders of the world's major industrialized countries to make economic decisions that can affect billions of people worldwide. How do such meetings reflect aspects of power and inequality on a global scale?

(Union of Concerned Scientists 2008). Instantaneous global communication has been crucial to the staggering reduction in the significance of distance and time.

■ *Transnational entities.* Globalization has led to the creation of new social structures to deal with the increase in social relations across national boundaries. Transnational corporations; economic organizations such as the International Monetary Fund, the World Trade Organization, and the World Bank; and political institutions such as the United Nations and the European Union are prominent transnational structures. International relief agencies such as the Red Cross/Red Crescent and Doctors Without Borders, and even international professional associations such as the International Sociological Association are part of this trend.

■ *Transnational identities.* Globalization has contributed to the emergence of new social identities. Ever more eclectic consumers mix cultural products from across the globe, including music, food, film, and clothing styles. It is not unusual to find, say, Jordanian teen girls in traditional hijab dress listening to American pop music or to find U.S. teens who are fans of Japanese anime and Indian food. Immigrants moving from one country to another often live a life of cultural hybrids, speaking one language at home and another at school or work; watching both native-language television programs via satellite and programs in the language of their adopted country; listening to both traditional music from their homelands and Western pop music; adopting values, behaviors, and dress that combine the cultures of their original and newly adopted homes. Websites often serve internationally diverse users. For example, the Google search engine, truly a global phenomenon, supports more than 100 languages, and the company's popular Gmail electronic mail system accommodates over 40 languages (Yunker 2008).

■ *Global cities.* As globalization disperses economic activity worldwide, these scattered economic processes are coordinated from a few key locations where managers, lawyers, financiers, and engineers navigate the legal and technical complexities of multinational

transactions (Sassen 1991, 2006). *Global cities* are home to many companies that provide key financial, legal, technical, and other high-level services and are thus strategic nodes in the networks that constitute the global economy. Among the most important global cities are New York, London, Tokyo, Paris, Frankfurt, Zurich, Amsterdam, Sydney, Hong Kong, Mexico City, and São Paulo. Global cities are also cosmopolitan, catering to sophisticated international workers through diverse restaurants, entertainment, religious and other cultural offerings. Global cities, then, are urban centers that transcend the nations in which they are located.

■ *Global social movements.* As social problems have gone global, so too have the responses of social movement

An Iraqi family joins hundreds of millions of other viewers to watch their national soccer team play Australia in a qualifying match for the 2010 FIFA World Cup.

CORE CONCEPTS CHALLENGE

How does the broadcast of such games worldwide exemplify the globalization of **culture***? What are other examples of global cultural events?*

activists (Smith and Johnston 2002). Environmental groups reach across national boundaries to tackle global climate change and the loss of wildlife habitat. Labor groups, including unions, work across national boundaries to protect employees of transnational corporations. Human rights groups try to mobilize worldwide support to pressure repressive governments to cease human rights abuses.

These developments represent some of the most significant changes that the world has undergone in the past century. The impact of these changes is raising a number of pressing sociological questions.

The Impact of Globalization on Culture, Structure, and Power

We conclude this section with a look at some of the issues resulting from the expansion of globalization, grouping them by sociology's core concepts.

CULTURE Has globalization improved understanding among people of different cultures? Or has it resulted in the homogenization of cultures as wealthier nations come to dominate in global relationships? These questions have driven the debate over globalization and its impact on culture.

Global culture has many dimensions (Berger 1997). Beyond *popular culture* in the form of music, movies, and clothing, the global economy has contributed to a common *business culture* of economic elites. In addition, *religious* organizations from wealthier nations—especially evangelical Protestants—have exported their beliefs and practices to other nations, another sort of cultural globalization. In the realm of *ideas*, Western intellectuals, through academic networks and nongovernment organizations, have advanced a culture rooted mostly in democratic egalitarian values. Combined, these processes have had a massive impact on how people around the globe are socialized.

When different cultures have contact, they exchange influences, such as when languages adopt foreign words and when music or literature integrates foreign traditions. Cross-cultural contact in turn can promote greater understanding, tolerance, and mutual appreciation, all of which can diffuse tensions, reduce conflict, and facilitate a more stable, peaceful world. It also paves the way to advances in knowledge that can potentially improve people's quality of life, as often happens when scholars share scientific advances.

But most cross-cultural contact also leads to challenges. First, some ideas and values from different cultures are incompatible. For example, a belief in full gender equality—a hallmark of most secular democratic societies—clashes with some patriarchal religious traditions that limit women's role in religion and sometimes even social and civic life. When one country promotes egalitarian and democratic principles, is it imposing its cultural values on the political culture of

A pedestrian in Beijing, China, passes a movie theater advertising the movie *Monsters University*. Unlike most foreign regimes, Chinese government censors allow only a handful of foreign films to be officially released each year, thereby limiting the impact of such cultural products on the local culture. How many foreign-made films have you seen in the past year? What does this suggest about the flow of pop culture into and out of the United States?

other peoples? Or is it asserting universal rights that unite humanity, irrespective of culture? The fact that different cultures offer different answers to such questions is one of the challenges societies face in a globalized world.

Patriarchy versus gender equality, and theocratic states versus secular democracies, are among the volatile issues that will continue to characterize the debate over global culture and that will be an ongoing source of conflict. Because of greater economic and political integration, the risk of a large-scale global conflict such as the two world wars of the twentieth century is probably reduced. However, insofar as globalization results in increased contact among cultures with irreconcilable differences, it will likely result in *more* conflicts than in the past.

Second, because the world's societies are not equally wealthy and powerful, their ability to be heard in a global exchange of culture is unequal. Although it is difficult to quantify, wealthy—predominantly Western—countries have exported most of the cultural goods traveling in the global economy. One report found that North America and Europe account for about 75 percent of all exports of cultural goods such as films, music, books, television, artwork, and video games. In contrast, all developing countries *combined* account for only 1 percent of such exports (UNESCO-Institute for Statistics 2005). At a time when most of the world can be exposed to the same media content, sometimes simultaneously, that content is most likely to come from wealthy Western societies. This situation raises the issue of cultural domination. Recall from Chapter 3 the concerns that sociologists have about the potential homogenizing effects of mass media and cultural products. Although many people around the world have embraced Western cultural products and values, others have resisted their influence. In some cases, such as in India, they have simply embraced locally produced films and music. In others, such as in China, governments have limited the import of Western films and censored the Internet.

STRUCTURE Has globalization reduced hierarchy and bureaucracy by promoting decentralized social networks and direct communication? Or have the large transnational entities that have emerged concentrated control more centrally and made hierarchy and bureaucracy increasingly resistant to change? These are among the questions sociologists and other observers debate in relation to the impact of globalization on structure and action.

Globalization has stimulated contradictory trends involving social structures and social action. On the one hand, new social structures have been created to facilitate and manage the increase in transnational relations. For example, on the economic front, the large transnational corporations that have emerged are massive global organizations employing thousands of people in many different countries and often organized into fairly traditional bureaucratic, pyramidal structures. On the other hand, the increased accessibility of new technologies has enabled communication and interaction that involve far fewer layers of bureaucratic hierarchies—that is, a flattened structure—because people interact more directly through networks (Castells 1996). Even small businesses can use the Internet, telephone, and overnight package delivery services to conduct business directly with consumers around the globe, cutting out the need for large corporate intermediaries.

Do such trends empower people and organizations to act more freely? Or does the unprecedented size of global companies restrict the practical options that are available to people? We do not yet have complete answers to these questions because these structures are still in transition.

POWER Does globalization help improve living standards throughout the world, or is it a new form of colonialism, reinforcing and even intensifying economic divisions? How has power shifted since globalization has become so pervasive? These two related questions are central to the ongoing debates over the effect of globalization on power and inequality.

It is difficult to answer questions about globalization and inequality definitively, in part because individual countries vary significantly in how much they have participated in globalization (see Table 17.1). Wealthier nations tend to be the most globalized, and poorer countries are the least integrated globally. Even within individual countries, generally only the relatively affluent can afford computers, broadband access, and other communications technologies that enable them to participate in aspects of globalization.

Deep inequalities and power imbalances among different countries and regions clearly have been intrinsic to globalization. Yet despite evidence that overall global poverty is declining, some of the world's poorest nations have experienced little or no benefit from globalization. Some critics in fact argue that less affluent developing nations have been seriously *harmed* by the economic policies associated with globalization (Kaplinsky 2007). Even workers in wealthier nations have experienced mixed results. Although they have benefited from the availability of cheaper goods, many have seen their jobs shift to low-wage countries where workers enjoy few if any labor rights or democratic freedoms. As transnational corporations continuously seek lower wages and lower production costs in what some critics call a "race to the bottom," workers lose their ability to maintain a living wage.

| TABLE 17.1 | MOST AND LEAST GLOBALIZED COUNTRIES, 2013 |

Most Globalized		Least Globalized	
Country	Globalization Index	Country	Globalization Index
1. Belgium	92.30	1. East Timor	24.35
2. Ireland	91.79	2. Kiribati	25.46
3. Netherlands	91.33	3. Equatorial Guinea	26.26
4. Austria	89.48	4. Laos	26.52
5. Singapore	88.89	5. Solomon Islands	26.72
6. Denmark	88.12	6. Eritrea	27.34
7. Sweden	87.63	7. Bhutan	27.91
8. Portugal	87.07	8. Liberia	30.81
9. Hungary	86.85	9. Comoros	31.05
10. Switzerland	86.28	10. Afghanistan	31.46
27. United States	74.76		

One globalization index, compiled at the KOF Swiss Economic Institute, combines measures of economic, political, and social globalization to score 187 countries on a scale of 0 (low) to 100 (high). This table shows the results for the 10 most globalized and the 10 least globalized countries, as well as for the United States. What similarities do you see among the 10 most globalized countries? How about among the 10 least globalized countries? *Source:* KOF Swiss Economic Institute (2013).

Sociologists arguing from the perspective of world systems theory maintain that wealthy "core" countries exert considerable influence over less affluent countries that are part of the poor "periphery" or middle-income "semi-periphery" of the world's economy. In this way, the dynamics inherent in the global economy maintain a significant imbalance of power and ensure continued inequality among wealthy and poor nations. Wealthy, powerful nations have created, and continue to enforce, the ground rules according to which global capitalism operates. A variety of international economic and political organizations implement these rules, including the World Bank, the International Monetary Fund, the World Trade Organization, and the United Nations (Peet 2009; Wallerstein 2004).

As a result of the actions of wealthier, more powerful nations, national governments in weaker countries now have less authority to regulate their own economies than they once did. To participate in the global economy, these countries must follow the ground rules established by the international economic organizations and must court investment from large multinational firms. To some observers, this situation represents a shift of power from national governments to transnational organizations. Since these transnational organizations in turn are dominated by wealthier countries, this shift has reinforced the power of wealthy countries over poorer ones.

This approach to economic globalization is known as *neoliberalism* (not to be confused with the liberal/conservative political spectrum) (Harvey 2007). **Neoliberalism** refers to *an economic philosophy that promotes markets, deregulation, privatization, and reduced government social expenditures.* Typical neoliberal policies include the deregulation of economic sectors, the reduction of taxes, the elimination of tariffs and trade barriers, opposition to labor unions, and the privatization of government-owned industries. Neoliberals favor a shift in power away from government and toward private enterprise.

In reality, critics point out, neoliberal policies are often applied selectively as the government intervenes to promote certain business interests. With respect to agriculture, for example, the United States and Europe provide farmers with subsidies that enable growers to sell their crops at a lower price than they otherwise could. Subsidization forces prices downward, sometimes harming nations whose major exports are agricultural products. Critics contend that neoliberalism ultimately favors policies that, first and foremost, protect the interests of investors. They note that neoliberal policies can be used to shift power from governments that are democratically elected and accountable to the people to corporations that are privately owned and accountable only to investors.

Supporters of neoliberal policies promote their version of economic globalization as the only legitimate form (Griswold 2009; Irwin 2009). They blast critiques of neoliberalism as "antiglobalization"—a label some activists use as well. But in reality, most of the critics oppose the

Global justice advocates march at a meeting of the World Social Forum in Mumbai, India. The forum is held as a counterpoint to the annual World Economic Forum held in Davos, Switzerland, which hosts elite business and political leaders. What do you think is meant by the slogan "Our world is not for sale"?

neoliberal version of globalization, not globalization itself. For example, rather than endorse unqualified "free trade," opponents of neoliberalism advocate "fair trade" policies that protect workers' rights and are environmentally sustainable. In effect, they argue for a globalization that would help reduce inequality and empower workers in the global economy.

The Limits of Globalization

Certain trends associated with globalization appear to be shifting (McGrew and Held 2007). For example, in the wake of the 9/11 terrorist strikes, the U.S. government increased efforts to restrict immigration, and divisive religious fundamentalism again became a major worldwide social force. In the early 2000s, global trade, capital flows, and foreign investments *declined* as countries tried to protect their domestic industries. The global economic crisis of the late 2000s further dampened the global economy and reduced economic globalization (KOF Swiss Economic Institute 2013). Nevertheless, globalization is resilient and will withstand the setbacks caused by changing political tides and temporary economic downturns.

It's important, though, to keep globalization in perspective. Billions of people live in poverty and are left out of globalization processes. In addition, local, regional, and national factors still heavily influence a nation's economic, political, cultural, and social life. In the future, social life will be neither exclusively local nor primarily global; instead, local and global issues and concerns will become increasingly intermeshed.

But the particular neoliberal policies associated with globalization may be subject to reform. The criticisms they have drawn have sparked a diverse "global justice" movement. Global justice activists are pursuing increased transparency (openness) in the operations of the organizations that oversee the global economy, as well as a greater focus on combating poverty. The real goal of these efforts to promote international justice, however, has been to minimize the negative effects of globalization on the environment—and especially on the world's poor and working classes.

These reform efforts are among a host of social movements promoting social change, a topic we examine later in the chapter. First, we consider another significant form of social change: the population shifts that are reshaping societies.

Some observers believe that although the United States will continue to play a major role globally, the country's importance has diminished as globalization has empowered other nations. Do you think U.S. influence in world affairs will decline in the twenty-first century? Why or why not?

Population Change

World War II created enormous uncertainty for young Americans. Because many had been drafted or had volunteered to serve in the military, their fate was in doubt for the war's duration. Millions of young people put off plans to get married and delayed having children until the future was clearer.

At the end of the war in 1945, the survivors of the conflict were able to carry out their marriage plans. Many couples were soon enjoying the economic good times that followed the war. They could now afford to have children, and the popular culture of the day encouraged attention to family life. Consequently, the number of marriages increased, and the percentage of childless marriages decreased. Individually, these people were simply starting the family life that they had put on hold during the war. Collectively, they were unintentionally creating one of the best-known social trends of the twentieth century: the post–World War II "baby boom."

The term *baby boomers* applies to people born in the postwar period roughly spanning 1946 to 1964, when the U.S. birth rate soared. Because the boomers' numbers are so much greater than usual, this cohort of Americans has had a powerful impact on the country throughout their lives. When they reached college age, they were part of an explosion in the size of higher education. When they had children, they created a *baby boomlet*—a smaller echo of the previous generation's baby boom. As they have aged and begun to retire, they are contributing to the "graying of America" and putting strains on the nation's health care and Social Security systems.

The baby boomers exemplify how social factors—war, economic good times, and cultural norms—can influence personal decisions. In turn, the changes in population that result from these individual actions can ripple throughout society for decades to come.

Demography is *the study of human population trends* such as the baby boom. It considers a wide array of population characteristics, including rates of birth, marriage, household occupancy, income, and education. In the United States, the Census Bureau is the agency responsible for collecting such data. (The Sociology in Action box examines the role of sociologists at the Census Bureau.) Internationally, the United Nations is a key clearinghouse for demographic data.

In studying human population trends, sociologists not only document patterns but also look for explanations as to *why* various developments occur. In this section, we examine population change, some social explanations for it, and the effects of this change on society.

The Population Explosion and Its Sources

The world is currently in the midst of a population explosion. The effects of this population surge are being felt globally and in many different ways, including as increased urbanization and the environmental crisis we examined in Chapter 15.

It took all of human history—tens of thousands of years—for the world's population to reach an estimated 1 billion people in about 1804. It rose to 2 billion people just 123 years later in 1927 and to 3 billion just 33 years after that, in 1960. In the ensuing 50 years—less than a single lifetime—the

SOCIOLOGY in ACTION

The U.S. Census Bureau

Sociology has made its way into almost every U.S. home—literally. That's because many sociologists work on the census that is mailed to every U.S. household. Sociologists help create the census questions, design the collection methods, and analyze the results. In these ways, sociological insights shape one of the best-known sources of data on population trends and countless other topics.

Administered by the U.S. Census Bureau, which employs many sociologists, the census is conducted every 10 years. Unlike a survey, in which information is gathered from a population sample, a census aims to reach every resident. The U.S. Constitution mandates this population count to determine the number of seats each state is allotted in the House of Representatives. Thus the census has been conducted every decade since 1790.

Over the years, the purpose of the census and the work of the U.S. Census Bureau have expanded significantly. Census data are now used to inform the allocation of billions of dollars in federal funds to local communities. The Census Bureau has many other data collection efforts that occur between the decennial census, including the annual American Community Survey. The information citizens provide is not traceable to individuals and cannot be used by law enforcement, the IRS, or immigration authorities.

In addition to their use by agencies at all levels of government, Census Bureau data are used by sociologists and other social scientists who study many aspects of society. The data are also a resource for activists and interest groups that advocate on behalf of certain groups, communities, and issues; and for businesses that study information such as population trends to predict changing markets and workforce educational levels to identify possible locations for new businesses.

Sociology has affected the range of topics the Census Bureau studies. In 2010, data on household size, age, sex, race, and ethnicity were collected through the census short form's 10 basic questions. Census Bureau questionnaires also explore income levels, employment patterns, household characteristics, business information, and education levels. The influence of sociology can be seen, too, in the Bureau's methods. In the 1940s, Census Bureau sociologists were involved in developing the basic sampling and statistical analysis techniques that are now a routine part of political polling, consumer satisfaction surveys, and biomedical research. Ever since, sociologists have helped design and refine the Census Bureau's sampling techniques and data collection methods. Sociologists also analyze the data the Bureau collects, writing issue briefs for the Bureau, presenting scholarly papers at the American Sociological Association's annual meetings, and publishing findings in sociological journals.

The impact of sociology on the Census Bureau is perhaps best symbolized by sociologist Robert Groves, Bureau director from 2009 to 2012. A sociologist who specializes in surveys and statistical analysis, Groves was a transitional figure, nudging the Census Bureau to adopt new technologies and techniques. He helped make the Bureau's data and analyses more readily accessible through the Internet, set up the Bureau to begin collecting data via the Internet instead of only paper surveys, and was the first director to maintain a blog to discuss his work and a range of data-related topics. Groves also stirred controversy by advocating that the Census Bureau supplement the traditional census count with sampling techniques that might more accurately capture the number of hard-to-reach populations such as the homeless and the poor. He argued that the Census Bureau needs to make better use of existing statistics already gathered by private industry and other government agencies, to promote cost efficiency. In the end, said Groves, "I don't think this is a job for political animals. . . . The most important thing to get right in this role is to make sure you're serving in a nonpartisan, objective nature" (Morello 2012). Visit census.gov to explore a treasure trove of information about the country, which was designed, collected, and analyzed with the help of sociologists.

think about it

1. *Have you ever filled out a census form? Did you know what the data would be used for?*

2. *Why do you think Congress might oppose using sampling techniques as part of the census?*

---

world's population has more than doubled, surpassing 7 billion in 2011. The earth's population is projected to continue growing, though at a slightly slower rate, reaching 10 billion in 2083 (Figure 17.1).

Why is the human population increasing so rapidly? You might think the obvious answer is that people are having more children than in the past. In fact, the rate at which women are bearing children has *declined* in many societies during the precise period in which the overall population has increased. Instead, the population explosion is due to two global developments.

First, more infants are surviving into childhood and then into adulthood than in the past. As a result of scientific advances and growing affluence, many infants now receive better nutrition and health care, factors that help them survive their critical early years. Thus the population boom is, in part, one of the unintended consequences of scientific progress. This trend is measured by looking at the **infant**

FIGURE 17.1 | WORLD POPULATION IN BILLIONS, 1 C.E. TO 2083 (PROJECTED)

Population in billions

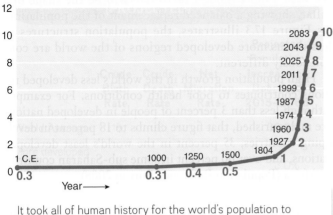

It took all of human history for the world's population to reach an estimated 1 billion people in about 1804, as the graph shows. What happened after that milestone was reached? *Source:* UN Department of Economic and Social Affairs, Population Division (2013).

mortality rate, *the number of infants less than a year old who die per 1,000 live births.* In recent decades, the infant mortality rate across the world has been declining significantly, though unevenly.

Second, around the world, people are living longer. The human life span has increased because of improved nutrition, medical care, and knowledge about the causes of disease and illness. **Life expectancy** refers to *the median number of years a person is likely to live given the current conditions.* This figure can be measured by nation, by sex, or by other subpopulations and can vary considerably by subpopulation even within a single country. When the life expectancy in a nation is low, it is a sign that many of its citizens are dying prematurely. Common reasons for early death include disease (AIDS is a major killer in some countries), lack of clean water, malnourishment, and famine.

As more infants survive into adulthood and more adults live longer, these two developments have combined into a powerful demographic trend that fuels population growth. But this trend has not occurred evenly across the planet, as we next consider.

The Demographic Divide

The term **demographic divide** refers to *the inequality in population and health conditions between rich and poor countries.* This divide includes stark differences in population growth, birth and death rates, and immigration patterns.

POPULATION GROWTH   Since 2007, the government of central Russia's Ulyanovsk region has sponsored "family contact day," encouraging couples to have sex. The government has offered prizes, including an SUV, to couples who produce a baby nine months later, on June 12, Russia's national day. The contest is one of many efforts by the Russian government to stem an annual population *decline* of about 700,000 (Haas 2008).

The **growth rate** *of a nation is the indicator that measures how quickly that country's population is increasing.* The growth rate combines two figures: the difference between births and deaths plus the difference between immigrants (those moving into a country permanently) and emigrants (those leaving a country permanently). In Russia, declining birth rates, high death rates, and significant emigration have combined to create a negative growth rate; the country's population is on course to decline by 22 percent by 2050. All of Europe and several dozen other relatively wealthy countries are also experiencing unprecedented negative population growth.

Russia's declining population contrasts starkly with trends in Uganda, an African nation whose population growth is among the world's highest. Uganda's population of about 40 million in 2015 is projected to rise to an astounding 126 million by 2060—more than tripling in size. It is these vast differences in population growth that underlie the demographic divide. Despite high infant mortality, the world's less developed countries continue to experience relatively high birth rates, resulting in high growth rates. The contrast in population trends between wealthier and poorer countries means that a greater percentage of the world's people live in less developed regions than in the past, and this trend is projected to continue. By 2050 roughly 9 out of 10 people will inhabit less developed—and therefore poorer—regions (Figure 17.2).

Differences in growth rates can be seen in a country's **population pyramid,** *a bar chart that shows the distribution of a population by age and sex.* The population structure of a country with a high birth rate

Percent of total population

Luxembourg	42.4
Israel	31.2
Switzerland	27.8
Australia	26.8
New Zealand	23.2
Canada	21.3
Sweden	16.8
Austria	16.7
Germany	16.4
Ireland	15.5
Spain	14.9
Belguim	14.4
United States	13.1
United Kingdom	12.9
France	12.6
Netherlands	11.2
Norway	10
Denmark	9.6
Russia	8.7
Portugal	7.3
Finland	3.7
Chile	1.9
Mexico	0.9
Brazil	0.4
India	0.4
China	0.1

The percentage of foreign-born individuals in the populations of different countries varies widely. How does the United States compare with other countries in this regard?

Source: OECD Factbook 2013.

benefits to stay solvent. It has reduced benefits and delayed the retirement age at which workers receive full benefits. This means fewer jobs for younger workers.

In addition, increased life expectancy has meant that many older Americans are living longer and suffering from the chronic illnesses typical of old age. The growing number of older Americans is driving up demand for health services and senior housing and causing a significant redeployment of medical facilities and resources to care for this aging population.

Other challenges facing a graying United States are more cultural. In the past, aging Americans often were isolated from mainstream life. But as their life expectancy increases and their health prospects improve, seniors' social role is in transition. Older Americans are healthier and more vigorous than previous generations, and many are enjoying active retirements. Some are even pursuing "encore careers" doing community service work.

The Threat of Overpopulation: The Neo-Malthusian View

The historian and political economist Thomas Robert Malthus published a book in 1798 arguing that the human population was growing faster than the available food supply. Although the details of his arguments are out of date, the insight that the earth's population growth is unsustainable remains relevant. A more contemporary analysis, known as the **neo-Malthusian perspective,** *warns that human overpopulation is threatening the planet.* As evidence, supporters of this perspective point to environmental degradation, the rampant consumption pursued by wealthier nations, and high birth rates in poorer nations (Ehrlich 1986). Such trends are unsustainable over time. The massive food shortages that Malthus and his later followers predicted were delayed by advances in agriculture, sometimes referred to as the "green revolution," but such technological advances cannot be maintained indefinitely. The dynamic of growth outpacing the supply of natural resources remains in effect.

To help correct ecological imbalances between the planet's population and its resources, neo-Malthusians support the empowerment of women. They maintain that women should have the right to make their own reproductive decisions, and they advocate the widespread availability and voluntary use of contraceptives. In addition, neo-Malthusians argue for a curb on rampant consumption and waste in wealthier societies.

What happens when the population grows at an unsustainable pace? Simply put, people die prematurely. In the world's poorer nations, infants and children are already dying at a frightening rate because they lack access to basic nutrition and medical care. Inequality and poverty are at the heart of this situation, but high birth rates make it worse. In such countries, nearly one out of five children dies before

younger workers supporting the benefits of a larger number of retirees. In 1965, when the baby boom ended, there were 4 workers for every Social Security beneficiary. By 2010, when the oldest boomers were beginning to retire, the ratio was 2.9 to 1, and it is projected to drop to 2.1 to 1 by 2050 (Social Security Board of Trustees 2013). With fewer workers paying into Social Security, the system has had to adjust age five, usually because of poverty-related conditions such as malnutrition and illnesses that could have been easily prevented (World Health Organization 2005b).

Demographic Transition

The threat of overpopulation should lessen as wealthier nations achieve negative growth and as more resources are put into stemming population growth in poorer countries. In fact, the rate of overall population growth globally has eased in recent years. This development is consistent with **demographic transition theory,** which suggests that *a society's population patterns are decisively influenced by its level of affluence and its adoption of new technology.* The theory originally focused on technological development but has evolved to reflect the fact that other factors associated with affluence—especially education and changing social norms— influence population patterns.

Although nations vary considerably and there are exceptions to this model, human societies have tended to move through four demographic stages. First, societies experienced high birth and death rates, a pattern yielding little overall change in population. In preindustrial societies throughout history, high death rates were the result of poor nutrition and hygiene, lack of knowledge about illness and disease, and the general difficulty of human survival. Because death rates were so high, people had no incentive to reduce birth rates. In fact, most cultures placed a high value on fertility, and families had large numbers of children as a source of needed labor in agricultural societies—and as insurance of survival.

Second, those societies that industrialized reduced their death rates at all age levels. Industrialization contributed to greater affluence, which in turn allowed for better nutrition and more sanitary living conditions. The scientific advances that led to industrialization also contributed to expanded knowledge about nutrition, sanitation, and disease. With the spread of such understanding and the adoption of healthier practices, infant mortality declined and adult illnesses became less deadly. But limited birth control options, along with cultural norms that discouraged contraception, kept birth rates high. Because the death rate declined while birth rates remained high, populations ballooned.

Third, as cultural norms changed and people developed more knowledge about and options for family planning—

and as societies amassed the resources needed to make contraception widely available—the birth rate gradually declined and the rate of population increase slowed. Fourth, societies achieved **zero population growth**—*a balance between birth rates and death rates, which maintains stable population numbers.*

About a third of the world's societies—the affluent nations—have moved through these stages and are in or approaching the fourth stage. They are growing at relatively modest rates or reducing their population in some cases. The remaining nations are mostly in the second stage and are contributing to the continuing increase in the global population.

Explaining the Demographic Divide

The social structure of a society influences birth rates. In agricultural societies, large families are highly valued since they provide labor for work on farms and in fields. Influenced by these structural conditions, agricultural societies have developed cultural norms that place great value—and confer high status—on large families.

As less developed nations industrialize, however, the cultural preference for large families begins to outlive its structural usefulness. Today, young people in such countries often work in factories, bringing needed income to the family from that source (as they did when Western nations first industrialized), but big families are not the economic asset they once were. In wealthier industrialized societies, in fact, having a large number of children is considered an expensive liability rather than an economic asset, and families feel pressure to reduce their reproduction rate. In this way, social structure and cultural norms interact to influence individual action.

The interaction of socioeconomic and cultural factors also influences growth rates. For example, the relative

SPOTLIGHT
on social theory

Demographic transition theory suggests that population patterns are affected by affluence and the adoption of new technology. What features of **functionalist theory** are reflected in this analysis?

TABLE 17.3	DEMOGRAPHIC TRANSITION MODEL OF TYPICAL SOCIETAL EVOLUTION		
	Birth Rates	Death Rates	Population
First phase	High	High	Steady
Second phase	High	Lower	Enormous growth
Third phase	Lower	Lower	Slowed growth
Fourth phase	Low	Low	Steady

Population Change

affluence of wealthy societies is associated with improved education, which in turn results in a more informed population and expanded access to effective birth control. In contrast, people in poorer societies are less likely to have access to reproductive health services and accurate information about family planning. Because more affluent societies also tend to have greater gender equality, women in such societies have more power to make their own decisions about reproduction. As women gain such rights, they tend to decide to have smaller families—or no children at all. Thus, increased affluence, higher levels of education, women's rights, and access to and cultural acceptance of birth control all contribute to lower birth rates. Securing equal rights for women is an example of the sorts of issues that spawn social movements, our next topic.

The Power of Social Movements

As we have seen, many social changes are unintentional and unanticipated. In this section, though, we examine efforts by people to promote change *deliberately* by participating in social movements.

Understanding Social Movements

On December 1, 1955, seamstress Rosa Parks was riding home on a bus in Montgomery, Alabama, when the driver told her to give up her seat for a white passenger and to move to the back in accordance with local segregation laws (Loeb 1999; Morris 1984). Tired from a long day at work, Parks refused—and was arrested. Her spontaneous act of individual defiance sparked the ensuing Montgomery bus boycott, a pivotal event in and catalyst for the U.S. civil rights movement.

At least, that is the usual story told about this famous incident. However, the real Rosa Parks and the actual bus boycott were more complicated, and they illustrate some common elements of social movement campaigns.

Parks's resistance did not happen without preparation. Parks was a civil rights activist long before her arrest. For over a decade, she had been active in a local chapter of the National Association for the Advancement of Colored People (NAACP), the leading civil rights group of the time, and had been mentored by E. D. Nixon, a labor union leader. A few months before her arrest, she had attended a 10-day training program at a labor and civil rights organizing school, where she had met like-minded activists and discusssed recent civil rights cases with them, including previous bus boycotts.

Shortly before Parks's arrest, the local NAACP had planned to challenge bus segregation in Montgomery using the case of Claudette Colvin, who had also been arrested for refusing to move to the back of the bus. Colvin's name is now largely lost to history; since she was unmarried and pregnant, the NAACP decided she would not be the right person to represent the message of their campaign. Rosa Parks, on the other hand, was perfect. Hardworking, dedicated, and churchgoing, she became the campaign's symbol—and an icon in the civil rights movement.

Parks could not have achieved change on her own. The power of the movement came from collective action by thousands of people. The local Women's Political Council took the lead in printing and distributing flyers encouraging a boycott. The newly formed Montgomery Improvement Association pooled money, automobiles, and all the resources necessary to sustain a year-long bus boycott. A young, relatively unknown preacher who was new in town and had not made any enemies was chosen to lead this group: Martin Luther King Jr. The NAACP took on the legal challenge and eventually won the court case that settled the dispute and ended segregation on Montgomery's buses.

The real story of the Montgomery bus boycott features many aspects of social movement activism that are familiar to sociologists (Bobo et al. 2010; Della Porta and Diani 2006; Jasper 1997; McAdam, McCarthy, and Zald 1996; Tarrow 2011; Tilly 2004a). Successful movements need to develop a clear message; have effective organizations that can recruit members, mobilize resources, nurture new leaders, and draw upon experienced activists; and be persistent, because most of their efforts fail until the right opportunities come along. Despite difficult odds, successful movements by ordinary citizens can help make history—a topic explored in the Through a Sociological Lens box.

In 1956, Montgomery bus boycott organizers used local churches for mass meetings such as this one to communicate with, organize, and encourage solidarity among thousands of African Americans. The meetings, an integral part of the civil rights movement, drew upon many aspects of black church culture, including religious songs, Bible readings, and speeches from pastors.

"Making Life" and "Making History"

The understanding that people create society is a basic principle of sociology. The idea that ordinary citizens should have both the right and the power to change society is the essence of democracy. An interesting thread connects sociology, democracy, and social change—a thread examined by sociologist Richard Flacks.

Flacks, a leader in the student and antiwar movements of the 1960s, became a sociologist and later wrote *Making History*, a now-classic book about social change. In the tradition of C. Wright Mills's analysis of the relationship between biography and history, Flacks highlights the difference between what he calls "making life" and "making history."

Most of us, most of the time, spend our time and energy "making life." We do household chores, shop, go to school or work, study, care for our families, enjoy leisure, pursue our hobbies—all the things we need to do to survive and to maintain and develop ourselves and our dependents.

"Making history" is different in that it involves the survival, maintenance, and development of *society*, not just individuals. More specifically, Flacks (1988) says, "Making history is the activity that influences the conditions and terms of everyday life of a collectivity" (p. 3). In other words, making history influences the rules that govern everyday life for groups of people. If Congress votes to provide publicly funded day care, if corporate executives close down a factory in your hometown, if students come together to successfully resist a tuition increase, each of these acts changes the terms and conditions under which people live—and each is thus making history.

History making is usually associated with those who have considerable power. In fact, Flacks argues that we can think of power as "the capacity to make history" (p. 5). People in powerful positions—such as political leaders and major corporate executives—make history as a routine part of their daily work lives. For them, "making life" and "making history" overlap substantially. The more that power is concentrated in the hands of such elites, the more that ordinary people feel like the objects of historical forces acting upon them, and the more *powerless* they feel to make history.

In fact, for most of us, history making is usually beyond our reach; we focus instead on making life. Democracy,

though, is the idea that power should *not* be highly centralized in the hands of elites. Instead, democratic ideals suggest that ordinary citizens should have the power to choose priorities and create the rules for society. A healthy democratic system is routinely responsive to people's wishes, generally carrying out the will of the people through elections, referenda, and other mechanisms. This democratic ideal is in fact a radical notion that challenges the concentrated power of elites wherever it exists—in local communities, universities, workplaces, corporate boardrooms, or the halls of political power.

Much of U.S. history has been driven by the tension between the ideal of democracy and a reality that has fallen far short. Democratic rhetoric, however, was and is inspirational, and it has motivated generations of social movement activists who have worked to change U.S. society so that it more closely resembles the democratic ideal.

But participation in social movements can be stressful, because social movement activists often carry out the task of "making history" at the expense of "making life." Participation in a social movement can require major commitments of time and energy, and sometimes dedicated activists neglect friends, family, jobs, and other relationships. Since this level of commitment is difficult to sustain in the long term, social movement activism often occurs in bursts. For a relatively short period of time, people will give priority to "making history," and an upturn of activism will result. But because the mundane responsibilities of "making life" eventually must be attended to, the higher level of commitment that activism requires becomes unsustainable over the long haul for many people. Nonetheless, these bursts of heightened social movement activity—lasting from days to a few years—can leave a permanent mark on social life. They "make history."

think about it

1. *How do "making life" and "making history" differ in sociological terms?*

2. *In what specific ways can you, as an ordinary citizen, get involved in "making history"?*

Defining Social Movements

Why don't corporate executives ever march in the streets holding picket signs? The answer is simple: they don't need to. Powerful executives have more conventional avenues by which to pursue their goals, such as hiring lobbyists, making campaign contributions, and networking with political officials. In the wake of the 2007–2009 financial crisis, for example, U.S. corporations received hundreds of billions of

dollars in taxpayer-funded assistance without needing to take to the streets to ask for it.

Most people do not command such significant resources. The halls of power are not routinely open to them, so when normal political channels fail, they must find other ways to be heard. One such mechanism is social movements.

Social movements are *organized, ongoing collective efforts by relatively powerless people engaging in extrainstitutional action to promote or resist change.* That formal definition highlights several characteristics that distinguish social movements from other forms of social and political action. For example, movements are organized and ongoing; they are not just spontaneous one-time actions (as might be the case, say, with a riot). Movements are collective; they are not just courageous acts by individuals or the cumulative effect of individual actions (as with a social trend).

The single biggest distinction between social movements and other kinds of politics is that social movement activists use *extrainstitutional* tactics—measures that are outside the regular, routine political processes of voting, lobbying, or making campaign contributions, for example. Extrainstitutional tactics include everything from boycotts and nonviolent street demonstrations to armed insurrection. The participants use such tactics because they typically lack access to routine channels of power and thus are relatively powerless compared to their opponents. At the turn of the twentieth century, for example, women agitating for the right to vote were shut out of mainstream politics and relied on unconventional tactics to advance their cause.

Movements can mobilize either to promote or to resist change. In fact, often a social movement will face off against a countermovement, as in the long-standing clash between the "pro-life" and "pro-choice" movements over abortion. The type, level, and degree of change that movements promote or resist all vary:

- The *type of change* being advocated or resisted can range from particular government policies (such as laws restricting gun ownership), to institutional practices (outsourcing of jobs), to cultural norms or behaviors (reducing drunk driving).

- The *level of change* at issue can vary from local concerns (teacher layoffs), to national issues (immigration reform), to global dynamics (war).

- The *degree of change* being advocated can involve everything from mild reform addressing a specific problem within the existing social system (banning smoking in public buildings) to complete social and political transformation (as sometimes occurs in civil wars).

In many cases, participants in social movements engage in conventional political action, such as voting and lobbying, in addition to their other activities on the movement's behalf. The line between social movement activism and conventional political participation can therefore be blurry. As well, many social movements have advocates within the political system. For example, Tea Party activists, in addition to holding demonstrations and other events, work with supporters in the Republican Party's conservative wing. These two elements are often mutually beneficial, as social movement agitation pressures elected officials and makes it possible for allies within the system to move an agenda forward. Support from insiders gives legitimacy to activists' efforts and helps ensure that their cause gets serious consideration (Meyer 2006).

Another major distinguishing feature of social movements is that they involve advocacy for social change—such as the passage of specific legislation or the enactment of institutional policies—rather than the provision of charity or social services (Table 17.4). For example, a homeless shelter might provide vital services that meet the immediate needs of those without a home. However, such short-term relief does not change the underlying conditions that created homelessness in the first place, such as the scarcity of low-income housing and the lack of adequate jobs that pay a living wage. Although social services are essential, making long-term improvements requires tackling the *underlying cause* of a given social problem, not just treating the symptoms.

This distinction is important because it helps explain the often different dynamics involved in social movements as opposed to social services or charities. Because social movements seek to change structural, institutional, or cultural conditions, they inevitably come into conflict with those resisting this change. This struggle is ultimately about power.

Power, Conflict, and Social Movements

Social movements typically face the dilemma that those who support (or resist) change through a social movement have

TABLE 17.4 SOCIAL SERVICE AND SOCIAL CHANGE

	Social Services/Charitable Efforts	Social Change
Primary goal is to . . .	Meet immediate needs	Change structural conditions, underlying causes of a problem, or the balance of power
Focus of activities is on . . .	Providing a direct service (often aimed at individuals)	Structural, institutional, or cultural change
Parties involved include . . .	A service provider (for example, social worker, expert, volunteer) Client (recipient of goods and/or services)	Change advocates and supporters "Target" group or institution (suggests conflict is likely)

little power, whereas those who have power and benefit from the current social structure generally resist movement efforts. As a result, when ordinary people advance their cause through social movements, they come into conflict with people in power. The conflict might be minimal and brief, or it might be violent and long-lasting. However, if conflict does not occur—if everyone already agrees on the issue at hand—then there is no social change.

A letter written in 1849 by Frederick Douglass (2003), the former slave and abolitionist leader, famously expresses this point. In his poetic prose, Douglass presents a sociological analysis of the role of power in enforcing order, and of ordinary people's potential to challenge that power:

> If there is no struggle there is no progress. Those who profess to favor freedom, and yet depreciate agitation, are men who want crops without plowing up the ground. They want rain without thunder and lightning. . . . Power concedes nothing without a demand. It never did and it never will. Find out just what people will submit to, and you have found the exact amount of injustice and wrong which will be imposed upon them; and these will continue until they are resisted with either words or blows, or with both. (p. 42)

As was the case with Douglass's fight against slavery, social movement organizers face daunting odds. By their nature, these movements are efforts by underdogs with little obvious power to challenge entrenched and powerful interests. Given this situation, it is not surprising that the vast majority of these efforts fail to achieve their stated aims. Yet sometimes social movements succeed and spark significant social change, often overcoming enormous odds. How is this possible?

As we saw in Chapter 5, power is the ability to bring about an intended outcome, even when it is opposed by others. Power is thus a social dynamic rather than a "thing" to be possessed. For a person or group to be given power over others, people must be convinced, rewarded, or threatened into obeying. But obedience is not inevitable; it is voluntary and can be withdrawn. So ordinary people have more power then they realize, because the orderly functioning of society requires their tacit cooperation to continue. This threat that noncompliance will disrupt a part of society is a major element of social movements' power. By **organizing**—*coordinating and directing the efforts of many individuals to work for a cause*—activists pool the power of individuals into a substantial collective force for change.

Those in positions of power who are being targeted by a specific social movement can resist in various ways. First, they can often prevail simply by relying on cultural norms and routines. For example, they might take advantage of the fact that most people have been socialized to "follow the rules" and "not rock the boat" and know that individuals generally do not want to take risks, be seen as deviant, or look foolish. To encourage compliant behavior, people in power often give activists labels with a negative social

Election Day!

FAST-FORWARD

Change and Social Movements

The women's suffrage movement of the late nineteenth and early twentieth centuries succeeded in 1920 with the ratification of the Nineteenth Amendment to the Constitution, which prohibited states from restricting women's right to vote. In its day, however, the suffrage movement was ridiculed by critics, who, as in the cartoon here, often stigmatized women as unnaturally neglectful of their proper role as homemakers for wanting to participate in politics. Today, women's right to vote is often taken for granted and women are central to the electoral process. Here, college students participating in the NAACP's "Vote Hard" campaign encourage people to vote in Alabama.

stigma, such as "outside agitators," "extremists," "romantic idealists," "troublemakers," "politically correct," "radicals," and "terrorists." Similarly, those in power can encourage

thinking about power

Name two or three present-day social movements that are seeking change.
What are the activists' goals? What gives these movements their **power**?
How successful do you think they have been?

common attitudes of cynicism, fatalism, or apathy, all of which discourage activism and are thus useful in preventing change. Activists often counter this tactic by linking their efforts to mainstream cultural values (democracy, freedom, justice, God) or by affirming a positive counterculture that promotes solidarity. Sometimes they even appropriate a "deviant" label once used against them, as in the case of the gay rights chant, "We're queer, we're here; get used to it."

Second, those in power can use material or political sanctions either to reward or punish individual activists. They can try to co-opt opponents—lure the activists to their side—by using rewards such as job offers or promotions, grants, and concessions on smaller issues. Or they can threaten to punish activists by, for example, firing them, expelling them from school, or fining them. Often merely the *threat* of such action is enough to secure compliance. In response, activists typically stress the importance of solidarity for success, try to protect individuals, and discourage the co-opting of members.

Third, as a last resort, those in power can use physical control, including arrests, beatings, and even the execution of individuals who participate in social movements. In opposing a movement's efforts, those in power must often be careful not to overreact and respond in an overly aggressive manner that might generate additional support for the movement. For their part, activists must reduce fears of participating in the movement—for example, by using Internet videos to publicize successful demonstrations by activists.

Movement Actors

Community organizers—activists who organize people to address local problems—have long noted that there are two basic sources of power: money and people. Powerful elites have few people among their ranks, but they do have lots of money and other resources with which to carry out their agendas. Social movements, on the other hand, may not have piles of money, but they have the potential to organize many people into a powerful force—and in this way to change the balance of power. To succeed, they need to develop viable organizations to coordinate their members' action.

Movements are usually made up of a number of different social movement organizations. For example, two of the most prominent social movement organizations within the human rights movement are Amnesty International and Human Rights Watch. The organizations that compose a movement usually have different goals, audiences, and tactics. But all such organizations must operate on a field that includes three groups of actors: supporters, opponents, and bystanders.

Supporters assist a movement and can be either *activists*, the core staff and volunteers who are directly involved in planning and carrying out the organization's goals, or *adherents*, those who agree with and occasionally assist the movement's efforts but with less intensity than the core activist supporters. A movement's *opponents* include the *target group*, the individuals and organizations that are being pressured, as well as any *countermovements*, social movements that have organized to oppose the movement's efforts. Finally, in any

given conflict, the vast majority of people are uninvolved *bystanders*, individuals with little or no stake in the outcome and who often know little or nothing about the issues. Nevertheless, bystanders play a potentially pivotal role, because the resolution of any conflict depends on whether they get involved, and, if they do, which side they support. It is especially important for social movements to enlist the support of bystanders since movements typically have less power in the conflict; with little money, they can win only by expanding their numbers. Those in power usually want to contain the conflict, not to expand it to include bystanders.

Movement Success: Message, Resources, and Opportunity

Sociologists highlight three important ingredients for social movement success: an effective message, adequate resources, and opportunity in the form of a favorable political environment.

FRAMING: ARTICULATING THE MESSAGE AND FORGING A COLLECTIVE IDENTITY

Are proposed cuts to the education budget a sensible step toward fiscal responsibility or an assault on students' future? In answering such a question, social movement activists engage in **framing**, *interpreting and assigning meaning to events and conditions in order to shape a movement's message and the collective identity that develops among members.* In framing issues and events, social movement activists try to mobilize support for their cause by communicating with the public (Johnston and Noakes 2005; Snow and Benford 1988).

A movement must communicate by framing the issue it is addressing in a way that is consistent with its goals (Snow et al. 1986). In particular, to be successful, a movement must

- Persuade people to see the condition they are concerned about as an injustice
- Advance a viable alternative
- Convince people that they are responsible for and capable of effecting change

Social movements attempt to spread these messages to the general public through one-on-one organizing, public events, their websites, and social media, as well as by mainstream media coverage.

Further, movements encourage the development of a collective identity through an organizational culture that involves shared values, music, logos, T-shirts, literature, and knowledge of movement history. A strong collective identity can be a crucial means of promoting solidarity and the willingness to sacrifice on behalf of a cause, both of which are essential if a movement is to be effective.

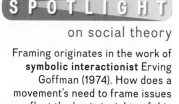

SPOTLIGHT

on social theory

Framing originates in the work of **symbolic interactionist** Erving Goffman (1974). How does a movement's need to frame issues reflect the basic insights of this theoretical perspective?

RESOURCE MOBILIZATION **Resource mobilization** is *the process by which social movements generate the assets necessary to build and sustain the movement.* This process, which is vital to the movement's success, includes raising money, recruiting members, developing tactics and strategies, finding people with necessary skills, and training leaders (McCarthy and Zald 1977).

The likelihood of a person's being successfully mobilized by a social movement is influenced by his or her structural location. Individuals are more likely to join a social movement effort if they

- Have prior contact with a movement activist, which provides a personal connection and a social incentive for participation

- Belong to other—even nonmovement—organizations, because such affiliations make them more likely to learn about movement issues and events and come into contact with activists

- Have few personal constraints, such as childrearing responsibilities, marriage, and full-time employment (parents acting specifically to protect the future of their children are an exception)

Middle-class college students typically have relatively high rates of participation in social movements. Why? Many often have few personal constraints, are involved in other organizations and activities, and live on campus—a common setting for social movement organization and mobilization.

POLITICAL OPPORTUNITY The environment in which a social movement operates can be critical to the success—or failure—of a movement (Jasper and Goodwin 2011; Tilly 2004a). **Political opportunities** are *the factors outside a social movement that can influence whether it emerges and is successful.*

Sometimes a dramatic event can create political opportunities. For example, the 2011 earthquake and tsunami that led to the Fukushima Daiichi nuclear crisis in Japan created a political opportunity for antinuclear power activists in Germany who had long warned of the dangers of nuclear power. Germany later adopted a plan to phase out its nuclear power plants by 2022.

External actors can also affect a movement's success or failure. A government, for example, can repress a movement, ignore it, or accommodate some of its demands, each of which will affect the movement differently. If a government is divided internally, movement activists are more likely to find political opportunities in aligning with allies within the halls of power.

A flare-wielding demonstrator in a Che Guevara T-shirt poses for news photographers during a demonstration for the Guy Fawkes World Day in Rio de Janeiro, Brazil, in 2013. What tactics do demonstrators use to attract media attention? How might such tactics help or harm the demonstrators' cause?

The mainstream media are also external players with the potential to exercise considerable influence over the outcome of a movement's efforts. Media coverage, along with social media messages, can help mobilize support and protect activists from violent government repression.

Finally, other social movement organizations can have an impact on the results of a movement's efforts. Countermovements can effectively undermine support for a movement. On the other hand, other organizations within a movement can often be allies in a broader struggle.

Movement Stages

Although each social movement is unique, successful movements tend to follow a cyclical pattern of birth, growth, success, and decline (Tarrow 2011; Taylor 1989). Movements often begin at the margins of society when a few activists—who are often influenced by earlier movement efforts—start raising an issue. These efforts attract the attention of a few others who are sympathetic to the cause. Over time, these contacts among individuals become routine, and the early activists create a social movement organization to coordinate and fund a movement campaign (Figure 17.5).

Most movements end at this stage, with an ineffectual organization that eventually disbands. But in successful cases, social movement organizations grow, drawing more supporters,

FIGURE 17.5 | A SUCCESSFUL MOVEMENT CYCLE.

A few people are concerned → Activists form a social movement organization → Movement grows to include many supporters → Change occurs—usually partial → Movement declines → A few activists remain committed to the cause

thinking sociologically about
Social Change

culture

- Changes in culture have contributed to the rise of globalization, and in turn globalization has changed the development and distribution of culture.
- The changing characteristics of a population influence changes in the culture.
- Culture plays an important role in the formation and character of social movements as they create a collective identity and promote their message of change.

structure

- Part of the change produced by globalization involves changes in the structure of organizations and communication.
- Changing populations contribute to changes in social structure.
- Social movement efforts often face the difficult task of changing social structures to achieve their goals.

power

- Globalization has shifted the amount of power held by various players, including national governments and transnational corporations.
- As populations change in a society, some communities become more powerful, while others become less so.
- Social movements involve struggles over power.

REVIEW, REFLECT, AND APPLY

Looking Back

1. Social change involves modification of social structure or cultural patterns. Change is a continuous process, is often unintended, occurs at different levels, and often produces conflict.

2. Sociological theories, such as Marx's theory emphasizing material factors and Weber's case for the influence of ideas, highlight differing causes of social change. However, change must be understood in the specific context within which it occurs, taking into account multiple sources.

3. *Globalization* is an umbrella term referring to the interaction or integration among various aspects of social life, including economies, cultures, political systems, and populations. This integration helps overcome the barriers of physical space and time.

4. Globalization is rooted in colonialism and is still characterized by deep global inequalities and controversies over the distribution of power, including concern about the homogenization of culture and about neoliberal policies that favor wealthy nations.

5. The world's population is growing rapidly, often due to improvements in health and life expectancy, and most of the growth is occurring in poorer nations. Meanwhile, many wealthier nations are experiencing stable or declining populations, producing a demographic divide. Explanations for this divide include socioeconomic and cultural factors.

6. Demographic trends include an increase in the share of the world's population in developing nations and in immigration to wealthier nations, as well as an overall aging population.

7. Social movements are efforts by relatively powerless people engaging in extrainstitutional action to promote or resist change. Unlike social services, social movement activism targets the causes of social problems, not just the symptoms, and involves conflict between opposing parties.

8. Successful social movements must frame their efforts effectively, mobilize resources, and navigate the political environment. An important goal is often to convince bystanders to support the movement.

9. Movements tend to operate in cycles, and even successful movements decline eventually. Social movements tend to start at the margins of society. When successful, their ideas become part of mainstream social life.

Critical Thinking: Questions and Activities

1. What do you think is more important as a cause of most social change: economic factors or ideas? Why?

2. What is globalization? Give examples of ways in which globalization has affected your life. Overall, do you think globalization has had a positive or negative impact on your life? Explain.

3. Do the earth's rapidly growing population and the demographic divide concern you? Why or why not? What challenge do they pose in the coming years? What, if anything, do you think should be done to address the issue?

4. Visit the website of a social movement organization of your choice. What cultural values and symbols is the movement invoking in communicating with readers?

Key Terms

contextual analyses (p. 478) analyses that take into account the particular historical and social context within which change is occurring and do not assume that a single factor is the most important in all situations.

crude birth rate (p. 488) the number of live births per 1,000 people in a population.

crude death rate (p. 488) the number of deaths per 1,000 people in a population.

demographic divide (p. 487) the inequality in population and health conditions between rich and poor countries.

demographic transition theory (p. 491) the view that a society's population patterns are influenced decisively by its level of affluence and its adoption of new technology.

demography (p. 485) the study of human population trends.

framing (p. 496) interpreting and assigning meaning to events and conditions in order to shape a movement's message and the collective identity that develops among members.

globalization (p. 478) the interaction or integration among various aspects of social life, including economies, cultures, political systems, and populations.

growth rate (p. 487) the indicator that measures how quickly a country's population is increasing.

historical materialism (p. 477) the part of Marx's work suggesting that the economic base of a society is the primary force driving change in other aspects of social life.

infant mortality rate (p. 487) the number of infants less than a year old who die per 1,000 live births.

life expectancy (p. 487) the median number of years a person is likely to live given the current conditions.

migration (p. 489) the movement of people from one place to another.

neoliberalism (p. 484) a set of economic policies that aim to allow private markets to operate with little or no government oversight or intervention.

neo-Malthusian perspective (p. 491) the view, derived from Malthus's thought, warning that overpopulation is threatening the planet.

organizing (p. 495) coordinating and directing the efforts of many individuals to work for a cause.

political opportunities (p. 497) factors outside a social movement that can influence whether it emerges and is successful.

population pyramid (p. 487) a bar chart showing the distribution of a population by age and sex.

resource mobilization (p. 497) the process by which social movements generate the assets necessary to build and sustain a movement.

social change (p. 475) the modification of structural or cultural patterns over time.

social movements (p. 493) organized, ongoing collective efforts by relatively powerless people engaging in extra-institutional action to promote or resist change.

social trend (p. 475) the direction a society takes when many individuals act independently but similarly.

unintended consequences (p. 476) results that are unplanned and unforeseen.

zero population growth (p. 491) a balance between birth rates and death rates, which maintains stable population numbers.

Glossary

A

absolute poverty (p. 237) a scarcity of resources so severe that it is life-threatening.

achieved status (pp. 90, 168) a position in a social system that a person attains voluntarily, to a considerable degree, as the result of his or her own efforts.

action (p. 87) the ability to behave independent of social constraints.

active audiences (p. 393) audiences that make choices about how they use the media and actively interpret media content.

affective action (p. 99) behavior guided by emotions and feelings.

affirmative action (p. 280) policies and programs that aim to avoid discrimination and redress past discrimination through the active recruitment of qualified minorities for jobs, promotions, and educational opportunities.

agenda-setting theory (p. 393) a theory that holds that media may not be able to tell people what to think, but they can significantly influence what people think about.

agents of social control (p. 208) the authorities and social institutions that enforce norms and rules, attempt to prevent rule violations, and identify and punish rule violators.

agents of socialization (p. 137) people and groups who teach us about our culture.

alienation (p. 402) the separation and isolation of workers as a result of the structure of capitalist society.

amalgamation (p. 263) the process by which a majority and a minority group blend or mix to form a new group.

anomie (p. 14) social normlessness, without moral guidance or standards.

anticipatory socialization (p. 144) the process by which individuals practice for a future social role by adopting the norms or behaviors associated with a position they have not yet achieved.

applied research (p. 33) the primary goal of this type of research is to directly address some social problem or need.

ascribed status (pp. 90, 168) a position in a social system, assigned to a person from birth, regardless of his or her wishes.

asexual (p. 311) people who experience no sexual attraction for anyone.

assimilation (p. 263) the process by which members of a minority group come to adopt the culture of the majority group.

authoritarian government (p. 445) a government that typically features self-appointed leaders who exert great control over the lives of citizens, which includes severely limiting their civil liberties.

B

basic research (p. 33) the primary goal of this type of research is to describe some aspect of society and advance our understanding of it.

behavioral targeting (p. 408) advertising sent to online users based on their earlier Internet activities.

behaviors (p. 68) the actions associated with a group that help reproduce a distinct way of life.

beliefs (p. 63) the specific convictions or opinions that a people generally accept as being true.

bilingual education (p. 367) instruction in both a student's first language and English.

biological determinism (p. 149) a theory that contends that biology, specifically our genetic makeup, almost completely shapes human behavior.

bisexual (p. 311) people who are attracted to others of both sexes.

breaching experiments (p. 91) social situations that intentionally break social rules, violating basic norms and patterns of behavior.

built environment (p. 415) the physical surroundings that humans create, including the buildings, roads, dams, homes, and consumer products we use every day.

bureaucracy (p. 178) a hierarchical administrative system with formal rules and procedures used to manage organizations.

C

capital (p. 225) money to invest in factories, real estate, and other businesses.

capital punishment (p. 216) the death penalty.

capitalism (p. 463) an economic system that emphasizes private ownership of the means of production, which are operated for profit.

capitalist class (or bourgeoisie) (p. 225) those who control major capital and own the means of production.

caste system (p. 127) stratification based on various ascribed characteristics determined at birth.

charismatic authority (p. 120) power whose legitimacy is derived from the extraordinary personal characteristics of an individual leader, which inspire loyalty and devotion.

charter schools (p. 367) public schools run by an organization that is independent from local school districts.

church (p. 337) formal religious organization with broad mainstream acceptance.

civil religion (p. 344) a set of common beliefs and ritual practices that bind people in a predominantly secular society.

class (pp. 123, 225) a group of people who share a roughly similar economic position and lifestyle.

class domination theory (p. 452) a theory that suggests that political power is concentrated in the hands of the rich, who own or control a large share of the nation's economic resources.

class mobility (p. 232) the ability to move from one social class to another.

class system (p. 128) stratification determined by economic position, which results from a combination of individual achievement and family of birth.

classism (p. 237) prejudice or discrimination based on social class.

coerce (p. 114) to force people's compliance by threatening, intimidating, pressuring, or harming them.

cohabitation (p. 325) a social relationship that can create family ties and typically involves sexual intimacy, in which people live together as unmarried partners.

collective bargaining (p. 375) negotiations between union representatives and an employer on questions of pay, benefits, and working conditions.

collective conscience (pp. 14, 193) the shared norms, beliefs, and values in a community.

colonialism (p. 248) the use of military, political, and economic power by one society to dominate the people of another society, usually for economic benefit.

color-blind racism (p. 283) a form of bias in which the promotion of race neutrality helps maintain existing racial and ethnic inequality.

commodification (p. 407) the process of transforming all things into a product to be bought and sold.

commodity fetishism (p. 402) consumers' failure to recognize the labor that created the value in the commodities they use.

community (p. 415) a set of social relationships, typically arising from living in a particular place, that give people a sense of identity and belonging.

community studies (p. 421) a field that typically looks at groups of people who share some common tie and engage in social interaction within a particular geographic area.

comparable worth (p. 372) a commitment to setting salaries for different job titles based on their value to an employer, regardless of the typical gender of those working in such jobs.

conflict theories (p. 20) social theories that focus on issues of contention, power, and inequality, highlighting the competition for scarce resources.

conspicuous consumption (p. 236) lavish spending, done to compete for status with others.

consumerism (p. 402) an emphasis on shopping and the possession of material goods as the route to personal happiness.

consumption (p. 400) the process of choosing, purchasing, and using goods.

content analysis (p. 45) a variety of techniques that enable researchers to systematically summarize and analyze the content of various forms of communication—written, spoken, or pictorial.

contextual analyses (p. 478) analyses that take into account the particular historical and social context within which change is occurring and do not assume that a single factor is the most important in all situations.

control theory (p. 208) a theory that suggests that our behavior is regulated by the strength of our connection to major social institutions, including family, school, and religion.

convention (p. 93) a practice or technique that is widely used in a particular social setting.

convergence (p. 394) the merging of different media forms.

convergence theory (p. 468) a theory that suggests capitalist and socialist economies are becoming increasingly similar.

conversation analysis (p. 92) a method of analyzing the patterns in face-to-face conversation that produce the smooth, back-and-forth turn-taking of such exchanges.

corporation (p. 462) a business that is treated legally as an entity separate from its owners.

correlation (p. 36) a relationship in which change in one variable is connected to change in another variable.

counterculture (p. 73) a subculture that champions values and lifestyles distinctly opposed to those of the dominant culture.

credentialing (p. 364) the process whereby those with advanced educational degrees and formal certificates monopolize access to the most rewarding jobs.

crime (p. 210) deviant behavior that violates a law.

crime rates (p. 211) statistics that measure the incidence of crime in relation to population size.

critical social science (p. 50) research carried out explicitly to create knowledge that can be used to bring about social change.

crude birth rate (p. 488) the number of live births per 1,000 people in a population.

crude death rate (p. 488) the number of deaths per 1,000 people in a population.

cult (p. 337) small religious communities whose beliefs and practices are at odds with the dominant culture.

cultivation theory (p. 393) a theory that argues that, by repeated and long-term exposure to the media's portrayal of the world (especially on television), people come to accept many of these depictions as reality.

cultural capital (pp. 239, 364) forms of knowledge, taste, preferences, and styles that high-status groups use to signal their status and to exclude others from their social circles.

cultural imperialism (p. 398) the tendency of media corporations from wealthier nations—especially the United States—to export so many of their media products that they come to dominate the local cultures of other, especially poorer, nations.

cultural lag (p. 65) the ways that new technological developments often outpace the norms that govern our collective experiences with these new technologies.

cultural object (p. 70) a physical item that is created by and associated with people who share a culture.

cultural relativism (p. 77) the practice of understanding a culture by its own standards.

culture (pp. 22, 59) the collection of values, beliefs, knowledge, norms, language, behaviors, and material objects shared by a people and socially transmitted from generation to generation.

culture shock (p. 64) the experience of being disoriented because of a lack of knowledge about an unfamiliar social situation.

culture war (p. 62) an intense disagreement about core values and moral positions.

D

decriminalization (p. 210) the process of making an illegal action legal.

deindustrialization (p. 250) the process by which investment in the nation's manufacturing capacity decreased.

democracy (p. 446) a political system in which the right to vote is widespread and government leaders are selected through multiparty elections.

demographic divide (p. 487) the inequality in population and health conditions between rich and poor countries.

demographic transition theory (p. 491) the view that a society's population patterns are influenced decisively by its level of affluence and its adoption of new technology.

demography (p. 485) the study of human population trends.

dependency theory (p. 248) a theory that attributes global inequality to the exploitation of weaker, poor nations by wealthy, more powerful ones.

dependent variable (p. 36) the entity that changes in response to the independent variable.

deviance (p. 193) behavior that does not conform to basic cultural norms and expectations.

deviant subculture (p. 200) a group in which membership is based on a shared commitment to specific nonconformist beliefs or behaviors.

dialect (p. 68) a variant of a language with its own distinctive accent, vocabulary, and in some cases grammatical characteristics.

differential association theory (p. 199) according to this theory, deviance is learned through interaction with other people involved in deviant behavior.

digital divide (p. 396) the gap between those who have the knowledge and resources needed to use digital information technology, especially computers and the Internet, and those who do not.

discrimination (pp. 124, 262) unequal treatment that gives advantages to one group of people over another without justifiable cause.

division of labor (p. 13) the way people specialize in different tasks, each requiring specific skills.

doing gender (p. 297) creating gender through interactions in particular social settings.

domestic violence (or intimate partner violence) (p. 307) a pattern of abusive behavior in any relationship that is used by one partner to gain or maintain power and control over another intimate partner.

dominant culture (p. 71) a culture that permeates a society and that represents the ideas and practices of those in positions of power.

dominant ideology (p. 70) a widely held and regularly reinforced set of assumptions that generally support the current social system and serve the interests of authorities.

dramaturgy (p. 170) an approach to the study of social interaction that uses the metaphor of social life as a theater.

dual product markets (p. 391) the situation that occurs when a company sells two completely different types of "products" to two completely different sets of buyers.

dysfunctional (p. 20) inhibiting or disrupting the working of a system as a whole.

E

economic security (p. 469) the condition of having a stable means of financial support adequate to maintain a given standard of living.

economy (p. 461) a social institution that includes a society's production, distribution, and consumption of goods and services.

education (p. 353) the social institution through which individuals acquire knowledge and skills and learn cultural norms and values.

emotional labor (p. 377) jobs that require employees to manage their feelings and to display specific feelings to their customers or clients.

empirical evidence (p. 36) data that can be observed or documented using the human senses.

empowerment (p. 111) an increase in the capacity of people to bring about an intended outcome.

endogamy (p. 325) legal restrictions or customs that limit marriage to people within the same social category.

environmental health (p. 437) the aspects of health, illness, and disease that result from environmental factors.

environmental justice (p. 432) the prevention of harmful practices that unfairly burden low-income people and racial minorities with disproportionate exposure to environmental hazards.

environmental security (p. 469) the safe management of natural resources to protect social stability.

environmental sociology (p. 429) the study of the interaction between social life, the built environment, and the natural environment.

epigenetics (p. 150) the study of changes in gene expression (some of which can be passed on to children) produced without changing the underlying genetic code.

equal opportunity (p. 238) the idea that all people should have the same chance to achieve success.

ethic of reciprocity (p. 338) the "golden rule" that encourages people to treat others as they would like to be treated.

ethnicity (p. 257) shared cultural heritage often deriving from a common ancestry and homeland.

ethnocentrism (p. 77) the practice of judging another culture by the standards of one's own.

ethnomethodology (p. 91) an approach that examines the methods people use to make sense of their daily activities, emphasizing the ways in which we collectively create social structure in our everyday activities.

exogamy (p. 325) marriage between people from different social categories.

experiment (p. 45) a data-gathering technique in which the researcher manipulates an independent variable under controlled conditions to determine if change in an independent variable produces change in a dependent variable, thereby establishing a cause-and-effect relationship.

extended family (p. 325) nuclear family plus other relatives who commonly live together.

F

faith (p. 336) belief grounded in personal conviction or divine revelation rather than scientific evidence.

family (p. 323) two or more people, related either by birth or through social commitment, who share resources, care for any dependents, and often maintain a close emotional relationship.

feminism (p. 316) a philosophy that advocates social, political, and economic equality for women and men.

feminization of poverty (p. 237) a trend in which women made up an increasingly large share of the poor.

fertility rate (p. 332) the average number of births per female.

field research (p. 44) a data collection technique in which the researcher systematically observes some aspect of social life in its natural setting.

folkways (p. 66) group habits or customs that are common in a given culture.

framing (p. 496) interpreting and assigning meaning to events and conditions in order to shape a movement's message and the collective identity that develops among members.

functionalist theories (p. 19) see "structural-functionalist theories."

fundamentalism (p. 345) a religious movement that advocates strict adherence to traditional principles in all aspects of social life, usually based on literal interpretation of a religion's infallible sacred texts.

G

Gemeinschaft (p. 419) social organization in which most relationships are based on the long-term personal ties of collective kinship, common tradition, and shared values.

gender (p. 291) the socially constructed cultural expectations associated with women and men.

gender convergence (p. 317) a trend toward increasing similarity in how women and men live.

gender division of labor (p. 372) differences between men and women in access to jobs.

gender expression (p. 293) the way a person communicates gender identity to others, through behavior, clothing, hairstyle, and other means.

gender identity (p. 293) a person's identification as a woman, a man, or some combination of the two.

gender role (p. 296) a set of social expectations regarding behavior and attitudes based on a person's sex.

operationalize (p. 36) t...

organizational environ...
the organization but t...

organizational structur...
and informal, that shap...

organizations (p. 177) s...
formal structure and a...

organizing (p. 495) coo...
many individuals to w...

out-group (p. 181) a soci...
negatively, considering...

outsourcing (p. 378) mo...
advantage of cheaper l...

overconformity (p. 204)...
excessive degree.

ownership concentratic...
outlets come to be ow...
corporations.

P

patriarchy (pp. 129, 301)...
tions and cultural prac...

peer group (p. 140) a gr...
who share similar inter...

peer-review process (p....
research manuscripts b...
ensure their quality.

persuade (p. 113) to obta...
them of the correctnes...

planned obsolescence (...
facture of consumer go...
relatively short period...

pluralism (p. 262) a situa...
groups coexist on equa...

pluralist theory (p. 451)...
is fragmented among n...

plurality voting (p. 447)...
which the candidate wi...
contested.

political opportunities (...
ment that can influenc...

political socialization (...
and expectations about...
volvement in politics.

politics (p. 445) the strug...

polygamy (p. 325) a marr...
allowed multiple spous...

popular culture (p. 74) c...
commonly embraced w...

population pyramid (p....
of a population by age...

positive deviance (p. 204...
response.

positivism (p. 11) a belief...
on the scientific metho...

positivist social science...
the social world, like th...
that can be identified th...
control human affairs.

postmodernity (p. 26) a l...
twentieth century chara...
economies and the frag...
of knowing.

poverty line (U.S.) (p. 237)...
ing the cost of a minimal...

gender stratification (p. 301) the systematic and unequal distribution of power and resources in society between women and men.

generalize (p. 42) the ability to describe patterns of behavior of a larger population based on findings from a sample.

generalized other (p. 155) the values and orientations of one's overall community rather than those of specific individuals.

genocide (p. 263) the systematic killing of a group of people, based on their race, ethnicity, nationality, or religion.

gentrification (p. 424) the process of rehabilitating older housing stock and investing in neighborhood development in a way that typically attracts new higher-income residents and displaces current middle- and low-income residents.

Gesellschaft (p. 419) social organization in which most social relationships are impersonal, temporary, and based primarily on the pursuit of individual rational self-interest.

glass ceiling (p. 305) the often invisible barrier created by individual and institutional sexism that prevents qualified women from advancing to higher levels of leadership and management.

global inequality (p. 244) the differences in wealth and power among the countries of the world.

globalization (p. 478) the interaction or integration among various aspects of social life, including economies, cultures, political systems, and populations.

government (p. 445) the system by which authority is exercised over a specific territory.

groupthink (p. 183) a form of uncritical thinking in which people reinforce a consensus rather than ask serious questions or thoroughly analyze the issue at hand.

growth machines (p. 424) a label for cities that highlights how powerful businesses and politicians work together to promote urban development, often while ignoring the interests of ordinary citizens.

growth rate (p. 487) the indicator that measures how quickly a country's population is increasing.

H

Hawthorne effect (p. 39) the fact that human beings will react differently because they know they are in a study.

health disparities (p. 435) persistent patterns of inequality in health.

hegemony (p. 119) a condition that exists when those in power have successfully spread their ideas—and marginalized alternative viewpoints—so that their perspectives and interests are accepted widely as being universal and true.

heterosexism (p. 312) attitudes and behavior that indicate an assumption that everyone is heterosexual.

heterosexual (p. 311) people who are attracted to people of a different sex.

hidden curriculum (pp. 139, 356) the lessons students learn simply by attending school, in contrast to the lessons from the formal subject-specific curriculum.

high culture (p. 74) cultural forms associated with—and especially valued by—elites.

historical materialism (p. 477) the part of Marx's work suggesting that the economic base of a society is the primary force driving change in other aspects of social life.

homophily (p. 173) social contact occurs at a higher rate among those who are similar than among those who are different.

homophobia (p. 312) the disapproval and fear of LGBT people.

homosexual (p. 311) people who are attracted to people of the same sex.

horizontal integration (p. 387) what occurs when a media company owns different forms of media.

human ecology (p. 422) the study of the links between the physical environment—natural and built—and social life.

human security (p. 469) concern for the health and rights of individual human beings rather than the security of nations.

hyperreality (p. 399) the condition in which media depictions of the world replace the experience of the "real" world.

hypothesis (p. 36) a statement about the relationship between variables that is to be investigated.

I

ideal culture (p. 68) what the members of a culture report to be their values, beliefs, and norms.

ideology (p. 70) a system of meaning that helps define and explain the world and that makes value judgments about that world.

illegitimate power (p. 119) a form of authority that relies on force or coercion to generate obedience.

incest taboo (p. 310) a norm restricting sexual relations between certain relatives.

income (p. 228) money received from sources such as wages, interest on savings, and dividends from stocks and bonds.

independent variable (p. 36) the entity that is associated with and/or causes change in the value of the dependent variable.

individual mobility (p. 232) a change in a person's class position that occurs without any change in the larger class structure.

individualism (p. 238) a system of beliefs that highlights the importance of the single person over any social group.

industrialization (p. 10) the use of large-scale machinery for the mass manufacture of consumer goods.

inequality (p. 123) the unequal distribution of resources among groups of people.

infant mortality rate (p. 487) the number of infants less than a year old who die per 1,000 live births.

informed consent (p. 47) the principle that subjects in any study must know about the nature of the research project, any potential benefits or risks that they may face, and that they have the right to stop participating at any time, for any reason.

in-group (p. 181) a social group with which a person identifies and toward which he or she feels positively; members have a collective sense of "us."

institutional discrimination (p. 277) unequal treatment that results from the structural organization, policies, and procedures of social institutions such as the government, businesses, and schools.

intensive interview (p. 44) a data-gathering technique that uses open-ended questions during somewhat lengthy face-to-face sessions.

interpretive social science (p. 49) an approach that focuses on understanding the meaning that people ascribe to their social world.

intersectionality theory (p. 125) a perspective that highlights the connections and interactions between various forms of inequality, especially race, class, and gender.

intersexual people (p. 291) individuals born with ambiguous reproductive or sexual anatomy.

intersubjectivity (p. 163) a common understanding between people about knowledge, reality, or an experience.

iron law of oligarchy (p. 184) the eventual and inevitable consolidation of power at the top of bureaucratic organizations.

J

job satisfaction (p. 372) the degree to which a person is content in his or her job.

K

kinship (p. 323) the bonds of family relationships.

knowledge (cultural) (p. 64) the range of information, awareness, and understanding that helps us navigate our world.

References

Aboud, Frances E. 1988. *Children and preju-dice*. Cambridge, MA: Basil Blackwell.

Adams, Michele, and Scott Coltrane. 2005. Boys and men in families: The domestic production of gender, power, and privilege. In *Handbook of studies on men & masculini-ties*, ed. Michael S. Kimmel, Jeff Hearn, and R. W. Connell, pp. 230–48. Thousand Oaks, CA: Sage.

Addams, Jane. (1895) 2007. *Hull House maps and papers*. Chicago: University of Illinois Press.

Addams, Jane. (1902) 2002. *Democracy and Social Ethics*. Urbana and Chicago: Univer-sity of Illinois Press.

Adler, Nancy E., and Katherine Newman. 2002. Socioeconomic disparities in health. *Health Affairs* 21 (2): 60–76.

Adler, Patricia A., and Peter Adler. 2005. Self-injurers as loners: The social organiza-tion of solitary deviance. *Deviant Behavior* 26 (4): 345–78.

Adorno, Theodor W., and Max Horkheimer. (1944) 2000. The culture industry: Enlightenment as mass deception. In *The consumer society reader*, ed. Juliet B. Schor and Douglas B. Holt, pp. 3–19. New York: New Press.

Akpabio, Eno, and Kayode Mustapha-Lambe. 2008. *Nollywood* films and the cultural im-perialism hypothesis. *Perspectives on Global Development and Technology* 7 (3): 259–70.

Alexander, Jeffrey, ed. 1985. *Neofunctionalism*. Beverly Hills, CA: Sage.

Alexander, Michelle. 2012. *The new Jim Crow: Mass incarceration in the age of colorblindness*. New York: New Press.

Alinsky, Saul. 1989. *Rules for radicals*. New York: Vintage.

Allen, Amy. 2000. *The power of feminist theory*. Boulder, CO: Westview Press.

Allen, Amy. 2005. Feminist perspectives on power. *Stanford Encyclopedia of Philosophy*, ed. Edward N. Zalta. Retrieved from http://plato.stanford.edu/archives/fall2008/entries/feminist-power.

Allen, Amy. 2008. *The politics of our selves: Pol-itics, autonomy, and gender in contemporary political theory*. New York: Columbia Uni-versity Press.

Allen, I. Elaine, and Jeff Seaman. 2013. *Changing course: Ten years of tracking online education in the United States*. Babson Sur-vey Research Group. Retrieved from www.onlinelearningsurvey.com/reports/chang-ingcourse.pdf.

Allen, James, Jon Lewis, Leon F. Litwack, and Hilton Als. 2000. *Without sanctuary: Lynching photography in America*. Santa Fe, NM: Twin Palms.

Allport, Gordon. 1954. *The nature of prejudice*. Cambridge, MA: Addison-Wesley.

Alon, Sigal. 2009. The evolution of class in-equality in higher education: Competition, exclusion, and adaptation. *American Socio-logical Review* 74 (October): 731–55.

Alon, Sigal, and Marta Tienda. 2007. Diver-sity, opportunity, and the shifting meritoc-racy in higher education. *American Sociological Review* 72 (August): 487–511.

Alper, Joseph. S. 2002. Genetic complexity in human disease and behavior. In *The double-edged helix: Social implications of genetics in a diverse society*, ed. Joseph S. Alper, Catherine Ard, Adrienne Asch, John Beck-with, Peter Conrad, and Lisa N. Geller, pp. 17–38. Baltimore, MD: Johns Hopkins University Press.

Alsop, Ruth, and Nina Heinsohn. 2005. Mea-suring empowerment in practice: Structur-ing analysis and framing indicators. World Bank Policy Research Working Paper 3510. Washington, DC: World Bank.

Altheide, David. 2006. *Terrorism and the poli-tics of fear*. Lanham, MD: AltaMira Press.

Altonji, Joseph G., and Rebecca M. Blank. 1999. Race and gender in the labor market. In *Handbook of labor economics*, vol. 3C, ed. Orley Ashenfelter and David Card, pp. 3143–259. New York: Elsevier Science.

Alvarez, Lizette. 2009a. More Americans joining military as jobs dwindle. *New York Times*, January 18, p. A1. Retrieved from www.nytimes.com/2009/01/19/us/19re-cruits.html.

Alvarez, Lizette. 2009b. Suicides of soldiers reach high of nearly 3 decades. *New York Times*, January 30, p. A19. Retrieved from www.nytimes.com/2009/01/30/us/30sui-cide.html.

Alvarez, R. Michael, Thad E. Hall, and Susan D. Hyde, eds. 2008. *Election fraud*. Washington, DC: Brookings Institution Press.

Amato, Paul R., and Alan Booth. 2000. *A generation at risk*. Cambridge, MA: Harvard University Press.

American Academy of Pediatrics. 2006. Chil-dren, adolescents, and advertising. Policy statement. *Pediatrics* 118 (6): 2563–69. Reaf-firmed March 2010. Retrieved from http://pediatrics.aappublications.org/cgi/content/full/118/6/2563#R2.

American Anthropological Association. 2011. *Race: Are we so different?* Retrieved from http://understandingrace.org/lived/global_census.html.

American Civil Liberties Union. 2010. LGBT rights: Lesbian, gay, bisexual, and transgender project. Retrieved from www.aclu.org/lgbt-rights.

American Council on Education. 2012. The American college president 2012. Retrieved from www.acenet.edu/news-room/Pages/ACPS-Release-2012.aspx.

American Folklife Center. 2013. What is folklife? Retrieved from www.loc.gov/folk-life/whatisfolklife.html.

American National Election Studies. 2007. *The ANES guide to public opinion and elec-toral behavior*. Ann Arbor: University of Michigan, Center for Political Studies. Retrieved from www.electionstudies.org.

American Social History Project. 2007. *Who built America?* New York: Bedford/St. Martin's.

American Society for Aesthetic Plastic Sur-gery. 2013. *Cosmetic Surgery National Data Bank 2012*. New York: American Society for Aesthetic Plastic Surgery.

American Society of Newspaper Editors. 2013. Newsroom census. Retrieved from http://asne.org/content.asp?admin=Y&contentid=121.

American Society of Plastic Surgeons. 2006. Abdominoplasty: Tummy tuck. Retrieved from www.plasticsurgery.org/public_edu-cation/ procedures/Abdominoplasty.cfm.

American Sociological Association. 1999. Code of ethics. Retrieved from www.asanet.org/page.ww?section=Ethics&name=Code+of+Ethics+Table+of+Contents.

American Sociological Association. 2005. Race, ethnicity and the health of Americans. Washington, DC: American Sociological Association. Retrieved from www2.asanet.org/centennial/race_ethnicity_health.pdf.

American Sociological Association. 2013a. ASA applauds Supreme Court's decision to overturn DOMA. June 26. Retrieved from www.asanet.org/press/asa_applauds_scotus_decision_to_overturn_doma.cfm.

American Sociological Association. 2013b. *Brief of Amicus Curiae American Sociological Association in Support of Respondent Kristin M. Perry and Respondent Edith Schlain Windsor.* Supreme Court of the United States. NOS. 12-144, 12-307.

Amnesty International. 2012. Death penalty facts. Retrieved September 19, 2013, from www.amnestyusa.org/pdfs/DeathPenalty-FactsMay2012.pdf.

Amnesty International. 2013. Death sentences and executions 2012. Retrieved September 19, 2013, from www.amnesty.org/en/library/asset/ACT50/001/2013/en/bbfea0d6-39b2-4e5f-a1ad-885a8eb5c607/act500012013en.pdf.

Anderson, Barbara A., Chris Provis, and Shirley J. Chappel. 2003. The selection and training of workers in the tourism and hospitality industries for the performance of emotional labour. *Journal of Hospitality and Tourism Management* 10 (1): 1–12.

Anderson, Elijah. 1999. *Code of the street.* New York: Norton.

Anderson, Jenny. 2011. Push for A's at private schools is keeping costly tutors busy. *New York Times*, June 7. Retrieved from www.nytimes.com/2011/06/08/education/08tutors.html? pagewanted=1&_r=1.

Anderson, Margaret, and Patricia Hill Collins, eds. 2013. *Race, class & gender: An anthology*, 8th edition. Belmont, CA: Cengage.

Anderson, Margaret, and Dana Hysock Witham. 2010. *Thinking about women: Sociological perspectives on sex and gender.* Boston Allyn & Bacon.

Andersson, Hilary. 2005. Born to be a slave in Niger. BBC, February 12. Retrieved from http://news.bbc.co.uk/1/hi/programmes/from_our_own_correspondent/4250709.stm.

Angwin, Julia. 2010. The web's new gold mine: Your secrets. *Wall Street Journal*, July 30. Retrieved from http://online.wsj.com/article/SB10001424052748703940409457539507351298940404.html.

Angwin, Julia, and Steve Stecklow. 2010. "Scrapers" dig deep for data on the web. *Wall Street Journal*, October 12. Retrieved from http://online.wsj.com/article/SB10001424052748703358504575544381288117888.html.

Appold, Stephen. 2007. Human ecology. In *21st Century sociology: A reference handbook*, ed. Clifton D. Bryant and Dennis L. Peck, pp. 444–54. Thousand Oaks, CA: Sage.

AP-Univision. 2010. The AP-Univision poll, May 7–12. Retrieved from http://surveys.ap.org/data%5CGfK%5CAP-Univision%20Poll%20May%202010%20Hispanic%20Topline_ALL _updated.pdf.

Arab American Institute. 2010. Demographics. Retrieved from www.aaiusa.org/pages/demographics/.

Arab American Institute. 2012. Demographics. Retrieved from http://b.3cdn.net/aai/44b17815d8b386bf16_v0m6iv4b5.pdf.

Aries, Philippe. 1965. *Centuries of childhood: A social history of family life*, trans. Robert Baldick. New York: Vintage.

Arnason, Johann P. 2001. History of civilizational analysis. In *International encyclopedia of the social and behavioral sciences*, ed. Neil J. Smelser and Paul B. Baltes. Oxford and New York: Elsevier.

Arnett, Jeffrey Jensen. 2004. *Emerging adulthood.* New York: Oxford University Press.

Arum, Richard. 2003. *Judging school discipline.* Cambridge MA: Harvard University Press.

Asch, Solomon E. 1952. *Social psychology.* Englewood Cliffs, NJ: Prentice Hall.

Asch, Solomon E. 1955. Opinions and social pressures. *Scientific American* 193 (5): 31–35.

Ashmawey, Rogaya. 2010. A write-in campaign. *Newsweek*, March 1. Retrieved from www.newsweek.com/2010/02/28/a-write-in-campaign.html.

Astin, Alexander W. 1998. The changing American college student: Thirty-year trends, 1966–1996. *Review of Higher Education* 21 (2): 115–35.

Attewell, Paul, David Lavin, Thurston Domina, and Tania Levey. 2007. *Passing the torch: Does higher education for the disadvantaged pay off across the generations?* New York: Russell Sage Foundation.

Aud, Susan, Sidney Wilkinson-Flicker, Paul Kristapovich, Amy Rathbun, Xiaolei Wang, and Jijun Zhang. 2013. *The condition of education 2013* (NCES 2013-037). Washington, DC: U.S. Department of Education, National Center for Education Statistics.

Austin, Algernon. 2013. The unfinished march: An overview. Washington, DC: Economic Policy Institute. Retrieved from http://s1.epi.org/files/2013/EPI-The-Unfinished-March-An-Overview.pdf.

Austin, Andrew. 2002. Advancing accumulation and managing its discontents: The U.S. antienvironmental countermovement. *Sociological Spectrum* 22: 71–105.

Babb, Sarah. 2004. Born to buy: Sarah Babb interviews Juliet Schor. In *Sociology speaks 2003–2004*. Chestnut Hill, MA: Boston College Department of Sociology.

Babbie, Earl. 2013. *The practice of social research*, 13th ed. Belmont, CA: Wadsworth.

Bagdikian, Ben. 2004. *The new media monopoly.* Boston: Beacon Press.

Bahrampour, Tara. 2010. Students raise the stakes against immigration's status quo. *Washington Post*, July 21, p. A3.

Baisnee, Olivier, and Dominique Marchetti. 2006. The economy of just-in-time television newscasting, trans. Fredline Laryea. *Ethnography* 7 (1): 99–123.

Bajaj, Vikas, and Ford Fessenden. 2007. What's behind the race gap? *New York Times*, November 4, 2007. Retrieved from www.nytimes.com/ 2007/11/04/weekinreview/04bajaj.html? _r=2&ref=business&oref=slogin&oref=slogin.

Baker, Wayne E. 2005. *America's crisis of values: Reality and perception.* Princeton, NJ: Princeton University Press.

Barabási, Albert-László. 2002. *Linked.* New York: Plume.

Baron-Cohen, Simon. 1999. *Mindblindness: An essay on autism and theory of mind.* Cambridge, MA: MIT Press.

Barr, Donald A. 2008. *Health disparities in the United States: Social class, race, ethnicity, and health.* Baltimore, MD: Johns Hopkins University Press.

Barres, Ben A. 2006. Does gender matter? *Nature*, July 13, pp. 133–36.

Barrett, Devlin, and Dan Fitzpatrick. 2013. J.P. Morgan, U.S. settle for $13 billion. *The Wall Street Journal*, November 19. Retrieved from http://online.wsj.com/news/articles/SB10001424052702304439804579207701974094982.

Barstow, Anne Llewellyn, ed. 2001. *War's dirty secret: Rape, prostitution, and other crimes against women.* Cleveland, OH: Pilgrim Press.

Bartiromo, Maria. 2009. Google's privacy. Retrieved from http://video.cnbc.com/gallery/?play=1&video=1372176413.

Battani, Marshall, John R. Hall, and Mary Jo Neitz. 2003. *Sociology on culture.* New York: Routledge.

Baudrillard, Jean. 1988a. Consumer society. In *Selected writings*, ed. Mark Poster, pp. 29–56. Stanford, CA: Stanford University Press.

Baudrillard, Jean. 1988b. For a critique of the political economy of the sign. In *Selected writings*, ed. Mark Poster, pp. 57–97. Stanford, CA: Stanford University Press.

Bauerlein, Mark. 2008. *The dumbest generation.* New York: Tarcher/Penguin.

Bauman, Zygmunt. 2001. *Community: Seeking safety in an insecure world.* Cambridge, UK: Polity Press.

Bawden, Tom. 2007. Buffett blasts system that lets him pay less tax than secretary. *Times (UK)*, June 28. Retrieved from www.timesonline.co.uk/tol/money/tax/article1996735.ece.

Baxter, Janeen, and Erik Olin Wright. 2000. The glass ceiling hypothesis: A comparative study of the United States, Sweden, and Australia. *Gender and Society* 14 (2): 275–94.

Bayat, Asef. 2007. *Making Islam democratic.* Stanford, CA: Stanford University Press.

BBC. 2010a. Suicide-hit Foxconn factory to in-crease wages. Retrieved from http://news.bbc.co.uk/2/hi/business/10184186.stm.

BBC. 2010b. Taiwan iPhone-maker Foxconn suffers another death. Retrieved from http://news.bbc.co.uk/2/hi/world/asia_pacific/10182824.stm.

Beaglehole, Robert. 1990. International trends in coronary heart disease mortality, morbidity, and risk factors. *Epidemiologic Reviews* 12: 1–16.

Becker, Howard. 1973. *Outsiders: Studies in the sociology of deviance.* New York: Free Press.

Beech, Hannah. 2012. China: Forced-abortion victim promised $11,200, but family fears for life. *Time*, July 13. Retrieved from http://world.time.com/2012/07/13/china-forced-abortion-victim-awarded-11200-fears-for-life/.

Beeghley, Leonard. 2011. *The structure of social stratification in the United States.* Boston: Allyn & Bacon.

Belknap, Joanne, and Heather Melton. 2005. *Are heterosexual men also victims of intimate partner abuse?* Harrisburg, PA: National Resource Center on Domestic Violence. Retrieved from http://new.vawnet.org/Assoc_Files_VAWnet/AR_MaleVictims.pdf.

Bell, Michael Mayerfield. 2012. *An invitation to environmental sociology.* Thousand Oaks, CA: Pine Forge Press/Sage.

Bellah, Robert N., Richard Madsen, William M. Sullivan, Ann Swidler, and Steven M. Tipton. 2007. *Habits of the heart: Individualism and commitment in American Life*, 3rd ed. Berkeley: University of California Press.

Benhabib, Seyla. 2002. *The claims of culture: Equality and diversity in a global era.* Princeton, NJ: Princeton University Press.

Benokraitis, Nijole V., ed. 2000. *Feuds about families: Conservative, centrist, liberal and feminist perspectives.* Upper Saddle River, NJ: Prentice Hall.

Benton, Ted. 1977. *Philosophical foundations of the three sociologies.* Boston: Routledge.

Berardo, Felix M., and Constance L. Shehan. 2004. Family problems in global perspective. In *Handbook of social problems: A comparative international perspective*, ed. George Ritzer, pp. 246–60. Thousand Oaks, CA: Sage.

Berbrier, Mitch. 1998. Being deaf has very little to do with one's ears: Boundary-work in the Deaf Culture movement. *Perspectives on Social Problems* 10: 79–100.

Berger, Joseph. 2006. For Hispanic parents, lessons on helping with the homework. *New York Times*, November 1, p. 11.

Berger, Peter. 1963. *Invitation to sociology.* New York: Doubleday.

Berger, Peter. 1967. *The sacred canopy.* Garden City, NY: Doubleday.

Berger, Peter. 1997. Four faces of global culture. *National Interest* 49 (Fall): 23–29.

Berger, Peter L., and Thomas Luckmann. 1966. *The social construction of reality.* New York: Doubleday.

Berlatsky, Noah. 2013. A self-published erotic novelist pioneers a new kind of porn. *Salon.* Retrieved from www.salon.com/2013/10/19/a_self_published_erotic_novelist_pioneers_a_new_kind_of_porn/.

Bernhardt, Amy M., Cara Wilking, Anna M. Adachi-Mejia, Elaina Bergamini, Jill Marijnissen, and James D. Sargent. 2013. How television fast food marketing aimed at children compares with adult advertisements. Retrieved from www.rwjf.org/en/research-publications/find-rwjf-research/2013/08/how-television-fast-food-marketing-aimed-at-children-compares-wi.html.

Bertrand, Marianne, and Sendhil Mullainathan. 2004. Are Emily and Greg more employable than Lakisha and Jamal? A field experiment on labor market discrimination. *The American Economic Review* 94 (4): 991–1013.

Best, Joel, and David F. Luckenbill. 1982. *Organizing deviance.* Englewood Cliffs, NJ: Prentice Hall.

Bianchi, Suzanne M., John P. Robinson, and Melissa A. Milkie. 2007. *Changing rhythms of American family life.* New York: Russell Sage Foundation.

Bielby, Denise D. 2006. Gender and family relations. In *Handbook of the sociology of gender*, ed. Janet Saltzman Chafetz, pp. 391–406. New York: Springer Science + Business Media.

Black, Dan, Gary Gates, Seth Sanders, and Lowell Taylor. 2000. Demographics of the gay and lesbian population in the United States: Evidence from available systematic data sources. *Demography* 37 (2): 139–54.

Black, Edwin. 2003. *War against the weak: Eugenics and America's campaign to create a master race.* New York: Four Walls Eight Windows.

Black, Ian. 2013. NSA spying scandal: What we have learned. *The Guardian*, June 10. Retrieved from www.guardian.co.uk/world/2013/jun/10/nsa-spying-scandal-what-we-have-learned.

Blackledge, Adrian. 2001. The wrong sort of capital? *International Journal of Bilingualism* 5 (3): 345–69.

Blackless, Melanie, Anthony Charuvastra, Amanda Derryck, Anne Fausto-Sterling, Karl Lauzanne, and Ellen Lee. 2000. How sexually dimorphic are we? Review and synthesis. *American Journal of Human Biology* 12: 151–66.

Blake, Mariah. 2005. Stations of the cross. *Columbia Journalism Review* (May/June): 32–39.

Blalock, Hubert M. 1989. *Power and conflict: Toward a general theory.* Newbury Park, CA: Sage.

Blanton, Hart, and James Jaccard. 2008. Unconscious racism: A concept in pursuit of a measure. *Annual Review of Sociology* 34: 277–97.

Blau, Joel, and Mimi Abramovitz. 2007. *The dynamics of social welfare policy.* New York: Oxford University Press.

Blau, Peter, and Otis D. Duncan. 1967. *The American occupational structure.* New York: Wiley.

Bleakley, Hoyt, and Aimee Chin. 2004. Language skills and earnings: Evidence from childhood immigrants. *Review of Economics and Statistics* 86: 481–96.

Bloom, Barbara, Barbara Owen, and Stephanie Covington. 2005. *Gender-responsive strategies for women offenders.* Washington, DC: National Institute of Corrections, U.S. Department of Justice.

Bluestone, Barry, and Bennett Harrison. 1982. *The deindustrialization of America.* New York: Basic Books.

Blumer, Herbert. 1986. *Symbolic interactionism: Perspective and method.* Berkeley: University of California Press.

Bob, Kim, Jackie Kendall, and Steve Max. 2010. *Organizing for social change: Midwest Academy manual for activists*, 4th ed. Santa Ana, CA: Forum Press.

Bobo, Kim, Jackie Kendall, and Steve Max. 2010. *Organizing for social change: Midwest Academy manual for activists.* Santa Ana, CA: Seven Locks Press.

Bobo, Lawrence, James R. Kluegel, and Ryan A. Smith. 1997. Laissez-faire racism: The crystallization of a kinder, gentler, anti-black ideology. In *Racial attitudes in the 1990s: Continuity and change*, ed. Jack K. Martin and Steven A. Tuch, pp. 15–42. Westport, CT: Praeger.

Boero, Natalie, and C. J. Pascoe. 2012. Pro-anorexia communities and online interaction: Bringing the pro-ana body online. *Body & Society* 18 (2): 27–57.

Boff, Leonardo, and Clodovis Boff. 1987. *Introducing liberation theology.* Maryknoll, NY: Orbis Books.

Bogaert, Anthony F. 2004. Asexuality: Prevalence and associated factors in a national probability sample. *Journal of Sex Research* 41 (August): 279–87.

Bogardus, Emory S. 1967. *A forty-year racial distance study.* Los Angeles: University of Southern California Press.

Boisjoly, Johanne, Greg J. Duncan, Michael Kremer, Dan M. Levy, and Jacque Eccles. 2006. Empathy or antipathy? The impact of diversity. *American Economic Review* 96: 1890–905.

Bonacich, Edna. 1972. A theory of ethnic antagonism: The split labor market. *American Sociological Review* 37 (5): 547–59.

Bonacich, Edna. 1976. Advanced capitalism and black/white relations in the United States: A split labor market interpretation. *American Sociological Review* 41 (1): 34–51.

Bond, Rod, and Peter B. Smith. 1996. Culture and conformity: A meta-analysis of studies using Asch's line judgment task. *Psychological Bulletin* 119: 111–37.

Bonilla-Silva, Eduardo. 2001. *White supremacy and racism in the post-civil rights era.* Boulder, CO: Lynne Rienner.

Bonilla-Silva, Eduardo. 2009. *Race without racists.* Lanham, MD: Rowman & Littlefield.

Bordo, Susan. 1993. *Unbearable weight.* Berkeley: University of California Press.

Bosso, Christopher J. 2005. *Environment Inc.: From grassroots to beltway.* Lawrence: University of Kansas Press.

Bourdieu, Pierre. 1986. The forms of capital. In *Handbook for theory and research for the sociology of education*, ed. J. G. Richardson, pp. 241–58. Westport, CT: Greenwood Press.

Bourdieu, Pierre, and Jean Claude Passeron. 1977. *Reproduction in education, society, and culture.* Thousand Oaks, CA: Sage.

Bourgois, Philippe. 2003. *In search of respect*, 2nd ed. New York: Cambridge University Press.

Bowen, William G., and Derek Bok. 1998. *The shape of the river.* Princeton, NJ: Princeton University Press.

Bowles, Samuel, and Herbert Gintis. 1976. *Schooling in capitalist America.* New York: Basic Books.

Bowles, Samuel, Herbert Gintis, and Melissa Osbourne Groves, eds. 2005. *Unequal chances: Family background and economic success.* Princeton, NJ: Princeton University Press.

Boyd, Emily M., John R. Reynolds, Kathryn Harker Tillman, and Patricia Yancey Martin. 2011. Adolescent girls' race/ethnic status, identities, and drive for thinness. *Social Science Research* 40: 667–84.

BRAC. 2010a. Community empowerment: Community rights awareness & legal literacy. Retrieved from www.brac.net/content/legal-empowerment-community-rights-awareness -legal-literacy.

BRAC. 2010b. Who we are. Retrieved from www.brac.net/content/who-we-are-0.

Braithwaite, John. 1989. *Crime, shame, and reintegration.* New York: Cambridge University Press.

Braverman, Harry. 1998. *Labor and monopoly capital.* New York: Monthly Review Press.

Brenner, Philip. 2011. Exceptional behavior or exceptional identity? Overreporting of church attendance in the U.S. *Public Opinion Quarterly* 75 (1): 19–41.

Bridges, J. S. 1993. Pink or blue: Gender-stereotypic perceptions of infants as conveyed by birth congratulations cards. *Psychology of Women Quarterly* 17: 193–205.

Briggs, Bill. 2013. Financial strain pushes many veterans to the breaking point. NBC News. Retrieved from http://inplainsight.nbcnews.com/_news/2013/05/04/17987594-financial-strain-pushes-many-veterans-to-the-breaking-point.

Brint, Steven. 2006. *Schools and societies,* 2nd ed. Palo Alto, CA: Stanford University Press.

Brint, Steven, Mary F. Contreras, and Michael T. Matthews. 2001. Socialization messages in primary schools. *Sociology of Education* 74 (July): 157–80.

Brooks, Abigail. 2004. Under the knife and proud of it: An analysis of the normalization of cosmetic surgery. *Critical Sociology* 30 (2): 207–39.

Brothers, Leslie. 1997. *Friday's footprint: How society shapes the human mind.* New York: Oxford University Press.

Brown, Callum G. 2009. *The death of Christian Britain: Understanding secularisation, 1800–2000.* New York: Routledge.

Brown, M. Christopher, II, and James Earl Davis. 2001. The historically black college as social contract, social capital, and social equalizer. *Peabody Journal of Education* 76 (1): 31–49.

Brown, Patricia Leigh. 2006. Supporting boys or girls when the line isn't clear. *New York Times,* December 2. Retrieved from www.nytimes.com/2006/12/02/us/02child .html?pagewanted=1&_r=1.

Brown, Susan I. 2005. How cohabitation is reshaping American families. *Contexts* 4 (3): 33–37.

Brownstein, Ronald. 2012. Poll: Public split on Dream Act, Rubio alternative. *National Journal,* May 8. Retrieved from www.nationaljournal.com/daily/poll-public-prefers-citizenship-for-dreamers-20120508.

Bruce, Steve. 2000. *Fundamentalism.* Malden, MA: Blackwell.

Bruce, Steve. 2002. *God is dead: Secularization in the West.* Malden, MA: Wiley-Blackwell.

Bruce, Steve. 2011. *Secularization: In defense of an unfashionable theory.* New York: Oxford University Press.

Bruinius, Harry. 2006. *Better for all the world: The secret history of forced sterilization and America's quest for racial purity.* New York: Knopf.

Brumfield, Ben. 2013. Selfie named word of the year for 2013. CNN. Retrieved from www.cnn.com/2013/11/19/living/selfie-word-of-the-year/.

Bruns, Axel. 2005. *Gatewatching: Collaborative online news production.* New York: Peter Lang.

Bruns, Axel. 2008. *Blogs, Wikipedia, Second Life, and beyond: From production to produsage.* New York: Peter Lang.

Budig, Michelle J., and Paula England. 2001. The wage penalty for motherhood. *American Sociological Review* 66 (2): 204–25.

Bugental, D. B., & Lewis, Jeffrey C. 1999. The paradoxical misuse of power by those who see themselves as powerless: How does it happen? *Journal of Social Issues* 55 (1): 51–64.

Bullard, Robert. 2000. *Dumping in Dixie: Race, class and environmental quality.* Boulder, CO: Westview Press.

Bumpass, Larry, and Hsien-Hen Lu. 2000. Trends in cohabitation and implications for children's family contexts in the U.S. *Population Studies* 54: 29–41.

Burawoy, Michael, William Gamson, Charlotte Ryan, Stephen Pfohl, Diane Vaughan, Charles Derber, and Juliet Schor. 2004. Public sociologies: A symposium from Boston College. *Social Problems* 51 (1): 103–30.

Bureau of Justice Statistics. 2009. Probation and parole in the United States, 2007 statistical tables. U.S. Department of Justice. August. Retrieved from www.bjs.gov/content/pub/pdf/ppus07st.pdf.

Bureau of Justice Statistics. 2012a. Arrests in the United States, 1990–2010. U.S. Department of Justice, October. Retrieved from www.bjs.gov/index.cfm?ty=pbdetail&iid=4515.

Bureau of Justice Statistics. 2012b. Correctional populations in the United States, 2011. U.S. Department of Justice, November. Retrieved from www.bjs.gov/index.cfm?ty=pbdetail&iid=4537.

Bureau of Justice Statistics. 2012c. Prisoners in 2011. U.S. Department of Justice, December. Retrieved from www.bjs.gov/index.cfm?ty=pbdetail&iid=4559.

Bureau of Justice Statistics. 2013a. Correctional populations in the United States, 2012. U.S. Department of Justice, December. Retrieved from www.bjs.gov/index.cfm?ty=pbdetail&iid=4843.

Bureau of Justice Statistics. 2013b. Prisoners in 2012. U.S. Department of Justice, December. Retrieved from www.bjs.gov/index.cfm?ty=pbdetail&iid=4737.

Burke, Meaghan. 2012. *Racial ambivalence in diverse communities: Whiteness and the power of color-blind ideologies.* Lanham, MD: Lexington Books.

Bush, George W. 2001. Address to a Joint Session of Congress and the American People. September 20. Office of the Press Secretary, White House. Retrieved from: http://georgewbush-whitehouse.archives.gov/news/releases/2001/09/20010920-8.html.

Butsch, Richard. 2005. Five decades and three hundred sitcoms about class and gender. In *Thinking outside the box: A contemporary television genre reader,* ed. Gary R. Edgerton and Brian G. Rose, pp. 111–35. Lexington: University Press of Kentucky.

Buttel, Frederick H. 2003. Environmental sociology and the explanation of environmental reform. *Organization & Environment* 16 (3): 306–44.

Buttel, Frederick H. 2004. The treadmill of production: An appreciation, assessment, and agenda for research. *Organization & Environment* 17 (3): 323–36.

Caldera, Y. M., A. C. Huston, and M. O'Brien. 1989. Social interaction and play patterns of parents and toddlers with feminine, masculine, and neutral toys. *Child Development* 60: 70–76.

Caldera, Y. M., and M. A. Sciaraffa. 1998. Parent-toddler play with feminine toys: Are all dolls the same? *Sex Roles* 39: 657–62.

Calhoun, Craig. 2012. *Classical sociological theory.* Malden, MA: Wiley-Blackwell.

Callero, Peter. 2003. The sociology of the self. *Annual Review of Sociology* 29: 115–33.

Campaign Finance Institute. 2013. Aggregated individual contributions by donors to 2012 presidential candidates. Retrieved from www.cfinst.org/pdf/federal/president/2012/Pres12Tables_YE12_AggIndivDonors.pdf.

Campbell, Donald, and Julian Stanley. 1963. *Experimental and quasi-experimental design for the social sciences.* Chicago: Rand McNally.

Campbell, Margaret, Gina S. Mohr, and Peeter W. J. Verlegh. 2013. Can disclosures lead consumers to resist covert persuasion? The important roles of disclosure timing and type of response. *Journal of Consumer Psychology* 23 (4): 483–95.

Carbaugh, Donal. 2005. *Cultures in conversation.* New York: Routledge.

Carbonaro, William. 2005. Tracking, students' effort, and academic achievement. *Sociology of Education* 78 (1): 27–49.

Carey, Nessa. 2012. *The epigenetics revolution: How modern biology is rewriting our understanding of genetics, disease, and inheritance.* New York: Columbia University Press.

Carli, Linda L. 1999. Gender, interpersonal power, and social influence. *Journal of Social Issues* 55 (1): 81–99.

Carlson, Nicholas. 2010. WARNING: Google Buzz has a huge privacy flaw. *Business Insider*, February 10. Retrieved from www.businessinsider.com/warning-google-buzz-has-a-huge-privacy-flaw-2010-2?op=1#ixzz2gsJ9YoMM.

Carnevale, Anthony P., and Stephen J. Rose. 2004. Socioeconomic status, race/ethnicity, and selective college admissions. In *America's untapped resource: Low-income students in higher education*, ed. Richard D. Kahlenberg. Washington, DC: Century Foundation Press.

Carnevale, Anthony P., and Jeff Strohl. 2013. Separate and unequal: How higher education reinforces the intergenerational reproduction of white racial privilege. Washington, DC: Georgetown Public Policy Institute. Retrieved from www9.georgetown.edu/grad/gppi/hpi/cew/pdfs/Separate&Unequal.FR.pdf.

Carr, Deborah, and Michael A. Friedman. 2005. Is obesity stigmatizing? Body weight, perceived discrimination, and psychological well-being in the United States. *Journal of Health and Social Behavior* 46 (3): 244–59.

Carr, Nicholas. 2010. *The shallows.* New York: Norton.

Carreiro, Joshua. 2005. Newspaper coverage of the U.S. labor movement: The case of anti-union firings. *Labor Studies Journal* 30 (3): 1–20.

Carvin, Andy. 2013. *Distant witness.* New York: CUNY Journalism Press.

Casanova, Jose. 1994. *Public religions in the modern world.* Chicago: University of Chicago Press.

Caspi, Avshalom, Joseph McClay, Terrie E. Moffitt, Jonathan Mill, Judy Martin, Ian W. Craig, Alan Taylor, and Richie Poulton. 2002. Role of genotype in the cycle of violence in maltreated children. *Science* 297: 851–54.

Castells, Manuel. 1983. *The city and the grass roots.* Berkeley: University of California Press.

Castells, Manuel. 1996. *The Rise of network society.* Oxford, UK: Blackwell.

Catalano, Shannon. 2007. Intimate partner violence in the United States. U.S. Bureau of Justice Statistics. Retrieved from www.ojp.usdoj.gov/bjs/intimate/ipv.htm.

Catalyst. 2013. 2013 Catalyst census: *Fortune* 500. Retrieved from www.catalyst.org/knowledge/2013-catalyst-census-fortune-500.

Center for American Women and Politics. 2013. Women in elective office 2013. Rutgers, NJ: Rutgers University Press. Retrieved from www.cawp.rutgers.edu/fast_facts/levels_of_office/documents/elective.pdf.

Center for Responsive Politics. 2013a. Donor demographics. Retrieved from www.opensecrets.org/bigpicture/donordemographics.php?cycle=2012.

Center for Responsive Politics. 2013b. Expenditures. Retrieved from www.opensecrets.org/pres12/expenditures.php.

Center for Responsive Politics. 2013c. The money behind the elections. Retrieved from www.opensecrets.org/bigpicture/index.php?display=T.

Cesari, Jocelyne. 2004. *When Islam and democracy meet.* New York: Palgrave Macmillan.

Chafetz, Janet Saltzman, ed. 1999. *Handbook of the sociology of gender.* New York: Kluwer Academic/Plenum.

Chalecki, Elizabeth. 2013. *Environmental security: A guide to the issues.* Santa Barbara, CA: Praeger.

Chandola, Tarani, Eric Brunner, and Michael Marmot. 2006. Chronic stress at work and the metabolic syndrome: Prospective study. *British Journal of Medicine* 332: 521.

Changemakers. 2009. Barefoot . . . and speaking up for her rights. Ashoka. Retrieved from www .changemakers.com/node/30060.

Chaves, Mark. 1994. Secularization as declining religious authority. *Social Forces* 72 (3): 749–44.

Chazan, David. 2010. Row over "torture" on French TV. BBC News, March 18, Retrieved from http://news.bbc.co.uk/2/hi/europe/ 8573755.stm.

Chazan, Guy, Benoit Faucon, and Ben Casselman. 2010. As CEO Hayward remade BP, safety, cost drives clashed. *Wall Street Journal*, June 29. Retrieved from http://online.wsj.com/article/SB1000142405274870396410457533515412672187 6.html.

Chen, Henglien Lisa. 2010. Welfare and long-term care in the East and West. *International Journal of Sociology and Social Policy* 30 (3/4): 167–81.

Cherlin, Andrew J. 2010. Demographic trends in the United States: A review of research in the 2000s. *Journal of Marriage and Family* 72 (3): 403–19.

Cherlin, Andrew J. 2013. *Public and private families.* New York: McGraw-Hill.

Cheshire, Tamara. 2006. American Indian families: Strength and answers from our past. In *Families in global and multicultural perspective*, 2nd ed., ed. Bron B. Ingoldsby and Suzanna D. Smith, pp. 315–27. Thousand Oaks, CA: Sage.

Chesler, Naomi C., and Mark A. Chesler. 2002. Gender-informed mentoring strategies for women engineering scholars: On establishing a caring community. *Journal of Engineering Education* 91 (9): 49–55.

Chesters, Jenny. 2011. Gender convergence in core housework hours. *Journal of Sociology* 49 (1): 78–96.

Chinn, Sarah. 2008. *Inventing modern adolescence.* Rutgers, NJ: Rutgers University Press.

Chomsky, Noam. 1989. *Necessary illusions: Thought control in democratic societies.* Cambridge, MA: South End Press.

Christakis, Nicholas A., and James H. Fowler. 2007. The spread of obesity in a large social network over 32 years. *New England Journal of Medicine* 357: 370–79.

Christakis, Nicholas A., and James H. Fowler. 2008. The collective dynamics of smoking in a large social network. *New England Journal of Medicine* 358: 2249–2258.

Christopher, Karen. 2002. Family-friendly Europe. *American Prospect* 13 (7): 60–64.

Chun, Jennifer Jihye. 2009. *Organizing at the margins: The symbolic politics of labor in South Korea and the United States.* Ithaca, NY: ILR/Cornell University Press.

Cialdini, Robert B., and Noah H. Goldstein. 2004. Social influence: Compliance and conformity. *Annual Review of Psychology* 55: 591–621.

Citizens for Tax Justice. 2011. Boeing's reward for paying no federal taxes over last three years? A $35 billion federal contract. Retrieved from www.ctj.org/pdf/boeing0211.pdf.

Clarke, Lee. 2006. Worst case Katrina. In *Understanding Katrina: Perspectives from the social sciences.* Retrieved from http://understanding katrina.ssrc.org/Clarke/.

Clawson, Dan, Alan Neustadtl, and Mark Weller. 1998. *Dollars and votes: How business campaign contributions subvert democracy.* Philadelphia, PA: Temple University Press.

Clawson, Dan. 2003. *The next upsurge: Labor and the new social movements.* Ithaca, NY: ILR/ Cornell University Press.

Clayman, Steven, and John Heritage. 2002. *The news interview.* New York: Cambridge University Press.

Clearfield, Melissa W., and Naree M. Nelson. 2006. Sex differences in mothers' speech and play behavior with 6-, 9-, and 14-month-old infants. *Sex Roles: A Journal of Research* 54 (1–2): 127–37.

Clendinen, D., and A. Nagourney. 1999. *Out for good: The struggle to build a gay rights movement in America.* New York: Simon & Schuster.

Cloward, Richard A., and Lloyd E. Ohlin. 1960. *Delinquency and opportunity.* New York: Free Press.

Cochran, John K., and Mitchell B. Chamlin. 2006. The enduring racial divide in death penalty support. *Journal of Criminal Justice* 34: 85–99.

Cohen, Patricia. 2010. Indian tribes go in search of their lost languages. *New York Times*, April 5, p. C1.

Cole, David, and James X. Dempsey. 2006. *Terrorism and the Constitution: Sacrificing civil liberties in the name of national security.* New York: New Press.

Coleman-Jensen, Alisha, Mark Nord, and Anita Singh. 2013. *Household food security in the United States in 2012.* Economic Research Report No. (ERR-155). Washington, DC: U.S. Department of Agriculture, Economic Research Service.

College Board. 2012. *Trends in student aid 2012.* College Board Advocacy & Policy Center. Retrieved from http://trends.collegeboard.org/sites/default/files/student-aid-2012-full-report.pdf.

Collins, Chuck, and Sam Pizzigati. 2010. *Resurrect the estate tax.* Washington, DC: Institute for Policy Studies. Retrieved from www.ips-dc.org/articles/resurrect_the_estate_tax.

Collins, Chuck, and Felice Yeskel. 2005. *Economic apartheid in America.* New York: New Press.

Collins, Patricia Hill. 2000. *Black feminist thought.* New York: Routledge.

Collins, Patricia Hill. 2009. *Black feminist thought.* New York: Routledge.

Collins, Randall. 1979. *Credential society.* New York: Academic Press.

Collins, Randall, Janet Saltzman Chafetz, Rae Lesser Blumberg, Scott Coltrane, and Jonathan H. Turner. 1993. Toward an integrated theory of gender stratification. *Sociological Perspectives* 36 (3): 185–216.

Coltrane, Scott. 1989. Household labor and the routine production of gender. *Social Problems* 36 (5): 473–90.

Comedy Central. 2013. Key and Peele: About the show. Retrieved from www.comedycentral.com/shows/key-and-peele.

Commission on Social Determinants of Health. (2008). *Closing the gap in a generation: Health equity through action on the social determinants of health. (Final report of the Commission on Social Determinants of Health.)* Geneva: World Health Organization.

Compa, Lance. 2004. *Unfair advantage: Workers' freedom of association in the United States under international human rights standards.* Ithaca, NY: ILR Press/Cornell University Press.

Conger, Dylan. 2010. Does bilingual education interfere with English-language acquisition? *Social Science Quarterly* 91 (4): 1103–22.

Congressional Budget Office. 2013. The distribution of major tax expenditures in the individual income tax system. Retrieved from www.cbo.gov/sites/default/files/cbo-files/attachments/43768_DistributionTaxExpenditures.pdf.

Conklin, John E. 2010. *Criminology,* 10th ed. Boston: Allyn & Bacon.

Conlin, Michelle. 2008. In the land of plenty, why pay? *BusinessWeek,* October 20, p. 56.

Connell, R. W. 2000. *The men and the boys.* Berkeley: University of California Press.

Connell, R. W. 2005. *Masculinities.* Berkeley: University of California Press.

Connell, Raewyn. 1987. *Gender and power.* Stanford, CA: Stanford University Press.

Conrad, Peter. 2005a. General introduction. In *The sociology of health and illness,* 7th ed., ed. Peter Conrad. New York: Worth.

Conrad, Peter. 2005b. The shifting engines of medicalization. *Journal of Health and Social Behavior* 46 (March): 3–14.

Conrad, Peter. 2007. *The medicalization of society.* Baltimore, MD: Johns Hopkins University Press.

Conrad, Peter, and Kristin K. Barker. 2010. The social construction of illness: Key insights and policy implications. *Journal of Health and Social Behavior* 51 (S): S67–S69.

Conrad, Peter, and Joseph Schneider. 1980. *Deviance and medicalization.* St. Louis, MO: Mosby.

Conway, Oliver. 2004. Congo word "most untranslatable." BBC News, June 22. Retrieved from http://news.bbc.co.uk/2/hi/africa/3830521 .stm.

Cookson, Peter, and Caroline Persell. 1985. *Preparing for power: America's elite boarding schools.* New York: Basic Books.

Cooley, Charles Horton. (1902) 1964. *Human nature and the social order.* New York: Schocken Books.

Coontz, Stephanie. 1992. *The way we never were: American families and the nostalgia trap.* New York: Basic Books.

Coontz, Stephanie. 2000. Historical perspectives on family studies. *Journal of Marriage and Family* 62: 283–97.

Coontz, Stephanie. 2006. *Marriage, a history: How love conquered marriage.* New York: Penguin.

Copen, Casey E., Kimberly Daniels, Jonathan Vespa, and William D. Mosher. 2012. *First marriages in the United States: Data from the 2006–2010 National Survey of Family Growth.* National Health Statistics Reports, No. 49. Hyattsville, MD: National Center for Health Statistics.

Cornell, Drucill, ed. 2000. *Feminism and pornography.* New York: Oxford University Press.

Cornell, Stephen, and Douglas Hartmann. 2007. *Ethnicity and race: Making identities in a changing world.* Thousand Oaks, CA: Pine Forge Press.

Cose, Ellis. 1995. *The rage of a privileged class.* New York: Harper Perennial.

Coser, Lewis. 1956. *The functions of social conflict.* New York: Free Press.

Costa-Font, Joan, David Elvira, and Oscar Mascarilla-Miro. 2009 "Ageing in place?" Exploring elderly people's housing preferences in Spain. *Urban Studies* 46 (2): 295–316.

Cottle, Simon. 2007. Ethnography and news production: New(s) developments in the field. *Sociology Compass* 1 (1): 1–16.

Cowie, Jefferson, and Joseph Heathcott, eds. 2003. *Beyond the ruins: The meanings of deindustrialization.* Ithaca, NY: Cornell University Press.

Cowley, Geoffrey, and Karen Springen. 2005. Designing heart-healthy communities. *Newsweek,* October 3, pp. 60–66.

Crockett, Alasdair, and David Voas. 2006. Generations of decline: Religious change in 20th-century Britain. *Journal for the Scientific Study of Religion* 45 (4): 567–84.

Cromartie, John. 2013. Nonmetro areas as a whole experience first period of population loss. *Amber Waves,* May 6. Washington, DC: United States Department of Agriculture. Retrieved from www.ers.usda.gov/amber-waves/2013-may/nonmetro-areas-as-a-whole-experience-first-period-of-population-loss.aspx#.U07hDvldV8E.

Cromartie, John, and Shawn Bucholtz. 2008. Defining the "rural" in rural America. *Amber Waves,* June. Retrieved from www.ers.usda.gov/AmberWaves/June08/Features/RuralAmerica.htm.

Croteau, David, and William Hoynes. 1994a. All the usual suspects: *MacNeil/Lehrer* and *Nightline.* In *By Invitation Only: How the Media Limit Political Debate,* pp. 105–37. Monroe, ME: Common Courage Press.

Croteau, David, and William Hoynes. 1994b. *By invitation only: How the media limit political debate.* Monroe, ME: Common Courage Press.

Croteau, David, and William Hoynes. 2006. *The business of media: Corporate media and the public interest.* Thousand Oaks, CA: Pine Forge Press.

Croteau, David, and William Hoynes. 2014. *Media/society: Industries, images, and audiences,* 5th ed. Thousand Oaks, CA: Sage.

Croteau, David, William Hoynes, and Kevin Carragee. 1996. The political diversity of public television. *Journalism and Mass Communication Monographs* 157: 1–55.

Croteau, David, William Hoynes, and Stefania Milan. 2011. *Media/society: Industries, images, and audiences,* 4th ed. Thousand Oaks, CA: Pine Forge Press.

Crothers, Lane. 2009. *Globalization and American popular culture,* 2nd ed. Lanham, MD: Rowman & Littlefield.

Crumley, Bruce. 2009. Will France impose a ban on the burqa? *Time,* June 19.

Curtis, Mary C. 2013. Backlash greets Cheerios ad with interracial family. *Washington Post,* May 31. Retrieved from www.washingtonpost.com/blogs/she-the-people/wp/2013/05/31/backlash-greets-cheerios-ad-with-interracial-family/.

Czaja, Ronald, and Johnny Blair. 2004. *Designing surveys,* 2nd ed. Thousand Oaks, CA: Pine Forge Press.

Dahl, Robert. 1957. The concept of power. *Behavioral Science* 2: 201–15.

Dahl, Robert. 1961. *Who governs? Democracy and power in an American city.* New Haven, CT: Yale University Press.

Dahrendorf, Ralf. 1959. *Class and class conflict in industrial society.* Stanford, CA: Stanford University Press.

Danaher, Kevin, and Anuradha Mittal. 2004. *10 Reasons to abolish the IMF and World Bank.* Westminster, MD: Seven Stories Press.

Daniels, Roger. 1997. *Not like us: Immigrants and minorities in America, 1890–1924.* Chicago: Ivan R. Dee.

Das, Satyajit. 2010. *Traders, guns, and money.* New York: Financial Times/Prentice Hall.

Davidov, Eldad, Bart Meuleman, Jaak Billiet and Peter Schmidt. 2008. Values and support for immigration: A cross-country comparison. *European Sociological Review* 24 (5): 583–99.

Davidov, Eldad, Peter Schmidt, and Shalom H. Schwartz. 2008. Bringing values back in. *Public Opinion Quarterly* 72: 420–45.

Davie, Grace. 1994. *Religion in Britain since 1945: Believing without belonging.* Oxford: Blackwell.

Davies, Karen. 2003. The body and doing gender: The relations between doctors and nurses in hospital work. *Sociology of Health & Illness* 25 (7): 720–42.

Davies, Scott, and Julian Tanner. 2003. The long arm of the law: Effects of labeling on employment. *Sociological Quarterly* 44 (3): 385–404.

Davis, Donna Z. 2013. A study of relationships in online virtual environments. In *Advancing research methods with new technologies*, ed. Natalie Sappleton, pp. 187–205. Hershey, PA: Information Science Reference.

Davis, Kathy, Monique Leijenaar, and Jantine Oldersma. 1991. *The gender of power.* Thousand Oaks, CA: Sage.

Davis, Kingsley. 1947. Final note on a case of extreme isolation. *American Journal of Sociology* 52 (5): 432–37.

Davis, Kingsley, and Wilbert Moore. 1945. Some principles of stratification. *American Sociological Review* 10: 242–49.

Davis, Shannon N., and Theodore N. Greenstein. 2004. Cross national variations in the division of household labor. *Journal of Marriage and Family* 66 (5).

Day, Dorothy. 1952. *The long loneliness.* New York: Harper & Row.

Death Penalty Information Center. 2013. National statistics on the death penalty and race. Retrieved September 19, 2013, from www.deathpenaltyinfo.org/race-death-row-inmates-executed-1976#racestat.

Deegan, Mary Jo. 1988. *Jane Addams and the men of the Chicago School, 1892–1918.* New Brunswick, NJ: Transaction.

Della Porta, Donatella, and Mario Diani. 2006. *Social movements: An introduction.* Malden, MA: Blackwell.

Demo, David H., Katherine R. Allen, and Mark A. Fine, eds. 2000. *Handbook of family diversity.* New York: Oxford University Press.

Denvir, Daniel. 2011. The 10 most segregated urban areas in America. Retrieved from http://politics.salon.com/2011/03/29/most_segregated_cities/slide_show/10/.

Denyer, Simon. 2013. Chinese families still at mercy of officials despite announced easing of one-child policy. *Washington Post*, November 22. Retrieved from www.washingtonpost.com/world/chinese-families-still-at-mercy-of-officials-despite-easing-of-one-child-policy/2013/11/21/f5a6db22-5215-11e3-9ee6-2580086d8254_story.html.

Derber, Charles, William A. Schwartz, and Yale Magrass. 1990. *Power in the highest degree.* New York: Oxford University Press.

Desilver, Drew. 2013. U.S. income inequality, on rise for decades, is now highest since 1928. Washington, DC: Pew Research Center. Retrieved from www.pewresearch.org/fact-tank/2013/12/05/u-s-income-inequality-on-rise-for-decades-is-now-highest-since-1928/.

Devlin, Bernie, Stephen E. Fienberg, Daniel P. Resnick, Kathryn Roeder, eds. 1997. *Intelligence, genes, and success: Scientists respond to the bell curve.* New York: Springer-Verlag.

Dey, Judy Goldberg, and Catherine Hill. 2007. *Behind the pay gap.* Washington, DC: American Association of University Women Educational Foundation.

DeYoung, Karen, and Scott Clement. 2013. Many Americans say Afghan war isn't worth fighting. *Washington Post*, July 25. Retrieved from www.washingtonpost.com/world/national-security/many-americans-say-afghan-war-isnt-worth-fighting/2013/07/25/d0447d44-f559-11e2-aa2e-4088616498b4_story.html.

Dill, Karen E., and Kathryn P. Thill. 2007. Video game characters and the socialization of gender roles. *Sex Roles* 57: 851–64.

Dines, Gail. 2010. *Pornland.* Boston: Beacon Press.

Dinovitzer, Ronit, Nancy Reichman, and Joyce Sterling. 2009. The differential valuation of women's work: A new look at the gender gap in lawyers' incomes. *Social Forces* 88 (2): 819–64.

Do, D. Phuong, Brian Karl Finch, Ricardo Basurto-Davila, Chloe Bird, Jose Escarce, and Nicole Lurie. 2008. Does place explain racial health disparities? *Social Science & Medicine* 67: 1258–68.

Dobbelaere, Karel. 1999. Towards an integrated perspective of the processes related to the descriptive concept of secularization. *Sociology of Religion* 60 (3): 229–47.

Domhoff, G. William. 2013. *Who rules America?* New York: McGraw-Hill.

Douglass, Frederick. 2003. *Frederick Douglass on slavery and the Civil War: Selections from his writings*, ed. Joslyn T. Pine. Mineola, NY: Dover.

Downes, David, and Paul Rock. 2011. *Understanding deviance*, 6th ed. New York: Oxford University Press.

Downie, Leonard, Jr., and Robert G. Kaiser. 2003. *The news about the news: American journalism in peril.* New York, Vintage.

Doyle, Thomas P., A. W. Richard Sipe, and Patrick J. Wall. 2006. *Sex, priests, and secret codes: The Catholic Church's 2,000 year paper trail of sexual abuse.* Los Angeles: Bonus Books.

Draper, Elaine. 2003. *The company doctor.* New York: Russell Sage Foundation.

Dreifus, Claudia. 2005. A sociologist confronts "the messy stuff" of race, genes and disease. *New York Times*, October 18, p. 2.

Drum, Kevin. 2013. The Google panopticon is set to become even more onsicient. *Mother Jones.* Retrieved September 20, 2013, from www.motherjones.com/print/234636.

Du Bois, W.E.B. (1899) 1996. *The Philadelphia negro: A social study.* Philadelphia: University of Pennsylvania Press.

Du Bois, W.E.B. (1903) 2005. *The souls of black folk.* New York: Simon & Schuster.

Du Bois, W.E.B. (1935) 1998. *Black reconstruction in the United States, 1860–1880.* New York: Free Press.

Duchrow, Ulrich. 2011. A European revival of liberation theology. *Tikkun* 26 (1): 74. Retrieved from www.tikkun.org/article.php/jan2011duchrow.

Dudley, Kathryn Marie. 1997. *The end of the line: Lost jobs, new lives in postindustrial America.* Chicago: University of Chicago Press.

Dugan, Máire A. 2003. Empowerment. In *Beyond intractability*, ed. Guy Burgess and Heidi Burgess. Boulder, CO: Conflict Research Consortium, University of Colorado. Retrieved from www.beyondintractability.org/essay/empowerment.

Duggan, Maeve. 2013. Photo and video sharing grow online. Washington, DC: Pew Research Center. Retrieved from www.pewinternet.org/~/media//Files/Reports/2013/PIP_Photos%20and%20videos%20online_102813.pdf.

Dugsin, R. 2001. Conflict and healing in the family experience of second-generation emigrants from Indian living in North America. *Family Process* 40 (2): 233–41.

Duhigg, Charles. 2007. For elderly investors, instant experts abound. *New York Times*, July 8, pp. 1, 14.

Dunlap, Riley E., and William R. Catton Jr. 1994. Struggling with human exceptionalism: The rise, decline and revitalization of environmental sociology. *American Sociologist* 25: 5–30.

Dunn, Robert G. 2000. Identity, commodification, and consumer culture. In *Identity and social change*, ed. Joseph E. Davis, pp. 109–34. New Brunswick, NJ: Transaction.

Durand, Jorge, Douglas S. Massey, and Rene Zenteno. 2001. Mexican immigration to the United States: Continuities and changes. *Latin American Research Review* 36 (1): 107–11.

Durkheim, Emile. (1893) 1997. *The division of labor in society.* New York: Free Press.

Durkheim, Emile. (1895) 1982. *The rules of sociological method*, trans. Sarah A. Solovay and John H. Mueller. New York: Free Press.

Durkheim, Emile. (1897) 1951. *Suicide*, trans. John A. Spaulding and George Simpson. New York: Free Press.

Durkheim, Emile. (1915) 2001. *Elementary forms of the religious life*, trans. Carol Cosman. New York: Oxford University Press.

Durkheim, Emile. (1922) 1956. *Education and sociology*, trans. D. F. Pocock. Glencoe, IL: Free Press.

Durkheim, Emile. (1925) 1961. *Moral education*, trans. Everett K. Wilson. Glencoe, IL: Free Press.

Durkheim, Emile. (1938) 1977. *The evolution of educational thought*, trans. Peter Collins. Boston: Routledge/Kegan Paul.

Duster, Troy. 2003. *Backdoor to eugenics*. New York: Routledge.

Dvorak, Petula. 2010. For bullied gay teens, the world is still far from accepting. *Washington Post*, October 4.

Dwoskin, Elisabeth. 2013. Google explores dropping cookies. *The Wall Street Journal*, September 19, p. B1.

Dyer, Gwynne. 2004. *War: The lethal custom*, revised ed. New York: Carol & Graf.

Dyson, Michael Eric. 2000. *I may not get there with you: The true Martin Luther King Jr.* New York: Free Press.

Eaton, Joe, and M. B. Pell. 2010. Analysis: Health lobbyists' powerful impact on reform bills. Kaiser Health News. Retrieved from www.kaiserhealthnews.org/Stories/2010/February/ 24/CPI-health-lobbying .aspx.

The Economist. 2007. A world wide web of terror. July 14, pp. 28–30.

Economist Intelligence Unit. 2013. Democracy Index 2012: Democracy at a standstill. *The Economist*. Retrieved from www.eiu.com/Handlers/WhitepaperHandler.ashx?fi=Democracy-Index-2012.pdf&mode=wp&campaignid=DemocracyIndex12.

Edelman, Laren B., and Mark C. Suchman. 1997. The legal environments of organizations. *Annual Review of Sociology* 23: 479–515.

Edin, Kathryn, and Maria Kefalas. 2005. *Promises I can keep: Why poor women put motherhood before marriage*. New York: Basic Books.

Education for All Global Monitoring Report. 2010. *Reaching the marginalized*. UNESCO Publishing. Retrieved from www.unesco.org/ new/en/education/themes/leading-the -international-agenda/efareport/reports/2010-marginalization/.

Edwards, Richard. 1982. *Contested terrain: The transformation of the workplace in the twentieth century*. New York: Basic Books.

Ehrlich, Paul R. 1986. *The population bomb*. New York: Ballantine Books.

Einstein, Albert. (1946) 1999. Quoted in *The Oxford Dictionary of Quotations*, ed. Elizabeth Knowles, p. 290. New York: Oxford University Press.

Elder, Glen. 1999. *Children of the Great Depression*. Boulder, CO: Westview Press.

Elder, Glen H., Jr. 2006. Life course perspective. In *The Blackwell encyclopedia of sociology*, ed. George Ritzer, pp. 2634–39. Boston: Blackwell.

Eller, Cynthia. 2001. *The myth of patriarchal prehistory*. Boston: Beacon.

Elson, Diane, and Hanke Keklik. 2003. *Progress of the world's women, 2002*, vol. 2. New York: UN Development Fund for Women.

Elwell, Craig K. 2013. Inflation and the real minimum wage: A fact sheet. Washington, DC: Congressional Research Service.

Retrieved from www.fas.org/sgp/crs/misc/R42973.pdf.

Emerson, Michael O., and David Hartman. 2006. The rise of religious fundamentalism. *Annual Review of Sociology* 32: 127–44.

Engels, Frederick. (1884) 1972. *The origin of the family, private property and the state*. New York: International.

Entman, Robert, and Andrew Rojecki. 2001. *The black image in the white mind*. Chicago: University of Chicago Press.

EPE Research Center. 2013. *Diplomas count 2013*. Editorial Projects in Education. Retrieved from www.edweek.org/ew/toc/2013/06/06/

Erickson, Kai. 1966. *Wayward puritans: A study in the sociology of deviance*. New York: Wiley.

Ericsson. 2013. *Ericsson mobility report*. June. Stockholm, Sweden. Retrieved from www .ericsson.com/res/docs/2013/ericsson-mobility-report-june-2013.pdf.

Eriksson, Malin, and Maria Emmelin. 2013. What constitutes a health-enabling neighborhood? *Social Science & Medicine* 97: 112–23.

Erlanger, Steven. 2010. France: Senate passes bill on facial veils. *New York Times*, September 15, p. A6.

Espenshade, Thomas J., Chang Y. Chung, and Joan L. Walling. 2004. Admission preferences for minority students, athletes, and legacies at elite universities. *Social Science Quarterly* 85 (5): 1422–46.

Esposito, John L., and John Voll. 2001. *Makers of contemporary Islam*. New York: Oxford University Press.

European Audiovisual Observatory. 2012. Focus 2012: World film market trends. Retrieved from www.obs.coe.int/oea_publ/market/focus-bis.html.

Evangelical Climate Initiative. 2006. Climate change: An evangelical call to action. Retrieved from http://christiansandclimate.org/learn/call-to-action.

Evans, Peter. 1997. Review of *The clash of civilizations and the remaking of the world order*. *Contemporary Sociology* 26 (6): 691–93.

Evans, Sarah. 1980. *Personal politics*. New York: Vintage.

Ewen, Stuart. 2001. *Captains of consciousness: Advertising and the social roots of consumer culture*. New York: McGraw-Hill.

Facebook. 2013. Facebook for business. Retrieved from www.facebook.com/business/overview .

Fadiman, Anne. 2012. *The spirit catches you and you fall down*. New York: Farrar, Straus & Giroux.

Farkas, Steve, Jean Johnson, and Tony Foleno with Ann Duffett and Patrick Foley. 2001. For goodness' sake: Why so many want religion to play a greater role in American life. New York: Public Agenda. Retrieved from www.publicagenda.org/files/pdf/for_goodness_sake.pdf.

Fass, Paula, and Mary Mason, eds. 2000. *Childhood in America*. New York: New York University Press.

Fastenberg, Dan. 2010. A brief history of international gay marriage. *Time*, July 22. Retrieved from www.time.com/time/world/article/0,8599,2005678,00.html.

Fausto-Sterling, Anne. 2000. *Sexing the body*. New York: Basic Books.

Feagin, Joe, and Hernan Vera. 2001. *Liberation sociology*. Boulder, CO: Westview Press.

Feagin, Joe R., and Eileen O'Brien. 2003. *White men on race power, privilege, and the shaping of cultural consciousness*. Boston: Beacon Press.

Feagin, Joe R., and Melvin P. Sikes. 1994. *Living with racism: The black middle class experience*. Boston: Beacon Press.

Federal Bureau of Investigation. 2012. Hate crime statistics 2011. Retrieved from www .fbi.gov/about-us/cjis/ucr/hate-crime/2011.

Federal Interagency Forum on Aging-Related Statistics. 2012. *Older Americans 2012: Key indicators of well-being*. Washington, DC: U.S. Government Printing Office. Retrieved from http://agingstats.gov/agingstatsdotnet/Main_Site/Data/2012_Documents/docs/EntireChartbook.pdf.

Federal Trade Commission. 2010. FTC approves final order settling charges that public relations firm used misleading online endorsements to market gaming apps. November 26. Retrieved from www.ftc .gov/opa/2010/11/reverb.shtm.

Fels, Anna. 2005. *Necessary dreams: Ambition in women's changing lives*. New York: Anchor.

Feng, Jing, Ian Spence, and Jay Pratt. 2007. Playing an action video game reduces gender differences in spatial cognition. *Psychological Science* 18 (10): 850–55.

Ferree, Myra Marx. 1990. Beyond separate spheres: Feminism and family research. *Journal of Marriage and Family* 52: 866–84.

Ferriss, Susan. 2003. Free trade's broken promises. (Austin) *American-Statesman*, November 5. Retrieved from www.statesman.com/specialreports/ content/specialreports/mexico_farms/1102 mexfactory.html.

Field, Kelly. 2010. Senators vow to crack down on "bad actors" in the for-profit sector. *Chronicle of Higher Education*, June 24. Retrieved from http://chronicle.com/article/Senators-Vow-to -Crack-Down-on/66058/.

Filson, Jennifer, Emilio Ulloa, Cristin Runfola, and Audrey Hokoda. 2010. Does powerlessness explain the relationship between partner violence and depression? *Journal of Interpersonal Violence* 25 (3): 400–15.

Financial Crisis Inquiry Commission. 2011. *The financial crisis inquiry report*. New York: Public Affairs.

Finberg, Howard I. 2005. Our complex media day. Retrieved from www.poynter.org/content/ content_view.asp?id=89510.

Fine, Gary Alan. 2006. Shopfloor cultures. *Sociological Quarterly* 47: 1–19.

Fiorina, Morris. 2011. *Culture war? The myth of a polarized America*, 3rd ed. Boston: Longman.

Fischer, Claude. 1992. *America calling: A social history of the telephone to 1940*. Berkeley: University of California Press.

Fischer, Claude, and Michael Hout. 2006. *Century of difference: How America changed in the last one hundred years.* New York: Russell Sage Foundation.

Fischer, Claude, Martin Sanchez Jankowski, Samuel R. Lucas, Ann Swidler, and Kim Voss. 1996. *Inequality by design: Cracking the bell curve myth.* Princeton, NJ: Princeton University Press.

Fischer, Claude, Michael Hout, Martin Sanchez Jankowski, Samuel R. Lucas, Ann Swidler, and Kim Voss. 1996. *Inequality by design: Cracking the bell curve myth.* Princeton, NJ: Princeton University Press.

Fischer, Kimberly, Muriel Egerton, Jonathan I. Gershuny, and John P. Robinson. 2007. Gender convergence in the American Heritage time use study. *Social Indicators Research* 82: 1–33.

Fishman, Mark. 1980. *Manufacturing the news.* Austin: University of Texas Press.

Flacks, Richard. 1988. *Making history.* New York: Columbia University Press.

Fletcher, Colin. 1974. *Beneath the surface.* Boston: Routledge.

Flew, Terry. 2007. *Understanding global media.* New York: Palgrave Macmillan.

Flint, Anthony. 2006. *This land: The battle over sprawl and the future of America.* Baltimore, MD: Johns Hopkins University Press.

Flora, Cornelia Butler, and Jan L. Flora. 2008. *Rural communities,* 3rd ed. Boulder, CO: Westview Press.

Floyd-Thomas, Stacy M., and Anthony B. Pinn, eds. 2010. *Liberation theologies in the United States.* New York: New York University Press.

Forsyth, Donelson. 2010. *Group dynamics.* Belmont, CA: Wadsworth.

Forsyth, Donelson. 2013. *Group dynamics.* Belmont, CA: Cengage Learning.

Foster, John Bellamy, and Fred Magdoff. 2009. *The great financial crisis: Causes and consequences.* New York: Monthly Review Press.

Foucault, Michel. 1979. *Discipline and punish,* trans. Alan Sheridan. New York: Vintage.

Foucault, Michel. 1980. *The history of sexuality,* vol. 1. New York: Vintage.

Foucault, Michel. 1995. *Discipline and punish: The birth of the prison,* trans. Alan Sheridan. New York: Vintage.

Fowler, Geoffrey A. 2005. In Asia, it's nearly impossible to tell a song from an ad. *Wall Street Journal,* May 31, pp. A1, A10.

Fowler, James H., and Nicholas A. Christakis. 2008. Dynamic spread of happiness in a large social network: Longitudinal analysis over 20 years in the Framingham Heart Study. *British Medical Journal* 337: a2338.

Fox, Greer Litton, and Velma McBride Murray. 2000. Gender and families: Feminist perspectives and family research. *Journal of Marriage and Family* 62: 1160–72.

Francis, Richard C. 2011. *Epigenetics: How environment shapes our genes.* New York: Norton.

Frank, Thomas. 1997. *The conquest of cool.* Chicago: University of Chicago Press.

Frankowski, Barbara L. 2004. Sexual orientation and adolescents. *Pediatrics* 113 (6): 1827–32.

Fraser, Nancy. 1992. Rethinking the public sphere: A contribution to the critique of actually existing democracy. In *Habermas and the Public Sphere,* ed. Craig Calhoun, pp. 109–42. Cambridge, MA: MIT Press.

Fraser, Steve, ed. 1995. *The bell curve wars.* New York: Basic Books.

Freedman, Robert. 2009. *Noise wars: Compulsory media and our loss of autonomy.* New York: Algora.

Freire, Paulo. 1970. *Pedagogy of the oppressed,* transl. Myra Bergman Ramos. New York: Seabury Press.

French, John R. P. Jr., and Bertram Raven. (1959) 2001. The bases of social power. In *The negotiation sourcebook,* ed. Ira G. Asherman and Sandra Vance Asherman, pp. 61–73. Amherst, MA: HRD Press.

Frey, William H. 2013. A big city growth revival? Washington, DC: Brookings Institution. Retrieved from www.brookings.edu/research/opinions/2013/05/28-city-growth-frey.

Fried, Mindy. 2008. The evaluator in the field as an outsider within. *Footnotes* 36 (3). Retrieved from www.asanet.org/footnotes/mar08_R/fn6 .html.

Friedland, Lewis A., and Shauna Morimoto. 2005. The changing lifeworld of young people: Risk, resume-padding, and civic engagement. CIRCLE Working Paper 40. Medford, MA: Center for Information and Research on Civic Learning and Engagement.

Friedland, N. 1976. Social influence via threats. *Journal of Experimental Social Psychology* 12: 552–63.

Friedman, Jeffrey, and Richard A. Posner, eds. 2009. *What caused the financial crisis.* Philadelphia: University of Pennsylvania Press.

Friedrichs, David O. 2009. *Trusted criminals: White collar crime in contemporary society,* 4th ed. Belmont, CA: Wadsworth.

Frumkin, Howard. 2003. Healthy places: Exploring the evidence. *American Journal of Public Health* 93 (9): 1451–56.

Fuchs, Christian. 2009. Social networking sites and the surveillance society: A critical case study of the usage of StudiVZ, Facebook, and MySpace by students in Salzburg in the context of electronic surveillance. Salzburg/Vienna: Research Group UTI.

Fussell, Elizabeth. 2006. Leaving New Orleans: Social stratification, networks, and hurricane evacuation. In *Understanding Katrina: Per-spectives from the social sciences.* Retrieved from http://understandingkatrina.ssrc.org/Fussell/.

Futrell, Robert, and Pete Simi. 2004. Free spaces, collective identity, and the persistence of U.S. white power activism. *Social Problems* 51 (1): 16–42.

Fuwa, Makiko. 2004. Macro-level gender inequality and the division of household labor in 22 countries. *American Sociological Review* 69 (6): 751–67.

Gaines, Donna. 1991. *Teenage wasteland.* New York: Pantheon.

Gaines, Donna. 2003. *A misfit's manifesto: The spiritual journey of a rock-and-roll heart.* New York: Villard.

Gallian, Joseph A. 2004. A conversation with Melanie Wood. *Math Horizons* (September): 13–14, 31.

Gallup, Cindy. 2011. *Make love, not porn: Technology's hard-core impact on human behavior.* TED Books.

Galtung, Johan. 1996. *Peace by peaceful means.* London: Sage.

Galtung, Johan. 2000. *Conflict transformation by peaceful means.* New York: United Nations.

Galtung, Johan. 2009. *The fall of the US empire–and then what?* TRANSCEND University Press, www.transcend.org/tup/index.php?book=5.

Gamson, William A., Bruce Fireman, and Steven Rytina. 1982. *Encounters with unjust authority.* Homewood, IL: Dorsey Press.

Gans, Herbert J. 1999. *Popular culture & high culture,* rev. ed. New York: Basic Books.

Gans, Herbert J. 2005. *Deciding what's news,* 25th anniversary ed. Chicago: Northwestern University Press.

Ganz, Marshall. 2009. *Why David sometimes wins: Leadership, organization, and strategy in the California farm worker movement.* New York: Oxford University Press.

Garcia, Marlen. 2009. At some schools, budget cuts put the kibosh on sports. *USA Today,* September 2. Retrieved from www.usatoday .com/sports/preps/2009-09-02-budget_sports _cuts_N.htm.

Gardner, Gary, Erik Assadourian, and Radhia Sarin. 2004. The state of consumption today. In *The state of the world, 2004* by the Worldwatch Institute, pp. 3–23 New York: Norton.

Garfinkel, Harold. 1967. *Studies in ethnomethodology.* New York: Prentice-Hall.

Garland, David. 1993. *Punishment and modern society.* Chicago: University of Chicago Press.

Garland, David. 2012. *Peculiar institution: America's death penalty in an age of abolition.* Cambridge, MA: Belknap Press.

Gaskell, Stephanie. 2013. America's longest war. *National Journal,* October 7. Retrieved from www.nationaljournal.com/national-security/america-s-longest-war-20131007.

Gates, Gary J. 2010. New Census Bureau data shows growth in same-sex couples outpacing population. Los Angeles: Williams Institute, UCLA School of Law.

Gates, Gary J. 2011. How many people are lesbian, gay, bisexual and transgender? Los Angeles: Williams Institute, UCLA School of Law.

Gauchat, Gordon. 2012. Politicization of science in the public sphere: A study of public trust in the United States, 1974–2010. *American Sociological Review* 77 (2): 167–87.

Gauchet, M. 1997. *The disenchantment of the world*. Princeton, NJ: Princeton University Press.

Gauntlett, David. 2002. *Media, gender and identity*. New York: Routledge.

Gaventa, John. 1982. *Power and powerlessness*. Urbana: University of Illinois Press.

Gazzaniga, Michael. 1998. *The mind's past*. Berkeley: University of California Press.

Gecas, Viktor. 2008. The ebb and flow of sociological interest in values. *Sociological Forum* 23 (June): 344–50.

Gelder, Ken, ed. 2005. *The subcultures reader*, 2nd ed. New York: Routledge.

Gerbner, George, Larry Gross, Michael Morgan, and Nancy Signorielli. 2008. Growing up with television: Cultivation processes. In *Media effects: Advances in theory and research*, ed. Jennings Bryant and Dolf Zillmann. Hillsdale, NJ: Erlbaum.

German Bundestag. 2014. Parliamentary groups, as of 3 March 2011. Retrieved from www.bundestag.de/htdocs_e/bundestag/groups/index.html.

Gerson, Kathleen. 2010. *Hard choices: How women decide about work, career, and motherhood*. Berkeley: University of California Press.

Gerson, Kathleen. 2010. *The unfinished revolution: How a new generation is reshaping family, work and gender in America*. New York: Oxford University Press.

Gibson, Campbell. 1998. Population of the 100 largest cities and other urban places in the United States: 1790 to 1990. Retrieved from www.census.gov/population/www/documentation/twps0027/twps0027.html.

Gibson, Campbell, and Kay Jung. 2002. Historical census statistics on population totals by race, 1790 to 1990, Table 1. Washington, DC: U.S. Census Bureau. Retrieved from www.census.gov/population/www/documentation/twps0056/twps0056.html.

Gibson, Margaret. 1988. *Accommodation without assimilation: Sikh immigrants in an American high school*. Ithaca, NY: Cornell University Press.

Gieryn, Thomas F. 2000. A space for place in sociology. *Annual Review of Sociology* 26: 463–96.

Gilbert, Dennis. 2011. *The American class structure in an age of growing inequality*, 8th ed. Thousand Oaks, CA: Pine Forge Press.

Gilens, Martin. 2005. Inequality and democratic responsiveness. *Public Opinion Quarterly* 69 (5): 778–96.

Gill, Rosiland. 2007. *Gender and the media*. Malden, MA: Polity Press.

Gilley, Brian Joseph. 2006. *Becoming two-spirit: Gay identity and social acceptance in Indian country*. Omaha: University of Nebraska Press.

Ginsborg, Paul. 2005. *Silvio Berlusconi: Television, power and patrimony*. London: Verso.

Gladwell, Malcolm. 1997. The coolhunt. *The New Yorker*, March 17.

Glanz, James, and Alissa Rubin. 2007. Blackwater shooting was "deliberate murder," Iraq says. *New York Times*, October 8. Retrieved from www.nytimes.com/2007/10/08/news/08iht-iraq.4.7803511.html.

Glass, Ira. 2008. The giant pool of money. *This American Life*, May 9. Retrieved from www.thisamericanlife.org/radio-archives/episode/355/the-giant-pool-of-money.

Glassner, Barry. 2009. *The culture of fear*, 10th anniversary ed. New York: Basic Books.

Goe, W. Richard, and Sean Noonan. 2007. The sociology of community. In *21st century sociology: A reference handbook*, ed. Clifton D. Bryant and Dennis L. Peck, pp. 455–64. Thousand Oaks, CA: Sage.

Goffman, Erving. 1959. *The presentation of self in everyday life*. Garden City, NY: Doubleday Anchor Books.

Goffman, Erving. 1961. *Asylums*. New York: Random House.

Goffman, Erving. 1963. *Stigma: Notes on the management of spoiled identity*. New York: Simon & Schuster.

Goffman, Erving. 1974. *Frame analysis*. New York: Harper & Row.

Goldsmith, Marshall. 2004. Why even thinking about retirement can be a bad idea. *Fast Company* 78 (January).

Goldsmith, Pat Antonio. 2004. Schools' racial mix, students' optimism, and the black-white and Latino-white achievement gaps. *Sociology of Education* 77 (2): 121–47.

Göle, Nilüfer. 2011. *Islam in Europe*. Princeton, NJ: Markus Weiner.

Gonzalez, Juan. 2000. *Harvest of empire: A history of Latinos in America*. New York: Penguin.

Goodman, Amy. 2007. Egyptian human rights activist Saad Eddin Ibrahim defies threats, arrests to challenge U.S.-backed Mubarak government. Retrieved from www.democracynow.org/2007/10/10/egyptian_human_rights_activist_saad_eddin.

Gordon, Colin. 2013. Growing together, growing apart. Washington, DC: Economic Policy Institute. Retrieved from www.epi.org/blog/growing-growing/.

Gordon, David M., Richard Edwards, and Michael Reich. 1982. *Segmented work, divided workers*. New York: Cambridge University Press.

Gorman, Siobhan, Evan Perez, and Janet Hook. 2013. U.S. collects vast data trove. *The Wall Street Journal*, June 7.

Gottdiener, Mark, and Ray Hutchison. 2010. *The new urban sociology*, 4th ed. Boulder, CO: Westview Press.

Gould, Kenneth A., David N. Pellow, and Allen Schnaiberg. 2008. *The treadmill of production: Injustice and unsustainability in the global economy*. Boulder, CO: Paradigm.

Government Accountability Office. 2008. Tax administration: Comparison of the reported tax liabilities of foreign- and U.S.-controlled corporations, 1998–2005. Retrieved from www.gao.gov/new.items/d08957.pdf.

Gramsci, Antonio. 1971. *Selections from the prison notebooks*, ed. and trans. Quintin Hoare and Geoffrey Nowell Smith. New York: International.

Granfield, Robert. 1992. *Making elite lawyers*. New York: Routledge.

Granfield, Robert, and Thomas Koenig. 1990. From activism to pro bono. *Critical Sociology* 17 (1): 57–80.

Granovetter, Mark. 1985. Economic action and social structure: The problem of embeddedness. *American Journal of Sociology* 91 (3): 481–510.

Granovetter, Mark S. 1973. The strength of weak ties. *American Journal of Sociology* 78 (6): 1360–80.

Granovetter, Mark S. 1974. *Getting a job*. Cambridge, MA: Harvard University Press.

Gray, Herman. 2004. *Watching race*. Minneapolis: University of Minnesota.

Gray, John. 2004. *Men are from Mars, women from Venus*. New York: Harper.

Greeley, Andrew. 2004. *Religion in Europe at the end of the second millennium: A sociological profile*. Edison, NJ: Transaction.

Green, Sara, Christine Davis, Elana Karshmer, Pete Marsh, and Benjamin Straight. 2005. Living stigma: The impact of labeling, stereotyping, separation, status loss, and discrimination in the lives of individuals with disabilities and their families. *Sociological Inquiry* 75 (2): 197–215.

Greenhouse, Steven. 2010. Ending strike, Mott's plant union accepts deal. *New York Times*, September 14, 2010, p. B6.

Greenwald, Glenn. 2014. *No place to hide: Edward Snowden, the NSA, and the U.S. surveillance state*. New York: Metropolitan Books.

Greider, William. 1999. *Fortress America*. New York: Public Affairs/Perseus.

Greider, William. 2010. *Come home, America*. New York: Rodale Press.

Griffin, Larry J. 2004. "Generations and collective memory" revisited. *American Sociological Review* 69 (4): 544–57.

Griswold, Daniel T. 2009. *Mad about trade: Why main street America should embrace globalization*. Washington, DC: Cato Institute.

Gross, Michael B. 2004. *The war against Catholicism*. Ann Arbor: University of Michigan Press.

Grubb, Ben. 2013. Do as we say, not as we do: Googlers don't telecommute. *The Sydney Morning Herald*. February 19. Retrieved from www.smh.com.au/it-pro/business-it/do-as-we-say-not-as-we-do-googlers-dont-telecommute-20130218-2eo8w.html.

Grusky, David B., and Manwai C. Ku. 2008. Doom, gloom, and inequality. In *Social stratification*, ed. David B. Grusky, pp. 2–28. Boulder, CO: Westview Press.

The Guardian. 2013. The NSA files. Retrieved July 23, 2013, from www.guardian.co.uk/world/the-nsa-files.

Guba, Egon, and Yvonna Lincoln. 1994. Competing paradigms in qualitative research. In *Handbook of Qualitative Research*, ed. N. Denzin and Yvonna Lincoln, pp. 105–17. Thousand Oaks, CA: Sage.

Guo, Guang. 2005. Twin studies: What can they tell us about nature and nurture? *Contexts* 4 (3): 43–47.

Gusfield, Joseph. 1996. *Contested meanings: The construction of alcohol problems.* Madison: University of Wisconsin Press.

Haas, Mark L. 2008. Pax Americana Geriatrica. *Miller-McCune*, August, pp. 31–39.

Habermas, Jurgen. 2002. *Religion and rationality*, trans. E. Mendieta. Cambridge, MA: MIT Press.

Hadaway, C. Kirk, Penny Long Marler, and Mark Chaves. 1993. What the polls don't show: A closer look at U.S. church attendance. *American Sociological Review* 58: 741–52.

Hadaway, C. Kirk, Penny Long Marler, and Mark Chavez. 1998. Overreporting church attendance in America. *American Sociological Review* 63: 122–30.

Hall, Richard, and Pamela Tolbert. 2004. *Organizations*, 9th ed. Englewood Cliffs, NJ: Prentice Hall.

Hamburger, Philip. 2002. *Separation of church and state.* Cambridge, MA: Harvard University Press.

Hamilton, Emily A., Laurie Mintz, and Susan Kashubeck-West. 2007. Predictors of media effects on body dissatisfaction in European American women. *Sex Roles* 56 (5–6): 397–402.

Hamm, Bernd, and Russell Smandych, eds. 2005. *Cultural imperialism.* Toronto, Ontario, Canada: University of Toronto Press.

Hanisch, Carol. 1970. The personal is political. In *Notes from the second year: Women's liberation.* Retrieved from www.carolhanisch.org/CHwritings/PIP.htm.

Hannigan, John. 2006. *Environmental sociology: A social constructionist perspective.* London: Routledge.

Haq, Naimul. 2011. Women find a way out of poverty. *Inter Press Service*, February 24. Retrieved from www.ipsnews.net/news.asp?idnews=54599.

Harding, Sandra. 1991. *Whose science? Whose knowledge?: Thinking from women's lives.* Ithaca, NY: Cornell University Press.

Harding, Sandra, ed. 2004. *The feminist standpoint theory reader.* New York: Routledge.

Hardisty, Jean. 1999. *Mobilizing resentment.* Boston: Beacon.

Harper, Charles L., and Kevin T. Leicht. 2007. *Exploring social change.* Upper Saddle River, NJ: Pearson.

Harper, Tim. 2007. Think you have it bad? Try a 240-km commute. *Toronto Star*, December 8. Retrieved from www.thestar.com/article/283771.

Hartsock, Nancy. 1983. *Money, sex, and power: Toward a feminist historical materialism.* Boston: Northeastern University Press.

Hartsock, Nancy. 1996. Community/sexuality/gender: Rethinking power. In *Revisioning the political: Feminist reconstructions of traditional concepts in Western political theory*, ed. Nancy J. Hirschmann and Christine Di Stefano, pp. 27–50. Boulder, CO: Westview Press.

Harvey, David. 1985. *The urban experience.* Baltimore, MD: Johns Hopkins University Press.

Harvey, David. 1990. *The condition of postmodernity.* Oxford: Blackwell.

Harvey, David. 2007. *A brief history of neoliberalism.* New York: Oxford University Press.

Hayim, Gila. 1980. *The existential sociology of Jean-Paul Sartre.* Amherst: University of Massachusetts.

He, Wan, and Mark N. Muenchrath. 2011. ACS-17, 90+ in the United States: 2006–2008. U.S. Census Bureau, American Community Survey Reports. Washington, DC: U.S. Government Printing Office.

Heckert, Alex, and Druann Maria Heckert. 2004. Using an integrated typology of deviance to analyze ten common norms of the U.S. middle class. *Sociological Quarterly* 45 (2): 209–28.

Heckert, Druann Maria, Carina Michelle Heckert, and Daniel Alex Heckert. 2005. Labeling theory and creative/alternative hair. *Sociological Imagination* 41 (2): 83–103.

Heclo, Hugh, Theda Skocpal, Mary Jo Bane, and Alan Wolfe. 2007. *Christianity and American democracy.* Cambridge, MA: Harvard University Press.

Heelas, Paul, and Linda Woodhead. 2005. *The spiritual revolution.* Malden, MA: Blackwell.

Heider, Don, ed. 2004. *Class and news.* Lanham, MD: Rowman & Littlefield.

Heiland, Frank, and Shirley H. Liu. 2006. Family structure and wellbeing of out-of-wedlock children: The significance of biological parents' relationship. *Demographic Research* 15 (September): 61–104.

Held, David, Anthony McGrew, David Goldblatt, and Jonathan Perreton. 1999. *Global transformations: Politics, economics, and culture.* Stanford, CA: Stanford University Press.

Held, Virginia. 1993. *Feminist morality: Transforming culture, society, and politics.* Chicago: University of Chicago Press.

Helft, Miguel. 2010. Anger leads to apology from Google about Buzz. *New York Times*, February 14. Retrieved from www.nytimes.com/2010/02/15/technology/internet/15google.html?_r=0.

Helft, Miguel, and Ashlee Vance. 2010. Apple passes Microsoft as no. 1 in tech. *New York Times*, May 27, p. B1. Retrieved from www.nytimes.com/2010/05/27/technology/27apple.html.

Henig, Robin Marantz. 2010. What is it about 20-somethings? *New York Times Magazine*, August 22. Retrieved from www.nytimes.com/2010/08/22/magazine/22Adulthood.

Henry, Neil. 2007. *American carnival: Journalism under siege in an age of new media.* Berkeley: University of California Press.

Herbenick, Debby, Michael Reece, Vanessa Schick, Stephanie A. Sanders, Brian Dodge, and J. Dennis Fortenberry. 2010. Sexual behavior in the United States: Results from a national probability sample of men and women ages 14–94. *Journal of Sexual Medicine* 7 (Suppl. 5): 255–65.

Herbert, Melissa. 2000. *Camouflage isn't only for combat: Gender, sexuality, and women in the military.* New York: New York University Press.

Herman, Edward S., and Noam Chomsky. 2002. *Manufacturing consent: The political economy of the mass media.* New York: Pantheon Books.

Herrnstein, Richard, and Charles Murray. 1996. *The bell curve: Intelligence and class structure in American life.* New York: Free Press.

Hertz, Tom. 2005. Rags, riches and race: The intergenerational economic mobility of black and white families in the United States. In *Unequal chances: Family background and economic success*, ed. Samuel Bowles, Herbert Gintis, and Melissa Osborne, pp. 165–91. Princeton, NJ: Princeton University Press.

Heuveline, Patrick, and Matthew Weinshenker. 2008. The international child poverty gap: Does demography matter? *Demography* 45 (1): 173–91.

Hills, Rachel. 2013. Ugly is the new pretty: How unattractive selfies took over the Internet. *New York* magazine, March 29. Retrieved from http://nymag.com/thecut/2013/03/ugly-is-the-new-pretty-a-rise-in-gross-selfies.html.

Hinduja, Sameer, and Justin W. Patchin. 2009. *Bullying beyond the shoolyard: Preventing and responding to cyberbullying.* Thousand Oaks, CA: Sage.

Hirsch, Barry T., and David A. Macpherson. 2013. Union membership and coverage database from the Current Population Survey. Retrieved from www.unionstats.com/. January 26.

Hirschfield, Paul. 2008. Preparing for prison? The criminalization of school discipline in the USA. *Theoretical Criminology* 12 (1): 79–101.

Hirschi, Travis. 1969. *Causes of delinquency.* Berkeley: University of California Press.

Hochschild, Arlie. 1979. Emotion work, feeling rules, and social structure. *American Journal of Sociology* 85: 551–75.

Hochschild, Arlie. 1983. *The managed heart.* Berkeley: University of California Press.

Hochschild, Arlie, with Anne Machung. 1989. *The second shift: Working parents and the revolution at home.* New York: Viking.

Hodson, Randy. 2001. *Dignity at work.* New York: Cambridge University Press.

Hof, Robert. 2005. It's a whole new web. *BusinessWeek*, September 26, pp. 76–79.

Hoffman, Lisa, and Brian Coffey. 2008. Dignity and indignation: How people experiencing homelessness view services and providers. *The Social Science Journal* 45: 207–22.

Hofstede, Geert. 1980. *Culture's consequences: International differences in work-related values.* Beverly Hills, CA: Sage.

Hogan, Dennis P. 1978. The variable order of events in the life course. *American Sociological Review* 43 (August): 573–86.

Hogan, Dennis P., and Nan Marie Astone. 1986. The transition to adulthood. *Annual Review of Sociology* 12: 109–130.

Hogan, Michael H. 1998. *A cross of iron: Harry S Truman and the origins of the national security state, 1945–1954.* New York: Cambridge University Press.

Hohler, Bob. 2009. Ill-equipped to compete. *Boston Globe,* June 24. Retrieved from www .boston.com/sports/schools/articles/2009/06/ 24/ill_equipped_to_compete/?page=1.

Hollander, Justin B. 2011. *Sunburnt cities: The Great Recession, depopulation and urban planning in the American Sunbelt.* New York: Routledge.

Holmes, Michael, and Mike Bloxham. 2007. An observational method for time use research: Advantages, disadvantages, and lessons learned from the Middletown Media Studies. Paper presented at the 2007 conference of the International Association of Time Use Researchers, Washington, DC.

Holsti, Ole. 1968. *Content analysis for the social sciences and humanities.* Reading, MA: Addison-Wesley.

Holton, Robert J. 1992. *Economy and society.* New York: Routledge.

Holyfield, Lori, Matthew Ryan Moltz, and Mindy S. Bradley. 2009. Race discourse and the U.S. Confederate flag. *Race, Ethnicity, and Education* 12 (December): 517–37.

Hook, Jennifer L. 2010. Gender inequality in the welfare state: Sex segregation in housework, 1965–2003. *American Journal of Sociology* 115 (5): 1480–523.

hooks, bell. 2000. *Feminist theory: From margin to center.* Boston: South End Press.

Hooper, Rowan. 2005. Television show scrambles forensic evidence. *New Scientist.* Retrieved from http://technology.newscientist.com/article/mg18725163.800.

Hoover, Kenneth, and Todd Donovan. 2007. *The elements of social scientific thinking,* 9th ed. Belmont, CA: Wadsworth.

Horsman, Reginald. 1981. *Race and manifest destiny: The origins of American Anglo-Saxonism.* Cambridge, MA: Harvard University Press.

Horton, James Oliver, and Lois Horton. 2005. *Slavery and the making of America.* New York: Oxford University Press.

Horvath, Miranda A. H., Llian Alys, Kristina Massey, Afroditi Pina, Mia Scally, and Joanna R. Adler. 2013. "Basically . . . porn is everywhere": A rapid evidence assessment on the effects that access and exposure to pornography has on children and young people. London: Middlesex University. Retrieved from www.mdx.ac.uk/Assets/ BasicallyporniseverywhereReport.pdf.

Hougham, Victoria. 2005. Sociological skills used in the capture of Saddam Hussein. *Footnotes* 33 (6): 3.

Howard, Philip N. 2005. *New media campaigns and the managed citizen.* New York: Cambridge University Press.

Hsieh, Elaine. 2007. Interpreters as co-diagnosticians. *Social Science & Medicine* 64: 924–37.

Hua, C. 2001. *A society without fathers or husbands: The Na of China.* New York: Zone Books.

Huber, Joan. 2007. *On the origins of gender inequality.* Boulder, CO: Paradigm.

Hughes, Everett C. 1945. Dilemmas and contradictions of status. *American Journal of Sociology* 50: 353–59.

Human Rights Campaign. 2013a. LGBT equality at the *Fortune* 500. Retrieved from www.hrc.org/resources/entry/ lgbt-equality-at-the-fortune-500.

Human Rights Campaign. 2013b. Marriage center. Retrieved from www.hrc.org/ campaigns/marriage-center.

Hunter, James Davison. 1991. *Culture wars: The struggle to define America.* New York: Basic Books.

Hunter, James Davison. 1994. *Before the shooting begins: Searching for democracy in America's culture war.* New York: Free Press.

Hunter, James Davison, and Alan Wolfe. 2006. *Is there a culture war?* Washington, DC: Brookings Institution Press.

Huntington, Samuel. 1993. The clash of civilizations? *Foreign Affairs* 72 (3): 22–49.

Huntington, Samuel. 1998. *The clash of civilizations and the remaking of world order.* New York: Simon & Schuster.

Huntington, Samuel. 2005. *Who are we? The challenges to America's national identity.* New York: Simon & Schuster.

Hurlbert, Jeanne S., Valerie A. Haines, and John J. Beggs. 2000. Core networks and tie activation: What kinds of routine networks allocate resources in nonroutine situations? *American Sociological Review* 65: 598–618.

Hutchison, William R. 2003. *Religious pluralism in America.* New Haven, CT: Yale University Press.

Hyde, Janet Shibley. 2005. Gender similarities hypothesis. *American Psychologist* 40 (6): 581–92.

Iceland, John, Matthew Hall, Kris Marsh, Luis Sanchez, and Gregory Sharp. 2010. Racial and ethnic residential segregation in the United States: Comparisons across racial and ethnic groups, 1970–2009. Retrieved from http://projects.pop.psu.edu/ canc/segregation/Cross-group-report-12-19-2010.pdf.

Ignatiev, Noel. 1996. *How the Irish became white.* New York: Routledge.

Inglehart, Ronald, and Pippa Norris. 2003. The true clash of civilizations. *Foreign Policy* 135: 62–70.

Institute for Women's Policy Research. 2013. The gender wage gap: 2012. IWPR #C350, March. Retrieved from www.iwpr.org/ publications/pubs/the-gender-wage-gap-2012.

Institute of Medicine. 2003. *Unequal treatment: Confronting racial and ethnic disparities of healthcare.* Washington, DC: National Academies Press.

Institute on Women and Criminal Justice. 2009. Quick facts—women and criminal justice—2009. Retrieved September 19, 2013, from www.wpaonline.org/pdf/ Quick%20Facts%20Women%20 and%20CJ_Sept09.pdf.

Interfaith Worker Justice. 2010. *A worker justice reader: Essential writings on religion and labor.* Maryknoll, NY: Orbis Books.

International Network on Cultural Policy. 2010. About us. Retrieved from www.incp-ripc.org/about/index_e.shtml.

Internet Crime Complaint Center. 2013. *2012 Internet crime report.* Retrieved from www .ic3.gov/media/annualreport/2012_ic3 report.pdf.

Internet World Stats. 2013. World Internet usage and population statistics. Retrieved from http://internetworldstats.com/stats.htm.

Inter-Parliamentary Union. 2013. Women in national parliaments. Situation as of July 31, 2011. Retrieved from www.ipu.org/ wmn-e/ classif.htmon.

Irwin, Douglas A. 2009. *Free trade under fire.* Princeton, NJ: Princeton University Press.

Irwin, Rachel. 2007. Culture shock: Negotiating feelings in the field. *Anthropology Matters* 9 (1): 1–11.

Jablonski, Nina G., and George Chaplin. 2002. Skin deep. *Scientific American* 287 (4): 74–82.

Jackson, John H. 2012. Preface. *A rotting apple: Education redlining in New York City.* The Schott Foundation for Public Education, April. Retrieved from http:// schottfoundation.org/publications-reports/ education-redlining.

Jackson, Maggie. 2008. *Distracted.* Amherst, NY: Prometheus Books.

Jackson, Pamela Braboy, and Alexandra Berkowitz. 2005. The structure of the life course: Gender and racioethnic variation in the occurrence and sequencing of role transitions. *Advances in Life Course Research* 9: 55–90.

Jackson, Philip. 1968. *Life in classrooms.* New York: Holt, Rinehart and Winston.

Jacobs, Lawrence R., and Theda Skocpol. 2007. *Inequality and American democracy.* New York: Russell Sage Foundation.

Jacobs, Sue Ellen, Wesley Thomas, and Sabine Lang, eds. 1997. *Two-spirit people: Native American gender identity, sexuality, and spirituality.* Urbana: University of Illinois Press.

Janis, Irving L. 1972. *Victims of groupthink: A psychological study of foreign-policy decisions and fiascoes.* Boston: Houghton Mifflin.

Janis, Irving L. 1989. *Crucial decisions.* New York: Free Press.

Janowitz, Morris, and Charles C. Moskos Jr. 1979. Five years of the all-volunteer force: 1973–1978. *Armed Forces and Society* 5 (2): 171–218.

Jasper, James M. 1997. *The art of moral protest.* Chicago: University of Chicago.

Jasper, James M., and Jeff Goodwin. 2011. *Contention in context: Political opportunities and the emergence of protest.* Stanford, CA: Stanford University Press.

Jensen, Per, Kirsten Fenger, Tom G. Bolwig, and Sven Asger Sorensen. 1998. Crime in Huntington's disease: A study of registered offences among patients, relatives, and controls. *Journal of Neurology, Neurosurgery, and Psychiatry* 65: 467–71.

Jhally, Sut, and Justin Lewis. 1992. *Enlightened racism.* Boulder, CO: Westview Press.

Johnson, Alan. 2007. A politics of inclusion: An interview with Saad Eddin Ibrahim. *Democratiya* 8 (Spring): 154–70. Retrieved from http://dissentmagazine.org/democratiya/article_pdfs/d8Interview.pdf.

Johnson, Allan G. 2005. *Privilege, power and difference.* New York: McGraw-Hill.

Johnson, Allen, and Timothy Earle. 2000. *The evolution of human societies: From foraging groups to agrarian state.* Stanford, CA: Stanford University Press.

Johnson, Bobbie. 2010. Privacy no longer a social norm, says Facebook founder. *The Guardian,* January 10. Retrieved from www.theguardian.com/technology/2010/jan/11/facebook-privacy.

Johnson, Bradley. 2007. 100 Leading media companies. *Advertising Age.* Retrieved from http://adage.com/article/mediaworks/100-leading-media-companies-report/120726/.

Johnson, Bradley. 2012. 100 leading companies 2012. *Advertising Age* 83 (35): 1.

Johnson, Carolyn Y. 2008. Study finds culture a factor in female math achievement. *Boston Globe,* October 10, p. A4.

Johnson, Charles, and Patricia Smith. 1999. *Africans in America: America's journey through slavery.* New York: Harvest Books.

Johnson, Stephen. 2004. *Mind wide open: Your brain and the neuroscience of everyday life.* New York: Scribner.

Johnston, David Cay. 2003. *Perfectly legal: The covert campaign to rig our tax system to benefit the super rich—and cheat everybody else.* New York: Portfolio/Penguin.

Johnston, David Cay. 2005. *Perfectly legal: The covert campaign to rig our tax system to benefit the super rich—and cheat everybody else.* New York: Penguin.

Johnston, David Cay. 2007. *Free lunch: How the wealthiest Americans enrich themselves at government expense.* New York: Penguin.

Johnston, Hank, and John A. Noakes, eds. 2005. *Frames of protest.* Lanham, MD: Rowman & Littlefield.

Jones, Jeffrey M. 2011. Americans divided on whether King's dream has been realized. Gallup. Retrieved from www.gallup.com/poll/149201/Americans-Divided-Whether-King-Dream-Realized.aspx.

Jones, Stephanie J., ed. 2007. *The state of black America, 2007.* Silver Spring, MD: Beckham Publications Group.

Jordan, Don, and Michael Walsh. 2008. *White cargo: The forgotten history of white slaves in America.* New York: New York University Press.

Jordan, Tim, and Steve Pile. 2002. *Social change.* Cambridge, MA: Blackwell.

Juergensmeyer, Mark. 2003. *Terror in the mind of God: The global rise of religious violence.* Berkeley: University of California Press.

Jung, Moon-Kie. 2006. *Reworking race: The making of Hawaii's interracial labor movement.* New York: Columbia University Press.

Jutte, Robert. 2008. *Contraception: A history.* Malden, MA: Polity Press.

Jylha, Marja, and Marja Saarenheimo. 2010. Loneliness and aging: Comparative perspectives. In *The Sage handbook of social gerontology,* ed. Dale Danaher and Chris Phillipson, pp. 317–28. Los Angeles: Sage.

Kahlenberg, Richard D. 1997. *The remedy: Class, race, and affirmative action.* New York: Basic Books.

Kahlenberg, Richard D., ed. 2010a. *Affirmative action for the rich: Legacy preferences in college admissions.* New York: Century Foundation Press.

Kahlenberg, Richard D. 2010b. Introduction. In *Rewarding strivers: Helping low-income students succeed in college,* pp. 1–16. New York: Century Foundation Press.

Kahlenberg, Richard D., ed. 2010c. *Rewarding strivers: Helping low-income students succeed in college.* New York: Century Foundation Press.

Kalleberg, Arne L. 2009. Precarious work, insecure workers: Employment relations in transition. *American Sociological Review* 74 (1): 1–22.

Kalleberg, Arne L. 2011. *Good jobs, bad jobs.* New York: Russell Sage Foundation.

Kalleberg, Arne L. 2012. Job quality and precarious work: Clarifications, controversies, and challenges. *Work and Occupations* 39 (4): 427–48.

Kandal, T. R. 1988. *The woman question in classical sociological theory.* Miami: Florida International University Press.

Kane, Emily W. 2000. Racial and ethnic variations in gender-related attitudes. *Annual Review of Sociology* 26: 419–39.

Kang, Cecilia. 2010. For the poor, cellphones can offer lifeline. *Washington Post,* September 8, p. A16.

Kant, Immanuel. (1784) 1999. An answer to the question: What is enlightenment? In *Practical Philosophy,* ed. Mary J. Gregor, pp. 11–22. Cambridge, UK: Cambridge University Press.

Kaplinsky, Raphael. 2007. *Globalization, poverty and inequality.* Malden, MA: Polity Press.

Karabel, Jerome. 2005. *The chosen: The hidden history of admissions and exclusion at Harvard, Yale, and Princeton.* New York: Houghton Mifflin.

Karen, David. 2005. No child left behind? Sociology ignored! *Sociology of Education* 78 (2): 165–69.

Karner, Christian, and Alan Aldridge. 2004. Theorizing religion in a globalizing world. *International Journal of Politics, Culture, and Society* 18 (1/2): 5–32.

Karp, David. 1996. *Speaking of sadness.* New York: Oxford University Press.

Karp, David. 2000. A decade of reminders: Changing age consciousness between fifty and sixty years old. In *Aging and everyday life,* ed. J. F. Grubium and J. A. Holstein, pp. 65–86. Malden, MA: Blackwell.

Karraker, Katherine Hildebrandt, Dena Ann Vogel, and Margaret Ann Lake. 1995. Parents' gender-stereotyped perceptions of newborns: The eye of the beholder revisited. *Sex Roles* 33 (9–10): 687–702.

Kasser, Tim. 2003. *The high price of materialism.* Cambridge, MA: MIT Press.

Kaufman, Jason, and Jay Gabler. 2004. Cultural capital and the extracurricular activities of girls and boys in the college attainment process. *Poetics* 32: 145–68.

Kaufman, Joan, Bao-Zhi Yang, Heather Douglas-Palumberi, Shadi Houshyar, Deborah Lipschitz, John H. Krystal, and Joel Gelernter. 2004. Social supports and serotonin transporter gene moderate depression in maltreated children. *Proceedings of the National Academy of Sciences* 101 (5): 17316–21.

Kay, Paul, and Willett Kempton. 1984. What is the Sapir-Whorf hypothesis? *American Anthropologist* 86 (1): 65–79.

Kayyali, Randa A. 2006. *The Arab Americans.* Westport, CT: Greenwood Press.

Kearns, Laura. 2014. Green Evangelicals. In *The new evangelical social engagement,* ed. Brian Steensland and Philip Goff, pp. 157–78. New York: Oxford University Press.

Keaten, Jamey. 2010. French polemic over fake game show electrocutions. Associated Press, March 17.

Keith, Jannette. 2003. *Rich man's war, poor man's fight.* Durham: University of North Carolina Press.

Kelly, Heather. 2013. Why Google loves "The Internship." CNN. Retrieved from www.cnn.com/2013/06/05/tech/innovation/internship-movie-google/.

Kelly, Sanja, and Sarah Cook. 2011. *Freedom on the Internet 2011.* Washington, DC: Freedom House.

Kephart, Ronald. 2003. Latin America and the Caribbean. In *Race and ethnicity: An anthropological focus on the United States and the world,* ed. Raymond Scupin, pp. 288–308. Upper Saddle River, NJ: Prentice Hall.

Kerbo, Harold. 2011. *Social stratification and inequality.* New York: McGraw-Hill.

Kerrey, Bob, and Larry Pressler. 2010. The biggest election winner: Big money. *USA Today,* November 6. Retrieved from www.usatoday.com/news/opinion/forum/2010-11-06-kerrey05_ST_N.htm.

Keshavarz, Somayeh, and Rozumah Baharudin. 2009. Parenting style in a collective culture of Malaysia. *European Journal of Social Sciences* 10 (1): 66–73.

Khan, Shamus Rahman. 2011. *Privilege: The making of an adolescent elite at St. Paul's School.* Princeton, NJ: Princeton University Press.

Khandelwal, M. S. 2002. *Becoming American being Indian: An immigrant community in New York City.* Ithaca, NY: Cornell University Press.

Kiel, Paul, and Dan Nguyen. 2013. Bailout tracker. New York: ProPublica. Retrieved from http://projects.propublica.org/ bailout/main/summary.

Kiernan, Ben. 2007. *Blood and soil: A world history of genocide and extermination from Sparta to Darfur.* New Haven, CT: Yale University Press.

Kim, Eunjung. 2005. Korean American parental control: Acceptance or rejection? *Ethos* 33 (3): 347–66.

Kim, Heejung, and Hazel Rose Markus. 1999. Deviance or uniqueness, harmony or conformity? A cultural analysis. *Journal of Personality and Social Psychology* 77 (4): 785–800.

Kim, Julia C., Charlotte H. Watts, James R. Hargreaves, Luceth X. Ndhlovu, Godfrey Phetla, Linda A. Morison, Joanna Busza, John D.H. Porter, and Paul Pronyk 2007. Understanding the impact of a microfinance-based intervention on women's empowerment and the reduction of intimate partner violence in South Africa. *American Journal of Public Health* 97 (10): 1–9.

Kimmel, Michael. 1996. *Manhood in America.* New York: Free Press.

Kimmel, Michael. 2007. *The gendered society.* New York: Oxford University Press.

Kimmel, Michael, and Michael Messner, eds. 2009. *Men's lives.* Boston: Allyn & Bacon.

Kimmel, Michael S., and Michael A. Messner. 2013. *Men's lives*, 9th ed. Boston, MA: Pearson.

Kinder, Donald R., and Lynn M. Sanders. 1996. *Divided by color: Racial politics and democratic ideals.* Chicago: University of Chicago Press.

Kinsey, Alfred C., Wardell B. Pomeroy, and Clyde E. Martin. (1948) 1998. *Sexual behavior in the human male.* Bloomington: Indiana University Press.

Kinsey, Alfred C., Wardell B. Pomeroy, Clyde E. Martin, and Paul H. Gebhard. (1953) 1998. *Sexual behavior in the human female.* Bloomington: Indiana University Press.

Klein, Alec. 2003. *Stealing Time: Steve Case, Jerry Levin, and the collapse of AOL Time Warner.* New York: Simon & Schuster.

Klinenberg, Eric. 2003. *Heat wave.* Chicago: University of Chicago Press.

Klinenberg, Eric. 2005. Convergence: News production in a digital age. *Annals of the American Academy of Political and Social Science* 597: 48–63.

Kluckhohn, Clyde. 1968. *Mirror for man.* New York: Fawcett Crest.

Koch, Pamela Ray, and Lala Carr Steelman. 2009. From molehills mountains made: An examination of red and blue state cultural stereotypes. *Cultural Sociology* 3 (1): 165–89.

Kochhar, Rakesh, Richard Fry, and Paul Taylor. 2011. Wealth gaps rise to record highs between whites, blacks, Hispanics. Washington, DC: Pew Research Center. Retrieved from www.pewsocialtrends.org/ files/2011/07/SDT-Wealth-Report_ 7-26-11_FINAL.pdf.

KOF Swiss Economic Institute. 2011. KOF index of globalization 2011: Economic crisis slows down globalization. Retrieved from http://globalization.kof.ethz.ch/ static/pdf/press_release_2011_en.pdf.

KOF Swiss Economic Institute. 2013. KOF index of globalization 2013. Retrieved from http://globalization.kof.ethz.ch/media/ filer_public/2013/03/25/press_release_ 2013_en.pdf.

Kohn, Melvin L. 1977. *Class and conformity: A study in values*, 2nd ed. Chicago: University of Chicago Press.

Kohn, Melvin L., Kazimierz M. Slomczynski, and Carrie Schoenbach. 1986. Social stratification and the transmission of values in the family: A cross-national assessment. *Sociological Forum* 1 (1): 73–102.

Kohut, Andrew. n.d. Andrew Kohut on polling at the Pew Research Center. Retrieved from www .pewtrusts.org/expert_qa_detail.aspx?id=29046.

Kollmeyer, Christopher. 2004. Corporate interests: How the news media portrays the economy. *Social Problems* 51 (3): 432–52.

Kosfeld, Michael, Markus Henrichs, Paul J. Zak, Urs Fischbacher, and Ernst Fehr. 2005. Oxytocin increases trust in humans. *Nature* 435 (2): 673–76.

Kozol, Jonathan. 2005. *The shame of the nation.* New York: Crown.

Kozol, Jonathan. 2012. *Savage inequalities.* New York: Broadway Books.

Krebs, Valdis. 2008. Social network analysis of terrorist networks. *Orgnet.com.* Retrieved from www.orgnet.com/ hijackers.html.

Kreider, Marilyn. 2007. Young adults living in their parents' home. Paper presented at the American Sociological Meeting, New York, NY, August 12. Retrieved from www.census .gov/population/www/ socdemo/hh-fam/young -adults-in-parents-home.pdf.

Kreider, Rose M., and Diana B. Elliot. 2009. America's families and living arrangements: 2007. U.S. Census Bureau, Department of Commerce. Retrieved from www. census.gov/population/www/socdemo/hh-fam/p20-561.pdf.

Kriesberg, Louis. 1982. *Social conflicts.* Englewood Cliffs, NJ: Prentice-Hall.

Kurutz, Steven. 2007. Not buying it. *New York Times,* June 21, p. F1.

LaFraniere, Sharon. 2005. Cellphones catapult rural Africa to 21st century. *New York Times,* August 25, p. A1.

LaFree, Gary. 1999. Declining violent crime rates in the 1990s: Predicting crime booms and busts. *Annual Review of Sociology* 25: 145–68.

LaFree, Gary, and Richard Arum. 2006. The impact of racially inclusive schooling on adult incarceration rates among U.S. cohorts of African Americans and whites since 1930. *Criminology* 44 (1): 73–103.

Lammers, J., A. D. Galinsky, E. H. Gordijn, and S. Otten. 2008. Illegitimacy moderates the effects of power on approach. *Psychological Science* 19: 558–64.

Landecker, Hannah, and Aaron Panofsky. 2013. From social structure to gene regulation, and back: A critical introduction to environmental epigenetics for sociology. *Annual Review of Sociology* 39: 333–57.

Lane, Robert E. 1994. The road not taken: Friendship, consumerism, and happiness. *Critical Review* 8 (4): 521–54.

Lang, Molly Monahan, and Barbara J. Risman. 2007. Blending into equality: Family diversity and gender convergence. In *Handbook of gender and women's studies,* ed. Kathy Davis, Mary Evans, and Judith Lorber, pp. 287–303. Thousand Oaks, CA: Sage.

Lareau, Annette. 2011, *Unequal childhoods: Class, race, and family life*, 2nd ed. Berkeley: University of California Press.

Lareau, Annette, and Elliot B. Weininger. 2003. Cultural capital in educational research. *Theory and Society* 32 (5–6): 567–606.

Laumann, Edward O., John H. Gagnon, Robert T. Michael, and Stuart Michaels. 2000. *The social organization of sexuality.* Chicago: University of Chicago Press.

Layton, Lyndsey, and Spencer S. Hsu. 2008. Letting the market drive transportation; Bush officials criticized for privatization. *Washington Post,* March 17, p. A1.

Lebowitz, Michael. 2010. *The socialist alternative.* New York: Monthly Review Press.

Lechner, Frank J. 1991. The case against secu- larization: A rebuttal. *Social Forces* 69 (4): 1103–19.

Lee, Jennifer, and Frank D. Bean. 2004. America's changing color lines: Immigration, race/ethnicity, and multiracial identification. *Annual Review of Sociology* 30: 221–42.

Lee, Valerie E., and Julia B. Smith. 1995. Effects of high school restructuring and size on early gains in achievement and engagement. *Sociology of Education* 68 (4): 241–70.

Leeland, John. 2006. A spirit of belonging, inside and out. *New York Times,* October 8. Retrieved from www.nytimes. com/2006/10/08/fashion/ 08SPIRIT.html?pagewanted=1&_r=1&ref= fashion.

Lemert, Edwin M. 1951. *Social pathology.* New York: McGraw-Hill.

Lenhart, Amanda. 2012. Teens, smartphones & texting. Washington, DC: Pew Internet and American Life Project. Retrieved from http://pewinternet.org/~/media//Files/Reports/2012/PIP_Teens_Smartphones_and_ Texting.pdf.

Lenski, Gerhard. 1966. *Power and privilege: A theory of social stratification.* New York: McGraw-Hill.

Leondar-Wright, Betsy. 2005. *Class matters.* Gabriola Island, BC: New Society.

Lethbridge-Cejku, Margaret, Jeannine S. Schiller, and Luther Bernadel. 2004. *Summary health statistics for U.S. adults: National Health Interview Survey, 2002.* Washington, DC: National Center for Health Statistics.

Levitt, Martin Jay. 1993. *Confessions of a union buster.* New York: Crown.

Levitt, Peggy. 2004. Salsa and ketchup: Transnational migrants straddle two worlds. *Contexts* 3 (2): 20–26.

Levitz, Jennifer. 2010. BP didn't provide fail-safe requirements. *Wall Street Journal*, May 12. Retrieved from http://online.wsj.com/article/SB10001424052748703393045752 40853617229196.html.

Levy, Frank. 1998. *The new dollars and dreams.* New York: Russell Sage Foundation.

Lewis, Bernard. 2004. *The crisis of Islam: Holy war and unholy terror.* New York: Random House.

Licoppe, Christian, and Zbigniew Smoreda. 2005. Are social networks technologically embedded? How networks are changing today with changes in communication technology. *Social Networks* 27: 317–25.

Lindberg, David C., and Ronald L. Numbers. 2008. *When science and Christianity meet.* Chicago: University of Chicago Press.

Linden, Greg, Kenneth L. Kraemer, and Jason Dedrick. 2007. Who captures value in a global innovation system? The case of Apple's iPod. Irvine, CA: Personal Computing Industry Center, UC Irvine.

Ling, Rich. 2008. *New tech, new ties.* Cambridge, MA: MIT Press.

Ling, Rich, and Scott W. Campbell, eds. 2012. *Mobile communication: Bringing us together and tearing us apart.* New Brunswick, NJ: Transaction.

Link, Bruce G., and Jo C. Phelan. 2001. Conceptualizing stigma. *Annual Review of Sociology* 27: 363–85.

Lobao, Linda. 2007. Rural sociology. In *21st Century sociology: A reference handbook*, ed. Clifton D. Bryant and Dennis L. Peck, pp. 465–75. Thousand Oaks, CA: Sage.

Loeb, Paul Rogat. 1999. *Soul of a citizen.* New York: St. Martin's Press.

Logan, John. 2006. The union avoidance industry in the United States. *British Journal of Industrial Relations* 44 (4): 651–75.

Logan, John. 2011. Separate and unequal: The neighborhood gap for blacks, Hispanics and Asians in metropolitan America. Providence, RI: Brown University. Retrieved from www.s4.brown.edu/us2010/Data/Report/report0727.pdf.

Logan, John R., and Harvey L. Molotch. 1987. *Urban fortunes: The political economy of place.* Berkeley: University of California Press.

Logan, John R., and Brian J. Stults. 2011. The persistence of segregation in the metropolis: New findings from the 2010 Census. Census brief prepared for Project US2010. Retrieved from www.s4.brown.edu/us2010/Data/Report/report2.pdf.

Logan, John R., Brian J. Stults, and Reynolds Farley. 2004. Segregation of minorities in the metropolis: Two decades of change. *Demography* 41 (1): 1–22.

Lonergan, Raymond. 1941. A steadfast friend of labor. In *Mr. Justice Brandeis, great American*, ed. Irving Dillard, pp. 42+. St. Louis, MO: Modern View Press.

Lorber, Judith, and Lisa Jean Moore. 2010. *Gendered bodies: Feminist perspectives.* New York: Oxford University Press.

Lubrano, Alfred. 2004. *Limbo: Blue-collar roots, white-collar dreams.* Hoboken, NJ: Wiley.

Lucas, Samuel. 1999. *Tracking inequality.* New York: Teachers College Press.

Lukes, Stephen. 2006. Questions about power: Lessons from the Louisiana hurricane. In *Understanding Katrina: Perspectives from the social sciences.* Retrieved from http://understanding katrina.ssrc.org/Lukes/.

Lukes, Steven. 2005. *Power: A radical view*, 2nd ed. Palgrave Macmillan.

Lustgarten, Abrahm. 2010. Furious growth and cost cuts led to BP accidents past and present. Retrieved from www.propublica.org/article/bp-accidents-past-and-present.

Lutendo, Malisha, Pranitha Maharaj, and Michael Rogan. 2008. Rites of passage to adulthood: Traditional initiation schools in the context of HIV/AIDS in the Limpopo Province, South Africa. *Health, Risk and Society* 10 (6): 585–98.

Lynch, Kevin. 1960. *The image of the city.* Cambridge, MA: MIT Press.

Lynch, Thomas. 2001. We should witness the death of McVeigh. *New York Times*, February 20, p. A21.

MacFarlane, S. Neil, and Yuen Foong Khong. 2006. *Human security and the UN.* Bloomington: Indiana University Press.

Macgregor, G. H. C. 1954. *The New Testament basis of pacifism.* Nyack, NY: Fellowship Publications.

MacLaury, Judson. 2011. *Government regulation of workers' safety and health, 1877–1917.* Washington, DC: U.S. Department of Labor. Retrieved from www.dol.gov/oasam/programs/history/mono-regsafeintrotoc.htm.

MacLeod, Jay. 2008. *Ain't no makin' it: Aspirations and attainment in a low-income neighborhood.* Boulder, CO: Westview Press.

MacMillan, Ross. 2005. The structure of the life course: Classic issues and current controversies. *Advances in Life Course Research* 9: 3–24.

Macoby, Eleanor E. 2007. Historical overview of socialization research and theory. In *Handbook of socialization: Theory and research*, ed. Joan E. Grusse and Paul D. Hasting, pp. 13–41. New York: Guilford Press.

Madden, Mary, Amanda Lenhart, Maeve Duggan, Sandra Cortesi, and Urs Gasser. 2013. Teens and technology 2013. Washington, DC: Pew Internet and American Life Project. Retrieved from www.pewinternet.org/~/media//Files/Reports/2013/PIP_TeensandTechnology2013.pdf.

Madden, Mary, Amanda Lenhart, Sandra Cortesi, Urs Gasser, Maeve Duggan, Aaron Smith, and Meredith Beation. 2013. Teens, social media, and privacy. Washington, DC: Pew Internet and American Life Project. Retrieved from http://pewinternet.org/~/media//Files/Reports/2013/PIP_TeensSocialMediaandPrivacy.pdf.

Maloney, Devon. 2013. The marketing tactics for *Hunger Games: Catching Fire* would make Panem's Capitol proud. *Wired*, November 22. Retrieved from www.wired.com/underwire/2013/11/catching-fire-marketing/.

Mann, Michael. 1986. *The sources of social power*, vol. 1. Cambridge, UK: University of Cambridge.

Mann, Michael. 2012. *The sources of social power.* New York: Cambridge University Press.

Mannheim, Karl. 1952. The problem of generations. In *Essays on the sociology of knowledge*, pp. 276–322. London: Routledge/Kegan Paul.

Manohar, Namita. 2008. "Sshh...!! Don't tell my parents": Dating among second generation Patels in Florida. *Journal of Comparative Family Studies* 39 (4): 571–88.

Mao Zedong. (1936) 2010. *Quotations from Chairman Mao Zedong during the Cultural Revolution.* Fairfax, CA: Intercultural.

Marcus, Mary Brophy. 2011. Bin Laden's death a turning point for Millennials. *USA Today*, May 4. Retrieved from http://your-life.usatoday.com/mind-soul/story/2011/05/Bin-Ladens-death-a-turning-point-for-Millennials-/46778218/1.

Marger, Martin N. 2013. *Social inequality.* New York: McGraw-Hill.

Mariampolski, Hy. 2001. *Qualitative market research: A comprehensive guide.* Thousand Oaks, CA: Sage.

Mariampolski, Hy. 2005. *Ethnography for marketers: A guide to consumer immersion.* Thousand Oaks, CA: Sage.

Marini, Margaret Mooney. 1984. The order of events in the transition to adulthood. *Sociology of Education* 57 (2): 63–84.

Marler, Penny Long, and C. Kirk Hadaway. 2002. "Being religious" or "being spiritual" in America: A zero-sum proposition? *Journal for the Scientific Study of Religion* 41 (2): 289–300.

Marquardt, Elizabeth, David Blankenhorn, Robert I. Lerman, Linda Malone-Colón, and W. Bradford Wilcox. 2012. The president's marriage agenda for the forgotten sixty percent. *The State of Our Unions.* Charlottesville, VA: National Marriage Project and Institute for American Values.

Marquart James W., Sheldon Ekland-Olson, and Jonathan R. Sorensen. 1994. *The rope, the chair, & the needle*. Austin: University of Texas Press.

Marsh, Charles. 2006. *The beloved community: How faith shapes social justice from the civil rights movement to today*. New York: Basic Books.

Marsh, Robert. 2009. How similar are the values of the people of China and Taiwan? *Comparative Sociology* 8: 39–75.

Martin, Christopher R. 2004. *Framed! Labor and the corporate media*. Ithaca, NY: ILR Press/Cornell University Press.

Martin, Joyce A., Brady E. Hamilton, Stephanie J. Ventura, Michelle J. K. Osterman, and T. J. Matthews. 2013. Births: Final data for 2011. *National Vital Statistics Reports* 62 (1).

Martin, Karin A. 1998. Becoming a gendered body: Practices of preschools. *American Sociological Review* 63(4): 494–511.

Martin, Steven P. 2004. Women's education and family timing: Outcomes and trends associated with age at marriage and first birth. In *Social inequality*, ed. Kathryn Neckerman, pp. 79–118. New York: Russell Sage Foundation.

Martineau, Harriet. (1837) 2009. *Society in America*. New York: Cambridge University Press.

Martineau, Harriet. (1838) 2009. *How to observe morals and manners*. Charleston, SC: BiblioLife.

Marx, Karl. (1844) 1978. Contribution to the critique of Hegel's *Philosophy of Right*: Introduction. In *The Marx-Engels reader*, ed. Robert C. Tucker, pp. 53–65. New York: Norton.

Marx, Karl. (1845) 1978. Theses on Feuerbach. In *The Marx-Engels Reader*, 2nd ed., ed. Robert C. Tucker. New York: Norton.

Marx, Karl. (1852) 1978. The eighteenth Brumaire of Louis Bonaparte. In *The Marx-Engels Reader*, 2nd ed., ed. Robert C. Tucker. New York: Norton.

Marx, Karl. (1859) 1978. Preface to *A contribution to the critique of political economy*. In *The Marx-Engels reader*, 2nd ed., ed. Robert C. Tucker, pp. 3–6. New York: Norton.

Marx, Karl. (1867) 1976. *Capital*, trans. Ben Fowkes. New York: Vintage.

Marx, Karl, and Friedrich Engels. 2008. *On religion*. Mineola, NY: Dover.

Massey, Douglas S., and Mary J. Fischer. 2006. The effect of childhood segregation on minority academic performance at selective colleges. *Ethnic and Racial Studies* 29 (1): 1–26.

Matsueda, Ross. L. 1992. Reflected appraisals, parental labeling, and delinquency. *American Journal of Sociology* 97 (6): 1577–611.

Maurer, Lora. 2009. Naomi Chesler: Teacher, researcher, mentor, mom. *The Connector* 23 (1): 8–9. Harvard-MIT Division of Health Sciences and Technology. Retrieved from http://hst.mit .edu/images/upload/Connector_Winter09.pdf.

Mayer, Jane. 2010. Covert operations. *The New Yorker*, August 30. Retrieved from www.newyorker.com/reporting/2010/08/30/ 100830fa_fact_mayer.

McAdam, Doug. 1989. The biographical consequences of activism. *American Sociological Review* 54 (5): 744–60.

McAdam, Doug, John D. McCarthy, and Mayer N. Zald, eds. 1996. *Comparative perspectives on social movements*. New York: Cambridge University Press.

McBride, Sarah. 2013. Yahoo telecommute ban is much ado about nothing: Silicon Valley. *Reuters*. February 28. Retrieved from: http://uk.reuters.com/article/2013/02/28/us-yahoo-telecommuting-idUSBRE91R17R20130228.

McCall, Leslie. 2013. *The undeserving rich: American beliefs about inequality, opportunity, and redistribution*. New York: Cambridge University Press.

McCarthy, John D., and Mayer N. Zald. 1977. Resource mobilization and social movements: A partial theory. *American Journal of Sociology* 82 (6): 1212–41.

McChesney, Robert, and John Nichols. 2010. *The death and life of American journalism*. Philadelphia, PA: Nation Books.

McConahay, John B. 1986. Modern racism, ambivalence, and the modern racism scale. In *Prejudice, discrimination and racism*, ed. John F. Dovidio and Samuel L. Gaertner, pp. 91–125. Orlando, FL: Academic Press.

McConkey, Dale. 2001. Whither Hunter's culture war? *Sociology of Religion* 62 (2): 149–74.

McCright, Aaron M., and Riley E. Dunlap. 2003. Defeating Kyoto: The conservative movement's impact on U.S. climate change policy. *Social Problems* 50: 348–73.

McCrummen, Stephanie. 2005a. Building unity in subdivisions. *Washington Post*, February 27, pp. A1, A13.

McCrummen, Stephanie. 2005b. Subdivisions impose social divide. *Washington Post*, May 1, pp. A1, A16.

McFarland, Daniel A., and Reuben J. Thomas. 2006. Bowling young: How youth voluntary associations influence adult political participation. *American Sociological Review* 71 (3): 401–25.

McGregor, Richard. 2010. *The party: The secret world of China's communist rulers*. New York: HarperCollins.

McGrew, Anthony, and David Held, eds. 2007. *Globalization theory*. Malden, MA: Polity.

McHale, Susan M., and Ann C. Crouter. 2003. How do children exert an impact on family life? In *Children's influence on family dynamics*, ed. Ann C. Crouter and Allan Booth, pp. 207–20. Mahwah: NJ: Erlbaum.

McIntosh, Peggy. 1988. *White privilege and male privilege: A personal account of coming to see correspondences through work in women's studies*. Wellesley, MA: Center for Research on Women.

McIntyre, Robert S., and T. D. Coo Nguyen. 2004. Corporate income taxes in the Bush years. Washington, DC: Citizens for Tax Justice and the Institute on Taxation and Economic Policy. Retrieved from www.ctj .org/corpfed04an.pdf.

McKenzie, Brian. 2013. Out of state and long commutes, 2011. Washington, DC: U.S. Census Bureau. Retrieved from www.census.gov/hhes/commuting/files/2012/ACS-20.pdf.

McKernan, Signe-Mary, Caroline Ratcliffe, Eugene Steuerle, and Sisi Zhang. 2013. Less than equal: Racial disparities in wealth accumulation. Washington, DC: Urban Institute. Retrieved from www.urban.org/UploadedPDF/412802-Less-Than-Equal-Racial-Disparities-in-Wealth-Accumulation.pdf.

McKinlay, John B., and Lisa D. Marceau. 2002. The end of the golden age of doctoring. *International Journal of Health Services* 32 (2): 379–416.

McKinlay, John B., and Sonja M. McKinlay. 1977. The questionable contribution of medical measures to the decline of mortality in the United States in the twentieth century. *The Milbank Memorial Fund Quarterly. Health and Society* 55 (3): 405–28.

McLanahan, Sarah, and Gary Sandefur. 2006. *Growing up with a single parent*. Cambridge, MA: Harvard University Press.

McLeod, Hugh. 2000. *Secularisation in Western Europe, 1848–1914*. New York: Palgrave Macmillan.

McLeod, Hugh. 2010. *The religious crisis of the 1960s*. New York: Oxford University Press.

McLeod, Hugh, and Werner Ustorf, eds. 2011. *The decline of Christendom in Western Europe, 1750–2000*. New York: Cambridge University Press.

McLuhan, Marshall. 1964. *Understanding media: The extensions of man*. New York: New American Library.

McPherson, Miller, Lynn Smith-Lovin, and James M. Cook. 2001. Birds of a feather: Homophily in social networks. *Annual Review of Sociology* 27: 415–44.

McQuail, Denis. 2005. *Mass communication theory*, 5th ed. Thousand Oaks, CA: Sage.

Mead, George Herbert. (1934) 1962. *Mind, self, and society*, ed. Charles W. Morris. Chicago: Chicago University Press.

Mehta, Chirag, and Nik Theodore. 2005. Undermining the right to organize: Employer behavior during union representation campaigns. Chicago: Center for Urban Economic Development, University of Illinois at Chicago.

Mendes, Elizabeth. 2011. In U.S., self-reported weight up nearly 20 pounds since 1990. Gallup Well-Being, November 23. Retrieved from www.gallup.com/poll/150947/Self-Reported-Weight-Nearly-Pounds-1990.aspx.

Merton, Robert. 1949. Discrimination and the American creed. In *Discrimination and the national welfare*, ed. R. M. MacIver, pp. 99–126. New York: Harper & Row.

Merton, Robert K. 1938. Social structure and anomie. *American Sociological Review* 3: 672–82.

Merton, Robert K. 1968a. The bearing of empirical research on sociological theory. In *Social Theory and Social Structure*, pp. 156–71. New York: Free Press.

Merton, Robert. 1968b. The Matthew effect in science. *Science* 159 (3810): 56–63.

Merton, Robert K. 1968c. *Social theory and social structure*. New York: Free Press.

Meyer, David. 2006. *The politics of protest*. New York: Oxford University Press.

Meyer, John W., David Tyack, Joane Nagel, and Audri Gordon. 1979. Public education as nation-building in America: Enrollments and bureaucratization in the American states, 1870–1930. *American Journal of Sociology* 85 (3): 591–613.

Meyrowitz, Joshua. 1985. *No sense of place: The impact of electronic media on social behavior*. New York: Oxford University Press.

Michener, H. A., and E. J. Lawler. 1975. The endorsement of formal leaders: An integrative model. *Journal of Personality and Social Psychology* 31: 216–33.

Milgram, Stanley. 1963. Behavioral study of obedience. *Journal of Abnormal and Social Psychology* 67 (4): 371–78.

Milgram, Stanley. 1965. Some conditions of obedience and disobedience to authority. *Human Relations* 18 (1): 57–76.

Milgram, Stanley. 1969. *Obedience to authority*. New York: HarperCollins.

Milkman, Ruth. 1997. *Farewell to the factory: Auto workers in the late twentieth century*. Berkeley: University of California Press.

Milkman, Ruth. 2006. *L.A. story: Immigrant workers and the future of the U.S. labor movement*. New York: Russell Sage Foundation.

Miller, Alan S., and Tmoko Mitamura. 2003. Are surveys on trust trustworthy? *Social Psychology Quarterly* 66 (1): 62–70.

Miller, Claire Cain, and Nicole Perlroth. 2013. Yahoo says new policy is meant to raise morale. *New York Times*. March 5. Retrieved from: www.nytimes.com/2013/03/06/technology/yahoos-in-office-policy-aims-to-bolster-morale.html?pagewanted=all.

Miller, Neil. 2006. *Out of the past: Gay and lesbian history from 1869 to the present*. Los Angeles, Advocate Books.

Miller, T. Christian. 2007. Private contractors outnumber U.S. troops in Iraq. *Los Angeles Times*, July 4.

Mills, C. Wright. 1948. *The new men of power*. New York: Harcourt.

Mills, C. Wright. 1952. *White collar*. New York: Oxford University Press.

Mills, C. Wright. 1956. *The power elite*. New York: Oxford University Press.

Mills, C. Wright. 1959. *The sociological imagination*. New York: Oxford University Press.

Miranda, Candice. 2003. In Kenya, television opens window mainly in the west. *Washington Post*, April 28, p. A19.

Mishel, Lawrence. 2012. Unions, inequality, and faltering middle-class wages. Washington, DC: Economic Policy Institute. Retrieved from www.epi.org/publication/ib342-unions-inequality-faltering-middle-class/.

Mohanty, Chandra Talpade, ed. 2003. *Feminism without borders: Decolonizing theory, practicing solidarity*. Durham, NC: Duke University Press.

Molm, L. D. 1997. Risk and power use: Constraints on the use of coercion in exchange. *American Sociological Review* 62: 113–33.

Molner, Alex, Faith Boninger, Michael D. Harris, and Ken M. Libby. 2013. Promoting consumption at school: Health threats associated with schoolhouse commercialism. Boulder, CO: National Education Policy Center. Retrieved from http://nepc.colorado.edu/files/commercialism-2012_0.pdf.

Molotch, Harvey L. 1976. The city as a growth machine. *American Journal of Sociology* 82 (2): 309–30.

Montejano, David. 1987. *Anglos and Mexicans in the making of Texas, 1836–1986*. Austin: University of Texas Press.

Moody, Harry R. 2010. *Aging: Concepts and controversies*, 6th ed. Thousand Oaks, CA: Pine Forge Press.

Moore, Christopher J. 2004. *In other words*. New York: Levenger Press/Walker & Company.

Moore, Ryan. 2005. Alternative to what? Subcultural capital and the commercialization of a music scene. *Deviant Behavior* 26 (3): 229–52.

Morello, Carol. 2012. Census chief Robert Groves: We've got to stop counting like this. *Washington Post*, August 5. Retrieved from http://articles.washingtonpost.com/2012-08-05/politics/35493263_1_census-bureau-census-records-census-questions.

Morello, Carol, and Ted Melnick. 2013. *Washington Post*, June 13. Retrieved from www.washingtonpost.com/local/white-deaths-outnumber-births-for-first-time/2013/06/13/3bb1017c-d388-11e2-a73e-826d299ff459_story.html.

Morgan, Stephen, David Grusky, and Gary Fields. 2006. *Mobility and inequality: Frontiers of research in sociology and economics*. Stanford, CA: Stanford University Press.

Morin, Rich, and D'Vera Cohn. 2008. Women call the shots at home; public mixed on gender roles in jobs. Pew Research Center. Retrieved from http://pewresearch.org/pubs/967/gender-power.

Morin, Richard. 1994. That misleading Holocaust survey; A flawed poll overstated the public's skepticism. *New York Times*, March 20, p. C3.

Morrill, Calvin, Mayer N. Zald, and Hayagreeva Rao. 2003. Covert political conflict in organizations: Challenges from below. *Annual Review of Sociology* 29: 391–415.

Morris, Aldon. 1984. *The origins of the civil rights movement*. New York: Free Press.

Morris, Allison, and Gabrielle Maxwell. 1998. Restorative justice in New Zealand: Family group conferences as a case study. *Western Criminology Review* 1 (1).

Mosco, Vincent. 2009. *The political economy of communication*, 2nd ed. Thousand Oaks, CA: Sage.

Motz, Lotte. 1997. *The faces of the goddess*. New York: Oxford University Press.

Mouw, Ted, and Barbara Entwisle. 2006. Residential segregation and interracial friendship in schools. *American Journal of Sociology* 112 (2): 394–441.

Mukhopadhyay, Carol C., Rosemary Henze, and Yolanda T. Moses. 2007. *How real is race?* Lanham, MD: Rowman & Littlefield.

Muller-Hill, B. 1988. *Murderous science: Elimination by scientific selection of Jews, Gypsies, and others, Germany, 1933–1945*. Oxford: Oxford University Press.

Mumford, Lewis. 1968. *The city in history*. New York: Harvest.

Murray, Pauli, ed. 1997. *States' laws on race and color*. Athens: University of Georgia Press.

Naff, Alixa. 1985. *Becoming American: The early Arab immigrant experience*. Cannondale: Southern Illinois University Press.

Napoli, Philip M. 2010. *Audience evolution*. New York: Columbia University Press.

National Alliance for Public Charter Schools. 2013. Back to school tallies: Estimated number of public charter schools & students, 2012–2013. January. Retrieved from http://dashboard.publiccharters.org/dashboard/home.

National CASA (Court Appointed Special Advocates). 2005. Cultural perspectives on child rearing Seattle, WA. management/diversity/cultural-child.htm.

National Center for Education Statistics. 2003. *Digest of education statistics 2003*. U.S. Department of Education. Retrieved from http://nces.ed.gov/pubsearch/pubsinfo.asp?pubid=2005025.

National Center for Education Statistics. 2010. What is the price of college? Retrieved from http://nces.ed.gov/pubsearch/pubsinfo.asp?pubid=2011175.

National Center for Education Statistics. 2013. *The condition of education 2013*. U.S. Department of Education. Retrieved from https://nces.ed.gov/pubsearch/pubsinfo.asp?pubid=2013037.

National Center for Health Statistics. 2013a. *Births: Final data for 2011*. Washington, DC: U.S. Department of Health and Human Services. Retrieved from www.cdc.gov/nchs/data/nvsr/nvsr62/nvsr62_01.pdf.

National Center for Health Statistics. 2013b. *Health, United States, 2012*. Hyattsville, MD: National Center for Health Statistics. Retrieved from www.cdc.gov/nchs/data/hus/hus12.pdf.

National Center for Victims of Crime. 2013. Intimate partner violence. Retrieved from www.victimsofcrime.org/docs/

ncvrw2013/2013ncvrw_stats_intimatepartner.pdf?sfvrsn=0.

National charter school study. 2013. Stanford, CA: Stanford University, Center for Research on Education Outcomes.

National Commission on the BP Deepwater Horizon Oil Spill and Offshore Drilling. 2011. *Deep Water: The gulf oil disaster and the future of offshore drilling recommendations*. Washington, DC: National Commission on the BP Deepwater Horizon Oil Spill and Offshore Drilling.

National Gay and Lesbian Task Force. 2011. Relationship recognition for same-sex couples in the U.S. Retrieved from www.thetaskforce.org/downloads/reports/issue_maps/rel_recog_6_28_11_color.pdf.

National Opinion Research Center. 2010. *General Social Survey, 2010*. Retrieved from www3.norc.org/GSS+Website/.

National Priorities Project. 2011. Military recruitment 2010. Retrieved from http://nationalpriorities.org/analysis/2011/military-recruitment-2010/.

National Priorities Project. 2014. President's 2015 budget in pictures. Retrieved from http://nationalpriorities.org/analysis/2014/presidents-2015-budget-in-pictures/.

Nelson, Charles A., Nathan A. Fox, and Charles H. Zeanah Jr. 2013. Anguish of the abandoned child. *Scientific American* 308 (4): 62–67.

Nelson, Margaret K. 2010. *Parenting out of control*. New York: New York University Press.

Neuman, W. Lawrence. 2009. *Social research methods: Qualitative and quantitative approaches*, 7th ed. Boston: Pearson.

New York Times. 2011a. Netizens gain some privacy. January 29. Retrieved from www.nytimes.com/2011/01/30/opinion/30sun3.html.

New York Times. 2011b. Rich district, poor district. March 26. Retrieved from www.nytimes.com/2011/03/27/opinion/27sun1.html?_r=2.

Newman, Katherine. 1988. *Falling from grace: The experience of downward mobility in the American middle class*. New York: Free Press.

Newman, Katherine S. 2004. *Rampage: The social roots of school shootings*. New York: Basic Books.

Newport, Frank. 2010. Tea Party supporters overlap Republican base. Gallup, July 2. Retrieved from www.gallup.com/poll/141098/Tea-Party-Supporters-Overlap-Republican-Base.aspx?version=print.

Newport, Frank. 2013a. Gulf grows in black-white views of U.S. justice system bias. Gallup. Retrieved from www.gallup.com/poll/163610/gulf-grows-black-white-views-justice-system-bias.aspx.

Newport, Frank. 2013b. In U.S., 87% approve of black-white marriage, vs. 4% in 1958. Gallup. Retrieved from www.gallup.com/poll/163697/approve-marriage-blacks-whites.aspx.

Ng, Sik H., and James J. Bradac. 1993. *Power in language*. Newbury Park, CA: Sage.

Ngowi, Rodrique. 2005. Africans adapt cell phone technology to suit continent's harsh realities. Associated Press Worldstream, September 16.

Nielsen. 2013. *Nielsen Entertainment & Billboard's 2013 mid-year music industry report*. Retrieved from www.nielsen.com/content/dam/corporate/us/en/reports-downloads/2013%20Reports/Nielsen-Music-2013-Mid-Year-US-Release.pdf.

Nimrod, Galit. 2009. Seniors' online communities. *Gerontologist* 50 (3): 382–92.

Noelle-Neuman, Elisabeth. 1974. The spiral of silence: A theory of public opinion. *Journal of Communication* 24 (2): 43–51.

Noelle-Neuman, Elisabeth. 1993. *The spiral of silence*. Chicago: University of Chicago Press.

Noonan, Mary C., Mary E. Corcoran, and Paul N. Courant. 2005. Pay differences among the highly trained. *Social Forces* 84 (2): 853–72.

Norris, Pippa, and Ronald Inglehart. 2012. *Sacred and secular: Religion and politics worldwide*. 2nd ed. New York: Cambridge University Press.

Nussbaum, Martha C. 2010. *Not for profit: Why democracy needs the humanities*. Princeton, NJ: Princeton University Press.

Nyberg, Renee Smith, and Trine C. Jensen. 2009. Honoring the Kun Lun way: Cross-cultural organization development consulting to a hospitality company in Datong, China. *Journal of Applied Behavioral Science* 45: 305–37.

Obama, Barack. 2009. Remarks by the president in address to the nation on the way forward in Afghanistan and Pakistan. Washington, DC: The White House. Retrieved from www.whitehouse.gov/the-press-office/remarks-president-address-nation-way-forward-afghanistan-and-pakistan.

O'Connell, Martin, Daphne Lofquist, Tavia Simmons, and Terry Lugaila. 2010. New estimates of same-sex couple households from the American Community Survey. Presented at the annual meeting of the Population Association of America, Dallas, Texas, April 15–17. Retrieved from www.census.gov/population/www/socdemo/hh-fam/SS_new-estimates.pdf.

O'Connor, Russell. 2013. What does feminist porn look like? *Role/Reboot*. Retrieved from www.rolereboot.org/sex-and-relationships/details/2013-02-what-does-egalitarian-porn-look-like.

Ogburn, William. 1922. *Social change*. New York: Huebsch.

Okin, Susan Moller. 1999. *Is multiculturalism bad for women?* Princeton, NJ: Princeton University Press.

Oliver, Melvin L., and Thomas M Shapiro. 2006. *Black wealth, white wealth: A new perspective on racial inequality*. New York: Routledge.

Orfield, Gary, and Chungmei Lee. 2006. *Racial transformation and the changing nature of segregation*. The Civil Rights Project. Cambridge, MA: Harvard University.

Orfield, Gary, John Kucsera, and Genevieve Siegel-Hawley. 2012. *E pluribus . . . separation deepening double segregation for more students*. The Civil Rights Project, September. Retrieved from http://civilrightsproject.ucla.edu/research/k-12-education/integration-and-diversity/mlk-national/e-pluribus...separation-deepening-double-segregation-for-more-students.

Organization for Economic Cooperation and Development (OECD). 2013. *OECD factbook 2010: Economic, environmental and social statistics*. Paris: OECD.

Organization for Economic Cooperation and Development. 2013. *Education at a glance 2013: OECD indicators*. OECD Publishing. Retrieved from http://dx.doi.org/10.1787/eag-2013-en.

Orme, Nicholas. 2003. *Medieval children*. New Haven, CT: Yale University Press.

Ortiz, Isabel, and Matthew Cummins. 2011. Global inequality: Beyond the bottom million. UNICEF. Retrieved from www.networkideas.org/featart/apr2011/Ortiz_Cummins.pdf.

Otto, Mary. 2007. For want of a dentist; Prince George's boy dies after bacteria from tooth spread to brain. *Washington Post*, February 28, p. B1.

Ovide, Shira. 2010. Watch Warren Buffet say "raise my taxes." *Wall Street Journal*, November 22. Retrieved from http://blogs.wsj.com/deals/2010/11/22/watch-warren-buffett-say-raise-my-taxes/.

Ozment, Steven. 2001. *Ancestors: The loving family in Old Europe*. Cambridge, MA: Harvard University Press.

Page, James S. 2007. Teaching peace to the military. *Peace Review* 19 (4): 571–77.

Pager, Devah. 2003. The mark of a criminal record. *American Journal of Sociology* 108 (5): 937–75.

Pager, Devah. 2007. *Marked: Race, crime, and finding work in an era of mass incarceration*. Chicago: University of Chicago Press.

Panagopoulos, Costas, ed. 2009. *Politicking online: The transformation of election campaign communications*. New Brunswick, NJ: Rutgers University Press.

Papper, Robert A., Michael E. Holmes, and Mark N. Popovich. 2004. Middletown Media Studies. *International Digital Media and Arts Association Journal* 1 (1).

Parker, Kim, and Wendy Wang. 2013. *Modern parenthood: Roles of moms and dads converge as they balance work and family*. March 14. Washington, DC: Pew Research Center.

Parrillo, Vincent N., and Christopher Donoghue. 2005. Updating the Bogardus social distance studies: A new national survey. *Social Science Journal* 42 (2): 257–72.

Parry, Marc. 2010. Tomorrow's college. *Chronicle of Higher Education*, October 31.

Retrieved from http://chronicle.com/article/Tomorrows-College/125120/.

Parsons, Talcott, and Robert F. Bales. 1955. *Family: Socialization and interaction process.* New York: Free Press.

Parsons, Talcott. 1949. The social structure of the family. In *The family: Its function and destiny*, ed. R. N. Asher, pp. 173–201. New York: Harper.

Parsons, Talcott. 1951. *The social system.* Glencoe, IL: Free Press.

Parsons, Talcott. 1954. An analytical approach to the theory of social stratification. In *Essays in sociological theory*, pp. 69–88. New York: Free Press.

Parsons, Talcott. 1960. The distribution of power in American society. In *Structure and process in modern societies.* New York: Free Press.

Pascoe, C. J. 2007. *Dude, you're a fag: Masculinity and sexuality in high school.* Berkeley: University of California Press.

Pascoe, C. J. 2011. *Dude, you're a fag: Masculinity and sexuality in high school.* Berkeley: University of California Press.

Passel, Jeffrey S., and D'Vera Cohn. 2008. *U.S. population projections: 2005–2050.* Washington, DC: Pew Research Center.

Passel, Jeffrey S., D'Vera Cohn, and Ana Gonzalez-Barrera. 2013. Population decline of unauthorized immigrants stalls, may have reversed. Washington, DC: Pew Research Center. Retrieved from www.pewhispanic.org/files/2013/09/Unauthorized-Sept-2013-FINAL.pdf.

Passel, Jeffrey S., Wendy Wang, and Paul Taylor. 2010. *Marrying out.* Washington, DC: Pew Research Center.

Patterson, Charlotte J. 2000. Family relationships of lesbians and gay men. *Journal of Marriage and Family* 62 (November): 1052–69.

Paules, Greta Foff. 1992. *Dishing it out.* Philadelphia: Temple University Press.

Pavlik, John V. 2008. *Media in the digital age.* New York: Columbia University Press.

Pearson, Jo. 2003. "Witchcraft will not soon vanish from this Earth": Wicca in the 21st century. In *Predicting religion: Christian, secular and alternative futures*, ed. Grace Davie, Paul Heelas, and Linda Woodhead, pp. 170–92. Burlington, VT: Ashgate.

Peet, Richard. 2009. *Unholy trinity: The IMF, World Bank, and WTO.* New York: Zed Books.

Pellow, David N., and Hollie Nyseth Brehm. 2013. An environmental sociology for the twenty-first century. *Annual Review of Sociology* 39: 229–50.

Pellow, David Naguib, and Robert J. Brulle, eds. 2005. *Power, justice, and the environment: A critical appraisal of the environmental justice movement.* Cambridge, MA: MIT Press.

Perl, Raphael F. 2006. *Terrorism and national security: Issues and trends.* CRS Issue Brief for Congress. Retrieved from http://fpc.state.gov/c17547.htm.

Persson, Henrik. 2011. Life from a freegan perspective. *E—The Environmental Magazine*, July. Retrieved September 16, 2013, from www.emagazine.com/magazine/life-from-a-freegan-perspective.

Peterson, Trond, and Ishak Saporta. 2004. The opportunity structure for discrimination. *American Journal of Sociology* 109 (4): 852–901.

Pettigrew, T., and M. Taylor. 2000. Discrimination. In *Encyclopedia of sociology*, vol. 1, ed. Edgar F. Borgatta, Rhonda J. V. Montgomery, pp. 688–95. New York: Macmillan.

Pew Center on the States. 2008. *One in 100: Behind bars in America 2008.* Washington, DC: Pew Charitable Trusts.

Pew Center on the States. 2009. *One in 31: The long reach of American corrections.* Washington, DC: Pew Charitable Trusts.

Pew Forum on Religion and Public Life. 2008a. Many Americans say other faiths can lead to eternal life. Washington, DC: Pew Research Center. Retrieved from http://pewforum.org/Many-Americans-Say-Other-Faiths-Can-Lead-to-Eternal-Life.aspx#1.

Pew Forum on Religion and Public Life. 2008b. *U.S. Religious Landscape Survey.* Washington, DC: Pew Research Center.

Pew Forum on Religion and Public Life. 2010a. *Religion among the millennials.* Washington, DC: Pew Research Center.

Pew Forum on Religion and Public Life. 2010b. U.S. religious knowledge survey. Washington, DC: Pew Research Center.

Pew Global Attitudes Project. 2013. Washington, DC: Pew Research Center. Retrieved from Question Database, www.pewglobal.org/question-search/?qid=408&cntIDs=&stdIDs=/.

Pew Research Center for the People and the Press. 2012b. Biennial Media Consumption Survey. Retrieved from www.people-press.org/files/legacy-questionnaires/News%20Consumption%20topline%20for%20release.pdf.

Pew Research Center. 2007a. *Blacks see growing values gap between poor and middle class.* Washington, DC: Pew Research Center.

Pew Research Center. 2007b. *Muslim Americans: Middle class and mostly mainstream.* Washington, DC: Pew Research Center.

Pew Research Center. 2010a. The decline of marriage and the rise of new families. Washington, DC: Pew Research Center. Retrieved from http://pewresearch.org/pubs/1802/decline-marriage-rise-new-families.

Pew Research Center. 2010b. Support for same-sex marriage edges upward; majority continues to favor gays serving openly in military. Retrieved from http://people-press.org/report/662/same-sex-marriage.

Pew Research Center. 2013a. Big racial divide over Zimmerman verdict. Retrieved from www.people-press.org/2013/07/22/big-racial-divide-over-zimmerman-verdict/.

Pew Research Center. 2013b. "Borders first" a dividing line in immigration debate. Washington, DC: Pew Research Center. Retrieved from www.people-press.org/2013/06/23/borders-first-a-dividing-line-in-immigration-debate/.

Pew Research Center. 2013c. Changing attitudes on gay marriage. Retrieved from http://features.pewforum.org/same-sex-marriage-attitudes/slide2.php.

Pew Research Center. 2013d. Modern parenthood: Roles of moms and dads converge as they balance work and family. Washington, DC: Pew Research Center.

Pew Research Religion & Public Life Project. 2012. "Nones" on the rise. October 9. Retrieved from www.pewforum.org/2012/10/09/nones-on-the-rise/.

Pew-Templeton Global Religious Futures Project. 2013. Pew Research Center's religion and public life project. Retrieved from www.globalreligiousfutures.org/.

Pfohl, Stephen. 2009. *Images of deviance and social control.* Long Grove, IL: Waveland Press.

Phelan, Jo C. 2005. Geneticization of deviant behavior and consequences for stigma: The case of mental illness. *Journal of Health and Social Behavior* 46: 307–22.

Phillips, D. R. 2000. *Ageing in the Asia-Pacific region: Issues, policies, and future trends.* New York: Routledge.

Picca, Leslie Houts, and Joe Feagin. 2007. *Two-faced racism: Whites in the backstage and frontstage.* New York: Routledge.

Pierce, Glenn L., and Michael L. Radelet. 2005. The impact of legally inappropriate factors on death sentencing for California homicides, 1990–1999. *Santa Clara Law Review* 46: 1–41.

Piketty, Thomas, and Emmanuel Saez. 2010. Income inequality in the United States. Supplemental updated data retrieved from http://elsa.berkeley.edu/~saez/Tab-Fig2008.xls.

Pinker, Steven. 2007. *The language instinct: How the mind creates language.* New York: Harper Perennial Modern Classics.

Piven, Frances Fox. 2008. *Challenging authority.* Lanham, MD: Rowman & Littlefield.

Pizzo, Stephen, Mary Fricker, and Paul Muolo. 1989. *Inside job: The looting of America's savings and loans.* New York: McGraw-Hill.

Poggi, Gianfranco. 2001. *Forms of power.* Malden, MA: Blackwell.

Polivka, Anne E., and Jennifer M. Rothgeb. 1993. Redesigning the CPS Questionnaire. *Monthly Labor Review* 116 (9): 10–28.

Pollin, Robert, and Stephanie Luce. 1998. *The living wage.* New York: New Press.

Polyani, Karl. 1977. *The livelihood of man.* New York: Academic Press.

Pompper, Donnalyn, Jorge Soto, and Laren Piel. 2007. Male body image and magazine standards: Considering dimensions of age and ethnicity. *Journalism and Mass Communication Quarterly* 83: 3 (Autumn): 525–45.

Popenoe, David. 2007. *The state of our unions: The social health of marriage in America.* Piscataway, NJ: The National Marriage Project.

Popenoe, David. 2009. *Families without fathers*. Piscataway, NJ: Transaction.

Population Reference Bureau. 2008. *2008 World population data sheet*. Washington, DC: Population Reference Bureau.

Portes, Alejandro. 2002. NAFTA and Mexican immigration. Working Paper, No. 351. Princeton University, Woodrow Wilson School of Public and International Affairs, Center for Migration and Development. Retrieved from http://cmd .princeton.edu/ papers/NAFTA%20and%20Mexican%20 Immigration.pdf.

Portes, Alejandro. 2011. English-only triumphs, but the costs are high. In *The structure of schooling: Readings in the sociology of education*, ed. Richard Arum, Irenee R. Beattie, and Karly Ford, pp. 567–71. Los Angeles: Sage.

Portes, Alejandro, and Rubin G. Rumbaut. 2001. *Legacies: The story of the immigrant second generation*. Berkeley: University of California Press.

Postman, Neil. 2005. *Amusing ourselves to death*. New York: Penguin.

Power, Matthew. 2006. The magic mountain: Trickle-down economics in a Philippine garbage dump. *Harper's*, September, pp. 57–68.

Powers, William. 2010. *Hamlet's BlackBerry*. New York: Harper.

Priest, Dana, and William M. Arkin. 2010. A hidden world, growing beyond control. *Washington Post*, July 19. Retrieved from http://projects.washingtonpost.com/ top-secret-america/articles/a-hidden-world-growing-beyond-control/.

Project for Excellence in Journalism. 2009. Covering the Great Recession. Retrieved from www.journalism.org/analysis_report/ covering_great_recession.

ProPublica. 2010. Disposable army: Civilian contractors in Iraq and Afghanistan. Retrieved from www.propublica.org/article/ civilian-contractors-the-story-so-far.

ProPublica. 2013. Bailout tracker. Retrieved from http://projects.propublica.org/ bailout/.

Prothero, Stephen. 2007. *Religious literacy*. New York: HarperCollins.

Pryor, John H., Sylvia Hurtado, Victor B. Saenz, José Luis Santos, and William S. Korn. 2007. *The American freshman: Forty year trends*. Los Angeles: University of California, Higher Education Research Institute.

Puette, William. 1992. *Through jaundiced eyes: How the media view organized labor*. Ithaca, NY: ILR Press.

Pugh, Allison J. 2009. *Longing and belonging: Parents, children and consumer culture*. Berkeley: University of California Press.

Puhl, Rebecca, and Kelly D. Brownell. 2001. Bias, discrimination, and obesity. *Obesity Research* 9 (12): 788–805.

Putnam, Robert, and David E. Campbell. 2010. *American grace: How religion divides and unites us*. New York: Simon & Schuster.

Putnam, Robert D. 2000. *Bowling alone: The collapse and revival of American community*. New York: Simon & Schuster.

Quillian, Lincoln. 2006. New approaches to understanding racial prejudice and discrimination. *Annual Review of Sociology* 32: 299–328.

Quillian, Lincoln, and Mary E. Campbell. 2003. Beyond black and white: The present and future of multiracial friendship segregation. *American Sociological Review* 68: 540–66.

Radelet, Michael L., and Marian J. Borg. 2000. The changing nature of death penalty debates. *Annual Review of Sociology* 26: 43–61.

Radelet Michael L., and Traci L. Lacock. 2009. Do executions lower homicide rates? The views of leading criminologists. *Journal of Criminal Law and Criminology* 99 (2): 489–508.

Radtke, Lorraine H., and Henderikus J. Stam. 1994. *Power/gender: Social relations in theory and practice*. Thousand Oaks, CA: Sage.

Rainey, James. 2006. Aiming for a more subtle fighting force. *Los Angeles Times*, May 9, p. A1.

Rainey, James. 2010. The news is, that pitch was paid for. *Los Angeles Times*, September 15. Retrieved from www.latimes.com/ entertainment/news/la-et-onthemedia-20100915,0,370372 .column.

Rainie, Lee, and Barry Wellman. 2012. *Networked: The new social operating system*. Cambridge, MA: MIT Press.

Rajan, Raghuram G. 2010. *Fault Lines: How Hidden Fractures Still Threaten the World Economy*. Princeton, NJ: Princeton University Press.

Ransford, Marc. 2005. Average person spends more time using media than anything else. Ball State University Center for Media Design. Middletown Media Studies II. Retrieved from www.bsu.edu/news/ article/0,1370,--36658,00 .html.

Rasinski, Kenneth. 1989. The effect of question wording on public support for government spending. *Public Opinion Quarterly* 53: 388–94.

Raven, Bertram H. 1965. Social influence and power. In *Current studies in social psychology*, ed. I. D. Stainer and M. Fishbein, pp. 399–444. New York: Wiley.

Ray, Rebecca, and John Schmitt. 2007. No-vacation nation. Washington, DC: Center for Economic Policy and Research.

Ray, Rebecca, Janet C. Gornick, and John Schmitt. 2009. Parental leave policies in 21 countries: Assessing generosity and gender equality. Washington, DC: Center for Economic and Policy Research. Retrieved from www.cepr.net/ documents/publications/parental_2008_09.pdf.

Rectanus, Mark. 2002. *Culture incorporated: Museums, artists, and corporate sponsorships*. Minneapolis: University of Minnesota Press.

Redmon, David. 2003. Playful deviance as an urban leisure activity. *Deviant Behavior* 24 (1): 27–51.

Reed, Brian J., and David R. Segal. 2006. Social network analysis and counter-insurgency operations: The capture of Saddam Hussein. *Sociological Focus* 39 (4): 251–64.

Rees, Courtney, and Sonia Ruiz. 2003. Compendium of cultural competent initiatives in health care. Menlo Park, CA: Henry J. Kaiser Family Foundation. Retrieved from www.kff.org/ uninsured/loader.cfm?url=/ commonspot/ security/getfile. cfm&PageID=14365.

Reese, William J. 2005. *America's public schools: From the common school to "No Child Left Behind."* Baltimore, MD: Johns Hopkins University Press.

Reiman, Jeffrey, and Paul Leighton. 2013. *The rich get richer and the poor get prison*, 10th ed. Boston: Allyn & Bacon.

Reinharz, Shulamit. 1992. *Feminist methods in social research*. New York: Oxford University Press.

Rendall, Steve, and Julie Hollar. 2006. Are you on the *NewsHour*'s guest list? Fairness and Accuracy in Reporting (FAIR). Retrieved from www.fair.org/index .php?page=2967.

Rendall, Steve, and Michael Morel. 2010. Does *NewsHour* "Help Us See America Whole"? Fairness and Accuracy in Reporting (FAIR). Retrieved from www.fair.org/ index.php?page=4177.

Renkema, Lennart J., Diederik A. Stapel, and Nico W. Van Yperen. 2008. Go with the flow: Conforming to others in the face of existential threat. *European Journal of Social Psychology* 38: 747–56.

Renzulli, Linda A., and Vincent J. Roscigno. 2011. Charter schools and the public good. In *The structure of schooling: Readings in the sociology of education*, ed. Richard Arum, Irenee R. Beattie, and Karly Ford, pp. 572–57. Los Angeles: Sage.

Reuben, Julie A. 1996. *The making of the modern university: Intellectual transformation and the marginalization of morality*. Chicago: University of Chicago Press.

Rhode Island Coalition Against Domestic Violence. 2000. *Domestic violence: A handbook for journalists*. Warwick, RI: RICADV.

Rice, LaVon. 2007. Shameless lackey or consumer advocate? *Footnotes* (January): 7.

Richeson, Jennifer A., Abigail A. Baird, Heather L. Gordon, Todd F. Heatherton, Carrie L. Wyland, Sophie Trawalter, and J. Nicole Shelton, 2003. An fMRI investigation of the impact of interracial contact on executive function. *Nature Neuroscience* 6 (12): 1323–28.

Rideout, Victoria J., Ulla G. Foehr, and Donald F. Roberts. 2010. *Generation M2: Media in the lives of 8- to 18-year olds*. Menlo Park, CA: Kaiser Family Foundation.

Riesebrodt, Martin. 2000. Fundamentalism and the resurgence of religion. *Numen* 47: 266–87.

Risman, Barbara, and Pepper Schwartz. 2002. After the sexual revolution: Gender politics in teen dating. *Contexts* 1 (1): 16–24.

Ritzer, George. 1975. *Sociology: A multiple paradigm science.* Boston: Allyn & Bacon.

Ritzer, George. 1993. *The McDonaldization of society.* Thousand Oaks, CA: Pine Forge Press.

Ritzer, George. 2013. *The McDonaldization of society,* 7th ed. Thousand Oaks, CA: Pine Forge Press.

Ritzer, George, and Nathan Jurgenson. 2010. Production, consumption, prosumption. *Journal of Consumer Culture* 10 (1): 13–36.

Ritzer, George, and J. Stepnisky. 2013. *Sociological theory,* 6th ed. New York: McGraw-Hill.

Robert Wood Johnson Foundation. 2008. *Where we live matters for our health: The links between housing and health.* Issue Brief 2, September.

Roberts, Donald, Ulla Foehr, and Victoria Rideout. 2005. *Generation M: Media in the lives of 8 to 18 year olds.* Menlo Park, CA: Kaiser Family Foundation.

Roberts, Sam, and Peter Baker. 2010. Asked to declare his race, Obama checks "black." *New York Times,* April 3, p. A9.

Rodriguez, Nestor. 2004. Workers wanted: Employer recruitment of immigrant labor. *Work and Occupations* 31 (4): 453–73.

Roediger, David R. 1999. *The wages of whiteness.* London: Verso.

Roethlisberger, Fritz Jules. 1939. *Management and the worker.* Cambridge, MA: Harvard University Press.

Rohter, Larry. 2006. Billboard ban in São Paulo angers advertisers. *New York Times,* December 12. Retrieved from www .nytimes.com/2006/12/12/world/ americas/12iht-brazil.html.

Roscigno, Vincent J., Sherry Mong, Reginald Byron, and Griff Tester. 2007. Age discrimination, social closure and employment. *Social Forces* 86 (1): 313–34.

Roscoe, Will. 1992. *The Zuni woman-man.* Albuquerque: University of New Mexico Press.

Rose, Mike. 2004. *The mind at work.* New York: Penguin.

Ross, Robert, and Kent Trachte. 1983. Global cites and global classes: The peripheralization of labor in New York City. *Review* 6 (3): 393–431.

Ross, Robert J. S. 2004. *Slaves to fashion: Poverty and abuse in the new sweatshops.* Ann Arbor: University of Michigan Press.

Rothenberg, Paula S. 2014. *Race, class, and gender in the United States,* 9th ed. New York: Worth.

Rothenberg, Paula S., ed. 2004. *White privilege: Essential readings on the other side of racism.* Boston: Worth.

Roy, Olivier. 1994. *The failure of political islam.* Cambridge, MA: Harvard University Press.

Roy, Olivier. 2004. *Globalized Islam.* New York: Columbia University Press.

Roy, Olivier. 2007. *Secularism confronts Islam.* New York: Columbia University Press.

Rubin, Beth A. 1996. *Shifts in the social contract.* Thousand Oaks, CA: Pine Forge Press.

Rubin, Herbert J., and Irene S. Rubin. 2004. *Qualitative interviewing.* Thousand Oaks, CA: Sage.

Rubin, J. Z., F. J. Provenzano, and Z. Luria. 1974. The eye of the beholder: Parents' views on sex of newborns. *American Journal of Orthopsychiatry* 44: 512–19.

Rupp, Deborah E., and Sharmin Spencer. 2006. When customers lash out: The effects of customer interactional injustice on emotional labor and the mediating role of discrete emotions. *Journal of Applied Psychology* 91 (4): 971–78.

Russell, Bertrand. 2004. *Power: A new social analysis.* New York: Routledge.

Saad, Lydia. 2011. To lose weight, Americans rely more on dieting than exercise. Gallup Well-Being, November 28. Retrieved from www.gallup.com/poll/150986/lose-weight-americans-rely-dieting-exercise.aspx.

Saad, Lydia. 2013. U.S. death penalty support stable at 63%. Gallup, January 9. Retrieved September 19, 2013, from www.gallup.com/poll/159770/death-penalty-support-stable.aspx?version=print.

Sabella, Russell. 2012. Cyberbullying: How school counselors can help. In *Cyberbullying prevention and response: Expert perspectives,* ed. Justin W. Patchin and Sameer Hinduja, pp. 72–92. New York: Routledge.

Sabella, Russell A., Justin W. Patchin, and Sameer Hinduja. 2013. Cyberbullying myths and realities. *Computers in Human Behavior* 29: 2703–11.

Sabia, Joseph J. 2008. There's no place like home: A hazard model analysis of aging in place among older homeowners in the PSID. *Research on Aging* 30 (1): 3–35.

Saez, Emmanuel. 2013. Striking it richer: The evolution of top incomes in the United States. Berkeley: University of California. Retrieved from http://elsa.berkeley.edu/ ~saez/saez-UStopincomes-2012.pdf.

Saguy, Abigail. 2013. *What's wrong with fat?* New York: Oxford University Press.

Saint, Nick. 2010. Outraged blogger is automatically being followed by her abusive ex-husband on Google Buzz. *Business Insider,* February 12. Retrieved from www .businessinsider.com/outraged-blogger-is-automatically-being-followed-by-her-abusive-ex-husband-on-google-buzz-2010-2#ixzz2gsOmM7mA.

Sallie Mae. 2013. How America pays for college 2013. Retrieved from www.salliemae.com/assets/Core/how-America-pays/howamericapays2013.pdf.

Sappleton, Natalie, ed. 2013. *Advancing research methods with new technologies.* Hershey, PA: Information Science Reference.

Sarracino, Carmine. 2009. *The porning of America.* Boston: Beacon Press.

Sassen, Saskia. 1991. *The global city: New York, London, Tokyo.* Princeton, NJ: Princeton University Press.

Sassen, Saskia. 2006. *Cities in a global economy,* 3rd ed. Thousand Oaks, CA: Pine Forge Press.

Sassen, Saskia. 2007. *A sociology of globalization.* New York: Norton.

Scharf, Deepti. 2003. *Melanie Wood: The making of a mathematician.* Durham, NC: Duke University Office of News and Communications. Retrieved from www.dukenews.duke.edu/2003/05/ melaniewood0503.html.

Schatzman, Leonard, and Anselm Strauss. 1973. *Field research.* Englewood Cliffs, NJ: Prentice Hall.

Scheufele, Dietram A., and Patricia Moy. 2000. Twenty-five years of the spiral of silence: A conceptual review and empirical outlook. *International Journal of Public Opinion Research* 12 (1): 3–28.

Schiller, Herbert I. 1989. *Culture, Inc.: The corporate takeover of expression.* New York: Oxford University Press.

Schiller, Herbert I. 1992. *Mass communications and American empire,* 2nd ed. Boulder, CO: Westview Press.

Schlesinger, Arthur. 1998. *The disuniting of America.* New York: Norton.

Schlozman, Kay, Benjamin Page, Sidney Verba, and Morris Fiorina. 2005. Inequalities of political voice. American Political Science Association Task Force on Inequality and American Democracy. Retrieved from www.apsanet.org/imgtest/ voicememo.pdf.

Schmidt, Alvin. 1997. *The menace of multiculturalism.* Westport, CT: Praeger.

Schnaiberg, Allan. 1980. *The environment.* New York: Oxford University Press.

Schneiberg, Marc, Marissa King, and Thomas Smith. 2008. Social movements and organizational form: Cooperative alternatives to corporations in the American insurance, dairy, and grain industries. *American Sociological Review* 73: 635–67.

Schneider, Joseph. 1978. Deviant drinking as a disease: Alcoholism as a social accomplishment. *Social Problems* 25 (4): 361–72.

Scholte, Jan Aart. 2005. *Globalization: A critical introduction,* 2nd ed. (New York: Palgrave Mcmillan).

Schor, Juliet. 1999. *The overspent American.* New York: Basic Books.

Schor, Juliet. 2004. *Born to buy: The commercialized child and the new consumer culture.* New York: Scribner.

Schrank, David, Bill Eisele, and Tim Lomax. 2012. *2012 urban mobility report.* College Station, TX: Texas A&M Transportation Institute. Retrieved from http://d2dtl5nn-lpfr0r.cloudfront.net/tti.tamu.edu/documents/mobility-report-2012.pdf.

Schudson, Michael. 1986. *Advertising: The uneasy persuasion.* New York: Basic Books.

Schulz, Amy J., and Leith Mullings, eds. 2005. *Gender, race, class and health: Intersectional approaches.* San Francisco: Jossey-Bass.

Schutz, Alfred. 1962. *Collected papers: The problem of social reality*, ed. Maurice Natanson. The Hague: Martinus Nijhoff.

Schwartz, Shalom H. 1992. Universals in the content and structure of values. *Advances in Experimental Social Psychology* 19: 255–65.

Schwartz, Shalom H. 1994. Are there universals in the content and structure of values? *Journal of Social Issues* 50: 19–45.

Schwartz, Shalom H., Gila Melech, Arielle Lehmann, Steven Burgess, Mari Harris, and Vicki Owens. 2001. Extending the cross-cultural validity of the theory of basic human values with a different method of measurement. *Journal of Cross-Cultural Psychology* 32: 519–42.

Schwedler, Jillian. 2006. *Faith in moderation.* New York: Cambridge University Press.

Scott, James. 1987. *Weapons of the weak.* New Haven, CT: Yale University Press.

Scott, James C. 1992. *Domination and the arts of resistance.* New Haven, CT: Yale University Press.

Scott, Joan Wallach. 2010. *The politics of the veil.* Princeton, NJ: Princeton University Press.

Scott, John P. 2000. *Social network analysis: A handbook.* London: Sage.

Scott-Clayton, Judith. 2011. The shapeless river: Does a lack of structure inhibit students' progress at community colleges? (CCRC Working Paper No. 25). Community College Research Center. New York: Columbia University Teachers College. Retrieved from http://ccrc.tc.columbia.edu/publications/lack-of-structure-students-progress.html.

Seidman, Steven, ed. 1996. *Queer theory/sociology.* Malden, MA: Blackwell.

Sengupta, Somini. 2007. Careers give India's women new independence. *New York Times*, November 23.

Sennett, Richard. 2000. *The corrosion of character: The personal consequences of work in the new capitalism.* New York: Norton.

Sennett, Richard. 2006. *The culture of the new capitalism.* New Haven, CT: Yale University Press.

Senter, Mary S., Nicole Van Vooren, and Roberta Spalter-Roth. 2013. Sociology majors: Before graduation in 2012. Washington, DC: American Sociological Association. Retrieved from www.asanet.org/documents/research/pdfs/BachBeyond_Sociology_Majors_Brief_2013.pdf.

Settersten, Richard A., Jr. 2002. Socialization and the life course. *Advances in Life Course Research* 7: 13–40.

Seymour, Diane, and Peter Sandiford. 2005. Learning emotion rules in service organizations. *Work, Employment and Society* 19 (3): 547–64.

Shaheen, Jack. G. 2009. *Reel bad Arabs: How Hollywood vilifies a people.* Northhampton, MA: Olive Branch Press.

Shanahan, Michael J. 2000. Pathways to adulthood in changing societies: Variability and mechanisms in life course perspective. *Annual Review of Sociology* 26: 667–92.

Shanahan, Michael J., and Scott M. Hofer. 2005. Social context in gene-environment interactions: Retrospect and prospect. *Journals of Gerontology, Series B* 60 (March): 65 (12).

Shapiro, Thomas, Tatjana Meschede, and Sam Osoro. 2013. The roots of the widening racial wealth gap: Explaining the black-white economic divide. Waltham, MA: Brandeis University, Institute on Assets and Social Policy. Retrieved from http://iasp.brandeis.edu/pdfs/Author/shapiro-thomas-m/racialwealthgapbrief.pdf.

Sharp, Gene. 1973. *Power and struggle.* Boston: Porter Sargent.

Sharp, Gene. 2010. *From dictatorship to democracy.* Boston: Albert Einstein Institute. Retrieved from www.aeinstein.org/organizations/ org/fdtd.pdf.

Sheehan, James. 2008. *Where have all the soldiers gone?* New York: Houghton Mifflin.

Sheffield, Hazel. 2012. Pasadena publisher launches a system for outsourcing local news. *Columbia Journalism Review*, August 27.

Shimberg, Elaine Fantle. 1999. *Blending families.* New York: Berkeley.

Short, James E. 2013. *How much media? 2013. Report on American consumers.* University of Southern California, Institute for Communications Technology Management. Retrieved from http://classic.marshall.usc.edu/assets/160/25918.pdf.

Shulman, Kevin A., Schulman, Kevin A., Jesse A. Berlin, William Harless, Jon F. Kerner., Shyrl Sistrunk, Bernard J. Gersh, Ross Dubé, et al. 1999. The effect of race and sex on physicians' recommendations for cardiac catheterization. *New England Journal of Medicine* 340 (8): 618–26.

Shweder, Richard A., Martha Minow, and Hazel Rose Marcus, eds. 2002. *Engaging cultural differences: The multicultural challenge in liberal democracies.* New York: Russell Sage Foundation.

Siebold, Guy L. 2001. Core issues and theory in military sociology. *Journal of Political and Military Sociology* 29 (1): 140–59.

Silver, Catherine B. 2002. Japanese and American identities: Values and their transmission in the family. *Sociological Inquiry* 72 (2): 195–219.

Simmel, Georg. (1903) 1950. The metropolis and mental life. In *The sociology of Georg Simmel*, trans. and ed., Kurt H. Wolff. New York: Free Press.

Simmel, Georg. (1922) 1955. *Conflict & the web of group affiliations.* Kurt H. Wolff and Reinhard Bendix, trans. and eds. New York: Free Press.

Simmel, Georg. 1964. *The sociology of Georg Simmel*, trans. Kurt H. Wolff. New York: Free Press.

Simon, Clea. 1997. Haunted by my family's madness. *Washington Post*, March 9, p. C1.

Simon, Clea. 1998. *Mad house: Growing up in the shadow of mentally ill siblings.* New York: Penguin.

Simpson, Miles. 1990. Political rights and income inequality: A cross-national test. *American Sociological Review* 55 (October): 682–93.

Simpson, Sally S. 2013. White-collar crime: A review of recent developments and promising directions for future research. *Annual Review of Sociology* 39: 309–31.

Simpson, Tim. 2008. The commercialization of Macau's cafes. *Ethnography* 9 (2): 197–234.

Skocpol, Theda. 2003. *Diminished democracy: From membership to management in American life.* Norman: University of Oklahoma Press.

Slater, Don. 1999. *Consumer culture and modernity.* Malden, MA: Polity/Blackwell.

Slavin, Robert E., Nancy Madden, Margarita Calderon, Anne Chamberlain, and Megan Hennessy. 2010. *Reading and language outcomes of a five-year randomized evaluation of transitional bilingual education.* Baltimore, MD: Johns Hopkins University.

Slivinski, Stephen. 2007. The corporate welfare state. *Policy Analysis* No. 542. Washington, DC: Cato Institute. Retrieved from www.cato.org/pubs/pas/pa592.pdf.

Sloan, Allan. 2007. House of junk: Junk mortgages under the microscope. *Fortune*, July 29.

Small, Meredith. 2005. Dare to bare. *New York Times*, October 11, p. A23.

Smedley, Audrey. 2007. *Race in North America: Origin and evolution of a worldview.* Boulder, CO: Westview Press.

Smith, Christian, ed. 2003. *The secular revolution.* Berkeley: University of California Press.

Smith, Dorothy. 1974. Women's perspective as a radical critique of sociology. *Sociological Inquiry* 44: 7–14.

Smith, Dorothy. 1987. *The everyday world is problematic: A feminist sociology.* Boston: Northeastern University Press.

Smith, Dorothy. 1989. *The everyday world as problematic: A feminist sociology.* Boston: Northeastern University Press.

Smith, Dorothy. 1990. *The conceptual practices of power.* Boston: Northeastern University Press.

Smith, Eliot R., and James R. Kluegel. 1986. *Beliefs about inequality.* Hawthorne, NY: Aldine Transaction.

Smith, Jackie, and Hank Johnston. 2002. *Globalization and resistance: Transnational dimensions of social movements.* Lanham, MD: Rowman & Littlefield.

Smith, Michael Peter, and Luis Gurnizo, eds. 1998. *Transnationalism from below: Comparative urban and community research*, vol. 6. Brunswick, NJ: Transaction.

Smith, Thomas S., and David D. Franks. 1999. Emergence, reduction and levels of analyses in the neurosociological paradigm. In *Mind, brain, and society: Toward a neurosociology of emotion*, ed. David D. Franks and Thomas S. Smith, pp. 3–17. Stamford, CT: JAI Press.

Smith, Tom W. 2007. *Job satisfaction in the United States.* Chicago: NORC/University of Chicago.

Smith-Lovin, Lynn, and Miller McPherson. 1993. You are who you know: A network perspective on gender. In *Theory on gender. feminism on theory,* ed. Paula England, pp. 223–51. New York: Aldine.

Smock, Pamela, Wendy Manning, and Meredith Porter. 2005. "Everything's there except money": How money shapes decisions to marry among cohabitors. *Journal of Marriage and Family* 67 (3): 680–96.

Snow, David A., E. Burke Rochford Jr., Steven K. Worden, and Robert D. Benford. 1986. Frame alignment processes, micromobilization, and movement participation. *American Sociological Review* 51: 464–81.

Snow, David A., and Robert D. Benford. 1988. Ideology, frame resonance, and participant mobilization. In *International social movement research,* pp. 197–217. Greenwich, CT: JAI Press.

Social Security Board of Trustees. 2013. *The 2013 annual report of the board of trustees of the Federal Old-Age and Survivors Insurance and Federal Disability Insurance trust funds.* Retrieved from www.socialsecurity.gov/OACT/TR/2013/trTOC.html.

Sorkin, Andrew. 2010. *Too big to fail: The inside story of how Wall Street and Washington fought to save the financial system—and themselves.* New York: Viking.

SourceWatch. 2011. Total Wall Street bailout cost. Retrieved from www.sourcewatch .org/index.php?title=Total_Wall_Street_Bailout_Cost.

Spaargaren, Gert, and Arthur P. J. Mol. 1992. Sociology, environment, and modernity: Ecological modernization as a theory of social change. *Society and Natural Resources* 5: 323–44.

Spalter-Roth, Roberta, and Nicole Van Vooren. 2008. *What are they doing with a bachelor's degree in sociology?* Washington, DC: American Sociological Association.

Spalter-Roth, Roberta, and Nicole Van Vooren. 2009. *Idealists versus careerists: Graduate school choices of sociology majors.* Washington, DC: American Sociological Association.

Spalter-Roth, Roberta, and Nicole Van Vooren. 2010. *Mixed success: Four years of experiences of 2005 sociology graduates.* Washington, DC: American Sociological Association.

Span, Paula. 2003. Marriage at first sight. *Washington Post Magazine,* February 23, pp. 16+.

Spencer, Wayne. 2003. Are the stars coming out? Secularization and the future of astrology. In *Predicting religion: Christian, secular and alternative futures,* ed. Grace Davie, Paul Heelas, and Linda Woodhead, pp. 214–28. Burlington, VT: Ashgate.

Squires, Gregory, and Chester Hartman. 2006. *There is no such thing as a natural disaster: Race, class and Katrina.* New York: Routledge.

Srinivasan, Shobha, Liam R. O'Fallon, and Allen Dearry. 2003. Creating health communities, healthy homes, and healthy people. *American Journal of Public Health* 93 (9): 1446–50.

Stanton, Elizabeth Cady. 1889. *A history of woman suffrage,* vol. 1. Rochester, NY: Fowler and Wells. Retrieved from www .fordham.edu/ halsall/mod/Senecafalls.html.

Stapinkski, Helene. 1998. Let's talk dirty. *American Demographics* 20 (11): 50–56.

Stark, Rodney. 1999. Secularization RIP. *Sociology of Religion.* 60: 249–273.

Stark, Rodney, and William Sims Bainbridge. 1985. *The future of religion: Secularization, revival, and cult formation.* Berkeley: University of California Press.

Starr, Paul. 1983. *The social transformation of American medicine.* New York: Basic Books.

Stearns, Elizabeth, Claudia Buchmann, and Kara Bonneau. 2009. Interracial friendships in the transition to college. *Sociology of Education* 82: 173–95.

Steel, Emily. 2010. Some data-miners ready to reveal what they know. *Wall Street Journal,* December 3. Retrieved from http://online.wsj.com/article/SB10001424052748704377004575650802136721966.html.

Stein, Ben. 2006. In class warfare, guess which class is winning. *New York Times,* November 26. Retrieved from www.ny-times.com/2006/11/26/business/yourmoney/26every.html.

Steinberg, Brian. 2013. Advertisers embrace gory shows like "Walking Dead." *Variety,* April 2. Retrieved from http://variety.com/2013/biz/news/advertisers-embrace-gory-shows-like-walking-dead-1200332162/.

Sterngold, James. 2010. How much did Lehman CEO Dick Fuld really make? *Bloomberg Businessweek,* April 29. Retrieved from www .businessweek.com/print/maga-zine/content/ 10_19/b4177056214833.htm.

Stevens, Mitchell. 2007. *Creating a class: College admissions and the education of elites.* Cambridge, MA: Harvard University Press.

Stewart, David W., Prem N. Shamdasani, and Dennis Rook. 2006. *Focus groups: Theory and practice,* 2nd ed. Thousand Oaks, CA: Sage.

Stiglitz, Joseph, and Andrew Charlton. 2007. *Fair trade for all.* New York: Oxford University Press.

Stock, Christianne, and Anne Ellaway. 2013. *Neighbourhood structure and health promotion.* New York: Springer.

Stockholm International Peace Research Institute. 2013. Trends in world military expenditure, 2012. Retrieved from http://books.sipri.org/files/FS/SIPRIFS1304.pdf.

Stockman, Farah. 2011. Bush program helped lay the groundwork in Egypt. *Boston Globe,* February 11. Retrieved from www.boston. com/news/nation/articles/2011/02/13/bush_program _helped_lay_the_ground-work_in_egypt/?rss_id=Boston. com+--+Top+political+stories.

Stockwell, Jamie. 2005. Defense, prosecution play to new "CSI" savvy. *Washington Post,* May 22, pp. A1, A10.

Stodghill, Alexis Garrett. 2012. Beyoncé L'Oréal ad controversy inspires black community backlash. The Grio. Retrieved from http://thegrio.com/2012/02/10/beyonce-describes-herself-as-african-american-native-american-french-in-new-loreal-ad.

Stohlberg, Carol Gay. 2011. Shy U.S. intellectual created playbook used in a revolution. *New York Times,* February 16. Retrieved from www.nytimes.com/2011/02/17/world/middleeast/17sharp.html.

Stoller, Robert. 1968. *Sex and gender: On the development of masculinity and femininity.* New York: Science House.

Story, Louise. 2008. To aim ads, web is keeping closer eye on you. *New York Times,* March 10. Retrieved from www.nytimes.com/2008/03/10/technology/10privacy.html.

Strasburger, Victor C., and Barbara J. Wilson. 2002. *Children, adolescents, and the media.* Thousand Oaks, CA: Sage.

Strasburger, Victor C., Barbara J. Wilson, and Amy B. Jordan. 2009. *Children, adolescents, and the media,* 2nd ed. Thousand Oaks, CA: Sage.

Straus, Murray A. 2004. Prevalence of violence against dating partners by male and female university students worldwide. *Violence Against Women* 10 (7): 790–811.

Sulik, Gayle. 2007. The balancing act: Care work for the self and coping with breast cancer. *Gender & Society* 21 (6): 857–77.

Sullivan, Dennis, and Larry Tifft. 2006. *Handbook of restorative justice: A global perspective.* New York: Routledge.

Sumner, William Graham. 1906. *Folkways.* Boston: Ginn.

Sutherland, Edwin H. 1947. *Principles of criminology,* 4th ed. Philadelphia: Lippincott.

Sutherland, Edwin H. 1949. *White collar crime.* New York: Dryden Press.

Sutherland, Edwin H., Donald R. Cressey, and David F. Luckenbill. 1992. *Principles of criminology,* 11th ed. Lanham, MD: General Hall.

Sweeney, Brigid. 2010. Luxury retailers cash in as affluent shoppers step up holiday buying. *Chicago Business,* November 15. Retrieved from www.chicagobusiness.com/article/20101113/ ISSUE01/311139970/luxury-retailers-cash-in-as-affluent-shoppers-step-up-holiday-buying.

Swisher, Kara. 2013. "Physically together": Here's the internal Yahoo no-work-from-home memo for remote workers and maybe more. *All Things D.* Retrieved from http://allthingsd.com/20130222/physically-together-heres-the-internal-yahoo-no-work-from-home-memo-which-extends-beyond-remote-workers/

Switzer, Kathrine. 2007. *Marathon woman.* New York: Carroll & Graf.

Syme, S. Leonard, and Lisa F. Berkman. 1976. Social class, susceptibility, and sickness. *American Journal of Epidemiology* 104: 1–8.

Szasz, Andrew. 2007. *Shopping our way to safety: How we changed from protecting the environment to protecting ourselves.* Minneapolis: University of Minnesota Press.

Sztompka, Piotr. 1993. *The sociology of social change.* Malden, MA: Blackwell.

Tahirih Justice Center. 2011. About us. Retrieved from www.tahirih.org/about-us/.

Takaki, Ronald. 2008. *A different mirror: A history of multicultural America.* New York: Back Bay Books.

Taley, Margaret. 2006. When nature calls, women in House hike. *Denver Post,* December 12. Retrieved from www.denverpost.com/rockies/ci_4911077.

Taormino, Tristan. 2013. Introduction: The politics of producing pleasure. In *The feminist porn book,* ed. Tristan Taormino, Constance Penley, Celine Parrenas Shimizu, and Mireille Miller-Young, pp. 9–20. New York: Feminist Press at the City University of New York.

Tarrow, Sidney. 2011. *Power in movement.* New York: Cambridge University Press.

Tavernise, Sabrina, and Robert Gebeloff. 2010. Immigrants make paths to suburbia, not cities. *New York Times,* December 14. Retrieved from www.nytimes.com/2010/12/15/us/15census.html?ref=nyregion.

Tax Policy Center. 2011a. Tax facts. Retrieved from www.taxpolicycenter.org/taxfacts/listdocs.cfm?topic2id=20.

Tax Policy Center. 2011b. Table T11-0005: Current law against baseline of pre-2009-stimulus law plus AMT patch, evaluated in 2011; distribution of federal tax change by cash income percentile, 2011. Urban Institute and Brookings Institution. Retrieved from www.taxpolicycenter.org/numbers/displayatab.cfm?DocID=2883&topic2ID=40&topic3ID=41&DocTypeID=2.

Taylor, Alan. 2001. *American colonies: The settling of North America.* New York: Penguin.

Taylor, Frederick Winslow. 1911. *The principles of scientific management.* New York: Harper Brothers.

Taylor, Verta. 1989. Social movement continuity: The women's movement in abeyance. *American Sociological Review* 54 (5): 761–75.

Taylor, Verta, Leila Rupp, and Nancy Whittier, eds. 2008. *Feminist frontiers.* New York: McGraw-Hill.

Teixeira, Ruy, and John Halpin. 2013. Building an all-in nation. Washington, DC: Center for American Progress. Retrieved from www.americanprogress.org/wp-content/uploads/2013/10/AllInNationReport.pdf.

TenHouten, Warren D. 1980. Social dominance and cerebral hemisphericity:

Discriminating social groups by performance on two lateralized tests. *International Journal of Neuroscience* 10: 223–32.

TenHouten, Warren D. 1999. Text and temporality: Patterned-cyclical and ordinary-linear forms of time consciousness, inferred from a corpus of Australian Aboriginal and Euro-Australian life-historical interviews. *Symbolic Interaction* 22: 121–37.

Tewksbury, Richard, and George E. Higgins. 2006. Examining the effect of emotional dissonance on work stress and satisfaction with supervisors among correctional staff. *Criminal Justice Policy Review* 17 (3): 290–301.

Thomas, Sarah. 2010. Students, teachers agog at New Newton North High School. Retrieved from www.boston.com/yourtown/news/newton/2010/08/students_leaders_agog_at_new_n.html.

Thomas, William I. 1923. *The unadjusted girl.* Boston: Little, Brown.

Thomas, William I., and Dorothy Swain Thomas. 1928. *The child in America: Behavior problems and programs.* New York: Knopf.

Thomson, Irene Taviss. 2010. *Culture wars and enduring American dilemmas.* Ann Arbor: University of Michigan Press.

Thorne, Barrie, and Marilyn Yalom, eds. 1992. *Rethinking the family: Some feminist questions.* Boston: Northeastern University Press.

Thrasher, Frederick Milton. 1927. *The gang.* Chicago: University of Chicago Press.

Tilly, Charles. 2004a. *Social movements 1768–2004.* Boulder, CO: Paradigm.

Tilly, Charles. 2004b. Terror, terrorism, terrorists. *Sociological Theory* 22 (1): 5–13.

Timberg, Craig. 2005. The rise of a market mentality means many go hungry in Niger. *Washington Post,* August 11, p. A17.

Timiraos, Nick. 2009. Mortgage deductions look less sacred. *Wall Street Journal,* February 27. Retrieved from http://online.wsj.com/article/SB123569898005989291.html.

Tjaden, Patricia, and Nancy Thoennes. 2000. *Full report of the prevalence, incidence, and consequences of violence against women.* Washington, DC: U.S. Department of Justice.

Tjaden, Patricia, and Nancy Thoennes. 2006. *Extent, nature, and consequences of rape victimization: Findings from the National Violence Against Women Survey.* Washington, DC: U.S. Department of Justice.

Tkaczyk, Christopher. 2013. Marissa Mayer breaks her silence on Yahoo's telecommuting policy. *Fortune.* April 19. Retrieved from: http://fortune.com/2013/04/19/marissa-mayer-breaks-her-silence-on-yahoos-telecommuting-policy/.

Tolson, A. 1977. *The limits of masculinity.* London: Tavistock.

Tomlinson, John. 2008. *Cultural imperialism: A critical introduction.* London: Continuum.

Tönnies, Ferdinand. (1887)/2001. *Community and civil society,* trans. Margaret Hollis. Cambridge, UK: University of Cambridge Press.

Toussaint, Eric, and Damien Millet. 2010. *Debt, the IMF, and the World Bank.* New York: Monthly Review Press.

Trescott, Jacqueline. 2010. Ant-covered Jesus video removed from Smithsonian after Catholic League complains. *Washington Post,* December 1.

Tschannen, Oliver. 1991. The secularization paradigm: A systematization. *Journal for the Scientific Study of Religion* 30 (4): 395–415.

Tuchman, Gaye. 1978. *Making the news.* New York: Free Press.

Tumin, Melvin. 1953. Some principles of stratification: A critical analysis. *American Sociological Review* 18: 387–94.

Turk, Austin T. 2004. Sociology of terrorism. *Annual Review of Sociology* 30: 271–86.

Turkle, Sherry. 1985. *The second self.* New York: Simon & Schuster.

Turkle, Sherry. 1995. *Life on the screen.* New York: Simon & Schuster.

Turkle, Sherry. 2008. Always-on/always-on-you: The tethered self. In *Handbook of mobile communication studies,* ed. James E. Katz, pp. 121–37. Cambridge, MA: MIT Press.

Turner, Darrell J. 2011. Religion: Year in review 2009. In *Britannica Book of the Year, 2010.* Retrieved from www.britannica.com/EBchecked/topic/1581715/religion-Year-In-Review-2009.

Turner, Jonathon. 1999. The neurology of emotion: Implications for sociological theories of interpersonal behavior. In *Mind, brain, and society: Toward a neurosociology of emotion,* ed. David D. Franks and Thomas S. Smith, pp. 81–108. Stamford, CT: JAI Press.

Turner, Jonathon. 2000. *On the origins of human emotions: A sociological inquiry into the evolution of human affect.* Stanford, CA: Stanford University Press.

Turner, Margery Austin, and Stephen L. Ross. 2005. How racial discrimination affects the search for housing. In *The geography of opportunity,* ed. Xaviar de Souza Briggs, pp. 81–100. Washington, DC: Brookings Institution Press.

Turow, Joseph, Jennifer King, Chris Jay Hoofnagle, Amy Bleakley, and Michael Hennessy. 2009. Contrary to what marketers say, Americans reject tailored advertising and three activities that enable it. Retrieved from http://papers.ssrn.com/sol3/papers.cfm?abstract_id=1478214.

Tweedie, Dale. 2013. Making sense of insecurity. *Work, Employment, and Society* 27 (1): 94–104.

Twenge, Jean M. 2006. *Generation me.* New York: Free Press.

Tyler, T. R. 2005. Introduction: Legitimating ideologies. *Social Justice Research* 18: 211–15.

Tyler, T. R., and S. L. Blader. 2003. The group engagement model: Procedural justice, social identity, and cooperative behavior. *Personality and Social Psychology Review* 7: 349–61.

Tynan, Dan. 2008. Thank you, porn! 12 ways the sex trade has changed the web. *PC World*. Retrieved from www.pcworld.com/article/155745/porn_on_the_web.html.

Tyron, Maida. 2007. Killed by a cavity. *Washington Post*, March 3, p. A14.

Ugochukwu, Chioma. 2008. Cultural resistance and resilience amid imported TV programming in Nigeria. *Africa Today* 55 (1): 35–58.

U.K. Parliament. 2014. Current state of the parties. Retrieved from www.parliament.uk/mps-lords-and-offices/mps/current-state-of-the-parties/.

UN Commission on Human Security. 2004. *Human security now*. New York: United Nations.

UN Department of Economic and Social Affairs, Population Division. 2011. *World population prospects: The 2010 revision*. Retrieved from esa .un.org/unpd/wpp/.

UN Department of Economic and Social Affairs, Population Division. 2012. *World urbanization prospects: The 2011 revision*. Retrieved from http://esa.un.org/unup/pdf/WUP2011_Highlights.pdf.

UN Department of Economic and Social Affairs, Population Division. 2013. *World population prospects: The 2012 revision*. Retrieved from http://esa.un.org/unpd/wpp/index.htm.

UN Development Fund for Women. 2007. Violence against women—facts and figures. Retrieved from www.unifem.org/attachments/gender_issues/violence_against_women/facts_figures_violence_against_women_2007.pdf.

UN Development Programme. 2005. *Human development report 2005*. New York: UN Development Programme.

UN Human Settlements Programme. 2003a. *The challenge of slums*. Sterling, VA: Earthscan Publications.

UN Human Settlements Programme. 2003b. *Slums of the world*. Nairobi, Kenya: UN Settlements Programme.

UN Office on Drugs and Crime. 2006. *Trafficking in persons: Global patterns*. Retrieved from www.unodc.org/documents/human-trafficking/HT-globalpatterns-en.pdf.

UN Population Fund. 2008. State of the world's population, 2007. Retrieved from www.unfpa.org/swp/2007/presskit/pdf/sowp2007_eng.pdf.

Underwood, Anne, and Jerry Adler. 2005. When cultures clash. *Newsweek*, April 25, pp. 68–72.

UNESCO. 2013. *Adult and youth literacy: National, regional, and global trends, 1980–2015*. June. Montreal, Quebec, Canada: UNESCO Institute for Statistics.

UNESCO-Institute for Statistics. 2005. *International flow of selected cultural goods and services, 1994–2003*. Montreal, Quebec: UNESCO Institute for Statistics.

Union of Concerned Scientists. 2008. UCS satellite database. Retrieved from www.ucsusa.org/nuclear_weapons_and_global_security/space_weapons/technical_issues/ucs-satellite -database.html.

Unitarian Universalist Association of Congregations. 2013. Existence of a higher power in Unitarian Universalism. Retrieved from www.uua.org/beliefs/welcome/higherpower/index.shtml.

United for a Fair Economy. 2012. Born on third base: What the *Forbes* 400 really says about economic equality & opportunity in America. Retrieved from http://faireconomy.org/sites/default/files/BornOnThirdBase_2012.pdf.

United Nations. 2005. *The inequality predicament: Report on the world situation 2005*. New York: United Nations. Retrieved from http:// daccessdds.un.org/doc/UNDOC/GEN/N05/ 418/73/PDF/N0541873.pdf?OpenElement.

Unnever, James D., and Francis T. Cullen. 2007. The racial divide in support for the death penalty. Does white racism matter? *Social Forces* 85 (3): 1281–301.

Unnever, James D., and Frances T. Cullen. 2010. Racial-ethnic intolerance and support for capital punishment: A cross-national comparison. *Criminology* 48 (3): 831–64.

Urban, Wayne J., and Jennings L. Wagoner Jr. 2009. *American education: A history*, 4th ed. New York: Routledge.

U.S. Bureau of Labor Statistics. 2012. Occupations with the largest job growth. Retrieved from www.bls.gov/emp/ep_table_104.htm.

U.S. Bureau of Labor Statistics. 2013a. Employment projections. Retrieved from www.bls.gov/emp/ep_chart_001.htm.

U.S. Bureau of Labor Statistics. 2013b. Labor force statistics from the Current Population Survey. "Employed persons by detailed occupation, sex, race, and Hispanic or Latino ethnicity." February 5. Retrieved from www.bls.gov/cps/cpsaat11.htm.

U.S. Bureau of Labor Statistics. 2013c. Occupational employment and wages—May 2012. BLS News Release USDL-13-0543, March 29. Retrieved from www.bls.gov/news.release/archives/ocwage_03292013.htm

U.S. Bureau of Labor Statistics. 2013d. Union membership. Retrieved from www.bls.gov/news.release/union2.toc.htm.

U.S. Bureau of Labor Statistics. 2013e. Women in the labor force: A data book. Retrieved from www.bls.gov/cps/wlf-data-book-2012.pdf.

U.S. Bureau of Labor Statistics. 2014. Current Employment Statistics—CES (National). Table B-3a. Average hourly and weekly earnings of all employees on private nonfarm payrolls by industry sector, seasonally adjusted. Retrieved from www.bls.gov/web/empsit/ceseeb3a.htm.

U.S. Census Bureau. 2010a. America's families and living arrangements. Retrieved from www.census.gov/population/www/socdemo/hh-fam/cps2010.html.

U.S. Census Bureau. 2010b. Income, poverty, and health insurance coverage in the United States: 2009. Retrieved from www.census.gov/prod/2010pubs/p60-238.pdf.

U.S. Census Bureau. 2010c. Race and Hispanic origin of the foreign-born population in the United States: 2007. Retrieved from www.census.gov/prod/2010pubs/acs-11.pdf.

U.S. Census Bureau. 2011a. Current Population Survey, March and annual social and economic supplements, 2010 and earlier, Table AD-1. Retrieved from www.census.gov/population/www/socdemo/hh-fam.html#ht.

U.S. Census Bureau. 2011b. The Hispanic population: 2010. Retrieved from www.census.gov/prod/cen2010/briefs/c2010br-04.pdf.

U.S. Census Bureau. 2011c. Overview of race and Hispanic origin: 2010. Retrieved from www.census.gov/prod/cen2010/briefs/c2010br-02.pdf.

U.S. Census Bureau. 2012a. Current Population Survey, March and annual social and economic supplements, 2012 and earlier. Retrieved from www.census.gov/hhes/www/poverty/publications/pubs-cps.html.

U.S. Census Bureau. 2012b. Current Population Survey, November. Retrieved from www.census.gov/hhes/www/socdemo/voting/publications/p20/2012/tables.html.

U.S. Census Bureau. 2012c. Current Population Survey, 2012 annual social and economic supplement. Retrieved from www.census.gov/hhes/www/poverty/publications/pubs-cps.html.

U.S. Census Bureau. 2012d. Most children under 1 are minorities, Census Bureau Reports. Retrieved from www.census.gov/newsroom/releases/archives/population/cb12-90.html.

U.S. Census Bureau. 2012e. *Statistical abstract of the United States*: 2012 . Table 1149: Cellular telecommunications industry: 1990–2010. Retrieved from www.census.gov/compendia/statab/cats/information_communications/telecommunications.html.

U.S. Census Bureau. 2013a. American Community Survey, 2012. Data retrieved from www.census.gov/acs/www/.

U.S. Census Bureau. 2013b. Current Population Survey, 2012 annual social and economic supplement. Retrieved from www.census.gov/hhes/socdemo/education/data/cps/2012/tables.html.

U.S. Census Bureau. 2013c. Educational attainment. Retrieved from www.census.gov/hhes/socdemo/education/.

U.S. Census Bureau. 2013d. Historical income tables: Mean household income received by each fifth and top 5 percent. Retrieved from www.census.gov/hhes/www/income/data/historical/inequality/.

U.S. Census Bureau. 2013e. Income, poverty, and health insurance coverage in the United States: 2012. Retrieved from www.census.gov/prod/2013pubs/p60-245.pdf.

U.S. Census Bureau. 2013f. Voting and registration in the election of November 2012. Retrieved from www.census.gov/hhes/www/socdemo/voting/publications/p20/2012/tables.html.

U.S. Department of Defense. 2013. *Base structure report, 2013.* Retrieved from www.acq.osd.mil/ie/download/bsr/Base%20Structure%20Report%202013_Baseline%2030%20Sept%202012%20Submission.pdf.

U.S. Department of Health and Human Services. 2010. *Healthy people 2020.* Retrieved from www.healthypeople.gov/2020/topics-objectives2020/overview.aspx?topicid=12.

U.S. Department of Housing and Urban Development. 2005. Discrimination in metropolitan housing markets: National results from phase I of HDS2000. Retrieved from www.huduser.org/portal/publications/hsgfin/phase1.html.

U.S. Department of Justice. 2008. About domestic violence. Retrieved from www.ovw.usdoj.gov/domviolence.htm.

U.S. Department of Justice. 2013. Criminal victimization, 2012. Bureau of Justice Statistics. Retrieved from www.bjs.gov/content/pub/pdf/cv12.pdf.

U.S. Department of State. 2012. Saudi Arabia: Country reports on human rights practices for 2012. Retrieved from www.state.gov/j/drl/rls/hrrpt/humanrightsreport/index.htm?year=2012&dlid=204381.

U.S. Equal Employment Opportunity Commission. 2010. Sexual harassment. Retrieved from www.eeoc.gov/laws/types/sexual_harassment.cfm.

U.S. Senate Permanent Subcommittee on Investigations. 2011. *Wall Street and the financial crisis.* April 13. Washington, DC. Retrieved from http://hsgac.senate.gov/public/_files/financial _crisis/financialcrisisreport.pdf.

Valian, Virginia. 1999. *Why so slow? The advancement of women.* Cambridge, MA: MIT Press.

Vallas, Steven Peter. 2007. Theorizing teamwork under contemporary capitalism. *Research in* the *Sociology of Work* 16: 3–24.

van Gennep, Arnold. (1909)/1961. *The rites of passage,* trans. Monika B. Vizedom and Gabrielle L. Caffee. Chicago: University of Chicago Press.

Vander Wal, Jillon S. 2012. Unhealthy weight control behaviors among adolescents. *Journal of Health Psychology* 17 (1): 110–20.

Varian, Hal R. 2007. An iPod has global value. Ask the (many) countries that make it. *New York Times,* June 28. Retrieved from www.nytimes.com/2007/06/28/business/worldbusiness/28scene.html.

Vartabedian, Ralph, and Ken Bensinger. 2010. Toyota's structure may be an issue. *Los Angeles Times,* February 23, p. A1.

Vaughan, Diane. 1996. *The* Challenger *launch decision.* Chicago: University of Chicago Press.

Vaughn, Diane. 2003. History as cause: *Columbia* and *Challenger. Report, Columbia Accident Investigation Board,* vol. 1, ch. 8.

Vaught, Charles, and David L. Smith. 2003. Incorporation and mechanical solidarity in an underground coal mine. In *The cultural study of work,* ed. Douglas Harper and Helene M. Lawson, pp. 96–115. Lanham, MD: Rowman & Littlefield.

Veblen, Thorstein. (1899)/1973. *The theory of the leisure class.* Boston: Houghton Mifflin.

Vedantam, Shankar. 2005. See no bias. *Washington Post Magazine,* January 23, pp. 12–17, 38.

Verba, Sidney, Kay Schlozman, and Henry Brady. 1995. *Voice and equality.* Cambridge, MA: Harvard University Press.

Vertovec, Steven. 2009. *Transnationalism.* New York: Routledge.

Vespa, Jonathan. Jamie M. Lewis, and Rose M. Kreider. 2013. America's families and living arrangements: 2012. U.S. Census Bureau. August. Retrieved from www.census.gov/prod/2013pubs/p20-570.pdf.

Vigil, James Diego. 1996. Street baptism: Chicano gang initiation. *Human Organization* 55 (Summer): 149–54.

Vogel, Joachim, and Töres Theorell. 2005. Social welfare models, labor markets, and health outcomes. In *Healthier societies: From analysis to action,* ed. Jody Heymann, Clyde Hertzman, Morris L. Barer, and Robert G. Evans, pp. 267–95. New York: Oxford University Press.

Vogel, Steve. 2007. *The Pentagon: A history.* New York: Random House.

von Clausewitz, Carl. (1832)/1976. *On war,* ed. and trans., Michael Howard and Peter Paret. Princeton, NJ: Princeton University Press.

Wade, Ann, and Tanya Beran. 2011. Cyberbullying: The new era of bullying. *Canadian Journal of Social Psychology* 26 (1): 44–61.

Wainright, Jennifer, Stephen Russell, and Charlotte Patterson. 2004. Psychosocial adjustment, school outcomes and romantic relationships of adolescents with same-sex parents. *Child Development* 75 (6): 1886–98.

Wajcman, Judy. 2008. Life in the fast lane? Toward a sociology of technology and time. *British Journal of Sociology* 59 (1): 59–77.

Wakefield, Sara, and Christopher Uggen. 2010. Incarceration and stratification. *Annual Review of Sociology* 36: 387–406.

Waldfogel, Jane. 1997. The effect of children on women's wages. *American Sociological Review* 62 (2): 209–17.

Waldinger, Roger, ed. 2001. *Strangers at the gates: New immigrants in urban America.* Berkeley: University of California.

Walker, Gordon. 2012. *Environmental justice: Concepts, evidence, and politics.* New York: Routledge.

Walker, Pat, ed. 1979. *Between labor and capital.* Boston: South End Press.

Wallerstein, Immanuel. 1974. *The modern world-system.* New York: Academic Press.

Wallerstein, Immanuel. 1979. *The capitalist world-economy.* New York: Cambridge University Press.

Wallerstein, Immanuel. 2004. *World systems analysis: An introduction.* Durham, NC: Duke University Press.

Wang, Marian. 2011. Magnetar deal prompts SEC settlement with JPMorgan Chase. June 21. ProPublica. Retrieved from www.propublica.org/blog/item/magnetar-deal-prompts-sec-settlement-with-jpmorgan-chase.

Wang, Wendy. 2012. The rise of intermarriage. Washington, DC: Pew Research Center. Retrieved from www.pewsocialtrends.org/files/2012/02/SDT-Intermarriage-II.pdf.

Ward, John T. 2010. Dissident in exile. *Drew Magazine.* Drew University. Retrieved from www.drewmagazine.com/2009/12/dissident-in-exile/.

Warner, Stephen. 1993. Work in progress toward a new paradigm for the sociological study of religion in the United States. *American Journal of Sociology* 98 (5): 1044–93.

Wartenberg, Thomas. 1990. *The forms of power: From domination to transformation.* Philadelphia: Temple University Press.

The Washington Post. 2013a. NSA secrets. Retrieved July 23, 2013, from www.washingtonpost.com/nsa-secrets.

Waskul, Dennis D., and Justin A. Martin. 2010. Now the orgy is over. *Symbolic Interaction* 33 (2): 297–318.

Wasserman, Stanley, Katherine Faust, and Dawn Iacobucci. 1994. *Social network analysis: Methods and applications.* Cambridge, UK: Cambridge University Press.

Watts, Duncan. 2004. The "new" science of networks. *Annual Review of Sociology* 30: 243–70.

Waxman, Sharon. 2005. Hollywood unions object to product placement on TV. *New York Times,* November 14. Retrieved from www.nytimes.com/2005/11/14/business/14guild.html.

Weber, Max. (1905)/1958. *The Protestant ethic and the spirit of capitalism,* trans. Talcott Parsons. New York: Scribner.

Weber, Max. (1915)/1946a. Religious rejections of the world and their directions. In *From Max Weber: Essays in sociology,* ed. H. H. Gerth and C. Wright Mills, pp. 323–59. New York: Oxford University Press.

Weber, Max. (1915)/1946b. The social psychology of world religions. In *From Max Weber: Essays in sociology,* ed. Hans Gerth and C. Wright Mills, pp. 267–301. New York: Oxford University Press.

Weber, Max. (1919)/1946a. Politics as a vocation. In *From Max Weber: Essays in sociology,* ed. H. H. Gerth and C. Wright Mills, pp. 77–128. New York: Oxford University Press.

Weber, Max. (1919)/1946b. Science as a vocation. In *From Max Weber: Essays in sociology,* ed. H. H. Gerth and C. Wright Mills, pp. 129–56. New York: Oxford University Press.

Weber, Max. (1922)/1978. *Economy and society,* ed. Guenther Rother and Claus Wittich. Berkeley: University of California Press.

Weber, Max. 1946. *From Max Weber: Essays in sociology*, trans. Hans Gerth and C. Wright Mills. New York: Oxford University Press.

Weber, Max. (1949)/2011. *Methodology of social sciences*, trans. Edward A. Shils and Henry A. Finch. New Brunswick, NJ: Transaction.

Wechsler Henry, Tobin F. Nelson, Jae Eun Lee, Mark Seibring, Catherine Lewis, and Richard P. Keeling. 2003. Perception and reality: A national evaluation of social norms marketing interventions to reduce college students' heavy alcohol use. *Journal of Studies on Alcohol* 64 (4): 484–94.

Weiner, Rachel. 2013. Black voters turned out at higher rate than white voters in 2012 and 2008. *The Washington Post*, April 29. Retrieved from www.washingtonpost.com/blogs/the-fix/wp/2013/04/29/black-turnout-was-higher-than-white-turnout-in-2012-and-2008/.

Weiss, Bari. 2011. A Democrat's triumphant return to Cairo. *Wall Street Journal*, February 26. Retrieved from online.wsj.com/article/SB10001424052748703408604576164482658051692.html.

Weiss, Jessica. 2000. *To have and to hold: Marriage, the baby boom and social change.* Chicago: University of Chicago Press.

Wellman, Barry. 2001. Physical place and cyberplace: The rise of personalized networking. *International Journal of Urban and Regional Research* 25 (2): 227–52.

Wellman, Barry, and Caroline Haythornthwaite. 2002. *The internet in everyday life.* Oxford, UK: Blackwell.

Wellman, Barry, and Scot Wortley. 1990. Different strokes from different folks: Community ties and social support. *American Journal of Sociology* 96 (3): 558–88.

Welzel, Christian, and Ronald Inglehart. 2010. Agency, values, and well-being: A human development model. *Social Indicators Research* 97: 43–63.

West, Candace, and Don H. Zimmerman. 1987. Doing gender. *Gender & Society* 1 (2): 125–51.

Western, Bruce. 2007. *Punishment and inequality in America.* New York: Russell Sage Foundation Publications.

Wharton, Amy S. 2009. The sociology of emotional labor. *Annual Review of Sociology* 35: 147–65.

Whitaker, Morgan. 2013. Interracial family in Cheerios ad sparks online backlash. MSNBC. June 3. Retrieved from: http://www.msnbc.com/politicsnation/interracial-family-cheerios-ad-sparks-onli.

White, Michael J., and Gayle Kaufman. 1997. Language usage, social capital, and school completion among immigrants and native-born ethnic groups. *Social Science Quarterly* 78: 385–98.

Whyte, William Foote. (1943)/1993. *Street corner society*, 4th ed. Chicago: University of Chicago Press.

Wikiinvest. 2013. News Corporation. Retrieved from www.wikinvest.com/wiki/Newscorp.

Wilcox, W. Bradford, ed. 2010. When marriage disappears. *The State of Our Unions.* Charlottesville, VA: National Marriage Project.

Wilcox, W. Bradford, ed. 2011. How parenthood makes life meaningful and how marriage makes parenthood bearable. *The State of Our Unions.* Charlottesville, VA: National Marriage Project.

Williams, Krissah. 2005. In hip-hop, making name-dropping pay. *Washington Post*, August 29, pp. D1, D9.

Williams, Robin M. 1970. *American society: A sociological interpretation.* New York: Knopf.

Williams, Terry. 1990. *The cocaine kids.* Boston: Addison-Wesley.

Willis, Paul. 1977. *Learning to labor.* New York: Columbia University Press.

Wilson, Clint C., Felix Gutierrez, and Lena Chao. 2003. *Racism, sexism, and the media.* Thousand Oaks, CA: Sage.

Wilson, Clint C., II, Féliz Gutiérrez, and Lena M. Chao. 2013. *Racism, sexism, and the media.* Thousand Oaks, CA: Sage.

Wilson, James Q. 2002. *The marriage problem.* New York: Harper.

Wilson, William Julius. 1973. *Power, racism, and privilege: Race relations in theoretical and socio-historical perspectives.* New York: Free Press.

Wilson, William Julius. 1980. *The declining significance of race.* Chicago: University of Chicago Press.

Wilson, William Julius. 1996. *When work disappears: The world of the new urban poor.* New York: Knopf.

Wolfe, Allan. 2005. *The transformation of American religion.* Chicago: University of Chicago Press.

Wolff, Edward N. 2012. *The asset price meltdown and the wealth of the middle class.* New York: New York University Press. Retrieved from http://appam.confex.com/data/extendedabstract/appam/2012/Paper_2134_extendedabstract_151_0.pdf.

Wolfinger, Nichaolas H. 2003. Family structure homogamy: The effects of parental divorce on partner selection and marital stability. *Social Sciences Research* 32 (1): 80–97.

Women's Prison Association. n.d. Luz's story. Retrieved from www.wpaonline.org/press/luz.htm.

Women's Prison Association Institute on Women & Criminal Justice. 2006. *Hard hit: The growth in the imprisonment of women, 1977–2004.* Retrieved from www.wpaonline.org/institute/hardhit/HardHitReport4.pdf.

Wong, Edward. 2013. Air pollution linked to 1.2 million premature deaths in China. *New York Times*, April 1. Retrieved from www.nytimes.com/2013/04/02/world/asia/air-pollution-linked-to-1-2-million-deaths-in-china.html?_r=0.

Wood, Molly. 2010. Google Buzz: Privacy nightmare. *CNET*. February 10. Retrieved from www.cnet.com/news/google-buzz-privacy-nightmare/.

Woodward, Bob. 2006. *State of denial: Bush at war, part III.* New York: Simon & Schuster.

World Bank. 2011. World development indicators: Literacy rate, adult total. Retrieved from http://data.worldbank.org/indicator/SE.ADT.LITR.ZS.

World Health Organization. 2004. *The global burden of disease.* Geneva, Switzerland: World Health Organization.

World Health Organization. 2005a. *WHO multi-country study on women's health and domestic violence against women.* Geneva: World Health Organization. Retrieved from www.who.int/gender/violence/who_multicountry_study/summary_report/summary_report_English2.pdf.

World Health Organization. 2005b. *World health report, 2005.* Geneva, Switzerland: World Health Organization.

World Health Organization. 2006. *Preventing disease through healthy environments.* Geneva, Switzerland: World Health Organization.

World Health Organization. 2007. *Male circumcision: Global trends and determinants of prevalence, safety and acceptability.* Retrieved from http://whqlibdoc.who.int/publications/2007/9789241596169_eng.pdf.

World Health Organization. 2010. Female genital mutilation. Retrieved from www.who.int/mediacentre/factsheets/fs241/en/.

World Health Organization. 2011. DALYs attributable to water, sanitation and hygiene (diarrhea), 2004. Retrieved from http://gamapserver.who.int/mapLibrary/Files/Maps/Global_wsh_daly_2004.png.

World Values Survey. 2005–2008. Online data analysis. Retrieved from www.wvsevsdb.com/wvs/WVSAnalizeSample.jsp.

Worldwatch Institute. 2006. *State of the world, 2006.* New York: Norton.

Wray, John. 2010. Lives: Acquired taste. *New York Times Magazine*, February 25, p. 50.

Wright, Daniel, Gail Self, and Chris Justice. 2000. Memory conformity: Exploring misinformation effects when presented by another person. *British Journal of Psychology* 91: 189–202.

Wright, Erik Olin. 1985. *Classes.* London: Verso Press.

Wrong, Dennis. 1979. *Power: Its forms, bases and uses.* New York: Oxford University Press.

Wuthnow, Robert. 2008. The sociological study of values. *Sociological Forum* 23 (June): 333–43.

Yamagata, Hisashi, Kuang S. Yeh, Shelby Stewman, and Hiroko Dodge. 1997. Sex segregation and glass ceilings: A comparative statics model of women's career opportunities in the federal government over a quarter century. *American Journal of Sociology* 103 (3): 566–632.

Yamane, David. 1997. Secularization on trial: In defense of a neosecularization paradigm. *Journal for the Scientific Study of Religion* 36 (1): 109–22.

Yeatmann, Anna. 1997. Feminism and power. In *Reconstructing political theory: Feminist perspectives*, ed. Mary Lyndon

Shanley and Uma Narayan, pp. 144–57. University Park: Pennsylvania State University Press.

Young, Iris Marion. 1992. Five faces of oppression. In *Rethinking power*, ed. Thomas Wartenberg, pp. 174–95. Albany: State University of New York Press.

Young, Jacob T. N., and Frank M. Weerman. 2013. Delinquency as a consequence of misperception: Overestimation of friends' delinquent behavior and mechanisms of social influence. *Social Problems* 60 (3): 334–56.

Yukl, G., H. Kim, and C. Falbe. 1996. Antecedents of influence outcomes. *Journal of Applied Psychology* 81: 309–17.

Yunker, John. 2008. The best global web designs of 2008. Retrieved from www.global-bydesign.com/ blog/2008/02/28/the-best-global-web-sites -of-2008/.

Zaimov, Stoyan. 2013. Pope Francis condemns big business idolatry, global economy for high unemployment. *The Christian Post*, September 24. Retrieved from www .christianpost.com/news/pope-francis-condemns-big-business-idolatry-global-economy-for-high-unemployment-105202/.

Zickuhr, Kathryn, and Aaron Smith. 2013. Home broadband 2013. Washington, DC: Pew Research Center. Retrieved from http://pewinternet.org/~/media//Files/Reports/2013/PIP_Broadband%20 2013_082613.pdf.

Zimmerman, Jonathan. 2002. *Whose America? Culture wars in the public schools*. Cambridge, MA: Harvard University Press.

Zinn, Maxine Baca, D. Stanley Eitzen, and Barbara Wells. 2011. *Diversity in families*, 9th ed. Boston, MA : Pearson.

Zinn, Maxinne Baca, and Bonnie Thornton Dill, eds. 1994. *Women of color in U.S. society*. Philadelphia, PA: Temple University Press.

Zukin, Sharon, and Jennifer Smith Maguire. 2004. Consumers and consumption. *Annual Review of Sociology*, 30: 173–97.

Zweig, Michael. 2011. *The working class majority*. Ithaca, NY: Cornell University Press.

Credits

Chapter 8

Page 194: Kai Erickson, *Wayward Puritans: A Study of the Sociology of Deviance*. New York, NY: Wiley, 1966, p. 6; **Fig. 8.1:** Bruce G. Link and Jo C. Phelan, "Conceptualizing Stigma," *Annual Review of Sociology*, vol. 27, 2001, pp. 363–385; **pp. 198–199:** Peter Conrad and Joseph Schneider, *Deviance and Medicalization*. St. Louis, MO: Mosby, 1980; **p. 200:** Robert Futrell and Pete Simi, "Free Spaces, Collective Identity, and the Persistence of U.S. White Power Activism," *Social Problems*, vol. 51, no. 1, 2004, pp. 16–42; 8.3: National Center for Health Statistics, *Health, United States, 2012*. 2013. www.cdc.gov; **p. 204:** American Society of Plastic Surgeons, "Abdominoplasty: Tummy Tuck." 2006. www.plasticsurgery.org; **p. 206:** Edwin H. Sutherland, *White Collar Crime*. New York, NY: Dryden Press, 1949; **p. 207:** Stephen Pfohl, *Images of Deviance and Social Control*. Long Grove, IL: Waveland Press, 2009; **p. 207:** Emile Durkheim, *Suicide*, trans. John A. Spaulding and George Simpson. New York, NY: Free Press, 1897, 1952; **p. 207:** "Video Surveillance Cameras in Downtown Boston." Source: www.notbored.org/boston.html; **p. 208:** Michel Foucault, *Discipline and Punish*, trans. Alan Sheridan. New York, NY: Vintage, 1979, p. 304; **p. 208:** Julia Angwin, "The Web's New Gold Mine: Your Secrets," *Wall Street Journal*, July 30, 2010. http://online.wsj.com; 8.4: U.S. Department of Justice, "Criminal Victimization, 2012," *Bureau of Justice Statistics*. 2013. www.bjs.gov; 8.5: FBI, "Uniform Crime Reports," *Crime in the United States;* **p. 213:** Jeffrey Reiman and Paul Leighton, *The Rich Get Richer and the Poor Get Prison*, 10th ed. Boston, MA: Allyn & Bacon, 2013, p. 111.; 8.6–8.7: Bureau of Justice Statistics, "Prisoners in 2011." 2012. www.bjs.gov; **Table 8.1:** U.S. Department of Justice, "Criminal Victimization, 2012." *Bureau of Justice Statistics*. 2013. www.bjs.gov; **p. 216:** James W. Marquart, Sheldon Ekland-Olson, and Jonathan R. Sorensen, *The Rope, the Chair, & the Needle*. Austin, TX: University of Texas Press, 1994, pp. x–xi; **Map 8.1:** Amnesty International, "Death Penalty Facts." September 19, 2013. www.amnestyusa.org; **p. 217:** Thomas Lynch, "We Should Witness the Death of McVeigh," *New York Times*, February 20, 2001, p. A21.

Chapter 9

Page 224–225: Alfred Lubrano, *Blue-Collar Roots, White-Collar Dreams*. Hoboken, NJ: Wiley, 2004, pp. 1, 5, 7–8; **p. 227:** Kinglsey Davis and Wilbert Moore, "Some Principles of Stratification," *American Sociological Review*, vol. 10, 1945, pp. 242–249; **Table 9.1:** Emmanuel Saez, "Striking it Richer: The Evolution of Top Incomes in the United States," *University of California*. 2013. http://elsa.berkeley.edu; **Fig. 9.2:** U.S. Census Bureau, "Income, Poverty, and Health Insurance Coverage in the United States: 2012," 2013. www.census.gov and Edward N. Wolff, *The Asset Price Meltdown and the Wealth of the Middle Class*. New York, NY: New York University Press, 2012; 9.3: U.S. Census Bureau, "Historical Income Tables: Mean Household Income Received by Each Fifth and Top 5 Percent." 2013. www.census.gov; **p. 232:** Jay MacLeod, *Ain't No Makin' It: Aspirations and Attainment in the Low-Income Neighborhood*. Boulder, CO: Westview Press, 2008, p. 239; **Table 9.2:** U.S Bureau of Labor Statistics, "Occupations with the Largest Job Growth," 2012. www.bls.gov; **Table 9.3:** Tom Hertz, "Rags, Riches, and Race: The Intergenerational Economic Mobility of Black and White Families in the United States," *Unequal Chances: Family Background and Economic Success*, ed. Samuel Bowles, Herbert Gintis, and Melissa Osborne. Princeton, NJ: Princeton University Press, 2005, pp. 165–191; 9.4: U.S. Census Bureau, "Voting and Registration in the Election of November 2012," 2013. www.census.gov; 9.5: U.S. Census Bureau, "Income, Poverty, and Health Insurance Coverage in the United States: 2012," 2013. www.census.gov; **Table 9.4:** U.S. Census Bureau, "Income, Poverty, and Health Insurance Coverage in the United States: 2012," 2013. www.census.gov; 9.6: U.S. Bureau of Labor Statistics, "Employment Projections," 2013. www.bls.gov; 9.7: Rebecca Ray and John Schmitt, *No-Vacation Nation*. Washington, DC: Center for Economic Policy and Research, 2007; **p. 242:** Shira Ovide, "Watch Warren Buffet say 'raise my taxes'," *Wall Street Journal*, November 22, 2010. http://blogs.wsj.com; 9.9: Isabel Ortiz and Matthew Cummins, "Global Inequality: Beyond the Bottom Million," *UNICEF*, 2011. www.networkideas.org; 9.10: Colin Gordon, "Growing Together, Growing Apart," *Economic Policy Institute*, 2013. www.epi.org.

Chapter 10

Map 10.1: Nina G. Jablonski and George Chaplin, "Skin Deep," *Scientific American*, vo. 287, no. 4, 2002, pp. 74–82; **Fig. 10.2:** American Anthropological Association, *Race: Are We So Different?*, 2011. http://understandingrace.org; **Table 10.1:** U.S. Census Bureau, "American Community Survey, 2012," 2013. www.census.gov; 10.3–10.4: U.S. Census Bureau, "Race and Hispanic Origin of the Foreign-Born Population in the United States: 2007," 2010. www.census.gov and U.S. Census Bureau, "American Community Survey, 2012," 2013. www.census.gov; 10.5: U.S. Census Bureau, "Current Population Survey, 2012 Annual Social and Economic Supplement," 2013. www.census.gov and U.S. Census Bureau, "Income, Poverty, and Health Insurance Coverage in the United States: 2012," 2013. www.census.gov; 10.6: Wendy Wang, "The Rise of Intermarriage," *Pew Research Center*, 2012. www.pewsocialtrends.org; **p. 284:** Comedy Central, "Key and Peele: About the Show," 2013. www.comedycentral.com.

Chapter 11

Page 293: Elizabeth Cady Stanton, *A History of Woman Suffrage*, vol. 1. Rochester, NY: Fowler and Wells, 1889, pp. 70–71; **p. 298:** Karen Davies, "The Body and Doing Gender: The Relations Between Doctors and Nurses in Hospital Work," *Sociology of Health & Illness*, vol. 25, no. 7, 2003, pp. 720–742; **p. 300:** Michele Adams and Scott Coltrane, "Boys and Men in Families: The Domestic Production of Gender, Power, and Privilege," *Handbook of Studies on Men & Masculinities*, ed. Michael S. Kimmel, Jeff Hearn, and R. W. Connell. Thousand Oaks, CA: Sage, 2005, pp. 230–248; **Fig. 11.1:** American Council on Education, "The American College President 2012," 2012. www.acenet.edu, Catalyst, "2013 Catalyst Census: *Fortune* 500," 2013, www.catalyst.org, and Center for American Women and Politics, "Women in Elective Office 2013," 2013, www.cawp.rutgers.edu; 11.2: U.S. Census Bureau, "Educational Attainment," 2013, www.census.gov; **Table 11.1:** U.S. Department of Labor, Women's Bureau, "20 Leading Occupations of Employed Women," 2010. www.dol.gov; **Table 11.2:** Inter-Parliamentary Union, "Women in National Parliaments," 2013. www.ipu.org; **p. 307:** U.S. Department of Justice, "About Domestic Violence," 2008. www.ovw.usdoj.gov; **p. 307:** World Health Organization, *WHO Multi-Country Study on Women's Health and Domestic Violence Against Women*, 2005. www.who.int; 11.3: World Health Organization, *WHO Multi-Country Study on Women's Health and Domestic Violence Against Women*, 2005. www.who.int; **p. 311:** Barbara L. Frankowski, "Sexual Orientation and Adolescents," *Pediatrics*, vol. 113, no. 6, 2004, pp. 1827–1832; **Map 11.1:** National Gay and Lesbian Task Force, "Relationship Recognition for Same-Sex Couples in the U.S.," 2011, www.thetaskforce.org; p. 315: Tristan Taormino, "Introduction: The Politics of Producing Pleasure," *The Feminist Porn Book*, ed. Tristan Taormino, Constance Penley, Celine Parrenas Shimizu, and Mireille Miller-Young. New York, NY: Feminist Press at the City University of New York, 2013, pp. 9–20; **p. 315:** Talcott Parsons, "An Analytical Approach to the Theory of Social Stratification," *Essays in Sociological Theory*. New York, NY: Free Press, 1954, pp. 69–88.

Chapter 12

Page 325–326: Felix M. Berardo and Constance L. Shehan, "Family Problems in Global Perspective," *Handbook of Social Problems: A Comparative International Perspective*, ed. George Ritzer. Thousand Oaks, CA: Sage, pp. 246–260; **Fig. 12.1:** U.S. Census Bureau, "Current Population Survey, March and Annual Social and Economic Supplements, 2012 and earlier," 2012, www.census.gov; 12.2: Bradford W. Wilcox, ed., "How Parenthood Makes Life Meaningful and How Marriage Makes Parenthood Bearable," *The State of Our Unions*. Charlottesville, VA: National Marriage Project, 2011; **p. 331:** Andrew J. Cherlin, *Public and Private Families*. New York, NY: McGraw-Hill, 2013; **p. 331:** Elaine Fantle Shimberg, *Blending Families*. New York, NY: Berkely, 1999, p. 207; **p. 333:** American Sociological Association, *Brief of Amicus Curiae American Sociological Association in Support of Respondent Kristin M. Perry and Respondent Edith Schlain Windsor*. Supreme Court of the United States. NOS. 12-144, 12-307, 2013; 12.3: U.S. Census Bureau, "Current Population Survey, March and Annual Social and Economic Supplements, 2012 and earlier," 2012, www.census.gov and Jonathan Vespa, Jamie M. Lewis, and Rose M. Kreider, "America's Families and Living Arrangements: 2012," *U.S. Census Bureau*, 2013. www.census.gov; 12.4: U.S. Census Bureau, "Current Population Survey, March and Annual Social and Economic Supplements, 2012 and earlier," 2012, www.census.gov; 12.5: Jonathan Vespa, Jamie M. Lewis, and Rose M. Kreider, "America's Families and Living Arrangements: 2012," *U.S. Census Bureau*, 2013. www.census.gov; **p. 338:** Emile Durkheim, *Elementary Forms of the Religious Life*, trans. Carol Cosman. New York, NY: Oxford University Press, 1915, 2001, p. 314; **p. 338:** Karl Marx, "Contribution to the critique of Hegel's *Philosophy of Right*: Introduction," *The Marx-Engels Reader*, ed. Robert C. Tucker. New York, NY: Norton, 1844, 1978, pp. 53–65; **p. 339:** Max Weber, *The Protestant Ethic and the Spirit of Capitalism*, trans. Talcott Parsons. New York, NY: Scribner, 1905, 1958, pp. 155, 331; **p. 339:** Max Weber, "The Social Psychology of World Religions," *From Max Weber: Essays in Sociology*, ed. Han Gerth and C. Wright Mills. New York, NY: Oxford University Press, 1919, 1946, pp. 129–156; 12.6: Pew-Templeton Global Religious Futures Project. *Pew Research Center's Religion and Public Life Project*. 2013. www.globalreligiousfutures.org; 12.7: World Values Survey. *Online Data Analysis*. 2005–2008. www.wvsevsdb.com; 12.8: National Opinion Research Center. *General Social Survey, 2010*. 2010. www3.norc.org; **Map 12.1:** Pew Research Center's Forum on Religion & Public Life, *U.S. Religious Landscape Survey*. 2008. http://religions.pewforum.org; **p. 346:** Michael O. Emerson and David Hartman, "The Rise of Religious Fundamentalism," *Annual Review of Sociology*, vol. 32, 2006, pp. 127–144.

Chapter 13

Table 13.1: Organization for Economic Cooperation and Development, *Education at a Glance 2013: OECD Indicators*. 2013. http://dx.doi.org; **Map 13.1:** UN Development Programme, *Human Development Report 2005*. New York, NY: UN Development Programme, 2005; **p. 354:** William J. Reese, *America's Public Schools: From the Common School to "No Child Left Behind."* Baltimore, MD: Johns Hopkins University Press, 2005, p. 3; **Fig. 13.1:** National Center for Education Statistics, *The Condition of Education 2013*. 2013. www.nces.ed.gov; 13.2: U.S. Census Bureau, "Current Population Survey, 2012 Annual Social and Economic Supplement." 2012. www.census.gov; **Table 13.2:** College Board, "Trends in Student Aid 2012." 2012. http://trends.collegeboard.org, National Center for Education Statistics, *Digest of Education Statistics 2003*. 2003. http://nces.edu.gov, National Center for Education Statistics, *The Condition of Education 2013*. 2013. http://nces.ed.gov; **p. 365:** Gary Orfield and Chungmei Lee, *Radical Transformation and the Changing Nature of Segregation*. Cambridge, MA: Harvard University, 2006, p. 29; **p. 367:** Alejandro Portes, "English-only Triumphs, but the Costs are High," *The Structure of Schooling: Readings in the Sociology of Education*, ed. Richard Arum, Irenee R. Beattie, and Karly Ford. Los Angeles, CA: Sage, 2011, pp. 567–571; **p. 369:** Sameer Hinduja and Justin W. Patchin, *Bullying Beyond the Schoolyard: Preventing and Responding to Cyberbullying*. Thousand Oaks, CA: Sage, 2009, p. 5; **Table 13.3:** U.S. Bureau of Labor Statistics, "Current Employment Statistics—CES (National). 2014. www.bls.gov; **p. 372:** Tom W. Smith, *Job Satisfaction in the United States*. Chicago, IL: NORC/University of Chicago, 2007, p. 1; **Table 13.4:** Tom W. Smith, *Job Satisfaction in the United States*. Chicago, IL: NORC/University of Chicago, 2007; 13.5: Institute for Women's Policy Research, "The Gender Wage Gap: 2012." March 2012. www.iwpr.org; **p. 373:** Ronit Donovitzer, Nancy Reichman, and Joyce Sterling, "The Differential Value of Women's Work: A New Look at the Gender Gap in Lawyers' Incomes," *Social Forces*, vol. 88, no. 2, 2009, pp. 819–864; **p. 375:** Steven Greenhouse, "Ending Strike, Mott's Plant Union Accepts Deal," *New York Times*, September 14, 2010, p. B6; 13.6: Barry T. Hirsch and David A. Macpherson, "Union Membership and Coverage Database from the Current Population Survey." 2013. www.unionstats.com; **p. 377:** Diane Seymour and Peter Sandiford, "Learning Emotion Rules in Service Organizations," *Work, Employment and Society*, vol. 19, no. 3, 2005, pp. 547–564.

Chapter 14

Page 385: Facebook, "Facebook for Business." 2013. www.facebook.com; **p. 388:** Ben Bagdikian, *The New Media Monopoly*. Boston, MA: Beacon Press, 2004, p. 3; **p. 393:** Barry Glasner, *The Culture of Fear*, 10th anniversary edition. New York, NY: Basic Books, 2009, p. xxi; **p. 393:** Robert Hof, "It's a Whole New Web," *BusinessWeek*, September 26, 2005, pp. 76–79; **Fig. 14.4:** Michael Holmes and Mike

Bloxham, "An Observational Method for Time Use Research: Advantages, Disadvantages, and Lessons Learned from the Middletown Media Studies," *Paper presented at the 2007 conference of the International Association of Time Use Researchers.* 2007; 14.5: Kathryn Zickuhr and Aaron Smith, "Home Broadband 2013," *Pew Research Center.* 2013. http://pewinternet.org; **Map 14.1:** Internet World Stats, "World Internet Usage and Population Statistics." 2013. http://internetworldstats.com; **p. 398:** International Network on Cultural Policy, "About Us." 2010. www.incp-ripc.org; **p. 401:** Stephanie Coontz, *The Way We Never Were: American Families and the Nostalgia Trap.* New York, NY: Basic Books, 1992, p. 170; **p. 402:** Peter Berger, *Invitation to Sociology.* New York, NY: Doubleday, 1963, p. 48; **p. 404:** Michael Schudson, *Advertising: The Uneasy Persuasion.* New York, NY: Basic Books, 1986, p. 238; **pp. 408–409:** American Academy of Pediatrics, "Children, Adolescents, and Advertising. Policy Statement," *Pediatrics,* vol. 118, no. 6, 2006, pp. 2563–2569; **pp. 408–409:** Sarah Babb, "Born to Buy: Sarah Babb Interviews Juliet Schor," *Sociology Speaks 2003–2004.* Chestnut Hill, MA: Boston College Department of Sociology, 2004; **pp. 408–409:** Juliet Schor, *Born to Buy: The Commercialized Child and the New Consumer Culture.* New York, NY: Scribner, 2004; **pp. 408–409:** Victor C. Strausburger and Barbara J. Wilson, *Children, Adolescents, and the Media.* Thousand Oaks, CA: Sage, 2002; **pp. 408–409:** Victor C. Strausberger, Barbara J. Wilson, and Amy B. Jordan, *Children Adolescents, and the Media,* 2nd edition. Thousand Oaks, CA: 2009; **Table 14.1:** Gary Gardner, Erik Assadourian, and Radhia Sarin, "The State of Consumption Today," *The State of the World, 2004.* New York, NY: Norton, 2004, pp. 3–23.

Chapter 15
Table 15.2: UN Department of Economic and Social Affairs, Population Division, *World Urbanization Prospects: The 2011 Revision.* 2012. http://esa.un.org; **p. 419:** Ferdinand Tonnies, *Community and Civil Society,* trans. Margaret Hollis. Cambridge, UK: University of Cambridge Press, 1887, 2001, p. 18.; **Fig. 15.3:** Daniel Denvir, "The 10 Most Segregated Urban Areas in America." 2011. http://politics.salon.com; 15.4: John R. Logan and Brian J. Stults, "The Persistence of Segregation in the Metropolis: New Findings from the 2010 Census." 2011. www.s4.brown.edu; **pp. 426–427:** Anthony Flint, *This Land: The Battle Over Sprawl and the Future of America.* Baltimore, MD: Johns Hopkins University Press, 2006, p. 29; 15.6: U.S. Census Bureau, "2010–2012 American Community Survey," 2012. www.census.gov; **p. 428:** Robert D. Putnam, *Bowling Alone: The Collapse and Revival of American Community.* New York, NY: Simon & Schuster, 2000, p. 213; **p. 433:** Evangelical Climate Initiative, "Climate Change: An Evangelical Call to Action." 2006. http://christiansandclimate.org; **p. 433:** Frederick H. Buttel, "Environmental Sociology and the Explanation of Environmental Reform," *Organization & Environment,* vol. 17, no. 3, 2004, pp. 306–344; **p. 434:** Peter Conrad, "General Introduction," *The Sociology of Health and Illness,* 7th ed., ed. Peter Conrad. New York, NY: Worth, 2005, p. 1; **p. 435:** John B. McKinlay and Lisa D. Marceau, "The End of the Golden Age of Doctoring," *International Journal of Health Services,* vol. 32, no. 2, 2002, pp. 379–416; **Map 15.1:** World Health Organization, "DALYs Attributable to Water, Sanitation, and Hygiene (Diarrhea), 2004." 2011. http://gamapserver.who.int.

Chapter 16
Page 444: Barak Obama, "Remarks by the President in Address to the Nation on the Way Forward in Afghanistan and Pakistan." 2009. www.whitehouse.gov; **p. 444:** Bill Briggs, "Financial Strain Pushes Many Veterans to the Breaking Point," *NBC News.* 2013. www.inplainsight.nbcnews.com; **Map 16.1:** Economist Intelligence Unit, "Democracy Index 2012: Democracy at a Standstill," *The Economist,* 2013. www.eiu.com; **Fig. 16.1:** Top right: Courtesy of the Libertarian Party; Middle: Courtesy of the Independence Party; Bottom right: Courtesy of the Socialist Party; Bottom left: Courtesy of the Reform Party; Top left: Courtesy of the Green Party; 16.2: Top: UK Parliament, "Current State of the Parties." 2014. www.parliament.uk. Bottom: German Bundestag, "Parliamentary Groups, as of March 3, 2011." 2014. www.bundestag.de; **p. 450:** Dietram A. Scheufele and Patricia Moy, "Twenty-Five Years of the Spiral of Silence: A Conceptual Review and Empirical Outlook," *International Journal of Public Opinion Research,* vol. 12, no. 1, 2000, pp. 3–28; 16.3: Center for Responsive Politics, "Expenditures." 2013. www.opensecrets.org; **p. 453:** Martin Gilens, "Inequality and Democratic Responsiveness," *Public Opinion Quarterly,* vol. 69, no. 5, 2005, pp. 778–796; 16.4: Congressional Budget Office, "The Distribution of Major Tax Expenditures in the Individual Income Tax System." 2013. www.cbo.gov; 16.5: Chuck Collins and Felice Yeskel, *Economic Apartheid in America.* New York, NY: New Press, 2005; **p. 455:** Carl von Clausewitz, *On War,* ed. and trans. Michael Howard and Peter Paret. Princeton, NJ: Princeton University Press, 1832, 1976, p. 87; **p. 456:** C. Wright Mills, *The Power Elite.* New York, NY: Oxford University Press, 1956, p. 202; **p. 456:** Dana Priest and William M. Arkin, "A Hidden World, Growing Beyond Control," *Washington Post,* July 19, 2010. http://projects.washingtonpost.com; 16.6: Stockholm International Peace Research Institute, "Trend in World Military Expenditure, 2012." 2013. www.sipri.org; 16.7: National Priorities Project, "President's 2015 Budget in Pictures." 2014. http://nationalpriorities.org; **p. 457:** "We'll be back after this commercial break, with more reasons why it's not safe to leave your home." © www.cartoonstock.com. Reprinted with permission. All rights reserved; **p. 460:** Raphael F. Perl, *Terrorism and National Security: Issues and Trends.* 2006. http://fpc.state.gov; **p. 461:** Austin T. Turk, "Sociology of Terrorism," *Sociological Review,* vol. 30, 2004, pp. 387–394; **Map 16.2:** U.S. Department of Agriculture Economic Research Service. 2013. www.ers.usda.gov.

Chapter 17
Table 17.1: KOF Swiss Economic Institute, "KOF Index of Globalization 2013." 2013. http://globalization.kof.ethz.ch; **Fig. 17.1–17.3:** UN Department of Economic and Social Affairs, Population Division, *World Population Prospects The 2012 Revision.* 2013. http://esa.un.org; **Table 17.2:** UN Department of Economic and Social Affairs, Population Division, *World Population Prospects The 2012 Revision.* 2013. http://esa.un.org; 17.4: Organization for Economic Cooperation and Development (OECD), *OECD Factbook 2010: Economic, Environmental and Social Statistics.* Paris, France: OECD, 2013; **p. 495:** Frederick Douglass, *Frederick Douglass on Slavery and the Civil War: Selections From His Writings,* ed. Joslyn T. Pine. Mineolo, NY: Dover, 2003, p. 42; 17.6: Pew Research Center, "Changing Attitudes on Gay Marriage." 2013. http://features.pewforum.org.

Photo Credits

Name Index

Subject Index

Applying Sociological Theory

Theory is integral to the discipline of sociology and is covered in every chapter of *Experience Sociology*. This list provides a sample of the application of sociology's major theoretical perspectives to key sociological issues. The numbers in parentheses indicate chapters.

OVERVIEW OF SOCIOLOGICAL THEORY

Role of theory in sociological research (2)
Sociology's common ground: culture, structure, and power (1)
Sociology's major theoretical perspectives (1)

STRUCTURAL FUNCTIONALISM

Addams and urban sociology (15)
And culture, structure, power (1)
Cultural lag (17)
Culture and prejudice (10)
Culture wars (3)
Debt and dissatisfaction (14)
Demography and population change (17)
Deviance: boundaries, solidarity, and innovation (8)
Durkheim (1)
Durkheim on deviance (8)
Economy and social cohesion (16)
Functions of class (9)
Functions of religion (12)
Functions of schooling (13)
Functions of the family (12)
Functions of the media (14)
Gender stratification (11)
Global culture, structure, and power (17)
Government regulation of media (14)
Groups and organizations (7)
Herbert Spencer (1)
Human ecology (15)
Ideas and change (17)
Institutional interrelationships (4)
Moral education (13)
Multiculturalism's critics (3)
Nature of work (4)
Organic and mechanical solidarity (15)
Organizations and structure (4)
Parsons and power (5)
Place, people, relationships (15)
Promoting values via socialization (6)
Religion (3)
Rituals (2)
Sacred/Profane (12)
Social cohesiveness (3)
Socialization (11)
Socialization and social control (8)
Solidarity and team success (2)
Statuses and roles (4)
Strain theory (8)
Tönnies (15)
Traditional gender roles (4)

CONFLICT THEORY

Addams and urban sociology (15)
Alienation and consumption (14)
And culture, structure, power (1)
Anti-corporate activism (3)
Arab societies (1)
Authority (5)
Bureaucracy (7)
Class inequality (5)
Competition for jobs (10)
Cultural capital (9, 13)
Cultural imperialism (14)
Culture wars (3)
Debt and dissatisfaction (14)
Demographic divide (17)
Digital divide (14)
Disenchantment (12)
Dominant ideology (3)
Domination and "power over" (5)
DuBois (1)
Educational inequality (13)
Eliminating sweatshops (4)
Environmental destruction (14)
Ethnocentrism (3)
Gender gap and division of labor (13)
Gender stratification (11)
Gender, power, and the family (12)
Global culture, structure, and power (17)
Globalization and colonialism (17)
Globalization of culture (3)
Globalization of work (4)
Hegemony and cultural power (5)
Historical materialism (17)
Ideas and change (17)
Inequality (1)
Inequality and consumption (14)
Institutional discrimination (10)
Leadership and oligarchy (7)
Marx (1)
Marx on class (9)
Marx on religion (12)
Media consolidation (14)
Multiculturalism (3)
New urban sociology (15)
Occupational status and prestige (13)
Organizations and structure (4)
Organizing for power (17)
Political power (5)
Politics of fear (16)
Power and crime (8)
Power and deviance (8)
Power and government (16)
Power and privilege (5)
Power in groups and organizations (7)
Power of disobedience (5)

Power on the job (13)
Promoting values via socialization (6)
Rationalization (4)
Sexual identities and inequality (11)
Social economy (16)
Socialization (11)
Socialization in school (13)
Status (5)
Stratification systems (5)
Sustainability and inequality (15)
Treadmill of production (15)
Urban growth machine (15)
Weber (1)
Weber and power (5)
Weber's concept of "life chances" (9)
Workplace control (7)

SYMBOLIC INTERACTIONISM

Addams and urban sociology (15)
And culture, structure, power (1)
Binge drinking (2)
Consumption and identity (14)
Conversation analysis (4)
Cooley and Mead (6)
Cultural capital (9, 13)
Culture and prejudice (10)
Developing a self (6)
Deviance: boundaries, solidarity, and innovation (8)
Differential association theory (8)
Doing gender (11)
Emotional labor (13)
Framing messages (17)
Humans without culture (6)
Individual prejudice (10)
Interaction and intersubjectivity (7)
Internet norms (3)
Learning gender (11)
Navigating communities (15)
Neurosociology (6)
Occupational status and prestige (13)
Online identity (6)
Peer group socialization (6)
Political socialization (16)
Power in groups and organizations (7)
Power tactics (5)
Religious symbols and interaction (12)
Rites of passage (6)
Sacred canopy (12)
Social construction of environmental problems (15)
Social construction of reality (7)
Socialization (11)
Socialization for war (16)
Socialization in school (13)
Status (5)
Statuses and roles (4, 7)
Subcultures and countercultures (3)
Symbols and language (3)
Team success (2)

Thomas theorem (7)
Transnational identities (17)
Workplace culture (13)

FEMINIST THEORIES

Addams (1)
Addams and urban sociology (15)
Breast cancer (2)
Defining political issues (16)
Doing gender (11)
Emotion work (7)
Emotional labor (13)
Empowerment and "power to" (5)
Feminist scholarship and activism (11)
Gender gap and division of labor (13)
Gender, power, and the family (12)
Inequality (11)
Intersectionality theory (5)
Learning gender (11)
Martineau (1)
Patriarchy (5)
Power and privilege (5)
Sexual identities and inequality (11)
Socialization (11)
Standpoint theory (5)
Team success (2)

OTHER THEORETICAL PERSPECTIVES

DEPENDENCY THEORY
Exploitation and global inequality (9)

DRAMATURGICAL THEORY
Racist "back-stage" behavior (10)
Role expectations and impression management (7)

ETHNOMETHODOLOGY
Conversation analysis (4)
Ethnomethodology (4)

FOUCAULT
Categorizing sexualities (11)
Foucault and power (5)
Power and the self (6)
Surveillance and social control (8)

LABELING THEORY
Deviance and stigma (8)

PLURALIST THEORY
Political power (5)

POSTMODERNISM
Postmodernism (1, 14)

RATIONAL CHOICE THEORY
Deviance as rational choice (8)
Religious marketplace (12)

WORLD SYSTEMS THEORY
Global economy (15, 17)